THE MUSICIAN'S BUSINESS AND LEGAL GUIDE

Edited and Compiled by
Mark Halloran, Esq.

Introduction by Gregory T. Victoroff, Esq.
Chairman, the Beverly Hills Bar Association
Committee for the Arts

PRENTICE HALL, Englewood Cliffs, NJ 07632

Library of Congress Cataloging-in-Publication Data

The Musician's business and legal guide/edited and compiled by Mark Halloran; introduction by Gregory T. Victoroff. -- Rev. 4th ed.

p. cm.
"A Jerome Headlands Press book."
Includes bibliography and index.
ISBN 0-13-605585-0
1. Music trade--Law and legislation--United States. 2. Musicians--legal status, laws, etc.--United States. 3. Music--Economic aspects--United States. 4. Copyright--Music--United States.
I. Halloran, Mark E.
ML3790.M84 1991
780' .23'73--dc20 91-23255
CIP
MN

Prentice-Hall, Inc.
A Simon & Schuster Company
Englewood Cliffs, NJ 07632

1979, 1980 and 1986 editions published under the title *The Musicians Manual*

Designed and Produced by:
Jerome Headlands Press
PO Box N
Jerome, Arizona 86331

Cover design by Julie Sullivan
Cover and still life photography by Michael Thompson
Index by Marc Savage, Savage Indexing Service

SPECIAL THANKS TO:
The staff at Jerome Headlands Press: Alberta Titonis, book design; Julie Sullivan, art director for still life photographs and book design edit; Susan Kinsella and Sue Tillman, editorial assistants; and George Glassman, copy editor and proof reader. Also to Mark Halloran and assistants, attorneys Marnie Glass and Joel Goldstein; Gregory Victoroff of the Beverly Hills Bar Association; and to Edward R. Hearn, attorney for Jerome Headlands Press.

Manufactured in the United States of America

10 9 8 7 6 5 4

ISBN 0-13-605585-0

Prentice Hall International (UK) Limited, *London*
Prentice-Hall of Australia Pty. Limited, *Sydney*
Prentice-Hall Canada Inc., *Toronto*
Prentice-Hall Hispanoamericana, S.A., *Mexico*
Prentice-Hall of India Private Limited, *New Delhi*
Prentice-Hall of Japan, Inc., *Tokyo*
Simon & Schuster Asia Pte. Ltd., *Singapore*
Editora Prentice-Hall do Brasil, Ltda., Rio de Janeiro

TABLE OF CONTENTS

PREFACE
by Mark Halloran, Esq.

As a musician, at some point in your professional career, you will learn that there are legal questions implicit in almost everything you do. Whether you write a song, perform a song, or sell a song, your actions give rise to rights and obligations that you should consider. The time to learn is now.

What is the purpose of this book? To impart knowledge. To demystify this seemingly monolithic business and the indecipherable body of law which shapes it. And to help you "make it" by explaining the music industry and music law.

This book is a collection of articles written by people who work in the music industry. Many are written by lawyers, others by musicians. We have tried to write in a style that is comprehensible to everyone, and have avoided presupposing a lot of knowledge on your part. Do not be insulted. We are not trying to patronize, but to inform.

For the most part the book follows a loose chronological scheme that parallels the typical development of a musician's career. It should be noted at the outset that the particular problems of musicians working in the fine arts---symphony orchestras, ballet, and opera to name a few---are not treated here.

At this point we must present a few warnings. First, there is no substitute for seeking competent help as you build your career. Talent agents, personal managers, lawyers and business managers are trained to guide you. Their expertise costs money, but in the long run you must think of the cost as an investment in your career. Also, those chapters written by lawyers are designed to guide you to identify problems, not to give specific solutions. Thus, if you have a legal problem, do not rely on the information contained in this book, but see an attorney. The chapters in this book are not the law, but merely describe legal applications, in general terms, in the music industry context. Additionally, do not automatically photocopy the forms for submittal, as many organizations require you to fill out their original forms. Discuss this in advance with the appropriate organization.

Although we have tried to give the most current information, the information set forth is subject to change. Finally, the views expressed by the authors, including me, are skewed in your favor, and do not necessarily reflect the views of the author's employers or partners.

One final note. Although this book should be a useful tool, musicians should write music, not contracts. Unless you devote your time and energy to developing and exploiting your talent, this book doesn't matter. Make it matter.

INTRODUCTION
By Gregory T. Victoroff, Esq., Beverly Hills Bar Association Committee for The Arts

Over ten years ago, a handful of idealistic and ambitious young lawyers and musicians compiled and published the first edition of The Musician's Manual, a product of the Committee for the Arts (CFTA) of the Barristers (young lawyers division) of the Beverly Hills Bar Association.

Over a decade later, CFTA has the same two basic objectives: to produce an educational and informative publication relating to music and law, of lasting value both to music professionals and lawyers, and to assist in the delivery of high quality legal services to musicians, singers, songwriters, arrangers, producers and others, at a nominal cost.

Over a decade later, it is significant to have many of the original volunteer authors, now heads of movie studios, record companies and respected law firms, revising their articles, reaffirming their dedication to the CFTA mission. New articles have been contributed by a flock of young new volunteers, maintaining CFTA's thirteen year tradition of helping to "make music" by demystifying what sometimes seems like a maze of legal formalities.

Over a decade later, exciting technological advances such as compact discs, music videos, MIDI, DAT and sampling have brought forth exciting new trends in music styles. In such a volatile, rapidly changing industry, there is something reassuring in the publication of this new edition. This restatement of laws protecting Americans' rights to play their guitars and sing their songs, echoes the wisdom of the founding fathers, embodied in the U.S. Constitution. Then and there, the first American laws respecting the arts, including music, were promulgated, as vital constitutional guarantees, essential for a free thinking society to flourish. Then and there the seeds of our rich American heritage of jazz, blues and rock and roll took root and began to grow.

In one way or another, music benefits everyone in our society. From birthdays, graduations and weddings, to inaugurations and revolutions, music helps define who we are. Yet few people ever appreciate how difficult it is for a musician, singer or songwriter to make a living working at their craft. Little attention is given to the years of study and practice, the enormous expense of musical instruments and equipment, the problems and paradoxes of auditions, "showcasing" and recording demo tapes, and the continual rejection of potential music buyers.

Musicians' awareness of their legal rights helps protect the free expression of political and social ideas as well as musicians themselves. Many of the legal rights described in this book were not created and guaranteed out of friendship. Musicians and lawyers together organized and fought for these laws. By enforcing their rights, musicians and songwriters exercise a degree of control over their individual careers and music's place in our culture.

The public interest is well served by fostering in musical artists an awareness of laws governing their musical endeavors. Moreover, by providing access to affordable legal information we hope to reinforce musicians' constitutional right to sing songs and play guitars and protect against self-serving politicians who would muzzle this lyrical form of social commentary.

"Music is essentially useless," said Santayana, "as life is."

GREENBACK DOLLAR

Getting Started: Music As A Business

- Entertainment Group Names: Selection & Protection
- Business Entities
- How to Set Up a Money Deal
- Music Attorneys

Entertainment Group Names: Selection & Protection

By Stephen Bigger

The first rule in selecting a name for an entertainment group is a simple one: Be original. It can be very difficult to put this rule into practice, however. The field is a very crowded one. A brief check of a trade reference such as the *Billboard International Talent & Touring Directory* shows, for example, that there are two different groups called "Full Circle," two different groups called "Lost & Found," etc.

One reason why it is important to create an entirely new or different name is to avoid being sued for infringing someone else's name. Rights in a group name or a trademark usually derive from priority of use. This means that a prior group, even a small one, can successfully stop a new and more successful group from using the same name, at least in the area of the prior group's reputation. Another good reason for being original is that it will be easier to protect the name if you are the first one to use that name or a similar name. If you know that there is already a group called "The Sledgehammers," it would be a poor choice to call your group something like "The Sledgehammer Band."

SERVICE MARKS

A group name used for entertainment services is legally known as a service mark. What is the difference between a service mark and a trademark? A trademark is a brand name used for a product. A trademark can be a word, or a logo design, or both together. A service mark is also a brand name, but is used for services rather than for physical goods. A group name, since it is used for services rather than for goods, is a service mark. Can a service mark also be used as a trademark? Yes. For example, a group name can be used as a trademark for clothing such as T-shirts as well as for toys and games or other merchandising items. However, use of a group name as a service mark for entertainment services will not necessarily entitle you to use the same mark as a trademark for goods. Again, in the U.S., trademark and service mark rights are usually created by use and therefore, in order to create rights in a trademark for a product, it is usually necessary to use the mark by actually selling the product bearing the trademark to the public.

Although the owner of a trademark for a particular product or service generally cannot stop someone else from using the same or similar name on a completely different type of product or service, there is an exception for famous names or trademarks. It would not be a good idea to call your new group something like "Pepsi-Cola," since to do so would be inviting a lawsuit from the owners of this famous name. No one would confuse a bottle of rum with a diamond ring, but the owners of the famous Bacardi name for rum were able to stop someone else from using that name on jewelry. There are exceptions. For example, a group called "The Cadillacs" is listed in the *Billboard Directory.* Still, it is not a good idea to court lawsuits by trading on someone else's famous name.

A trademark for a record label can usually coexist with the same or similar name for an entertainment group, publishing company, talent agency and so forth without problems. For example, there is a Genesis record label and also a group by that name. It would be best, however, for a group to find a completely original name so that no confusion would exist between a record company or publishing company and that group name. There is the famous trademark exception: if someone were to adopt the name RCA or EMI or MCA for the name of their group, you can be sure that they would quickly find themselves on the wrong end of a lawsuit brought by the owner of a famous trademark.

In coining a group name, some special problems may arise if the name is going to be used together with the name of a star performer. If, for example, the star performer is named Lucky Starr and the backup group is called "The Sledgehammers," some thought should be given as to whether the star performer should have any rights in the group name or whether that name should belong separately to the group, whether or not they continue to perform with the star. A later section *Who Owns the Name?* also discusses this issue , as does the chapter "Group Breakups."

Until recently, it was not possible to obtain a federal service mark registration (which is granted by the U.S. Patent and Trademark Office) for the name of an individual performer. That was changed a few years ago when Johnny Carson was able to convince the Patent Office that he was entitled to register his name, but he was able to do so only upon proving that the name was used together with the words "in concert" in connection with entertainment services.

A common question is whether anyone can use his or her name as a performer, even if it conflicts with the name of someone else who has an earlier claim to fame. The answer is, not necessarily. If your name happens to be Neil Diamond, you would have a difficult time convincing a court that you were entitled to use that name as a singer in view of the likelihood of confusion with the famous Neil Diamond.

It's best for a group to find a completely original name so that no confusion will exist between a record company or publishing company and that group name.

RESEARCHING THE NAME

As soon as you have selected a name for the group, and before it is used, it is extremely important that a search be conducted to see whether the proposed name conflicts with any prior name. As mentioned above, rights in a group name or trademark usually derive from priority or use. Therefore, if a group prior to yours has used the same or a similar name, they are entitled to object to the use of the name by your group, at least for the area of their reputation.

Trade references that are easily checked include the American Federation of Musicians (AFM), the *Billboard International Talent & Touring Directory* (which has a section on performing artists), and a phonographic record directory, such as *Phonolog Reports*, which is published triweekly and includes a section on pop artists.

The AFM in New York will tell you over the telephone whether they currently have on file an exclusive agency contract for a group with the name you propose to use. The *Billboard Directory* is a fairly good listing of active performing groups, but it only includes those who wish to be listed (by responding to an annual questionnaire) and is not necessarily complete. A record album directory such as *Phonolog Reports* (available at some larger record stores) will list performing artists whose records are currently being sold.

In addition, a search should be conducted through a professional searching bureau to see whether the name has been registered as a trademark or service mark either with the U.S. Patent and Trademark Office in Washington, D.C. (federal registration) or in any one of the fifty states with the local Secretary of State (state registration). A comprehensive search by a professional searching bureau will cover the federal trademark register, all of the state trademark registers, and common law rights (that is, trademarks and names used but not necessarily registered) reflected in trade directories, etc. It is advisable to have the results of such a search reviewed by an attorney who is experienced in trademark law to give you some sense of the relative importance of the various references turned up in the search.

CREATING RIGHTS IN THE NAME

In the U.S., at least, rights in a group name, trademark or service mark are usually created by use and not by registration or any other kind of filing or claim. How can you "reserve" the name before you use it? It is now possible to do so in the U.S. by means of a federal "intent to use" trademark or service mark application (see the section titled *U.S. Trademark Registration*).

Reserving a name for incorporation with the Secretary of State of your particular state, registering the name with the AFM, or filing a fictitious business name statement will not create any rights in the name which you can enforce against a prior user of the same or a similar name.

The U.S. is a common law jurisdiction where you have trademark rights by using the mark quite apart from any statutory registration procedure. In other countries, it is a different story. Thus, in several European and Latin American countries, trademark rights are created solely by registration rather than use, a concept more fully discussed in the section *U.S. Trademark Registration*. The U.S. system is really designed to protect the "little guy" who has created some reputation in a name by using it even if he or she cannot afford to register the name. This positive aspect, whereby a prior user cannot lose their rights as long as they continue to use the name, in spite of any subsequent user who may be bigger or more famous, also includes a definite element of uncertainty. If your group is a newcomer, even if you conduct an extensive search, you cannot be absolutely certain that you are not infringing on the local rights of some other prior group that may be performing in some backwater. There is nothing you can do to dislodge the rights of such a group, provided that they continue to use the name and maintain some kind of public reputation.

What do you do if you search the name you wish to use for your group and find another group with the same or a similar name? At that point, you have two choices: (1) use a different name or (2) try to buy out the rights to the name from the prior group. What you should not do is ignore the rights of the prior group, even if you are about to sign a big recording contract and they have never recorded their music. To try to "roll over" a prior relatively unknown group because you are bigger, more famous, or better financed, could be a fatal mistake.

What if, on searching a proposed group name, you discover that there was a prior group of the same or similar name, but they are no longer performing? Do they still have any rights in the name? That depends on the circumstances. If the prior group still has some kind of "residual reputation," even though they are not currently performing, it could be very dangerous to go ahead and use the name without coming to terms with them, either by obtaining their permission to use the name or (preferably) an assignment of their rights. Rights in a group name, like other property rights, can be sold or transferred to someone else, even though such rights are not "physical" property.

A prior user cannot lose their rights as long as they continue to use the name, in spite of any subsequent user who may be bigger or more famous.

In a recent case involving the group name "The Buckinghams," the "residual reputation" of a group that had disbanded some five years ago was protected by the court. Although the group had not performed for that period of time, there was no intention by the group to abandon the name, and they continued to collect royalties from their records which were currently being sold. "The Buckinghams" were therefore entitled to stop another group from using the name, even though the prior group had stopped performing and making records.

Territoriality

Another basic concept in trademark and service mark law is that of "territoriality." In the entertainment area, this means that it is possible for two groups to operate under the same name in different parts of the country and for each of them to own the name in its own territory. Of course, everyone wants to own his own group name for the entire country, if not the entire world. However, if two separate groups, without knowledge of the other, independently adopt the same name, then both are entitled to use it in their respective territories. It is even possible for each of the parties to obtain a separate federal registration, with an appropriate limitation to the area of the group's reputation. If, however, you are aware of a group in another part of the country with the name you wish to use, then you cannot, without risking a lawsuit, use the name in the other group's territory, either by performing there, distributing records, or even engaging in advertising or other promotional activities for your group. Since every group hopes to be successful nationwide, and to perform and distribute records on a national basis, it makes no sense when starting out to pick a name used by another group even if the other group is purely local, unrecorded, and in a different part of the country. Further, if it can be shown that you were aware of the other group's name before you began use of the same name, and your adoption of the name was therefore not "innocent", a court may rule against your right to use the name even in your own territory, especially if the prior group is expanding or can show a likelihood of expansion into your territory.

Who Owns the Name?

After selecting the name and searching it, the next important step in protecting the name is to decide who is going to own it and to put this decision in writing. If you cannot afford a lawyer, confirm your agreement in writing. The basic agreement can be as simple as a signed and dated statement which says that if Tom, Dick, or Harry leaves the group, then the departing member will have no right to use the group name, which shall continue to be owned by the remaining members of the group. A simple agreement along these lines can help avoid complicated hassles and problems in the future.

Doesn't the person who thought up the name own it? No. Remember, the group name is like a brand name for a product. It identifies to the public the services provided by the group. Rights in the name are only created when it is used to create a public reputation. (With the single exception of a federal "intent to use" trademark or service mark application which must be validated by actual commercial use of the name before registration is granted.) If one member of the group thinks up the group name, that person individually does not "own" the name. Rather, the entity that actually uses the name ordinarily owns it, subject to some agreement to the contrary. It would be possible, although not usual, for some other party to own the group name, such as the manager of the group, the record company, or the financial backer. However, any such unusual ownership arrangement should be confirmed by an agreement in writing. If nothing is in writing to the contrary, the general assumption would be that the members of the group together own the group name and any one member leaving the group would have no further rights in the use of the name.

There are some interesting decisions in this area. In the "Rare Earth" case, a federal district court held that in the event of a group breakup where the group was organized as a corporation, the faction having working corporate control would prevail in a dispute over the right to use the name. In a Michigan state court decision involving "The Dramatics" name, the court held that upon dissolution, where a partnership made no advanced disposition of the group name, the group name became "the property of the partners in common and belongs to each of them with a right to use it in common, but not the exclusion of the other partners." In other words, after the breakup of the group, you could have three or four different individuals calling themselves "The Dramatics." Such a result seems in the interests of no one and points again to the advisability of have a written agreement as to the ownership of the group name at the outset.

Typically, a group first performing under a name will be a partnership so that each of the members of the group will own the group name in common. In other words, they will have the right to use the group name together, but not separately. The question of ownership can be simplified to some degree by having the members of the group form a corporation that will own the name. Then, if a federal registration is obtained in the name of the corporation, and one or more members leave the group, this will not affect the title to the registration.

The situation can also become complicated if you have a solo performer who is working with the group and the performer and the group use separate names. The solo performer may believe, if there is no agreement settling the point, that he

THE LITTLE GUY PREVAILS

THE FOLLOWING EXAMPLES OF HOW THE "LITTLE GUY" PREVAILED AGAINST LARGER AND BETTER FINANCED OPPONENTS IS A LESSON THAT SHOULD NEVER BE FORGOTTEN IN THE AREA OF GROUP NAMES AND THEIR PROTECTION.

In the landmark Bigfoot case, a large tire company knew of a smaller company on the West Coast that had been using the trademark Bigfoot. They very effectively wiped out the reputation of the smaller company by blitzing the media on a nationwide basis, so that by the time they were through, Bigfoot meant only one thing to the public and that was the tire sold by the larger company. When the case came before the court, it resulted in the largest award ever given in a U.S. trademark case: over $19,000,000 dollars in damages, in view of the deliberate infringement by the larger company of the smaller company's trademark rights. (In the trial court, there was a punitive damage award by the jury of $16,800,000 and an actual damage award of $2,800,000, both of which were upheld on post trial motions. However, on appeal, the higher court reduced the awards to something over $4,000,000 for punitive damages and $600,000 for actual damages.)

In a more recent decision, which cited the Bigfoot case, a court awarded $250,000 in damages to a little-known group called "The Rubberband", which had prior use and a federal registration and had objected to a later use of the name by the well-known group, "Bootsy's Rubber Band." The court noted that the later group's fame had effectively wiped out any reputation that the earlier group had, and held that the little-known group was entitled to receive all of the profits earned by the willful infringement of their name, although the newcomer was allowed to keep its name.

Another pertinent case, also in the entertainment area, concerned the right to use the group name "Flash." A California group by that name had performed in the San Francisco Bay Area but had never recorded an album. There was also an English group called "Flash" which had recorded with a major company. When the records bearing their group name were distributed in the San Francisco area, the unrecorded Bay Area group was able to stop the distribution of the record based on their prior use and reputation for that territory.

or she has some rights to the ownership of the group name. Imagine the situation where a solo performer named Lucky Starr and a backup group called "The Sledgehammers" perform together. They sign their first contract with a record company, and the record company designs a composite logo for the entire performing unit including the words "Lucky Starr & the Sledgehammers." Then the solo performer and the group together obtain a federal registration for the composite mark (including both names and the logo design). When the parties have a falling-out, you can imagine how difficult it might be to untangle the question of who owns what. Just how tangled this situation can become is humorously addressed in the chapter titled "Group Breakups."

On the question of ownership of the copyright in a logo design prepared, for example, by an artist hired by the record company, it would be advisable to have an agreement with the artist and the record company confirming that the ownership in the copyright for the logo design belongs to the group, or at least that the record company makes no claim to the words which are included in the logo design. Otherwise, if there is a falling-out between the record company and the group, the record company may claim that they own the logo design. Generally, the fact that the record company's artist designed the logo would not give them any ownership rights in the name, since the group would own the name in whatever form it is depicted.

If one member of the group thinks up the group name, that person individually does not "own" the name. Rather, the entity that actually uses the name ordinarily owns it, subject to some agreement to the contrary.

U.S. TRADEMARK REGISTRATION

Although trademark rights are usually created and must be maintained by use rather than by registration, it is advisable to register a trademark. State trademark registrations are obtained with the local Secretary of State and a federal registration may be obtained at the U.S. Patent and Trademark Office in Washington, D.C. The rights conferred by federal registration are so much wider than those afforded by a state registration that normally a federal registration, which covers the entire country, would be the only registration of the group name that you would want and need.

Under a new provision of the U.S. Federal Trademark Law effective November 16, 1989, it is now possible to "reserve" a name in advance of any actual commercial use by filing an "intent to use" trademark or service mark application for federal registration - so long as there is a bona fide intention to use the mark on the specific goods or services covered by the application. The simple filing of such an application will create superior rights in the name, even if some other party begins later use of the same or a similar name before the applicant begins commercial use. For this reason, it is now <u>very</u> important to <u>search</u> a group name to see whether a federal application for registration might have been filed for the same or a similar name (even in the absence of any public use by the applicant) which may bar the use of a new group name. The filing of such a federal "intent to use" trademark or service mark application must be validated by filing evidence of actual commercial use of the name before the registration is granted. If such evidence of actual commercial use is not filed within a period of up to approximately four years after the filing of such an application, the application will be declared invalid.

A federal trademark or service mark registration provides very important procedural rights in court (i.e., rights having to do with how and where you can bring a lawsuit), including the right to sue for trademark infringement in federal district court, and an arsenal of procedural weapons that can be used against an infringer, including extensive discovery procedures (which allow you to discover the evidence and information available to the other side in a lawsuit). Significantly, a federal registration also provides "constructive notice," so that any subsequent user of the same or a similar name is deemed to have knowledge of your rights. Someone with constructive notice cannot claim that he innocently adopted the name and is entitled to use it notwithstanding your prior registration. Only a federal registration entitles the owner to use the ® symbol denoting a federally registered mark.

The ™ symbol is unofficial and without any legal meaning or definition under federal or state statutes. It has been used on an optional basis to indicate a claim to trademark ownership for an unregistered trademark. Sometimes the ™ symbol is used to indicate a service mark. It is not essential to use either symbol and, in fact, their use is not especially popular in the entertainment world. It is advisable to use the ® symbol if you have a federally registered mark since it puts other parties on actual notice of your federal registration and may affect the question of damages in suing an infringer (i.e. whether the damages should be counted from the beginning of the infringement or later on when the infringer is notified in writing by you or your lawyer).

Registration Procedure

The procedure for obtaining a federal trademark or service mark registration begins with the filing of an application for registration with the U.S. Patent and Trademark Office in Washington, D.C. Before that application can be filed, it is necessary to have use of the mark in interstate commerce (that is, commerce across state lines) - or to base the application on a bona fide "intent to use" the mark on the goods or services specified in the application (which must later be validated in actual commercial use of the mark before registration is granted). This requirement of use in interstate commerce for a federal application is met if there is a public performance by the group under the group name in a place that attracts an interstate clientele or where the group performance is advertised in a newspaper or publication which crosses state lines. If based on pre-application use, a federal application also requires the submission of specimens showing the use of the name, and these usually would be in the form of advertisements or promotional materials for the public performance of the group. The Patent Office usually will not accept album covers bearing the group name as specimens of use for entertainment services. This seems a very narrow view, but it has been established practice at the Patent Office for some time. (Someday, someone, I hope, will challenge this practice by an appeal to the Trademark Trial and Appeal Board or the courts, and win.)

If no special problems are encountered, it usually takes about one year to obtain a federal registration after filing the application. The application procedure is in two stages. The first stage involves an official examination by the Patent Office both for registrability of the mark and for any prior registrations for similar marks, which may be cited against the new application as barring registration. The second stage is the opposition period, during which the application is published in the *U.S. Official Gazette* and may be opposed by any party wishing to do so within a term of thirty days following the publication date. *The U.S. Official Gazette* (Trademark Section) is issued weekly and may be ordered by writing the Superintendent of Documents, Government Printing Office, Washington, D.C. 20402.

The cost of obtaining a federal registration without any special problems is a few hundred dollars, including official filing fees and legal fees. If an application is opposed by a determined adversary, the defense of the application is tantamount to fighting a lawsuit in federal court, including discovery under the federal rules of civil procedure (whereby both sides can interrogate and find out information and evidence held by the other side). This could cost several thousand dollars. The applicant, of course, has the option of defending against the opposition or simply withdrawing the application without incurring any additional expense.

After a federal registration is obtained, it is necessary to continue use of the name in order to preserve the validity of the registration. A federal registration may be canceled for abandonment of the name, and the statute provides that two years' nonuse constitutes *prima facie* (that is, a legally sufficient case on its face) abandonment. Further, it is necessary after the fifth anniversary of the registration to file an affidavit confirming that the use of the name has been continued. At the same time, it is highly advisable to also file an affidavit of incontestability, provided that the name has been used continuously for the past five years, which will make the registration incontestable (meaning, it cannot be canceled by someone else based on a prior registration or on a claim of prior use). Renewal of the registration is also required every ten years.

Foreign Registration

Generally, you will want to go to the expense of foreign registration only for those countries where you have some real commercial interest either now or in the future. The first country which comes to mind is Canada. Many groups starting out will search the name in the U.S. and Canada at the same time, and if the name is clear, file in both countries.

The U.S. is a member country of the Paris Convention, the "magna carta" of the international patent and trademark field. It is possible under this convention to file foreign applications within a six-month term following the filing of a U.S. application, claiming the priority date of the U.S. application. This can be very helpful for a new group that becomes famous overnight, and is faced with infringements in other countries where other parties try to register the name before the new group has had the opportunity to get applications on file. Foreign applications must be filed sometime within the six-month convention priority term to claim the U.S. priority date. Applications filed after the term expires will not be entitled to do so.

If your urge is to own the group name worldwide, you will no doubt be sobered by the fact that there are approximately 175 trademark jurisdictions in the world. The cost of registering the name as a trademark or service mark in all of these jurisdictions, without any special problems, could easily cost something like $150,000. If you run into Patent Office or third-party objections, the cost could easily escalate to over $200,000. Further, in these 175 or so jurisdictions, only about sixty countries provide for the registration of service marks, which is what you really want, rather than a trademark registration. Some rather important countries including Japan, Ireland, and Switzerland have no provisions for the registration of service marks. In these countries, you can only register a trademark for a product. It is expected that in the near future legislation will be approved providing for service mark registration in Japan and Ireland.

Further, a significant number of countries, particularly those in Latin America and Europe (such as France, Germany, Italy, and Spain) are among the "first to file" countries, where trademark and service mark rights derive basically from registration rather than from use. In other words, the first to register the name is the one to own it. The exception is for the famous name (famous if it can be proven by evidence of local reputation), which, under the Paris Convention, may be entitled to special protection in the country concerned even in the absence of registration.

What happens if someone else has filed first in a country like France for your group name, and you then try to perform or sell records in that country? The answer is that the owner of the registration would be entitled to stop you from performing in France under that name, <u>and,</u> chances are, from selling records bearing the group name as well. In other words, in a country like France, if you do not own a registration, you do not own the name.

Prior use is not required for filing trademark or service mark applications in most foreign countries. In some countries, such as Canada and Australia, and more recently the U.S., an application can be filed either on the basis of prior use or proposed use. It is therefore possible to reserve a name in foreign countries by filing a trademark or service mark application, even before you use the name. However, many of these countries also have user requirements after registration, so that if you do not use the name for a certain period of time after registration, your registration may be subject to cancellation for nonuse.

MINIMUM PROTECTION: DOING IT YOURSELF

If your group is starting out on a shoestring budget and you cannot afford a lawyer, you can still take some of the most important steps in selecting and protecting the group name.

First, you can engage in some minimal searching which will entail little or no expense, including telephoning the AFM and checking the pop artists section in the *Phonolog Reports* which you may be able to find in a local record store. You can also check the *Billboard Directory* to see if there are names listed which are the same or similar to yours. Further, you may be able to check an annual publication called *The Trademark Register* which lists all federal registrations currently in force in an abbreviated fashion, by class. The classes you should check are International Class 41, which covers entertainment services, and the prior U.S. Class 107. *The Trademark Register* may be ordered by writing that publication at the National Press Building, Suite 1297, Washington, D.C. 20045. Some larger libraries carry this as a reference work.

You can make an informal survey of people you know in the entertainment area to see whether they have heard of any name which is the same or similar to the one you propose to use. You could order a search report directly from a professional searching bureau at a cost of approximately $200 for a comprehensive search covering federal and state registrations and common law rights, or something like $100 for a more limited search restricted to the federal register. It is advisable to have a trademark lawyer review such a search. Professional searching bureaus are listed in the telephone yellow pages under "Trademark Agents" or "Trademark Consultants."

After you have satisfied yourself as best you can that the use of the proposed name will not infringe on the rights of some other group, the most important thing you can do is to go ahead and use the name publicly so that you create rights in the name. Keep a careful record of the performance places, dates and publicity, so that you can, if necessary, prove that you used the name, in what territory and for how long. It is also helpful in protecting the name to use it consistently and with some continuity. If the name is unused for a period of time so that you no longer have a public reputation in the name, then you will have lost your rights in the name.

Stand up for your rights once you have used the name, notwithstanding any "big" group that comes along later on and tries to bluff you into discontinuing the name because they are famous and you are not.

Finally, you can stand up for your rights once you have used the name, notwithstanding any "big" group that comes along later on and tries to bluff you into discontinuing the name because they are famous and you are not. Remember the Bigfoot case and the Flash decision mentioned earlier. Do not let your group be pushed around if, in fact, you are the prior user. As the prior user, you have superior rights, at least for the area of your reputation, and you can enforce them against any subsequent user no matter how big or how famous.

MAXIMUM PROTECTION

Even if you have just become famous and have signed a big recording contract, you will want to decide how extensively you should protect the group name by way of registration. Of the 175 or so foreign trademark jurisdictions, you will want to focus on the 60 or so jurisdictions where service marks can be registered for entertainment services. Of these, the dozen or so most important foreign service mark registration jurisdictions would include: Australia, the Benelux area, Brazil, Canada, France, Great Britain, Germany, Italy, Mexico, South Africa, Spain, Denmark, Finland, Norway, and Sweden.

You can also get trademark registrations in the other jurisdictions (such as Ireland, Japan, and Switzerland), where service mark registrations are not available, covering merchandising items such as T-shirts, toys and games or whatever. Generally, however, it is not worthwhile to spend the money on trademark registrations for merchandising items unless you have a real commercial interest in merchandising the name in those jurisdictions. Many of these countries have user requirements, so that a registration is subject to cancellation for five years' nonuse (or some lesser period). That includes countries such as Japan, Ireland, Switzerland and several others. In other words, if you obtain a registration for your name covering T-shirts, and you do not use the mark in the jurisdiction, your registration may become subject to attack after five years nonuse.

If, on the other hand, you intend to merchandise the group name actively, then it is highly advisable to obtain trademark registrations for the merchandising items, especially in those jurisdictions where trademark rights derive from registration rather than from use. Otherwise, without a trademark registration for the goods concerned, you really have nothing to license to another party who will be manufacturing the goods and selling them in the local jurisdiction. The chapter "Merchandising in the Music Industry" discusses this issue more fully.

You may also want to consider "defensive merchandising" registering the mark for merchandising items, simply to prevent someone else from doing so. For example, a famous performer may not wish to merchandise his or her name in order to sell T-shirts or whatever, but may be plagued by unscrupulous persons who capitalize on the name by emblazoning it on T-shirts anyway. The famous performer has two choices in these cases. He or she can ignore the infringements or try to stop them.

The most effective way of stopping infringements of this kind is to register the name for merchandising items and then license the name on a selective basis in order to create trademark rights in the area of most active infringements. A recent case in point is that of the unauthorized sale of T-shirts in Great Britain bearing the group name "Abba." In that case, the merchandising company representing the famous Swedish group was not able to stop the sale of the unauthorized T-shirts, since they were being sold by the first user, notwithstanding the fact that they had no connection or authorization from the famous group. The English court indicated that the fame of the Abba name for entertainment services in Great Britain (where at the time service marks were not yet registrable) was not enough to entitle the group or its merchandising company to a perpetual right to use the name on T-shirts as against some unauthorized party who was the first user of the name on the goods in the jurisdiction.

There is some question, by the way, whether the use of a group name on the front of a T-shirt is, in fact, trademark use. It would be better, from the standpoint of trademark protection, if the group name were also to appear on the neck label to indicate that it is the brand name for the shirt itself, since otherwise an infringer may be able to claim that the use of the group name only on the front of the shirt is an ornamental use (which anyone can use) and therefore not a "trademark" use (which only the trademark owner is entitled to use or authorize). Also, the addition of the "TM" symbol to the group name shown on the front of the shirt may be helpful to show that trademark rights are being claimed.

Finally, a maximum approach to protection of a group name should certainly include some kind of system for watching for infringements of the name. There are services available which provide surveillance of trademark journals where applications are published for opposition purposes in something like 150 countries. These services are typically called "Trademark Surveillance Services." Costs average $200 per year for surveillance on an international basis. In this way, you will be informed of someone in Peru or France or Sweden who files to appropriate the group name for entertainment services or merchandising items or whatever and you will have the opportunity to oppose the applications or cancel the resulting registration before it can be used to damage or block your rights in the name in that country.

Business Entities

By Edward R. Hearn

There are mainly three forms of business that can be used to organize your music business affairs. These are (1) sole proprietorship (a single self-employed individual running the business); (2) partnership (two or more self-employed people running the business); and (3) corporation (which can be owned by one or more individuals and is organized under specific state laws). Each of these forms has special features that should be examined when making a decision about how to organize your business. These features include, among others, expenses, personal liability, and taxes. You should seek professional advice to determine the best form for your particular situation before investing too much time and money in your enterprise. The cost of planning in advance to minimize problems is much less than the cost of trying to cure those problems after they have materialized.

SOLE PROPRIETORSHIP

A sole proprietorship is a business conducted by one individual who is the sole owner. If you have your own business for the purpose of making money, whether by making or selling records, writing and publishing songs, operating a recording studio or performing solo, you have a proprietorship business, and this material applies to you.

A proprietorship is the simplest form of business to start because it generally requires no contracts (contracts require at least two people) and only a few special papers have to be prepared. These papers include a fictitious business name statement, commonly called a DBA ("doing business as"), which identifies you as the owner by your name and address and the name under which the proprietor is doing business (see the sample DBA at the end of this chapter). Note, however, that a DBA need only be filed if you use a name other than your own to do business. That statement must be filed with the county recorder located in your local county court house. After filing with the county recorder, you must publish a legal notice statement of your doing business. You can inquire at your county recorder's office to find out which local newspapers publish the notices and have the least expensive legal notice rates. Certain local governments may require the proprietor to obtain a separate business license or that license may be covered by the fictitious business name filing. Your county recorder's office can fill you in on this.

If you resell goods, you will need a resale permit issued by the appropriate tax authority. This is discussed later in this chapter in the section titled *General Obligations as a Business.*

You, as the sole proprietor, are the only one who makes decisions on how the business should operate and what its focus should be. With a proprietorship, you enjoy all the profits, but must absorb all the losses. Employees do not participate in the ownership. A proprietor who has employees must withhold income and social security taxes, unemployment, and other insurances required by state and federal law and must submit the withheld sums to the appropriate government collecting agent. While a proprietorship usually has fewer regulatory and record-keeping requirements than a partnership or corporation, the ones on which you must focus are the reports to be filed with the local, state, and federal taxing authorities. If you are going to start your own proprietorship and hire employees, be certain to contact each of those authorities to obtain the required forms and instructional booklets that tell you what to do. Frequently, a good bookkeeper or accountant will be able to assist you with that part of your business. These requirements are discussed in more detail later in this chapter.

As a proprietorship, you are responsible for your acts and, in general, the acts of your employees. If, for example, you or one of your employees should injure someone in a car accident while promoting your record to radio stations, you would be responsible to compensate the injured party. A judgement against you would enable the judgement creditor (the person who won the suit and to whom you owe the money) to look to all your assets, both business and personal, to recover on the judgement.

Business creditors must exhaust all of the property and money of the partnership before they can look to your car, stereo, or instrument, and the person you still owe for the car, stereo, or instrument has to be paid before the business creditor can claim any of these prized items.

The entire income of a proprietor, assuming there is no loss, is taxable income, while business expenses and losses are deductible from income. Proprietors, as self-employed, must file quarterly estimated income tax returns and make prepayment of anticipated taxes with the Internal Revenue Service and the state taxing authorities. The estimated tax is based on a projection of expected income during your first year of business and thereafter on your prior years taxes. You should consult an accountant who has a tax orientation to assist you in these matters.

PARTNERSHIPS

Assuming that your band of one, or your one-person record or publishing company has grown to two or more people who share the profits and losses, and you plan to stay in business for a while, you now have a partnership. A partnership is defined as an association of two or more persons conducting a business on a continuing a basis as co-owners for profit. The relationship among the partners usually is governed by a written partnership agreement that details the rights and responsibilities of each partner. Although you do not need a written contract to be considered a partnership, obtaining a written partnership agreement is recommended. If there is no written partnership agreement, then state statutes control the relations of the partners with each other. The partners can be individuals, other partnerships, corporations, or a combination of each. Each partner contributes property, services, and/or money to the business of the partnership. Partners also may loan property, money, or services to the partnership.

General Partnership

In a partnership, each of the partners has an undivided interest in all of the partnership property. Essentially, each partner owns the assets in common with the other partners and has a duty to each of the other partners to take care of that property and not to dispose of it without the consent of the other partners.

Each person who is a partner may act on behalf of the partnership and that act binds all of the partners in the partnership. Each person in the partnership is liable for the business obligations of the partnership incurred by any of the partners. In other words, if your partner signs a business commitment to pay for advertising for the business, you as a partner are responsible with the other partners for making payment. On contract actions, the creditor can sue all of the partners, but cannot single out any one partner to sue exclusive of the others. A tort claim (inflicting harm on another person or property) for injuries is different. If, for example, a partner runs a car through a record store display window while delivering records in the normal course of partnership business, each partner is severally (individually) liable and the store owner could sue any individual partner or all the partners in the partnership.

The personal assets of the partners can be taken by the creditors of the business, but only after all of the partnership assets have been taken and the personal creditors of the individual partners have satisfied their claims out of the partners' personal assets. For example, the business creditors must exhaust all of the property and money of the partnership before they can look to your car, stereo, or instrument, and the person you still owe for the car, stereo, or instrument has to be paid before the business creditor can claim any of these prized items. Some States' laws will allow certain "necessary" property of the debtor to be exempt from creditor's claims, such as food and clothing.

Death or withdrawal of a partner (or some other specified event set out in a partnership agreement) will dissolve the partnership. By written agreement, however, the partners can provide that the partnership will continue despite a partner's death or withdrawal. In that case the agreement establishes distribution rules to determine how the departing partner is to be compensated (this is called a buy out) and how the partnership is to continue without the deceased or withdrawn partner.

As with a proprietorship, a partnership must file a fictitious business name statement (if all the partners' surnames are not in the partnership name) and publish a doing-business statement in a local county newspaper. You also must file a form SS-4 with the Internal Revenue Service to obtain an employer identification tax number <u>even if you do not employ anybody</u>. These forms can be obtained by writing your regional Internal Revenue Service center. The performing rights organizations, such as BMI, ASCAP, and SESAC, ask publisher members to include their employer identification tax numbers on their membership applications. You also must secure any local licenses or permits required.

In a general partnership, all of the partners participate in the control of the business. Partners may agree among themselves to assign specific duties to each other according to ability. Voting on business decisions may be equal, or may be weighted according to capital contribution (money and property contributed to making the partnership work), or on some other basis.

The profits, losses, and risks are shared equally among the partners unless they agree to a different division.

At income tax time, the partnership files an informational tax return, describing losses or profits, but the partnership itself pays no taxes. Rather, the losses or profits are passed through to the individual partners for reporting on their individual tax returns (thus, a partnership is often described as a tax conduit) and again, unless the agreement provides otherwise, losses or profits are shared equally. As with a proprietorship, the partners must file quarterly returns and personal income tax prepayments.

On dissolution of the partnership, the assets of the partnership are liquidated (turned into cash) and the creditors of the partnership are paid first. The balance of the liquidated assets, if any, is distributed to the partners, first to cancel any loans of each of the partners to the partnership, secondly to return any money or assets contributed by the partners, and finally to the partners according to how they share profits.

Joint Venture

A joint venture is a form of business relationship consisting of an association of two or more persons, partnerships, or corporations or some combination thereof, for the purpose of accomplishing a single or limited series of business transactions for profit rather than carrying on a continuous business. A venture is a partnership with respect to all the applicable rules discussed above and the terms of the relationship should be governed by a written agreement. Examples of a musical joint venture include recording a single album project, producing one (1) video, or promoting a concert.

Limited Partnership

A limited partnership is another form of partnership that functions as a financing vehicle to raise capital to fund identified business goals. A limited partnership consists of a least two people, corporations or partnerships, or some combination thereof. A limited partnership requires at least one general partner, whether a person, another partnership, or a corporation, and one or more limited partners as investors. The limited partners contribute capital but take no part in the management of the business and have no liability beyond the amount of money that each of them contributed to the partnership. Should a limited partner become involved in the management of the business then he or she would lose this limited liability status. Generally, the limited partnership is for an established duration and must be set out in a written limited partnership agreement. State and federal securities laws regulating investments apply to limited partnerships and a discussion of these laws is addressed in the chapter entitled "How To Set Up A Money Deal."

CORPORATIONS

At some point in your career, you may decide that it is time to incorporate, either because you have reached a high income level, or because you wish to protect your personal assets from the claims of your business creditors. Frequently, successful entertainers form what in the business is known as a "loan-out" corporation. In other words, you have yourself incorporated and that corporation agrees

WHEN THERE ARE NO WRITTEN PARTNERSHIP AGREEMENTS

An issue frequently raised by bands is how to structure the business arrangements among the members of the band. Whenever two or more musicians get together and form a band, they have formed a general partnership. While it is important at some point to have a written agreement, most struggling bands cannot afford to hire a lawyer to prepare an agreement for them. If this is the case, it is important for the members of the band to work out their answers among themselves. Communicate with each other. Seek professional help. Don't be afraid to follow your instincts on what seems fair and reasonable to you. A good issue on which to focus is to determine at what point your band should make an effort to have a written agreement. It is far less expensive to plan your business properly in the beginning before problems arise, than it is to resolve those problems after the fact, especially if the resolution takes the form of expensive litigation. If you cannot reach an agreement, maybe that is a sign you should not be in business together. Given this problem, here are some issues to focus on.

Legal Presumptions

If the members of a band have formed a partnership by working together but do not have a written agreement, then generally the state statutes presume that certain conditions apply to the band's arrangements. These conditions are that each partner: (a) has an equal vote in the affairs of the partnership and a majority vote determines the decision of the partners; (b) owns an equal share in the assets of the partnership, which includes equipment purchased by the band, and the name of the band, and income rights; (c) shares equally in the profits and losses of the partnership; and (d) is responsible for the acts of all of the other partners performed in pursuing the partnership business. If a partner, for example, delivers the band's independently produced record to record stores for sale and in the course of making a delivery has a car accident, then all of the partners are liable for any damages.

Leaving Members

When there is no written agreement and a partner leaves the partnership, willingly or at the demand of the other partners, then the band's partnership terminates automatically. The band has a responsibility to pay all of the debts of the partnership and if necessary to sell the partnership's assets to do so. If thereafter, the remaining members of the partnership wish to continue performing as a band they may, but in effect they form a new partnership and start over again. If the band's creditors cooperate, you usually are able to avoid having to liquidate the band's assets so long as the remaining band members continue paying the creditors. You need to work out with the departing member their continuing responsibility to make payments owed or to receive payments due.

Taxes

The partnership does not pay taxes on income earned by the band. Instead, the band files an informational tax return on Federal Partnership Return of Income, Form 1065, wherein each partner states his or her distributive share of income or loss. Then each partner lists that share of income or loss on their individual tax returns filed by April 15 of each year. The amount of loss or profit is then added or subtracted from other sources of income.

PARTNERSHIPS: CRITICAL WRITTEN AGREEMENTS

Acquisition of Property

The band acquires expensive property, such as sound or lighting system. The band and each of its individual members assume a share of that system's cost. Each partner should be aware of their payment responsibilities and what happens if somebody leaves the band. For example, will the departing member have to continue to make payment or will they be relieved of that responsibility? Do the remaining members of the band have any obligation to pay the departing members some value for the equipment based on the market value of the equipment or the share of money paid by the departing member if the band is going to keep that equipment.

Name

The band is becoming well-known and its name is recognizable to a large audience. Who will have the rights in the name of the band if the band should break up, or individual members should leave the band? The partnership agreement generally states that the group as a whole owns the name. A provision should be included in the agreement that if any member leaves the group, whether voluntarily or otherwise, that member surrenders the right to use the band name, which will stay with the remaining members of the group. Any incoming member would have to acknowledge in writing that the name of the band does belong to the partnership and that the new member does not own any rights in the band's name greater than their partners' interests.

If a group should completely disband, then the partnership agreement could provide that none of the band members may use the name or that any one of the members could buy from the other partnership members the right to use the name at a value to be established, for example, by binding arbitration with expert testimony concerning the valuation of the band's name if the members cannot agree among themselves. The other members of the now defunct band would then abandon any further right to use the name. Negotiating the issue after a band breaks up, however, could be very difficult if the members are not cooperative or are not on good terms with each other.

When a group disbands but its product still sells, most likely no former member will be allowed to use the band's name in forming a new group.

Leaving Members

If the band is going to sign contracts that will last for a long period of time, such as recording or publishing agreements, there are certain rights of departing and new band members under those agreements concerning services already performed or commitments that still have to be met. Determining how to resolve those issues is generally less costly before the fact than after.

Song Rights

Can the departing member take their songs when they leave the group? If the songs were co-written with remaining band members, the band can continue to use the songs and record them, as can the departing member, but each will have to report to the other their share of income earned from such usages. If the departing member is the sole author of certain compositions, that could prevent the band from recording them if they had not already been released on commercially distributed phonorecords, and from performing them if they had not been licensed to a performing rights society like BMI or ASCAP. Sometimes bands will form a publishing company as part of the asset of the partnership, the terms of which will control what happens when a writer member leaves the band, but usually the band will continue to be able to use the songs, and likely the departing member will be able to also.

THE CASE OF DEEP PURPLE

An example of the issues involved when a group disbands but its product still sells involved the group "Deep Purple," which has not been performing as a band for many years. Its records, however, still sell. Recently, one of the original members of that band formed a new group. None of the other members of that new group had been members of "Deep Purple" except that original member.

This new group began to perform under the name "Deep Purple." The corporation owned by the members of "Deep Purple" when they broke up and their management still owned the rights to the name "Deep Purple." They sued the new "Deep Purple" to stop them from performing under that name and were awarded damages of $672,000; $168,000 of that sum was for what is known as compensatory damages (that is, actual damages suffered by the corporation) and the remaining $504,000 was for punitive damages.

to make your services available to other parties (for example, record companies) in any particular deal.

What does it mean to be a corporation? Corporations differ substantially from proprietorships and partnerships. A corporation is an artificial, separate, legal entity recognized by state law, the formation of which is regulated by procedures established by state law. Ownership of a corporation is obtained by buying shares of stock for value. A corporation can be owned by one or more persons (including a partnership) or other corporations. A corporation can be owned privately (the stock is not traded on the stock market) or publicly (with the corporation's stock being sold on the stock market and being held by the public at large).

The corporation is a separate legal entity with a life apart from the persons who own and operate it. Corporations raise capital by selling shares for a sum of dollars. The issuance of shares in the corporation is a security subject to state and, under some circumstance, federal securities laws. Like an individual or a partnership, a corporation can own, buy, or sell property in its own name, enter into contracts, borrow money, raise capital, and do the various kinds of activities that a proprietorship or a partnership can do.

The corporation is governed by a board of directors elected by the shareholders. In turn, the corporation is managed by officers (such as a president and treasurer) who are employees of the corporation hired by the board of directors. In loan-out corporations, the officers and directors usually are the individuals who form the corporation and who are the shareholders. If the corporation was formed by one person, then that person usually holds all of the officer positions and is the sole director.

Risks of the business are borne by the corporation. The shareholders' liabilities are limited to the amounts invested in the corporation. The investments are usually evidenced by issued shares (or stock).

The corporation must file annual tax returns and pay taxes on profits. After taxes, profits can be retained for operating capital or distributed to shareholders as dividends, which are taxable to shareholders as income. Profits are shared among shareholders in proportion to their ownership participation. There is no passing of profits and losses from a corporation to the individual owners of shares except for a Chapter S corporation.

With a Chapter S corporation, the shareholders get the benefits of a partnership by passing profits and losses through to the shareholders for tax purposes, while retaining the benefit of the corporation's limited liability status. Losses passed through to the shareholders cannot exceed amounts invested by the shareholders.

The corporation is brought into existence by filing a document known as the articles of incorporation (or charter or articles of association in some states), the filing of which, for example costs approximately $100 in California, plus a prepayment of an annual minimum franchise tax payment, currently $600 and scheduled to increase to $900 in 1990. Other states have similar fees that range in amount from state to state. Forming a corporation, however, will cost more than this because of attorney's fees. In addition, there may be local fees for permits and business licenses.

With publicly held companies, shares of such companies generally are transferable from one owner to a subsequent owner on the open market. With nonpublic corporations, there is no ready market for the shares and the shareholders generally have to seek out specific buyers. Also, the law restricts the sale of shares, and requires that certain procedures established by state and federal statutes be followed before the shares can be sold. This is a complex area that requires professional counsel on securities, tax, and accounting issues and is too involved a topic to examine in this chapter. You should be aware that these are considerations that require some attention and you need professional counsel when it comes time for you to focus on them.

The rules that govern the operation of the corporation are known as the bylaws and are adopted at the beginning of the life of the corporation. Generally, the officers of the corporation are empowered to operate the daily affairs of the corporation, subject to approval or disapproval by the board of directors, who in turn answer to the shareholders. The board of directors will hold periodic meetings to review the acts of the officers. The shareholders will hold periodic meetings to review the board of directors.

Voting among shareholders is based on the number of shares owned - generally one vote per share. Shareholders are sometimes divided into different classes. Some classes of shares may be nonvoting. Some corporations' bylaws provide for "cumulative" voting for the directors of the board. In other words, a shareholder can multiply the number of his or her shares (e.g. 100 out of 500) by the number of board positions (e.g. 3) and apply all of the total (e.g. 300) to one candidate on the board, and thereby insure placing a representative on the board.

The corporation's existence is perpetual unless the shareholders vote to terminate the corporation or the corporation cannot continue financially. On dissolution, creditors, such as banks, trade creditors, employees, and taxing bodies, are paid first, and then shareholders receive a return on capital (that is, they get back what they paid for their shares), and, finally, a distribution of profits, if any.

The need to get professional counsel when you begin your own business cannot be stressed too strongly. Your lawyer or accountant will help you determine which form will be best for your situation and thereafter will monitor the operation of your business to determine whether you should switch to another form as your needs change.

LEGAL OBLIGATIONS OF EMPLOYERS AND OF BUSINESS

As an individual involved in the music business, you may find it necessary or advisable to hire others to work for you. If you hire employees you must satisfy certain obligations imposed on employers by state and federal laws. This section briefly identifies those obligations and also identifies other concerns of which you should be aware in running a business. In any event, if you start your own business and hire others as employees, consult with an attorney or accountant, or at least with the appropriate government officials to make certain that the federal and state laws regarding wages, benefits, hours, compensation, insurance, taxes, licenses, and other matters are satisfied.

Employer's Tax Obligations

Becoming an employer imposes a host of form-filling and form-filing obligations, some of which are described here. One of the first things an employer must do is to obtain an employer identification number from the Internal Revenue Service. This number must be shown on all federal tax returns, statements, and other documents. Application for this number is made on form SS-4, which may be obtained from your local IRS office. The completed form SS-4 must be filed with your local IRS office.

Generally, employers must withhold federal income and social security taxes as well as state income taxes from the wages paid to their employees. Call or write your nearest IRS office and the local office of your state taxing bureau to obtain the necessary information on the procedures for withholding such taxes.

The employer must have all employees complete the employee withholding allowance certificate (form W-4). If the employee had no federal income tax liability for the preceding year and anticipates no liability for the current year, the employee withholding exemption certificate form W-4E should be completed. The form should be returned to your local IRS office. Based on the information contained in the W-4 forms and in tax tables (which should be included in the information you receive from the federal and state taxing authorities) you will be able to determine the amount of income and social security taxes to be withheld from each wage payment and the amount of the employer's matching contributions for social security taxes.

The withheld income and social security taxes are deposited along with federal tax deposit form 501 at the authorized commercial bank depository or the federal reserve bank in your area. The deposits are required on a semimonthly, monthly, or quarterly basis, depending on the amount of the tax involved. Further, a return form 941, which describes the amounts withheld, must be filed on a quarterly basis.

The employer must furnish to each employee two copies of the annual wage and tax statement form W-2 for the calendar year no later than January 31 following the end of the calendar tax year. If the service of the employee is terminated before the end of the year the form W-2 must be submitted to the employee not later than thirty days after the last payment of wages to that employee. This form W-2 is an informational one for the purpose of advising the employee how much was withheld and may be combined with state and city withholding statements. It must be used by the employee in filing annual income tax returns.

It is important to remember that if you are the person responsible for withholding taxes on behalf of employees (yourself or others), you may become personally liable for a 100% penalty on the amount that should have been withheld for your failure to comply with these obligations.

Note also that the employer may be subject to federal and state unemployment taxes and to withholding on state disability insurance taxes. You should consult your accountant or the local office of the IRS, the state unemployment compensation bureau, and the state disability insurance office to find out the details on unemployment taxes and disability insurance. Generally, the procedures for withholding money on these programs are similar to those for withholding federal and state income taxes and social security taxes.

If you hire someone as an independent contractor, who will be responsible for making their own tax payments, then it should be clear that that person is operating their own business, has been retained by you to perform a service, is not under your control or direction, and will be performing the same or similar services for others. Also, you should file a Form 1099 with the IRS by February 28th of each year identifying the independent contractor and the amount paid for the services. Examples of independent contractors include: a sound person to set up and engineer the sound for a showcase concert; a producer to oversee and produce a sound recording of the masters for your albums; an arranger to arrange your original compositions to be recorded for your album.

Other Employer Obligations

Most employers are subject to state workers' compensation laws. These laws impose liability on the employer for industrial accidents sustained by employees regardless of the employer's negligence and provide a schedule of benefits to be paid to the employees for injuries or to their heirs if the employees are killed in an accident. It is important that you obtain sufficient workers' compensation liability insurance from an authorized insurer or a certificate of consent from your state's director of industrial relations if you are going to self-insure. Generally, insurance coverage may be obtained through the local office of your state's compensation insurance fund or may be placed with a licensed workers' compensation private carrier.

Both state and federal laws impose minimum obligations on the employer concerning wages, hours, and working conditions. You can obtain detailed information on these obligations by contacting the Department of Labor, Department of

Industrial Welfare or Department of Industrial Relations in your state as well as the Department of Labor for the federal government. Both state and federal laws impose obligations on the employer to refrain from discrimination in hiring and in the conditions of employment. You must be careful to comply with these laws.

GENERAL BUSINESS OBLIGATIONS

As a business you have certain additional obligations. We will not go into detail here, but will simply identify problem areas with the advice that you become aware of them either by consulting with your local, state, and federal authorities or with an attorney.

If you engage in retail sales to consumers you must comply with state sales and use taxes. Generally, this tax is imposed on the consumer but the seller is obligated to collect the tax. On the seller's failure to collect, he or she will be obligated to pay the sums to the state that should have been collected from the consumer. Also, as a seller of retail goods, you generally must obtain a seller's permit from the local office of your state taxing authority. If you sell your product to a distributor who will in turn sell to retailers or if you sell directly to a retailer, then you need to obtain a resale tax certificate exemption from the state.

Note that businesses in most states must pay personal property tax on certain items of personal property that the business owns or possesses at a certain point in time in each calendar year. Generally, a business must file a property statement with its county assessor within the period of time required by state law. You should check with your accountant or state's business property tax department to obtain the necessary information to enable you to comply with the state's laws on such taxes.

Governmental requirements are unquestionably a burden, particularly for a small business. While it may be possible to ignore them and try to "fly below radar" for awhile, the odds are against doing it for long. The more successful the enterprise, the sooner it will become visible.

It is generally advisable to obtain casualty and public liability insurance and you should consult with local insurance agents to give you advice on this matter.

Many trades, occupations, and businesses are required by states to obtain state and sometimes local business licenses. Again you should consult with your local and state governmental authorities to determine what your obligations are.

It should be clear from the list of items discussed here that starting a business involves numerous filings and much record keeping. These governmental requirements are unquestionably a burden, particularly for a small business. Nonetheless, they are unavoidable. While it may be possible to ignore them and try to "fly below radar" for awhile, the odds are against doing it for long. The more successful the enterprise, the sooner it will become visible.

The recommended approach is to comply from the outset. If the requirements seem confusing or you do not have sufficient business experience to feel confident that you have undertaken all the proper steps, have an accountant, business person or lawyer look over what you have done and advise you. Once your bookkeeping and reporting systems are established, they are not difficult to maintain.

This chapter will explore some of the alternative forms of financing that may be available to you as a musician, as well as showing you how to analyze and structure a financial package to obtain the money for your dream project. The suggestions made below apply whether you are tomorrow's rock star, the next Hemingway, or a budding filmmaker hoping to follow in the footsteps of George Lucas. The examples used will draw on common experiences in the music industry, but the concepts and the manner of structuring the deal apply whether you are a musician, writer, actor, or, for that matter, if you want to establish your own instrument manufacturing company.

DEVELOPING THE BUSINESS PLAN

A business plan tells potential investors who you are, your professional goals, what you plan to do to achieve those goals, and how that achievement can generate income to be used to pay back the investor and further finance your career. An outline of the general headings of a business plan is at the end of this article.

Identifying Your Goals

The first and most important thing to be done is to clearly identify the reasons you need to raise money. To establish a clear focus, you must identify your career goals, your immediate project goals, and your strengths and weaknesses. Identifying your goals—for example, securing a recording contract or getting a name artist to record your songs—will assist you in determining a feasible project to undertake to achieve that end. The project might take the form of producing an independent record so you can market it and demonstrate that there is an audience for your product or preparing a publishing demo to shop your songs.

In identifying your goals, you also need to analyze your strengths and weaknesses. What is your best selling point? Identifying your strongest talents will also assist in determining the project that would be most appropriate to achieve your goals. If your best skill is songwriting, perhaps you should raise funds to do a publishing demo of some of your songs to send to publishers and to performers who record material written by others. If your best talent is performance skill, perhaps you should develop a video package that will show the style you use to slay your audience. Money also can be raised for other projects, such as producing a master sound recording, backing a tour for promotional or showcase purposes, buying equipment to enhance your stage show, or hiring a publicist to orchestrate a media blitz before you storm into Los Angeles.

Reaching a final decision on your goals and the projects designed to achieve them is a precondition to figuring out how much money you will need to raise and what kind of information to include in a business plan that you will need to present to prospective investors.

Preparing the Budget

Once you have decided on the project that will be the best vehicle for achieving your goals, your next step is to determine the costs of the project. You must develop a budget for the amount of money you need and how it will be spent. To do this, you must determine the cost of the various elements of your project. If you plan to record your own album, you must budget the cost of studio time, tape, musicians, arrangers, producer and engineer, mixing, mastering, pressing, cover art, design, packaging, distribution, advertising and marketing. Each project has its own cost items. If you are going to raise money from others, it is your responsibility to develop a clear and accurate picture of what those costs will be. The section entitled *Identifying and Evaluating Sources Of Income*, discusses approaches on analyzing future income sources to be used in scheduling pay back arrangements with investors.

Preparing the Proposal

Having identified your goals, the project, and the amount of money you will need, you must next reduce all that information to a proposal or business plan that you can submit to individuals who may have an interest in funding your project. The proposal should itemize the elements we have just explored, as well as explain what the end product will be like, how the business operates, how marketing the product or implementing the service will assist you in developing your career, and how money will be earned to repay the investors. The proposal should also contain information on your background and the current status of your career, and a clear statement of your goals. There is no better way to force yourself to develop a clear focus than having to articulate it to others, especially if you are asking them for money.

RAISING CAPITAL

Your project, most likely, will be financed by one of three methods: self-financing, borrowing or profit sharing. This section will discuss these methods and the advantages and drawbacks inherent in each.

Self-financing

The best way to retain full control of your project is to use your own money. It is the only technique that allows you to be free of financial obligations to lenders and gives you maximum artistic and financial control. Although it means that you must bear all the risk of the project, it also means that you will enjoy the benefits.

Self-financing also minimizes the paperwork, record keeping, and other business complications involved in other ways of raising money. Until you are able to devote full time to managing the business, it is advisable to keep your record keeping requirements to a minimum.

Borrowing

If you are not in a position to self-finance, borrowing is the second basic technique for raising funds. Borrowing means accepting a loan for a fixed sum of money and agreeing to repay that sum plus a specified percentage of interest by a certain time. Arrangements where the return to the lender depends on the success of the project will be discussed under the section on profit sharing.

Loans usually are absolute obligations that must be repaid whether or not the project is successful. If the rate of interest is high, you will have to earn a substantial amount of money from the project before you make any profit. For example, on a loan of $10,000 from a commercial establishment at 18% annual interest payable in two years, your interest obligation would be more than $3,600. To pay back the principal and interest on a self-produced album that sells for $5.00 (average wholesale price), you would have to sell about 2,720 albums, plus an additional number to cover your cost of sales. Only then would you be able to sell for a profit. As costs climb, of course, the number of records you must sell to break even also rises.

Loan Sources

There are two possible sources of loans. The first are commercial sources. They include banks, finance companies, savings and loan associations, and credit cards with cash advance provisions.

Interest on commercial loans secured by such collateral as a home, an auto, or recording or performing equipment or even a cosignature of a person in whom the bank has confidence will usually be lower than interest on unsecured loans. The reason is obvious: the risk is lower. Loans backed up with collateral or the cosignature of a credit worthy individual are also easier to secure.

In deciding whether or not to give you a personal loan, a bank will look at your credit rating and at whether you own property that can be used as collateral for the loan. Unfortunately, musicians' credit ratings aren't always good, because of the fluctuating conditions of their employment. But if you have a credit card or two and have lived in the same place for a couple of years without having trouble paying the rent, you may be able to convince a bank to loan you a modest amount of money—between $1,000 and $5,000. Some banks, however, state that they will sometimes loan more than this amount if the borrower's credit rating is good. Banks may want to see your income tax returns for the last couple of years.

Some banks refuse to make a personal loan of more than $5,000 unless the loan is secured by collateral, which generally means a house that you are buying. If you're looking for a loan to buy new keyboard equipment, you'll find that banks generally will not consider securing the equipment itself as collateral for the loan. Some banks will let you use an automobile as collateral, however, provided you have title to it.

In the event you don't qualify for a personal loan yourself, you can ask a relative or a friend to act as a cosigner for the loan, which means that they promise to make the payments if you are unable to. The bank will be more concerned with their credit rating than with yours, but will still want to make sure that you actually have the ability to make the payments.

In addition to personal loans, banks regularly make commercial loans to businesses. You may feel that since music is your business, you belong in this category, but you'll find that commercial loans have their own rules and regulations. If you have a solidly established band with established income, a commercial loan might be your best option. But if what you have in mind is borrowing money to start a project, you'll probably have to go with a personal loan. When you become more established, some banks will lend money secured by the copyrights in your songs, master recordings, and other intellectual property.

A commercial loan package usually contains your business plan, the profit and loss statements of your business and tax returns for the last two or three years, and a personal financial statement. Banks will check your credit history. They need to know you have a sound financial plan and that you are financially responsible. They will generally insist that you put up 50% of the money for improving the business out of your own pocket, with the loan supplying the other 50%.

Since commercial lenders make money lending money, you should shop for the best deal.

The best way to retain full control of your project is to use your own money.

A second source for loans is family and friends. Usually they will lend money at a rate lower than that of a commercial lender. The important thing to consider when borrowing from friends, because of the close relationship and the potential for straining it, is the strong pressure for timely repayment that may result, which often is more burdensome than the legal obligation to repay.

When you borrow from friends, the usury laws of most states come into play. These statutes limit the amount of interest a private lender can charge a borrower. Banks and other commercial lenders are generally exempt from the usury limits and can charge higher rates.

Whether you borrow from friends or from commercial lenders, you will want to structure a written repayment plan that states the amount lent, the rate of interest, and the method of repayment.

This can be a simple written promissory note: "On or before June 15, 1991, John Debtor promises to pay Sally Lender the sum of $2,500 plus 9% interest from January 1, 1990, (signed) John Debtor."

The note from a commercial lender is more complex, but it will contain the same elements. Sometimes commercial loans are structured so that you pay a smaller monthly amount the first two years and a larger one the next two to three years. Once again, you should shop for the most favorable terms, interest and monthly pay back amounts.

INVESTMENTS

Another source of money is investment from a financial backer. The arrangement can take several forms, depending on whether the investor is "active" or "passive."

Active Investors

Active investors are individuals who put up money to finance a project for another person and become involved in the project (or fail to take adequate action to insulate themselves from responsibility). They assume all of the risks of the business, including financial liability for all losses, even if the losses go beyond the amount invested. Generally, such persons are responsible for the obligations of the business even if they have not given their approval or have not been involved in incurring business debts.

The forms of business in which the financing participants are active include a general partnership, a joint venture or a corporation. The profits or losses of such businesses are shared among the participants according to the nature of their agreement. These are discussed more fully in the chapter titled "Business Entities."

A general partnership is co-ownership of an ongoing enterprise in which the partners share both control and profits. A joint venture is a general partnership which either has a very short term or a limited purpose. For example, the production of a single record could be termed a joint venture.

The general partners and the joint venturers are each personally liable for all the debts of the enterprise. The liability is not limited to the amount that they invested nor to the debts which were incurred with their approval. All of the personal assets of each of the general partners or joint venturers are liable for repayment of the debts incurred by the enterprise.

If a corporation is formed, then even if the project is a total failure, only the assets of the corporation are vulnerable to the business creditors. A corporation is a separate entity formed under state laws. Its ownership is divided among its shareholders. A corporate structure provides limited liability to the shareholders. If you are thinking about setting up a corporation, you'll need some sound legal advice.

If you are interested in learning more about the structuring of partnerships or corporations, your local library should have some good books on setting up a small business that will provide the basic information.

Passive Investors

A more complex category of investments is that in which backers provide money for the project but take no role in the management and affairs of the project. Such backers are passive investors who are hoping for a return on their money based on the success of the project.

The primary advantage of profit sharing arrangements from the point of view of the person getting the money is that the downside risks are shared. If a project fails to recoup the money invested, you are not obligated to repay the investors. Offsetting this advantage are several problems that make profit sharing the most complicated form of financing a project.

The foremost of the problems are the security law requirements. Any time one enters into an agreement in which someone gives money for a project with the understanding that part of the profits are to be shared with them and the investors do not actively participate in the management of the funds or the operation of the business, a "security" has been sold. A security can be a promissory note, stock, points or any other form of participation in a profit sharing arrangement, whether written or oral, where the investor's role in the business is passive. Because general partners and joint venturers are actively involved in the business, their participation is generally not considered a security.

Limited partnerships, promissory notes structured with profit sharing, corporate stock and contracts providing for points participation are securities, and the securities laws of state and federal statutes must be satisfied when these types of funding are used. Failure to comply may have serious civil and perhaps even criminal consequences.

What does this legal talk mean to you? Why should you have to worry about it if all you want to do is raise some money to record some music or finance a performance tour? The securities laws were enacted to protect investors from being harmed by the fraud of others, by their lack of sophistication or even their inability to afford to lose the money they invest in the project. The legal burden falls on the one seeking to raise the money to make certain the investor is getting a fair deal and fully understands the risks involved. "Let the seller beware", is the rule that operates.

If you want someone else to invest money in your project without allowing them a hand in controlling the project, then you should be willing to accept some responsibility to them. Willing or not, state and federal statutes places responsibility on you.

Investment Loans Conditional on the Success of the Venture

In these types of loans, the debt is evidenced by a promissory note and repayment is conditional on the success of the funded project. Because such a loan is a security, the note should set out the terms of repayment, including interest rates and payment schedules.

A common form of this kind of loan is a 'point' arrangement in which a percentage (called "points") of sales from the funded project are shared with an investor who only puts in time or some other investor who only puts in money. Another form is a percent interest in the income (or losses) generated by the business. This arrangement can be provided in a written contract rather than in the form of a conditional promissory note.

The primary advantage of profit sharing arrangements from the point of view of the person getting the money is that the downside risks are shared. If a project fails to recoup the money invested, you are not obligated to repay the investors. Offsetting this advantage are several problems that make profit sharing the most complicated form of financing a project.

Limited Partnerships

Like a general partnership, a limited partnership also has co-ownership and shared profits, but only some of the participants are entitled to control or manage the enterprise. Those persons are termed the general partners. The other investors are called limited partners and their only involvement is the passive one of putting funds into the project.

A partner receives that percentage of the business profits or losses set out in the agreement between the partners, for example, 10% of the net profits up to $10,000 and 5% of the net profits after the first $10,000. The term of the partnership is often limited to a specified period, for example three to five years. If the project has not earned the hoped for return by the end of the term, the investor has to absorb the loss.

There also are rules in the federal law and in several states that apply to limited partnerships and other security investments structured as private offerings, which are easier to qualify under the law than are public offerings.

Corporate Shares

A third way to raise investment capital is through the sale of shares in a corporation. Corporate shares are securities and usually are sold for a stated number of dollars per share. That money is then used to operate the business or pay for a specific project. Shareholders own whatever percentage of the corporation their shares represent of the total number of shares sold.

Shareholders participate in the profits of the corporation when they are distributed as dividends and vote on shareholder issues according to their percentage of ownership.

Whatever method of financing your project uses, it is wise to check with your lawyer and to set up a good financial record keeping system with your bookkeeper.

COMPLYING WITH LEGAL STATUTES

After having reached a decision on the legal structure to use in raising the money for your project, you must make certain that your efforts to raise money comply with state and federal law. California statutes, for example, require that, unless an exemption applies, the party raising and accepting investment capital must file documents with the Commissioner of Corporations explaining in part the proposed investment project, how the money will be used, all of the risks in the venture, the financial ability of the investors, and the background of the persons seeking the funding. The commissioner must conclude that the proposed offer and sale is "fair, just and equitable." On an affirmative finding, the commissioner will issue a permit authorizing the sale. A negative conclusion would bar the sale. Most states have statutes imposing similar requirements.

Fundamental in any offering of a security, whether a public or a nonpublic offering, is the disclosure to the potential investors of all the risks involved in the project, including the risk that the project may fail, that no profit may be made, and that the investors may never have their investment returned. In seeking the investment money, you must disclose in writing to the potential investors the nature of the project, the risks, the background of the principals (the people starting and running the business), the nature of the proposed business, the manner in which the money will be used, and the way that the investor will share in any profits (or losses). Also, under certain circumstances an offer and sale of securities involving an interstate transaction may require registration of the securities with the Securities and Exchange Commission (SEC) in Washington, D.C. Knowledgeable legal counsel should be obtained before seeking to offer any securities.

State Law Exemptions

Under the securities statutes and regulations of most states, there are certain exemptions for the requirement to obtain a permit. These exemptions occur only in very specific situations. For example, three common exemptions are the nonpublic partnership interest, the limited number of shareholder exemptions for corporations, and the nonpublic debt security (note for a loan). In California, a limited partnership interest or other security will be presumed to be a nonpublic offering not requiring a permit from the commissioner provided that (1) there is no advertising of the investment; (2) there are no more than 35 investors contributing to the project; (3) the investor represents that he or she is purchasing the interest for his or her own account and not with the intent to distribute the interest to others it; (4) either the persons investing the money have a pre-existing business or personal relationship with you, or their professional financial advisor can reasonably be presumed to have the ability to protect their own interests because of their business experience. Also a notice detailing information about the investment must be filed with the Commissioner's Office, which establishes the kind of information that must be presented.

If the structure of the financing arrangement is to be in the form of a debt secured with a note with payment to the investor to come from the proceeds, if any, of the venture, then the requirements just described, must be met under California law to qualify the arrangements as an exempt nonpublic debt offering except that the investments may not be taken from more than 10 persons. This description is overly simplified and is not intended to be a full explanation of all the nuances and requirements of the security statutes and regulations. Its purpose is merely to give you a sense of how the laws operate.

IDENTIFYING AND EVALUATING SOURCES OF INCOME

If you lack your own money for your project, and do not have the credit necessary to borrow money, then you must face the reality of raising the investment capital and complying with the appropriate securities statutes discussed above. Probably the most frustrating aspect of this will be your quest to identify the angel who will give you the money you need. Frequently investors are attracted by the idea of putting money into entertainment projects because of the mistaken impression that it is a glamorous business and they desire to be associated with the glamour, or because they have read that the entertainment industry can generate a substantial amount of money and wish to take a risk that they will earn a great return if your project is successful.

Frequently investors are attracted by the idea of putting money into entertainment projects because of the mistaken impression that it is a glamorous business and they desire to be associated with the glamour.

For the most part, the money usually comes from family, friends, or interested persons who have seen your talents and wish to be involved in developing your potential. Even if the money is coming from family and friends, however, it is critical that you keep the relationship on a business level to preserve the personal relationship.

Unfortunately, there is no magic source of money. It will be up to you to identify who has enough faith in your talents and future that they will make their money available to you. Another possible source of money is investment counselors and accountants who are searching for reasonable business opportunities for their clients. In reviewing proposals for investments, financial advisors analyze the possibilities of eventual return on the investment and the tax benefits, if any, that may be made available to the investors.

Educating Investors About Risk

Once you have identified individuals who would be willing to put money into your project, it is very important that you examine their expectations and how they compare with your own perspective. It is critical that you clearly educate your investors about the risks, the rewards, and all the problems and variables that can arise over which you may have little or no control. Investors need to know how much money they need to put into your project in order to evaluate whether they can afford it. If they have any reservations, you should uncover them. If the reservations cannot be resolved, you probably should not accept money from them. Spend time talking with them and make certain that you really understand each other and that they are people to whom you want to be committed.

Fair Return

In discussing pay back with the investor, you need to identify and explore three specific areas. What will be the share of the investor's participation? For how long will the investor participate? And from what sources of income will the investor be repaid? The argument that the investor can make, and it's a good one, is that he or she is taking a substantial risk in putting money into your project that could be invested in other ways for a more certain return. As a consequence, the investor will insist on a very healthy return. This is not unreasonable, provided that the return taken by the investor leaves you with enough of a share to continue your life and career.

Measuring a fair return to the investor is a function of how badly you need the money and how eager the investor is to put money into your project. This point alone will frequently determine how much either side is willing to offer. Investors who have alternative places to put their money for a good return are not going to be as willing to invest, and if you have no other source of income for a project, you may not be in a position to do a lot of arguing. A rule of thumb to follow is that if you have to give up an amount that you feel will hurt your business or your ability to fund your career, then you should not accept the money; go look for another investor.

Unfortunately, there is no magic source of money. It will be up to you to identify who has enough faith in your talents and future that they will make their money available to you.

Another, perhaps more constructive way of measuring a reasonable return to the investor is by looking at the amount of risk assumed by the investor in relation to the amount of money invested; the smaller the number of dollars and the smaller the risk of failure, the smaller the return. For example, if your project cost $2,000 it would be hard to justify returning to an investor 10% of your income for life. If however, the investor put $200,000 into your project, it is easier to justify committing a reasonable percentage of your income to the investor for a substantial period of time.

You can determine the proper percentage to offer to an investor by looking at how much you can afford to give up. Remember, there are only so many slices in the money pie, and if you give up more slices than you have, there will be nothing left for you to eat. Consequently, you should identify the parties to whom you already have made commitments, such as managers, attorneys, other investors, partners, and the like. After you have paid those people, you will still need money to run your business and take home money to support your private needs. You must carefully analyze your income potential and anticipated expenses.

You must identify the sources of income from which the investor will be repaid. Will the money be coming from the revenue generated by the project itself or will it be coming from other sources such as record sales, live performances, music publishing, or merchandising? These points must be clearly and carefully thought out before you commit to a participation with an investor.

CONCLUSION

There are no simple answers. Deals can be structured in many ways. The key to your decision requires a business analysis of your funding sources, the urgency of your need for money, the risks the investor is making and his or her alternative investment choices, and your other money commitments. You should take the time to do your homework and be very careful about the commitment you are making. When in doubt, seek advice. If the deal doesn't make sense or doesn't feel good to you, then you should trust your instincts and walk away from it, rather than let yourself be pressured into a commitment that may later hinder your career. In any event, be honest with yourself, identify your goals, your value system, what you are willing and not willing to give up. Only by taking all these factors into account can you arrive at a financial package that will work for you. Once you set up such a package, however, you may be able to accomplish career objectives that would otherwise have remained beyond your reach.

EXHIBIT 1
BUSINESS PLAN OUTLINE

Here are the topics usually covered in business plans. Even if you are not using a business plan to find financing for your project, it will help identify your goals, outline the strengths and weaknesses of your project, and help determine when your project will make a profit. In short, a business plan is the map that shows how to get from an idea stage to project completion and profit.

When you want to borrow money, the business plan is a vital sales tool that will impress prospective investors with your planning ability and general competence as a manager.

I Summary of your project, including the money you need to successfully launch the project and reach your market.

II Company description (History, background and management).

III Description of your background.

IV Description of industry you are operating in.

V Project description and planning schedule.

VI Description of the market for your project.
- A. Market Size
- B. Market Trends
- C. Competition

VII Marketing plan.
- A. Estimated sales and market share
- B. Strategy
- C. Pricing
- D. Sales and distribution
- E. Publicity and advertising

VIII Operations: (If project is a "Product" i.e. a compact disc or new software, describe how product will be manufactured).

IX Project time line.

X Critical risks and problems.

XI Financial information.
- A.Financing required
- B.Current financial statements
- C.Financial projection (three year profit and loss, cash flow and balance sheet projections).

As this book reflects, musicians face myriad legal problems throughout their careers. Only with the help of a competent attorney knowledgeable in the music business can a musician effectively solve these problems. The following discussion will attempt to answer common questions concerning music attorneys — who they are, what they do, what they cost, and what their obligations are to you.

An attorney or lawyer is a professional with legal training who is licensed to practice law in a particular state or states. Typically, an attorney must be a college graduate and also graduate from law school. Full-time law schools have a broad-based curriculum which lasts three years. After graduation, the student must pass the state's "bar exam" before admission to practice law. The "bar" is a state sponsored monopoly—only attorneys can practice law. The traditional professional activities of lawyers fall into roughly four categories: consulting with clients; drafting and negotiating legal documents; representing clients before the courts; and insuring compliance by clients with local, state and national laws and contracts (such as union agreements) governing the client's business activities. For musicians by far the most important of these four functions is the lawyer's drafting and negotiating legal documents.

SPECIALIZATION

Most attorneys specialize in particular fields of practice. The primary reason for specialization is the complexity of the problems that confront the professional and the sophistication and training necessary to apply the correct problem-solving tools. The law is far too complex for a lawyer to have adequate competence in all legal areas. A specialist, at least in theory, can do a better job for his client because of his acquired experience in a particular area.

Due to the growth and complexity of the entertainment field, a specialty has arisen among lawyers —"entertainment" lawyers. Music lawyers are entertainment lawyers specializing in legal and business aspects of the music business.

A recent trend is the certification of lawyers who practice a specialty. In California, for example, there are five certified specialties: criminal law; worker's compensation; taxation; patent law; and family law. Entertainment law is not one of the certified specialties. Thus, at this time, there are no state certified music lawyers in California (or elsewhere that I am aware of). This does not mean lawyers can't specialize in representing music industry clients. They can and do. What distinguishes a music attorney, then, is not certification, but that he or she has more experience in solving the problems musicians encounter. It is not necessary for an attorney to specialize exclusively in music to have enough expertise to help you. In fact, only a handful of lawyers (largely in Los Angeles, New York and Nashville) are exclusively music attorneys. Many entertainment lawyers concentrate on film and TV as well as music.

MUSIC ATTORNEY FUNCTIONS

The notion that music entertainment attorneys do nothing but attend record company parties is a myth. There is little glamour in drafting and negotiating contracts. Both recording and publishing agreements can be incredibly complex, and proper drafting and negotiating require not only superior legal skills, but also a thorough knowledge of music business practice.

In addition to negotiating and drafting a wide variety of agreements for songwriters, recording artists, record companies, music publishers, record producers, personal managers and music investors, a few music attorneys also actively solicit deals for their clients by "shopping" (distributing) demo tapes. Over time they develop relationships with people and companies in the industry, and their recommendation of a music client is sometimes influential in obtaining a contract. An attorney's role in shopping deals does not fall squarely within the four traditional professional activities categories set out above. Most music attorneys do not find deals for their clients. That task is left to the musician and his manager. The attorney's first and foremost function is involvement in structuring, negotiating and documenting the deal to maximize its benefit to the client.

Another important function of the music attorney is to act as a business hub in coordinating the activities of your other representatives, such as your agent, personal manager and business manager. Because music attorneys deal with these representatives, they develop a working knowledge of their functions in the music industry. A competent music attorney helps insure that these persons are acting in your best interests.

Music attorneys are sometimes empowered to be attorneys-in-fact for their clients. In this regard, they collect and receive all monies due you or your companies from all sources relating to your agreements with them. They deposit into a client trust account all checks and other monies payable to you and your companies and deduct any monies for attorney compensation before remitting the remainder to you or your companies.

A further service a music attorney may provide is that of a general career adviser, rendering the kind of advice you would expect from a personal manager. This advice can be crucial in the early stage of your career, as musicians often are unable to attract competent, experienced personal managers until they are signed to a major label.

FINDING A MUSIC ATTORNEY

Music attorneys, like other attorneys, work alone (a "sole practitioner"), or as a part of a law firm. The size of a law firm can range from two to as many as several hundred lawyers. In the large firms that have entertainment divisions, the entertainment division is often divided into two departments: TV/film and music. Generally, the more experienced lawyers (who often are partners, that is, own part of the firm), negotiate the big deals, while the nonpartners (associates) negotiate the smaller deals. Associates usually do the lion's share of the often tedious task of drafting and negotiating agreements.

In recent years the large firms with entertainment divisions have lost much of their business to smaller "boutique" entertainment law firms, which typically have

10-20 lawyers. These firms, unlike large multi-service firms, usually handle only entertainment clients. More and more of the boutique entertainment firms charge on a percentage basis of 5% of the dollar value of the deal negotiated, rather than on an hourly basis. Although percentage arrangements may be advantageous when you are unable to afford hourly rates, on large dollar deals you may end up paying more than the hourly rate. Also, remember that your income is already being diminished by your personal manager (10-25%), agent (10%) and your business manager (5%).

Few music lawyers will take clients "on the come" (i.e., do free work until the client is successful and can pay the bills). Simple economics justify this policy. Because the music industry is overcrowded and fiercely competitive, the odds of the music lawyer ever collecting delayed fees for work done by an aspiring client are negligible.

You should see a number of different lawyers before retaining one. Lawyers have various personalities, legal skills, and music business experience and contacts. It is important to retain an attorney who specializes in entertainment law and knows how the industry works. A working knowledge of the standard (and nonstandard) contracts is mandatory—attorneys who don't have this knowledge will spend a lot of your money researching or buying time from another entertainment attorney, or could steer you entirely wrong. Do not be afraid to "interview" a lawyer, but make sure you have made your intention clear when making the appointment, and also confirm you will not be charged for the time. Be prepared to ask pointed questions about the lawyer's music business experience. Don't expect, however, that you can use the interview as a ruse for getting free legal help—that's not fair and will put off the attorney. It is best to talk to successful musicians and managers who can recommend specific lawyers who have done good work for them. If you call to set up an appointment, the fact that your acquaintance has an ongoing relationship with the attorney should help you get in the door. It is also helpful if your lawyer likes your music—he or she will be more motivated to work for you.

There are various ways to find a music attorney. Some well-known practitioners command coverage in the music industry press.

Another way to meet music lawyers is to attend music conferences. A number of prominent music attorneys are invited to appear at music symposia, and some business relationships are started as a result of meeting at such functions. However, it may not be advisable to retain an attorney far beyond your status in the industry, because high-powered music lawyers must first serve their existing clients—if it's your telephone call or Michael Jackson's, the choice is clear!

Lawyer Referral Services

In recent years many lawyer referral services have been established in California. The usual procedure is for a prospective client in need of legal assistance to call a central referral office. The referral person discusses the caller's problem, and then refers the caller to an attorney on the lawyers referral panel. The panel attorney then interviews the referral client for a moderate fee. After the first interview, the fee arrangement and the legal services to be rendered are left up to the lawyer and client. Often the fee is split between the referral panel and the lawyer. For

A few music attorneys also actively solicit deals for their clients by "shopping" (distributing) demo tapes. Over time they develop relationships with people and companies in the industry, and their recommendation of a music client is sometimes influential in obtaining a contract.

example, California Lawyers for the Arts attorneys remit 15% of all fees generated in excess of $100 to CLA. This nonprofit organization based in San Francisco is a well-known lawyer referral service of approximately 125 lawyers devoted exclusively to the arts. CLA has been authorized by the California State Bar Association to refer clients statewide.

In Los Angeles, you can call the Lawyer Referral Service (LRS) of the Los Angeles County Bar Association for recommendations. The Beverly Hills Bar Association Committee for the Arts (CFTA) Lawyer Referral and Information Service (LRIS) offers lawyer referrals to those with entertainment-related legal problems. These referral panels only provide you with the name of an attorney who has registered with it and who claims to have some experience in your area of concern. The panels do not rate lawyers; thus, you cannot be guaranteed that the panel attorney will have the skills and experience you need. It should also be noted that the "heavy weights" usually are not on these panels.

Another source of music attorneys is the National Academy of Songwriters (NAS). For its members, NAS makes referrals to music attorneys who have agreed to charge reduced fees. Any one hour consultation on a new matter is $50, the next four hours are also $50, with additional hours at the lawyer's normal rate.

If you live outside California, check with the state or a local bar association on lawyer referral services that may be available to you.

WHEN TO SEE A MUSIC ATTORNEY

The cardinal rule in seeking legal representation is: see a lawyer before you sign anything except autographs. In essence, when you sign a contract, you are setting up your own law (with the other party) that will govern your relationship with that party. Even though in some instances a lawyer may not be able to negotiate more favorable contract terms for you, at the very least he or she can explain the agreement so you know what you are getting into. Most likely, however, the lawyer can help by negotiating terms more favorable to you. These terms might include higher advances and royalty rates (in recording contracts), partial ownership of your copyright and a participation in the "publisher's share" of revenue (in publishing contracts), and a way to get you out of a contract if it doesn't work out. Also, you should consult with an attorney when establishing contracts with your other advisors, such as your talent agent and especially your personal manager. A word of warning: don't sign a contract assuming you can get out.

Be wary of people who give you form or standard contracts to sign, saying that "everybody accepts these terms." Although standard contracts exist, they are drafted by attorneys who are out to protect their clients' interest, not yours. Odds are that an attorney representing you also has a standard contract—but it's much more favorable to you. The negotiating process consists of each side making specific demands, and seeing if the other side will agree. If you retain a lawyer, the other side may give in to at least some of the demands. Together the opposing lawyers can identify issues and potential problems the parties may have overlooked. The result is a contract that is different from the original form contract and more favorable to you.

MEETING WITH YOUR ATTORNEY

Your first meeting with an attorney will probably be arranged over the phone. Before meeting you should be prepared to talk about two things: your specific legal needs and your fee arrangement with the attorney.

Fees

Lawyers cost money. Many lawyers cost a lot. Fees can exceed $300 an hour or be 5% of the money value of your deal. Nonsuperstar music attorneys normally charge in the range of $100-$200 per hour. For example, the legal fee for negotiation of an agreement with a major record company, even by a relatively low priced attorney, will be at least in the $2,000 - $4,000 range.

Be wary of people who give you form or standard contracts to sign, saying that "everybody accepts these terms."

You must realize that a lawyer, unlike a shoe salesman, is selling his services. In order to make money, they must cover the overhead (rent, employee salaries, insurance, taxes, etc.) and make a decent profit. Overhead often exceeds 50% of the billing rate, so don't get the impression that lawyers are putting $300 an hour into their pockets. They're not, especially if the bill is unpaid.

You should also realize that in retaining a lawyer you are making a contract even if your agreement is not written. In return for his fee, the lawyer promises to render legal services on your behalf. Both parties should do their best to fulfill their obligations.

It is preferable for the fee agreement to be written. The basic rule in California is that if the bill will likely exceed $1,000, the fee arrangement must be written.

Not all lawyers charge on a per hour basis. Some will charge a set fee, such as $500, to negotiate or draft a contract. As discussed above, others will set their charge as a percentage of the money you receive under contracts they negotiate. This fee generally runs 5% of the deal, although the percentage and structure of these types of arrangement vary greatly. You should check around to see if the fee arrangement proposed by the lawyer is competitive, although price (whether low or high) is not necessarily an accurate indication of the value or quality of the attorney's work. Cautious lawyers will remind you that you have the right to seek the advice of another lawyer as to the propriety of the fee arrangement. Many lawyers will represent you on a percentage basis only for negotiating a specific contract. Additional services, such as tax advice, formation of corporations, etc., will have a separate, and additional charge.

Lawyers also generally ask reimbursement for their out-of-pocket costs, which may include long-distance telephone calls, photocopies, word processing, postage, messenger service, fax, etc. These are not considered part of the hourly fee, which only covers the lawyer's services.

Committee for the Arts, Beverly Hills Bar Association Barristers, from left to right: Esteban Gallegos, James Sedivy, Teri R.C. Williams, Linda Newmark, Mark Halloran, Greg Victoroff and Larry Blake. Photo by Hadi Salehi.

Fee Payment

The quickest way to sour your attorney-client relationship is not to pay your bill. Lawyers on an hourly basis will render a monthly statement which sets out the services rendered, date of services, the costs, and the total bill. If you can't pay the bill, you should at least call to say you can't pay it, and arrange some payment schedule. Some music attorneys will accept some minimum payment to continue working for you.

In the good ol' days lawyers rarely sued their clients for nonpayment. Now they are doing so with increasing regularity. In California you have the right to a fee arbitration if the lawyer's claim exceeds $1,500 (the small claims court limit). The lawyer will send you a notice advising you of your right to arbitrate, and you must respond within 30 days or you lose your arbitration right.

Retainers

Many lawyers require an initial payment of money, or a retainer. Most retainers are credited against your bill, but make sure that is your agreement. Thus, if you retain an attorney and give him a $500 check, usually that $500 will be credited to your account. Until your lawyer renders legal services sufficient to justify his right to the money, he holds these funds "in trust" for you. In theory, at least, he can't take these funds until he earns them by doing sufficient work for you. For example, in the first month your attorney negotiates a publishing contract, and spends six hours at $100 an hour doing it. He will send you a bill showing $500 received and $600 due for services rendered. Thus, you owe $100 at that point. Some attorneys also will require that you keep replenishing the retainer. In the foregoing example, they would bill you $600 so the retainer would be brought back up to $500. A reminder: keep a record of all legal bills so you can try to deduct them as a business expense. You should also keep copies of all documents and correspondence.

Conflicts of Interest

In return for the monopoly on practicing law, lawyers are constrained by very special ethical obligations to you. Like all agents, lawyers have a "fiduciary" obligation to their "principal": you. The heart of this obligation is that they must act with your best interests as the goal - not their own or those of third parties.

As part of this obligation lawyers have an ethical duty to avoid so-called "conflicts of interest." In every situation where you think your attorney may be representing conflicting interests you should seriously question whether you should retain a different lawyer. You should closely scrutinize the conflict, especially in recording contract situations. The most prevalent conflict of interest of occurs when a lawyer concurrently represents multiple clients with potentially adverse interests. For example, assume your attorney represents XYZ Records, and XYZ Records wants to sign you to a recording contract. XYZ wants to give you as little as they can; you want as much as you can get. This is a conflict of interest, as your interest, and XYZ's interest are opposed to one another, or "adverse."

Under the California Rules of Professional Conduct (3-310), if a conflict arises, the lawyer must disclose his relationship with the adverse party and obtain the client's written consent to dual representation. A lawyer cannot represent both

Remember your lawyer's time is money. If you are organized in your legal and business affairs, it makes the lawyer's job easier, and therefore cheaper to you.

Keep accurate records, and don't hesitate to communicate in writing. People read faster than they talk, and written communication provides a record.

Always be honest with your lawyer. Lawyers operate more efficiently on facts, not lies.

Pay your bills on time.

Keep your lawyer informed, so he can prevent difficulties. The old adage that an ounce of prevention is worth a pound of cure is appropriate in music business legal affairs.

Prepare for your meetings with your lawyer. Bring all documents that might be useful, such as letters and your calendar.

Don't sign anything until your lawyer has reviewed it.

parties except with the written consent of all parties concerned. Lawyers violating this rule are subject to discipline by the state bar, as well as malpractice claims by clients whose interests were damaged by the lawyer with the conflict. Similar legal controls are in effect in other states.

A lawyer may represent multiple clients with adverse interests if (1) it is obvious that he can adequately represent the interests of each; and (2) each client consents to the representation after full disclosure of the possible effect of such representation on the exercise of the lawyer's independent professional judgement on behalf of each. The conflict of interest situation extends to all members of a law firm. Under the American Bar Association's Code of Professional Responsibility, a lawyer cannot avoid a conflict by referring you to someone else in the firm.

In our previous hypothetical situation, it may be that the attorney for XYZ Records can adequately represent you in your negotiations with XYZ. After discussing the conflict, he may present you with what is known as a "conflict" letter. This letter will say (1) the lawyer informed you of the conflict; (2) he suggested you seek independent counsel; (3) the agreement is fair to you; (4) you consent to his representation of the other party; and (5) you will not claim in the future that your lawyer breached his "fiduciary" duty (i.e., trust) to you in regard to the conflict. This letter, at least in theory, protects the attorney from your future claim that he did not fairly represent you. The ethical lawyer will act in accordance with the terms of the conflict letter, which he will ask you to sign. You should feel free to have another lawyer look at it.

What if the conflict cannot be overcome? You have to get another lawyer. The lawyer with the conflict may suggest specific counsel, or, preferably, provide you with a list of competent lawyers and leave the choice to you. The fact you are referred to another lawyer does not mean the lawyer with the conflict cannot subsequently represent you. He or she just can't represent you with regard to the conflict situation.

Confidentiality

Your lawyer is under a duty to keep your communication with him confidential. Frequently negotiations are secret, and it is in your best interest to keep them that way. News often gets out, though, as when the trades note that a particular record company is negotiating with a specific act. Conceivably, this can help you: if more than one company is interested in you, your lawyer can play them one against another. However, if a lawyer is going to "leak" information, he needs your consent.

Changing Lawyers

Although many attorney-client relationships are long-lasting, you may well find that you want to change attorneys. If you do, you should inform your new attorney of your previous relationship. Your new lawyer cannot represent you simultaneously in a matter that is being handled by another lawyer.

The technical description used by the bar is that you "discharge" your lawyer. By law, a client has an absolute right to discharge his attorney at any time, regardless of the reason. This does not mean, however, that you don't have to pay the discharged lawyer for the reasonable value of the services already provided to you. As an initial step, your new lawyer will want to have your previous files turned over to him. Your former lawyer has an ethical duty to let the successor counsel inspect and copy the documents in the file. Because much of the information in the files is confidential, you must authorize that the files be copied. The fact you may owe your old lawyer money is irrelevant as far as turning over the files is concerned. Your previous lawyer still has a duty to represent your best interests, which includes turning over the files and cooperating with your new lawyer.

You should note that your attorney can also sever his relationship with you (except in litigation). However, he must avoid prejudicing your rights by giving you notice, time to hire another lawyer, and deliver all your papers and unearned retainer to you.

CONCLUSION

Developing an effective music lawyer-musician relationship can be a valuable step in your career. Your decision in selecting an attorney is crucial—it should be an <u>informed</u> decision and should be done as early in your career as possible.

EXHIBIT 1
ATTORNEY/CLIENT FEE LETTER AGREEMENT
HOURLY ARRANGEMENT

Dear Client:

It is a pleasure to undertake your representation in connection with the above referenced matter.

We are writing this letter to set forth the basis under which our firm will represent you, your related entities and any other persons or entities which you request us to represent with respect to this matter.

Our fees on all matters will be based on the guidelines set forth in the Rules of Professional Conduct of the State Bar of California. Our hourly rates range between $45.00 and $175.00 per hour, depending on which attorney or paralegal performed the work. Fees for services will be charged on a minimum quarterly-hourly basis and, when services are rendered outside our office, you will be charged on a portal-to-portal basis. We will be sending you itemized monthly statements which will be due upon receipt, and which will also include our costs advanced in connection with your representation. Such cost charges include, but are not limited to, messenger service, shipping, postage, copying expenses and telephone charges.

An initial retainer fee in the sum of $_______is due at the commencement of our representation. * The retainer will be applied to fees and costs as they are incurred. You will not receive any interest on the retainer, and upon completion of our work, any remaining balance will either be refunded to you or applied toward future legal services rendered by our firm on your behalf. At this time, the services contemplated will encompass representing you in connection with:

(specific contract or project is outlined here)

It is the policy of our firm to look to clients jointly and severally regarding any fees incurred either on their behalf or at their direction on behalf of any person, firm or entity for which our clients request we render services. This firm reserves the right to withdraw from this matter at any time should fees and costs not be paid as agreed. In the event it becomes necessary for this firm to take legal action for the collection of fees and costs due, the prevailing party in such action shall be entitled to collect attorneys' fees from the other party.

If the foregoing agrees with your understanding, please execute the enclosed copy of this letter and return it in the return envelope provided, together with your check in the sum of $___________as our retainer, as explained above.

If you have any questions concerning this agreement, please do not hesitate to contact me. Additionally if at any time you have questions regarding anything relating to our services or fees charged, we encourage you to bring such matters to our attention so that we may discuss and resolve them at once.

We look forward to the opportunity of working with you on this matter.

*Optional? We acknowledge receipt of the sum of $______and will proceed on your behalf at once.

EXHIBIT 2: PERCENTAGE FEE LETTER AGREEMENT

Dear Client:

This letter will confirm our agreement with you whereby we agree to render our services as your attorneys in connection with your professional career.

You engage us during the period of this agreement as your attorneys and will cause any companies connected with your professional career in which you have any controlling interest to engage us as their attorneys in connection with all legal matters pertaining to your professional career in the entertainment industry. The term of this agreement shall commence on the date hereof, and shall continue until terminated by either of us by written notice, which shall be personally delivered or mailed by certified or registered mail, postage prepaid, to the respective address set forth on this page (or to such other address as either of us may notify the other of). No termination shall affect our right to be paid our percentage fee described below.

For our services to be rendered during the term of this Agreement you and each of your companies (but not both regarding the same gross consideration) will pay us as and when received by you or such companies, respectively, beginning as of the date hereof, five percent (5%) of all gross consideration (including salaries, bonuses, percentages, commissions, royalties, profit shares, stock interests, and all other forms of compensation of any nature and from any source), prior to any withholding or deductions, earned, accrued, paid or payable (directly or indirectly) to you or your companies from and after the date hereof, for your services or the services of such companies in connection with any facet of your professional career in the entertainment industry rendered during the term hereof, or for such services rendered by you or such companies pursuant to any agreement (oral or written) (and any extensions, renewals, substitutions, or resumptions thereof) substantially negotiated or entered into during the term hereof (irrespective of when such services under such agreement were or are to be rendered), whether such gross consideration is received by you or your companies (or any third party on your or its behalf) during or after the term hereof.

Notwithstanding anything in the preceding paragraph to the contrary, the aforesaid percentage shall be ten percent (10%) (not five percent (5%) with respect to gross consideration as defined above which is not subject to being commissioned by a licensed artist's manager (commonly referred to as an "agent"). Our additional compensation with respect to such uncommissioned gross consideration arises out of situations where no licensed artist's manager is involved, resulting in greater responsibility on our part in connection with the negotiations in connection therewith. There shall be no inference from this increase that we in any way agree to seek personal employment for you.

The services which we shall be expected to render in return for the above compensation shall include reviewing, drafting, modifying, negotiating and otherwise assisting you in connection with all agreements, contracts or other legal matters in connection with your professional career in the entertainment industry, and consulting with you and advising you regarding all other legal aspects of your professional career in the entertainment industry; but the services we shall be expected to render in return for the above compensation shall not include matters which involve litigation, arbitration or other contested proceedings, planning or the preparation of tax returns, preparation or administration of pension or profit sharing plans, or matters pertaining to your personal life or other businesses as opposed to your professional career.

You understand, of course, if we represent you in any such matter involving litigation, arbitration or other contested proceedings, the preparation of administration of profit sharing plans, or matters pertaining to your personal life or other businesses, as opposed to your professional career, we shall be paid an additional reasonable fee for such services, to be agreed upon between us, and costs reasonably incurred in connection therewith.

You are hereby authorizing us and empower us, and appoint us as your attorneys-in-fact and as attorney-in-fact for your companies to collect and receive all monies due you or your companies from all sources relating to this agreement, to negotiate and endorse your (or your companies') name upon and deposit into our client's trust account all checks and other monies payable to you or your companies, to deduct therefrom our compensation as set forth above, together with any costs advanced by us and to remit the remainder to you or your companies as the case may be.

The terms "you" and "your", as used herein, shall refer to you or any firm, partnership, corporation or other entity owned or controlled by you.

If the foregoing meets with your approval, please sign and return the original and one copy of this letter; the other copy is for your files.

Inasmuch as this letter constitutes an agreement between us, we cannot, of course, advise you concerning it, and we suggest that you retain outside counsel to advise you concerning this agreement.

EXHIBIT 3
ATTORNEY CONFLICT OF INTEREST WAIVER LETTER

Dear Client:

We understand that you have been representing and continue to represent each of us in connection with a variety of matters. We also understand that you have and may in the future represent one of us in matters involving the other and in which the other has been or will be represented by his own counsel.

We would like your firm to represent us in connection with the following matters:

(description of project/contract, etc.)

In connection with the above, you have advised us of the following terms of the provisions of Section 3-310 of the California State Rules of Professional Conduct[1]:

"(A) If a member has or had a relationship with another party interested in the representation, or has an interest in its subject matter, the member shall not accept or continue such representation without all affected clients' informed written consent.

"(B) A member shall not concurrently represent clients whose interests conflict, except with their informed written consent.

You have also advised us of the following provisions of California Evidence Code Section 962 relating to the attorney-client privilege[2]:

"Where two or more clients have retained or consulted a lawyer upon a matter of common interest, none of them, nor the successor in interest of any of them, may claim a privilege under this article as to a communication made in the course of that relationship when such communication is offered in a civil proceeding between one of such clients (or his successor in interest) and another of such clients (or his successor in interest)."

Notwithstanding such joint representation and any actual or potential conflict of interest, we hereby request that you represent both of us in connection with the aforesaid matters and consent to such representation. Furthermore, we acknowledge and agree that at no time will your representation of us be construed, claimed or deemed to be a breach of a fiduciary relationship, a conflict of interest or a violation of any other obligation to wither of us. We each agree that at no time shall we claim or contend that you should be or are disqualified from representing either of us in connection with said matter or any other matter, related or unrelated.

[1] This is similar to other states' rules of professional conduct.

[2] This is similar to other states' rules of professional conduct.

3
C
G7
C
C7
G7
C
C7
F
G7
Dm7
G7
C
C7
F
G7
C
F
C7

- Copyrights: The Law & You
- Copyright Infringement

A copyright is a property right comprised of a set of legally enforceable privileges granted by law to creators of artistic works such as songs and recordings. There are a variety of these privileges ("exclusive rights") and they vary depending on the type of creation. The most important is the exclusive right to make and sell copies of the creation, and especially in the case of music, the exclusive right to publicly perform it. The copyright owner makes money by selling or licensing these rights to others, or by exploiting the music rights himself.

WHAT CAN BE COPYRIGHTED?

Although the copyright law recognizes that artistic creations ("works") other than music are copyrightable, the most important artistic creation for a musician is what the law terms a "musical work," that is, a musical composition such as a song or instrumental piece. For simplicity's sake, we will refer to a musical work as a "song."

Two prerequisites must be met before a song can be protected by copyright. The song must be: original to the author, and fixed in a tangible medium of expression. "Original" means only that you yourself created the work (rather than copied it). "Fixed in a tangible medium of expression" means you put your song on paper or on tape, or in any other medium from which it can be perceived for more than a very short period of time. Singing a song in a club does not fix that song in order for you to have a copyright in it. Once you have recorded a demo, or written a lead sheet, the song is fixed. Copyright law terms you the "author" of the song.

WHAT CANNOT BE COPYRIGHTED?

Songs Not Fixed

Unless you put a song on paper or record it, the song cannot be copyrighted. You may have been humming a song identical to "Send in the Clowns" by Stephen Sondheim a year before he wrote it, and perhaps you even performed the song at a nightclub, but unless you put the song on paper or tape, you cannot claim a valid copyright.

Ideas

Ideas are not copyrightable. The originators of rap could not copyright one rap song and then say that everyone is forbidden to write rap songs. Only the expression of the idea, that is, what has been put on paper or tape, is protected. Thus you are free to write a rap song even if they did not originate the rap mode. You cannot, however, steal a previous rap song note for note and beat for beat.

Song Titles

Song titles are not copyrightable, as they do not possess sufficient expressive content. However, this does not mean you could write a new song and entitle it "Like A Rolling Stone" with total impunity. The owners of "Like a Rolling Stone" might have legal recourse, but this recourse would be under laws other than copyright law.

Public Domain Songs

Not all songs are copyrighted. Songs that are not protected by a copyright (e.g. songs whose copyright has expired) fall into what is called the "public domain;" they are owned by the public. You are free to use a song in the public domain in any way you choose. Many "new" songs take material liberally from the public domain.

If you are unsure as to whether a song is public domain, you can have the Copyright Office or a private search service check the copyright status. The Copyright Office charges $20/hr and normally takes 6 weeks to do a search. A private service, such as The Clearing House, charges a sliding scale, but is quicker than the Copyright Office and usually has more complete and current information.

For information on copyright searches you can call the Reference & Bibliography Section of the Copyright Office.

WHAT'S THE DIFFERENCE BETWEEN COPYRIGHTS, PATENTS, AND TRADEMARKS?

Copyright protects works that are artistic in nature, such as songs and sound recordings (discussed below.) Patents protect new and useful inventions, such as new processes and machines. Trademarks are words or symbols used in association with products or services, which distinguish the goods or services in the marketplace. A registered trademark's notice is ®. Don't confuse it with the copyright notices, which include the symbols © or ℗.

Copyrights, patents, and trademarks make up the bulk of what is known as "intellectual property law." This body of law recognizes that the products of people's minds that are in tangible form have a value that should be protected.

WHAT MUSICAL CREATIONS ARE COPYRIGHTABLE?

Generally, in the music field, you can get a copyright for two types of creations: musical works and sound recordings. Although dramatic works (such as a musical play, e.g. "Phantom of the Opera") may include accompanying music, these are beyond the scope of this discussion.

Musical Works

Interestingly, the copyright law does define "musical works." However, what most people consider a song is a musical work. Both the music and the lyrics (or each of them separately) can constitute a musical work.

Sound Recordings

A sound recording is a work comprised of a series of recorded sounds. Thus, the sounds on an album, cassette or compact disc constitute a sound recording. You must distinguish between the musical work and the sound recording. When Linda Ronstadt recorded Roy Orbison's song "Blue Bayou," her rendition of the song, which you hear when the album is played, is a sound recording. However, "Blue Bayou" is the musical work, which is separate and distinct from Ronstadt's performance as "embodied" in the sound recording.

This distinction is important when it comes to public performance income. There is no exclusive right to publicly perform a sound recording, even if you own it, but there is as to a musical work. Accordingly, public performance royalties (distributed by ASCAP, BMI, and SESAC) are paid to the writer and publisher of the musical work, not the performer or owner of the sound recording. Thus, the public performance income generated by Ronstadt's version of "Blue Bayou" is paid to the writer and publisher of the song, not to Ronstadt or her record company.

Congress has considered, but not yet passed, bills that would create public performance right in sound recordings. A system similar to the ASCAP and BMI monitoring systems would probably be used to compute frequency of performances, and the money would be distributed among record companies, producers, writers, and performers. It should be noted that public performance income from exploitation of sound recordings is currently paid in some countries outside the United States.

What is a Phonorecord?

Many provisions of the Copyright Act refer to "phonorecords." A phonorecord is the physical object (typically a tape, cassette, record or compact disc) which embodies the sounds of a sound recording. When you buy an album, you have purchased a phonorecord that embodies a sound recording. However, you do not own the sound recording—the copyright owner has only parted with the physical embodiment of the copyrighted work, not ownership in the sound recording.

HOW TO OBTAIN A COPYRIGHT

Some people are under the misapprehension that you send off to Washington, D.C. to get a copyright. What you send off for is not a "copyright"—which you get as soon as you fix the work in a tangible medium of expression—but a copyright registration, a very valuable piece of paper that is not only evidence of your claim to copyright, but also makes it easier for you to sue when someone infringes your copyright. In general, failure to register does not invalidate the copyright. Also, although under the old copyright law you could lose your copyright if you failed to put a proper copyright notice on published copies of your work, as of March 1, 1989, you are no longer legally required to put a copyright notice on published copies.

Obtaining Copyright Registration Forms

Copyright registration forms can be ordered by writing or calling the Copyright Office. The forms are free. Allow at least two to four weeks for delivery. This time does vary, however, so you are well advised when calling to ask the person at the Copyright Office how long you will have to wait. The Copyright Office is also very helpful with any questions you have regarding registration. Sample forms are duplicated at the end of this chapter. Please note the forms (as filled out) are merely illustrative, and should not be followed word for word. Also, you should keep at least one original form on file, so you have an original to photocopy. You may also order Copyright Office circulars, which are written in plain English and are very helpful.

What to Submit to the Copyright Office

To register a copyright in a song, you submit the appropriate form plus one lead sheet or cassette if the work is not published. The cassette need only contain words, basic melody and rhythm; it doesn't have to be a fully arranged and beautifully produced demo. You must submit two lead sheets or cassettes if the work is published (i.e., copies have been distributed to the public). The appropriate form for registering a song is form PA (performing arts), or SR (sound recording). If you use form SR and own both the song and the sound recording, the registration covers both the song and the sound recording of the song. Please note: the Copyright Office keeps the materials you submit, and stores them as a national artistic treasure of the Library of Congress.

For free copyright registration forms write The Library of Congress, Washington, D.C. 20559, or call the Copyright Office at (202) 479-0700 (if you're not sure which form you need) or (202) 707-9100 (if you know the specific form you want).

Can I Register More Than One Song by Submitting a Tape?

You may register many songs for a single fee by putting them on a tape and registering the sound recording and the songs simultaneously using form SR. The biggest drawback of this method is that since the songs are clumped together as one song it is more difficult to identify just one of the songs.

What are the Alternative Registration Methods?

Because of the high cost of copyright registration (currently $20 per song) and technical requirements of the copyright office, alternative forms of registration have arisen. The primary reason for using alternative registration methods is to provide proof of the date of creation (fixation) of a song, which is crucial in determining who first created the song copyright. At the outset it should be emphasized that <u>no</u> alternative means of registration will protect your songs to the extent formal registration with the Copyright Office will provide.

So-called "poor man's copyright" consists of enclosing a copy of your song in an envelope, sending it registered mail to yourself, and not opening the envelope. The idea is that the postmark serves as proof as to the date of creation of the song. Some variations of the "poor man's copyright" theme include having a notary public stamp a lead sheet with a signature and date, placing lead sheets or tapes of the song in a safe deposit box, and having people listen to a song so that they may testify that the song had been created as of a certain date.

An Alternative Registration Service

National Academy of Songwriters in Hollywood, California (NAS) provides a registration service "song book" for a very modest fee and keeps a record of your song on file. This service is similar to script deposits kept by the Writer's Guild of America for screenplay writers. NAS's "song bank" is designed as an interim measure before you register your song with the Copyright Office, which NAS does <u>not</u> do for you.

WHAT IS PROPER COPYRIGHT NOTICE?

Proper notice of a claim to copyright in a song or sound recording is an important step in protecting your rights, since it puts people on notice that you claim the copyright. Failure to attach proper notice to published copies, however, no longer invalidates your copyright. There are separate symbols for notice of copyright in songs © and in sound recordings ℗. The copyright notice for songs and sound recordings must include three elements: the symbol C or P in a circle, the year of publication, and the name of the copyright owner. An incorrect copyright notice that appeared on an independently produced cassette read: "All material © 1991."

Why Are There Different Copyright Symbols?

The word "Copyright," the abbreviation "Copr.," or the symbol © is used on copies. ℗ is used on phonorecords. What's the distinction? © (or the word "Copyright" or the abbreviation "Copr.") protects works that are visually perceptible (e.g. sheet music).   protects sound recordings; they are not visually perceptible. When you look at what the law terms a "phonorecord" (a record or tape), you can neither see the song nor hear the sounds embodied in the record or tape. Here's a simple rule to apply: Put a © notice on lead sheets, and put a ℗ notice on cassettes and records. Proper notices are illustrated below.

What is the Proper Copyright Notice for Songs?

A copyright notice for a song fixed on sheet music should look something like this:

© 1991 Sally Songwriter.
All rights reserved.

Notices that vary from this form are common. A popular one is "Copyright © 1991 Sally Songwriter," or "© Copyright Sally Songwriter 1991." All the law requires is that these three symbols "give reasonable notice of the claim of copyright."

The words "All Rights Reserved" are not suggested by United States copyright law, but they are recommended because they provide additional copyright protection in certain South American countries.

What is the Proper Notice for Sound Recordings?

The notice for sound recordings fixed in tapes, records, or CDs is the same as for songs, except that a ℗ is used instead of a ©. Thus, the notice for a claim to copyright in a sound recording looks something like this:

℗ 1991 XYZ Records.
All Rights Reserved.

This notice may be put on the surface, label, or container of the phonorecord.

What If I Omit The Notice on Published Copies or Phonorecords?

Under the pre-1978 U.S. Copyright law omission of a copyright notice in published copies was fatal to a claim of copyright. This is not true under the present law. However, if you omitted the notice between January1,1978 and February 28, 1989 the law allows you to take certain corrective actions. These curative provisions may be invoked when the notice was omitted from a small number of copies, if the song was registered within five years of publication and a reasonable effort is made to add the notice to the copies of phonorecords already distributed to the public, or if the notice has been omitted in violation of a written requirement that published copies bear the required notice. There are also curative provisions if your song is published with inaccurate information (for example, the wrong publication date).

Do I Have To Put a Copyright Notice on Demos?

Legally you don't have to put any copyright notice on demos, that is, unpublished lead sheets, demonstration tapes, or demonstration 45s. However, the more prudent thing to do is put the appropriate notice on your song or tape.

My advice: put a © notice on every lead sheet or lyric sheet as soon as you write it down. And put a ℗ notice on every tape or record you submit or loan. It puts people on notice that you are claiming copyright in your songs and recordings, and reflects that you take your craft seriously.

WHAT IS PUBLICATION?

A song is published when it is distributed to the public by means of a sale or some other means of transferring ownership. The most common way songs are first published is when records containing the songs are distributed. Whenever a song is published, it should have the appropriate copyright notice affixed to the record, tape, sheet music or other physical embodiment of the work.

WHAT IF I WANT TO RECORD A COPYRIGHTED SONG?

The copyright law gives the owner of a copyrighted song the exclusive right to make the first sound recording of the song. However, once the song has been recorded and distributed to the public, others are entitled to make their own recordings of that work.

If you want to record a song for a record, you have two alternatives: you may negotiate a license (called a "mechanical license") from the copyright owner; or you may use the "compulsory mechanical license" provision of the copyright law, which does not require that you gain permission of the copyright holder, but does require you to account to the copyright holder and to pay fixed rates per song for each record manufactured and sold. In practice, however, the vast majority of mechanical licenses are negotiated, primarily through The Harry Fox Agency in New York. Mechanical license fees are paid to that agency, which deducts its administration fee, and remits the balance to the copyright holder (usually a publisher) on a quarterly basis.

HOW LONG DO COPYRIGHTS LAST?

Beginning in 1978, the revised copyright law gave songwriters some extra protection by extending the lifetime of copyrights. Under the pre-1978 law, a copyright began at the date of publication, and lasted for an initial period of twenty-eight years, with a twenty-eight year renewal period, for a maximum of fifty-six years.

Under the revised law, however, copyright protection dates from the date of creation (i.e., fixation in a tangible medium of expression) and, in most cases, lasts for the lifetime of the author plus fifty years. Thus, if you write a song in 1990, and die in the year 2010, the copyright lasts until 2060. Under the old law, if the song had been published in 1990, the copyright would have expired in 2018 if not renewed, and 2046 if it had been renewed.

For "works made for hire" (discussed below), as for anonymous works, the term is seventy-five years from the date of publication, or one hundred years from the date of creation (fixation), whichever is shorter.

CAN COPYRIGHT OWNERSHIP BE TRANSFERRED?

Copyrights, like tangible things, can be divided up and bought and sold. For example, when you license ASCAP to collect public performance royalties you have, in effect, transferred part of your copyright to ASCAP. You still own the rest of the copyright, however. Also, in typical music publishing and record deals, you transfer your copyright to the label or publisher, in return for their promise to pay you royalties.

What is a License?

You can also give permission to someone to exploit your copyright without transferring ownership. This is called a "license." For example, someone may record your song under a mechanical license—but you still own the song.

Should a Transfer Of Copyright Be Recorded with the Copyright Office?

If you transfer your copyright, or any exclusive right under copyright, the transfer of ownership must be written and signed by the copyright owner (you). The transfer should be recorded in the Copyright Office. Recording is important to the person to whom the copyright is transferred, as it is a prerequisite for bringing a copyright infringement suit. Also, conflicts may emerge between persons who claim the same copyright. In such cases, the first to record the transfer will prevail in a lawsuit arising from a dispute over copyright ownership. Failure to register the transfer, however, does not invalidate the transfer.

Can I Get My Copyright Back After Transferring It?

Because a newly created song is hard to value, the copyright law formerly provided that after the initial twenty-eight year term, despite assignment of the copyright to others, the renewal copyright would revert to the author, or the author's heir(s) if the author had died.

The present law does not provide for a renewal period. Instead, it provides that the author or the author's heirs may get the copyright back between the thirty-fifth and fortieth years after transferring their copyright by serving a written notice on the person who then currently holds the copyright. They then regain ownership of the copyright for the rest of its duration. Note this does not apply to "works made for hire" as your employer or the person commissioning the song is deemed the author of the song (discussed below).

Obviously for you or your heir to take advantage of this provision you must keep good records and a prospective calendar. Your business manager should be helpful.

WHAT IF I CO-WRITE A SONG?

If you co-write a song with another songwriter, that musical work generally is a "joint work." Both authors co-own the entire work. Thus, Lennon and McCartney both owned all of "Michelle," before they transferred it to a publishing company. The copyright lasts for 50 years from the death of the last surviving co-author.

WHAT IF I'M HIRED TO WRITE A SONG?

Songwriters are frequently hired to write songs. In such a case, the songwriter is described in the songwriter contract as an "employee for hire" or "writer for hire." The significance of this is that the employer (the person who hired the writer) is deemed the author of the song, and owns the song unless the contract states otherwise. If the work is not prepared by an employee in the course of his or her employment, the work will only be considered a "work made for hire" if there is a written agreement to consider it such and the song falls into the specific list of "specially ordered or commissioned works" listed in the Copyright Act. The most important category for songwriters is that if you write a song for a film it can be "specially ordered or commissioned." Remember, in the work-made-for-hire situation, you cannot get your copyright back between the thirty-fifth and fortieth years after transferring the copyright, as the employer is the author of the song.

WHAT IS COPYRIGHT INFRINGEMENT?

A work is infringed when any of the exclusive rights in a copyright are violated. Persons who infringe copyrights are subject to both civil and criminal penalties. Here are some examples:

You write a song, and the sheet music is sold in a store. An infringer purchases the sheet music, duplicates it and sells it. This is an infringement of your right to reproduce the work and your exclusive right to distribute copies of the work to the public.

Another example is when you record an album containing your songs, and the infringer dubs hundreds of cassettes, and sells them. Again, this violates your exclusive reproduction and distribution rights. This is also an infringement of your rights in both your song and the sound recording fixed in the album. Consequently, both you (as the song owner) and your record company could sue for infringement.

Didn't George Harrison's "My Sweet Lord" Infringe "He's So Fine?"

George Harrison was found to have infringed the 1962 Chiffons classic "He's So Fine" with his 1970 hit "My Sweet Lord." The court found the music of the two songs to be identical. Even though the lyrics and concepts of the song were different, and even though Harrison only subconsciously took from "He's So Fine," this was still an infringement.

When Should I Sue for Copyright Infringement?

The copyright law, like most other laws, has a statute of limitations. This means you have only a limited amount of time to bring suit. In cases of infringement you have three years from the infringement date to bring suit. Any delay, however, can harm you. As soon as you learn of an unauthorized use of your song, see a lawyer immediately.

Can I Infringe the Original Sound Recording Performance by Doing a Cover?

As long as you have permission to re-record a song (whether from the copyright owner or by filing the compulsory mechanical license), you can try to sound like the original performance. As discussed above, you get permission to record the song by getting a compulsory license by complying with copyright law formalities, or by obtaining a negotiated license from the copyright owner of the underlying song. You don't have to have the permission of the original performer unless that performer happens to have the rights to the song. If you want to record "Born in The U.S.A." you can try to sound like Bruce Springsteen, but you must have permission to record the song.

You should be careful, however, if an advertising agency hires you to directly imitate the sound of a well-known performer. Recent cases involving Bette Midler and Tom Waits have led to substantial judgments against advertising agencies who deliberately had singers imitate the voices of Midler and Waits.

What Can I Win in an Infringement Suit?

The remedies provided by law in an infringement suit include both injunctions and money damages. If you can prove infringement at a preliminary stage of the suit the court will make the infringer stop.

This is a form of injunction—that is, a court order against the infringer. The court can also order the impounding of the allegedly infringing copies or phonorecords as well as the machinery used to produce them.

Since proving money damages is difficult the law sets out what are termed "statutory damages," which generally run from $500 to $20,000 for a single act of copyright infringement.

If you win your infringement suit you may elect to receive either your actual damages which you suffer plus the profits of the infringer from the infringement, or statutory damages. In certain instances the court will also award court costs and attorneys' fees. Remember, statutory damages and attorney's fees will be awarded only if you make timely registration of your copyright with the Copyright Office.

The copyright law also provides for criminal penalties.

What's "Fair Use?"

As discussed above, the copyright owner has certain exclusive privileges in the copyright. Thus, a person who wishes to use the copyrighted material usually must seek permission of the copyright holder. However, the law recognizes certain limited uses of copyrighted material without permission as "fair use." In broad terms, the doctrine of "fair use" means that in some circumstances where the use is reasonable and not harmful to the copyright owner's rights, copyrighted material may be used to a limited extent without permission of the copyright owner. For example, under this doctrine critics have been held to be free to publish short extracts or quotations for purposes of illustration or comment. Record reviewers frequently quote from songs and this is considered a fair use.

The line between fair use and infringement is unclear and not easily defined. There is no specific number of words, lines, or notes that can be safely taken without permission. Acknowledging the source of the copyrighted material does not avoid infringement. The safe course is to get permission before using copyrighted material. The Copyright Office cannot give this permission. It can, however, supply information regarding copyright ownership as disclosed by a search of its records for an hourly fee. For information about Copyright Office searches write to the Copyright Office Reference Division of the Copyright Office. Copyright searches are also done by some private law firms and by The Clearing House (Los Angeles).

When it is difficult to obtain permission, use of copyrighted material should be avoided unless it seems clear that the doctrine of "fair use" would apply to the situation. If there is any doubt or question, it is advisable to consult an attorney.

How Much Of An Old Song Can I Take Without Infringing?

We all know that new songs frequently incorporate parts of old songs. One pervasive myth is that you can graft four bars from a copyrighted song without subjecting yourself to a lawsuit by the copyright owner, as taking four bars is a "fair use." In fact, there is no such provision in the law. The test is whether the amount of the old song that was taken was substantial. This rather loose standard is applied by a judge or jury when listening to your song. Again, remember there is no standard measure of how much music, or how many of the lyrics can be incorporated in a new song without infringing the old song.

CONCLUSION

Copyright law is complex. As a performing musician or songwriter you should have a basic understanding of copyright law. When you write or record a song, you have certain valuable rights in that song that you can exploit. By knowing your rights you can protect them; when you have a specific problem, you should consult an attorney for guidance.

EXHIBIT 1: SUMMARY OF COPYRIGHT NOTICES APPEARING ON A RECORD ALBUM

Item	Location	Purpose
℗, year, owner	Typically on label and rear of cover	Gives notices of owner of sound recording; also gives notices of owner of album art and text unless another owner is identified.
©, year, owner	Label, rear of cover	Provides extra notice of ownership of the art and text on the cover and label when the owner of the sound recording is the same.
©, year, owner	Beside specific text or art on cover	Identifies ownership of specific text or art when they are owned by another.
©, year, owner	At end of written lyric	Provides notice of ownership of songs.
All rights reserved	After each © notice.	Provides notice required for copyright protection in certain foreign countries.
Used by permission	After certain © notices	Used whenever permission to use another's copyrighted work is granted.
Unauthorized reproduction prohibited, etc.	Rear of cover	Optional warning designed to deter infringement; can take various forms.
Songwriter names	Adjacent to song titles	Not required by copyright law when songwriters have assigned songs to music publishers or others, but it is customarily added as a matter of courtesy or may be required by contract as it facilitates payment of songwriter royalties.
BMI/ASCAP/SESAC	Next to song title	Not part of the copyright notice, but services to identify the performing rights society that licenses the song for public performances and collects royalties on behalf of the songwriter and publisher.
Playing time	Next to song title	Not part of the copyright notice but convenient for disc jockeys who have to squeeze in those 10 second commercial spots.

FORM PA
UNITED STATES COPYRIGHT OFFICE

REGISTRATION NUMBER

PA PAU

EFFECTIVE DATE OF REGISTRATION

Month Day Year

DO NOT WRITE ABOVE THIS LINE. IF YOU NEED MORE SPACE, USE A SEPARATE CONTINUATION SHEET.

1

TITLE OF THIS WORK ▼

PREVIOUS OR ALTERNATIVE TITLES ▼

NATURE OF THIS WORK ▼ See instructions

2

a

NAME OF AUTHOR ▼

DATES OF BIRTH AND DEATH
Year Born ▼ Year Died ▼

Was this contribution to the work a "work made for hire"?
☐ Yes
☐ No

AUTHOR'S NATIONALITY OR DOMICILE
Name of Country
OR { Citizen of ▶ ____ / Domiciled in ▶ ____ }

WAS THIS AUTHOR'S CONTRIBUTION TO THE WORK
Anonymous? ☐ Yes ☐ No
Pseudonymous? ☐ Yes ☐ No
If the answer to either of these questions is "Yes," see detailed instructions.

NATURE OF AUTHORSHIP Briefly describe nature of the material created by this author in which copyright is claimed. ▼

b

NAME OF AUTHOR ▼

DATES OF BIRTH AND DEATH
Year Born ▼ Year Died ▼

Was this contribution to the work a "work made for hire"?
☐ Yes
☐ No

AUTHOR'S NATIONALITY OR DOMICILE
Name of country
OR { Citizen of ▶ ____ / Domiciled in ▶ ____ }

WAS THIS AUTHOR'S CONTRIBUTION TO THE WORK
Anonymous? ☐ Yes ☐ No
Pseudonymous? ☐ Yes ☐ No
If the answer to either of these questions is "Yes," see detailed instructions.

NATURE OF AUTHORSHIP Briefly describe nature of the material created by this author in which copyright is claimed. ▼

c

NAME OF AUTHOR ▼

DATES OF BIRTH AND DEATH
Year Born ▼ Year Died ▼

Was this contribution to the work a "work made for hire"?
☐ Yes
☐ No

AUTHOR'S NATIONALITY OR DOMICILE
Name of Country
OR { Citizen of ▶ ____ / Domiciled in ▶ ____ }

WAS THIS AUTHOR'S CONTRIBUTION TO THE WORK
Anonymous? ☐ Yes ☐ No
Pseudonymous? ☐ Yes ☐ No
If the answer to either of these questions is "Yes," see detailed instructions.

NATURE OF AUTHORSHIP Briefly describe nature of the material created by this author in which copyright is claimed. ▼

NOTE

Under the law, the "author" of a "work made for hire" is generally the employer, not the employee (see instructions). For any part of this work that was "made for hire" check "Yes" in the space provided, give the employer (or other person for whom the work was prepared) as "Author" of that part, and leave the space for dates of birth and death blank.

3

a **YEAR IN WHICH CREATION OF THIS WORK WAS COMPLETED** **This information must be given in all cases.**
____ ◀ Year

b **DATE AND NATION OF FIRST PUBLICATION OF THIS PARTICULAR WORK**
Complete this information ONLY if this work has been published.
Month ▶ ____ Day ▶ ____ Year ▶ ____
____ ◀ Nation

4

COPYRIGHT CLAIMANT(S) Name and address must be given even if the claimant is the same as the author given in space 2.▼

See instructions before completing this space

TRANSFER If the claimant(s) named here in space 4 are different from the author(s) named in space 2, give a brief statement of how the claimant(s) obtained ownership of the copyright.▼

DO NOT WRITE HERE
OFFICE USE ONLY

APPLICATION RECEIVED

ONE DEPOSIT RECEIVED

TWO DEPOSITS RECEIVED

REMITTANCE NUMBER AND DATE

MORE ON BACK ▶
- Complete all applicable spaces (numbers 5-9) on the reverse side of this page
- See detailed instructions
- Sign the form at line 8

DO NOT WRITE HERE

Page 1 of ______ pages

EXAMINED BY

FORM PA

CHECKED BY

☐ CORRESPONDENCE Yes

FOR COPYRIGHT OFFICE USE ONLY

DO NOT WRITE ABOVE THIS LINE. IF YOU NEED MORE SPACE, USE A SEPARATE CONTINUATION SHEET.

5

PREVIOUS REGISTRATION Has registration for this work, or for an earlier version of this work, already been made in the Copyright Office?

☐ **Yes** ☐ **No** If your answer is "Yes," why is another registration being sought? (Check appropriate box) ▼

a. ☐ This is the first published edition of a work previously registered in unpublished form.

b. ☐ This is the first application submitted by this author as copyright claimant.

c. ☐ This is a changed version of the work, as shown by space 6 on this application.

If your answer is "Yes," give: **Previous Registration Number ▼** **Year of Registration ▼**

6

DERIVATIVE WORK OR COMPILATION Complete both space 6a & 6b for a derivative work; complete only 6b for a compilation.

a. Preexisting Material Identify any preexisting work or works that this work is based on or incorporates. ▼

See instructions before completing this space

b. Material Added to This Work Give a brief, general statement of the material that has been added to this work and in which copyright is claimed. ▼

7

DEPOSIT ACCOUNT If the registration fee is to be charged to a Deposit Account established in the Copyright Office, give name and number of Account.

Name ▼ **Account Number ▼**

CORRESPONDENCE Give name and address to which correspondence about this application should be sent. Name/Address/Apt/City/State/Zip ▼

Area Code & Telephone Number ▶

Be sure to give your daytime phone ◀ number

8

CERTIFICATION* I, the undersigned, hereby certify that I am the

Check only one ▼

☐ author

☐ other copyright claimant

☐ owner of exclusive right(s)

☐ authorized agent of ________________

Name of author or other copyright claimant, or owner of exclusive right(s) ▲

of the work identified in this application and that the statements made by me in this application are correct to the best of my knowledge.

Typed or printed name and date ▼ If this application gives a date of publication in space 3, do not sign and submit it before that date.

date ▶

Handwritten signature (X) ▼

9

MAIL CERTIFICATE TO

Name ▼

Number/Street/Apartment Number ▼

City/State/ZIP ▼

Certificate will be mailed in window envelope

YOU MUST:
- Complete all necessary spaces
- Sign your application in space 8

SEND ALL 3 ELEMENTS IN THE SAME PACKAGE:
1. Application form
2. Nonrefundable $20 filing fee in check or money order payable to *Register of Copyrights*
3. Deposit material

MAIL TO:
Register of Copyrights
Library of Congress
Washington, D.C. 20559

* 17 U.S.C. § 506(e) Any person who knowingly makes a false representation of a material fact in the application for copyright registration provided for by section 409, or in any written statement filed in connection with the application, shall be fined not more than $2,500.

February 1991—200,000

☆U.S. GOVERNMENT PRINTING OFFICE: 1991—282-170/20,014

FORM SR
UNITED STATES COPYRIGHT OFFICE

REGISTRATION NUMBER

SR SRU

EFFECTIVE DATE OF REGISTRATION

Month Day Year

DO NOT WRITE ABOVE THIS LINE. IF YOU NEED MORE SPACE, USE A SEPARATE CONTINUATION SHEET.

1

TITLE OF THIS WORK ▼

PREVIOUS OR ALTERNATIVE TITLES ▼

NATURE OF MATERIAL RECORDED ▼ See instructions
☐ Musical ☐ Musical-Dramatic
☐ Dramatic ☐ Literary
☐ Other ______

2

a **NAME OF AUTHOR ▼**

DATES OF BIRTH AND DEATH
Year Born ▼ Year Died ▼

Was this contribution to the work a "work made for hire"?
☐ Yes
☐ No

AUTHOR'S NATIONALITY OR DOMICILE
Name of Country
OR { Citizen of ▶ ______ / Domiciled in ▶ ______

WAS THIS AUTHOR'S CONTRIBUTION TO THE WORK
Anonymous? ☐ Yes ☐ No
Pseudonymous? ☐ Yes ☐ No
If the answer to either of these questions is "Yes," see detailed instructions

NATURE OF AUTHORSHIP Briefly describe nature of the material created by this author in which copyright is claimed. ▼

b **NAME OF AUTHOR ▼**

DATES OF BIRTH AND DEATH
Year Born ▼ Year Died ▼

Was this contribution to the work a "work made for hire"?
☐ Yes
☐ No

AUTHOR'S NATIONALITY OR DOMICILE
Name of country
OR { Citizen of ▶ ______ / Domiciled in ▶ ______

WAS THIS AUTHOR'S CONTRIBUTION TO THE WORK
Anonymous? ☐ Yes ☐ No
Pseudonymous? ☐ Yes ☐ No
If the answer to either of these questions is "Yes," see detailed instructions

NATURE OF AUTHORSHIP Briefly describe nature of the material created by this author in which copyright is claimed. ▼

c **NAME OF AUTHOR ▼**

DATES OF BIRTH AND DEATH
Year Born ▼ Year Died ▼

Was this contribution to the work a "work made for hire"?
☐ Yes
☐ No

AUTHOR'S NATIONALITY OR DOMICILE
Name of Country
OR { Citizen of ▶ ______ / Domiciled in ▶ ______

WAS THIS AUTHOR'S CONTRIBUTION TO THE WORK
Anonymous? ☐ Yes ☐ No
Pseudonymous? ☐ Yes ☐ No
If the answer to either of these questions is "Yes," see detailed instructions

NATURE OF AUTHORSHIP Briefly describe nature of the material created by this author in which copyright is claimed. ▼

NOTE

Under the law, the "author" of a "work made for hire" is generally the employer, not the employee (see instructions). For any part of this work that was "made for hire" check "Yes" in the space provided, give the employer (or other person for whom the work was prepared) as "Author" of that part, and leave the space for dates of birth and death blank.

3

a **YEAR IN WHICH CREATION OF THIS WORK WAS COMPLETED** **This information must be given in all cases.**
______ ◀ Year

b **DATE AND NATION OF FIRST PUBLICATION OF THIS PARTICULAR WORK**
Complete this information ONLY if this work has been published.
Month ▶ ______ Day ▶ ______ Year ▶ ______
______ ◀ Nation

4

COPYRIGHT CLAIMANT(S) Name and address must be given even if the claimant is the same as the author given in space 2.▼

See instructions before completing this space.

TRANSFER If the claimant(s) named here in space 4 are different from the author(s) named in space 2, give a brief statement of how the claimant(s) obtained ownership of the copyright.▼

DO NOT WRITE HERE OFFICE USE ONLY
APPLICATION RECEIVED
ONE DEPOSIT RECEIVED
TWO DEPOSITS RECEIVED
REMITTANCE NUMBER AND DATE

MORE ON BACK ▶
- Complete all applicable spaces (numbers 5-9) on the reverse side of this page
- See detailed instructions
- Sign the form at line 8

DO NOT WRITE HERE

Page 1 of ______ pages

EXAMINED BY

FORM SR

CHECKED BY

☐ CORRESPONDENCE Yes

☐ DEPOSIT ACCOUNT FUNDS USED

FOR COPYRIGHT OFFICE USE ONLY

DO NOT WRITE ABOVE THIS LINE. IF YOU NEED MORE SPACE, USE A SEPARATE CONTINUATION SHEET.

PREVIOUS REGISTRATION Has registration for this work, or for an earlier version of this work, already been made in the Copyright Office? 5

☐ **Yes** ☐ **No** If your answer is "Yes," why is another registration being sought? (Check appropriate box) ▼

☐ This is the first published edition of a work previously registered in unpublished form.

☐ This is the first application submitted by this author as copyright claimant.

☐ This is a changed version of the work, as shown by space 6 on this application.

If your answer is "Yes," give: **Previous Registration Number ▼** **Year of Registration ▼**

DERIVATIVE WORK OR COMPILATION Complete both space 6a & 6b for a derivative work; complete only 6b for a compilation. 6

a. Preexisting Material Identify any preexisting work or works that this work is based on or incorporates. ▼

See instructions before completing this space.

b. Material Added to This Work Give a brief, general statement of the material that has been added to this work and in which copyright is claimed. ▼

DEPOSIT ACCOUNT If the registration fee is to be charged to a Deposit Account established in the Copyright Office, give name and number of Account. 7

Name ▼ **Account Number ▼**

CORRESPONDENCE Give name and address to which correspondence about this application should be sent. Name/Address/Apt/City/State/Zip ▼

Area Code & Telephone Number ▶

Be sure to give your daytime phone ◀ number.

CERTIFICATION* I, the undersigned, hereby certify that I am the 8

Check one ▼

☐ author

☐ other copyright claimant

☐ owner of exclusive right(s)

☐ authorized agent of ________________

Name of author or other copyright claimant, or owner of exclusive right(s) ▲

of the work identified in this application and that the statements made by me in this application are correct to the best of my knowledge.

Typed or printed name and date ▼ If this application gives a date of publication in space 3, do not sign and submit it before that date.

date ▶

Handwritten signature (X) ▼

MAIL CERTIFICATE TO 9

Name ▼

Number/Street/Apartment Number ▼

City/State/ZIP ▼

Certificate will be mailed in window envelope

YOU MUST:
- Complete all necessary spaces
- Sign your application in space 8

SEND ALL 3 ELEMENTS IN THE SAME PACKAGE:
1. Application form
2. Nonrefundable $20 filing fee in check or money order payable to *Register of Copyrights*
3. Deposit material

MAIL TO:
Register of Copyrights
Library of Congress
Washington, D.C. 20559

* 17 U.S.C. § 506(e): Any person who knowingly makes a false representation of a material fact in the application for copyright registration provided for by section 409, or in any written statement filed in connection with the application, shall be fined not more than $2,500.

December 1990—100,000

☆U.S. GOVERNMENT PRINTING OFFICE: 1990—282-170/20,006

To establish a claim of copyright infringement, the plaintiff (person who files the lawsuit) must first demonstrate that he or she is the owner of the copyright of the song that they believe was copied by the composer of the defendant's song. The plaintiff must then demonstrate that the composer of defendant's song in fact copied from plaintiff's song and that the material that was copied results in a finding of copyright infringement. Once infringement is established, then the question becomes what remedies are available to the plaintiff.

ESTABLISHING OWNERSHIP

Copyright of a song is established when the work is first fixed in a tangible form — for example, notated on paper or recorded on tape. In other words, registration of the song with the Copyright Office is not a prerequisite to the song being protected by copyright. However, before an infringement case can be filed in court, the owner of the copyright must, as a general rule, register the song with the Copyright Office.

The copyright owner will typically be either the composer of the song, the employer of the composer (if the composer wrote the song during the course and scope of employment as a "work for hire") or a person or company to whom the original owner of the song (i.e., the composer or their employer) transferred a copyright interest in the song.

Plaintiff's proof of ownership may become complicated where the plaintiff is not the composer of the song but, instead, claims ownership either as the employer of the composer or by virtue of a transfer in ownership. Further, the fact that the plaintiff has registered the song with the Copyright Office and has claimed ownership of the song on the registration certificate does not conclusively establish that the plaintiff is, in fact, the true owner of the copyright in the song.

ESTABLISHING COPYING

A composer charged with copyright infringement rarely admits copying from plaintiff's song. And it is very unusual for there to be what the law calls "direct" evidence of copying, such as testimony by a business associate of the composer of defendant's song that they observed the composer listening to plaintiff's song while writing defendant's song.

Since admissions of plagiarism and other forms of direct evidence of copying are hard to come by, the law permits a copyright plaintiff to prove copying through "circumstantial" evidence — by showing that the composer of defendant's song had "access" to plaintiff's song and that the two songs in issue are "substantially similar."

Access

Access means that the composer of defendant's song had a "reasonable opportunity" to hear plaintiff's song or view a print version of it before writing defendant's song. If the plaintiff can establish only that there was a "bare possibility" that the composer of defendant's song heard or viewed a printed version of plaintiff's song before defendant's song was written, then plaintiff has not established access and, with one exception discussed below, plaintiff's case will be dismissed from court.

A plaintiff can establish access by showing that the composer of defendant's song, as a member of the general public, had a reasonable opportunity to have been exposed to plaintiff's song. For example, where plaintiff's song was a major hit before defendant's song was written, access would ordinarily be established. This is true even if the composer of defendant's song denies having heard plaintiff's song since, in the eyes of the law, there was a reasonable possibility that they would have heard plaintiff's song on the radio or on television. If, on the other hand, plaintiff's song received only limited airplay in one region of the country and little other exposure, and the composer of defendant's song could show that he or she never visited that region while plaintiff's song was being played, access would, ordinarily, not be established. As another example, if plaintiff's song was played by plaintiff during only a few club dates, access would ordinarily not be established unless it could be shown that the composer of defendant's song frequented one or more of the clubs where plaintiff's song was performed.

There is a second way of establishing access. If the plaintiff can establish that plaintiff's song was auditioned for or submitted to the composer of defendant's song before defendant's song was written, then access would be established. Access might also be established where plaintiff's song was auditioned for or submitted to a business associate or close friend of the composer of defendant's song. More difficult questions arise where plaintiff's song was auditioned for or submitted to a large company, such as a major record label, with which the composer of defendant's song has a business relationship.

In the end, the question of whether access is established is usually one of degree which raises interesting and difficult issues for lawyers and judges. However, it is clear that the stronger the showing of access, the greater the chance plaintiff will have of proving copying by circumstantial evidence.

Substantial Similarity

As mentioned above, to prove copying by circumstantial evidence, the plaintiff must, ordinarily, show not only access, but also that the two songs in issue are "substantially similar."

There is no precise definition of "substantially similar." Clearly, "substantially similar" means something less than "identical" and something more than "a little bit alike." Probably the best way of defining "substantially similar" is "so similar that an ordinary listener to music would believe that there was a strong possibility that one song, or at least an important part of it, was copied from the other."

Even where the two songs in issue are substantially similar, the plaintiff's case will ordinarily be dismissed from court if the plaintiff cannot also present evidence of access. There is, however, one exception to the general rule that both access and substantial similarity must be proved to establish copying by circumstantial evidence. Where an expert witness will testify that the similarity between plaintiff's song and defendant's song is so overwhelming that there is no explanation for the similarity other than that one was copied from the other, access will be "inferred" from the similarity and the plaintiff will not be required to present any other evidence showing access, so long as there is some evidence that plaintiff's song was written before defendant's. It should, however, be pointed out that it is a rare case where this exception — known as the "striking similarity" doctrine — to the general rule would be applicable.

ESTABLISHING INDEPENDENT CREATION

It is important to note that the plaintiff has not conclusively established copying by presenting evidence showing both access and substantial similarity. Presentation of this evidence merely means that the issue of copying will be presented to the jury. However, even if the plaintiff proves both access and substantial similarity, the defendant will win if they can convince the jury that defendant's song was created independently of plaintiff's song. This stems from the fact that no matter how similar the two songs in issue are, if the composer of defendant's song did not in fact copy from the plaintiff's song, there can be no finding of copyright infringement. This is true even if the two songs are identical — without copying there cannot be infringement. This is the law's way of recognizing that two composers could conceivably compose the very same song without either having heard the other's composition.

To establish independent creation, which simply means a lack of copying, defendant will attempt to show a number of things. First, defendant will try to prove that the composer of defendant's song had solid musical training and a substantial background in music. This supports the conclusion that they did not need to copy from anything to write a good song. Second, defendant will attempt to show that the composer of defendant's song wrote several hit songs before writing defendant's song. This supports the conclusion that he or she was a skilled and successful composer who had no motivation or need to copy.

Third, and of great importance in persuading a jury that the similarity between the songs in issue did not result from copying, defendant will try to present music researchers and expert witnesses who can testify, using examples, that several songs written before both plaintiff's song and defendant's song are similar to each of them. This evidence is used to show that the musical elements which result in the aural similarity between the two songs in issue are elements that are commonly used by composers of popular music, which increases the likelihood that the similarities between the songs in issue are coincidental and, thus, decreases the likelihood that defendant's song was copied from plaintiff's song or, for that matter, any other song.

The law has long recognized that there are limits on the abilities of songwriters to combine notes and chords so as to make music that will be relatively easy for most musicians to play, as well as both pleasing and accessible to the musically-untrained, popular ear. Because of these limits, courts recognize that simple musical elements are likely to recur in popular songs spontaneously — that is, not as the result of one composer copying from a song composed by another. Consequently, defendant will also attempt to prove, through expert witnesses, that the musical elements in defendant's song upon which the plaintiff's claim of copying is based are simple musical elements, which are pleasing to the musically-unsophisticated ear of the audience for contemporary popular songs and relatively easy for most musicians to perform.

Finally, defendant will attempt to show that the composer of defendant's song wrote several earlier songs that contained the musical elements supposedly copied from plaintiff's song. If defendant had used these musical elements in songs written before he or she could possibly have heard plaintiff's song, it would be unlikely that in composing defendant's song they copied from plaintiff's song. It is, after all, ordinarily permissible to copy from one's own compositions, and composers of contemporary music often write songs that are very much like their earlier works. If, however, a composer copies from one of their earlier written songs that is owned by someone else, a problem may arise.

In the final analysis, assuming that plaintiff puts on evidence of access and substantial similarity, and defendant puts on evidence of independent creation, it will be for the jury to determine whether the composer of defendant's song in fact copied from plaintiff's song.

ESTABLISHING INFRINGEMENT

Even if the plaintiff establishes ownership of plaintiff's song and that the composer of defendant's song copied from it, still more must be shown to establish infringement.

The plaintiff must establish that more than a minimal amount of material contained in defendant's song was copied from plaintiff's song. Contrary to what many musicians believe, there is no legal rule that establishes that a composer may freely borrow four bars, or six notes, or any other set amount of material from a copyrighted work without being found liable for infringement. Indeed, the copying of a very brief musical passage from plaintiff's song may result in a finding of infringement if that passage is qualitatively important to both of the songs in issue. For example, the copying of a very brief melodic "hook" might well result in infringement if that hook was the centerpiece of plaintiff's song and important in defendant's song.

Defendant will not be able to avoid being held liable for infringement by showing that there is much material in defendant's song that is not in any way similar to, and thus could not have been copied from, plaintiff's song. For example, if the basis of plaintiff's claim is a strong musical similarity between the choruses of plaintiff's and defendant's songs, defendant cannot avoid a finding of infringement by showing that the music in the verses and bridges of the two songs is totally dissimilar and that there is no similarity whatsoever in lyrics throughout the two songs.

Since the copyright law does not protect ideas, but rather only their expression, in order to establish infringement, plaintiff must demonstrate that the composer of defendant's song copied not only the musical ideas contained in plaintiff's song, but also the manner in which the composer of plaintiff's song expressed those ideas. The line between a musical idea and the manner in which a musical idea is expressed is a very, very difficult one to draw, and the distinction between musical ideas and the manner in which they are expressed is puzzling to musicians, lawyers and judges. Nevertheless, it is a distinction which is central to United States copyright law.

For there to be infringement, the material that was copied from the plaintiff's song must have been original to its composer. That is so because the copyright in a song protects only those musical elements, and combinations of musical elements, in a song that were original to its composer. If certain elements of a copyrighted song were original to its composer and others were not, but were instead copied from an earlier written song, the copyright in the song is valid, but the copyright protection in the song extends only to those elements that were original to its composer. It must, however, be understood that "original" does not mean novel or unique. If a composer writes a theme that is similar (or, for that matter, identical) to an earlier written theme without copying that earlier written theme, then, under copyright law, the composer's theme is considered their "original" theme.

Finally, plaintiff is not required to show that the composer of defendant's song deliberately infringed the copyright in plaintiff's song. In fact, plaintiff need not even establish that the copying from plaintiff's song was a conscious act by the composer of defendant's song. Several courts have concluded that even subconscious copying will result in a finding of infringement.

Significantly, if defendant's song is found by the jury to be an infringing copy of plaintiff's song, everyone who commercially exploits defendant's song will be liable for infringement, regardless of whether they had any reason to suspect that defendant's song infringed plaintiff's. Thus, a record company that innocently puts out a record containing a performance of defendant's song will be held liable for copyright infringement even if it does not have any possible way of knowing that the song is infringing, and even if the person or company that supplied it with the recording represented and warranted that the song did not infringe any other musical work. The same would be true with respect to both a motion picture company that innocently included defendant's song in the soundtrack of one of its films, and a manufacturer which innocently employed the music from defendant's song in a television commercial used to sell its products.

The fact that companies in this position will be treated as infringers despite their lack of knowledge that defendant's song infringes plaintiff's is of great consequence, since the remedies available to a winning plaintiff will apply to these companies.

REMEDIES

It is important to note that a losing defendant cannot avoid the remedies discussed below by, after being charged with infringement, expressing a willingness either to negotiate a "fair" license with plaintiff to use plaintiff's song or to pay plaintiff the prevailing "statutory rate" for a compulsory mechanical license, assuming the defendant could have avoided liability in the first place by paying plaintiff the statutory rate.

The four most important remedies available to a winning plaintiff are: 1) injunctive relief; 2) statutory damages; 3) actual damages; and, what is often perceived as the pot of gold at the end of the rainbow, 4) the profits of each of the infringing defendants that is attributable to their use of infringing musical material.

Injunctive Relief

Injunctive relief is a court order enjoining (i.e., prohibiting) each of the defendants from further distributing and selling works that contain material which infringes plaintiff's song. For example, if one of the defendants is a record company that has released an album containing a song that is found to infringe plaintiff's song, the record company will be enjoined from further distributing and selling the album until the infringing song is removed. Similarly, if one of the defendants is a motion picture company that has released a film containing infringing music, the company will be ordered to discontinue distribution and exhibition of the film unless the infringing music is removed from the soundtrack.

Where a plaintiff is able to obtain an order enjoining a defendant from commercially exploiting a work — such as a successful album or film — which is producing substantial revenues for that defendant, plaintiff will have enormous economic leverage, permitting plaintiff to then, as a practical matter, dictate the terms of a monetary settlement with that defendant.

Statutory Damages

Statutory damages are a form of damages provided for in the Copyright Act. They are calculated by multiplying a set amount of money times the number of infringements. This calculation can, however, become very complicated. Ordinarily, statutory damages are not nearly as meaningful to a plaintiff as any of the other remedies. Nevertheless, if an infringement action is contemplated or pursued, the option of statutory damages should be discussed between the lawyer and his client.

Actual Damage

Actual damages are those damages actually suffered by the plaintiff as the result of the infringement of plaintiff's song. For example, if an infringing song were comprised of music copied from plaintiff's song, coupled with obscene or distasteful lyrics, plaintiff might find it difficult to commercially exploit plaintiff's song. Or if a song that infringed plaintiff's song was included on the soundtrack of a successful film, plaintiff might well find it difficult to license plaintiff's song to a motion picture company. In sum, any use of an infringing song that tends to either make plaintiff's song "old news" or to tarnish plaintiff's song is damaging to the plaintiff, and the plaintiff, often through the use of expert witnesses, will attempt to prove the monetary extent of those damages.

Award of Profits

Often, the most significant remedy available to a prevailing plaintiff is an award of the profits of each of the defendants that are attributable to the use by each of infringing material. Profits, simply put, means revenues minus properly deductible costs and expenses. The issues, however, relating to the calculation of an award of profits are among the most challenging faced by lawyers involved in copyright cases.

In establishing the profits of an infringing defendant, the plaintiff is only required to present proof of the gross revenues realized by the defendant from its exploitation of the infringing song or, where the infringing song is embodied in a larger work, such as a motion picture or an album containing a number of other songs, from defendant's exploitation of that larger work. Defendant is then required to prove his, her or its properly deductible costs and expenses, which gives rise to a series of complicated accounting questions too complex to be treated in this chapter.

Since a prevailing plaintiff is entitled only to the profits attributable to the use of infringing material, two separate issues frequently arise. First, a determination must be made as to what extent the commercial success of the infringing song is attributable to its inclusion of infringing material, as distinguished from other factors, such as, for example, its use of noninfringing material and/or the talents of the performer who sings it. This question will often be the subject of expert testimony, with the plaintiff trying to prove that the infringing material was crucial to the popularity of the infringing song, and the defendant trying to prove that the infringing material played an insignificant role in the infringing song's success.

Second, where the infringing song is embodied in a work (such as an album or a motion picture) which includes other material that has no connection with plaintiff's song, another question becomes how much of the profits realized from the exploitation of that work is attributable to the infringing song and how much to the other material. For example, where the infringing song is one of ten cuts on an album, more than 10% of the profits realized by the record company from its sales of the album would be attributable to the infringing song if it was the hit, or one of the hits, that drove up the sales of the album, and less than 10% if it was not one of the hits and it therefore received little airplay.

Where an infringing song is used on the soundtrack of a motion picture, a question is how much of the motion picture studio's profits from its distribution of the film were attributable to the song's presence on the soundtrack. If the infringing song's inclusion on the soundtrack constituted an incidental or minor use, only a minuscule percentage of the film's profits would be attributable to its inclusion. If, on the other hand, the song was the film's title song, which was released on a record that was successfully used to promote the film and keep the radio-listening public reminded that the film was in theatres, the plaintiff's case for profits would be much better.

A very difficult question arises where an infringing song is used in a commercial for a product, such as a beer. The question then becomes how much of the company's profits from beer sales were attributable to the use of the song in the commercial.

In dealing with the difficult questions regarding attribution of profits discussed above, both plaintiff and defendants will rely upon statistics, sales figures and expert testimony in their attempts to maximize (in the case of the plaintiff) or minimize (in the defendants' case) the significance of the song in "selling" the album, the film or the beer.

Punitive Damages/Attorneys' Fees

Finally, there is the question of whether punitive damages and/or attorneys' fees are available as remedies. The Copyright Act does not provide for punitive damages and the prevailing, but not universally held, view is that punitive damages are not a remedy available to a successful plaintiff. However, in most cases a winning plaintiff will be able to recover attorneys' fees from the defendant. Less frequently, a winning defendant will be able to recover attorneys' fees from the plaintiff.

THREE DAY TICKET
Aug. 15, 16, 17
1969

Live Performance

- **Club Contracts**
- **Showcasing**
- **On the Road: A Primer for Touring Musicians**
- **Publicity: There's Never Enough**

This chapter deals with issues on which you should focus when dealing with clubs where you perform. Generally, there are three kinds of clubs: draw clubs, clubs with walk-in trades and lounge act clubs.

The draw club books acts with recognizable names to attract an audience. This could be a national recording act—or a local act with a following that will fill the house. Sometimes these clubs will use an opening act to reinforce the lead act's draw and ensure a full house.

The walk-in trade club depends on a regular crowd that frequents the club and normally will hire "club bands" that play Top 40 and maybe some of their own material. Lounge act clubs focus on groups that have highly polished performances of popular music (sometimes also called "copy music") and are prevalent in major cities' hotels, casinos, and resort areas. Many new bands get their start in these clubs, "slipping" in original tunes as they achieve popularity.

As some clubs are signatories of agreements with the American Federation of Musicians (AFM) find out if you need to be a member of the AFM before a club who is a signatory can book you.

Sometimes bands or their managers book their acts into clubs for showcase purposes, that is to "show" the group's talents to industry people who have promised to attend— or to generate enthusiasm. For example, a Midwest group who has a huge regional following books themselves into a Los Angeles club for almost no pay to showcase for record companies, publishers or even prospective managers. Or a record company may fill (or paper) a club when a new record is released to generate enthusiasm for a particular group being pushed by the record company or they may be filled by the group's personal manager or talent agency to influence record companies to develop an interest in the group.

A "casual" is a club or hotel room booked by a private party for a special occasion such as weddings, bar mitzvahs, anniversaries, industrial conventions.

APPROACHING THE CLUB

Before playing the club route, you should study the various kinds of clubs in which you could perform and decide which best suit your act. You should tailor your presentation to the club to fit your act and the club's style. It is important that you understand the reputation of the club and the makeup of the audience who is likely to enjoy your performance.

Club owners want a band that will please their audience and are professional. The club owner wants to know whether or not the artist will work as promised, show up on time, and make money for the club.

The more clubs in which you perform and the more reliable a track record you develop, the easier the bookings should become, particularly if you are able to show a consistent (and growing) draw.

Most club owners also expect you to have publicity materials that they can use to help promote the performance. The chapter "Publicity: There's Never Enough" discusses publicity issues in detail.

CLUB CONTRACTS

When dealing with clubs, you should understand that even a casual agreement to show up and play for free to see what happens is a contract. This section will focus on the various points you should review with the club owner in order to arrive at a performing contract. These same points are relevant for standard AFM contracts that are used when bands are booked into clubs that are affiliated with the AFM.

Remember that the contractual relationship with the club is only as good as the relationship between the club owner and the group itself. You should therefore make a threshold determination of whether the owners of the club are people with whom you really wish to deal. Counterbalancing that, if they are not people with whom you wish to deal, but the club is an important milestone in the development of your band and the band's credibility to the music industry, then that point has to be given fair consideration.

The contract with the club can be either oral or written. The problem with an oral contract is that in the event of a dispute, it is difficult to prove the terms agreed to between the club owner and the band. If the contract is written, then the agreed-to points are much easier to document. Rather than treating the written contract as an awesome legal document, consider it a checklist of important points that should be covered between the club owner and the group. Look to the contract as a way of making clear the relationship between the club and you, and of bringing to light all of the issues that are important to both parties. This way, everyone will focus on those issues at the very beginning and hopefully eliminate any later surprises. Contract discussions are an indication to the club owner of how professional you are.

Compensation

Your compensation could come in a number of forms. It could be from door receipts, in which case you should identify with the club owner the number of tickets to be sold, the prices of those tickets, and the number of freebees to the owner and to the performers. With that information, you will have some idea of the range of dollars to expect based on the percentage of the door receipts you have agreed to accept. Your compensation could be a flat sum, in which case the door receipts are not a problem. Reach an agreement on the form of compensation (i.e., whether it is in cash or cashier's check). The norm is cash, but insist on at least a cashier's check. Part of the money should be paid if not at the beginning, then at least partway through the performance with the balance due, if any, immediately at the conclusion of the performance.

Sound and Lights

An audience's perception of how good a performance is often depends on the quality of sound and lights. Make sure that the club has equipment adequate to your needs and that the club owner understands what these needs are.

If you (or the club) wishes to supplement the club's system with your own (or rented) equipment, work out the additional expense as part of your contract and arrange for a load in time. If you are using an acoustic piano, your contract should state that it be tuned prior to performance. Sample performance contracts will be found at the end of this chapter. Even if you don't use the contract, it is a good check list and can be used during contract negotiations with the club owner.

If the club has a resident sound engineer whose job is setting up and operating the house sound reinforcement system, establish a harmonious relationship by providing a plot plan of how the stage looks when your equipment is set up. Communicate your priorities regarding sound and provide the sound person with a set list. Ask whether your sound person can sit with him or her and provide direction about the mix.

AFM UNION CONTRACTS

Certain clubs have signed collective bargaining agreements with the American Federation of Musicians (AFM) which establishes the scale and working conditions that the club must pay and provide union musicians who perform at that club based on the time they are playing and the number of sets being performed. The contracts with the union are most prevalent with hotels, pit orchestras, house bands, and major clubs in larger cities.

The musician members of the AFM also sign a contract with the AFM which requires that members deal only with clubs that meet the AFM contract requirements. Technically, a musician member of the AFM should not play in the nonunion clubs at less than union scales, since to do so would be a violation of the contract between the AFM and the musician member.

It is not uncommon for clubs that have signed with the AFM to file with the union local what is known as a "dummy" contract between the performer and the club by which the club commits to pay at AFM scale, with the musician and the club owner agreeing (under the table) that the musician will perform at a lower price. This approach is taken so that the AFM will not bother the club or the musician and the musician can get the work. The net effect of this is that the musician gets the short end and, if he or she wants to be hired back, accepts the fall guy position.

Another common problem is that union clubs are barred by the AFM contract from hiring nonunion musicians. If you examine the sample AFM booking contract, you will note that there is a provision which says "All employees covered by this agreement must be members in good standing of the Federation." Musicians who are engaged by the club and are not members of the union must become members of the union no later than the thirtieth day following the beginning of their employment or the effective date of the agreement, whichever of the two is later. Consequently, if you are not a union member when you start performing with a union club, you may find yourself in a situation where you must become a member of the union if you are going to continue to play in the club over a period of time - depending on the extent to which the AFM or the particular club enforce this provision.

Other points which should be considered in your relationship with a club when using the AFM contract are as follows:

1. The wage should be at least union minimum scale. Consider the costs that have to be paid from that wage, such as sound system, special instruments, and

lighting. These points should be discussed with the owner of the club and can be made part of any contract (see list of items above) including a union contract.

2. The customary union procedure is to pay half of the agreed-to wages in advance of the engagement and the remaining amount prior to the performance on the evening of the engagement. The AFM may demand that the entire amount be paid in advance or that a bond be posted.

3. The union contract gives the club owner complete control, supervision, and direction over the musicians, including the manner, means, and details of the performance. This is more often than not a matter of bargaining power and the more popular the group, the less power the owner has over the group. As a practical matter, most club owners prefer not to be involved in decisions on a group performance or the kind of materials to be performed. Presumably, if you have properly

A CHECKLIST
OF THE IMPORTANT ITEMS IN A CLUB CONTRACT.

Identity of the performer and club name.

Dates and times of the performance.

Number of sets to be performed and the length of those sets.

Duration of the breaks between the sets.

Special arrangements that need to be made in terms of equipment, stage settings, space for performance, and lighting.

Refreshments (the house policy on drinks and food/snacks).

Setup time and the time for sound checking.

Whether any recording or broadcasting is to take place, and who controls the by-product of that effort.

The advertising image of the group to be displayed by the club.

What happens if the gig does not take place.

Your compensation.

identified your style, then the club owner will have decided that you are the kind of act desired, and will be expecting that kind of performance.

4. Any disputes between the club owner and the musician under a union contract usually are resolved by the AFM arbitration proceeding and the results can be enforced by a court.

5. If the performance is to be recorded or broadcast, the contract requires AFM approval. The AFM may demand additional compensation for the musician in that event. At the same time, the club owner may insist on additional compensation for use of the club if the performance is to be recorded by a record company or broadcast over a radio station. These are points that should be negotiated in advance.

Many of the smaller clubs do not sign contracts with the union and therefore have no obligation to pay union scale. Union musicians, however, often perform in nonunion clubs if it is on the "QT" or they file a dummy contract so that the AFM can get their "cut."

When the club has no contract with the AFM, however, then the only leverage that a union musician has is to refuse to perform in the club unless that scale is paid. The economic realities of the business, however, are such that the musician frequently has no bargaining power to force the club to pay union scale. Generally, the musician is glad to get any kind of work and will not be touchy about whether union scale is paid.

Many of the points raised in the checklist on the considerations to be clearly identified between the group and the club owner also can be made a part of the AFM contract with the club, such as the billing credits to be used by the club in its advertisement of the group and the rights of the parties in the event of a cancellation by either the club owner or the group.

WHO SIGNS THE CONTRACT?

One further point that should be considered is: Who should sign the contract on behalf of a group? One of the members of the group? All of the members of the group? The group manager? Or some other party? As a practical matter, one of the members of the group should be given authority to sign on behalf of all of the members of the group since performing groups for all practical purposes are partnerships and one partner has the power to bind the other partners. Sometimes, a manager will be authorized to sign contracts on behalf of a group. The extent of that authority depends on the agreements reached between the manager and the group and is another point to be considered carefully.

TAXES

Remember your tax obligations on your compensation. Generally, club owners will treat you as an independent contractor and you will be responsible for your own federal income tax and social security payment as well as any state, unemployment, or workman's compensation insurance that must be paid. The IRS may impose the responsibility on the club owner for withholding if it determines that there was an employer-employee relationship, but you should take responsibility for setting aside a portion of your payment so that you can pay the IRS when the time comes.

WHEN THE CLUB DOESN'T PAY YOU

Generally speaking, if you are owed money by the club owner and the owner refuses to pay, you have recourse to the courts (and to your AFM local if it's a union club). This obviously can be an expensive proposition, and is not one to be pursued too lightly. California law in general provides if the claim is no more than $2000 or if you are willing to limit your claim to that amount, you can bring your own action in the small claims court in the county where you reside or where the club is located. The small claims court procedure requires you to go to the county clerk for your local court system and pay a small fee for filing, stamping, and serving the complaint. The sheriff then serves the complaint on the defendant, setting forth a date, time, and place for a hearing. The defendant can file a counterclaim within forty-eight hours of the hearing, but it has to be verified, or sworn to. (Your complaint does not have to be sworn to.) At the appointed date, time, and place, both parties must appear at the court and explain their stories to the judge. The judge can then order the club to pay you. If the judge does rule in your favor, the club owner can appeal to a higher level court. If you lose, you cannot appeal, and that is the end of the case. Similar small claims procedures are in effect in most states.

If you are not a union member when you start performing with a union club, you may find yourself in a situation where you must become a member of the union if you are going to continue to play in the club over a period of time - depending on the extent to which the AFM or the particular club enforce this provision.

CONCLUSION

Making arrangements for performing in a club deserves special consideration and planning. You should keep in mind that your ability to get your music out there will be enhanced by getting your business act together.

The simple performance agreement below can be modified by adding additional terms, called "Riders" to the Agreement. These usually specify specialized needs such as lighting, stage size and height, backstage food, beer policy of the club and so forth.

EXHIBIT 1: PERFORMANCE AGREEMENT

Agreement made as of (month/day/year) between the parties identified below.

In consideration for the following covenants, conditions, and promises, the Employer identified below agrees to hire the below-identified Artist to perform an engagement and the Artist agrees to provide such performance services, under the following terms and conditions:

This agreement for performance services is entered into by the musician(s) known as:

(now referred to as Artist)

and employer known as (club, production company, etc.)

(now referred to as Employer)

Names of musicians

Mr/Ms

Mr/Ms

Mr/Ms

Mr/Ms

Employer hires musicians on the terms and conditions set forth in this contract.

Place of engagement

Place

Street

City/State/Zip

Phone (   )

Date, Time and Duration of Engagement

Date(s)

Time (AM/PM)

Number of sets Duration

Type of engagement (dance, stage show, etc.)

Wages and Deposit

Guaranteed Fee $

Deposit Amount/Date to be paid

Percentage (specify how it is to be calculated: gross/net of ticket sales/door/bar etc.)

Sound System to be provided by (Club owner, promoter, sound reinforcement company)

Description of Sound System (Use checklist in Sound Reinforcement Contract.)

Sound Check. The set up and sound check time with full access to stage and P.A. equipment on the date of performance shall be at: _______ AM/PM.

Security. Employer will provide sufficient security so that no unauthorized persons will have access to the stage area or the backstage area. The band will provide names of persons or guests authorized to be backstage. Employer shall be responsible for any theft or damage to the equipment of Artist that may occur during the time that the equipment is located on Employer's premises.

Transcription. No performance and/or this performance shall not be recorded, video taped, reproduced, transmitted or disseminated in or from the place of engagement in any manner or by any means whatsoever in the absence of a specified written agreement with the Employee.

Promotion and production. Employer shall be responsible for all matters pertaining to the promotion and production of the scheduled engagement, including but not limited to venue rentals, security, and advertising. Employer agrees to promote the scheduled performance(s) and will use its best efforts to obtain calendar listings, feature articles, interviews of the Artist, reviews of the performance and Artist's records in all local print, radio and television media.

Merchandising. Artist shall have the option to sell albums, books, and/or merchandising material at the performance and shall retain the proceeds of such sales.

Free tickets. _____ free tickets shall be provided by the employer for the band.

Insurance. Employer agrees to retain any and all necessary personal injury or property damage liability insurance with respect to the activities of Artist on the premises of Employer or at such other location where Employer directs Artist to perform. Employer agrees to indemnify and hold Artist harmless from any and all claims, liabilities, damages, and expenses arising from any action or activity of Employer or Artist while Artist is rendering the contracted services except for claims arising from Artist's willful misconduct or gross negligence.

Cancellation. In the event that Employer cancels any performance less than five (5) weeks before the date of such performance, Employer will pay Artist, as liquidated damages, one-half of the guaranteed fee. In the event that Employer cancels any performance less than two (2) weeks before the date of such performance, Employer will pay Artist, as liquidated damages, the full guaranteed fee agreed to be paid for such performance.

The agreement that musicians perform is subject to detention by sickness, accident, riot, strikes, epidemic, acts of God or other legitimate conditions beyond their control.

Disputes. In the event any dispute arises under this Agreement that results in litigation or arbitration, the prevailing party shall be paid its reasonable attorneys' fees and costs by the losing party.

This contract shall be governed by _______ (state) law, may be modified only by signed writing, and is binding and valid only when signed by the parties below, and Artist has received the deposit specified no later than ________ (date).

______________________________ ______________________________

Artist **Employer**

EXHIBIT 2: SOUND REINFORCEMENT CONTRACT

This contract for sound reinforcement services is entered into by:

____

Name of sound reinforcement company, now referred to as the Employee

____________________ ____________________

Employee address/city/state/zip — Phone

____________________ ____________________

and name of (band, club, promoter), now referred to as the Employer

____________________	____________________
Name of club/performing venue	Date of event
____________________	____________________
Address	Number of sets and duration
____________________	____________________
City/state/zip	Type of event
____________________	____________________
Phone	Maximum audience expected

Load-in. Hall is available for load-in and set up and sound check at:

____________________	____________________
Load in date and time	Sound check date and time

Sound System. Employee agrees to provide a complete sound system consisting of:

____________________	____________________
Amplifiers	Speakers
____________________	____________________
Mixers	Monitors

____

Microphones and stands

____

Other special equipment

____

Any alterations or deviations from the above items involving extra cost of equipment or labor, or substitutions of equipment, are subject to written agreement.

Employee agrees to provide the following personnel to operate the equipment:

____

____

____

Power. Employer agrees to provide at least____________amps single phase and_________volts of power.

Speaker space. Employer agrees to provide adequate space for placement of loud speakers. The space needed for the speakers will be ____ feet by ____feet. This area must be capable of supporting the weight (weight) of the speakers safely.

Mixing Platform. Employer agrees to provide a safe platform or space in the audience within 50 to 100 feet of the stage in order to set up mixers to mix the sound for the show. Platform or area should be_____________feet by___________feet.

Security. Employer agrees to hire adequate security for stage area and accepts full liability for any stolen articles and/or destruction of employee's equipment.

Payment. Employer agrees to pay employee

$ ______________________ Deposit required $ ______________________

By (date) ____

Date and time balance in cash or cashier's check to be paid by:

____

Cancellation. Employer agrees that unless _____(number of weeks) prior written notice is given, cancellation will result in employee's retaining all deposits. Failure of employee to perform services is subject to proven detention by accidents, accidents to means of transportation, riots, strikes, epidemics, acts of God or any other legitimate conditions beyond its control.

____

Employee Signature

Showcasing

By John Braheny

Performing in live showcases, either alone or in the context of a group, is a great way to expose your songs and your act to get feedback from an audience; to network with other songwriters and find collaborators; to audition for record companies or other industry people (producers, managers, publishers); and to audition for booking agents and club owners to get live performing gigs.

Most cities, regardless of how small, have a club where you can play a few original songs. Though most professional club gigs require that you play predominantly contemporary hits or standards, depending on the audience, you can usually get by with throwing in a few of your own over the course of an evening. This is a good way to get audience reaction to your songs. You don't always get it right away, but after they hear them a few times, you'll see which ones start to get requests.

Pick a showcase that wants the kind of music you enjoy playing or you're wasting your time. If the audience doesn't like you the gig will get old very fast. The attitude "we'll make them love what we do" is admirably ambitious but chances are the owner knows the audience better than you do.

Audition Nights

In the major music centers, "writers nights" or "open mike nights" are often held in local clubs. These are either fairly loose, informal gatherings where you just show up and play or are prescheduled, organized events that you may have to audition for in advance. Talk to whomever's in charge of organizing the talent and get the real story so you don't sign up late and end up showcasing for two drunks and a bartender at 3 am. For these types of showcases you rarely, if ever, get paid. Occasionally a club owner might split part of the "gate" collected at the door with the performers, but don't count on it. There is always the potential for a difference of opinion on this point. The deciding factor is the degree of benefit you get out of it. If you do it just for fun and performing experience, that may be enough. If you're a working band and you have to give up a paying gig somewhere to showcase without pay, you're going to want some assurance that someone will be listening who will be worth showcasing for.

Pay to Play

There has been some controversy, particularly on the L.A. club scene over "pay to play," a system in which the act is required to purchase and resell a specific amount of tickets to their gig in order to play the club. Generally, it means paying the sound and light persons. It was instituted by some (but not all) club owners who felt that they were taking a loss on bands that had no following and did nothing to promote themselves. On the other hand, bands and many music industry people feel that it's the clubs' job to book acts for their talent and help them build an audience rather than booking them on their ability to pay for tickets. Whether or not you decide to "pay to play" is a tough decision but, before making it, check out the clubs that don't have that policy.

Club Buy Outs

Another way to approach showcasing is a club "buy out," renting the club exclusively for the whole night, booking your own opening act, hiring sound and lighting operators, sending invitations to music industry people and doing your own publicity.

Established Showcases

Established, well publicized showcases in major music centers that regularly draw industry people are always worth playing at (and attending regularly, even if you don't play). These showcases are sponsored by local clubs or musician or songwriter organizations and are publicized in the events sections of local newspapers or in local musician newspapers or newsletters.

Choosing Your Showcase Material

Here are some questions to ask that will help you tailor your performance to the needs of the club or organization sponsoring a showcase.

BENEFITS OF SHOWCASING

Networking is the most important benefit. You not only have an opportunity to meet and be heard by industry pros, but an amazing amount of career opportunities are generated by meeting, hearing and being heard by other writers and artists. Here are some I've experienced and seen happen on a regular basis.

Someone likes the way you sing and wants you to play on a demo or master session — or vice versa.

Someone likes your songs, lyrics or music and wants you to collaborate with them — or vice versa.

You make new friends and become part of a mutual support group.

You find out about resources, organizations, services that can further your career.

You get the gossip about local movers and shakers, recording sessions and other projects needing material.

You get inspired and motivated by being around other creative people who are being inspired and motivated.

The more people you meet, the more possibilities can open up for you. One person introduces you to a few more who, in turn, introduce you to others. All of these contacts increase your odds of finding whatever you're looking for.

What does the club owner want? All Top 40 stuff? Top 40 standards? Top 40 with some originals?

Who will be in the club's audience? Under 18? A singles' bar drinking crowd?

OPTIMIZING YOUR SHOWCASE (OR GIG)

If you're doing a one shot, one night showcase at a club you haven't played before:

1. Make sure your appearance is listed on their mailer if the club has one. If it's a regularly scheduled showcase night that promotes itself generically it may not mention specific acts. See if the club has a place to display your photos.

2. Check with the people who run the showcase for any tips that will help you come off well in their club. Remember, they've seen lots of acts win or lose in their place and that perspective can be very valuable to you.

3. If you have a band make sure the stage is big enough to accommodate your instruments, amps etc. with enough room for whatever stage movement you need to show yourself off to best advantage. If there isn't enough room, look for another club.

4. If there is a house P.A. system, speak to whoever runs it. Generally, if you have a sound person you work with regularly (who knows your music) and the house system is adequate, it's better for him or her to work with the club's sound person who's used to getting the best sound out of the room. If the club's sound system isn't adequate, and you bring in your own, the procedure is riskier. Your sound person had better be one who can tailor the sound output to the acoustic properties of the room with the right EQ (treble/bass adjustments) and speaker placement and who is willing to accept advice from the club's sound person. I've seen some good groups empty the house because they wouldn't listen to advice and played too loudly for the room. Volume must be tailored according to the size and shape of the room and whether the walls are reflective or absorbent. If you're doing a record company showcase, being able to hear clean vocals is important, so start there and mix around it. Make sure you have a sound check to work out all the problems and to set your instrument levels.

5. Show up on time for sound checks and performances.

6. Make sure the lighting is adequate. Will someone be running the lights? Make sure they're aware of any lighting cues you might need. Write them down.

7. Know ahead of time exactly how much time you can have for your set and stick to it. Plan your set(s) carefully, consider the length of the set, pacing, and where you should place your strongest material. Generally, if you have a potential hit single, or other very commercial material, begin and end with it. If you're going to be the last set, put it at the beginning of your performance. Record people frequently have other places to go and are anxious to leave. If you play a couple of

less commercial tunes to open with and think you'll "finish strong," you'll find when you hit the heavy ones that they have already gone.

8. Be cooperative with everyone at the club, including the waitresses. It may make the difference between your coming back to the club or not, having the employees tell everyone to come and see you or telling everyone you're losers.

9. Talk with the owner about guest lists and guest policies beforehand so you'll know where you and your guests stand. This will avoid bad scenes created at the door with your guests whom you want to be in a receptive state of mind toward your group.

10. Dress with some conscious thought about how you look as a group on stage. No matter what you decide to wear, make it a calculated choice rather than looking like you just got off work as a mechanic and didn't bring along a change.

11. Make sure that all information concerning the showcase is conveyed to the whole group.

12. If you're auditioning for record companies, it's imperative that you perform primarily original material. A&R people are not interested in the way you play the hits. If you're working a Top 40 gig, make sure to check with the owner to see if you can throw in a set made up predominantly of originals to play when you know the company reps will be there. Invite the appropriate music industry people that you've got on your mailing list. The development of industry mailing lists are covered in the chapter titled "Publicity, There's Never Enough." Make sure your letter and press releases inform them of the time you'll be doing your original set.

13. Try and fill the house with fans who appreciate your music. Get flyers printed and send them to your fan mailing list. If you're working a regular gig at a club, try to get the owner to kick in some bucks for the flyers. After all, the owner has a vested interested in showing off the club. You distribute the flyers at your expense, and make sure they are seen in the right places.

14. Remember: if you're good at performing your own songs, live showcases are not only a great way to present them, but an excellent way to network.

Sooner or later, all artists have to take their music to the people. One day, you too are going to have to hit the road.

It may well be the most lonely, costly, frustrating, irritating, infuriating, exasperating experience of your life, but - for all the problems involved - once you've been home for 3 or 4 weeks, you'll want to be out there again! The call of the open road has been a siren song for centuries; now musicians travel into unknown places where danger, hilarity, and - hopefully - friendly strangers lurk.

Here are some simple steps to make sure that your next tour will be more profitable, and maybe, just a bit more fun.

ADVANCE PLANNING

Before you do anything, get out your calendar. When's the best time to tour? Most experts agree that the best time is between two and four months after the release of your last record. Other factors depend on who your audience is: don't tour colleges in midsummer (they're closed); don't plan a festival tour in midwinter; avoid the two weeks before Christmas and the next three weeks afterwards (people are buying holiday presents, not entertainment, beforehand; afterwards they're wishing they hadn't spent the money).

ROUTING GIGS AND TOURS

If you're booking your own tour, do it with a road map and an airline schedule at hand. If your agent is doing it, remind him that you do not wish to be told that "you can sleep on the plane," or it's "only eight hundred miles" to the next gig. Initially, look for gigs close to home, and then move on. A circular route that covers the areas or cities where you already have a measure of support makes the best sense, and is the most economical way to go. You'll never get the routing perfect, but at least make the effort.

BUDGET

Well-planned tours demand a budget. What are your basic costs for equipment and instruments? What are your players' salaries? How long will you be gone? What kind of hotels will you be staying in? And, how are you traveling? Remember to budget for the miscellaneous disasters that will certainly occur. Carry at least two major credit cards, a telephone credit card, two different gasoline cards (if you're travelling by car or bus), and a cash float.

TRAVEL

Some bands have toured in cars with U-Haul trailers, but for groups who can't afford tour buses, mini-vans or larger window vans are preferable; rentals are reasonably economic. Don't forget to get the most complete insurance coverage available. Lease from a company that will repair or replace the vehicle if anything goes wrong. Join AAA (they'll provide good maps and road condition advice).

Check to see whether air or automobile offer the best economies. You'll probably get exhausted in either case, by driving, or hanging about airports.

CONTRACTS AND RIDERS

You will have a contract for every gig on your upcoming tour. They must be signed before you leave - there are endless horror stories of bands who've travelled hundreds of miles to discover another band already on stage and a club owner with a short memory.

Contract riders are the subject of much creativity (The Chieftains like to have Harp Lager in the dressing rooms; another band specifies removal of brown M&Ms from the mix), but they are vital unless you wish to exist solely on the presumed generosity of club owners and concert promoters.

Make sure that your rider defines your needs for power, lighting and sound, equipment, stage size and food and refreshment. Since the cost of supplying the rider is a cost of the show, and you may well be on a percentage of the box office after the show costs are covered, remember that you are paying for what's requested in the rider. But you can't expect a club or a promoter to provide what you need unless they know what it is. Finally, make the rider part of the contract.

PACKING

Make sure that you have all the supplies you'll need. It is sometimes hard to find your particular guitar strings or drumsticks in Fargo, ND or Thibodeaux, CA; spare parts for amps are not stocked in many small towns. If you have stage clothes, make sure that they're easy to care for, and have special cases for them. Cram as much stuff into the cases as you can, so you don't have dozens of additional bags to lose on the tour. Take plenty of records, photos, bios, 3/4 inch videos, and singles - a tour is a movable promotion opportunity, and you need all the promotional material that will help build your career.

LIFE ON THE ROAD

If you're in a group, a tour can cement friendships and solidify the music you play, or can tear you all apart. The longer the tour, the greater the risks of a band falling apart. You will discover a soundman who snores, a bass player who is always late (so, leave him behind; he'll catch up, and he won't be late again), a singer who drinks too much, and a horn player who whines about absolutely everything. Make personnel changes, or learn to live with your musicians!

Late night parties on the bus should only be held when there isn't a gig the next day (and always check your visitors who may disappear with some of your possessions). Bring humidifiers to prevent sore throats, and a cellular phone to keep in touch. Pack junky novels, video games, your address book, and some postcards and postage stamps. Pick up guide books for all the major cities you'll visit.

TRUCK STOPS

In rural areas, truck stops (or all-night burger joints) can be in a twilight zone. Long hair (or very short hair), pink socks, and highly fashionable clothing can be regarded with suspicion. Send the straightest looking member of your party to check, especially if it's late at night.

LIFE AS AN OPENING ACT

If you're touring as an opening act (the fate of most bands at one time or another), make friends with the headliner and (more importantly) the headliner's road manager. Is there room on one of their trucks for your gear? How much of their sound and lights can you use? Can you get to eat some of their food? Remember that you get more flies with honey (and more food and beer and sound and lights); ask nicely and make no demands. When you're the headliner in the future, remember the particular miseries of the early days, and make your opening act welcome.

BACKSTAGE

Life's a cabaret, and nowhere more than backstage. There'll be people from the record company (you hope) and you should treat them with special respect; let them in first, give them a beer, and then hide the rest before the horde arrives - the guys from the radio station, a gaggle of new fans, a free-lance writer who isn't sure who he's going to be writing this piece for, the young lady who wants a ride to the next gig (where her father, and the police, will be waiting), and a songwriter with a demo tape of a new song that's just perfect for you. Make sure that valuable instruments, equipment, clothes, wallets, and purses are safely locked away.

THREE WORDS ABOUT SEX ON THE ROAD

Resist the temptation. Everything they say about AIDS, broken relationships, and strange lesions in unlikely places is almost all true.

HOME

Write letters, send postcards, make telephone calls. Writing thank you letters isn't difficult. A signed promo shot and a warm letter to a club owner or a promoter makes a return trip all that much easier. Remember that you've got to do this all over again, and again, and again. Until you become a superstar. Then - if you do have to do it - you'll do it in greater comfort and for a great many more dollars.

Publicity: There's Never Enough

By Diane Rapaport

Playing to an empty house is every musician's nightmare. It means the band didn't draw.

Draw is a band's ability to fill a club, concert hall or arena with paying customers. A band's draw determines the pay scale it can demand, and club owners and concert producers make or lose fortunes by their ability to accurately predict what a band will draw on a particular day at a given price.

No matter what a band's potential draw is, one thing is certain: if no one knows about a gig, no one will attend. The purpose of publicity is to let people know where and when a gig is happening and persuade them to attend. Publicity can be as simple as calling up fans or, in the case of a major tour by a Top 100 recording artist, a national media campaign that will include print, radio and television.

Well-placed publicity persuades people whose opinions are respected to share information and enthusiasm with others: fans call up their friends and persuade them to attend a performance; DJs play cuts from a record, cassette or CD; critics review a performance. This "heat" stimulates interest and enthusiasm as well as credibility, because it's not presented as advertising.

"Free" publicity seldom happens by chance. In fact, millions of dollars are spent yearly by public relations firms and publicists to guarantee that "free" publicity happens. These people understand that newspaper reporters, radio and television news directors, reviewers and critics often wait for news to be brought to them. They expect to be courted, cajoled and pleaded with to talk or write about an event or to play a record, cassette or CD.

Fortunately, you don't have to spend a fortune on public relations firms to help you get publicity. If you know the techniques and tools involved, diligence and a professional approach should always gain good results. It can be done by anyone willing to spend time, a little money and perseverance.

Success depends on how well the following are accomplished: assembling effective publicity materials; researching publicity outlets; planning and carrying out a campaign.

Once you understand the basics of a successful publicity campaign, you can apply the techniques to publicizing <u>any</u> business, whether it be a record label, recording studio or sound reinforcement company.

PUBLICITY RESPONSIBILITY

In an ideal situation, publicity is a shared effort. A representative from the band will sit down with the club owner or promoter six to eight weeks prior to a performance and figure out who's doing what. In an ideal situation, the band provides photos, press releases and flyers; the club owner or promoter sends them to the media, following many of the steps described in this article. Many concert promoters also reinforce their publicity efforts with colorful posters which they have designed and which they pay for and distribute.

The band usually takes responsibility for mailings to fans and to music professionals they would like to impress, such as record executives, other club owners and promoters.

Unfortunately, this ideal situation doesn't always occur. Many club owners aren't very knowledgeable about courting the media, nor desirous of putting out the effort and money it takes. Sometimes, in order to save money, club owners and promoters will bunch several gigs into one press release and your band can get lost in the shuffle.

Unless you are working with a club owner or promoter who has a glorious reputation for publicity, do your own. Even if they do some publicity, your efforts will enhance theirs. What really matters is that the club or concert hall is full.

Doing your own publicity is mandatory when you are a second or third band on a concert lineup. Most of the publicity will be directed towards the main draw. Your interest is best served by using the main draw as a springboard to gain publicity and attention for your band. Make sure that you remind sympathetic critics and other people who intend to show up to hear the headliner to arrive early enough to hear your band.

If you are signed to a record label (large or small), the record company may not always be interested in providing publicity for performances, particularly when the performance is not accompanied by a new record release. They may, however, be willing to tag record advertisements with news about the performance. This is something you or your manager should ask for.

PUBLICITY MATERIALS

Publicity materials and demo tapes are your ambassadors: they deliver information, stimulate excitement, and imprint the name and image of your band in people's minds. They help create a draw for your performances and sell your records, cassettes or CDs.

The basics are a year's supply of letterhead stationery and envelopes; black and white photographs of the band; bios; flyers and posters; and postcards.

Letterhead Stationery

Letterhead stationery helps establish your band as a business and makes communication with the media and other businesses more professional. The lettering style and colors you use, and your symbol (logo) have a great deal to say about your image. You will use them repetitively in all your publicity materials to highlight and dramatize your band's name and image, etching them in the minds of people who see them.

A creative "image" for your band "on paper" is accomplished by a skilled graphic designer. Notice how many different (and creative ways) just the name, address and phone number have been arranged on business cards, and you'll begin to get some idea of the skill that it takes to accomplish this "image" with a logo.

Mediocre work creates bad impressions that are hard to erase. Well executed visual materials induce those who receive them to come to your performances or listen to your music. If your publicity materials seem amateurish, you create the impression that your music is amateurish—even if it isn't.

Photographs

Black and white glossy photographs are important promotional tools. They're often the first visual people see and they must help answer the question "What kind of music do you do?" For this reason, photographs should instantaneously communicate the number of people in your band and the kind of music they create.

If you have a record, it is also a good idea to have a black and white photograph of the cover as well.

Most of the photographs that you see reproduced in magazines and newspapers have been provided by the bands (or their management). Only when a band has become a major headliner will a newspaper or magazine bother to send a photographer to a performance.

Photographs should be no larger than 8" x 10" and no smaller than 5" x 7". They must be able to be successfully reduced or "cropped" to fit narrow newspaper columns. This means tight groupings of people and instruments. Five musicians spread out over a big field of poppies won't cut it. For good reproduction in newsprint, photos must be in sharp focus and shot against an uncluttered background that doesn't compete with the musicians (plain white or very light grey backgrounds are best). Good, sharp black and white tones in the photograph are mandatory.

Hire a professional photographer. The positioning of musicians and their instruments; lighting and camera angle are very important. A good photographer will be able to relax band members so that they don't feel and look self-conscious.

A good photograph can be used to create flyers, posters and postcards—and record, cassette and CD covers.

Photographers can be found by reading the credits for photos you like in a local music magazine and requesting the photographer's phone number from that magazine. Record and CD jackets are also good places to look for names of photographers and graphic designers. You can look in the yellow pages, but make sure that the graphic designer or photographer is experienced in working with musical groups.

Graphic designers and professional photographers are expensive to hire. Fortunately, the success rate of good publicity materials is so high that the initial costs will be worth it when you get great results; better gigs at better pay; airplay for your music and so forth. Frankly, if you have to choose between putting out money for a competent graphic designer or a great photographer, or upgrading your amplifier, spend the money on getting great publicity materials.

Bios

Another primary publicity tool is a well written bio. This contains information about the music and the musicians. It is used by the media to help write reviews, stories, gig information, and to stimulate interest.

Bios should directly answer the questions almost always asked about your group: what kind of music; what instrumentation; what experience has the band had (what gigs; what records; how long has the band been performing/recording). It should also contain one or two complimentary key quotes (if you have them) from reviews. Information about the birthplaces of musicians or what high school they attended is irrelevant. Try to keep bios to one page, double spaced.

Many musicians have difficulty describing their music. Those who can have a huge advantage over those who categorize their style with such ambiguities as "unique" or "it's a blend of many styles." Vague responses give people the feeling that if you don't know, or care, why should they take the trouble to find out? Vague answers arouse resistance, not curiosity.

One easy way to start being specific is to name the approximate genre e.g. (classical, jazz, country, rock, rap) and then to specifically state what makes your music different in this genre. The more innovative your music is, the more important it becomes to give people a handle on what it is all about.

If you're really at a loss for words, ask a professional writer to help you out.

Flyers, Posters and Postcards

Once a creative image is created and photographs taken, these materials can be used to create flyers, posters and postcards to help you advertise your gigs or cassettes and CDs. The cost of reproduction is low. You can have 1000 sheets of letterhead stationery and envelopes, or flyers, for under $100, 100 black and white reproductions of a photograph for under $40.

RESEARCHING PUBLICITY OUTLETS

Fan Mailing Lists

Fans should be the first to know where and when a gig is happening and to receive news about other important events, such as a new record deal or the release of a record. They're the ones that have followed you from gig to gig and dragged their friends to hear you. They're the ones that have talked your band up to others and played your records and tapes. Their loyalty should be repaid with care and regard.

Fans are a major source of support. Ask the Grateful Dead, whose list of "Deadheads" now numbers well into the hundreds of thousands. The Deadheads have been primarily responsible for the Dead's ability to fill concert halls with virtually no hit records to their name. This list has also allowed the Dead to set up their own in-house (and very successful) merchandising company.

According to Will Ackermann, President of Windham Hill Records, his first fan list enabled him to raise the money that funded "Turtle's Navel," Windham Hill's very first release (and Will's first record).

When your band releases a record, fan lists are an important source of mail order sales.

Start a fan list with these established methods: Leave an attractive card on every table in each night club or bar you work with room for names and addresses. You might also ask people to name the magazine or newspaper they most regularly read and radio station they listen to most. Leave a guest book in an obvious place every place you perform. Pass a guest book around during band breaks.

During every performance, mention that you are assembling a fan mailing list so that you can let people know when and where you are playing.

Once you have a substantial mailing list, you might offer to exchange it with other bands who also keep fan lists. The sum of two or more good mailing lists will help bands draw greater followings—especially if their music appeals to similar audiences.

Media Lists

Next, research how word about musical events in your community gets around. The most common outlets are newspapers, magazines, organizational newsletters, community bulletin boards, storefront windows, radio and television.

You'll need names, addresses and phone numbers of the people responsible for listings, reviews, interviews, stories, airplay, talk shows, etc. Once assembled, such a list is officially known as a press list.

To assemble a press list you'll need to research sources by spending a few afternoons at the local library reading magazines and newspapers or visiting bookstores or record stores that stock them. You should also spend time listening to radio stations in your area and looking at TV news and talk shows.

Most major city newspapers and local magazines have a number of people writing about music: one may review only the big shows; another may concentrate on club performances; still another may specialize in interviews and feature stories; several might write special columns. Spend time reading their "work." You'll discover that all writers have special biases—and the ones who are biased towards your particular kind of music will be the ones to spend time cultivating. By reading their work, you'll also be able to personalize your approach. Just as you like to know that a critic hears and likes your music, they in turn enjoy knowing that you read and pay attention to their words.

Editorial information, addresses and phone numbers of magazines are listed in the magazine's "masthead," usually located within a few pages of the table of contents. You may also find it useful to request a "media kit" from a newspaper, magazine (or radio station's) advertising sales person. The media kit will contain important information about the readership (or size of listening audience), advertisers and so on.

One person's name may crop up on several different magazines and newspapers, identifying him or her as a free-lance writer. Like musicians competing for club gigs, free-lancers compete for space (and pay) in newspapers and magazines by coming up with good ideas and performing them well. They are good people to know since they are always on the lookout for scoops, interesting events, side issues, and special news.

In addition to specific writers, many newspapers, magazines, radio stations, and television news programs feature special events as a community service. Listings are almost always free. The only rule is to get your information to the right people on time (called "lead time"). When you notice a newspaper or magazine listing, call and ask for the name of the person to whom you should send information and what the lead time is. For some monthly publications, lead time is sometimes 4-8 weeks in advance of publication; for Sunday papers, 10-14 days.

Next, research names and addresses of local organizations that send newsletters to their membership. These may be as obvious as organizations catering to a particular genre of music (for example, folk or jazz clubs) or simply a membership of people that seems similar to those attending your performance. This might be anything from a religious organization to political groups, historical societies and specialty clubs.

Finally, if you are thinking of putting out a record, be sure to get the names of program directors who might consent to add your music to playlists. Include the names of DJs who have personal latitude to slip in cuts from music not normally on their playlists (late night shows and special programs are good bets).

Research carefully. Find out the preferred radio play format at each station. Airplay for bands not recording for major labels is difficult to obtain. Stations most open to new music are college radio stations and public broadcast stations with special music programming. However, even radio stations playing only major label music may have event listings, open to any band getting information to them on time.

The names of producers for special television programming may be obtained by simply calling the television station and asking. Also ask for the names of the "Assignment Editors" who are responsible for scheduling news programming.

ORGANIZING YOUR LIST

This research (perhaps three days of work) should net you over 100 names. Split the list into these categories: (1) events reviewers; (2) record reviewers; (3) freelance writers; (4) feature writers; (5) program directors; (6) television talk show producers; (7) event listings people. Note people you feel will be the most sympathetic: they're the ones you will concentrate your publicity efforts on.

One more list of names to research: the names, addresses and phone numbers of people who might help further your career. These include club owners, concert promoters, booking agents, managers, entertainment lawyers, and record company executives. This list won't help your draw, but after six months or a year of sending information about your band to these people, they'll be a lot easier to court. You might call this list your "blue-ribbon" list.

I put these names on computer so that I can easily update the lists. You should update your lists every three months. You'll be surprised at how many changes there will be.

PLANNING AND CARRYING OUT A CAMPAIGN

Now that you have your basic tools—mailings lists and publicity materials—here's how to use them.

Send fans postcard invitations to gigs, or a whole month's worth of performance listings, if the amount of performances warrants. Also send announcements about items you have for sale, such as records, T-shirts, posters and so forth.

Send press and blue-ribbon mailing lists announcements of important gigs or other important events, such as the signing of a record contract or the release of a new record.

Press Releases

Announcements to media and other professionals are almost always sent in the form of a press release.

Press releases capsulize information. They are factual mini-stories that tell who, what, where, when and how, directly and simply. A good press release anticipates basic questions and answers them. They are organized so that the most important information comes first and the least important last. Hype should be omitted—with this exception. You can use one or two judicious quotes from favorable reviews or articles.

The form of a press release is important. It should be double spaced on your letterhead stationery. Double spacing makes it easy for the press to edit copy and make changes. At the upper right hand side, you should type the words "For Immediate Release" and directly underneath a date. On the upper left, you should write the words "Contact Person" and his or her name and phone number so that if further information is needed, people will know whom to call.

The title is almost always centered and should be keyed to what the release is about. "New Record Released by The KiX" or "KiX to Perform at Central Stadium." The body of the release should stay factual and informative. Plainly written press releases work best.

This plain press release format works for almost any kind of announcement. I've used them for announcing the release of a new scientific instrument, the opening of a new business, a record release and so forth.

Press releases usually get sent as part of a larger package which should include a personal letter, photo and bio, and any other graphic that you use, such as a poster. If you have them, you should always include copies of favorable reviews and lists of radio stations where your music has been played. This information is placed into special folders. They can be plain file folders, or ones that are imprinted with your logo and lettering design, and are called "press kits."

A special note: handwritten and hand stamped envelopes almost always get opened and paid attention to. For this reason, I never use mailing labels for mailings, even for rather large ones. Business and media people are deluged with junk mail: anything that looks like that very often goes directly to the wastebasket.

Mailings to press people are vitally important. The most common misconception bands (and many new managers) have regarding being reviewed or written about is that newspaper, magazine and radio people are on the prowl, out there searching for the next superstar. Truth is, media people are deluged with information and don't have to go out at all.

You should recognize that most often newspapers and magazines cover bands that are, in the eyes of their readers, famous or notorious. When Metallica, The Boston Pops, Pink Floyd or the Rolling Stones come to town, that's where you'll find your media people.

If you want critics/writers and other media people to come to your performances, either get yourself booked with a name band that these people are likely to see anyway, or ask them to come to your performance on weekend nights at a reasonable hour.

Newspapers and magazines devote space to community news, new bands, old area bands with new players, or new phenomena, such as independent records. They write about gigs in advance (thus helping publicize them) and sometimes show up and review gigs (this gives you ammunition to court other critics, writers, club owners and record people). However, remember this: the actual time writers have to attend performances for groups just starting out is often no more than one night a week.

The choice of what to write about, publicize, or review is made in the newspaper's or magazine's offices and is based on eyes, minds and ears being captured by what arrives in the form of press releases, invitations, records, cover letters etc. Hot tips fed by long-time business contacts (other managers, promoters, secretaries and friends) also influence the choices.

Mailings to people on your blue-ribbon list should always be followed with a telephone call. The purpose of the call is to make sure the person received the invitation, establish personal contact and to pitch your cause personally. It's the perfect time to introduce yourself and your work and ask if you can provide any additional information. Spend no more than a minute or two on the phone. Phone calls are also the way to correct misinformation or make changes (such as a different starting time for the performance). Professionalism demands that you be polite—and stay polite, even if well-intentioned promises to show up never materialize. Media people are not ogres, just overworked (and often underpaid) people in demand. In the long run, a friendly attitude and cooperative manner will help you gain support.

Finally, remember this: there's no such thing as too much publicity. There's only not enough.

PRESS RELEASE FORMAT

Contact Person: (name and phone number)

For Immediate Release
Date

Title of Release

(Name of band) will be giving a concert at (name of club/hall/other venue) on (date), at (time). Price of admission will be (price)

(Name of band) is best known for (type of music played). Featured musicians will be (name of musician) on (name of instrument) and (name of musician) on (name of instrument). At their last performance, (name of reviewer or critic) had this to say ("favorable quote ")

(Name of band) has been performing in (name two or three important gigs).

(Name of band) has (made a record, is making a record, is about to record, has received an award or any other important news you might care to mention).

TIMING A PUBLICITY CAMPAIGN

3-4 Weeks Prior to Performance

Mail out a press release and bio to everyone on your media and blue-ribbon list. Follow this mailing with a phone call, two to three days after you think your materials have been received.

Put up posters and flyers.

If you have a record send it along with a press release and bio to radio stations that your research has indicated might play it. Include a personal invitation to the gig. When you make your follow up phone call, ask if the station might be interested in interviewing a key person in your band.

2-3 Weeks Prior to Performance

Send out the same release (or a longer one with more information) and a photograph, captioned with time, place, date and price), and other graphic materials. Include a personal letter of invitation. The personal letter might also contain a sentence or two of blatant hype pleading for attention and saying why it is important for the person to show up. Keep it short. This is also the time to request an interview or longer feature story.

Send postcards to your fans.

To other than media people (i.e. club owners, record company executives), send a personal letter inviting them to the performance, together with the press release and other publicity materials.

Follow up with phone calls.

Check the places where you placed flyers and posters to make sure that they are still there. Repeat if necessary.

Day of Performance

Make sure that people who are invited are on the "guest list" (at the entrance to the bar or club or at the gate or ticket booth). I've seen quite a few embarrassing situations where key people showed up only to find that band had forgotten to place their names on the list.

When you get reviews, reprint them on your letterhead stationery. Include them in mailings. Hype breeds hype. When the media sees favorable reviews and articles on your band, it stimulates them to join the bandwagon.

Two other nice ways to use reviews: make up a page of favorable quotes; blow up a review so that words are more easily read. Use favorable quotes in posters, flyers and on recording materials.

Persevere

Do these steps for every gig until you get results. Perseverance and repetition works. The eighth time a club owner or record company executive sees a press release about a band, they will realize that you are consistently performing. The fifth time a critic is invited to a gig, they may actually show up. The tenth time you send a press release and photograph announcing a gig, you may be surprised to open up the newspaper and see it printed word for word.

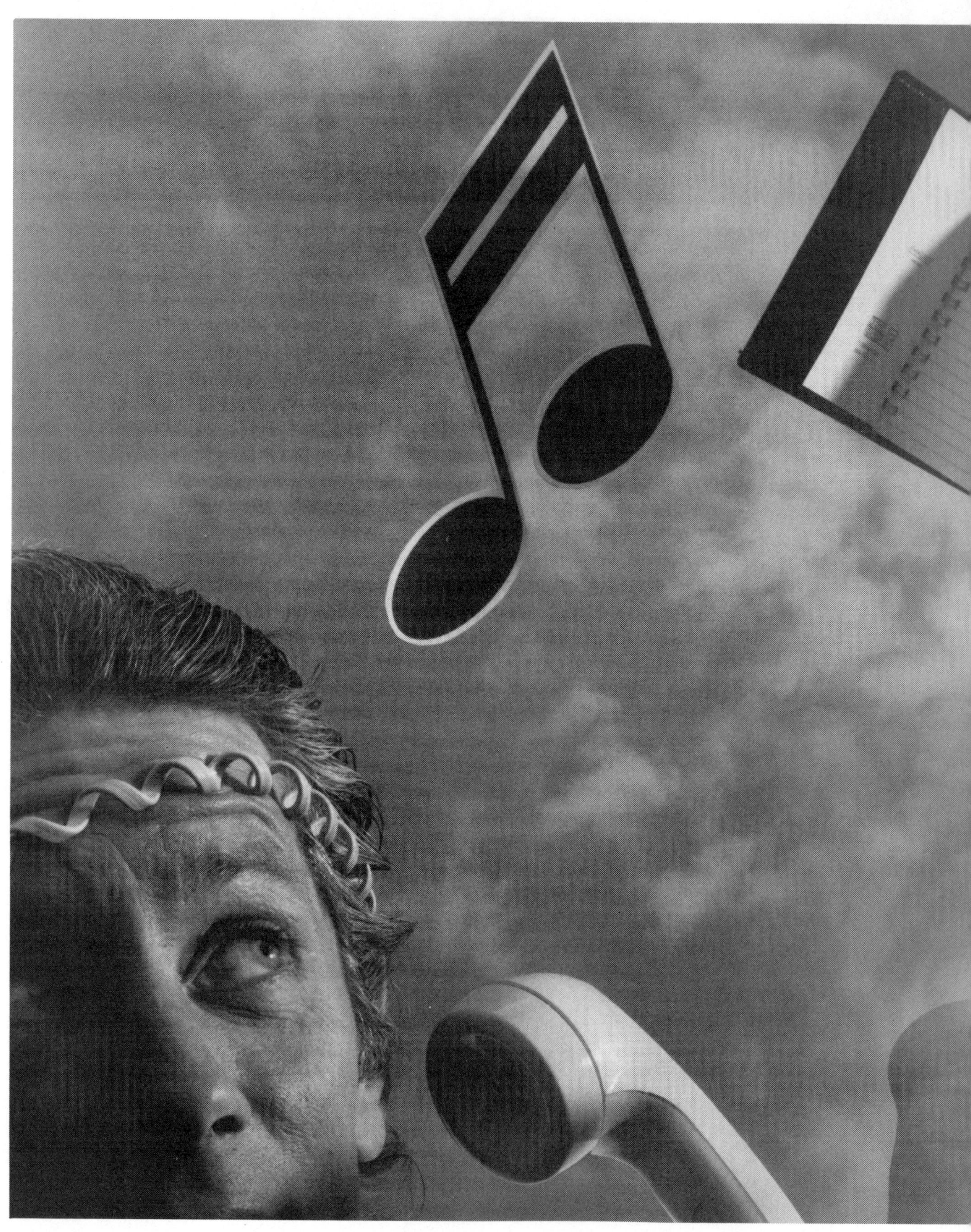

Managers and Agents

- What Does A Manager Do?
- Analysis of a Personal Management Contract
- Talent Agencies
- Business Managers

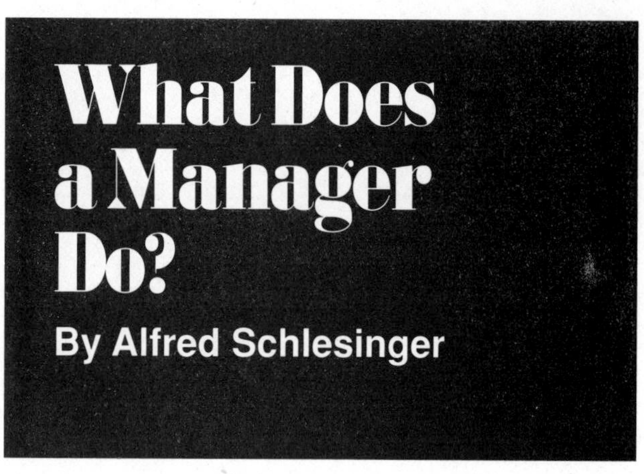

What Does a Manager Do?

By Alfred Schlesinger

Let's say you are an artist who says to a prospective manager, "OK, I'm a talent, here I am, here's what I look like, here's what I do. Are you interested?" And the manager says "Yes!"

First off, your manager will probably say to you, "Look, approximately one hundred percent of our energies have to go toward getting a record contract. Anything else we do is more or less avoiding the main issue. You are not going to make it, you are not going to become a star, you won't make good money and nothing monumental will happen to you as a musical performer without a record. Let's get a record contract!"

Now the presumption I am going to make is that the manager, whether an individual or a company, has honesty and integrity, knowledge and capability. If any one of these attributes is missing, the manager will not be effective.

WHAT ARE YOU LOOKING FOR IN A MANAGER?

The manager-artist relationship comes down to the fact that your manager (whether a single person or an organization) represents and works for you. This person or organization is your right hand, handling all your day-to-day business while you create.

The manager represents, advises and counsels, and for that, receives a percentage of your earnings. If you make money, your manager makes money. If not, your manager will have spent an awful lot of time and effort for nothing.

When considering a manager, check out their reputation. People have reputations because they have earned them. Nobody can be liked by everybody, but if a person is spoken of as being genuine and honest, you can assume this is probably true.

However, a good reputation means nothing unless there is a trust and good feeling between artist and manager. I don't see how anyone can have a personal manager they don't like.

The manager's enthusiasm and belief in you are essential for a successful relationship. A manager cannot and should not represent you if he or she doesn't understand your motives, priorities, beliefs, way of life and what's important to you.

The personality of the manager must be considered. Some managers can break down doors (literally and figuratively), scream, holler, demand and be very effective. Some artists might like that, others might want someone more laid back. The object is to enable the artist to write, rehearse and perform; to create with a free, clear mind. The idea is not, however, to remove the artist from business entirely, but rather to free them from the nitty-gritty work-a-day affairs. Artists should know what is going on with their careers and be familiar with the agent, record company personnel, business manager, attorney, public relations people and whoever else has a hand in their success or failure. Managing an artist is a tremendous job; an artist choosing to do it alone will have great difficulty finding time to create music and run their business.

THE MANAGER'S ROLE

A manager provides knowledge, judgement and objectivity in the following key areas:

Record Companies

It's a manager's job to know the record companies.

Certain record companies are better for certain types of music. Some record companies are stronger on the West Coast than on the East. Certain companies have political problems, and you don't want to get into the midst of a political situation. Some record companies are losers and can't give their records away; others are hot. Some own their own branch distribution centers while others depend on several independent distributors.

It's up to the manager to know which companies are in trouble, financially or politically. Some of the rather well-known and respected record companies are in financial straits, and though the vast majority of record companies are honest, there are some that are very shy about paying royalties.

The artist usually doesn't know these things. He or she usually goes to the manager and says, "You know, I like the way that company promotes their records. I like their covers, their roster, the way they handle this and that." The artist's opinions along these lines are very important, and most managers will want to know what the artist fancies and why. It's a happy situation when the manager agrees with the artist and it all sounds good. But, like the artist, the record company has an image to maintain, and sometimes that's all the artist will see. The manager has to know the truth behind the company's image and if the record company is the right one for a particular artist.

One of the most devastating things that can happen to a recording artist is having a manager get a very heavy commitment from a record company for a certain number of albums to be released each year. If the artist can't handle that many albums or that kind of pressure, the contract can wind up being virtually a contract for life.

Scheduling

It's also important for a manager to help schedule an artist's life, structuring recording and gigging contracts appropriately.

Some performers schedule sixteen months of activity into a year. There is no way that can be done. A manager has to help the artist plan ahead, sometimes a year or more at a time. Time should be set aside for creative activity, for vacation, for recording and for touring. To help the artist do that, the manager has to be very sensitive to the artist's habits and needs. For example, if the artist is a songwriter, the manager must realize that songs take a certain amount of time to produce. It's difficult for some artists to write songs while recording, while on the road or on vacation. It's important to set aside enough time out of the year for this kind of creativity.

Recording Habits

It's very important for a manager to understand the artist's recording habits.

The manager must know how long the recording is likely to take. Some artists can spend two days at a recording studio, and come out with ten tracks, a flawless, marvelous album. Others will take anywhere up to eighteen months in the studio. One of the most devastating things that can happen to a recording artist is having a manager get a very heavy commitment from a record company for a certain number of albums to be released each year. If the artist can't handle that many albums or that kind of pressure, the contract can wind up being virtually a contract for life.

For example, say you are committed to delivering two albums a year for five years. But in the first year only one album is made. In the second year three albums must be delivered. If only one is done that year, the next year four are due, etc. It's possible under some circumstances and in some jurisdictions for you to be recording for a company ten years - longer if less than one album per year is produced.

Recording Package

The manager should help put together a recording package. Instrumentation, musicians and singers, a producer and engineer must be selected. (The role of the engineer has long been overlooked, but is very significant in the recording process today.) Presumably, the manager knows the top people and studios in the business and can help select a package appropriate for the artist.

Selecting the best kind of material to record is another part of the manager's function. If the artist is a writer, he or she may have a great wealth of material. Which of that material put on the demo or subsequent album will best represent the artist's talent?

All of these are critical decisions which should be made before the process of getting a contract is started. The manager then seeks out the record company that can combine all the elements of the recording package that the manager has put together on the artist's behalf.

Objectivity

The manager provides objectivity.

One reason an artist needs help in all these areas is that they often lack objectivity. Is the artist capable of stepping back and saying, "This is great; this is bad; this is OK"? Sometimes yes, but more often than not, no.

Most of the people in the business are reasonably sensitive, even the strictly business people. They will never tell an artist, "I hated your last album, it stunk." The record company executive may sugarcoat his remarks to the artist, but he will level with the manager. Then it is the job of the manager, who one hopes is also a sensitive person, to get the story across to the artist.

The artist who deals directly with this sort of feedback is making a serious error. Moreover, show business is an image business. A great deal of time, effort and money is spent to create an image. It can be very damaging to an artist's image to get in there and do battle. The artist should always be the hero, the good guy. The manager should always be the fall guy. If, as sometimes happens, bad feeling is created, the artist should never suffer by it.

THE RECORDING TEAM

The manager's role in helping to successfully negotiate a recording contract is only the beginning. With the signing of the contract, the manager becomes the captain of an incredibly varied team of people, both inside and outside of the record company. The manager works with these people on behalf of the artist.

Record Company

The most important of all the relationships an artist maintains (after his or her personal manager) is with the record company. It can be the artist's best friend or worst enemy. If the record company is not with the artist all the way, their career is definitely going to suffer delays and setbacks.

A manager has to have a lot of insight concerning the people within the record company that he or she is dealing with. Keeping them friendly and committed to furthering the artist's career is important.

If the president of the record company is behind a record, that album has a much greater chance of "happening." A manager must have access to the top person and be able to intelligently discuss situations and gain their support.

Artist Relations

A creative, very important member of the team, the artist relations person, takes the artist's part and stands up for the artist in the company - even though the A&R person is employed by the company. The artist relations person introduces the artist and manager to all the other employees in the record company, acting as a general communications liaison and information resource.

Promotion Representative

The national promotion representative does all the long distance calling to the key top forty radio markets and has a feel for what's happening in the field. Remember, air play is absolutely essential for success.

Sales and Marketing

The head of sales and marketing helps choose the sales tools that supplement live performances and airplay. These tools range from store displays and merchandising accessories to ads in Sunday supplements, co-op deals with leading record dealers, radio time, etc.

Relationships should be maintained with local sales and promotion representatives who can help get that important extra push.

At the appropriate time, the manager will want to work with the person in charge of international sales and promotion to help set up foreign tours and release the record in other countries.

ALBUM RELEASE AND TOURING

The best time for a record to be released is when it's going to get the most attention and when a tour has been set up to support that release.

Arguments can be made for bringing out an album alone, and for coming out with a group of albums by various artists on the same label. For example, if the label has a release of 10 albums, the company is likely to spend a lot more promotional money and do a lot more for that 10 album package. But bringing out an album alone will give it more individual attention, even if less money is spent.

Some managers believe that there are times during the year when you shouldn't release an album. Generally, those times are November and December, and perhaps June and July. Disc jockeys rarely add records to their play lists during the last part of the year. They're playing Christmas records and the top 100 of the year or the top 400 of the century, and new records, particularly those by new artists, don't get much attention. Also, record dealers are busy selling; they're not going to take the time to order a new record unless it's moving at a tremendous clip. Albums just released in November or December aren't going to be in that position yet. In June and July, kids are getting out of school, finishing their exams, going away on vacations. It's just not the time when anything is going to get the best possible push. On the other hand, a June-July release might mean that a record will be released alone and the record company can put its full strength behind it.

The most important of all the relationships an artist maintains (after his or her personal manager) is with the record company. It can be the artist's best friend or worst enemy. . . Keeping the record company friendly and committed to furthering the artist's career is important.

Tour Timing

Anywhere between three and four weeks after an album is released is considered a good time for an artist to start a tour. When an album is released, it will take a few weeks for it to go through all the channels of distribution, including a couple of weeks for reviews to start happening and a couple more weeks before the radio stations get it, give it a listen, and, with luck, start to play it.

It's very important for a manager to know when the album will be released, so that a tour can be planned and booked. For example, say you go into the recording studio in the beginning of January. Figure maybe it's going to be a May release. The manager should know by February whether that release date will be met. If it is, the booking agent is asked to begin the tour in June. On the other hand, if February comes around and you have only one track down, your manager knows to forget the May release, stay on the safe side and look for the album sometime in August. Around March or April the manager will get together with the booking agent and plan a tour for the fall.

Sometimes a tour is not necessary until after a few records have been released. The first single, the second single, maybe the first or even the second album may sell without the buying public knowing that you are a working, touring act. But after these first few albums, it's important for the public to see your face and equate the sounds they hear on the record with a live human being.

Your manager should also know what you can handle as far as touring is concerned. Some artists are "touring fools" who go out 300, 325 days a year. An average act will tour at least 50 to 100 days a year; 300 days might show dedication, but I personally feel it's absolutely devastating.

Clout

Whether a manager's opinions about when to start a tour or when to have a record released carry any weight depends on whether or not the record company is enthusiastic about the album. If everybody at the record company is excited beyond belief, your manager's opinion is going to carry some muscle. But if the attitude of the company is, "Look, it's not bad for a first album; we'll put it out and see what happens," then the manager has hardly any influence at all.

Nevertheless, if the manager can go in with a good working plan for coordinating a tour with an album release, then he or she will have a shot at being heard. The management at many record companies is extremely astute, intelligent and willing to listen. They recognize that they are dealing with as many as forty or fifty acts and that the manager focuses on only a few. As in many other areas of business, the manager can perform an extremely important function by doing some of the record companies' homework for them.

MANAGEMENT ORGANIZATIONS

There are one-person firms and small and large organizations.

A one-person organization has its limitations because the manager can't always be supported by one talent and probably will manage other clients. But a good manager will not take on more clients than can be served effectively.

Some management companies consist of more than one person with others working for them. Selecting a large company like this can be a mistake for a young performer. An artist might think, "John/Jane Doe who runs this organization is the heaviest manager in the business and I'm going to get Doe's personal attention." Usually this doesn't happen. Probably they will get the services of someone working for the firm instead of those of the top person. This is not necessarily bad if the right relationship is established with this person, and the muscle of a large organization is behind the artist.

But if you sign a contract thinking that Ms. A will be representing you, only to find after six months or so that you're dealing with Mr. B, you should be able to terminate the contract.

Again, it depends on feelings. Many performers enter the offices of a large organization and immediately turn and walk out. They don't feel comfortable and don't want to get involved with a machine, no matter how well oiled.

MANAGEMENT CONTRACTS

If something is important to you, get it in the contract. If a manager will not put a provision in writing, then the manager probably has no intention of living up to it.

The Term of the Contract

Management contracts vary in term from one to five years. What's important here is for the artist to decide what goals should be reached and in what time. Some contracts state that if the artist doesn't have a recording contract in six months, he or she can terminate; another might require two network variety performances in the first year. If the manager agrees, those terms can be put into the contract.

The artist should understand, however, that the manager needs a fair length of time to help the artist towards success. It sometimes takes as long as two years or more before the artist starts to make any real money. It would be unfair for a hard working, honest and reasonably effective manager to be terminated at the end of a year after laying the groundwork and not be around to collect the rewards. Artists must be realistic about the time in which they can expect to reach their goals.

Unfortunately, there are rarely outs in contracts for someone who no longer loves their manager. The personal relationship is so important and quite hard to define on paper. It's very difficult to frame a contract saying, "Notwithstanding the fact that we have a five-year contract, if at any time during that contract I don't like you, I can terminate."

POWER OF ATTORNEY

In standard management contracts, managers are given a blanket power of attorney, meaning that they can sign and approve anything regarding the artist's career without the consent or knowledge of the artist. Certainly, the artist should work to limit that power if they are available to sign; or specify the circumstances under which the manager has that power, e.g. not being able to sign for engagements longer than a certain period of time or for a certain amount of money. At the very least, the artist can have a clause requiring consultation and approval, if only verbal, before the manager signs anything on behalf of the artist.

It's very difficult to frame a contract saying, "Notwithstanding the fact that we have a five-year contract, if at any time during that contract I don't like you, I can terminate."

Normally, a manager makes day-to-day decisions, but leaves major ones open for discussion and consultation. But artist and manager should develop a *modus operandi,* an understanding of what can be done without consultation.

Percentages and Expenses

Manager percentages usually fall between 15 and 20%, although there are exceptions. For instance, if the manager invests large sums of money in the artist at a risk, they might receive 25%.

In standard contracts, the manager is not specifically obligated to advance or lend money, but many artists expect it. If a manager does advance money, the artist must repay.

Sometimes a manager is excluded from receiving percentage commissions on publishing, songwriting or monies from ASCAP or BMI, recording, etc. My feeling is that the manager promotes all the artist's causes and, if you limit the income, you may find it detrimental in the long-run - if only as an erosion of feeling between you.

Costs expended on behalf of the artist by the manager (other than normal overhead like office, secretary, etc.) should be paid by the artist. This includes travel, phone calls made on the artist's behalf, publicity photographs, etc.

Many artists include clauses in their management contracts limiting the circumstances and amounts which a manager can spend on their behalf without the artist's consent.

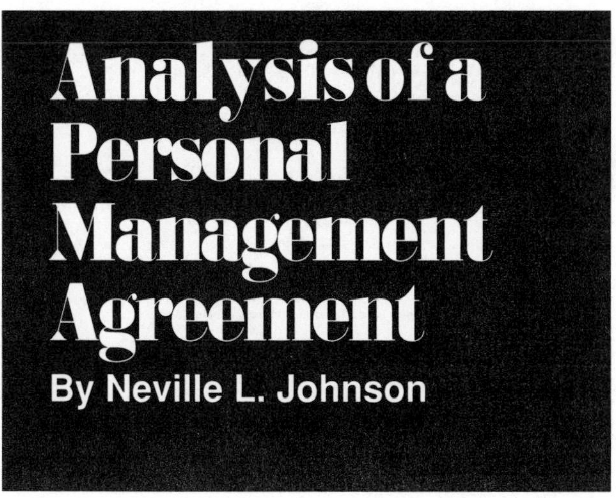

Analysis of a Personal Management Agreement

By Neville L. Johnson

It is often necessary and difficult for a musician to find a good personal manager. Personal managers are the supervisors and coordinators of the business and career activities of professional entertainers. They are the liaison to those who do business with the artist. Depending on the needs of the client, personal managers must at times motivate, direct, market, make demands, and advise. Managers are involved in such issues as which employment to seek and accept, the artist's public "mystique" or image, and generally the marketing and promotion of the artist's career. In most instances, communications with agents, attorneys, business managers, publicists, record companies and music publishers are routed through the personal manager.

Many artists are unwilling, incapable, or unable to devote the time necessary to supervise and coordinate the many services required from those who build and maintain their careers. Virtually all successful recording artists have personal managers, while songwriters and record producers rarely do, although in the latter case, the trend for doing so is increasing.

Some personal managers invest money, in addition to time, into the acts they represent. Their profession is risky and costly.

Fledgling or unsigned acts have difficulty obtaining qualified personal managers because those who are desirable are busy with successful acts and do not have the time or interest to focus on a developing talent. Being a personal manager is often a thankless job, sometimes lucrative, and always difficult.

Personal managers, are in effect, employees of the acts they represent and operate in a fiduciary capacity to the artist. Thus, the artist is always boss—but has usually engaged the manager because of their superior knowledge of and capabilities in the business arena. A "fiduciary" is one in whom a special trust is placed and who, consequently, owes special duties to the client. Like an attorney or accountant, personal managers must place their own interests in a position subordinate to that of the client. The client's best interests always come first.

A personal manager is the eyes and ears of the artist and must disclose completely all business dealings involving said artist. The personal manager must never obtain an unfair economic advantage with respect to the client, must exercise no undue influence over the client's affairs, and must always operate with the highest standards of good faith and fair dealing. Personal managers must always use their best efforts to see that the client has independent advice when necessary, as in, for example, a conflict of interest situation where the manager seeks to be an employer or partner with the client and the manager may be biased in the giving of advice to the artist.

A personal manager relationship is the business equivalent of a marriage. The relationship must be entered into with sobriety, intelligence and forethought. The successful artist will understand, appreciate and supervise the myriad duties of the personal manager. Similarly, the artist will understand and fulfill their obligation to the personal manager. They need each other so that collectively they can make money by the contribution of their respective services and abilities to the mutual enterprise of advancing the artist's career.

MANAGERS AT PERIL

Although the personal manager is the chief executive responsible for the promotion and marketing of the artist, procuring of labor for a musician is a difficult and treacherous area for all personal managers who operate in California. (The only other state where procurement of labor may be a problem is New York.) California's Labor Code, in a section called the Talent Agencies Act, regulates the offer, promise, procurement or attempted procurement of employment for entertainers. There has been much controversy about this law over the years. Except with respect to the procurement of recording agreements, personal managers are not allowed to so act without a state license giving them permission to operate as a talent agency. Most personal managers have failed to obtain such licenses because of various state rules and union regulations. For example, anyone with a talent agency license must operate in an office, not a residence.

The AFM, AFTRA and SAG allow union members to terminate agency agreements if work is not secured within a specified period of time. Many managers cannot operate within these structures. There have been various attempts over the years to produce a workable arrangement satisfactory to all parties but the matter has yet to be resolved to the satisfaction of all. For example, a personal manager may not solicit a live engagement for an entertainer unless he or she possess a talent agency license. Most talent agencies are not interested in musical acts that do not have record agreements with major labels. Thus personal managers representing talent in that position effectively are required to seek such employment, or at least deal with offers that come in, but may violate state law if they do so. (If the manager takes no commission, his conduct is probably lawful.) The Talent Agencies Act has been used by many musicians over the years as a legal maneuver to terminate management agreements.

EXHIBIT 1
PERSONAL MANAGEMENT AGREEMENT

1. TERM

Manager is hereby engaged as Artist's exclusive personal manager and advisor. The agreement shall continue for three (3) years (hereinafter the "initial term") from the date thereof, and shall be renewed for one (l) year periods (hereinafter "renewal period(s)") automatically unless either party shall give written notice of termination to the other not later than thirty (30) days prior to the expiration of the initial term or the then current renewal period, as applicable, subject to the terms and conditions hereof.

> ***Commentary:*** *Most personal management agreements have a three year term, although some can last up to five years, at the manager's discretion. Artists sometimes insert provision providing for minimum floor of earnings which the artist must earn during the period before any option period may be exercised. Most personal management agreements with newer acts provide that if a recording agreement is not secured within a period of up to eighteen months, after commencement of the term, then the management agreement may be terminated by either party.*

2. SERVICES

(a) Manager agrees during the term thereof, to advise, counsel and assist Artist in connection with all matters relating to Artist's career in all branches of the music industry, including, without limitation, the following:

(i) in the selection of literary, artistic and musical material;

(ii) with respect to matters pertaining to publicity, promotion, public relations and advertising;

(iii) with respect to the adoption of proper formats for the presentation of Artist's artistic talents and in determination of the proper style, mood, setting, business and characterization in keeping with Artist's talents;

(iv) in the selection of artistic talent to assist, accompany or embellish Artist's artistic presentation, with regard to general practices in the entertainment industries;

(v) with respect to such matters as Manager may have knowledge concerning compensation and privileges extended for similar artistic values;

(vi) with respect to agreements, documents and contracts for Artist's services, talents, and/or artistic, literary and musical materials, or otherwise;

(vii) with respect to the selection, supervision and coordination of those persons, firms and corporations who may counsel, advise, procure employment, or otherwise render services to or on behalf of Artist, such as accountants, attorneys, business managers, publicists and talent agents; and

(b) Manager shall be required only to render reasonable services which are called for by this Agreement as and when reasonably requested by Artist. Manager shall not be required to travel or meet with Artist at any particular place or places, except in Manager's discretion and following arrangements for cost and expenses of such travel, such arrangements to be mutually agreed upon by Artist and Manager.

Commentary: *The foregoing details what managers do. Travel requirements should be negotiated on a case by case basis. An artist might resist paying for travel and long distance phone charges when the manager chooses to live in a location remote from the residence of the artist. Travel should be necessary and the cost reasonable. An artist may also require an allocation of costs if the manager, when traveling, does other business unrelated to the artist.*

As far as "advising and counseling" - although it is a vague job description, this is as far as most agreements go. Further, it is difficult to articulate the efforts that may be required.

3. AUTHORITY OF MANAGER

Manager is hereby appointed Artist's exclusive, true and lawful attorney-in-fact, to do any or all of the following, for or on behalf of Artist, during the term of this Agreement:

(a) approve and authorize any and all publicity and advertising, subject to Artist's previous approval;

(b) approve and authorize the use of Artist's name, photograph, likeness, voice, sound effects, caricatures, and literary, artistic and musical materials for the purpose of advertising any and all products and services, subject to Artist's previous approval;

(c) execute in Artist's name, American Federation of Musicians contracts for Artist's personal appearances as a live entertainer, subject to Artist's previous consent to the material terms thereof; and

(d) without in any way limiting the foregoing, generally do, execute and perform any other act, deed, matter or thing whatsoever, that ought to be done on behalf of the Artist by a personal manager.

Commentary: *The key modifier in the above paragraph is "subject to Artist's approval." An artist will usually want to delete any last clause which gives the manager the right to execute documents on behalf of the artist. The intelligent artist always supervises and understands his contractual relations. Too much control - and the possibility of abuse - reside in any manager who has unchecked freedom to bind the artist. Managers should only be appointed to execute AFM agreements as noted in subparagraph 3 (c) and when the artist is reasonably not available to do so, which will be rare, given the existence of courier services and fax machines.*

4. COMMISSIONS

(a) Since the nature and extent of the success or failure of Artist's career cannot be predetermined, it is the desire of the parties hereto that Manager's compensation shall be determined in such a manner as will permit Manager to accept the risk of failure as well as the benefit of Artist's success. Therefore, as compensation for Manager's services, Artist shall pay Manager, throughout the full term hereof, as when received by Artist, the following percentages of Artist's gross earnings (hereinafter referred to as the "Commission"):

(i) Fifteen percent (15%) of Artist's gross earnings or received in connection with Artist providing their services as a recording artist for the recording of master recordings to be manufactured and marketed as phonograph records and tapes during the term hereof. Manager shall receive said Commission in perpetuity on the sale of those master recordings recorded during the term hereof. In no event shall the term "gross earnings" be deemed to include payments to third parties, (which are not owned or controlled substantially or entirely by Artist), in connection with the recordings of master recordings prior to or during the term hereof;

Commentary: *Most managers in the music business take a 15% or 20% commission of an artist's earnings. Tom Parker, manager of Elvis Presley, purportedly was paid as much as 50% of his earnings.*

(ii) Fifteen percent (15%) of the Artist's gross earnings from live performances;

Commentary: *The artist should seek to limit the manager's compensation on live engagements to the artist's "net" derived from such engagements: i.e. after the deductions of travel, lights, and other out-of pocket payments that an artist makes to third parties, including agents and musicians.*

(iii) Fifteen percent (15%) of the Artist's gross earnings derived from any and all of Artist's activities in connection with music publishing, or the licensing or assignment of any compositions composed by Artist alone or in collaboration with others (it being understood that no commissions shall be taken with respect to any compositions that are the subject of any separate music publishing agreement between Artist and Manager).

Commentary: *Some managers seek to administer the compositions of their artists and/or take a higher percentage from music publishing royalties. Although nothing is inherently wrong with such practices, the personal manager will be subjected to extra scrutiny as to the fairness of the agreements if the artist has no independent advice or unless the circumstances otherwise dictate that the arrangement is fair.* *See discussion after Paragraph 12.*

(b) The term "gross earnings" as used herein shall mean and include any and all gross monies or other consideration which Artist may receive, acquire, become entitled to, or which may be payable to Artist, directly or indirectly (without any exclusion or deduction) as a result of Artist's activities in the music industry, whether as a performer, writer, singer, musician, composer, publisher, or artist.

Commentary: *Note that virtually all aspects of entertainment are covered. Artists can and do limit the authority of a manager and his or her compensation in certain areas.*

This must be decided on a case by case basis. For example, if an artist has a thriving jingle or soundtrack business, or is an established actor, then the artist may desire to exclude these areas from the manager's commission.

(c) Manager shall be entitled to receive his full commission as provided herein in perpetuity on Artist's gross earnings derived from any agreements entered into during the term of this agreement, notwithstanding the prior termination of this agreement for any reason. Artist also agrees to pay Manager the commission following the term hereof upon and with respect to all of Artist's gross earnings received after the expiration of the term hereof but derived from any and all employments, engagements, contracts, agreements and activities, negotiated, entered into, commenced or performed during the term hereof relating to any of the foregoing, and upon any and all extensions, renewals and substitutions thereof and therefore, and upon any resumptions of such employments, engagements, contracts, agreements and activities which may have been discontinued during the term hereof and resumed within one (1) year thereafter;

Commentary: *This is a tricky area. In the music business, many personal managers are limited to a commission derived from activities performed during the term of the agreement, and not with respect to activities performed after the personal management agreement but pursuant to agreements that were entered into during the term of the management agreement. For example, should the manager get a commission on records recorded after the management term pursuant to a record deal entered into during the term? There are two views. The manager will argue that if he or she is responsible for building up the career of the artist, the fruits of the manager's labor should be enjoyed for as long as that "contractual tree" bears fruit and it would not be fair to build up an artist's career over a five album period, so that the artist was about to "break" on a major scale, only to be excised from the deal on the next album when the artist achieves major success. The artist will attempt to limit the compensation to only employment activity by the artist rendered to third parties during the term of the management agreement. Artists will argue that they will be forced to pay two commissions: one to the previous manager and one to a new manager, which would be unduly onerous. Moreover, what if the failure to achieve success theretofore was in some part the manager's fault? Possible compromises are a reduced percentage for the manager, an "override" that extends for a limited period, or that the parties will negotiate a fee or override at the end of the term, and if they cannot agree, a third party can decide a fair buy out.*

(d) Manager is hereby authorized to receive, on Artist's behalf, all "gross monies and other considerations" and to deposit all such funds into a separate trust account in a bank or savings and loan association. Manager shall have the right to withdraw from such account all expenses and commissions to which Manager is entitled hereunder and shall remit the balance to Artist or as Artist shall direct. Notwithstanding the foregoing, Artist may, at any time, require all "gross monies or other considerations" to be paid to a third party, provided that such party shall irrevocably be directed in writing to pay Manager all expenses and commissions due hereunder.

Commentary: *This is a subject near and dear to both parties. The manager wants to be assured of getting paid; the artist needs to be sure of a fair count. In early days of a* *career, when there is little to be made, most managers collect and disburse revenue. Any artist who becomes successful should have an accountant or business manager who supervises the financial activities of the artist. The artist must have the absolute right to audit the books of the manager at reasonable intervals.*

It also would be a good idea to have the manager acknowledge that he is a fiduciary to the artist, particularly with respect to the financial aspects of the relationship. (The penalties are much stronger for one who violates a fiduciary relationship, as opposed to a mere contractual relationship. If a fiduciary breaches a relationship, punitive or exemplary damages may be claimed—they may not in an ordinary breach of contract situation. Most managers would balk at placing such provision in the agreement, even though that is the true nature of the agreement).

(e) The term "gross monies or other considerations" as used herein shall include, without limitation, salaries, earnings, fees, royalties, gifts, bonuses, share of profit and other participations, shares of stock, partnership interests, percentages music related income, earned or received directly or indirectly by Artist or Artist's heirs, executors, administrators or assigns, or by any other person, firm or corporation on Artist's behalf. Should Artist be required to make any payment for such interest, Manager will pay Manager's percentage share of such payment, unless Manager elects not to acquire Manager's percentage thereof.

Commentary: *Sometimes artists are offered deals which, for example, would include a stock purchase at a reduced price in return for services. The manager may want to - and should have the right to - get in on the deal.*

5. LOANS AND ADVANCES

Manager will make loans or advances to Artist or for Artist's account and incur some expenses on Artist's behalf for the furtherance of Artist's career in amounts to be determined solely by Manager in Manager's best business judgement. Artist hereby authorizes Manager to recoup and retain the amount of any such loans, advances and/or expenses, including, without limitation, transportation and living expenses while traveling, promotion and publicity expenses, and all other reasonable and necessary expenses, from any sums Manager may receive on behalf of Artist. Artist shall reimburse Manager for any expenses incurred by Manager on behalf of Artist, including, without limitation, long-distance calls, travel expenses, messenger services, and postage and delivery costs. Notwithstanding the foregoing, no travel expenses and no single expense in excess of fifty dollars ($50.00) shall be incurred by Manager without the prior approval of Artist. Manager shall provide Artist with monthly statements of all expenses incurred hereunder and Manager shall be reimbursed by Artist within fourteen (14) days of receipt by Artist of any such statement. Notwithstanding the foregoing, any loans, advances or payment of expenses by Manager hereunder shall not be recoupable by Manager hereunder until Artist has earned revenue in the entertainment industry and there is sufficient such revenue to so recoup, repay and compensate Manager without causing Artist hardship or leaving insufficient funds for Artist to pursue his career.

Commentary: *This is another area of controversy. The artist must be careful to see that they are not being sent to the poor house by the manager. A cap on expenses, such as $50.00 per transaction as aforesaid is the best type of insurance. It does cost money to promote and further the career of an artist, however, so it makes sense that a manager should* *be reimbursed for their out-of-pocket expenses occurred on behalf of an artist. Most publicists, attorneys, accountants and business managers charge and obtain reimbursement for out-of-pocket expenses.*

6. NONEXCLUSIVITY

Manager's services hereunder are not exclusive. Manager shall at all times be free to perform the same or similar services for others, as well as to engage in any and all other business activities.

Commentary: *The artist may wish to insert a clause guaranteeing that the manager will have sufficient time to devote to the career of the artist or a "key man" clause guaranteeing that the manager, not some employee, will be primarily rendering services to and on behalf of the artist.*

7. ARTIST'S CAREER

Artist agrees at all times to pursue Artist's career in a manner consistent with Artist's values, goals, philosophy and disposition and to do all things necessary and desirable to promote such career and earnings therefrom. Artist shall at all times utilize proper theatrical and other employment agencies to obtain engagements and employment for Artist. Artist shall consult with Manager regarding all offers of employment inquiries concerning Artist's services. Artist shall not, without Manager's prior written approval, engage any other person, firm or corporation to render any services of the kind required of Manager hereunder or which Manager is permitted to perform hereunder.

Commentary: *The manager/artist relationship is built on trust and mutual agreement. All major decisions should be mutually agreed upon, especially concerning those who will work closely with the manager and artist.*

8. ADVERTISING

During the term hereof, Manager shall have the exclusive right to advertise and publicize Manager as Artist's personal manager and representative with respect to the music industry.

Commentary: *Managers have businesses too, which may benefit from promotion. The artist might want to approve any advertising or publicity in which his name is used.*

9. AGENT

Artist understands that Manager is licensed as a "talent agency" and that this agreement shall remain, in full force and effect subject to any applicable regulations established by the Labor Commissioner of California, and Artist agrees to modify this agreement to the extent necessary to comply with any such laws.

Commentary: *You wouldn't see this clause in most management agreements. Most provide that the manager is not licensed as a talent agency. Further, an artist would want additional guarantees that employment and offers would be obtained over specified periods, and that the manager would be "franchised" by any union of which the artist was a member.*

10. ENTIRE AGREEMENT

This constitutes the entire agreement between Artist and Manager relating to the subject matter hereof. This agreement shall be subject to and construed in accordance with the laws of the State of California applicable to agreements entered into and fully performed therein. A waiver by either party hereto or a breach of any provision herein shall not be deemed a waiver of any subsequent breach, nor a permanent modification of such provision. Each party acknowledges that no statement, promise or inducement has been made to such party, except as expressly provided for herein. This agreement may not be changed or modified, or any covenant or provision hereof waived, except by an agreement in writing, signed by the party against whom enforcement of the change, modification or waiver is sought. As used in this agreement, the word "Artist" shall include any corporation owned (partially or wholly) or controlled (directly or indirectly) by Artist and Artist agrees to cause any such corporation to enter into an agreement with Manager of the same terms and conditions contained herein.

11. LEGALITY

Nothing contained in this agreement shall be construed to require the commission of any act contrary to law. Whenever there is any conflict between any provision of this agreement and any material law, contrary to which the parties have no legal right to contract, the latter shall prevail, but in such event the provisions of this agreement affected shall be curtailed and restricted only to the extent necessary to bring them within such legal requirements, and only during the time such conflict exists.

12. CONFLICTING INTERESTS

From time to time during the term of this agreement, acting alone or in association with others, Manager may package an entertainment program in which the Artist is employed as an artist, or Manager may act as the entrepreneur or promoter of an entertainment program in which Artist is employed by Manager or Manager may employ Artist in connection with the production of phonograph records, or as a songwriter, composer or arranger. Such activity on Manager's part shall not be deemed to be a breach of this agreement or of Manager's obligations and duties to Artist. However, Manager shall not be entitled to the commission in connection with any gross earnings derived by Artist from any employment or agreement whereunder Artist is employed by Manager, or by the firm, person or corporation represented by Manager as the package agent for the entertainment program in which Artist is so employed; and Manager shall not be entitled to the commission in connection with any gross earnings derived by Artist from the sale, license or grant of any literary rights to Manager or any person, firm or corporation owned or controlled by Manager. Nothing in this agreement shall be construed to excuse Artist from the payment of the commission upon gross earnings derived by Artist from Artist's employment or sale, license or grant of rights in connections with any entertainment program, phonograph record, or other matter, merely because Manager is also employed in connections therewith as a producer, director, conductor or in some other management or supervisory capacity, but not as Artist's employer, grantee or licensee.

***Commentary**: Many managers also act as producers or packagers of television shows, live concerts or operate production companies, record companies or music publishing companies. For this reason, a manager might find himself in a partnership with a client, or as the employer of a client. There is nothing inherently wrong with this, but because* *the manager may have control in excess of that ordinarily granted to them in the management agreement, or greater compensations than would ordinarily be paid in their capacity as manager, it is incumbent upon the manager to insure that the artist is provided for fairly. First, the manager should not obtain "double commissions;" that is, a fee and percentage as a producer or employer, in addition to a management commission from the artist from the same activity which the manager is compensated as an employer or partner. Second, the artist's participation should be negotiated by an independent third party. Sometimes, the artist and manager will have the same attorney. This is the kind of situation where the artist should hire their own attorney.*

13. SCOPE

This agreement shall not be construed to create a partnership between the parties. Each party is acting hereunder as an independent contractor. Manager may appoint or engage any other persons, firms or corporations, throughout the world, in Manager's discretion, to perform any of the services which Manager has agreed to perform hereunder except that Manager may delegate all of his duties only with Artist's written consent. Manager's services hereunder are not exclusive to Artist and Manager shall at all times be free to perform the same or similar services for others as well as to engage in any and all other business activities. Manager shall only be required to render reasonable services which are provided for herein as and when reasonably requested by Artist. Manager shall not be deemed to be in breach of this agreement unless and until Artist shall first have given Manager written notice describing the exact service which Artist requires on Manager's part and then only if Manager is in fact required to render such services hereunder, and if Manager shall thereafter have failed for a period of thirty (30) consecutive days to commence the rendition of the particular service required.

Commentary: *An independent contractor may also be a type of employee. As noted above, the personal manager effectively works for the artist (and hopefully is effective).*

14. ASSIGNMENT

Manager shall have the right to assign this agreement to any and all of Manager's rights hereunder, or delegate any and all of Manager's duties to any individual, firm or corporation with the written approval of Artist, and this agreement shall inure to the benefit of Manager's successors and assigns, provided that Manager shall always be primarily responsible for rendering of managerial services, and may not delegate all of his duties without Artist's written consent. This agreement is personal to Artist, and Artist shall not assign this agreement or any portion thereof, and any such purported assignment shall be void.

Commentary: *The artist will want the manager to be always personally responsible and liable, notwithstanding any assignment or delegation of any rights and duties, and as noted previously, this responsibility can and should be provided.*

15. NOTICES

All notices to be given to any of the parties hereto shall be addressed to the respective party at the applicable address as follows:

("Artist") and ("Manager")

All notices shall be in writing and shall be served by mail or telegraph, all charges prepaid. The date of mailing or of deposit in a telegraphy office, whichever shall be first, shall be deemed the date such notice is effective.

16. ARTIST'S WARRANTIES

Artist represents, warrants and agrees that Artist is over the age of eighteen, free to enter into this agreement, and that Artist has not heretofore made and will not hereafter enter into or accept any engagement, commitment or agreement with any person, firm or corporation which will, can or may interfere with the full and faithful performance by Artist of the covenants, terms and conditions of this agreement to be performed by Artist or interfere with Manager's full enjoyment of Manager's rights and privileges hereunder. Artist warrants that Artist has, as of the date hereof, no commitment, engagement or agreement requiring Artist to render services or preventing Artist from rendering services (including, but not limited to, restrictions on specific musical compositions) or respecting the disposition of any rights which Artist has or may hereafter acquire in any musical composition or creation, and acknowledges that Artist's talents and abilities are exceptional, extraordinary and unique, the loss of which cannot be compensated for by money.

17. ARBITRATION

In the event of any dispute under or relating to the terms of this agreement or any breach thereof, it is agreed that the same shall be submitted to arbitration by the American Arbitration Association in Los Angeles, California in accordance with the rule promulgated by said association and judgement upon any award rendered by be entered in any court having jurisdiction thereof. Any arbitration shall be held in Los Angeles County, California, if possible. In the event of litigation or arbitration arising from or out of this agreement or the relationship of the parties created hereby, the trier thereof may award to any party any reasonable attorneys fees and other costs incurred in connection therewith. Any litigation by Manager or Artist arising from or out of this agreement shall be brought in Los Angeles, County, California.

Commentary: *Another alternative is the "Rent a Judge" program, a type of arbitration which provides that controversies be heard by retired judges. Litigation is expensive and time consuming. A typical case in the Superior Court of California may take up to four years and cost hundreds of thousands of dollars. Arbitration or "Rent a Judge" is private, swift, and less expensive than our court trial system, but many people do not like these programs because they believe that the best form of justice is that meted out in the court system. Notwithstanding any arbitration clause, the Labor Commissioner will have exclusive jurisdiction over any dispute where the Talent Agencies Act is alleged to have been violated.*

IN WITNESS WHEREOF, the parties hereto have signed this agreement as of the date hereinabove set forth.

("Artist") ("Manager")

____________________________ ____________________________

Talent Agencies

By Steven H. Gardner and Brad Gelfond

Talent agents in today's music industry are highly specialized employment agencies. As agents (persons authorized by others to act for them), they are restricted in their relationship with their clients by law and by provisions in various trade union collective bargaining agreements. Leaving the day-to-day rigors of career planning to the personal manager, the talent agent's main task is to procure and negotiate contracts of employment, including bookings, for their clients. California and New York have, historically, been the center of the entertainment industry, and this discussion focuses on these states. A review of each state's licensing laws is beyond the scope of this introductory article. The first part of the article will explore the legal reins that define the role of the talent agent (hereafter "agent"), while the second portion discusses the considerations in choosing an agent.

THE LEGAL REINS

Every state has a system for licensing and regulating of talent/employment agencies. Some license their talent agencies under general employment agency laws while others have statutes tailored to the entertainment field. For instance, when the California legislature began its regulation of employment agencies in 1913, the first distinction between "general agencies" and "theatrical employment agencies" was made. Until 1967, there were four categories of talent agents licensed by California: employment agent; theatrical employment agent; motion picture employment agent; and artist's manager.

The Talent Agencies Act (first passed in 1978) attempts to provide the talent agent with the exclusive right to procure, offer, promise, or attempt to procure employment for an artist. In addition, talent agencies (like personal managers) may counsel or direct artists in the development of their professional careers.

In affording this exclusive status, California has set up a variety of agent licensing regulations, including requirements for the filing of detailed applications, posting of a $10,000 bond, logging of fingerprint cards, and, most importantly, acquiring the Labor Commissioner's prior approval of all form contracts between the agent and the client. This prior approval must appear on the contract itself—look for it. Moreover, each agent must post in their office a schedule of fees, and a description of what to do if a dispute arises. In any event, if a problem between the agent and the client does occur, and cannot be worked out informally, the office of the Labor Commissioner should be the artist's first stop.

Under California Labor Code Section 1700.45, the contract between the artist and the talent agent may contain a provision which refers disputes to a system of arbitration other than one conducted by the Labor Commissioner. However, under the statute, notice of such arbitration must be given to the Labor Commissioner, and the Labor Commissioner (or his/her representative) has the right to attend the arbitration proceedings. Arbitration is a dispute-resolution forum outside the court system. Many states, including California, are experiencing a clogged judicial system which severely delays the decision-making process (sometimes up to five years). Arbitration is designed to avoid such delays by limitations on prehearing discovery, quick setting of hearings, and binding decisions. Also, rules of evidence, which are guidelines to the court system as to what may and may not be said in court, are generally not applicable to arbitrations, unless agreed to by all sides.

Fees and Commissions

Talent agents located in the state of New York are governed by New York's general business law. Classified as "theatrical employment agencies," the agents are subject to a statutory fee ceiling which does not have a California counterpart. In New York, for any single theatrical engagement (including employment as an actor, performer, or entertainer), the agent may take no more than 10% of the gross compensation payable to the client, except that for engagements in the orchestral, operatic or concert field, the agent's commission may go as high as 20%.

Unlike New York, California sets no maximum on fees which the agent may charge for services. This and other fee ceilings are imposed by the various entertainment guilds, (i.e. AFM, AFTRA) in the form of constitutions and bylaws. Agents are then "franchised" (recognized) by these guilds, and the agents agree to abide by the rules set forth by the guilds. Artist members of the craft guilds are required to utilize only franchised agents, or face disciplinary action by their guild in the form of suspension or fines.

The union franchise stringently regulates in at least two major areas: the term (length) of the agent's employment agreement with the client, and the maximum compensation payable to the agent. The franchise is essentially an agreement between the agent and the guild that commits the agent to abide by particular regulations as to the representation of their members.

For example, the American Federation of Musicians (AFM) franchise rules allow variable lengths of contract terms dependent upon the services rendered by an agent. A booking agent (one who primarily arranges such personal appearances as clubs, tours, Las Vegas shows) is restricted to a term of three years, while a general agent (one who represents a client for film, television, recording, personal appearance, commercials, writing, etc.) can sign a client for up to seven years, regardless of the franchise or the services rendered, as this is the longest period allowable for a personal service contract in California. However, the artist may always renew the contract after the seven years are up, if the artist so desires.

Fees are also governed by guild franchises. Although the norm is a 10% maximum on general services, increased fees can be obtained by the agent. For instance, the AFM uses a variable fee scale relative to the length of the engagement booked. These scales escalate from 10% up to 20% for an engagement of only one day, but in no event can the commission reduce the artist's net income below that specified as scale by the particular guild. These fee specifications represent only the amount of money available and others may be entitled to other chunks of the gross compensation earned on a performance date. Normally, agents do not charge commissions on BMI or ASCAP performance income received by an artist.

The incentive for the licensing of one as a talent agent is the almost monopolistic status bestowed upon them to procure employment for artists in the entertainment field. From 1982 to December 31, 1985, the California Talent Agencies Act provided that the activities of producing, offering or promising to procure recording contracts for an artist would not, of itself, require licensing under the act. This exception was to be repealed as of January 1, 1986, however, it is continued in the present law. This was an experiment in the law to allow traditionally unlicensed personal managers, who normally perform the duties involved in the procurement of recording contracts, to operate free from the fear of retribution by the Labor Commissioner.

New York law does permit a personal manager whose business "only incidentally involves the seeking of employment" to remain unlicensed. For the nonlicensed individual who acts in the procurement of employment (recording contract or otherwise), one of the severest sanctions is the power of the Labor Commissioner to order the return of all commissions obtained while the representative was unlicensed. This result was most dramatically presented by the Jefferson Airplane case of *Buchwald v. Katz* where the personal manager was ordered by the Labor Commissioner to return $40,000 in commissions which he had received while managing the group, and was also denied reimbursement for all monies advanced by him for the group. A new trial was ordered in this particular case, however, and certain portions of the management agreement were upheld while other publishing agreements were voided. These cases are important in two respects: first, they ratify the powerful role of the Labor Commissioner in determining controversies in the talent agent arena; and second they ultimately fail to provide a clear and precise definition of "unlicensed procurement activity." No clear guideline has yet been established.

SEEKING PERSONAL APPEARANCE TALENT AGENCY REPRESENTATION

An agent is a valuable member of the artist's "career team," and it is worthwhile to spend some time examining the elements involved in the agency selection process. As you begin seeking personal appearance representation by a talent agency, you will discover that there are many talent agencies, all seemingly providing the same services. A closer look will reveal that each agency has their own areas of expertise and services they can offer an artist. Because the selection can be a difficult decision, the following questions should be taken into consideration when you select an agent.

How enthusiastic are the agents?

First and foremost, it is important to be represented by people who are excited about the kind of music (or art) you perform. Agents who are passionate about their clients and their art are always more formidable representatives than those who are not. Even the best agency is useless to an artist unless the artist finds agents there he or she can trust and communicate with.

Many people compare selecting an agent to selecting a spouse. It is important that you have a good feeling about the person who is about to become your agent. You must be able to communicate artistic ideas and business strategy with this person. Since your agent is representing you in business deals, make sure that this is someone you trust to act in your best interest when you are absent. Also, make sure that your agent will project an attitude and demeanor that you want to be associated with.

Sometimes when searching for an agency, you will talk to a specific person, or be pursued by a specific person. Other times, you will be talking with more than one person. If you find a particular person whom you like, make sure that this person becomes your responsible agent. An artist's responsible agent is his conduit to the agency. It is through this agent (or team of agents in rare cases) that the artist will communicate with the entire agency. The responsible agent's ability to motivate the other agents in the agency determines in large part whether the agency will succeed on behalf of the artist. You should be certain that your responsible agent is not spread so thin by overwhelming client responsibilities that he will not be able to pay attention to your needs. Sign with someone who has time to devote to you and with whom you expect to spend many years together. While it is important to insure you have the best responsible agent possible, it is important to consider your relationship with all the agents. When you are signing with an agency, you are not just signing with one agent, but with the entire agency. You should evaluate the company from the top executives to the newest agent. An agency should encourage personnel stability, as it is important to insure continuity of your personal appearance career. Even the largest agencies with the most impressive client lists can become ineffectual if their personnel changes too dramatically.

Developing Acts

Check an agency's client list as you meet with them, as it can yield valuable information. A new artist should be compatible with at least some of the artists on the agency's list. For example, it might be a mistake to be a country artist in an agency dominated by heavy metal clients. There are exceptions to this rule, especially if an agency is making concerted forays into new areas.

It is also important to examine carefully what successes the agency has had. If you are a new act, just about to begin your personal appearance career, it wouldn't be wise to sign with an agency who only booked arena headliners. It is also important for an agent to know the proper places to play as you are developing your personal appearance career. There are some clubs that are better for metal acts, others better for alternative acts, etc. For example, if you are a group that plays ethnic music, there are some venues where your performance will be more successful. Your agent must know this information.

Packaging

Packaging generally refers to the practice of placing a support act(s) on a headliner's tour. This can happen in clubs, theaters, arenas, and stadiums. In the past, agents wielded tremendous influence in placing opening acts on key tours. While agents still maintain some control over packaging, today the headliner makes the final decision on the selection of supporting acts. However, agents have great input on this decision, and usually the inside track on upcoming support slots. It is foolish for a developing band to sign with an agency because they are interested in doing a tour with another of the agency's headliners as these things are never guaranteed. You should listen to the prospective agents' ideas on how he or she feels you would be best packaged, and with which acts. Check to see if the agency has had success packaging their clients with other agencies, both as support and headliners, and with their own clients as well.

Making Deals

If you are a headline act, you should check to see if the agency has experience making building (venue) deals. As the business becomes more competitive, agents are now involved in negotiating venue expenses like rent, ticket commissions, and merchandising deals for their clients. Favorable deals can yield you additional tour revenue.

What kind of person is my prospective agent? Is this person someone who I feel understands what I do? Does this agent represent my values and business attitude? What kind of reputation does the agency have? Who will my responsible agent be? How long has he or she been with the company? Can this agent motivate other company agents? How many clients does the agent have?

Clout

Clout is a product of the special relationship between agencies and major music business "players." Large agencies make repeated deals with buyers, enabling buyers many opportunities to make money. This creates a solid business relationship. An agent who delivers several money-making concerts to any given talent buyer generally has more leverage with that buyer to command maximum guarantees, more favorable deals, and to create career opportunities for his developing acts. Concert promoters attempt to protect their relationships with the major agencies. They are often worried that the agency will begin to do business with a different promoter in the marketplace, and that they won't get the opportunity to play some of the agencies' acts. By playing an agency's developing acts, a promoter hopes to be benefited in two ways. First, if they help develop an act by playing it in its early stages, they will develop a relationship and be given the opportunity to play the act in the future. Second, they hope to develop good will with the agency by helping in the development process. It is possible for small agencies to develop relationships like those mentioned above with promoters, but this generally doesn't happen to the same degree as with a large agency.

Small Agencies

Small agencies do have their advantages. In a small agency, the artist/agent ratio tends to be lower (there are exceptions at large agencies). This allows each agent the opportunity to spend more time booking and working for each client. The work load of agents in a small agency allows them to initiate special projects, and to spend as much time as is needed for any given client.

Coverage

Coverage refers to the number of buyers that any given agent will be responsible for servicing. In an agency the "buyer pie" (buyers can be defined as concert promoters, club owners, college buyers, etc.) is divided up among all the agents. Obviously, in a large agency, each agent will have fewer buyers to deal with, so they can become more specialized. Typically, the buyers are divided up geographically and/or by type (contemporary buyers, middle of the road buyers, country buyers, etc.). Large agencies are doing more business, so they tend to have a more thorough awareness of the concert business and any individual market.

What makes this agency special? What are the agency's strengths? What experience and successes has the agency had in developing acts, packaging, making deals? How much clout does my agent and agency have with promoters and with the music business community Should I be represented by a large agency or a small agency? What kind of coverage will I get?

Can the agency service my needs if I cross over into other creative areas like film and television?

There are certain structural differences between agencies that an artist should consider. The differences relate to the scope of representation which the agencies offer. A specialized agency offers representation in one area; personal appearance representation is one example. Full service agencies, on the other hand, offer a much broader range of services, representing television, film, & commercial actors, producers, directors, writers, and even editors, and other "below-the-line" personnel, as well as personal appearance clients (musicians, bands, singers, etc.). Full service agencies offer representation to any client in whichever areas they chose to create. This is especially useful for musicians who choose to explore acting or are interested in scoring films.

What kind of system of working does the agency have?

Whether large or small, full service or specialized, another consideration of an agency is its ability to manage data and efficiently communicate that data to its clients or clients' representatives. In order to maximize efficiency, innovative agencies have turned to computer technology to help them assimilate data. This technology has created the opportunity for thorough and efficient inner office data sharing as well as new methods for sharing information with clients.

CONCLUSION

Hopefully these questions will lead the way and initiate other questions. It is important to consider carefully as many variables as possible. You should also research the agency with some of the agency's clients and their managers, some talent buyers, record company executives and attorneys. You should know how the agency you select to represent you is regarded by the rest of the music business. Ask for a copy of the agency's client list. The best recommendation for an agency is a history of long associations with their clients. Good luck.

EXHIBIT 1: AFM EXCLUSIVE AGENT-MUSICIAN AGREEMENT FOR USE IN THE STATE OF CALIFORNIA ONLY

______________________	______________________
Name of Agent	Legal Name of Musician
______________________	______________________
Address of Agent	Professional Name of Musician
	______________________
	Name of Musician's Group or Orchestra
______________________	______________________
AFM Booking Agent Number	Musician's AFM Locals

This Agreement Begins on _________19___ and Ends on _____ 19_____.

1. SCOPE OF AGREEMENT

Musician hereby employs Agent and Agent hereby accepts employment as Musician's exclusive artist manager throughout the world with respect to musician's services, appearances and endeavors as a musician. As used in this Agreement "Musician" refers to the undersigned musician and to musicians performing with any orchestra or group which Musician leads or conducts and whom Musician shall make subject to the terms of this agreement; "AFM" refers to the American Federation of Musicians of the united States and Canada. Also, as used in this agreement, the word "Agent" shall refer to "Artists' Manager" as that term is defined in Section 1700.4 of the Labor Code of the State of California.

> ***Commentary:*** *Note that this is an exclusive agreement. The musician may not enter into other agreements covering the specific area of concern (music); however, it would not prohibit the musician from hiring an agent for commercials, broadcasting, etc.*

2. DUTIES OF AGENT

(a) Agent agrees to use reasonable efforts in the performance of the following duties: assist Musician in obtaining, obtain offers of, and negotiate, engagements for Musician; advise, aid, counsel and guide Musician with respect to Musician's professional career; promote and publicize Musician's name and talents; carry on business correspondence in Musician's behalf relating to Musician's professional career; cooperate with duly constituted and authorized representatives of Musician in the performance of such duties.

(b) Agent will maintain office, staff and facilities reasonably adequate for the rendition of such services.

(c) Agent will not accept any engagements for Musician without Musician's prior approval which shall not be unreasonably withheld.

(d) Agent shall fully comply with all applicable laws, rules and regulations of governmental authorities and secure such licenses as may be required for the rendition of services hereunder.

> ***Commentary:*** *These are renditions of the classic duties of the talent agent. Reasonable efforts (rather than the stricter "best efforts" found in some contracts), however, are required of the agent. Note also that although the contract provides that the duties of the agent are to "advise, aid, counsel and guide Musician" with respect to his professional career, this is an area usually left to the personal manager.*

3. RIGHTS OF AGENT

(a) Agent may render similar services to others and may engage in other businesses and ventures, subject, however, to the limitations imposed by paragraph 8 below.

> ***Commentary:*** *Note the nonexclusivity of the agent to your professional career - the agent can take on as many clients as he or she can handle (but see below).*

(b) Musician will promptly refer to Agent all communications, written or oral, received by or on behalf of Musician relating to the services and appearances by Musician.

(c) Without Agent's written consent, Musician will not engage any other person, firm or corporation to perform the services to be performed by Agent hereunder nor will Musician perform or appear professionally or offer so to do except through Agent.

> ***Commentary:*** *(b) & (c) Everything concerning music employment must go through the agent - to accept a free-lance job may be in breach of the agreement (and your agent will get his or her commission anyway). It is to the artist's best interests to refer job queries to their agent because the agent can often negotiate more favorable terms than the artist. However, stay on top of the negotiations in the event the agent is unable to close the deal.*

(d) Agent may publicize the fact that Agent is the exclusive agent for Musician.

(e) Agent shall have the right to use or to permit others to use Musician's name and likeness in advertising or publicity relating to Musician's services and appearances but without cost or expense to Musician unless Musician shall otherwise specifically agree in writing.

> ***Commentary:*** *You may find an awful picture of yourself in a brochure or on a poster. Negotiate for the right to approve all publicity releases whenever possible.*

(f) In the event of Musician's breach of this agreement, Agent's sole right and remedy for such breach shall be the receipt from Musician of the commissions specified in this agreement, but only if, as, and when, Musician receives moneys or other consideration on which such commissions are payable hereunder.

Commentary: *If you violate the contract, the agency may not enjoin (i.e., get a court order to stop) your performance - the agency is limited to the remedy of damages determined by the amount of commissions due it.*

4. COMPENSATION OF AGENT

(a) In consideration of the services to be rendered by Agent hereunder, Musician agrees to pay to Agent commissions equal to the percentages set forth below of the gross moneys received by Musician, directly or indirectly, for each engagement on which commissions are payable hereunder:

(i) Ten percent (10%)

(ii) In no event, however, shall the payment of any such commissions result in the retention by Musician for any engagement of net moneys or other consideration in an amount less than the applicable minimum scale of the AFM or of any local thereof having jurisdiction over such engagement.

(iii) In no event shall the payment of any such commissions result in the receipt by Agent for any engagement of commissions, fees or other consideration, directly or indirectly, from any person or persons, including the Musician, which in aggregate exceed the commissions provided for in this agreement. Any commission, fee, or other consideration received by Agent from any source other than Musician, directly or indirectly, on account of, as a result of, or in connection with supplying the services of Musician shall be reported to Musician and the amount thereof shall be deducted from the commissions payable by the Musician hereunder.

Commentary: *While the commission percentages are fairly clear,* ***(ii)*** *makes sure that you will always earn at least scale. This, however, does not take into consideration amounts which you may be obligated to pay to personal managers, business managers and the like. The AFM has little control over these.*

(b) Commissions shall become due and payable to Agent immediately following the receipt thereof by Musician or by anyone else in Musician's behalf.

Commentary: *Normally, the check will be sent to the agency prior to the engagement, after which monies (less commission) will be paid to you.*

(c) No commissions shall be payable on any engagement if Musician is not paid for such engagement irrespective of the reasons for such nonpayment to Musician, including but not limited to nonpayment by reason of the fault of Musician. This shall not preclude the awarding of damages by the International Executive Board to an agent to compensate him for actual expenses incurred as the direct result of the cancellation of an engagement when said cancellation was the fault of the member.

Commentary: *If you are not paid, your agent isn't paid. But note, if you are the cause of the cancellation, you may be liable for the actual expenses incurred by the agent resulting from the cancellation.*

(d) Agent's commissions shall be payable on all moneys or other considerations received by Musician pursuant to contracts for engagements negotiated or entered into during the term of this agreement; if specifically agreed to by Musician by initialing the margin hereof, to contracts for engagements in existence at the commencement of the term hereof (excluding, however, any engagements as to which Musician is under prior obligation to pay commissions to another agent); and to any modifications, extensions and renewals thereof or substitutions therefor regardless of when Musician shall receive such moneys or other considerations. However, to be entitled to continue to receive commissions on the aforementioned contracts after the termination of this agreement, agent shall remain obligated to serve Musician and to perform obligations with respect to said employment contracts or to extensions or renewals of said contracts or to any employment requiring musician's services on which such commissions are based.

Commentary: *The agent is entitled to commissions on engagements negotiated during the term of this agreement, even if the monies are actually received at a later time. You can exclude commissions to the agent on current engagements by not initialing the margin.*

(e) As used in this paragraph and elsewhere in this agreement, the term "gross earnings" shall mean the gross amounts received by Musician for each engagement less costs and expenses incurred in collecting amounts due for any engagement, including costs of arbitration, litigation and attorney's fees.

(f) If specifically agreed to by Musician by initialing the margin hereof, the following shall apply:

(i) Musician shall advance to Agent against Agent's final commissions an amount not exceeding the following percentages of the gross amounts received for each engagement, 15% on engagements of three (3) days or less; 10% on all other engagements.

(ii) If Musician shall so request and shall simultaneously furnish Agent with the data relating to deductions, the Agent within forty-five (45) days following the end of each twelve (12) month period during the term of this agreement and within forty-five (45) days following the termination of this Agreement, shall account to and furnish Musician with a detailed statement itemizing the gross amounts received for all engagements during the period to which such accounting relates, the moneys or other considerations upon which Agent's commissions are based, and the amount of Agent's commissions resulting from such computations. Upon request, a copy of such statement shall be furnished promptly to the Office of the President of the AFM.

(iii) Any balances owed by or to the parties shall be paid as follows: by the Agent at the time of rendering such statement; by the Musician within thirty (30) days after receipt of such statement.

Commentary: *If you initial this clause, you agree to pay to your agent monies against commissions to be earned. (i) This is usually not to your advantage. The trade-off, however, is the detailed itemization of account which you can demand of the agent (ii).*

5. DURATION AND TERMINATION OF AGREEMENT

(a) The term of this agreement shall be as stated in the opening heading hereof, subject to termination as provided in paragraphs 5(b), 6 and 10 below.

(b) In addition to termination pursuant to other provisions of this agreement, this agreement may be terminated by either party, by notice as provided below, if Musician

(i) is unemployed for four (4) consecutive weeks at any time during the term hereof; or

(ii) does not obtain employment for at least twenty (20) cumulative weeks of engagements to be performed during each of the first and second six (6) month periods during the term hereof; or

(iii) does not obtain employment for at least forty (40) cumulative weeks of engagements to be performed during each subsequent year of the term hereof.

(c) Notice of such termination shall be given by certified mail addressed to the addressee at their last known address and a copy thereof shall be sent to the AFM. Such termination shall be effective as of the date of mailing of such notice. Such notice shall be mailed no later than two (2) weeks following the occurrence of any event described in (i) above; two (2) weeks following a period in excess of thirteen (13) of the cumulative weeks of unemployment specified in (ii) above; and two (2) weeks following a period in excess of twenty-six (26) of the cumulative weeks of unemployment specified in (iii) above. Failure to give notice as aforesaid shall constitute a waiver of the right to terminate based upon the happening of such prior events.

(d) Musician's disability resulting in failure to perform engagements and Musician's unreasonable refusal to accept and perform engagements shall not be themselves either deprive Agent of its right to or give Musician the right to terminate (as provided in (b) above).

(e) As used in this agreement, a "week" shall commence on Sunday and terminate on Saturday. A "week of engagements" shall mean any one of the following:

(i) a week during which Musician is to perform on at least four (4) days; or

(ii) a week during which Musician's gross earnings equals or exceeds the lowest such gross earnings obtained by Musician for performances rendered during any one of the immediately preceding six (6) weeks; or

(iii) a week during which Musician is to perform engagements on commercial television or radio or in concert for compensation equal at least to three (3) times the minimum scales of the AFM or of any local thereof having jurisdiction applicable to such engagements.

Commentary: *Although the agreement is for three years, you can call it quits if any of the circumstances contained in this clause occur. You must give timely notice, however, and strictly follow the method outlined in (c). Note the various definitions of "week."*

6. AGENT'S MAINTENANCE OF AFM BOOKING AGENT AGREEMENT

Agent represents that Agent is presently a party to an AFM Booking Agent Agreement which is in full force and effect. If such AFM Booking Agent Agreement shall terminate, the rights of the parties hereunder shall be governed by the terms and conditions of said Booking Agent Agreement relating to the effect of termination of such agreements which are incorporated herein by reference.

7. NO OTHER AGREEMENTS

This is the only and the complete agreement between the parties relating to all or any part of the subject matter covered by this agreement. There is no other agreement, arrangement or participation between the parties, nor do the parties stand in any relationship to each other which is not created by this agreement, whereby the terms and conditions of this agreement are avoided or evaded, directly or indirectly, such as, by way of example but not limitation, contracts, arrangements, relationships or participations relating to publicity services, business management, music publishing, or instruction.

Commentary: *Any oral representations of the agent to "puff" the contract may not be binding due to this warranty. "Puffing" is representing more than what is written in the contract. Typical representations such as "Don't worry, we never enforce that provision" should be disregarded. Specifically, certain relationships are directly prohibited by way of example.*

8. INCORPORATION OF AFM CONSTITUTION, BY-LAWS, ETC.

There are incorporated into and made part of this agreement, as though fully set forth herein, the present and future provisions of the Constitution, By-laws, Rules, Regulations and Resolutions of the AFM and those of its locals which do not conflict therewith. The parties acknowledge their responsibility to be fully acquainted, now and for the duration of this agreement, with the contents thereof.

Commentary: *The AFM constitution, bylaws, rules, regulations, and resolutions run numerous pages. They are, however, controlling as to the terms of this document.*

9. SUBMISSION AND DETERMINATION OF DISPUTES

(a) Every claim, dispute, controversy or difference arising out of, dealing with, relating to, or affecting the interpretation or application of this agreement, or the violation or breach, or the threatened violation or breach thereof shall be submitted, heard and determined by the International Executive Board of the AFM in accordance with the rules of such Board (regardless of the termination or purported termination of this agreement or of the Agent's AFM Booking Agent Agreement), and such determination shall be conclusive, final and binding on the parties.

(b) This provision is inserted herein by AFM, a bona fide labor union, in connection with the regulation of the relations of its members to Musician's agents and managers. Under this agreement, Agent undertakes to endeavor to secure employment for the Musician. Reasonable written notice shall be given to the Labor Commissioner of the State of California of the time and place of any arbitration hearing hereunder. The said Labor Commissioner or his authorized representative has the right to attend all arbitration hearings. The provisions of this agreement relating to said Labor Commissioner shall not be applicable to cases not falling under the provisions of Section 1700.45 of the Labor Code of the State of California. Nothing in this agreement nor in the AFM Constitution, By-laws, Rules, Regulations, and Resolutions shall be construed so as to abridge or limit any rights, powers or duties of said Labor Commissioner.

> ***Commentary:*** *You may not get to court immediately when a dispute occurs. A grievance procedure is outlined and adhered to, and you and the agent are bound to abide by it. Legal representation is not prohibited, and if you think you need it, get legal counsel early in the dispute.*

10. NO ASSIGNMENT OF THIS AGREEMENT

This agreement shall be personal to the parties and shall not be transferable or assignable by operation of law or otherwise without the prior consent of the Musician and of the AFM. The obligations imposed by this agreement shall be binding upon the parties. The Musician may terminate this agreement at any time within ninety (90) days after the transfer of a controlling interest in the Agent.

> ***Commentary:*** *You cannot assign (i.e., transfer) this agreement to your piano player, and the agent cannot pawn you off to "Skylab Booking Agency." Also, if the controlling interest (and this can be less than 51%) in the agency is transferred, you can get out.*

11. NEGOTIATION FOR RENEWAL

Neither party shall enter into negotiations for or agree to the renewal or extension of this agreement prior to the beginning of the final year of the term hereof.

12. APPROVAL BY AFM

This agreement shall not become effective unless, within thirty (30) days following its execution, an executed copy thereof is filed with and is thereafter approved in writing by the AFM.

IN WITNESS WHEREOF,
he parties hereto have executed this agreement the _____ day of ______ 19__

_________________________	_________________________
Agent	Musician
	_________________________
	Residence address
By_______________________	_________________________
Title or Capacity	City/state/zip

OTHER PROVISIONS TO BE CONSIDERED

Agent representing no more than two clients: The agent may make the representation that he will handle you and one other client, exclusively. The trade-off is that the agent gets a larger cut, subject, of course, to your getting at least scale.

Note: Other provisions which can be negotiated in connection with this agreement and other agency contracts:

1. *Simultaneous ending of all agreements with the agency when any one (i.e. group member) is terminated or expires. This is important to a group.*
2. *Exclusion of commissions for performances already set, or in the areas of music publishing, literary fields, etc.*
3. *No double commissions on employment arising under different agreements, or when agent receives a commission from a buyer of talent.*
4. *No commissions on residuals or repeats of TV programs or films.*
5. *Specific maximum commissions as to all agency contracts.*
6. *Commission computation on "net receipts" rather than "gross receipts."*
7. *Termination if agent hasn't procured employment resulting in offers exceeding a specific dollar amount.*

EXHIBIT 2: STANDARD AFTRA EXCLUSIVE AGENCY CONTRACT UNDER RULE 12-B

THIS AGREEMENT, made and entered at ______________________ by and between

____, hereinafter

called the "AGENT" and ______________________, hereinafter called the "ARTIST."

1. SCOPE OF AGREEMENT

The Artist employs the Agent as his sole and exclusive Agent in the transcription, radio broadcasting and television industries (hereinafter referred to as the "broadcasting industries") within the scope of the regulations (Rule 12-B) of the American Federation of Television and Radio Artists (hereinafter called AFTRA), and agrees not to employ any other person or persons to act for him in like capacity during the term hereof, and the Agent accepts such employment. This contract is limited to the broadcasting industries and to contracts of the Artist as an artist in such fields and any reference hereinafter to contracts or employment whereby the Artist renders his services, refers to contracts or employment in the broadcasting industries, except as otherwise provided herein.

Commentary: *This clause limits the scope of the representation to broadcasting engagements within the purview of the guild.*

2. MEMBERSHIP

The Artist agrees that prior to any engagement or employment in the broadcasting industries, he will become a member of AFTRA in good standing and remain such a member for the duration of such engagement or employment. The Artist warrants that he has the right to make this contract and that he is not under any other agency contract in the broadcasting fields. The Agent warrants that he is and will remain a duly franchised agent of AFTRA for the duration of this contract. This paragraph is for the benefit of AFTRA and AFTRA members as well as for the benefit of the parties to this agreement.

Commentary: *You must maintain your membership in good standing in AFTRA.*

3. TERM

The term of this contract shall be for a period of ______________ commencing on the __________ day of _____________, 19__.

NOTE - The term may not be in excess of three years.

4. AGENT COMPENSATION

(a) The Artist agrees to pay to the Agent a sum equal to _______ per cent (not more than 10%) of all moneys or other consideration received by the Artist, directly or indirectly, under contracts of employment entered into during the term specified herein as provided in the Regulations. Commissions shall be payable when as such moneys or other consideration are received by the Artist or by anyone else for or on the Artist's behalf.

(b) Any moneys or other consideration received by the Artist or by anyone for or on his behalf, in connection with any termination of any contract of the Artist on which the Agent would otherwise be entitled to receive commission, or in connection with the settlement of any such contract, or any litigation arising out of such contract, shall also be moneys in connection with which the Agent is entitled to the aforesaid commissions; provided, however, that in such event the Artist shall be entitled to deduct arbitration fees, attorney's fees, expenses and court costs before computing the amount upon which the Agent is entitled to his commissions.

(c) Such commissions shall be payable by the Artist to the Agent, as aforesaid, during the term of this contract and thereafter only where specifically provided herein.

(d) The agent shall be entitled to the aforesaid commissions after the expiration of the term specified herein, for so long a period thereafter as the Artist continues to receive moneys or other consideration under or upon employment contracts entered into by the Artist during the term specified herein, including moneys or other consideration received by the Artist under the extended term of such employment contracts, resulting from the exercise of an option or options given an employer under such employment contracts, extending the term of such employment contracts, whether such options be exercised prior to or after the expiration of the terms specified herein.

(e) If after the expiration of the term of this agreement and during the period the Agent is entitled to commissions, a contract of employment of the Artist be terminated before the expiration thereof, as said contract may have been extended by the exercise of options therein contained, by joint action of the Artist and employer, or by the action of either of them, other than on account of an Act of God, illness or the like and the Artist enters into a new contract of employment with said employer within a period of sixty (60) days, such new contract shall be deemed to be in substitution of the contract terminated as aforesaid. In computing the said sixty (60) day period, each day between June 15th and September 15th shall be counted as three-fifths (3/5) of a day only. No contract entered into after said sixty (60) day period shall be deemed to be in substitution of the contract terminated as aforesaid. Contracts of substitution have the same effect as contracts for which they were substituted; provided however, that any increase or additional salary, bonus or other compensation payable to the Artist (either under such contract of substitution or otherwise) over and above the amounts payable under the contract of employment entered into prior to the expiration of the term of this agreement shall be deemed an adjustment and unless the Agent shall have a valid Agency contract in effect at the time of such adjustment the Agent shall not be entitled to any commissions on any such adjustment. In no event may a contract of substitution with an employer entered into after the expiration of the term of this agreement, extend the period of time during which the Agent is entitled to commission beyond the period that the Agent would have been entitled to commission had no substitution taken place except to the extent, if necessary, for the Agent to receive the same total amount of commission he would have received had no such substitution taken place; provided, however, that in no event shall the Agent receive more than the above percentages as commissions on the Artist's adjusted compensation under the contract of substitution. A change in form of an employer for the purpose of evading this provision, or a change in the corporate form of an employer resulting from reorganization or like, shall not exclude the application of these provisions.

(f) So long as the Agent receives commissions from the Artist, the Agent shall be obligated to service the Artist and perform the obligations of this contract with respect to the services of the Artist on which such commissions are based, subject to AFTRA's Regulations Governing Agents.

(g) The Agent has no right to receive money unless the Artist receives the same, or unless the same is received for or on his behalf, and then only proportionate in the above percentages when and as received. Money paid pursuant to legal process to the Artist's creditors, or by virtue of assignment or direction of the Artist, and deductions from the Artist's compensation made pursuant to law in the nature of a collection or tax at the source, such as Social Security or Old Age Pension taxes, or income taxes withheld at the source, shall be treated as compensation received for or on the Artist's behalf.

Commentary: *Both the length of this contract and the commission payable under it are negotiable up to the maximums specified.*

5. EMPLOYMENT OFFERS

Should the Agent, during the term or terms specified herein negotiate a contract of employment for the Artist and secure for the Artist bona fide offer of employment, which offer is communicated by the Agent to the Artist in reasonable detail and writing, which offer the Artist declines, and if, after the expiration of the term of this agreement and within ninety (90) days after the date upon which the Agent gives such written information to the Artist, the Artist accepts said offer of employment on substantially the same terms, then the Artist shall be required to pay commissions to the Agent upon such contract of employment. If an Agent previously employed under a prior agency contract is entitled to collect commissions under the foregoing circumstances, the Agent with whom the present contract is executed waives his commission to the extent that the prior agent is entitled to collect the same.

6. DURATION AND TERMINATION

(a) If during any period of ninety-one (91) days immediately preceding the giving of the notice of termination hereinafter mentioned in this paragraph, the Artist fails to be employed and receive, or be entitled to receive, compensation for fifteen (15) days' employment, whether such employment is from fields under AFTRA's jurisdiction or any other branch of the entertainment industry in which the Agent may be authorized by written contract to represent the Artist, then either the Artist or the Agent may terminate the employment of the Agent hereunder by written notice to the other party. (1) For purposes of computing fifteen (15) days' employment required hereunder, each separate original radio broadcast, whether live or recorded, and each transcribed program, shall be considered a day's employment, but a rebroadcast, whether recorded or live, or an off-the-line recording, or a prior recording or time spent in rehearsal for any employment in the radio broadcasting or transcription industry, shall not be considered such employment. (2) During the months of June, July and August, each day's employment in the radio broadcasting industry, shall, for purposes of computing fifteen (15) days' employment under this subparagraph "(a)" and for no other purpose, be deemed one and one-half (1 1/2) days' employment. (3) For the purposes of computing the fifteen (15) days' employment required hereunder, each separate television broadcast (including rehearsal time) shall be considered two and one-half (2 1/2) days' employment. However, any days spent in rehearsal over three days inclusive of the day of the telecast, and any days of exclusivity over three days inclusive of the day of telecast, will automatically extend the ninety-one (91) day period by such coverage. (4) During the months of June, July and August, each day's employment in the television broadcasting field shall, for the purpose of computing fifteen (15) days' employment under this subparagraph "(a)" and for no other purpose, be deemed three and three-quarters (3 3/4) days' employment. (5) Each master phonograph record recorded by the Artist shall be one (1) day's employment.

(b) The ninety-one (91) day period which is the basis of termination shall be suspended during any period of time which the artist has declared himself to be unavailable or has so notified the agent in writing or has confirmed in writing a written communication from the agent to such effect. The said ninety-one (91) day period which is the basis of termination shall also be suspended (1) during the period of time in which the artist is unable to respond to a call for his services by reason of physical or mental incapacity or (2) for such days as the artist may be employed in a field in which the artist is not represented by the agent.

(c) In the event that the Agent has given the Artist notice in writing of a bona fide offer of employment as an Artist in the entertainment industry and at or near the Artist's usual places of employment at a salary and from an employer commensurate with the Artist's prestige (and there is in fact such an offer), which notice sets forth the terms of the proposed employment in detail and the Artist refuses or negligently fails to accept such proffered employment, then the period of guaranteed employment specified in said offer, and the compensation which would have been received thereunder shall be deemed as time worked or compensation received by the Artist in computing the money earned or time worked with reference to the right of the Artist to terminate under the provisions of this paragraph.

(d) No termination under paragraph 6 shall deprive the Agent of the right to receive commissions or compensation on moneys earned or received by the Artist prior to the date of termination, or earned or received by the Artist after the date of termination and during the term or terms specified herein, or commission or compensation to which the Agent is entitled pursuant to paragraphs 4(e) and 5 hereof.

(e) The Artist may not exercise the right of termination if at the time he attempts to do so, either:

(i) the Artist is actually working under written contract or contracts which guarantee the Artist employment in the broadcasting industries for at least one program each week for a period of not less than thirteen (13) consecutive weeks. For the purposes of this subparagraph a "program" shall be either (i) a regional network program of one-half (1/2) hour length or more; (ii) a national network program of one-quarter (1/4) hour length or more; or (iii) a program or programs the aggregate weekly compensation for which equals or exceeds the Artist's customary compensation for either (i) or (ii), or

(ii) the Artist is under such written contract, as described in the preceding subparagraph (i) or in subparagraph (v) below, and such contract begins within forty-five (45) days after the time the Artist attempts to exercise the right of termination, or

(iii) where the Artist attempts to exercise the right of termination during the months of August or September, and the Artist is under such written contract as described in the preceding subparagraph (i) or in subparagraph (v) below and such contract begins not later than the following October 15th, or

(iv) if during any period of ninety-one (91) days immediately preceding the giving of notice of termination herein referred to, the Artist has received, or has been entitled to receive, compensation in an amount equal to not less than thirteen (13) times his past customary compensation for a national network program of one-half (1/2) hour's length, whether such employment or compensation is from the broadcasting industries or any other branch of the entertainment industry in which the agent may be authorized by written contract to represent the Artist.

(v) The Artist is actually working under written contract or contracts which guarantee the Artist either (a) employment in the television broadcasting field for at least one (1) program every other week in a cycle of thirteen (13) consecutive weeks where the program is telecast on an alternative week basis, or (b) employment for at least eight (8) programs in a cycle of thirty-nine (39) consecutive weeks, where the program is telecast on a monthly basis or once every four (4) weeks.

Commentary: *In the cases referred to in subparagraphs (i), (ii), (iii) and (v) above, the ninety-one (91) day period begins upon the termination of the contract referred to in such subparagraphs; and for the purpose of such subparagraphs any local program which under any applicable AFTRA collective bargaining agreement is the equivalent of a regional or national network program, shall be considered a regional or national network program as the case may be.*

(f) Where the Artist is under a contract or contracts for the rendition of his services in the entertainment industry in any field in which the agent is authorized to act for the artist, during the succeeding period of one hundred and eighty-two (182) days after the expiration of the ninety-one (91) day period in question, at a guaranteed compensation for such services of twenty-five thousand ($25,000.00) dollars or more, or where the Artist is under a contract or contracts for the rendition of his services during said 182 day period in the radio phonograph recording and/or television fields at a guaranteed compensation for such services of twenty thousand dollars ($20,000.00) or more, then the artist may not exercise the right of termination.

(g) Periods of layoff or leave of absence under a term contract shall not be deemed to be periods of unemployment hereunder, unless under said contract the Artist has the right during such period to do other work in the radio or television field or in any other branch of the entertainment industry in which the Agent may be authorized by written contract to represent the Artist. A "term contract" as used herein means a contract under which the Artist is guaranteed employment in the broadcasting industries for at least one program each week for a period of not less than thirteen (13) consecutive weeks, and also includes any "term contract" as defined in the Regulations of the Screen Actors Guild, Inc. in respect to the motion picture industry, under which the Artist is working. Also, a "term contract" as used herein relating to the television field means a contract under which the Artist is guaranteed employment in the television field as set forth in subparagraph (e) (v) above.

(h) Where the Artist has a contract of employment in the broadcasting industries and either the said contract of employment, or any engagement or engagements thereunder, are cancelled by the employer pursuant to any provision of said contract which does not violate any rule or regulation of AFTRA, the Artist shall be deemed to have been employed and to have received compensation for the purposes of paragraph 6(a) for any such cancelled broadcasts, with the following limitation - where a contract providing for more than one program has been so cancelled, the Artist shall not be deemed to have been employed or to have received compensation under such contract, with respect to more than one such program on and after the effective date of cancellation of such contract.

(i) For the purposes of this paragraph 6, where the Artist does not perform a broadcast for which he has been employed but nevertheless is compensated therefor, the same shall be considered employment hereunder.

(j) If at any time during the original or extended term of this contract, broadcasting over a majority of both the radio stations as well as a majority of the television broadcasting stations shall be suspended, the ninety-one (91) days period mentioned in this paragraph 6 shall be extended for the period of such suspension.

> ***Commentary:*** *Generally, the artist must be ready, willing and able to accept employment of at least 15 days duration, every 90 days. The exact provisions and exceptions pertaining hereto are complicated, but the guild will help you sort out the time requirements if you are really interested in terminating the contract.*

7. AGENT REPRESENTATION

The Agent may represent other persons. The Agent shall not be required to devote his entire time and attention to the business of the Artist. The Agent may make known the fact that he is the sole and exclusive representative of the Artist in the broadcasting industries. In the event of a termination of this contract, even by the fault of the Artist, the Agent has no rights or remedies under the preceding sentence.

8. ARTIST'S AGENCY REPRESENTATIVES

The Agent agrees that the following persons, and the following persons only, namely (HERE INSERT NO MORE THAN FOUR NAMES) shall personally supervise the Artist's business during the term of this contract. One of such persons shall be available at all reasonable times for consultation with the Artist at the city or cities named herein. The Agent, upon request of the Artist, shall assign any one of such persons who may be available (and at least one of them always shall be available upon reasonable notice from the Artist), to engage in efforts or handle any negotiations for the Artist at such city or its environs and such person shall do so. Employees of the Agent who have signed the AFTRA covenant and who are not named herein may handle agency matters for the Artist or may aid any of the named persons in handling agency matters for the Artist.

9. AGENCY CONTINUITY

In order to provide continuity of management, the name or names of not more than four (4) persons connected with the Agent must be written in the following space, and this contract is not valid unless this is done:

(HERE INSERT NOT MORE THAN FOUR NAMES)

In the event three (3) or four (4) persons are so named, at least two (2) of such persons must remain active in the Agency throughout the term of this contract. In the event only one (1) or two (2) persons are so named, at least one (1) such person must remain active in the Agency throughout the term of this contract. If the required number of persons does not remain active with the Agency, the Artist may terminate this contract in accordance with Section XXIII of AFTRA's Regulations Governing Agents.

> ***Commentary:*** *This clause insures continuity of representation within the agency, which many of the other agency agreements do not provide for.*

10. USE OF ARTIST'S NAME

The Artist hereby grants to the Agent the right to use the name, portraits and pictures of the Artist to advertise and publicize the Artist in connection with Agent's representation of the Artist hereunder.

11. AGENT WARRANTIES

The Agent agrees:

(a) To make no deductions whatsoever from any applicable minimums established by AFTRA under any collective bargaining agreement.

(b) At the request of the Artist, to counsel and advise him in matters which concern the professional interests of the Artist in the broadcasting industries.

(c) The Agent will be truthful in his statements to the Artist.

(d) The Agent will not make any binding engagement or other commitment on behalf of the Artist, without the approval of the Artist, and without first informing the Artist of the terms and conditions (including compensation) of such engagement.

(e) The Agent's relationship to the Artist shall be that of a fiduciary. The Agent, when instructed in writing by the Artist not to give out information with reference to the Artist's affairs, will not disclose such information.

(f) That the Agent is equipped, and will continue to be equipped, to represent the interests of the Artist ably and diligently in the broadcasting industry throughout the term of this contract, and that he will so represent the Artist.

(g) To use all reasonable efforts to assist the Artist in procuring employment for the services of the Artist in the broadcasting industries.

(h) The Agent agrees that the Agent will maintain an office and telephone open during all reasonable business hours (emergencies such as sudden illness or death excepted) within the city of __________ or its environs, throughout the term of this agreement, and that some representative of the Agent will be present at such office during such business hours. This contract is void unless the blank in the paragraph is filled in with the name of a city at which the Agent does maintain an office for the radio broadcasting and television agency business.

(i) At the written request of the Artist, given to the Agent not oftener than once every four (4) weeks, the Agent shall give the Artist information in writing, stating what efforts the Agent has rendered on behalf of the Artist within a reasonable time preceding the date of such request.

(j) The Agent will not charge or collect any commissions on compensation received by the Artist for services rendered by the Artist in a package show in which the Agent is interested, where prohibited by Section VIII of AFTRA's Regulations.

12. SUBMISSION AND DETERMINATION OF DISPUTES

This contract is subject to AFTRA's Regulations Governing Agents (Rule 12-B). Any controversy under this contract, or under any contract executed in renewal or extension hereof or in substitution herefor or alleged to have been so executed, or as to the existence, execution or validity hereof or thereof, or the right of either party to avoid this or any such contract or alleged contract on any grounds, or the construction, performance, nonperformance, operation, breach, continuance or termination of this or any such contract, shall be submitted to arbitration in accordance with the arbitration provisions in the regulations regardless of whether either party has terminated or purported to terminate this or any such contract or alleged contract. Under this contract the Agent undertakes to endeavor to secure employment for the Artist.

(FOR CALIFORNIA ONLY)

This provision is inserted in this contract pursuant to a rule of AFTRA, a bona fide labor union, which Rule regulates the relations of its members to agencies or artists managers. Reasonable written notice shall be given to the Labor Commissioner of the State of California of the time and place of any arbitration hearing hereunder. The Labor Commissioner of the State of California, or his authorized representative, has the right to attend all arbitration hearings. The clauses relating to the Labor Commissioner of the State of California shall not be applicable to cases not falling under the provisions of Section 1647.5 and/or Section 1700.45 of the Labor Code of the State of California.

Nothing in this contract nor in AFTRA's Regulations Governing Agents (Rule 12-B) shall be construed so as to abridge or limit any rights, powers or duties of the Labor commissioner of the State of California.

WHETHER OR NOT THE AGENT IS THE ACTOR'S AGENT AT THE TIME THIS AGENCY CONTRACT IS EXECUTED, IT IS UNDERSTOOD THAT IN EXECUTING THIS CONTRACT EACH PARTY HAS INDEPENDENT ACCESS TO THE REGULATIONS AND HAS RELIED AND WILL RELY EXCLUSIVELY UPON HIS OWN KNOWLEDGE THEREOF.

IN WITNESS WHEREOF, the parties hereto have executed this agreement the _____ day of __________ , 19__.

______________________________ ARTIST

______________________________ AGENT

EXHIBIT 3: GENERAL SERVICES AGREEMENT

1. SCOPE OF AGREEMENT

I hereby employ you as my sole and exclusive representative, talent agency and agent in the entertainment, literary and related fields throughout the world for a period of ( ) years from the date hereof. You accept said employment and agree to counsel and advise me during normal business hours at your office in the advancement of my professional career and to use reasonable efforts to negotiate employment and other contracts providing for the rendition of my services in those branches of the entertainment, literary, music, and related fields throughout the world, in which I am now or hereafter shall be willing and qualified to render services, including without limitation motion pictures, television and radio, publishing, audio and video recordings, personal appearances, concerts, theater, merchandising, testimonials and commercial tie-ins, whether or not using my name, voice or likeness.

Commentary: *This is a general services agreement which goes beyond areas traditionally covered by union contracts. It authorizes representation in all areas of the entertainment industry, but you can exclude areas where you feel the agent may not be particularly helpful or needed (i.e., music publishing, where you may already have another established relationship). It is also exclusive (i.e., you cannot have general services representation by more than one agency).*

2. WARRANTIES

I have the right to enter into this agreement. I have not entered into and will not hereafter enter into any agreement which will conflict with the terms and provisions hereof. I agree that you may have interests of any kind either in your own or in the activities of others as well as the right to render your services for others during the term hereof either in the capacity in which you are employed by me hereunder or otherwise, whether similar to or competitive with the interests and activities for which you are employed to represent me hereunder, including without limitation, on behalf of the owners of package programs or other productions in which my services are used. Such representation shall not constitute a violation of your fiduciary or other obligations hereunder. With respect to the rendition of my services outside of the continental United States, you shall have the right to designate without my consent any one or more persons, firms or corporations to carry out or do any or all acts or things hereunder otherwise to be performed by you. No breach of this agreement by you or failure to perform the terms hereof shall be deemed a material breach of this agreement unless within thirty (30) days after I learn of such breach I serve written notice upon you of such breach and you do not remedy such breach within fifteen (15) days, exclusive of Saturdays, Sundays and holidays, after receipt by you of such written notice; provided, however, that the provisions of this sentence shall not be applicable to the provisions of Paragraph 6 of this agreement.

Commentary: *Packaging is allowed by the agent, as is the representation of other (possibly competing) clients. Ask for a list of the agent's other clients. Note the warranty that you are free to enter into this agreement (meaning that you have not signed with another agent for representation in the same areas).*

3. COMPENSATION

I agree to pay you 10%, as and when received by me or by any person, firm or corporation on my behalf, directly or indirectly, or by any person, firm or corporation owned or controlled by me, directly or indirectly, or in which I now have or hereafter during the term hereof acquire any right, title, or interest, directly or indirectly, or by my successors and assigns, of the gross compensation paid or payable to me or for my account, during or after the term hereof, pursuant to or as a result of or in connection with (a) any employment or contract now in existence or negotiated or entered into during the term hereof (or within six months after the term hereof, if any such employment or contract is on terms similar or reasonably comparable to any offer made to me during the term hereof and is with the same offeror thereof or any person, firm or corporation directly or indirectly connected with such offeror) whether procured by you, me or any third party; and (b) all modifications, extensions, renewals, replacements, supplements or substitutes for such employment or contract or pertaining thereto whether procured by you, me or any third party; however, it is expressly understood that to be entitled to continue to receive the payment of compensation on the aforementioned contracts during or after the termination of this agreement you shall remain obligated to serve and to perform obligations with respect to said employment contracts and to extensions or renewals of said contracts and to any employment requiring my services on which such compensation is based. Commissions on considerations other than money shall be payable, at your election, either in money based on the fair market value of such other considerations, or in pro rata share in kind of such other considerations.

> ***Commentary:*** *The commission amount varies, depending upon a maximum established in union-regulated areas or that negotiated by the client. At the time of signing a series of agreements, the artist may want to negotiate an "across the board commission," applicable to all areas of representation - AFM, AFTRA, general services, etc. Also, commissions may be figured either on gross receipts (all amounts paid to or on behalf of the artist) or net receipts (gross receipts less the deduction of certain expenses, such as travel, weekly guarantees to artist, or such artificial amount as 10% on monies earned after the first $50,000).*

4. OTHER ARTIST BUSINESSES

If any firm, corporation, partnership, joint venture or other form of business entity now or hereafter owned or controlled by me in which I now or hereafter have any right, title or interest has or hereafter during the term hereof acquires directly or indirectly any right to my services in the entertainment, literary, music and related fields, then said firm, corporation, etc., shall be deemed to have engaged you as its sole and exclusive agent and shall confirm such engagement by executing an agency agreement in the same form as this agreement or your then standard form pertaining to such activity. Regardless of whether such business entity executes any such agreement with you, such agency agreement shall be deemed executed and shall be of full force and effect, and I shall remain primarily liable, jointly and severally, with such third party, to pay commission to you as provided in paragraph 3 above, based upon the gross compensation paid and/or payable to such third party, to pay commission to you as provided in Paragraph 3 above, based upon the gross compensation paid and/or payable to such third party, directly or indirectly, for furnishing my services, as fully and effectively as if such gross compensation were paid and/or payable to me. For the purposes of Paragraph 3 above, the term "gross compensation" shall be deemed to include such gross compensation paid and/or payable to such third party. If such third party does not, for whatever reason, execute such agreement with you, you shall nevertheless remain my exclusive agent to represent me in connection with my services on the terms and conditions as herein contained and I shall remain liable to pay commissions to you as provided in this contract and in the preceding sentence hereof.

Commentary: *This clause attempts to cover the situation where artists form other business entities, usually for tax purposes, which "loan-out" the services of the artist. Due to the legal fiction which separates the identities of a corporation from that of its shareholders, this paragraph insures that not only the artist but also his loan-out corporation is firmly bound to the representation agreement.*

5. COMPENSATION DEFINITION

As used herein, "gross compensation" means all monies, properties, considerations and other things of value of every kind and character whatsoever including but not limited to salaries, earnings, fees, royalties, rents, bonuses, gifts, proceeds, rerun fees and stock (without deductions of any kind) and shall likewise include, without limitations, any gross compensation paid and/or payable to me or for my account on a so-called "pay-or-play" basis, as a guarantee or otherwise in lieu of the rendition of my services; "services" shall include any and all of my services in any capacity whatsoever, whether as an employee, independent contractor or otherwise; "employment" and "contract" shall include any and all employment or contracts (including contracts to refrain from services or activities) of every kind whatsoever whether written or oral, in any way pertaining to services, materials or interests in any branch of the entertainment, literary, music and related fields.

6. DURATION AND TERMINATION

If I do not obtain a bona fide offer of employment from a responsible employer during a period in excess of four (4) consecutive months, during all of which time I have been ready, willing, able and available to accept employment, either party hereto shall have the right to terminate this contract by notice in writing to that effect sent to the other party by registered mail, provided no such bona fide offer has been obtained subsequent to the expiration of said four (4) month period and before the giving of said notice. The exercise of my right to terminate under this paragraph shall not affect your rights under Paragraph 3 hereof with respect to employment or contracts in existence or negotiated for prior to the effective date of such termination.

Commentary: *This is your "out" - if no bona fide offer of employment is received by you during at least four consecutive months during the term of the contract, you can fire the agency and they can cancel you.*

7. ASSIGNMENT OF REPRESENTATION

You shall have the right to assign this agreement or any part thereof to any persons, firms or corporations ("companies") now or hereafter controlling, controlled by or under common control with you, any companies resulting from a merger or consolidation with you, any companies succeeding to a substantial part of your assets, or any parent, affiliated or subsidiary companies.

Commentary: *This clause allows the agency to assign your representation to another affiliated company. This should be looked at carefully, especially when you are signing because of the lure of one particular agent. The artist should include a "key-man" clause specifying that if a particular agent leaves the agency, the artist can follow the agent.*

8. DISPUTES

Controversies arising between us under the provisions of the California Labor Code relating to Talent Agencies and under the rules and regulations for the enforcement thereof, shall be referred to the Labor Commissioner of the State of California, as provided in Section 1700.44 of said Code.

> ***Commentary:*** *The Labor Code permits controversies to be submitted to either the Labor Commissioner or arbitration. This clause opts for the Labor Commissioner.*

9. SIGNEES

In the event this agreement is signed by more than one person, firm, corporation, or other entity, it shall apply to the undersigned jointly and severally, and to the activities, interests and contracts of each of the undersigned individually. If any one of the undersigned is a corporation or other entity, the pronouns "I," "me" or "my" as used in this agreement shall refer to the undersigned corporation or other entity, and the undersigned corporation or other entity agrees that it will be bound by the provisions hereof in the same manner and to the same extent as it would, had its name been inserted in the place of the pronouns.

10. ORAL PROMISES AND EXTENSIONS OF TERM

This instrument constitutes the entire agreement between us and no statement, promises or inducements made by any party hereto which is not contained herein shall be binding or valid and this contract may not be enlarged, modified or altered except in writing, signed by both parties hereto. The term of this agreement stated in Paragraph 1 hereof shall be automatically extended for one (1) year, unless I shall give you written notice to the contrary no later than thirty (30) days prior to the end of such term. The termination of any other agency agreement between us for any reason shall not affect this agreement in any respect.

> ***Commentary:*** *This is an all-inclusive clause disavowing any oral promises made. Moreover, all changes in the agreement must be made in writing. Note the automatic extension for one year of the term of the contract unless the artist gives notice 30 days before the term ends.*

Very truly yours,

____

AGREED TO AND ACCEPTED:

By______________________

____

____

Business Managers

By Marshall M. Gelfand and Wayne C. Coleman

Business managers administer the financial functions and activities necessary to their clients' daily business life. The business manager overseas the flow of income, expenditures, investments, plans and budgets insurance coverage, taxes and estates, while at the same time monitoring the tax consequences of each transaction. Artists normally engage a business manager after having some success, for example a gold album or a series of moderately selling albums.

There are no licensing or education requirements which must be met in order to become a business manager. However, anyone who offers his services as a business manager must be qualified to deal with the complex problems involved in structuring a complete financial program. For these reasons, most business managers are certified public accountants (CPA's), attorneys, or businessmen with other financial backgrounds. CPA's dominate the field.

Business management, as described herein, is unique to the entertainment industry. It began in the 1930's in Los Angeles, primarily because of the tremendous incomes earned in the movie industry. After World War II, with the growth of the television and music industries, business management grew rapidly in Los Angeles, and spread to New York, Nashville, and San Francisco. Business management is in its infancy in Europe and other major entertainment markets outside the United States.

BUSINESS MANAGER'S RELATIONSHIP TO OTHER CLIENT ADVISERS

As stated earlier, business managers administer the financial activities of their clients' business life. This responsibility makes them an important factor in the client's advisory team. The other members of the team are:

The personal manager who structures the career.

The talent agent who seeks employment and books the dates for the artist's performances.

The lawyer who in addition to providing normal legal advice may also become involved in career planning. The lawyer is crucial in making deals on behalf of the artist.

These four people act as a team advising their clients on all facets of their careers. The client remains the captain of this team and usually makes the final decisions.

It is advisable to have a system of checks and balances so that no person or entity can unduly dominate or control an artist's career. It may cost more (often 25 percent to 30 percent of total gross income) to have a personal manager, an attorney, and a business manager, but in the long run it will provide greater financial stability to have the complete team working on your behalf.

BUSINESS MANAGER FUNCTIONS

In administering the financial activities of the client, the business manager performs many functions. These may be summarized as follows:

Accounting and Bookkeeping

Bookkeepers and staff bear the basic day-to-day responsibility for reviewing and paying bills, collecting and accounting for income, and recording all the data required to issue monthly financial statements to each client. In many firms, the statements are generated by computer and show income and expenses for each month and cumulatively for the year to date. They also list each deposit for the month and all checks issued during the month. These statements are reviewed by the professional staff, who then prepare cash flow statements, tax projections, and other special reports based on individual client needs.

Collection of Income

Once the client enters into a contract, the business manager then has the responsibility of enforcing or following up on the contractual payment provisions to make sure that the income is received. Once income is received, the business manager is responsible for budgeting the outflow of the income and assuring that unnecessary expenditures are avoided. This will involve tax planning, both before a deal is made and after the income is received.

Most contracts call for the income to be reported to the artist on a periodic basis. The business manager has to know the types of income which are to be reported and the expected time of reporting.

It takes a sophisticated accounting and monitoring system to ensure that income is collected on a timely basis. For example, in the music industry today, many recording artists perform songs written by themselves. Many also own their own publishing companies which may receive income from many different sources around the world. Business managers have to know when the various sources of income should flow in. They monitor the receipts and contact delinquent income sources to assure the client receives the money that is due.

Budgeting

The business manager will consult with the artists about the expenditures necessary to maximize the artists' long-range financial security. For example, adequate insurance coverage is a must.

The business manager must also be concerned with personal discretionary expenditures. Expenditures for personal capital items are a large portion of spending by an entertainer. The business manager can be very helpful in finding a house or automobile the client can afford, helping to minimize costs and recommending financing, if appropriate. In the area of personal expenses, the role the business manager plays depends upon the individual client. The era of the credit card has eliminated strong financial control on personal spending, so a manager is unlikely to be able to set budget restraints in this area on clients who will not or cannot restrain themselves.

Investments

The business manager develops with the client an investment philosophy designed for the client's individual needs. A conservative approach would be to protect capital and avoid speculative risk by investing in quality real estate with a potential for appreciation and eventual capital gains. It is also the business manager's responsibility to assist in the purchase, construction, and financing of clients' homes. Separate investment policies may be determined for their clients' pension and profit sharing plans.

Tax Planning

The tax planning program includes determination of the type of entity to be used (sole proprietorship, partnership or corporation), structuring the proper pension or profit-sharing plan, and estate planning in conjunction with attorneys, pension administrators and insurance representatives. The business manager also has the responsibility for tax compliance, preparation and review of all tax returns, and representation of all clients in examinations by the IRS or state tax agencies.

Publishing Administration

For songwriter clients, some business managers have the facility to copyright, license, and administer the songwriter's compositions. This includes scheduling and reviewing royalty statements received from domestic licensees and performing rights societies and issuing royalty statements to other writers and publishers. Some firms also assist personal management in structuring and administering foreign subpublishing deals throughout the world.

Royalty Examinations

Some business management firms have separate departments to examine the records of companies which are the source of income. These separate specialized departments perform examinations of United States record companies and music publishers and their foreign licensees and affiliates, to determine if there have been any underpayments of income. Their examinations may take place in all the major world markets, for both individual artists and United States companies who have foreign distribution deals. Additionally, they may examine both the production and distribution records of motion pictures and television shows for clients who are profit participants. They may also perform due diligence investigations for clients interested in purchasing other catalogs of copyrights for investment purposes.

Tour Accounting

The business manager may assist in budgeting for United States and foreign tours by their clients. For example, in conjunction with the personal manager, the business manager may help a concert touring artist to project income and expenses on a national tour. In the past, touring was done for career enhancement and financial rewards. Today where sales of two million albums and tapes are not uncommon, touring often becomes an effective method of increasing record sales, rather than a major source of financial profit itself. Business management firm staff and partners travel on tours when necessary to assist in settlements with promoters and concert halls. They may also help in structuring and negotiating the most favorable tax burden state by state and around the world.

STRUCTURE OF A BUSINESS MANAGEMENT FIRM

The functions and services outlined above are sometimes performed by one business manager with a support team of one staff person and a bookkeeper. However, in large companies, those functions are performed by several bookkeepers, staff personnel, supervisors and partners. In this respect, each client has their own minicorporate organization to handle financial activities.

Specialized departments, such as tax, audit, or investment departments, may be called upon to provide the expertise necessary to handle the more technical and complex matters.

In the organizations described above, clients have the best of two worlds; the first being that of the personal attention of a sophisticated and trained professional to oversee their general affairs; and second, the availability of a complete range of specialized services necessary to service their needs.

BUSINESS MANAGEMENT FEES

Most professional fees are based upon time billings. However, in the business management field the general rule is a percentage fee, usually 5 percent of the client's income. In some cases where appropriate, a ceiling may be placed upon a total fee collected. A third method used by some business managers is to have a retainer fee with their clients. The fee structure is usually set out in the initial meeting between the potential client and the business manager.

Most business managers do not have written contracts with their clients because they feel that a good personal relationship between the client and the manager is imperative, and either party should feel free to leave at any time they desire.

GENERAL CAREER ADVICE

Typically, the business aspect of a successful artist's career displays a number of crucial elements. Although not all of these elements may be present in any one career, their importance will be evident to any aspiring young musician-singer-songwriter who is serious about their career.

If You Record Your Own Composition, Keep Your Own Publishing

Artists that have a large and growing catalog of recordings will learn that they can earn substantially more money if they write the songs they record and own their own publishing company.

Currently the worldwide gross mechanical royalty income for a typical album can average approximately 50 to 70 cents. In the United States, for songs licensed at full statutory rates, the amount for a normal album is currently 57 cents (if there are 10 songs on the album, 51.3 cents if there are 9, etc.), while in Germany, after paying the subpublisher his share, the net mechanical royalty rate is in the area of 75 to 85 cents per album. (A subpublisher is a foreign publisher who publishes musical materials on behalf of a U.S. publisher. Most charge a fee before remitting the monies they have collected to the U.S. publisher.) Thus, when artists sell two million albums around the world, they could receive over $1,000,000 in gross mechanical royalty income alone. (The terms gross and net mechanical royalty are discussed in the chapter, "Music Publishing.")

These examples demonstrate the importance of recording one's own songs and controlling one's own publishing, in terms of potential income derived from songs which have had worldwide success. Indeed, mechanical royalties outside North America are calculated according to the album's price. As the price rises, so does the level of royalty income. This is not true in North America, as in the U.S. and Canada mechanical royalty rates are based on fixed fees.

If, for any reason, young artists decide to give up a share of their publishing, for example, to launch their career, they should consider limiting the agreement to two or three years. Copyrights are one of an artist's most valuable assets and should be retained if possible.

Don't Be A Jumper

A good record company has a nurturing loyalty to its artists: it is important for artists to have a reciprocal loyalty to the company that has supported them and contributed substantially to their success. The relationship rests upon mutual respect. Successful artists should think twice before moving to a different company which may, for instance, simply be willing to pay higher advances. Of course, if the artist is not selling then it may be advisable not to renew their deal with the same company.

Today, reputable companies desire to pay their artists promptly and correctly according to their recording agreements. It is rare for deliberate errors to be uncov-

ANALOGIES THAT MAY BE HELPFUL IN UNDERSTANDING THE BUSINESS MANAGEMENT FIRM.

The bookkeeper in a business management firm may be compared to the bookkeeping and accounting department of a corporation.

The staff accountants, who usually have a minimum of two years of experience, perform the functions of the assistant controllers. The supervisors or managers, who are usually all certified public accountants, can be compared to the treasurer or controller.

The partner, who has the overall responsibility of the financial planning, is the client's vice president and chief financial officer.

The client may be compared to the president or chairman of the board. The client must be the final judge in important financial decisions that affect his future.

ered during a royalty examination. Mistakes may occur because the recording agreement may specify unique or complex royalty provisions that may be unclear or difficult to handle by the computer system which calculates payments due the artist.

Record income can be substantial, so artists should consider most carefully with which company to sign. They will want to stay with that company for a long time if the relationship is successful.

It is not always the object to make a great deal of money from performing, but to provide maximum exposure and accessibility, which boosts record sales . . .Today where sales of two million albums and tapes are not uncommon, touring often becomes an effective method of increasing record sales, rather than a major source of financial profit itself.

You Should Tour Periodically

It is essential for recording artists to support their record sales by touring. They must be out there so that the consumer can see them. It is not always the object to make a great deal of money from performing, but to provide maximum exposure and accessibility, which boosts record sales. The personal manager will lead the team in working out the detailed plans well in advance - particularly if a complicated worldwide tour is contemplated.

Do Not Forget The Overseas Market

Many big acts today have up to 50% or more of their recordings sold overseas. This is in contrast to the early 1960's when a 95%/5% division between the United States and overseas sales was typical. Ultimately artists may be paid a full artist royalty rate in every territory where their material is released. However, today it remains common for the record company to pay the artist between 50% and 75% of the domestic royalty rate on sales outside the domestic market.

Be Involved In Making Your Own Career Decisions

Final decisions as to which record company to sign with, when to tour, whether to record their own or other's compositions and when to put out greatest hits compilations should be made by the artist. They should be involved in every aspect of their career. To have time for this involvement, they must be willing to delegate responsibility for other decisions.

CONCLUSION

The business manager's primary function is to maximize clients' earnings while safeguarding their capital. Thus, their clients may concentrate on their artistic efforts with a feeling of financial security and that their business affairs are being attended to.

To accomplish the goals of planning for short-term and long-term financial security, the business managers must recognize that they are providing personal services for clients who are generally not experienced business people. Therefore, they must have integrity, sound decision-making abilities, and a talent for simplifying the communications concerning their clients' tax and business affairs. Finally, they must remember that the most important persons they must protect and provide services for are their clients.

AWARD
DINNER
BMI
HILLS CALIFORNIA
1981
CONSTITUTION
and
BY-LAWS
of the
LOCAL No. 6
INFORMATION FOR
WRITERS AND
SESAC...more than you

Music Organizations

- **Music Unions**
- **Performing Rights Organizations: An Overview**
- **ASCAP/BMI Primer**

The information in this article is subject to change without notice as union collective bargaining agreements are amended and renegotiated from time to time. Union chapters or locals in your city may have rules, benefits and minimum pay scales which are different from those quoted in this article. Rules, scales and benefits may change or differ as a result of a number of variables, including the specific geographic area where musical services are performed, pay escalation provisions within existing union agreements or entirely new collective bargaining agreements. Advances in musical technology and differing interpretations of union rules as governed by local union officials, custom and practice may also be significant factors. Local union personnel can be extremely helpful in answering particular questions you may have.

Other songwriters' and musicians' organizations such as The Songwriter's Guild of America, The National Academy of Songwriters and The Society of Composers and Lyricists are not discussed herein because they are not recognized as collective bargaining units for their members.

WHAT'S A MUSIC UNION?

A music union is a labor union whose membership is comprised of musicians. A labor union is a group of people who band together (no pun intended) to demand better pay and working conditions. Bargaining as a group, union members have greater negotiating strength than as individuals. This article discusses in some detail many of the rules and benefits of membership in the two major U.S. music unions, the American Federation of Musicians (AFM) and the American Federation of Television and Radio Artists (AFTRA).

American Federation of Musicians of the United States and Canada, AFL-CIO, CLC.

The AFM is one of the world's largest unions of performing artists, with over 400 Locals and over 200,000 members.

AFM members are instrumentalists, leaders, contractors, orchestrators, copyists, music librarians, arrangers and proof readers working in all mediums of music performance: live performance, television, movies, etc.

American Federation of Television and Radio Artists, AFL-CIO.

AFTRA members are singers, sound effects artists, actors, announcers and narrators, working in radio, television and phonograph recording.

Screen Actors Guild, (SAG)

Vocalists singing in theatrical motion pictures are governed by SAG's 1983 Theatrical Motion Picture Agreement.

Locals

The AFM and AFTRA are comprised of local unions and governing organizations known as the "International Executive Board" (for AFM) and the "National Board" (for AFTRA). The International Executive Board and National Board grant charters to "Locals" in certain geographic areas, like Los Angeles, Detroit or Nashville. AFTRA locals are usually referred to by the name of the community, whereas AFM locals are given a number. Each local is basically autonomous and independent from other locals and the International Board or National Board, so some pay rates, such as live performance rates, and benefits vary from local to local.

SIGNATORY COMPANIES

Like General Motors and the United Auto Workers, about every 2-5 years music employers such as record companies, television and movie producers negotiate contracts called Agreements with the AFM, AFTRA and SAG. A music employer who signs an Agreement promises to hire only union members and to provide at least the minimum pay and working conditions set forth in the Agreement. The employer signing the Agreement is called a signatory company. If you are employed by a nonsignatory company, such as a small record label or nonunion bar or restaurant, you may be violating union rules and receiving less than union approved pay or scale. In so doing, you may also be undermining the bargaining strength of the union and its members. Union locals can tell you whether or not your employer is a signatory company.

WHY JOIN?

No union can promise professional success, especially in the highly competitive music industry, which is subject to ever changing tastes and trends. Nevertheless, union membership does offer certain opportunities for career advancement and some very real benefits. One of the most important benefits of union membership is your eligibility for employment by signatory companies.

Membership Benefits

The benefits you get by joining a union depend on the strength of the particular union and local. For example, among the benefits provided by AFM Local 47 in Los Angeles are: job referrals for professional bands and musicians; death benefit group insurance; legal counsel and representation in grievance and arbitration proceedings; credit union membership; notary public service and business discounts; scholarship and awards programs; listings and information on agents, managers, record companies, "casual leaders," nightclubs, studio contractors and community orchestras; club memberships, social activities and monthly membership meetings; a disabled musicians' fund; subscription to Local 47's monthly newspaper and International Musician, the AFM newspaper; a 24 hour telephone assistance line; contract preparation and consulting in areas concerning your musical career; free published help wanted and audition notices; rehearsal space; and, low cost instrument insurance. If a person fails to pay you for you services, the union will attempt to collect your money without any cost to you. Also, through the Booking Agent Agreement, commissions charged by booking agents are limited to 15 - 20%.

Recording Contracts

Another good reason to join a music union is a common provision in recording contracts between musicians and record companies who are signatories to AFM or AFTRA Agreements:

"Artist represents that during the term of this recording agreement, Artist is and will remain or will promptly become and remain a member in good standing of any applicable guild and/or union to the extent that Company may legally require such membership. All applicable provisions of the collective bargaining Agreement to which Company is a party shall be deemed a part of this Agreement and shall be incorporated herein by reference."

This provision obligates a signatory record company to pay you at least minimum union pay or scale for recording sessions, (as well as providing other benefits described later in this article), after you become a union member.

AGREEMENTS

The following sections discuss most of the major AFM and AFTRA Agreements controlling phonograph recordings, movies, television, commercials and live performance. In calculating your minimum scale be sure to refer to the correct and current Agreement. Also, different payments for recording, production, sideline musicians, contractors, leaders, instrumentalists and vocalists are found in each Agreement. Although the scales change periodically, many of the "terms of art" have the same meaning from one Agreement to another. When an Agreement expires, if not extended, the expired terms and conditions are usually followed until a new Agreement can be negotiated and signed.

Funds

In addition to pay scales, some union Agreements also require employers to pay money to various "Funds." Depending on the particular fund, the money is used for pension, welfare and retirement benefits, payments to recording members, to members who perform in videos, and to members who perform free live public concerts in parks, veteran's hospitals, schools and other public places.

TERMS OF ART

As with all professions, union musicians share certain "terms of art:" ordinary words that have special meanings which derive from the various union Agreements discussed in this article. A few common terms of art used throughout the AFM Agreements are:

Contractor

A contractor's duties are to locate and hire musicians for a particular job. The contractor will prepare the contracts and make sure that they are filed with the union. A contractor need not be an instrumentalist, but must attend the engagement. Contractors may also be responsible for rehearsals.

Leader

When a musical group is hired one of the members is designated as the leader. The leader is responsible for the group and is the person who deals directly with the employer. The leader must file the contracts with the union and collect payment from the employer. If the leader fails to collect payment and fails to report the uncollected payment to the union, the leader may be personally liable to the other union members for the uncollected amount.

Arranging

This is the art of preparing and adjusting an already written composition for presentation in other than its original form. This includes reharmonization, paraphrasing and/or development of a composition so that it fully represents the melodic, harmonic and rhythmic structure.

Orchestrating

This is the labor of scoring the various voices and/or instruments of an arrangement without changing or adding to the melodies, counter-melodies, harmonies and rhythms.

AFM SCALE: RECORDINGS

One of the fundamental things a union does is establish minimum pay rates for its members. Always remember that these rates are minimum and you are free to negotiate higher pay. Called "scales" (again, no pun intended) "rates," union "fees," or "minimums," they all mean basically the same thing: money - paid to you, the "member" - at a variable minimum pay rate established in the applicable Agreement. For the sake of consistency, throughout this article, these minimum payments will generally be called "scales." Examples of various scales appearing throughout this article are current only as of this writing, are included for illustrative purposes only and should not be relied upon. Always consult your local for current scale.

The AFM Phonograph Record Labor Agreement sets scale for instrumentalists, leaders, contractors, arrangers, orchestrators and copyists working in the phonograph recording industry. Vocalists are paid by AFTRA.

Session Scales

For instrumentalists, leaders, or contractors the AFM sets basic scale and overtime scale for regular sessions (3 hours) and special sessions (1 1/2 hours). You can also get premium scale for work during specified holidays, at odd hours, (between midnight and 8:00 a.m.), and after 1:00 p.m. on Saturdays and Sundays. The rates are different for symphonic and nonsymphonic work. As of this writing the basic regular session scale is $220.94. Leaders and contractors get double scale.

Doubling, Cartage and Electronic Instruments

Additional payments may be paid if you play more than one instrument during a session. This is called doubling. If you play an electronic device to simulate sounds of instruments in addition to the normal sound of the instrument to which the electronic device is attached or applied, such use is treated as a double. For the first double you get an additional 20% of the applicable session scale, and 15% more for each additional double. You may also be entitled to compensation for cartage (hauling) if an employer requires you to bring a heavy instrument to a session. If you bring a large or heavy piece of equipment, such as a harp, you are entitled to an additional $30.00. If you bring a string bass, tuba, drum set or amplifier you are entitled to an additional $6.00.

Orchestrators, etc.

Arrangers, orchestrators and copyists' scales are set according to a detailed pay schedule based on the extent of the work done, per page or per line, and sometimes hourly. For example, page rates for orchestrators depend on what you do: for transcribing a melody from voice, instrument or mechanical device, including chords, symbols and lyrics (one staff) you get $35.00 for the first page (up to 32 bars) and $25.00 for each additional page. Arrangers usually negotiate their own rates, based in part on orchestrators' rates. Copyists get paid at least $14.80 per hour, or per page, according to certain detailed criteria set forth in the Agreement.

Dubbing

The AFM seeks to discourage dubbing [using recordings not originally released in phonograph records (such as a film soundtrack) in a phonograph recording or using a recording made at an earlier time in a present recording]. These rules relate to recordings containing performances by persons covered by any AFM Phonograph Record Labor Agreement since January 1954. Dubbing is allowed where the record company notifies the union and pays the current scale to the artist who made the original recording that is now being used.

Royalty Artists

When it comes to overdubbing, tracking, sweetening or playing multiple parts there are special provisions for "royalty artists." The AFM considers you a royalty artist if you record pursuant to a recording contract which (a) pays you royalties of at least 3% of the suggested retail price of records sold or (b) if you are a member of a self contained group of two or more performing together in fields other than phonograph records under a group name (like a band or orchestra which also performs live) and the group is under a recording agreement which provides for a royalty payment of at least 3% of the suggested retail price of records sold. As a royalty artist you receive the basic session rate per song for the first session at which you perform in respect to each song. This applies whether or not you play multiple parts, double, overdub or sweeten.

Personal Services Contract

The AFM bylaws do not allow you to enter into any personal service contract (such as a recording contract) for any period of more than 5 years without the approval of the AFM. This is true even in states such as California, where the maximum length of a personal service contract is allowed by law to be longer.

Recoupable Payments

Most recording agreements allow the recording company to recoup recording costs from the artist's royalties. The record company may seek to include all payments made to the AFM as recoupable recording costs. However, payments made by the record company under the Phonographic Record Trust Agreement and

Phonograph Record Manufacturers Special Fund Agreement, which are based on record sales, are not properly recoupable as recording costs.

Music Performance Trust Fund

The Phonographic Record Trust Agreement requires signatory record companies to pay the trustee of the Agreement .315% of the suggested retail price of records, tapes and compact discs (to a maximum suggested retail price of $8.98) for each record sold; (or in the case of compact discs, a maximum retail price of $10.98). This money is then used for the presentation of free live public concerts in parks, veterans' hospitals, schools and other public places. During a recent fiscal year, the Music Performance Trust Fund paid union musicians over $10 million to perform free public concerts, making the AFM the largest employer of musicians in the world.

Phonographic Record Manufacturers Special Payments Fund Agreement (February 1987) (PRMSP Fund)

This Agreement requires record companies to pay a small percentage of the price of each record sold (about 5¢ for a top priced LP) to the PRMSP Fund. The money in this fund is paid to members annually in amounts determined by the number of union recording sessions each has played during the year. For example, during a recent fiscal year the Special Payments Fund paid over $10 million to approximately 40,000 recording musicians. That's an average of over $250 each.

Video Promo Supplement

The Phonograph Record Labor Agreement also provides that musicians appearing in music videos be compensated when the video incorporates a recording produced by a signatory record company.

Musicians other than royalty artists who perform on camera are paid $157.48 per day.

If the record company receives money from the licensing, sale, or leasing of the video, the company pays the AFM 1% of revenues received after the company has recouped $75,000. The funds paid to the AFM are then distributed among all the musicians involved in producing the recording used in the video.

If the record company sells the video as a video disc or video cassette in the consumer market, the record company must pay $500 to the AFM after the company has received $5,000 in revenues from sales. The $500 is considered an advance against the 1% payment revenue required after $75,000 is recouped.

AFM SCALE: MOVIES

The AFM Theatrical Motion Picture Agreement defines and sets different scales for recording, production, and sideline musician members.

Recording Scale

If you play on the recording of a movie soundtrack, you are entitled to receive recording scale. The scale depends on the number of musicians employed, with the highest rate being for a group of 23 musicians or less. There are separate rates for single sessions (3 hours or less) and double sessions (6 hours or less) with overtime rates as well. You are also entitled to additional pay if you are asked to double (see section on doubling above). If there are 23 or fewer musicians employed, you currently get $191.50 for a single session. For a double session, the scale is $383.

Production Scale

Musicians are paid production scale when performing at rehearsals for the movie. These musicians do not record on the soundtrack or appear on camera and are paid either single session or double session scale. For longer rehearsal periods, 30 or 40 hour per week, scales are quoted in the Agreement. For a single session, you currently get $101.03; for a double session, $181.86. For a 30 hour week the current scale is $808.21; for a 40 hour week, scale is $969.85.

Sideline Scale

Sideline musicians appear on camera but do not record. The basic scale is $118.40 for a minimum of 8 hours. You are also paid extra for time spent in costume fittings, interviews, wardrobe and makeup.

Orchestrators, etc.

Scale for orchestrators, copyists, proofreaders and music librarians, per page, hourly and weekly, are set forth in the Theatrical Motion Picture Agreement. Consult the text of the Agreement for applicable rates.

Music Sound Consultant

If you are not a conductor, leader or contractor and are assigned by the producer to advise on the sound quality of the music being recorded you are entitled to $38.97 per hour.

Overscale Employees

By individual negotiations between you and the producer, it can be agreed that any payment you receive which is in excess of the minimum scale may be applied to any of the minimum payments, premiums, allowance, doubling, penalties, overtime or other minimum requirements of the Agreement.

Theatrical Motion Picture Special Payments Fund

This Agreement requires a signatory movie producer to make residual payments to the AFM on behalf of musicians who perform on the film soundtrack. 1% - 1 2/3% of the producer's accountable receipts from the exhibition of the motion picture on free television and supplemental markets (i.e. video cassettes, pay-type CATV, pay television) must be paid to the Theatrical Motion Picture Special Payments Fund. The Administrator of the fund then pays you a percentage of these receipts based on a detailed formula set forth in the Agreement.

AFM SCALE: TELEVISION

The AFM Television, Video Tape Agreement sets scale for network and syndicated television, both live and taped.

Types of Programs

In this Agreement, the AFM sets rates according to the type and length of the television program. Signatory producers of 30, 60 or 90 minute television programs, classified as variety programs, strip variety programs, nonprime time children's variety shows, and other types, pay different rates to AFM members.

Recording Scale

As with movies, you are entitled to recording scale if you actually play on the recording of the television program soundtrack. Scale is set according to the length of the program and session. For example, for a 90 minute variety program, not a strip show (i.e. not a daily program like The Tonight Show), such as a Bob Hope Special, the scale is $459.50.

Production Scale

If you play for rehearsals only, do not record on the program soundtrack and do not appear on camera, you are entitled to production scale. The hourly rate, for a minimum session of 2 hours is $53.55.

Orchestrators, etc.

If you render services as an orchestrator or copyist, you are entitled to per page or hourly scale set forth in the Agreement.

Reuse Fees

The AFM Video Tape Agreement also requires employers to pay reuse fees for reruns of the program. If the program is rerun in the United States or Canada, the instrumentalists, leader, contractor and music sound consultant receives 75% of the original scale payment for the second and third run; 50% for the fourth, fifth and sixth runs; 10% for the seventh run and 5% for each additional run. There are separate schedules covering payments for foreign broadcasts.

AFM SCALE: MOVIES MADE FOR TELEVISION

The AFM Television Film Labor Agreement sets rates for movies made for TV, situation comedies and dramatic series (i.e. "Dallas"). These programs are shot on film or tape and broadcast on free commercial television first. As with the Basic Theatrical Motion Picture and Television Video Tape Agreements, the TV Film Labor Agreement has separate wage scales for recording, production and sideline musicians, orchestrators, copyists and music librarians.

Recording Scale

If you play on the soundtrack recording of a program covered by this Agreement, you are entitled to recording scale. For a single session of 3 hours, the current scale is $166.52. For a double session you get $333.04.

Production Scale

As with movies, if you play at rehearsals but are not recorded and do not appear on camera, you are entitled to receive nonrecording production scale. Scale for a single session (less than 3 hours) is $101.03. A double session (less than 6 hours) is $181.86.

Sideline Scale

As with the Motion Picture Agreement, if you appear on camera, but are not recorded, you are a sideline musician and you currently are entitled to $118.40 for a minimum 8 hour session.

Orchestrators, etc.

If you render services as an orchestrator, arranger, copyist, music librarian or proofreader on a TV movie, situation comedy or dramatic series you are entitled to minimum rates set forth in the Agreement.

Television Film Producers Special Payments Fund

Residuals of 1% of the producer's accountable receipts from the distributor of TV movies in supplemental markets (i.e. cassettes, pay-type CATV and pay television) are paid by the producer to the Motion Picture and Television Producers Special Payments Fund. Such funds are then distributed to you according to the formula set forth in the Fund Agreement.

AFM NONSTANDARD TELEVISION (PAY TELEVISION) AGREEMENT

This agreement covers cable TV, pay or subscription TV, pay cable TV and closed circuit TV. It provides rates for recording and production musicians, orchestrators, arrangers, copyists and music librarians, calculated in the same manner as the Television and Video Tape Agreement. For example, for a 1 hour variety program, other than a strip program, for a minimum 8 hour session, the recording scale is $306.75. The production scale is $53.55 per hour, with a 2 hour minimum.

AFM NATIONAL PUBLIC TELEVISION AGREEMENT

This Agreement sets minimum rates for the services of instrumentalists, leaders, contractors (varying as to the length of the program) and arrangers, orchestrators, copyists and librarians.

Supplemental Market Fees

This Agreement calls for supplemental market fees [i.e. cassettes, pay-type CATV pay television and in-flight (commercial airlines, trains, ships and busses) exhibitions].

Reuse Fees

Reuse payments must also be made by signatory producers to the AFM for subsequent broadcast cycles. If the producer elects to pay the instrumentalist under a higher of two wage scales, he may exhibit the program for a longer initial release. Following the initial release, the producer must pay reuse fees to the AFM on behalf of the musicians. The exact amounts are calculated according to a formula set forth in the Agreement.

AFM SCALE: COMMERCIALS

The AFM Television and Radio Commercial Announcements Agreement sets forth pay scales usually paid by the signatory advertising agency making the commercial.

Session Scale

The Commercials Agreement calls for a minimum session for instrumentalists, leaders and contractors of 1 hour, during which 3 different commercial announcements may be recorded, the total length of which may not exceed 3 minutes. The maximum rate varies as to the number of musicians at the session. For example, for the minimum session, for 1 musician, you are entitled to $156, if there are 2 - 4 musicians, $84.30, and 5 or more musicians earns you $78.

Synthesizers Prohibited

This Agreement, (like the Theatrical Motion Picture Agreement) also provides that electronic synthesizers and similar devices cannot replace performances of instrumentalists.

Reuse Fees

The initial scale payment allows the commercial producer to broadcast the commercial by television or radio, but not both, during a period of 13 weeks from the date of first broadcast. Thereafter, you should be paid reuse fees for each additional 13 week cycle. The reuse fee for an instrumentalist who does not double, playing in a combo of 2 - 4 musicians, for a national broadcast, is $63.25.

Orchestrators, etc.

You are entitled to specific scale payments set forth in the Agreement if you render services as an arranger, orchestrator, copyist or music librarian.

AFM SCALE: LIVE PERFORMANCE

The AFM represents instrumentalists and vocalists when they perform live concerts. The individual locals set minimum wage scales and working conditions for nightclubs, hotels and other venues where live music is performed.

Booking Agents Agreement

The AFM Booking Agents Agreement sets limits on the commissions agents may charge members for securing live performance engagements. Approved agent commissions range from 15% - 20% depending on the duration of the employment secured by the agent, provided your net pay after deducting the agent's commission is never below scale.

Union Form Contracts

Members are required to use union approved form contracts for their live performances. One advantage of using the union form contracts is the union contract provision requiring the concert promoter or venue owner to pay you interest and attorneys fees in addition to other damages if he fails to pay you for your services or otherwise violates the contract. In California, if you bring an action against the promoter for a breach of the contract and you lose, you will have to pay for the promoter's attorney fees.

Recording or Broadcasting Prohibited

You are entitled to additional payments if your live performance is recorded (either on audio or video or both), or transmitted on television or radio. For this reason, no live performances may be recorded, reproduced or transmitted without making prior arrangements with the AFM.

Casuals

Casual engagements are one or two night performances. The locals negotiate minimum scale for rehearsals and various types of shows including dance only; dance with an incidental act; show and dance; cocktail hour, tea dance, fashion shows; show with accompanying act; casual concert where admission is charged; and park concerts.

The scale is based on the number of musicians performing and length of show and includes payment by the employer to the union pension and welfare funds.

Continuous/Extended Engagements

The locals also negotiate scale for musicians who are hired for extended live performances. There are separate scales for hotel nightclubs, freestanding nightclubs, and beer and wine establishments. Within each of these scale structures the pay is based upon the number of days per week you perform, the length of each performance and the number of musicians performing.

Arbitration

The union form contract provides that if any dispute or claim arises out of the engagement covered by the contract, the parties shall submit the matter to either the local's trial board or to an arbitrator who is picked by the parties. In a recent California lawsuit between Bill Graham, a concert promoter and Leon Russell, a performer, the Court ruled that union arbitration provisions must provide the parties with an opportunity to obtain an unbiased and neutral arbitrator.

AFM DUES

Membership

If you play a musical instrument of any kind or are a vocalist or render musical services for pay, you are classified as a professional musician and you are eligible for membership in the AFM. You may apply for membership in any local in the area in which you live.

Initiation Fees

You must pay initiation fees to both the AFM local and to the International Federation. Each local sets its own initiation fee and the Federation initiation fee varies according to the amount of the local initiation fee. You pay the total initiation fees to the local and the local then forwards the Federation initiation fee to the International Secretary-Treasurer.

Indoctrination

When you apply for AFM membership you must participate in an indoctrination procedure administered by the local. This will introduce you to the rules and benefits of the AFM. The local also holds examination and audition meetings.

Dues - Periodic

You are required to pay annual or quarterly dues to the local and the Federation. For Local 47 the rates are $82 per year or $21 if paid quarterly. These payments include AFM dues. The dues for Local 47 include death benefit group insurance.

Work Dues

You must pay work dues based on your total earnings for all musical services performed. Upon joining the AFM, you must authorize all employers to deduct from your pay the work dues owed, and to remit that amount to your local.

Work dues are a minimum of 1% of scale wages, half of which is paid to the Federation with the remainder payable to the local in whose jurisdiction the services were performed.

Locals may impose additional work dues. However, the maximum amount of work dues payable depends on whether you are a traveling member (a member of another local), or a local member. Maximum dues payable if you are a traveling member performing services within the jurisdiction of a local of which you are not a member, cannot exceed 4% of scale wages. The maximum work dues payable if you are performing services within your own local's jurisdiction cannot exceed 5% of scale wages earned.

Health and Welfare Funds

Locals use Health and Welfare Funds to provide health insurance benefits for members. To be eligible for these benefits, a total of $200 must be contributed to the Fund by your employers every 6 months.

Employers Pension and Welfare Fund, Strike Fund

Members can also participate in a Employers Pension and Welfare Fund. Should it be necessary for the union to call a strike, the AFM also maintains a Strike Fund for its members.

Fines, Defaulters List

Members are not allowed to render services for an employer who is on the AFM's Defaulters List. It is also improper for a member to record or perform for a company which is not a signatory to the AFM Agreement. The union feels that musicians who play for defaulters condone unfair practices and undermine the bargaining power of the union and each of its members. Also, an AFM member is not permitted to render musical services outside of Canada or the United States, or their territories or possessions, without the approval of the union.

AFTRA SCALE: RECORDINGS

AFTRA Code of Fair Practice for Phonograph Records sets the following scales for the recording industry.

Hourly and Side Scale

Scale under this agreement is determined per hour or per side, whichever is greater. A Side is defined as 1 song or a bonafide medley on a single record not exceeding 3 1/2 minutes, and for each 60 second portion thereof over 3 1/2 minutes playing time, an additional 50% of the applicable per side unit is paid. For soloists and duos, the minimum scale is $120.25 per person per hour or side, whichever is greater.

Solo and Group Scale

The individual scale is the same for soloists and duos but is lower for groups of 3 or more singers. If, however, as a singer in a group of 3 or more vocalists, you step out and sing 16 or more cumulative bars on a particular side, then you are paid at the soloist and duo scale. There are also separate scales for vocalists making classical recordings or original cast show albums.

Dubbing

Under AFTRA rules "dubbing" is allowed where the record company notifies AFTRA and pays scale to the artists involved in making the original recording that is now being used at a later time. The company must also obtain the consent of any "star," "featured" or overscale artist.

Royalty Artists

The minimum rates mandated by AFTRA are payable even if you are a royalty artist. AFTRA considers you a royalty artist if your recording contract pays you record royalties. As a "royalty artist" you are not entitled to more than 3 times the minimum scale per side.

AFTRA SCALE: TELEVISION

AFTRA National Code of Fair Practice for Network Television Broadcasting Agreement, with its supplement for pay television and video discs and cassettes, sets rates for AFTRA members' services in the television industry.

Solo or Group Scale

The AFTRA Code sets different wage rates for soloists, duos and chorus singers.

Program Scale

The scale increases for programs with a longer running time. Another variable affecting scale is whether the program is a single performance or multiple performances during a calendar week. The specific scale varies for work that is done on camera, or off camera, and whether or not the program is a dramatic prime time program. For instance, if you sing, on camera, in a group of 3 to 8 singers, in a prime time dramatic program, you are entitled to a program fee of $393 per person for a minimum session of 3 hours.

Replay Fees

This Agreement also provides for replay fees. For the first and second network replay, you are paid 75% of the applicable minimum program fee plus 20% of the rehearsal and doubling fees for programs originally telecast after November 16, 1976. For all other replays you are paid 75% of the applicable basic minimum program fee for the first and second replay fees; 50% for the third, fourth and fifth replays, 10% for the sixth replay and 5% for each replay thereafter.

Supplemental Market Fees

Supplemental Market Fees must be paid by the producer of a program when the program is exhibited on pay television, basic cable or in-flight. The producer pays 2% of the distributor's gross receipts in the supplemental markets. This 2% is paid for the benefit of all performers, except walk-ons and extras. If the program is a network prime time dramatic program and produced after July 1, 1983, the producer pays 3.6% of the distributor's gross receipts, rather than 2%. You will receive your portion of these payments either directly from the producer or the producer will deposit the fees with AFTRA for distribution to you.

AFTRA SCALE: TELEVISION COMMERCIALS

Signatories to AFTRA Television Recorded Commercials Agreement pay the following fees for commercials:

Session Scale

Signatories to the AFTRA 1985 Television Recorded Commercials Agreement pay session scale based on an 8 hour day. Scale varies for soloists and duos and groups of different sizes where you work on camera. If you work off camera, the minimum session scale is for 2 hours. For a solo or duo, the off camera scale for a single 2 hour session is currently $250.60.

Use Scale

Scale for use of program commercials is divided into classes, according to the number of cities in which the commercial is telecast, (Class C is 1 - 5 cities, Class B is 6 - 20 cities, Class A is over 20 cities.) New York, Chicago and Los Angeles each count as 11 cities.

Principals, Group Rates

Use payments for each class have separate scales for principal performers and group performers and within each of those scales are different rates for on camera and off camera performances, each time the commercial is reused. For example, if you are an off camera solo vocalist, your session fee ($250.60) includes payment for the first class A use. For the second class A use, you get an additional $96. For the third through the 13th uses you receive $76.35 each, thereafter you are entitled to $34.65 for each additional use.

AFTRA SCALE: RADIO COMMERCIALS

Signatories to AFTRA Radio Recorded Commercials Agreement pay for sessions of 90 minutes in duration. Reuse fees under this Agreement are affected by many variables, including special scale for wild spots, dealer commercials, network program commercials, regional and network program commercials, single market commercials and foreign uses. Scales are determined according to complex formulas set forth in the Agreement.

AFTRA MEMBERSHIP DUES

You are eligible for AFTRA membership if you have performed or intend to perform as a singer in the fields of radio, television or phonograph recording. AFTRA does not regulate the musical services of its members outside the U.S.

Initiation Fees

AFTRA's Los Angeles Local imposes an initiation fee of $600, however, this need not be paid when you first work. You have 30 days from your first engagement before the initiation fee and dues are payable.

Dues

Dues are payable semi-annually and based on the performer's gross earnings under AFTRA's jurisdiction for the previous year as follows:

Gross Income in AFTRA's Jurisdiction			Semi-Annual Dues (AFTRA Parent)	Semi-Annual Dues (Other Parent)
$ 0	to	2,000	$42.50	$37.50
2,000	to	5,000	60.00	50.00
5,000	to	10,000	85.00	75.00
10,000	to	15,000	115.00	100.00
15,000	to	20,000	137.50	132.50
20,000	to	25,000	175.00	170.00
25,000	to	37,500	225.00	NO DISCOUNT
37,500	to	50,000	325.00	NO DISCOUNT
50,000	to	75,000	425.00	NO DISCOUNT
75,000	to	100,000	600.00	NO DISCOUNT
100,000	to	150,000	875.00	NO DISCOUNT
150,000	and	over	1,000.00	NO DISCOUNT

As this chart shows, if your parent union (the first performing union you join) is not AFTRA, there is a discount in your dues if your income from AFTRA performances is under $25,000 per year.

Other AFTRA Benefits

Benefits of the AFTRA Welfare Fund are available if you have $1,000 in earnings within AFTRA's jurisdiction, during any one of four consecutive twelve month earning periods. This Fund includes life insurance, accidental death insurance and medical insurance.

The AFTRA Pension Fund provides benefits determined by the number of years you are active with AFTRA and your earnings during those years.

A Dental Assistance Plan is available if you have earnings of $2,500 within AFTRA's jurisdiction, during any one of four consecutive twelve month earning periods. A credit union is also available to AFTRA members.

Discipline

As an AFTRA member, if you violate union rules, you may be "disciplined" by means of fine, suspension or expulsion from the union.

CONCLUSION

For a union to be successful, its members must respect its rules. By reporting unfair practices and conscientiously participating in union activities and elections you help protect other union members and, to an extent, you exercise a degree of control over how the union represents you and protects your interests. The complex array of union scales and payments for royalties, reuses and supplemental markets, were not guaranteed to musicians by employers out of friendship. Unions organized and fought for these payments. As long as enthusiastic and ethical professionals are involved in unions, they will help to ensure fair treatment for all musicians.

Members of the Phoenix Symphony Orchestra. Photo by Brant Seegmiller.

Performing Rights Organizations: An Overview

By Mark Halloran

If a song you write is commercially recorded, you will want to join a performing rights organization so you can collect money for the public performance of your song.

This chapter will give you a basic overview of the three U.S. performing rights organizations— the American Society of Composers, Authors and Publishers (ASCAP), Broadcast Music Incorporated (BMI) and SESAC (formerly called the Society of European Stage Authors and Composers). For a more in-depth discussion of ASCAP and BMI, consult the following chapter, "An ASCAP/BMI Primer." We will briefly discuss performing rights, how television and blanket licenses work, the agreements you enter with ASCAP and BMI, collaboration, money generated by ASCAP and BMI, and the issue of nondramatic versus dramatic public performance rights.

COPYRIGHT LAW UNDERPINNING

To understand exactly how performing rights organizations work, you must understand one fundamental tenet of copyright law: a copyright owner in a musical work (song) has the exclusive right to perform the work publicly. The concept "performance" includes not only live performances, but also the rendering of previous performances that are fixed in records, videotape, or film. Thus, when a radio station broadcasts a song, that song is being publicly performed. As such, the radio station must be licensed by the copyright owner to play the song. The radio station normally obtains this license from ASCAP, BMI, or SESAC for a fee. The same is true for songs included in television programs. When a television program is broadcast, the songs in the program are being publicly performed. The network or local station must be licensed to publicly perform the songs.

Radio and TV are not the only kinds of public performance. When you are dancing to "Walk This Way" sung by Run DMC in a nightclub, is the playing of that song by the disc jockey a public performance? Yes. But at this point you should consider an absolutely crucial distinction. What exactly is being performed? The answer is that the musical composition in the record is being performed, not the sound recording. (A sound recording is a series of sounds. Its copyright is separate from the copyright in the song.) If the disc jockey is playing "Walk This Way," then the song "Walk This Way," not Run DMC's recording, is being publicly performed. To do this without violating copyright law, the nightclub must have a license to perform this song. That is where ASCAP, BMI and SESAC step in. They negotiate licenses (permissions) with radio and TV stations, nightclubs, cabarets, discos and the like, enabling them to perform publicly the musical compositions contained in the performing rights catalogues.

The essence of the agreement between the performing rights organizations and the nightclub is simple: the performing rights organization grants the right to the nightclub to use the song (perform the song publicly), and in return the performing rights organization is paid a fee by the nightclub. This fee is ultimately divided among the songwriters and publishers who create and publish the songs. You should note that the company that publishes "Walk This Way" and the writers must authorize ASCAP, BMI or SESAC to license the public performance . Run DMC, who perform the song, and their label, which owns the recording, do not license the public performance of the song. They are not the copyright holder of "Walk This Way," but merely the performer of the song and owner of the sound recording respectively. As such they do not collect public performance royalties in the U.S. In certain foreign territories, performing rights organizations also license public performances of sound recordings, but ASCAP, BMI and SESAC do not.

A main exception to the blanket license procedure are U.S. motion picture theaters. As a result of an antitrust case brought on behalf of theater owners, ASCAP and BMI do not license the public performance of musical works in U.S. motion picture theaters. However, certain foreign performing rights organizations do in their respective territories.

PERFORMING RIGHTS ORGANIZATIONS

A performing rights organization licenses the public performance of copyrighted musical compositions. Here is the trade-off that constitutes the license: the users of copyrighted songs pay a fee to the performing rights organizations in order to perform the copyrighted songs publicly. In the United States the phrase "performing rights organization" is synonymous with the three organizations: the American Society of Composers, Authors and Publishers (ASCAP) , Broadcast Music Incorporated (BMI), and SESAC (formerly known as the Society of European Stage Authors and Composers). The vast majority of U.S. copyrighted songs are in the repertory of either ASCAP (with a total of over 3,000,000 songs) or BMI (with 2,000,000 songs).

ASCAP

In 1914 Victor Herbert and a handful of other composers organized ASCAP because performances of copyrighted music for profit were so numerous and widespread, and most performances so fleeting, that as a practical matter it was impossible for individual copyright owners to negotiate with and license the music users and to detect unauthorized public performance of their songs. ASCAP was organized to serve as a clearinghouse for copyright owners and users to solve these problems associated with the licensing of public performances of music. Today ASCAP is a membership society which represents approximately 33,000 composers and 14,000 publishers. ASCAP collected $360,000,000 in 1990, and distributed over $188,000,000 to its members.

BMI

BMI, a corporation operating on a not-for-profit basis whose stock is owned by members of the broadcasting industry, was organized in 1939. BMI represents some 42,000 publishing companies and 75,000 songwriters and composer, and operates in much the same manner as ASCAP. In 1990, BMI collected more than $244,000,000 and distributed over $200,000,000 to its affiliates.

SESAC

SESAC is the second oldest U.S. performing rights organization. The formation of SESAC in 1931 predated the ASCAP radio strike by approximately 9 years. During this strike, radio stations would not play ASCAP licensed music. SESAC has approximately 2,500 - 3,000 writer/publisher affiliates. Although traditionally known for its strength in country, gospel, and band music, it is now moving into Jazz, New Age, and Pop. SESAC is different from ASCAP and BMI in that it is much smaller and its service is much more personalized.

TELEVISION AND RADIO LICENSING

The bulk of money paid to the performing rights organizations comes from radio and television broadcasters. The performing rights organizations negotiate "blanket" licenses that cover all the works in their catalogues. Thus, the television or radio station does not have to check the music before it is broadcast—the station can be confident the song being played is somewhere in the performing rights organizations catalogue. The granting of blanket licenses makes sense when you consider the vast number of songs in the performing rights organizations catalogues. If a broadcaster or nightclub individually negotiated with the copyright holder each time a song was played, chaos could result. Blanket licenses also benefit writers and publishers, as they do not have the means to enforce their exclusive right to public performance of their songs: the performing rights organizations do it for them. The performing rights organizations also sue broadcasters, clubs and others who publicly perform songs without a license. Bringing infringement suits is one of their most important functions.

After a performing rights organization issues its blanket license, the license holder may use any of the works of any of the members of that organization as often as desired during the license term. The performing rights organizations figure out to whom the money should go, and they use sampling techniques to compute the division of income based on the frequency and the kind of public performance of songs. The computation and payment of royalties is discussed more fully in the article which follows.

Broadcast blanket licenses have been under fire by nonnetwork television stations in both the courts and Congress. Although the legal and legislative attacks have been unsuccessful, nonnetwork television stations are increasingly negotiating for a "per program" use fee in lieu of a blanket license.

What exactly is being performed? The musical composition in the record is being performed, not the sound recording. (A sound recording is a series of sounds. Its copyright is separate from the copyright in the song.) If the disc jockey is playing "Walk This Way," then the song "Walk This Way," not Run DMC's recording, is being publicly performed.

ASCAP and BMI Contracts With Songwriters

Assuming you qualify for membership in ASCAP, BMI or SESAC you will then be asked to enter a contract with them. In entering either the ASCAP, BMI or SESAC songwriter contract, you are giving ASCAP, BMI or SESAC the right to license the public performance of songs that you write in return for their promise to pay you royalties for the reported performances of your songs.

Publishers can also join ASCAP, BMI or SESAC. Their contracts with ASCAP, BMI or SESAC are much the same as for writers. However, performing rights organizations pay writers and publishers separately so both must join.

Collaboration

If an ASCAP writer collaborates with a BMI or SESAC writer, the song is licensed concurrently by both organizations. Thus, you will notice on some record albums that a song listing for the performing rights organization will list both ASCAP and BMI or SESAC.

Foreign Collections

ASCAP, BMI and SESAC also collect money from affiliated foreign performing rights organizations. However, the vast majority of income comes from the U.S. For example, in 1989 ASCAP's U.S. receipts were $260,000,000 and foreign receipts $57,000,000. Both ASCAP and BMI charge a service fee for such collections. Many U.S. publishers, however, have subpublishers or agents overseas who collect and remit monies to American publishers directly.

DRAMATIC VERSUS NONDRAMATIC RIGHTS

ASCAP, BMI and SESAC do not license dramatic performance rights.

Dramatic performing rights ("grand rights") must be distinguished from nondramatic performance rights ("small rights"). The Copyright Act grants the exclusive right to perform publicly a dramatic work to the copyright owner. Dramatic works include, among other things, plays (both musical and dramas), dramatic scripts for radio, television, ballets and operas. A musical composition (a song), in and of itself, is a nondramatic work.

Drawing the line between a dramatic and nondramatic performance is difficult, if not impossible. Both the standard ASCAP and BMI contracts state they license only nondramatic performances of the compositions they license. Thus radio and television licensees must be careful to make sure their ASCAP or BMI blanket license covers their use of a song from a play or opera. The industry practice is that radio stations play unlimited numbers of instrumentals from cast albums, or will play a sequence of up to two vocals and an instrumental from the cast album. Some record companies and publishers, however, avoid this licensing problem by obtaining clearance from the copyright holder for unrestricted radio use of songs from cast albums, and notify broadcasters of such a clearance.

Dramatic performances are usually licensed directly from the writers of the music, lyrics, and book of the play, or their agents. Writers usually reserve dramatic rights in their contracts with publishers. A sample illustration: if a theater company wants to do A Chorus Line, they must seek permission directly from the writers of the play to perform the play and the accompanying music. On the other hand, if a radio wants to play only the song "At the Ballet" from the cast album, this is not a dramatic performance, and ASCAP and BMI license this sort of performance.

GRIEVANCE PROCEDURES

If you have a dispute with ASCAP or BMI (for example, you don't agree with your royalty statement), you have recourse through the ASCAP or BMI grievance procedures. The ASCAP grievance procedure is set out in their articles of association. These articles are provided to you by ASCAP when you join. BMI grievances are submitted to the American Arbitration Association in New York City. SESAC has no formally established grievance procedure.

One of the most important business decisions that a songwriter and a music publisher make is choosing which performing rights organization to join. This chapter is devoted to an overview of performing rights organizations in general and an examination of the methods of operation of the two major American performing rights organizations, the American Society of Composers, Authors and Publishers (ASCAP), and Broadcast Music Incorporated (BMI). A third, significantly smaller American performing rights organization, SESAC, will not be discussed.

WHAT IS A PERFORMING RIGHT?

Since 1897, United States copyright law has included the "public performing right," extending to the copyright owner (generally the songwriter and/or publisher) the right to perform the composition in public. The copyright owner may in turn grant the performing right to another party (generally in exchange for a licensing fee). A "public performance" in this context does not include singing in the shower, for example.

WHAT IS A PERFORMING RIGHTS ORGANIZATION?

ASCAP and BMI fulfill songwriters' and publishers' need for a comprehensive method to license public performing rights and charge fees for widespread performances of their compositions in saloons, nightclubs, hotels and fairs throughout the country.

Thus, by virtue of the policy of the performing rights organizations and the principle of vicarious liability, licensing fees are collected from the venue of performance, not the performer. Public performing rights royalties are paid only to the writer and publisher of the performed composition, and not, for example to a recording artist who has included a version of the composition on his or her sound recording. For example, Daryl Hall receives BMI writer royalties for broadcast performances of "Every Time You Go Away," while Paul Young, as the recording artist "covering" Halls' composition, is paid royalties on album sales by his record company.

Rather than licensing rights and charging performance royalties or fees on a song-by-song basis, ASCAP and BMI collect licensing fees pursuant to so-called "blanket licenses" which entitle the licensee to perform any composition in the ASCAP or BMI catalog for the duration of the license. In addition to those venues already mentioned, blanket licenses are granted for network and local television and radio, cable television, restaurants, malls and stores, concert halls, bars, background music services, colleges, circuses, ice shows, airplanes and others, essentially for any user who performs music publicly. Users may also select alternative per-program licenses that provide unlimited catalog use with the fee based on the programs that actually use the music.

The two major exceptions to the blanket license are the use of compositions for distant signal cable transmissions and domestic motion picture theaters. Under the 1976 Copyright Law, cable systems pay fees for distant signal transmissions directly to the Copyright Tribunal who then distribute them to all copyright claimants, including the performance rights organizations, the film industry, etc.

Additionally, although foreign motion picture theaters are subject to performing rights organization licensing, ASCAP is prohibited from licensing domestic theaters, originally as a result of a United States antitrust case [*Alden Rochelle v. ASCAP, 80 F. Supp. 888* (S.D.N.Y. 1948)] brought on behalf of domestic theater owners. In 1960, the antitrust suit was vacated and replaced with provisions of a Consent Decree. BMI has not sought to license domestic theaters, although it is not legally prohibited from doing so.

The licensing of performing rights is a big business as evidenced by ASCAP's collection of almost $360,000,000 in domestic fees in 1990, and BMI's collection of more than $244,000,000. After deduction of administrative costs, approximately 80% of these fees were distributed by the organizations as royalties to publisher and songwriter members.

ASCAP and BMI license nondramatic ("small") performing rights only. "Grand" performing rights for dramatic performances, such as musicals, operas and plays are generally licensed directly by the publisher. Additionally, the organizations' consent decrees, discussed later, allow member copyright owners to directly license these performing rights to anyone without involvement by ASCAP or BMI.

MEMBERSHIP

Performing rights organizations represent both writers and publishers, and even where a writer is represented by a third party publisher, that writer needs to also join a performing rights organization. As performing rights organizations pay writers and publishers separately, both must join or become affiliated

A writer may only belong to one performing rights organization at a time. When a writer is affiliated with a performance rights organization, the writer affiliation, rather than publisher affiliation, determines the organization administering the composition (e.g. ASCAP administers the performing rights to musical compositions written and registered by ASCAP members). When the writer is unaffiliated, the publisher's membership determines the organization administering the writer's composition. It is common for music publishers acting as publishers for more than one writer to establish both ASCAP and BMI publishing companies (under separate names for separate legal entities) so that both ASCAP and BMI writers can be represented (e.g., ASCAP will only pay the publisher share of performing rights royalties to an ASCAP publisher).

ASCAP Membership

A writer or publisher may be elected to ASCAP when one of his or her compositions is published, recorded, or is performed publicly. Once elected, new writer members are eligible to begin collecting royalties on the same basis as existing writer members.

New writer members are eligible to collect a portion of royalties for performances occurring as many as six calendar quarters prior to election, and to be fully paid royalties for performances occurring as recently as three calendar quarters prior to election. New publisher members are eligible to collect full royalties for performances occurring two calendar quarters prior to election.

ASCAP writer and publisher applications and respective instruction sheets are included as Exhibits l-4, the writer biographical sketch is included as Exhibit 5, the membership agreement (application for both writer and publisher) is included as Exhibit 6, and the publisher warranty letter and designation of representative letter are included as Exhibits 7 and 8.

ASCAP has approximately 33,000 writer members, 14,000 publisher members and licenses many millions of compositions in its catalog.

BMI Affiliation

BMI's "Open Door" policy offers affiliation to writers or publishers with a musical work either published, recorded, or likely to be performed publicly. New BMI affiliates are eligible to commence collecting royalties only on performances concurrent with the effective date of the affiliation agreement which may be backdated to allow for retroactive payment for performances during a period for which BMI has not yet made a royalty payment to its affiliates (i.e., currently no more than three prior quarters). BMI writer and publisher applications and instruction sheets are included as Exhibits 11-14; respective affiliation agreements are included as Exhibits 15 and 16. BMI has approximately 75,000 writer affiliates, 42,000 publisher affiliates and licenses more than 2 million compositions in its catalog.

REGISTRATION OF COMPOSITIONS

Prior to choosing which performing rights organization to join, most attorneys advise registration with the United States Copyright Office in order to definitively establish authorship and ownership of a composition. Whether or not they are registered with the U.S. Copyright Office, compositions are registered with the performing rights organization of choice.

ASCAP requires a magnetic tape, floppy diskette or 8 1/2 x 11 form (Exhibit 10) which is used to input data to a magnetic tape. If music is performed on a television program, a music cue sheet (Exhibit 9) should be filed for every composition (cue).

BMI's registration (clearance) form (Exhibit 17), like ASCAP's index card, must be completed for each composition. Cue sheets are required for television background, theme, and cue music.

When compositions are co-written by members of different performing rights organizations (e.g. ASCAP and BMI, or members of performing rights organizations of different countries), special registration procedures may be required.

METHOD FOR DETERMINING PERFORMANCES PAID

With minor exceptions, it is impractical to monitor and thus pay for performances not on television or radio (e.g. bars or nightclubs) or used as cable foreground/background music services. Accordingly, there are no significant royalties paid for nontelevision/radio performances per se, and royalties for radio and television performances are derived from licensing fees from radio, television and nontelevision/radio licensees such as bars and nightclubs.

It is important to note that samples referred to below may include compositions in the repertory of the opposite organization, and/or compositions that cannot be identified by the respective organization, and may therefore actually encompass fewer real hours of the respective organization's compositions than it would seem.

Radio

ASCAP annually samples some 60,000 hours of AM and FM radio in producing a model of the music broadcast on radio, with larger stations sampled more heavily. This model is then applied to weighted multipliers to calculate radio royalties.

BMI annually samples some 500,000 hours of selected AM and FM radio stations to develop their model, with the information coming in the form of detailed listings or "logs." BMI's model is weighted only to the extent that the multiplier used for stations in the top 25% according to size of license fee is larger than that used for those in the bottom 75%.

The independent statisticians developing the models do not forewarn the performing rights organizations as to which stations and periods will be surveyed. Although surveying substantially fewer hours than BMI, ASCAP prefers actual "off-the-air" audiotapes to avoid any potential influence by the survey itself on the stations. BMI prefers to survey, by log, nearly six times as many hours as ASCAP to provide for inclusion and identification of many more compositions (particularly "nonhits") spot checking the written logs submitted for accuracy. Which sampling system provides a more accurate accounting is debatable.

The following schedule estimates ASCAP/BMI writer royalties payable for surveying radio performances of a pop song reaching the peak position indicated (the rating of songs refer to commonly accepted charts in the music industry such as Billboard Magazine, Radio and Records and Cashbox). The number of performances of the composition, rather than the chart position however, determines the amount of performance royalties paid by ASCAP and BMI. These royalties fluctuate depending on the music category itself (e.g., pop country, rhythm and blues, religious, gospel, symphonic), and the ability of the composition to "cross over" to other music charts or categories.

#1	Song:	$70,000 - 100,000
#5	Song:	$40,000 - 70,000
#10	Song:	$30,000 - 40,000
#20	Song:	$15,000 - 30,000

Network Television

Both ASCAP and BMI receive cue sheets prepared and submitted by the networks' television and program producers which detail the seconds of music used in a program. ASCAP and BMI also do audio and video taping of network television to spot check information provided by the networks.

Local Television

ASCAP uses cue sheets from the producer, a sample of regional TV Guides, audio tapes and inquiry letters to the local television stations to statistically sample 30,000 hours of local television performances. This sampling is then applied to

COMPARISONS: ASCAP/BMI

ASCAP	BMI
Agreements	
Writer and publisher-current term until 1995-provisions nonnegotiable. May be terminated annually by letter of resignation received by September 30.	Writer 2 years, publisher 5 years-provisions nonnegotiable. Writer agreements may be terminated by letter of resignation submitted by certified mail not more 6 months and not less than 60 days prior to contract renewal; otherwise, self-renewing. Publisher resignations are generally similar.
Organization	
ASCAP is a membership society owned by writers and publishers who elect its 12 member writer and publisher Board. Regulated by Consent Decree.	BMI is a corporation acting on a not for profit basis on behalf of affiliates. Stock is held by broadcasting organizations. Regulated by Consent Decree.
Dues	
Annual dues: writer - $10, publisher - $50.*	BMI has no dues. One-time publisher administration fee - $25.
Method for Determining Performances Paid	
A. Radio - statistical sample.	A. Radio - statistical sample.
B. Network TV - complete count of program logs and cue sheets	B. Network TV - complete count of program logs and cue sheets.
C. Local TV - statistical sample using a combination of local TV Guides, cue sheets, and audio tape.	C. Local TV - computerized system with regional TV Guide information- with supplemental sample and use of cue sheets to aid in further identification of local or syndicated productions.
D. Jingles - requires unique performance information, certification and contractual provisions.	D. Jingles - must have required number of seconds of music without voice over for feature jingle payment; no lack of voice-over qualification for network jingle payment.

**ASCAP dues are used to aid needy members; any monies not expended for that purpose go into the General Fund and are distributed back to the members.*

ASCAP	BMI
Payment Dates	
Publisher - two quarters after first performance, paid at end of each calendar quarter. Writer - three quarters after first performance, paid on "running four quarters" basis in Feb., May, Aug., Nov. (Being phased out in November 1991, at which date writers will receive all payments three (3) quarters after first performance.)	Publisher/writer paid during same quarter, 7-8 months after the close of the calendar quarter in which the performance occurred.
Payment Rates	
Credit value and performance credits.	Minimum rates usually increased by quarterly rate bonuses.
Performance Bonuses	
System for designating 'qualifying works' based on numbers of feature performances results in higher credit values for those works when used as background music or themes.	A bonus system is applied for compositions frequently performed on radio and local television, or written for theatrical or full-length TV, film, Broadway shows.
Advances	
None granted since Sept. 1982 -no immediate plans for future advances.	None granted since August 1982.
Foreign Royalties	
"Collection agent" for 42 foreign performing rights organizations, 3-4% fee. Canada, United Kingdom, France, Spain and Japan paid July and December. Other countries July or December.	"Collection agent" for 42 foreign performing rights societies, 3% fee paid June and/or December.
Internal Procedures	
Board of review- if not resolved, can be appealed to American Arbitration Association.	If not internally resolved, arbitration by American Arbitration Association.

mathematical multipliers to calculate local television royalties payable to writers and publishers whose compositions were "picked up" in the survey. BMI also uses cue sheets from producers in conjunction with a complete computerized account of regional TV Guides and added program listings from local television to provide a virtual census of syndicated television. (Since syndicated programs are typically easier to identify, BMI also uses a sample to aid in identifying certain local productions). Payment is then made to the BMI writer and publisher for each performance.

TELEVISION MUSIC

There are three main categories of television music— theme, background, and feature performances.

Theme music appears at the opening and/or closing of each television program, as well as segments within programs. ASCAP pays the same rate for each performance of theme music regardless of where it appears. BMI will only pay at the full theme rate if it appears at both the opening and closing of the program; otherwise BMI pays one half the full rate. BMI's full theme rate is per half-hour show (e.g., a theme for a 60 minute program earns a double rate and a two hour movie earns a quadruple rate); the ASCAP full theme rate is not dependent upon length of the program. Once a theme is aired for 13 weeks or more on prime time network television, it is sometimes referred to as a "supertheme" and yields higher rates.

Background music is played to enhance the program, but is not intended as the focus of the program. There is typically about 10 (although some animated programs often contain up to 20) minutes of background music in a 30 minute program. While ASCAP pays on the actual total minutes of background music, BMI will not pay for background music in excess of 1/2 the length of the program (e.g., BMI would pay for a maximum of 15 minutes of background music on a 30 minute program).

A feature performance is music that is the visual focus of the program. For instance, a composition sung on camera is considered a feature performance. ASCAP and BMI require that a feature performance exceed 44 seconds to be paid at the full rate. Features less than 45 seconds are paid at specified lower rates with this ASCAP exception: If a work has had at least five feature performances in the most recent five survey years, it does not have to meet the minimum time criteria.

The following illustrates approximately average ASCAP/BMI per-performance writer royalties payable for network and syndicated television programs. The rates specified below are for reference only and will fluctuate depending on many factors (some of which only apply to network programs), including time of day, and program type (e.g., series, soaps, quiz shows, movies) causing significant differences in royalties paid by ASCAP or BMI for the same performance.

Network Television Rates*	Syndicated Television Rates**	Local Television Rates***
Theme - $250-275	Theme - $55	Theme - $100-260
Background (1 minute) - $150-200	Background (1 min.) - $50	Background (1 min.)-$60
Feature performance - $1,500-2000	Feature performance - $165	Feature performance - $700

**Average ASCAP/BMI Prime-time rates per 30 minute show.*

***BMI rates based on performances on 100 stations.*

****ASCAP rates for local television, based on one surveyed performance.*

PAYMENT OF ROYALTIES

The actual amount of royalties paid varies between the organizations due to many factors, including but not limited to differences in rates and survey methods. Generally, each organization divides the revenues derived from licenses and fees such that 50% is available for publisher distribution and 50% for writer distribution. For purposes of calculating performance royalty distributions, ASCAP and BMI assign varying credit values to publishers, factoring in the size and dollar value of their catalogs.

ASCAP

ASCAP's method of paying royalties is to "follow the dollar" (e.g., radio licensing fees are paid out only as radio royalties). ASCAP's survey year begins on June 1 and royalties are calculated on a quarterly basis.

As of November 1, 1991, ASCAP discontinued what was known as the "running four quarters" method of payment. Writers and publishers are now paid in four quarterly installments, two quarters following the actual quarter of performance of the composition (Current Performance system). The same performances in each quarter will result in different royalties payable to writers and publisher during those distributions which reflect differences in the credit values assigned, as well as the different numbers of credits being processed for writers and publishers in each distribution.

As a protection to the writer, ASCAP does not normally pay writer royalties to anyone other than the writer himself or his personally controlled corporation, unless such royalties have been assigned to legitimate creditors as collateral.

Qualifying Works

Works that have generated specified amounts of feature performances over time (for example, the accumulation of 20,000 feature performances, or a specified amount of feature performances during a five year survey period) are called 'qualifying works' and are assigned higher credit values in determining performance royalties for background music.

Four Funds

A unique aspect of ASCAP's writer royalties is the "Four Funds" method of payment (as opposed to the "Current Performance" system described above), which is only available to writer members of three years or more. In this method, a writer may elect to delay payment of 80% of the royalties due in any one period and average them in to their quarterly payments over a 5-10 year period. A projection should be requested from ASCAP before a decision is made to enter into Four Funds, since the Current Funds basis is the preferable system for most composers; the Four Funds formula is generally advantageous only to those who have been long-time members with many years of success.

BMI

BMI pays quarterly, seven to eight months (television features and radio performances are paid first by separate statement; theme and background performances

ASCAP
EXAMPLE OF WRITER/PUBLISHER PERFORMANCE STATEMENT

February Distribution 1991
April 1, 1990 - June 30, 1990

Network Television (9)

CURRENT DISTRIBUTION'S CREDIT VALUE =

MEMBER NAME

MEMBER CODE

TITLE (1)	T-CODE (2)	CA % (3)	SHARE (4)	NETWK (5)	D P (6)	PROGRAM (7)	EPISODE TITLE	# PLAYS	PERF. TYPE	DURTN. MN:SC	# CREDITS (8)
								1	THEME	*	106.250
								2	FEATURE	*	
								1	BKG	0.26	
								8	PROMO	*	
								4	THEME	*	
									ETC	ETC	ETC ETC

SUBTOTALS # CREDITS:

**Under ASCAP's Weighting Formula, the credits for this performance were calculated without regard to its duration.*

Radio

TITLE	T-CODE	CA %	SHARE	# CREDITS
			50.0%	
			50.0%	
			33.3%	
			16.0%	

SUBTOTALS # CREDITS:

(1) Title of the member's work being credited.
(2) ASCAP code for this title.
(3) If a work is a copyrighted arrangement of a work in the public domain, this shows the percentage at which it is credited (from 2% up).
(4) The members' percentage interest in the work.
(5) ABC, CBS, or NBC.
(6) D = daytime; P = prime time.
(7) Name of show (e.g. "Cheers").
(8) Credits generated by performance which are subsequently converted into dollars. The figure given is only an example; in an actual statement, the # of credits would show for each performance type logged.
(9) The statements for surveys of cable, local, PBS and radio performances are very similar. For cable television, the abbreviation "SRVCE" replaces "NETWK" and references HBO, MTV etc. For local television, the program name is given, but not the episode. Other types of performances are indicated by the word "ORIGIN", e.g. MUZAK, Circus, etc. When there are no surveyed performances in a particular medium, the statement will contain the words: "NO PERFORMANCES OF YOUR CATALOG WERE SURVEYED IN THIS MEDIUM DURING THIS PERFORMANCE PERIOD."

are paid in subsequent statements) after the end of the calendar quarter in which the performance occurred, based upon a published rate schedule prescribing minimum rates for each quarter. Actual rates paid are typically larger than the minimums prescribed due to quarterly rate bonuses. Royalties are paid simultaneously to writer and publisher in equal lump sums. In the absence of a publisher, payment of the full amount of royalties may be made to the writer, or by agreement between the writer and publisher, payment may be split unequally, with the writer receiving the larger share (but not vice-versa). Additionally, PBS payments are made in the fourth performance quarter distribution. Jingles are payed in a special distribution in February of each year. Cable payments are made in the second and fourth performance quarter distributions.

As a protection to the writer, BMI does not normally pay writer royalties to anyone other than the writer himself or his personally controlled corporation, unless such royalties have been assigned to legitimate creditors as collateral.

Bonuses

BMI recognizes frequently performed works by awarding bonuses to both writers and publishers for songs reaching a certain number of performances. Bonuses can range from 1.5 times the standard rate, to almost 17 times the standard rate.

ADVANCES

At one time, both ASCAP and BMI routinely paid advances (nonrefundable, recoupable prepayments of estimated future royalties) to composers and publishers in an effort to stabilize their incomes and woo major musical stars to their respective organization. In 1982, the Buffalo Broadcasting decision* found that ASCAP and BMI's blanket licenses to local television stations constituted an unreasonable restraint of trade in violation of antitrust laws (a ruling that might have removed the performing rights organizations from the local television world). ASCAP and BMI ceased advances to writers and publishers due to the serious potential financial consequences from this threat to approximately one-third of their revenue.

Although the Buffalo Broadcasting decision was overturned in 1984, both organizations remain wary of advances. Consequently, ASCAP has no announced plans to grant advances; BMI is reviewing its policy, but has no immediate plans to resume advances.

As an alternative to advances, both organizations allow assignments of royalties as collateral against bank loans to the composer or publisher. BMI and ASCAP also accept assignment of writer royalties against advances made to the writer by his or her publisher. As the paper work for such assignments is complex, assignments are usually only practical for composers and publishers with substantial projected royalties.

FOREIGN COLLECTION

Foreign performing rights organizations (unlike the United States, only one performing rights organization exists in the majority of countries) monitor foreign per-

**For a more detailed discussion, see the author's article, "Beyond Buffalo Broadcasting: A Brave New World, Or An Impossible Mission?", A.B.A. Entertainment and Sports Lawyer (Winter, 1991,*

formances of compositions in the ASCAP/BMI domestic repertories, and direct royalties for such performances to the United States writer and publisher through ASCAP and BMI (ASCAP and BMI charge a "collection agent" fee of approximately 3% for this service, used to process analyses of performances). The lag in payment of such royalties can range from as little as concurrent payment (for example, the Canadian performing rights organization, SOCAN, typically pay on the same basis as their American counterparts) to as much as 5 years, when there are unusual problems.

Additionally, unless the foreign writer/publisher specifies differently, their United States royalties are collected by ASCAP or BMI and paid to their domestic organization for payment to the writer/publisher. ASCAP and BMI currently have reciprocal relationships with 42 foreign performing rights organizations.

A United States writer's or publisher's foreign performing rights royalties may be diluted by the payment of royalties by the foreign performing rights organization to translators of popular United States compositions. Monies not distributed to ASCAP or BMI are generally forfeited to the foreign organizations general fund (sometimes referred to as "black box") for disbursement to its members. For this and other reasons, most publishers prefer to have their foreign royalties collected "at the source" by foreign publishers (i.e., subpublishers). By giving the subpublisher a vested interest in the collection of such royalties, a quicker and more conscientious effort to collect such royalties is likely to result. Writer royalties, however, must flow from the foreign performing rights organization to the domestic organization.

GRIEVANCE PROCEDURES

In the event of a grievance, ASCAP's consent decree provides for a proceeding with its Board of Review (4 elected composers and 4 elected writers). The complaint must be filed within nine months after the most recent annual statement to preserve claims for performances shown on that statement, and the board is required to specify the facts and underlying grounds for its decision. Any decision of such a proceeding may be appealed to the American Arbitration Association. Because of its joint Consent Decree with the U.S. Justice Department , ASCAP cannot effect certain major changes without Justice Department and/or federal court approval and advance notice to its members. Additionally, ASCAP operates under Articles of Association, which outline their membership rules.

BMI's rules and regulations with respect to distributions and/or grievances are decided by its management. Although also operating under a consent decree entered into with the Justice Department in 1966, any BMI grievances unresolved by management must be arbitrated in New York by the American Arbitration Association.

ORGANIZATION MEMBERSHIP TRANSFERS

There are many considerations in resigning from one performing rights organization to join another, including ease of resignation, catalog transfer (if applicable), timing, forfeiture and/or delay of royalties, and existing advances or assignments of royalties.

Resignations of ASCAP writer and/or publisher membership must be received by September 30 to take effect the following January 1. BMI writer termination letters must be received between 60 days and 6 months in advance of the expiration of the agreement; a publisher termination letter must be received by BMI between 90 days and 6 months prior to the expiration of the agreement.

Since most publishers have both ASCAP and BMI publishing companies, it is seldom necessary for publishers to resign from an organization. Writer transfer from BMI to ASCAP for new works and catalog is not difficult. For new works, writer transfer from ASCAP to BMI is also not difficult. However, many attorneys feel that the procedures for the transfers of catalog are complex with potential payment delays and/or forfeitures.

CONCLUSION

The commendable performances of both organizations has caused performing rights revenues to become the major source of income for writers and publishers in the music industry. As a result, informed selection of a performing rights organization is an important, but not irreversible, writer decision. A good working knowledge of the organizations' procedures not only helps streamline the organizations' efforts, but also aids in the proper and timely payment of royalties.

The Los Angeles Songwriters Showcase (LASS) Expo 89. Sitting at the piano Len Chandler (LASS co-founder and Showcase Director) and Brenda Russell. Above l. to r. Jeff "Skunk" Baxter, Tony Haynes, Diane Warren, Tom Kelly, Martin Page, John Braheny (LASS co-founder and Showcase Director) and Billy Steinberg.
Photo by Richard Aaron.

EXHIBIT 1
ASCAP INSTRUCTIONS FOR WRITER MEMBERSHIP

Dear Writer Applicant:

Enclosed is an application for writer membership in ASCAP. (PLEASE READ THE FOLLOWING PARAGRAPHS BEFORE FILLING OUT THE APPLICATION.)

Composers and authors (lyricists) may join ASCAP as either ASSOCIATE or FULL members. The requirements for each category of membership are explained below.

FULL membership in ASCAP is available to any composer or author who has had at least one original work commercially recorded, printed as sheet music which is available for sale in commercial outlets, available as a score or rental, or performed in ASCAP licensed media (e.g., on a local radio station or nightclub). As a FULL member, you will receive royalties for performances of your compositions included in the ASCAP sample survey. If your works do appear in the survey during any survey year, you will also have the right to vote in ASCAP's elections in the succeeding year and thereby participate in the governing and operations of the Society. As a FULL member you will receive distributions on a Current Performance basis for three full survey years after which you will have an option to switch to the "Four Funds" basis for receiving distributions.

Dues for FULL members are $10.00 per year (PLEASE DO NOT SEND YOUR DUES PAYMENT NOW.) Membership dues will be deducted automatically from your earnings. Should your earnings not cover the membership dues, you will be billed accordingly.

If you are the composer or author of a copyrighted musical composition which has not been commercially recorded or published, you may join the Society as an ASSOCIATE member; you will not pay membership dues and, of course, you will not have voting rights. Your status will be changed from ASSOCIATE to FULL membership as soon as you have had a composition commercially published or recorded or have had a performance in media licensed by the Society. If you do not meet the requirements for FULL membership three years after you have been elected to Associate Membership, your membership will be terminated automatically. If you subsequently qualify for FULL membership you may then re-apply for such membership, but not for ASSOCIATE membership.

In completing the application, please indicate whether you are applying for ASSOCIATE or FULL membership. In order to help you fill in the other blanks at the top of the form, please note that the STANDARD category refers to composers and authors of works performed in symphony and concert halls and educational institutions, and to composers of sacred music; the POPULAR PRODUCTION category includes all other kinds of music (e.g., "Pop," country, jazz, gospel etc.) and "production" music (i.e., music written for films or for stage productions). Please indicate if you are a composer, author (lyricist) or both.

Please print your full name in the space provided at #1 on the application and sign the application with your full name. Both your name and business address (if any) should be provided in #3 and please do not forget to check which address you wish to have your mail sent. (YOU SHOULD NOTIFY THE SOCIETY IMMEDIATELY IN WRITING OF ANY CHANGE OF ADDRESS.) Please indicate in the space provided on the application if you are currently a publisher member of the Society.

Please list all of your published works (title, author and composer, publisher and year published) in the space provided on the application (List of Works).

BOTH copies of the enclosed Membership Agreements should be signed where it says "Owner," using the same signature as on the application. THIS WILL BE THE NAME UNDER WHICH YOU WILL BE ELECTED TO MEMBERSHIP. Please be sure to return BOTH copies of the Membership Agreement.

If you are applying for FULL Membership the completed forms, along with a commercial recording, or a sales or rental copy of one of the compositions listed on your application should be returned to the Membership Department. If your application for Membership is based on a performance of a composition in media licensed by the Society, please indicate, giving particulars such as time, date, city, place of performance (e.g. radio station call letters or nightclub name) title of program, title of composition. Proof of performance indicating information listed above should be submitted on letterhead of the licensee.

If your composition is available in rental form only, a copy of the orchestration, score, or similar document (including a publisher's catalogue price list showing the availability of the score for rental) should be submitted with your application. This can be returned to you after your application has been processed. If you are applying for ASSOCIATE membership the completed forms, along with proof of copyright of one composition should be returned with BOTH copies of the Membership Agreement, signed where it says "Owner." A copy of the Copyright Office Certificate of Registration is sufficient for this purpose.

Please do NOT send lead sheets or demo tapes.

Enclosed are two different Recording cards: one for albums, one for singles. If the basis for your membership is an album release we need a completed album card; we also need an individual card for each single from the album. These cards should be submitted to the Society in duplicate so that one may be returned to you for your records. If you have any questions on how to fill them out, please do not hesitate to get in touch with the Society.

If your application is in order, it will be presented to the Membership Committee and the Board of Directors and you will be advised of their action.

With best wishes for your success as a writer.

Sincerely yours,

MEMBERSHIP DEPARTMENT

TITLE OF SINGLE **RECORDING INFO CARD**

(Duration in Min.)

WRITERS

PUBLISHERS

PERFORMING ARTIST(S)

INDICATE RECORD CO & NO

ALBUM TITLE IF ANY

TITLE OF ALBUM **RECORDING INFO CARD**

RECORDING ARTIST(S)

RECORDING CO & NO

LIST OF INDIVIDUAL SONG TITLES AND WRITERS

CONTINUE REVERSE SIDE

EXHIBIT 2
ASCAP APPLICATION FOR WRITER MEMBERSHIP

I hereby apply for membership as a FULL ☐ STANDARD ☐ AUTHOR ☐
ASSOCIATE ☐ POPULAR PRODUCTION ☐ COMPOSER ☐

in the American Society of Composers, Authors and Publishers. If elected, I agree to be bound by the Society's Articles of Association, as now in effect and as they may be amended, and I agree to execute agreements in such form and for such periods as the Board of Directors shall have approved or shall hereafter approve for all members.

The following information is submitted in support of this application.

1. Full Name: Mr. Miss
Mrs. Ms. ______________________________

(First name) (Middle Name/Initial) (Last Name)

2. Pseudonyms, if any (no more than four)

____

3. Home Address

____

(Street) (City) (State) (Zip Code) (Area Code & Tel. #)

Business Address (if same as above, write "same"):

____

(Street) (City) (State) (Zip Code) (Area Code & Tel. #)

Please check to which address your mail is to be send

4. Date of Birth ______________________________

Place of Birth ______________________________

5. Citizen of: ______________________________

6. Social Security #: ______________________________

7. I am ☐, or have been ☐, a writer or publisher member or affiliate of ASCAP, BMI or SESAC, or of a foreign performing rights licensing organization (Check one of applicable). If you have checked on the boxes above, please state the name of the organization with which you were affiliated, relationship, and the period of your affiliation, and attach a copy of your release if applicable:

____

If publisher member or affiliate, please list firm name: ______________________________

8. I have ☐, or do not have ☐, a relative (including brother, sister, husband, wife, child or any other relation) who is affiliated with an organization referred to in item 7. (Check the applicable box.) If you have answered affirmatively, please give the name of any such person, relationship to you and organization with which affiliated.

____

9. I have ☐, have not ☐, paid to have the works submitted by me on behalf of this application published or recorded. (Check the applicable box.) If you have answered affirmatively, please indicate which works submitted by you were the subject of such payment and to whom payment was made. ______________________________

____

10.The musical works of which I am composer of author are listed on the opposite page. I represent that there are no existing assignments of licenses, direct or indirect of nondramatic performing rights in or to any of the works so listed, except with publishers of such works. If there are assignments of licenses other than with publishers, I have attached true copies. I have read the Society's Articles of Association and make this application with full knowledge of their contents.

I warrant and represent that all of the information furnished in this application is true. I acknowledge that any contract between ASCAP and me will be entered into in reliance upon the representations contained in this application, and that the contract will be subject to cancellation if the information contained in this application is not complete and accurate.

Signature ____________________ Date __________

SCHEDULE A: WRITER'S LIST OF WORKS

List of Domestic Copyrighted Musical Compositions Owned by the Applicant

Title	Year of Copyright	Composer	Author	Publisher

Note: --For works based on compositions in the public domain, the title, author and composer of the public domain source must be indicated.

EXHIBIT 3
ASCAP INSTRUCTIONS FOR PUBLISHER MEMBERSHIP

Dear Applicant:

Enclosed are the documents necessary to complete your election to publisher membership in ASCAP. Please return them at your earliest convenience along with ONE of the following (a) a regular piano sales copy of a work in your catalogue, (b) an orchestration, or (c) a commercial recording of one of the works in your catalogue. If your application for membership is based on a performance of a composition in media licensed by the Society, please indicate, giving particulars such as time, date, city, place of performance (e.g., radio station call letters or nightclub name), title of program, and title of composition. Proof of performance indicating information listed above should be submitted on the letterhead of the licensee. If your composition is available in rental form only, a copy of the orchestration, score, or similar document including a publisher's catalogue price list showing the availability of the score for rental should be submitted with your application. This can be returned to you after your application has been processed.

Dues for Publisher Members are $50.00 per year; (PLEASE DO NOT SEND YOUR DUES PAYMENT NOW). Membership dues will be deducted automatically from your earnings. Should your earnings not cover the membership dues, you will be billed accordingly. BEFORE SUBMITTING YOUR APPLICATION PLEASE CONTACT THE MEMBERSHIP DEPARTMENT TO MAKE SURE THAT THE NAME YOU WISH TO USE FOR YOUR COMPANY IS AVAILABLE, IF YOU HAVE NOT ALREADY DONE SO.

The documents enclosed are:

(1) An application for publisher membership
(2) A copy of ASCAP's Articles of Association
(3) Membership Agreements
(4) A Designation of Publisher Representative form (for use by Corporations and Partnerships)
(5) Duplicate copies of a "Warranty Letter"
(6) Separate schedules marked "A" and "B," and
(7) A supply of Index Cards and Recording Cards with an explanation on how they should be completed.

Please read the following explanation carefully so that each document is completed correctly.

I. THE APPLICATION FOR MEMBERSHIP

1. In the space provided please indicate the appropriate category of membership: the '"STANDARD" category includes publishers of works performed in symphony and concert halls, or works performed in educational institutions, and to sacred music; the "POPULAR" category includes publishers of rock, gospel, country or jazz music and "production music" (i.e., music written for films or for stage productions).

2. A division of a corporation is not a legal entity and therefore cannot be elected to membership. If you are applying as a corporation and it operates a music division, the application must be made in the corporation's name. For example "XYZ CORP." (123 Music Division).

3. Print or type your company name at the bottom of the application, and then sign on the line "BY" (PLEASE PRINT OR TYPE THE NAME SIGNED UNDERNEATH THE LINE) and indicate the signer's title (for example, "Partner," "President," or "Owner"). The application must be signed by a corporate officer, partner or individual owner as the case may be. If any corrections have to be made on the document, they must be initialed by the person signing the application.

4. Please make sure that you include the zip code after you indicate the state in which your company is located. REMEMBER TO NOTIFY US PROMPTLY OF ANY CHANGE OF ADDRESS.

5. Please indicate on the application if you are correctly a writer or publisher member of the Society or another performing right licensing organization. If not applicable, please indicate.

II. THE MEMBERSHIP AGREEMENT

1. Date, sign and return BOTH copies of the Agreement. The company name and signer's name should go on to the lines headed "Owner" and the names should be the same as on the application for membership. A full executed copy will be returned to you.

2. If the company is a corporation, the name of the corporation, e.g., "XYZ Corp., Inc.," should appear next to the word "Owner" on the third page of the "Agreement. A corporate officer must sign the agreement, indicating his or her title.

3. If the company is a partnership, the partners' names, e.g., "John Doe" and "Richard Roe" partners, d/b/a "XYZ Music," should appear next to the word "Owner,": on the third page of the Agreement. All the partners' names should be shown. A partner must sign the Agreement, indicating that he or she is a "Partner."

4. If the company is an individual ownership, the company name, e.g., "John Doe d/b/a XYZ Music" should appear next to the word "Owner" on the third page of the Agreement. The individual must sign the Agreement.

5. Do not enter any information on the front page of the Agreement.

III. THE DESIGNATION OF PUBLISHER REPRESENTATIVE

1. Each publisher member, other than an individual ownership, must file with the Society's Secretary, the name of the person who shall be the company's representative in the Society for all purposes. Please complete the accompanying form, and return it with your application and both copies of your agreement.

2. If your company is a partnership the representative must be a partner; if it is an association or corporation, the representative must be an officer of the association or corporation. Each publisher member may have only one representative at a time. The designation of representative may be revoked at any time, as long as a new representative is designated.

3. The company's name and that of the representative should be printed or typed on the bottom of the designation form and the designated representative should sign the form on the line indicated.

IV. THE WARRANTY LETTER AND SCHEDULES "A" AND "B"

1. Read and sign the Warranty Letter and return BOTH copies. The Schedule A (listing all domestic copyrights owned by your company) and the Schedule B (listing all foreign copyrights for which your company controls United States performing rights as subpublisher) should be completed.

2. If any of the compositions listed on the Schedule A were originally published by someone other than your company, please be sure to attach a coy of the assignment (or other appropriate document) to your company as recorded in the United States Copyright Office.

V. INDEX CARDS AND RECORDING CARDS

Enclosed is a separate explanation on how to fill out the Society's publisher index cards. Also enclosed are two different Recording cards: one for albums, one for singles. If you are reporting an album release, we also need an individual card for each single from the album.*

Please submit each card in duplicate, indicating title, at least one writer, or one publisher, and the performing artist(s). Index cards as well as Recording cards should be submitted to the Society in duplicate so that one may be returned to you for your records. If you have any questions on how to fill out these cards after reviewing the instructions please do not hesitate to get in touch with the Society.

We look forward to your election to membership in ASCAP.

Sincerely yours,

MEMBERSHIP DEPARTMENT

*Examples of index and recording cards follow Exhibit 1, ASCAP Writer Membership Instructions.

EXHIBIT 4
ASCAP APPLICATION FOR PUBLISHER MEMBERSHIP

I (we) hereby apply for membership as a ☐ Standard/ ☐ Popular Production Music Publisher, in the American Society of Composers, Authors and Publishers. If elected I (we) agree to execute agreements in such form and for such periods as the Board of Directors shall have approved or shall hereafter approve for all members.

The following information is submitted in support of this application:

1. Firm Name ______________________________
2. Business address ______________________________
   ____
   Telephone Number (   ) ______________________________
3. Check and complete one of the following to indicate organization of company:
   A. CORPORATION __________ Corporate I.D. No. __________
   State of corporation __________ Date of Charter __________ Percent/ownership __________

Name	Stockholders (list all stockholders)	Soc. Sec. No.	Home Address & Zip	Office held

Name	Officers (list all officers)	Soc. Sec. No.	Home Address & Zip	Office held

B. PARTNERSHIP (list all partners) Year Business Established __________ Percentage __________

Name	Soc. Sec. No.	Home Address & Zip	of ownership

C. INDIVIDUAL OWNERSHIP Year Business Established __________

Name ______________________________ Soc. Sec. No. __________

Home Address ______________________________

____

Telephone Number (   ) ______________________________

If owner is or has been a member of affiliate of ASCAP, BMI or SESAC, or of a foreign performing right licensing organization please state the name of the organization with which owner is affiliated and relationship.

____

If publishing company, please indicate firm name ______________________________

4. Cities in which branch offices are maintained ______________________________
5. If any owner, stockholder, officer, or employee with any executive responsibilities, has been or is now connected with any publishing company, songwriter's agency, recording company, performance rights licensing organization (as an employee), or any other organization engaged in the solicitation, publication or exploitation of music, please fill in the information requested below:

Name of Individual	Telephone	Name of Company	If Publishing Co. Indicate Performance Rights Affiliation	Position Held	Years of Association

6. If you have made, or intend to make, any charge to an author (lyricist), or composer in connection with the examination, publication, recording or exploitation of any composition published or to be published by you, please state the nature of the charge and the service to be performed.

7. I (we) have read ASCAP's Articles of Association and make this application with full knowledge of their contents. I (we) understand that any agreement entered into between ASCAP and me (us) will be in reliance upon the information contained in this application and attached schedules I (we) understand that the agreement will be subject to cancellation if any information contained in this application is not fully and correctly provided or if the true name of each owner, stockholder and officer is not provided as requested.

Firm Name ______________________________

By ______________________________ Title ______________________________ Date __________

EXHIBIT 5
BIOGRAPHICAL DATA REQUESTED BY ASCAP

1. NAME ______________________________

2. ADDRESS ______________________________

3. PLACE AND DATE OF BIRTH ______________________________
   If you do not want year of birth publicized, please indicate.
   However, kindly include this information for our files.

4. FATHER'S NAME ______________________________

5. MOTHER'S MAIDEN NAME ______________________________

6. MARRIED OR SINGLE ______ IF MARRIED, DATE OF MARRIAGE ______________

7. NAME OF SPOUSE ______________________________

8. CHILDREN (if any) ____ NAMES AND ADDRESSES ______________________________

9. EDUCATION (SCHOLASTIC AND MUSICAL) ______________________________

10. MEMBERSHIP IN MUSICAL ASSOCIATION, SCHOLARSHIPS, FELLOWSHIPS AND SIMILAR HONORS ______________________________

11. KINDLY OUTLINE BRIEF SKETCH OF YOUR CAREER WITH PARTICULAR REFERENCE TO ACTIVITIES IN MUSIC, AND CITING FACTORS THAT LED YOU TO MUSIC.

12. LIST YOUR IMPORTANT WORKS

13. PRINCIPAL HOBBIES

14. WILL YOU PLEASE ENCLOSE A RECENT PICTURE OF YOURSELF FOR OUR FILES?

EXHIBIT 6
ASCAP WRITER OR PUBLISHER MEMBERSHIP AGREEMENT (1986-1995)

AGREEMENT made between the Undersigned (for brevity called "*Owner*") and the AMERICAN SOCIETY OF COMPOSERS, AUTHORS AND PUBLISHERS (for brevity called "*Society*"), in consideration of the premises and of the mutual covenants hereinafter contained, as follows:

1. The *Owner* grants to the *Society* for the term hereof, the right to license nondramatic public performances (as hereinafter defined), of each musical work:

Of which the *Owner* is a copyright proprietor; or

Which the *Owner*, alone, or jointly, or in collaboration with others, wrote, composed, published, acquired or owned; or

In which the *Owner* now has any right, title, interest or control whatsoever in whole or in part; or

Which hereafter, during the term hereof, may be written, composed, acquired, owned, published or copyrighted by the *Owner* alone, jointly or in collaboration with others; or

In which the *Owner* may hereafter, during the term hereof, have any right, title, interest or control, whatsoever, in whole or in part.

The right to license the public performance of every such musical work shall be deemed granted to the *Society* by this instrument for the term hereof, immediately upon the work being written, composed, acquired, owned, published or copyrighted.

The rights hereby granted shall include:

(a) All the rights and remedies for enforcing the copyright or copyrights of such musical works, whether such copyrights are in the name of the *Owner* and/or others, as well as the right to sue under such copyrights in the name of the *Society* and/or in the name of the *Owner* and/or others, to the end that the *Society* may effectively protect and be assured of all the rights hereby granted.

(b) The nonexclusive right of public performance of the separate numbers, songs, fragments or arrangements, melodies or selections forming part or parts of musical plays and dramatico-musical compositions, the *Owner* reserving and excepting from this grant the right of performance of musical plays and dramatico-musical compositions in their entirety, or any part of such plays or dramatico-musical compositions on the legitimate stage.

(c) The nonexclusive right of public performance by means of radio broadcasting, telephony, "wired wireless," all forms of synchronism with motion pictures, and/or any method of transmitting sound other than television broadcasting.

(d) The nonexclusive right of public performance by television broadcasting; provided, however, that:

(i) This grant does not extend to or include the right to license the public performance by television broadcasting or otherwise of any rendition or performance of (a) any opera, operetta, musical comedy, play or like productions, as such, in whole or in part or (b) any composition from any opera, operetta, musical comedy, play or like production (whether or not such opera, operetta, musical comedy, play or like production was presented on the stage or in motion picture form) in a manner which recreates the performance of such composition with substantially such distinctive scenery or costume as was used in the presentation of such opera, operetta, musical comedy, play or like production (whether or not such opera, operetta, musical comedy, play or like production was presented on the stage or in motion picture form): provided, however, that the rights hereby granted shall be deemed to include a grant of the right to license nondramatic performances of compositions by television broadcasting of a motion picture containing such composition if the rights in such motion picture other than those granted hereby have been obtained from the parties of interest.

(ii) Nothing herein contained shall be deemed to grant the right to license the public performance by television broadcasting of dramatic performances. Any performance of a separate musical composition which is not a dramatic performance, as defined herein, shall be deemed to be a nondramatic performance . For the purposes of this agreement, a dramatic performance shall mean a performance of a musical composition on a television program in which there is a definite plot depicted by action and where the performance of the musical composition is woven into and carries forward the plot and its accompanying action. The use of dialogue to establish a mere program format or the use of any nondramatic device merely to introduce a performance of a composition shall not be deemed to make such performance dramatic.

(iii) The definition of the terms "dramatic" and "nondramatic" performances contained herein are purely for the purposes of this agreement and for the term thereof and shall not be binding upon or prejudicial to any position taken by either of us subsequent to the term hereof or for any purpose other than this agreement.

(e) The *Owner* may at any time and from time to time, in good faith, restrict the radio or television broadcasting of compositions from musical comedies, operas, operettas and motion pictures, or any other composition being excessively broadcast, only for the purpose of preventing harmful effect upon such musical comedies, operas, operettas, motion pictures or compositions, in respect of other interests under the copyrights thereof; provided, however, that the right to grant limited licenses will be given, upon application, as to restricted compositions, if and when the *Owner* is unable to show reasonable hazards to his or its major interests likely to result from such radio or television broadcasting; and provided further that such right to restrict any such composition shall not be exercised for the purpose of permitting the fixing or regulating of fees for the recording or transcribing of such composition and provided further that in no case shall any charges, "free plugs," or other consideration be required in respect of any permission granted to perform a restricted composition; and provided further than in no event shall any composition, after the initial radio or television broadcast thereof, be restricted for the purpose of confining further radio or television broadcasts thereof to a particular artist, station, network or program. The *Owner* may also at any time and from time to time, in good faith, restrict the radio or television broadcasting of any composition, as to which any suit has been brought or threatened on a claim that such composition infringes a composition not contained in the repertory of *Society* or on a claim by a non-member of *Society* that *Society* does not have the right to license the public performance of such composition by radio or television broadcasting.

2. The term of this agreement shall be for a period commencing on the date hereof and expiring on the 31st day of December, 1995.

3. The *Society* agrees, during the term hereof, in good faith to use its best endeavors to promote and carry out the objects for which it was organized, and to hold and apply all royalties, profits, benefits and advantages arising from the exploitation of the rights assigned to it by its several members, including the *Owner*, to the uses and purposes as provided in its Articles of Association (which are hereby incorporated by reference), as now in force or as hereafter amended.

4. The *Owner* hereby irrevocably, during the term hereof, authorizes, empowers and vests in the *Society* the right to enforce and protect such rights of public performance under any and all copyrights, whether standing in the name of the *Owner* and/or others, in any and all works copyrights by the *Owner*, and/or by others, to prevent the infringement thereof, to litigate, collect and receipt for damages arising from infringement, and in its sole judgment to join the *Owner* and/or others in whose names the copyright may stand, as parties plaintiff or defendants in suits or proceedings, to bring suit in the name of the *Owner* and/or in the name of the *Society*, or others in whose name the copyright may stand, or others, and to release, compromise, or refer to arbitration any actions, in the same manner and to the same extent and to all intents and purposes as the *Owner* might or could do, had the instrument not been made.

5. The *Owner* hereby makes, constitutes and appoints the *Society*, or its successor, the *Owner*'s true and lawful attorney, irrevocably during the term hereof, and in the name of the *Society* or its successor, or in the name of the *Owner*, or otherwise to do all acts, take all proceedings, execute, acknowledge and deliver any and all instruments, papers, documents, process and pleadings that may be necessary, proper or expedient to restrain infringements and recover damages in respect to or for the infringement or other violation of the rights of public performance in such works, and to discontinue, compromise or refer to arbitration any such proceedings or actions, or to make any other disposition of the differences in relation to the premises.

6. The *Owner* agrees from time to time, to execute, acknowledge and deliver to the *Society*, such assurances, power of attorney or other authorizations or instruments as the *Society* may deem necessary or expedient to enable it to exercise, enjoy and enforce, in its own name or otherwise, all rights and remedies aforesaid.

7. It is mutually agreed that during the term hereof the Board of Directors of the *Society* shall be composed of an equal number of writers and publishers respectively, and that the royalties distributed by the Board of Directors shall be divided into two (2) equal sums, and one (l) each of such sums credited respectively to and for division amongst (a) the writer members, and (b) the publisher members, in accordance with the system of distribution and classification as determined by the Classification Committee of each group, in accordance with the Articles of Association as they may be amended from time to time, except that the classification of the *Owner* within his class may be changed.

8. The *Owner* agrees that his classification in the *Society* as determined from time to time by the Classification Committee of his group and/or The Board of Directors of the *Society*, in case of appeal by him, shall be final, conclusive and binding upon him.

The *Society* shall have the right to transfer the right of review of any classification from the Board of Directors to any other agency or instrumentality that in its discretion and good judgment it deems best adapted to assuring to the *Society*'s membership a just, fair, equitable and accurate classification.

The *Society* shall have the right to adopt from time to time such systems, means, methods and formulae for the establishment of a members' status in respect of classification as will assure a fair, just and equitable distribution of royalties among the membership.

9. "Public Performance" Defined. The term "*public performance*" shall be construed to mean vocal, instrumental and/or mechanical renditions and representations in any manner or by any method whatsoever, including transmissions by radio and television broadcasting stations, transmission by telephony and/or "wired wireless"; and/or reproductions of performances and renditions by means of devices for reproducing sound recording in synchronism or timed relation with the taking of motion pictures.

10. "Musical Works" Defined. The phrase "*musical works*" shall be construed to mean musical compositions and dramatico-musical compositions, the words and music thereof, and the respective arrangements thereof, and the selections therefore.

11. The power, rights, authorities and privileges by this instrument vested in the *Society*, are deemed to include the World, provided, however, that such grant of rights for foreign countries shall be subject to an agreements now in effect, a list of which are noted on the reverse side hereof.

12. The grant made herein by the *Owner* is modified by and subject to the provisions of (a) the Amended Final Judgment (Civil Action No. 13-95) dated March 14, 1950 in U.S.A. v ASCAP as further amended by Order dated January 7, 1960, (b) the Final Judgment (Civil Action No. 42-245) in U.S.A. v ASCAP dated March 14, 1950, and (c) the provisions of the Articles of Association and resolutions of the Board of Directors adopted pursuant to such judgments and order.

SIGNED, SEALED AND DELIVERED, ON THIS___ day of ____________, 19 ______

Owner ____________________

AMERICAN SOCIETY OF COMPOSERS,
AUTHORS AND PUBLISHERS

Society

BY ____________________

____________________ President

ASCAP
FOREIGN AGREEMENTS AT THIS DATE IN EFFECT
(SEE PARAGRAPH 11 OF THE WITHIN AGREEMENT)

COUNTRY	WITH (Name of Firm)	EXPIRES	REMARKS

EXHIBIT 7
ASCAP WARRANTY LETTER

American Society of Composers,
Authors and Publishers
One Lincoln Plaza
New York, New York 10023

Gentlemen:

I (we) make the following representations:

1. Schedule A (Writer's List of Works) attached is a true and correct list of the domestic copyrighted musical compositions owned by me (us) as of this date.

2. Schedule B (Foreign Agreements at this date) attached is a true and correct list of the foreign copyrights of which performing rights for the United States are owned by me (us) (showing in each case the countries represented by me (us)).

I (we) hereby represent that there are no existing assignments or licenses, direct or indirect, of nondramatic performing rights in or to any of the works listed on Schedules A and B except for the assignments or licenses of which I (we) have attached true copies.

Firm Name ____________________

By ____________________

Title ____________________

ASCAP: SCHEDULE A

List of Domestic Copyrighted Musical Compositions Owned by the Applicant

Title	Year of Copyright	Composer	Author	Publisher

Note: --For works based on compositions in the public domain, the title, author and composer of the public domain source must be indicated

ASCAP: SCHEDULE B

List of Foreign Copyrights of which Performing Rights for the United States are owned by Applicant. (Please indicate in each case the countries represented by applicant.)

TITLE	COUNTRY REPRESENTED*	COMPOSER	AUTHOR

*For instance, if applicant subpublishes the work for the United States and Canada, then those countries should be indicated in this column. Do no list country of the original publisher.

EXHIBIT 8
ASCAP DESIGNATION OF PUBLISHER REPRESENTATIVE

Section II of Article III of the Society's Articles of Association provides that;

"Each publisher member, if a co-partnership, firm, association or corporation shall file with the secretary of the Society, from time to time, the name of a person who shall be deemed to be its representative in the Society for all purposes, and wherever in these Articles of Association there shall be reference to publisher members relating to election as directors, holding other office or serving in any other capacities, the same shall have reference to such representative. <u>If a co-partnership or firm, such representative shall be a member thereof and if an association or corporation, such representative shall be an officer thereof.</u> No such co-partnership, firm, association or corporation shall have more than one representative at any one time. Such designation may be revoked at any time by notice in writing given to the Society provided that a new representative shall be named, subject to the restrictions above contained."

In accordance with the above, if you are a co-partnership, firm, association or corporation, please indicate below the name of your representative, whose signature must also appear on the line indicated.

____

Publisher (please print)

____

Name of Representative (please print) and Title

____

Signature of Representative

____

Date

EXHIBIT 9
MUSIC CUE SHEET*

PRODUCERS: Productions R Us — AIR DATE: November 20, 1989

SERIES: Road to Performing Rights — LENGTH: 1 hour

NETWORK: NBC — TIME; 9 P.M. to 10 P.M.

TITLE "Cue Sheet Preparation"

TYPE OF USE	COMPOSER(S)	PUBLISHER (AFFILIATION)	TIME
OPENING THEME	I am Composer ASCAP	Best Publishing (ASCAP)	1:10
CLOSING THEME	I am Composer ASCAP	Best Publishing (ASCAP)	:30
BACKGROUND MUSIC CUES (39)	I am Composer ASCAP	Best Publishing (ASCAP)	20:50
VISUAL PERFORMANCES Pop Song	I am Composer ASCAP	Best Publishing (ASCAP)	3:50

*Author's recommended form, not a form supplied by ASCAP.

EXHIBIT 10
ASCAP TITLE REGISTRATION TRANSMITTAL

Date of Transmittal: ______________

Transmitting Publisher: ____

Address: ____
____

Type of Medium
( ) Tape: Density _______ Track ______ No. of Reels ________
( ) Diskette: Software ______________ No. of Diskettes ______
Delimiter used ( )Yes ( )No
( ) Paper Data Entry Form

Number of Registrations: ________

Comments: ____
____

Person to Contact: ____
Tel. No.: ( ) ____________

- -

Index Dept.: Date Received: _____
By: ____
Control No: _____

ASCAP TITLE REGISTRATION DATA ENTRY FORM

(To be used when "Paper Data Entry Form" is checked on ASCAP's "Title Registration Transmittal" form)

TITLE (40 POSITIONS) ____

ALTERNATE TITLE, IF ANY (40 POSITIONS) ____

RECORDING ARTIST-1 (30 POSITIONS) RECORDING ARTIST 2 (30 POSITIONS)

COMPOSER/AUTHOR NAME - 1 (30 POSITIONS)	AFFILIATION	SOC. SEC. NO.	PCT. CLAIMED
COMPOSER/AUTHOR NAME - 1 (30 POSITIONS)	AFFILIATION	SOC. SEC. NO.	PCT. CLAIMED
COMPOSER/AUTHOR NAME - 1 (30 POSITIONS)	AFFILIATION	SOC. SEC. NO.	PCT. CLAIMED
COMPOSER/AUTHOR NAME - 1 (30 POSITIONS)	AFFILIATION	SOC. SEC. NO.	PCT. CLAIMED

*Note: The form supplied by ASCAP allows up to 12 titles to be registered in this manner.

EXHIBIT 11
BMI INSTRUCTIONS FOR WRITER AFFILIATION

We are delighted that you have expressed interested in affiliation as a BMI writer. You will find enclosed a handbook for BMI writers which will undoubtedly answer many questions you may have with respect to affiliation. There is no fee for writer affiliation with BMI.

We should like to bring to your attention the fact that affiliation with BMI is likely to be of practical financial benefit to you only if you currently have one of more musical compositions which are being performed or are likely to be performed by broadcasting stations or publicly. If you have no such composition at this time, we would suggest that you delay applying for writer affiliation.

You will find enclosed the following documents:

1. Application for writer affiliation
2. Two copies of standard basic writer agreement
3. One clearance form
4. Copy of current payment schedule
5. Various pamphlets of general information

COMPLETING THE APPLICATION:

ALL QUESTIONS MUST BE ANSWERED. Your FULL LEGAL NAME must be given in Question 1 and again in your signature at the bottom of the application. Your name must appear exactly the same in both places.

SIGNING THE AGREEMENTS:

BOTH copies of the agreement should be signed by you with your full legal name (exactly as your application is signed) under the words "ACCEPTED AND AGREED TO." We will type in the date, your name and address and the period of the contract in Paragraph 1. The contract will be effective at the beginning of the calendar quarter in which we receive your completed documents in acceptable form.

If you are under eighteen years of age, a parent or legal guardian must co-sign with you on BOTH the application and agreements. If the co-signer is a legal guardian, we must have some documentation of the guardianship.

COMPLETING THE CLEARANCE FORM:

All information must be listed, including the title of the song, all writers, their percentages of the song, all publishing companies and their percentages of the song, the record label and the release date.

RETURNING THE PROPER DOCUMENTS:

YOU MUST RETURN THE FOLLOWING DOCUMENTS (An envelope is enclosed for your convenience.)

1. THE COMPLETED APPLICATION
2. BOTH COPIES OF THE SIGNED AGREEMENT
3. THE COMPLETED CLEARANCE FORM

Upon receipt of the properly completed documents, there will be a delay of 2 to 3 weeks before you will receive your copy of the fully executed agreement.

Proper forms, instructions and additional clearance forms for reporting your works to BMI's Clearance Department will be mailed with your full executed agreement. Please DO NOT SUBMIT ANY SONGS for registration to BMI, EXCEPT THE SONG LISTED ON THE CLEARANCE FORM AND RETURNED WITH YOUR APPLICATION, until you have received additional forms and instructions.

We suggest that you keep the enclosed payment schedule available for your reference.

If you have any questions with respect to the application or the agreement, please do not hesitate to communicate with us.

EXHIBIT 12
BMI WRITER APPLICATION

APPLICATION WILL NOT BE ACCEPTED UNLESS ALL QUESTIONS ARE FULLY ANSWERED

PLEASE PRINT

DATE: ____________

1. FULL LEGAL NAME: MR. MS. MISS MRS. ______________________________
(First Name) (Middle Name or Initial) (Last Name)

2. HOME ADDRESS:
____
(Street) (City) (State) (Zip Code) (Phone Number)

3. BUSINESS ADDRESS (If same as above, write "same"):
____
(Street) (City) (State) (Zip Code) (Phone Number)
(Check one address to which all mail is to be sent)

4. DATE OF BIRTH: ______________________ CITIZENSHIP: ______________
(Month) (Day) (Year) (Country)
RESIDENCE: ______________
(Country)

5. LIST ALL PEN NAMES WHICH YOU HAVE USED OR WILL USE AS A WRITER:
____

6. Are you now or have you ever been a writer-member or writer-affiliate of BMI, ASCAP, SESAC, or of any foreign performing rights licensing organization? If so, state name of organization and the period which you were a member or affiliate:
____

7. Is your spouse, parent, brother, sister, child or any other relative a writer-member or writer-affiliate of any organization specified in Paragraph 6? If so, give name, relationship to you and organization:
____

8. COMPLETE THE ENCLOSED CLEARANCE FORM listing one composition written by you, either alone or in collaboration with others, which is commercially recorded or being performed or likely to be performed and return it to BMI with the application. A supply of clearance forms for reporting other songs will be sent to you when the processing of your application has been fully completed.

9. SOCIAL SECURITY NUMBER: ______________________________
(If no Social Security Number is listed, application WILL NOT BE ACCEPTED.
Foreign nationals should request Form 1001 from BMI for completion.)

I warrant and represent that all of the information furnished on this application is true. I acknowledge that any contract consummated between me and BMI will be entered into in reliance upon the representations contained in this application, and that the contract will be subject to cancellation if any question herein contained is not answered fully or accurately.

SIGNATURE: ______________________________
(Full Legal Name in Ink)
(If applicant is under 18 years of age, the parent or legal guardian must sign below)

Guardian Signature: ______________________________

PLEASE RETURN APPLICATION, AGREEMENTS AND CLEARANCE FORM TO THE BMI OFFICE FROM WHICH THEY WERE RECEIVED.

EXHIBIT 13
BMI INSTRUCTIONS FOR PUBLISHER AFFILIATION

We are delighted that you have expressed interest in affiliation as a BMI publisher. We should like to bring to your attention the fact that affiliation with BMI is likely to be of practical financial benefit to you only if you currently have some musical compositions which are being performed or are likely to be performed either by broadcasting stations or publicly. If you have no such compositions at this time, we would suggest that you delay applying for publisher affiliation.

You will find enclosed the following documents:

1. Application for publisher affiliation
2. Two copies of standard basic publisher agreement
3. One clearance form
4. Copy of current payment schedule
5. Instructions for completing the application

COMPLETING THE APPLICATION AND SIGNING THE AGREEMENTS:

Please use the step-by-step instructions provided for completing your application and signing your contracts.

RETURNING THE PROPER DOCUMENTS:

YOU MUST RETURN THE FOLLOWING DOCUMENTS (An envelope is enclosed for your convenience.)

1. **THE COMPLETED APPLICATION**
2. **BOTH COPIES OF THE SIGNED AGREEMENT**
3. **THE COMPLETED CLEARANCE FORM**
4. **CASHIER'S CHECK, MONEY ORDER OR PERSONAL CHECK PAYABLE TO BMI FOR $25.00**

Upon receipt of the properly completed documents, there will be a delay of 8 to 12 weeks before you will receive your copy of the fully executed agreement.

Proper forms, instructions and additional clearance forms for reporting your works to BMI's Index Department for clearance will be mailed with your fully executed agreement. Please DO NOT SUBMIT ANY SONGS for registration to BMI, EXCEPT THE SONG LISTED ON THE CLEARANCE FORM AND RETURNED WITH YOUR APPLICATION, until you have received additional forms and instructions.

Applying for affiliation with BMI as a writer is done separately from the publishing company. If you need applications for writers, please advise the name and address of each writer and we will forward the necessary forms.

We suggest that you keep the enclosed payment schedule available for your reference.

If you have any questions with respect to the application or the agreement, please contact the Publisher Administration Department.

BMI
INSTRUCTIONS FOR COMPLETING PUBLISHER APPLICATION

ALL QUESTIONS MUST BE ANSWERED

QUESTION 1: Complete with five name choices for your firm. (NOTIFICATION OF YOUR FIRM'S NAME CLEARANCE WILL TAKE **APPROXIMATELY TWO WEEKS** UPON RECEIPT OF THE APPLICATION.)

QUESTION 2: Indicate your business address and phone number.

QUESTION 3: You must complete and return one clearance form listing one song commercially recorded and released or publicly performed during the past year or one that will be performed in the near future. **THE APPLICATION WILL NOT BE PROCESSED WITHOUT THE COMPLETED CLEARANCE FORM.** All information must be listed, including the title of the song, all writers, their percentages, all publishing companies, their percentages, the record label and the release date or information regarding a public performance.

QUESTION 4: COMPLETE ONLY <u>ONE SECTION</u> IN QUESTION 4, EITHER A, B, OR C. THE APPLICATION WILL NOT BE PROCESSED IF MORE THAN ONE SECTION IS COMPLETED.

SECTION A: INDIVIDUALLY OWNED: Complete this section if you are the SOLE OWNER of the firm. You must list your full legal name, birth date, Social Security Number and HOME address. If your business address is a Post Office Box, you must list a different address for your home address. You must also indicate if you were ever a writer member of any other performing rights licensing organization.

SECTION B: PARTNERSHIP: Complete this section if the firm is owned by TWO OR MORE PEOPLE. You must list the partners' full legal names, their home addresses, Social Security Numbers and their percentages of ownership of the firm. YOU MUST ALSO HAVE A FEDERAL TAX ACCOUNT NUMBER. You may obtain a number from the IRS on Form SS #4.

SECTION C: CORPORATION: Complete this section if the firm is a FORMALLY ORGANIZED CORPORATION which has been finalized through the Secretary of State. A photocopy of the **Certificate of Incorporation** must be returned with the application. Complete the full legal names of the stockholders, their home addresses and their percentages of ownership of the firm. You must also list all officers of the company, their home addresses and the office held. YOU MUST HAVE A FEDERAL TAX ACCOUNT NUMBER. You may obtain a number from the IRS on form SS #4.

QUESTION 5: All executive employees should be listed, such as professional managers, contact persons, etc.

QUESTION 6: You must complete this question if any owner, stockholder, officer or executive employee of this firm is connected with any record company, publishing company, songwriters agency or any other organization engaged in the solicitation, publication or exploitation of music.

SIGNING THE APPLICATION: The application must be signed (not printed) in ink by an owner or officer in their full legal name.

SIGNING THE AGREEMENTS: BOTH COPIES of the agreement should be signed on the back page, bottom line by an owner or officer of the firm exactly as signed on the application in their full legal name and returned with the application, clearance form and fee. We will type in the date, your company name and address and the period of the contract in Paragraph 1. The contract will be effective at the beginning of the calendar quarter in which we receive your completed documents in acceptable form.

EXHIBIT 14
BMI PUBLISHER APPLICATION

NOTE:
ALL QUESTIONS MUST BE ANSWERED.
APPLICATION MUST BE SIGNED ON LAST PAGE AND RETURNED TO THE BMI OFFICE FROM WHICH IT WAS RECEIVED WITH A $25 CHECK OR MONEY ORDER FOR ADMINISTRATION FEE.
(NOTE THIS AMOUNT IS NOT REFUNDABLE.)

1. NAME OF YOUR PROPOSED PUBLISHING COMPANY:

(In order to eliminate confusion it is necessary to reject any name identical with, or similar to, that of an established publishing company. Also, any name using INITIALS as part of your company name cannot be accepted.)

1st Choice: ______________________________

2nd Choice: ______________________________

3rd Choice: ______________________________

4th Choice: ______________________________

5th Choice: ______________________________

2. BUSINESS ADDRESS:

____

______________________________ ZIP CODE   [ ] AREA CODE   [ ] TELEPHONE NO.

3. COMPLETE THE ENCLOSED CLEARANCE FORM listing one composition owned by your publishing company which has been commercially recorded within the past year or is likely to be broadcast or performed in concerts or otherwise publicly performed and return it with the application.

IF CUE SHEETS ARE NECESSARY, PLEASE SUBMIT

4. COMPLETE A, B OR C TO INDICATE HOW YOUR COMPANY IS ORGANIZED:

A. INDIVIDUALLY OWNED:

Name of Individual ______________ Date of Birth ______________

Home Address ______________ Soc. Sec. No. ______________

______________ Zip Code ______________

Are you now or have you ever been a writer-member or writer-affiliate of BMI, ASCAP, SESAC, or of any foreign performing rights licensing organization? If so, state name of organization and the period during which you were a member or affiliate.

____

B. PARTNERSHIP: Fed. Tax Acct. No. ____________
If not available, request form SS4 from I.R.S.

List all Partners

NAME	HOME ADDRESS & ZIP CODE	SOC. SEC. NO.	PERCENTAGE OF OWNERSHIP

C. FORMALLY ORGANIZED CORPORATION: Fed. Tax Acct. No. ____________
(Complete only if corporation is now in existence)
If not available, request form SS4 from I.R.S.

State in which incorporated ____________

NOTE: PHOTOCOPY OF CERTIFICATE OF INCORPORATION MUST BE SUBMITTED WITH THIS APPLICATION.

List all Stockholders

NAME	HOME ADDRESS & ZIP CODE	PERCENTAGE OF OWNERSHIP

List all Officers

NAME	HOME ADDRESS & ZIP CODE	OFFICE HELD

5. LIST ALL EXECUTIVE EMPLOYEES: professional manager, contact man, etc.

NAME	HOME ADDRESS & ZIP CODE	POSITION HELD

6. If any owner, stockholder, officer or executive employee has been or is connected with any record company, publishing company, songwriters agency, or any other organization engaged in the solicitation, publication or exploitation of music, please give the following information.

NAME OF INDIVIDUAL	NAME OF COMPANY	IF PUBLISHING CO., IS IT BMI?	POSITION HELD	YEARS OF ASSOCIATION FROM	TO

NOTICE:

IT IS ACKNOWLEDGED THAT ANY CONTRACT CONSUMMATED BETWEEN APPLICANT AND BMI WILL BE ENTERED INTO IN RELIANCE UPON THE REPRESENTATION CONTAINED IN THIS APPLICATION AND THE REPRESENTATION THAT ALL OWNERS, INCLUDING PARTNERS, ARE OVER THE AGE OF EIGHTEEN. THE CONTRACT WILL BE SUBJECT TO CANCELLATION IF ANY QUESTIONS HEREIN CONTAINED ARE NOT ANSWERED FULLY AND ACCURATELY OR IF THE TRUE NAME OF EACH OWNER, STOCKHOLDER, OFFICER AND/OR EXECUTIVE EMPLOYEE IS NOT REPORTED IN QUESTIONS 4, 5 AND 6 HEREOF.

DATE ____________ SIGNATURE ____________

SIGN IN INK

(PLEASE PRINT NAME OF PERSON SIGNING)____________

EXHIBIT 15
BMI AGREEMENT WITH WRITER

Dear

The following shall constitute the agreement between us:

1. As used in this agreement:

(a) The word "period" shall mean the term from to , and continuing thereafter for additional terms of two years each unless terminated by either party at the end of said initial term or any additional term, upon notice by registered or certified mail no more than six months or less than sixty (60) days prior to the end of any such term.

(b) The word "works" shall mean:

(i) All musical compositions (including the musical segments and individual compositions written for a dramatic or dramatico-musical work) composed by you alone or with one or more collaborators prior to the period, except those in which there is an outstanding grant of the right of public performance to a person other than a publisher affiliated with BMI.

2. You agree that:

(a) Within ten (10) days after the execution of this agreement you will furnish to us two copies of a completed clearance sheet in the form supplied by us with respect to each work heretofore composed by you which has been published in printed copies or recorded commercially or which is being currently performed or which you consider as likely to be performed.

(b) In each instance that a work for which clearance sheets have not been submitted to us pursuant to subparagraph (a) hereof is published in printed copies or recorded commercially or in synchronization with film or tape or is considered by you as likely to be performed, whether such work is composed prior to the execution of this agreement or hereafter during the period, you will promptly furnish to us two copies of a completed clearance sheet in the form supplied by us with respect to each such work.

(c) If requested by us in writing, you will promptly furnish to us a legible lead sheet or other written or printed copy of the work.

3. The submission of clearance sheets pursuant to paragraph 2 hereof shall constitute a warranty by you that all of the information contained thereon is true and correct and that no performing rights in such work have been granted to or reserved by others except as specifically set forth therein in connection with works heretofore written or co-written by you.

4. Except as otherwise provided herein, you hereby grant to us for the period:

(a) All the rights that you own or acquire publicly to perform, and to license others to perform, anywhere in the world, any part or all of the works.

(b) The nonexclusive right to record, and to license others to record, any part or all of any of the works on electrical transcriptions , wire, tape, film, or otherwise, but only for the purpose of performing such work publicly by means of radio and television or for archive or audition purposes and not for sale to the public or for synchronization (i) with motion pictures intended primarily for theatrical exhibition or (ii) with programs distributed by means of syndication to broadcasting stations.

(c) The nonexclusive right to adapt or arrange any part or all of any works for performance purposes, and to license others to do so.

5. (a) The rights granted to us by subparagraph (a) of paragraph 4 hereof shall not include the right to perform or license the performance of more than one song or aria from a dramatic or dramatico-musical work which is an opera, operetta, or musical show or more than five minutes from a dramatic or dramatico-musical work which is a ballet if such performance is accompanied by dramatic action, costumes or scenery of that dramatic or dramatico-musical work.

(b) You, together with the publisher and your collaborators, if any, shall have the right, jointly, by written notice to us, to exclude from the grant made by subparagraph (a) of paragraph 4 hereof performances of works comprising more than thirty minutes of a dramatic or dramatico-musical work, but this right shall not apply to such performances from (i) a score originally written for and performed as part of a theatrical or television film, (ii) a score originally written for and performed as part of a radio or television program, or (iii) the original cast, sound track or similar album of a dramatic or dramatico-musical work.

(c) You retain the right to issue nonexclusive licenses for performances of a work or works (other than to another performing rights licensing organization), provided that within ten (10) days of the issuance of such license we are given written notice of the titles of the works and the nature of the performances so licensed by you.

6. (a) As full consideration for all rights granted to us hereunder and as security therefor, we agree to pay to you, with respect to each of the works in which we obtain and retain performing rights during the period:

(i) For performances of a work on broadcasting stations in the United States, its territories and possessions, amounts calculated pursuant to our then current standard practices upon the basis of the then current performance rates generally paid by us to our affiliated writers for similar compositions. The number of performances for which you shall be entitled to payment shall be estimated by us in accordance with our then current system of computing the number of such performances.

It is acknowledged that we license the works of our affiliates for performance by non-broadcasting means, but that unless and until such time as feasible methods can be devised for tabulation of and payment for such performances, payment will be based solely on broadcast performances. In the event that during the period we shall establish a system of separate payment for nonbroadcasting performances, we shall pay you upon the basis of the then current performance rates generally paid by us to our other affiliated writers for similar performances of similar compositions.

(ii) In the case of a work composed by you with one or more collaborators, the sum payable to you hereunder shall be a pro rata share, determined on the basis of the number of collaborators, unless you shall have transmitted to us a copy of an agreement between you and your collaborators providing for a different division of payment.

(iii) All monies received by us from any performing rights licensing organization outside of the United States, its territories and possessions, which are designated by such performing rights licensing organization as the author's share of foreign performance royalties earned by your works after the deduction of our then current handling charge applicable to our affiliated writers.

(b) We shall have no obligation to make payment hereunder with respect to (i) any performance of a work which occurs prior to the date on which we have received from you all of the information and material with respect to such work which is referred to in paragraphs 2 and 3 hereof, or (ii) any performance as to which a direct license as described in subparagraph (c) of paragraph 5 hereof has been granted by you, your collaborator or publisher.

7. We will furnish statements to you at least twice during each year of the period showing the number of performances as computed pursuant to subparagraph (a) (i) of paragraph 6 hereof and at least once during each year of the period showing the monies due pursuant to subparagraph (a) (iii) of paragraph 6 hereof. Each statement shall be accompanied by payment to you, subject to all proper deductions for advances, if any, of the sum thereby shown to be due for such performances.

8. (a) Nothing in this agreement requires us to continue to license the works subsequent to the termination of this agreement. In the event that we continue to license any or all of the works, however, we shall continue to make payments to you for so long as you do not make or purport to make directly or indirectly any grant of performing rights in such works to any other licensing organization. The amounts of such payments shall be calculated pursuant to our then current standard practices upon the basis of the then current performance rates generally paid by us to our affiliated writers for similar performances of similar compositions. You agree to notify us by registered or certified mail of any grant or purported grant by you directly or indirectly of performing rights to any other performing rights organization within ten (10) days from the making of such grant or purported grant and if you fail so to inform us thereof and we make payments to you for any period after the making of any such grant or purported grant, you agree to repay to us all amounts so paid by us promptly on demand. In addition, if we inquire of you by registered or certified mail, addressed to your last known address, whether you have made any such grant or purported grant and you fail to confirm to us by registered or certified mail within thirty (30) days of the mailing of such inquiry that you have not made any such grant or purported grant, we may, from and after such date, discontinue making any payments to you.

(b) Our obligation to continue payment to you after the termination of this agreement for performances outside of the United States, its territories and possessions shall be dependent upon our receipt in the United States of payments designated by foreign performing rights organizations as the author's share of foreign performance royalties earned by your works. Payment of such foreign royalties shall be subject to deduction of our then current handling charge applicable to our affiliated writers.

(c) In the event that we have reason to believe that you will receive or are receiving payment from a preforming rights licensing organization other than BMI for or based on United States performances of one or more of your works during a period when such works were licensed by us pursuant to this agreement, we shall have the right to withhold payment for such performances from you until receipt of evidence satisfactory to us of the amount so paid to you by such other organization or that you have not been so paid. In the event that you have been so paid, the monies payable by us to you for such performances during such period shall be reduced by the amount of the payment from such other organization. In the event that you do not supply such evidence within eighteen (18) months from the date of our request thereof, we shall be under no obligation to make any payment to you for performances of such works during such period.

9. In the event that this agreement shall terminate at a time when, after crediting all earnings reflected by statements rendered to you prior to the effective date of such termination, there remains an unearned balance of advances paid to you by us, such termination shall not be effective until the close of the calendar quarterly period during which (a) you shall repay such unearned balance of advances, or (b) you shall notify us by registered or certified mail that you have received a statement rendered by us at our normal accounting time showing that such unearned balance of advances has been fully recouped by us.

10. You warrant and represent that you have the right to enter into this agreement; that you are not bound by any prior commitments which conflict with your commitments hereunder; that each of the works, composed by you alone or with one or more collaborators, is original; and that exercise of the rights granted by you herein will not constitute an infringement of copyright or violation of any other right of, or unfair competition with, any person, firm or corporation. You agree to indemnify and hold harmless us and our licensees from and against any and all loss or damage resulting from any claim of whatever nature arising from or in connection with the exercise of any of the rights granted by you in this agreement. Upon notification to us or any of our licensees of a claim with respect to any of the works, we shall have the right to exclude such work from this agreement and/or to withhold payment of all sums which become due pursuant to this agreement or any modification thereof until receipt of satisfactory written evidence that such claim has been withdrawn, settled or adjudicated.

11. (a) We shall have the right, upon written notice to you, to exclude from this agreement, at any time, any works which is in our opinion (i) is similar to a previously existing composition and might constitute a copyright infringement, or (ii) has a title or music or lyric similar to that of a previously existing composition and might lead to a claim of unfair competition, or (iii) is offensive, in bad taste or against public morals, or (iv) is not reasonably suitable for performance.

(b) In the case of works which in our opinion are based on compositions in the public domain, we shall have the right, upon written notice to you, either (i) to exclude any such work from this agreement, or (ii) to classify any such work as entitled to receive only a fraction of the full credit that would otherwise be given for performances thereof.

(c) In the event that any work is excluded from this agreement pursuant to paragraph 10 or subparagraph (a) or (b) of this paragraph 11, all rights in such work shall automatically revert to you ten (10) days after the date of our notice to you of such exclusion. In the event that a work is classified for less than full credit under subparagraph (b) (ii) of this paragraph 11, you shall have the right, by giving notice to us, within ten (10) days after the date of our letter advising you of the credit allocated to the work, to terminate our rights therein, and all rights in such work shall thereupon revert to you.

12. In each instance that you write, or are employed or commissioned by a motion picture producer to write, during the period, all or part of the score of a motion picture intended primarily for exhibition in theaters, or by the producer of a musical show or revue for the legitimate stage to write, during the period, all or part of the musical compositions contained therein, we agree to advise the producer of the film that such part of the score as is written by you may be performed as part of the exhibition of said film in theaters in the United States, its territories and possessions, without compensation to us, or to the producer of the musical show or revue that your compositions embodied therein may be performed on the stage with living artists as part of such musical show or revue, without compensation to us. In the event that we notify you that we have established a system for the collection of royalties for performance of the scores of motion picture films in theaters in the United States, its territories and possessions, we shall no longer be obligated to take such action with respect to motion picture scores.

13. You make, constitute and appoint us, or our nominee, your true and lawful attorney, irrevocably during the term hereof, in our name or that of our nominee, or in your name, or otherwise, to do all acts, take all proceedings, execute, acknowledge and deliver any and all instruments, papers, documents, process or pleadings that may be necessary, proper or expedient to restrain infringement of and/or to enforce and protect the rights granted by you hereunder, and to recover damages in respect to or for the infringement or other violation of the said rights, and in our sole judgment to join you and/or others in whose names the copyrights to any of the works may stand; to discontinue, compromise or refer to arbitration, any such actions or proceedings or to make any other disposition of the disputes in relation to the works, provided that any action or proceeding commenced by us pursuant to the provisions of this paragraph shall be at our sole expense and for our sole benefit.

14. You agree that you, your agents, employees or representatives will not, directly or indirectly, solicit or accept payment from writers for composing music for lyrics or writing lyrics to music or for reviewing, publishing, promoting, recording or rendering other services connected with the exploitation of any composition, or permit use of your name or your affiliation with us in connection with any of the foregoing. In the event of a violation of any of the provisions of this paragraph 14, we shall have the right, in our sole discretion, by giving you at least thirty (30) days' notice by registered or certified mail, to terminate this agreement. In the event of such termination no payments shall be due to you pursuant to paragraph 8 hereof.

15. No monies due or to become due to you shall be assignable, whether by way of assignment, sale or power granted to an attorney-in-fact, without our prior written consent. If any assignment of such monies is made by you without such prior written consent, no rights of any kind against us will be acquired by the assignee, purchaser or attorney-in-fact.

16. In the event that during the period (a) mail addressed to you at the last address furnished by you pursuant to paragraph 19 hereof shall be returned by the post office, or (b) monies shall not have been earned by you pursuant to paragraph 6 hereof for a period of two consecutive years or more, or (c) you shall die, BMI shall have the right to terminate this agreement on at least thirty (30) days' notice by registered or certified mail addressed to the last address furnished by you pursuant to paragraph 19 hereof and, in the case of your death, to the representative of your estate, if known to BMI. In the event of such termination no payments shall be due you pursuant to paragraph 8 hereof.

17. You acknowledge that the rights obtained by you pursuant to this agreement constitute rights to payment of money and that during the period we shall hold absolute title to the performing rights granted to us hereunder. In the event that during the period you shall file a petition in bankruptcy, such a petition shall be filed against you, you shall make an assignment for the benefit of creditors, you shall consent to the appointment of a receiver or trustee for all or part of your property, or you shall institute or shall have instituted against you any other insolvency proceeding under the United States bankruptcy laws or any other applicable law, we shall retain title to the performing rights in all works for which clearance sheets shall have theretofore been submitted to us and shall subrogate your trustee in bankruptcy or receiver and any subsequent purchasers from them to your right to payment of money for said works in accordance with the terms and conditions of this agreement.

18. Any controversy or claim arising out of, or relating to, this agreement or the breach thereof, shall be settled by arbitration in the City of New York, in accordance with the Rules of the American Arbitration Association, and judgment upon the award of the arbitrator may be entered in any Court having jurisdiction thereof. Such award shall include the fixing of expenses of the arbitration, including reasonable attorney's fees, which shall be borne by the unsuccessful party.

19. You agree to notify our Department of Performing Rights Administration promptly in writing of any change in your address. Any notice sent to you pursuant to the terms of this agreement shall be valid if addressed to you at the last address so furnished by you.

20. This agreement cannot be changed orally and shall be governed and construed pursuant to the laws of the State of New York.

21. In the event that any part or parts of this agreement are found to be void by a court of competent jurisdiction, the remaining part or parts shall nevertheless be binding with the same force and effect as if the void part or parts were deleted from this agreement.

ACCEPTED AND AGREED TO:

Very truly yours,
BROADCAST MUSIC, INC.

____

By ______________________________

EXHIBIT 16
BMI AGREEMENT WITH PUBLISHER

AGREEMENT made on ______________________ between BROADCAST MUSIC, INC. ("BMI"), a New York corporation, whose address is 320 West 57th Street, New York, N.Y. 10019 and

____

a______________________________ doing business as______________________________ ______________________ ("Publisher"), whose address is ______________________

WITNESSETH:

FIRST: The term of this agreement shall be the period from______________________ to______________________, and continuing thereafter for additional periods of five (5) years each unless terminated by either party at the end of such initial period, or any such additional five (5) year period, upon notice by registered or certified mail not more than six (6) months or less than three (3) months prior to the end of any such term.

SECOND: As used in this agreement, the word "works" shall mean:

A. All musical compositions (including the musical segments and individual compositions written for a dramatic or dramatico-musical work) whether published or unpublished, now owned or copyrighted by Publisher or in which Publisher owns or controls performing rights, and

B. All musical compositions (including the musical segments and individual compositions written for a dramatic or dramatico-musical work) whether published or unpublished, in which hereafter during the term Publisher acquires ownership or copyright or ownership or control of the performing rights, from and after the date of the acquisition by Publisher of such ownership or control.

THIRD: Except as otherwise provided herein, Publisher hereby sells, assigns and transfers to BMI, its successors or assigns, for the term of this agreement:

A. All the rights which Publisher owns or acquires publicly to perform, and to license others to perform, anywhere in the world, any part or all of the works.

B. The nonexclusive right to record, and to license others to record, any part or all of any of the works on electrical transcriptions, wire, tape, film or otherwise, but only for the purpose of performing such work publicly by means of radio and television or for archive or audition purposes and not for sale to the public or for synchronization (1) with motion pictures intended primarily for theatrical exhibition or (2) with programs distributed by means of syndication to broadcasting stations.

C. The nonexclusive right to adapt or arrange any part or all of any of the works for performance purposes, and to license others to do so.

FOURTH:

A. The rights granted to BMI by subparagraph A of paragraph THIRD hereof shall not include the right to perform or license the performance of more than one song or aria from a dramatic or dramatico-musical work which is an opera, operetta, or musical show or more than five (5) minutes from a dramatic or dramatico-musical work which is a ballet if such performance is accompanied by the dramatic action, costumes or scenery of that dramatic or dramatico-musical work.

B. Publisher, together with all the writers and co-publishers, if any, shall have the right jointly, by written notice to BMI, to exclude from the grant made by subparagraph A of paragraph THIRD hereof performances of works comprising more than thirty (30) minutes of a dramatic or dramatico-musical work, but this right shall not apply to such performances from (1) a score originally written for and performed as part of a theatrical or television film, (2) a score originally written for and performed as part of a radio or television program, or (3) the original cast, sound track or similar album of a dramatic or dramatico-musical work.

C. Publisher retains the right to issue nonexclusive licenses for performances of a work or works (other than to another performing rights organization), provided that within ten (10) days of the issuance of such license BMI is given written notice of the titles of the works and the nature of the performances so licensed by Publisher.

FIFTH:

A. As full consideration for rights granted to BMI hereunder and as security therefor, BMI agrees to make the following payments to Publisher with respect to each of the works in which BMI has performing rights:

(1) For performances of works on broadcasting stations in the United States, its territories and possessions BMI will pay amounts calculated pursuant to BMI's then standard practices upon the basis of the then current performance rates generally paid by BMI to its affiliated publishers for similar performances of similar compositions. The number of performances for which Publisher shall be entitled to payment shall be estimated by BMI in accordance with its then current system of computing the number of such performances.

It is acknowledged that BMI licenses the works of its affiliates for performance by nonbroadcasting means, but that unless and until such time as feasible methods can be devised for tabulation of and payment for such performances, payment will be based solely on broadcast performances. In the event that during the term of this agreement BMI shall establish a system of separate payment for nonbroadcasting performances, BMI shall pay Publisher upon the basis of the then current performance rates generally paid by BMI to its other affiliated publishers for similar performances of similar compositions.

(2) For performances of works outside of the United Sates, its territories and possessions BMI will pay to Publisher all monies received by BMI in the United States from any performing rights licensing organization which are designated by such organization as the publisher's share of foreign performance royalties earned by any of the works after the deduction of BMI's then current handling charge applicable to its affiliated publishers.

(3) In the case of works which, or rights in which, are owned by Publisher jointly with one or more other publishers who have granted performing rights therein to BMI, the sum payable to Publisher under this subparagraph A shall be a pro rata share determined on the basis of the number of publishers, unless BMI shall have received from Publisher a copy of an agreement or other document signed by all of the publishers providing for a different division of payment.

B. Notwithstanding the foregoing provisions of this paragraph FIFTH, BMI shall have no obligation to make payment hereunder with respect to (1) any performance of a work which occurs prior to the date on which BMI shall have received from Publisher all the material with respect to such work referred to in subparagraph A of paragraph TENTH hereof, and in the case of foreign performances, the information referred to in subparagraph B of paragraph FOURTEENTH hereof, or (2) any performance as to which a direct license as described in subparagraph C of paragraph FOURTH hereof has been granted by Publisher, its co-publisher or the writer.

SIXTH: BMI will furnish statements to Publisher at least twice during each year of the term showing the number of performances of the works as computed pursuant to subparagraph A (1) of paragraph FIFTH hereof, and at least once during each year of the term showing the monies received by BMI referred to in subparagraph A (2) of paragraph FIFTH hereof. Each such statement shall be accompanied by payment of the sum thereby shown to be due to Publisher, subject to all proper deductions, if any, for advances or amounts due to BMI from Publisher.

SEVENTH:

A. Nothing in this agreement requires BMI to continue to license the works subsequent to the termination of this agreement. In the event that BMI continues to license any or all of the works, however, BMI shall continue to make payments to Publisher for so long as Publisher does not make or purport to make directly or indirectly any grant of performing rights in such works to any other licensing organization. The amounts of such payments shall be calculated pursuant to BMI's then current standard practices upon the basis of the then current performance rates generally paid by BMI to its affiliated publishers for similar performances of similar compositions. Publisher agrees to notify BMI by registered or certified mail of any grant or purported grant by Publisher directly or indirectly of performing rights to any other performing rights organization within ten (10) days from the making of such grant or purported grant and if Publisher fails so to inform BMI thereof and BMI makes payments to Publisher for any period after the making of any such grant or purported grant, Publisher agrees to repay to BMI all amounts so paid by BMI promptly on demand. In addition, if BMI inquires of Publisher by registered or certified mail, addressed to Publisher's last known address, whether Publisher has made any such grant or purported grant and Publisher fails to confirm to BMI by registered or certified mail within thirty (30) days of the mailing of such inquiry that Publisher has not made any such grant or purported grant, BMI may, from and after such date, discontinue making any payments to Publisher.

B. BMI's obligation to continue payment to Publisher after the termination of this agreement for performances outside of the United States, its territories and possessions shall be dependent upon BMI's receipt in the United States of payments designated by foreign performing rights licensing organizations as the publisher's share of foreign performance royalties earned by any of the works. Payment of such foreign royalties shall be subject to deduction of BMI's then current handling charge applicable to its affiliated publishers.

C. In the event that BMI has reason to believe that Publisher will receive or is receiving payment from a performing rights licensing organization other than BMI for or based on United States performances of one or more of the works during a period when such works were licensed by BMI pursuant to this agreement, BMI shall have the right to withhold payment for such performances from Publisher until receipt of evidence satisfactory to BMI of the amount so paid to Publisher by such other organization or that Publisher has not been so paid. In the event that Publisher has been so paid, the monies payable by BMI to Publisher for such performances during such period shall be reduced by the amount of the payment from such other organization. In the event that Publisher does not supply such evidence within eighteen (18) months from the date of BMI's request therefor, BMI shall be under no obligation to make any payment to Publisher for performances of such works during such period.

EIGHTH: In the event that this agreement shall terminate at a time when, after crediting all earnings reflected by statements rendered to Publisher prior to the effective date of such termination, there remains an unearned balance of advances paid to Publisher by BMI, such termination shall not be effective until the close of the calendar quarterly period during which (A) Publisher shall repay such unearned balance of advances, or (B) Publisher shall notify BMI by registered or certified mail that Publisher has received a statement rendered by BMI at its normal accounting time showing that such unearned balance of advances has been fully recouped by BMI.

NINTH:

A. BMI shall have the right, upon written notice to Publisher, to exclude from this agreement, at any time, any work which in BMI's opinion (1) is similar to a previously existing composition and might constitute a copyright infringement, or (2) has a title or music or lyric similar to that of a previously existing composition and might lead to a claim of unfair competition, or (3) is offensive, in bad taste or against public morals, or (4) is not reasonably suitable for performance.

B. In the case of works which in the opinion of BMI are based on compositions in the public domain, BMI shall have the right, at any time, upon written notice to Publisher, either (1) to exclude any such work from this agreement, or (2) to classify any such work as entitled to receive only a stated fraction of the full credit that would otherwise be given for performances thereof.

C. In the event that any work is excluded from this agreement pursuant to subparagraph A or B of this paragraph NINTH, or pursuant to subparagraph C of paragraph TWELFTH hereof, all rights of BMI in such work shall automatically revert to Publisher ten (10) days after the date of the notice of such exclusion given by BMI to Publisher. In the event that a work is classified for less than full credit under subparagraph B (2) of this paragraph NINTH, Publisher shall have the right, by giving notice to BMI within ten (10) days after the date of BMI's notice to Publisher of the credit allocated to such work, to terminate all rights in such work granted to BMI herein and all such rights of BMI in such work shall revert to Publisher thirty (30) days after the date of such notice from Publisher to BMI.

TENTH:

A. With respect to each of the works which has been or shall be published or recorded commercially or synchronized with motion picture or television film or tape or which Publisher considers likely to be performed, Publisher agrees to furnish to BMI:

(1) Two copies of a completed clearance sheet in the form supplied by BMI, unless a cue sheet with respect to such work is furnished pursuant to subparagraph A (3) of this paragraph TENTH.

(2) If such work is based on a composition in the public domain, a legible lead sheet or other written or printed copy of such work setting forth the lyrics, if any, and music correctly metered; provided that with respect to all other works, such copy need be furnished only if requested by BMI pursuant to subsection (c) of subparagraph D (2) of this paragraph TENTH.

(3) If such work has been or shall be synchronized with or otherwise used in connection with motion picture or television film or tape, a cue sheet showing the title, composers, publisher and nature and duration of the use of the work in such film or tape.

B. Publisher shall submit the material described in subparagraph A of this paragraph TENTH with respect to works heretofore published, recorded or synchronized within ten (10) days after the execution of this agreement with respect to any of the works hereafter so published, recorded, synchronized or likely to be performed prior to the date of publication or release of the recording, film or tape or anticipated performance.

C. The submission of each clearance sheet or cue sheet shall constitute a warranty by Publisher that all of the information contained thereon is true and correct and that no performing rights in any of the works listed thereon has been granted to or reserved by others except as specifically set forth therein.

D. Publisher agrees:

(1) To secure and maintain copyright protection of the works pursuant to the Copyright Law of the United States and pursuant to the laws of such other nations of the world where such protection is afforded; and to give BMI prompt written notice of the date and number of copyright registration and/or renewal of each work registered in the United States Copyright Office.

(2) At BMI's request:

(a) To register each unpublished and published work in the United States Copyright Office pursuant to the Copyright Law of the United States.

(b) To record in the United States Copyright Office in accordance with the Copyright Law of the United States any agreements, assignments, instruments or documents of any kind by which Publisher obtained the right to publicly perform and/or the right to publish, co-publish or subpublish any of the works.

(c) To obtain and deliver to BMI copies of: unpublished and published works; copyright registration and/or renewal certificates issued by the United States Copyright Office; any of the documents referred to in subsection (b) above.

E. Publisher agrees to give BMI prompt notice by registered or certified mail in each instance when, pursuant to the Copyright Law of the United States, (1) the rights granted to BMI by Publisher in any work shall revert to the writer or the writer's representative, or (2) copyright protection of any work shall terminate.

ELEVENTH: Publisher warrants and represents that:

A. Publisher has the right to enter into this agreement; Publisher is not bound by any prior Commitments which conflict with its undertakings herein; the rights granted by Publisher to BMI herein are the sole and exclusive property of Publisher and are free from all encumbrances and claims; and exercise of such rights will not constitute infringement of copyright or violation of any right of, or unfair competition with, any person, firm, corporation or association.

B. Except with respect to works in which the possession of performing rights by another person, firm, corporation or association is specifically set forth on a clearance sheet or cue sheet submitted to BMI pursuant to subparagraph A of paragraph TENTH hereof, Publisher has exclusive performing rights in each of the works by virtue of written grants thereof to Publisher signed by all the authors and composers or other owners of such work.

TWELFTH:

A. Publisher agrees to defend, indemnify, save and hold BMI, its licensees, the advertisers of its licensees and their respective agents, servants and employees, free and harmless from and against any and all demands, loss, damage, suits, judgments, recoveries and costs, including counsel fees, resulting from any claim of whatever nature arising from or in connection with the exercise of any of the rights granted by Publisher in this agreement; provided, however, that the obligations of Publisher under this paragraph TWELFTH shall not apply to any matter added to, or changes made in, any work by BMI or its licensees.

B. Upon receipt by any of the parties herein indemnified of any notice, demand, process, papers, writ or pleading, by which any such claim, demand, suit or proceeding is made or commenced against them, or any of them, which Publisher shall be obliged to defend hereunder, BMI shall, as soon as may be practicable, give Publisher notice thereof and deliver to Publisher such papers or true copies thereof, and BMI shall have the right to participate by counsel of its own choice, at its own expense. Publisher agrees to cooperate with BMI in all such matters.

C. In the event of such notification of claim or service of process on any of the parties herein indemnified, BMI shall have the right, from the date thereof, to exclude the work with respect to which a claim is made from this agreement and/or to withhold payment of all sums which may become due pursuant to this agreement or any modification thereof until receipt of satisfactory written evidence that such claim has been withdrawn, settled or adjudicated.

THIRTEENTH: Publisher makes, constitutes and appoints BMI, or its nominee, Publisher's true and lawful attorney, irrevocably during the term hereof, in the name of BMI or that of its nominee, or in Publisher's name, or otherwise, to do all acts, take all proceedings, and execute, acknowledge and deliver any and all instruments, papers, documents, process or pleadings that may be necessary, proper or expedient to restrain infringement of and/or to enforce and protect the rights granted by Publisher hereunder, and to recover damages in respect of or for the infringement or other violation of the said rights, and in BMI's sole judgment to join Publisher and/or others in whose names the copyrights to any of the works may stand, and to discontinue, compromise or refer to arbitration, any such actions or proceedings or to make any other disposition of the disputes in relation to the works; provided that any action or proceeding commenced by BMI pursuant to the provisions of this paragraph THIRTEENTH shall be at its sole expense and for its sole benefit.

FOURTEENTH:

A. It is acknowledged that BMI has heretofore entered into, and may during the term of this agreement enter into, contracts with performing rights licensing organizations for the licensing of public performing rights controlled by BMI in territories outside of the United States, its territories and possessions (hereinafter called "foreign territories"). Upon Publisher's written request, BMI agrees to permit Publisher to grant performing rights in any or all of the works for any foreign territory for which, at the time such request is received, BMI has not entered into any such contract with a performing rights licensing organization; provided, however, that any such grant of performing rights by Publisher shall terminate at such time when BMI shall have entered into such a contract with a performing rights licensing organization covering such foreign territory and shall have notified Publisher thereof. Nothing herein contained, however, shall be deemed to restrict Publisher from assigning to its foreign publisher or representative the right to collect a part or all of the publisher's performance royalties earned by any or all of the works in any foreign territory as part of an agreement for the publication, exploitation or representation of such works in such territory, whether or not BMI has entered into such a contract with a performing rights licensing organization covering such territory.

B. Publisher agrees to notify BMI promptly in writing in each instance when publication, exploitation or other rights in any or all of the works are granted for any foreign territory. Such notice shall set forth the title of the work, the country or countries involved, the period of such grant, the name of the person, firm, corporation or association entitled to collect performance royalties earned in the foreign territory and the amount of such share. Within ten (10) days after the execution of this agreement Publisher agrees to submit to BMI, in writing, a list of all works as to which Publisher has, prior to the effective date of this agreement, granted to any person, firm, corporation or association performing rights and/or the right to collect publisher performance royalties earned in any foreign territory.

C. In the event that BMI transmits to Publisher performance royalties designated as the writer's share of performance royalties earned by any of the works in any foreign territory, Publisher shall promptly pay such royalties to the writer or writers of the works involved. If Publisher is unable for any reason to locate and make payment to any of the writers involved within six (6) months from the date of receipt, the amounts due such writers shall be returned to BMI.

FIFTEENTH:

A. Publisher agrees that Publisher, its agents, employees, representatives or affiliated companies, will not directly or indirectly during the term of this agreement:

(1) Solicit or accept payment from or on behalf of authors for composing music for lyrics, or from or on behalf of composers for writing lyrics to music.

(2) Solicit or accept manuscripts from composers or authors in consideration of any payments to be made by or on behalf of such composer or authors for reviewing, arranging, promotion, publication, recording or any other services connected with the exploitation of any composition.

(3) Permit Publisher's name, or the fact of its affiliation with BMI, to be used by any other person, firm, corporation or association engaged in any of the practices described in subparagraphs A (1) and A (2) of this paragraph FIFTEENTH.

(4) Submit to BMI, as one of the works to come within this agreement, any musical composition with respect to which any payments described in subparagraphs A (1) and A (2) of this paragraph FIFTEENTH have been made by or on behalf of a composer or author to any person, firm, corporation or association.

B. Publisher agrees that Publisher, its agents, employees or representatives will not directly or indirectly during the term of this agreement make any effort to ascertain from, or offer any inducement or consideration to, anyone, including but not limited to any broadcasting licensee of BMI or to the agents, employees or representatives of BMI or any such licensee, for information regarding the time or times when any such BMI licensee is to report its performances to BMI, or to attempt in any way to manipulate performances or affect the representative character or accuracy of BMI's system of sampling or logging performances.

C. Publisher agrees to notify BMI promptly in writing (1) of any change of firm name of Publisher, and (2) of any change of twenty percent (20%) or more in the ownership thereof.

D. In the event of the violation of any of the provisions of subparagraphs A, B or C of this paragraph FIFTEENTH, BMI shall have the right, in its sole discretion, to terminate this agreement by giving Publisher at least thirty (30) days' notice by registered or certified mail. In the event of such termination, no payments shall be due to Publisher pursuant to paragraph SEVENTH hereof.

SIXTEENTH: In the event that during the term of this agreement (1) mail addressed to Publisher at the last address furnished by it pursuant to paragraph TWENTIETH hereof shall be returned by the post office, or (2) monies shall not have been earned by Publisher pursuant to paragraph FIFTH hereof for a period of two consecutive years or more, or (3) the proprietor, if Publisher is a sole proprietorship, shall die, BMI shall have the right to terminate this agreement on at least thirty (30) days' notice by registered or certified mail addressed to the last address furnished by Publisher pursuant to paragraph TWENTIETH hereof and, in the case of the death of a sole proprietor, to the representative of said proprietor's estate, if known to BMI. In the event of such termination, no payments shall be due Publisher pursuant to paragraph SEVENTH hereof.

SEVENTEENTH: Publisher acknowledges that the rights obtained by it pursuant to this agreement constitute rights to payment of money and that during the term BMI shall hold absolute title to the performing rights granted to BMI hereunder. In the event that during the term Publisher shall file a petition in bankruptcy, such a petition shall be filed against Publisher, Publisher shall make an assignment for the benefit of creditors, Publisher shall consent to the appointment of a receiver or trustee for all or part of its property, Publisher shall file a petition for corporate reorganization or arrangement under the United States bankruptcy laws or any other applicable law, or, in the event Publisher is a partnership, all of the general partners of said partnership shall be adjudged bankrupts, BMI shall retain title to the performing rights in all works for which clearance sheets shall have theretofore been submitted to BMI and shall subrogate Publisher's trustee in bankruptcy or receiver and any subsequent purchasers from them to Publisher's right to payment of money for said works in accordance with the terms and conditions of this agreement.

EIGHTEENTH: Any controversy or claim arising out of, or relating to, this agreement or the breach thereof, shall be settled by arbitration in the City of New York, in accordance with the Rules of the American Arbitration Association, and judgment upon the award of the arbitrator may be entered in any court having jurisdiction thereof. Such award shall include the fixing of the expenses of the arbitration, including reasonable attorney's fees, which shall be borne by the unsuccessful party.

NINETEENTH: Publisher agrees that it shall not, without the written consent of BMI, assign any of its rights hereunder. No rights of any kind against BMI will be acquired by the assignee if any such purported assignment is made by Publisher without such written consent.

TWENTIETH: Publisher agrees to notify BMI's Department of Performing Rights Administration promptly in writing of any change in its address. Any notice sent to Publisher pursuant to the terms of this agreement shall be valid if addressed to Publisher at the last address so furnished by Publisher.

TWENTY-FIRST: This agreement cannot be changed orally and shall be governed and construed pursuant to the laws of the State of New York.

TWENTY-SECOND: In the event that any part or parts of this agreement are found to be void by a court of competent jurisdiction, the remaining part or parts of this agreement shall nevertheless be binding with the same force and effect as if the void part or parts were deleted from this agreement.

IN WITNESS WHEREOF, the parties hereto have caused this agreement to be duly executed as of the day and year first above written.

BROADCAST MUSIC, INC.

By ____

Assistant Vice President

By ____

(Title of Signer) ________________________

EXHIBIT 17
BMI CLEARANCE FORM

COMPLETE FORM IN ACCORDANCE WITH INSTRUCTIONS ON THE REVERSE SIDE AND RETURN BOTH COPIES TO BMI. DO NOT USE THIS FORM TO CORRECT OR REVISE INFORMATION ON A PREVIOUSLY CLEARED WORK. SEND DETAILS IN A LETTER.

FOR BMI USE
DO NOT WRITE BELOW

ENTERED VIA SCOPE ______
DATE ______
BY ______

TITLE-ONE WORK PER FORM

IF BASED ON PUBLIC DOMAIN GIVE ORIGINAL TITLE, WRITER AND SOURCE

CREDIT RATE	MULTP CREDIT	CLEAR-ANCE	BMI	LOG US/CAN

CHECK IF WORK IS FROM:
- ☐ MOTION PICTURE OR TV FILM
- ☐ BROADWAY SHOW
- ☐ OFF BROADWAY SHOW

GIVE TITLE OF PICTURE, FILM OR SHOW

WRITER(S) NAME(S) LAST FIRST MIDDLE	WRITER(S) ADDRESSES	PERF. RTS. ORGN.	PERCENTAGE SHARE	MODE OF PAY-MENT	WH
SOC. SEC. NO.					
SOC. SEC. NO.					
SOC. SEC. NO.					
SOC. SEC. NO.					
SOC. SEC. NO.					
PUBLISHER(S) NAME(S)					

	PERF. RTS. ORGN.	PERCENTAGE SHARE	CREDIT U.S.	CREDIT CAN	ORIG. PUB.	WORLD RIGHTS
☐ CHECK HERE IF NO RIGHTS GRANTED BY WRITER(S) TO ANY PUBLISHER. ☐ CHECK HERE IF PUBLISHER IS ADMINISTRATOR ONLY. DO NOT CHECK THIS BOX IF PUBLISHER OWNS PART OR ALL OF COPYRIGHT AND/OR PERFORMING RIGHTS.						
NAME(S) OF U.S. ORIGINAL PUBLISHER(S):						
IF WORK IS OF FOREIGN ORIGIN, COMPLETE BELOW AND ATTACH AN ADDITIONAL COPY OF THIS FORM:						
U.S. SUB-PUBLISHER(S): (PLEASE GIVE TERRITORIES)						
FULL NAME OF FOREIGN ORIGINAL PUBLISHER:						

PLEASE DO NOT SUBMIT NONMUSICAL WORKS. THEY CANNOT BE CLEARED BY BMI. FOR SPOKEN WORD MATERIAL WITH A MUSICAL BACKGROUND, SEE INSTRUCTIONS ON REVERSE SIDE.

TYPE OR PRINT NAME AND ADDRESS OF SUBMITTING BMI AFFILIATE.

MAIL CONFIRMATION TO:

CLEARED IN ACCORDANCE WITH TERMS ON REVERSE SIDE

RECORD LABEL & NO. OF IST RECORD RELEASE
ARTIST   RELEASE DATE
DATE SUBMITTED TO BMI
AUTHORIZED SIGNATURE

INSTRUCTIONS

Fill out columns on left side of page and RETURN TO BMI CLEARANCE DEPARTMENT. DO NOT fill in columns in shaded area. (BOTH COPIES OF THIS FORM MUST BE RETURNED TO BMI).

TITLE

Give complete title of work you are submitting for clearance. If also known under another title, please indicate a/k/a (also known as) and give other title. (ONLY ONE WORK PER FORM.)

If this work is based on a Public Domain work. GIVE ORIGINAL TITLE, WRITER AND SOURCE, A LEAD SHEET OR RECORDING MUST BE SUBMITTED WITH THIS CLEARANCE FORM IF THIS WORK IS BASED ON A PUBLIC DOMAIN WORK.

If this work was written for a Full Length Feature Motion Picture or a Film made for TV, or a Broadway or Off-Broadway Show, check appropriate box and give complete title of Motion Picture, Film or Show. Enclose program, name of theatre and/or additional details

PERCENTAGE SHARES

Indicate share of each writer. All writers' shares should total 100.

Indicate share of each publisher. All publishers' shares should total 100%.

IF NO RIGHTS HAVE BEEN ASSIGNED TO ANY PUBLISHER, CHECK THE BOX PROVIDED, IN SUCH CASE FULL PUBLISHER SHARE WILL BE DIVIDED BETWEEN WRITERS IN SAME PERCENTAGE AS WRITER SHARES.

If part of publisher share has been granted, indicate percentage due to publisher and percentage retained by writer(s).

WRITER(S)

Give complete name and address of each writer. If pseudonym, give complete name of writer under his pseudonym: Last Name first followed by First Name and Middle Name or Initial. Give Social Security No. of each writer.

Give name of PERFORMING RIGHTS ORGANIZATION (Perf. Rts. Orgn.) with which each writer is affiliated.

PUBLISHER(S)

Give complete name of all publishers and co-publishers.

If publisher acquired this work from a publisher outside the United States, give complete name of the original foreign publisher, territories for which subpublishing rights were acquired and ATTACH AN ADDITIONAL COPY OF THIS FORM.

Give name of PERFORMING RIGHTS ORGANIZATION (Perf. Rts. Orgn.) with which each publisher is affiliated.

SPOKEN WORD MATERIAL

Spoken word material with a musical background will be cleared only if the music is original (not based on a Public Domain work) and if a substantial part of the recording contains background music. A recording must be submitted with this Clearance Form if this is spoken word material.

RECORD

If this work has been recorded, give the record label and number, artist and date it was or will be released.

DATE

Give the date you are submitting this work to BMI.

SIGNATURE

This form must be signed by an affiliated writer or an authorized representative of the submitting publisher.

IF ALL OF THE ABOVE INSTRUCTIONS ARE NOT FOLLOWED, THIS WORK WILL NOT BE REGISTERED FOR LOGGING PURPOSES AND THE FORM WILL BE RETURNED TO YOU FOR CORRECTION OR COMPLETION.

CLEARANCE TERMS

THE RETURN OF A STAMPED COPY OF THIS FORM INDICATES THAT THE WORK LISTED ON THE REVERSE SIDE HAS BEEN CLEARED.

A writer submitting this form warrants and represents that (s)he is the writer or co-writer of the work to the extent indicated and that (s)he has not acquired his or her interest in such work by virtue of purchase or assignment from the writer or writers thereof.

Please note that in the event that a work cleared is published or recorded with lyrics which we, in our sole judgment, regard as unsuitable for broadcast use or with musical or lyrical material which we, in our sole judgment, regard as an infringement, we reserve the right at any time to exclude this work in its entirety from the provisions of our agreement and to withdraw the clearance.

We bring to your attention that in the event a clearance form submitted does not properly indicate in the space provided therefor that a work is based on public domain source, we reserve the right, if at any time such work is found to have a public domain source, to allocate to such work a percentage of the normal logging credit or, in the case of a work having little or no original material, to give no logging credit to such work.

SYNTHESIZER
START/STOP

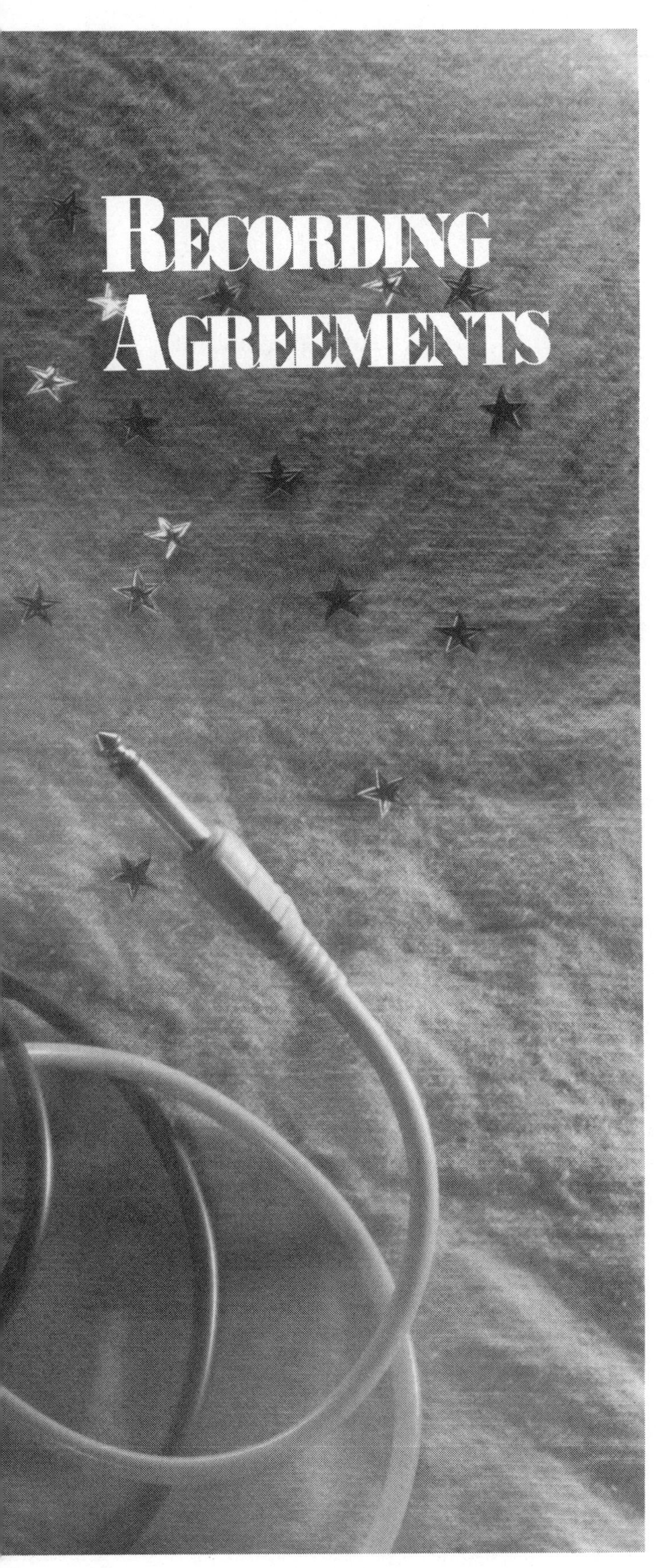
RECORDING
AGREEMENTS

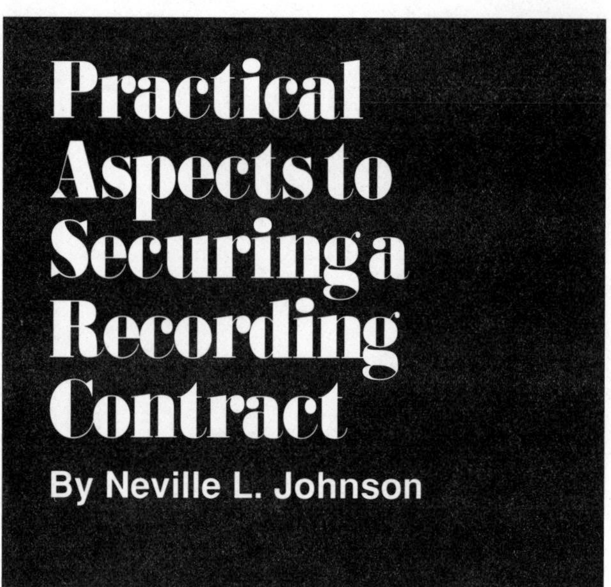

There is no standard method for obtaining a recording agreement with a major record company, but here are some guidelines. Approach record companies with a "physical package." Utilize a "human package" as an integral element of the presentation, and be familiar with the business practices and marketing philosophy of the record company to which presentation is made. After discussing the components of a "physical package" and a "human package," I will analyze the best method of presenting a "total package" to a record company, and the important factors to be considered in selecting a company.

THE PHYSICAL PACKAGE

The "physical package" consists of the artist, the act, a demonstration tape, and additional materials such as lyric sheets, pictures, reviews, biographical information, and letters and invitations.

A demonstration tape ("demo tape") is a necessity for most acts that have not had a record deal prior to the time of the presentation. A demo tape, most importantly, must contain music that is unique, creative, and "commercial." The majors want music that can sell large quantities. These days, it's rock and roll, heavy metal, pop, adult oriented rock (AOR), middle of the road (MOR), country, R&B, jazz and classical, with the latter two categories being particularly difficult to break into because their market share is so limited. Most executives want to get a million seller. An A&R executive who doesn't deliver hot acts that get on the radio will not have a job for long. "A and R" is an abbreviation for Artists and Repertoire. A major function is talent acquisition.

The artist should keep in mind that the ultimate sale will not be to a record company, but to the public. Music executives evaluate music, in large part, on the basis of its sales potential. Record companies are not philanthropic organizations: they are in business to make money, and can only do so with records that have commercial appeal.

Besides great music, a demo tape should have the following characteristics:

Cassette Tape

Always send cassette tape.

Good Tape Quality

The tape used should be the best available. Good quality tape will allow the listener to hear the performances clearly. Never send the master tape. Although most demo tapes are eventually returned, delays are common, and some are simply lost or forgotten.

Good Performance

The artist performing on a demo tape must sound as though they are ready to cut tapes of master quality. Although high quality production is not a decisive factor to record companies, over the years, the quality of demo tapes has measurably improved, especially with the "MIDI" revolution. Today many acts are recording demo tapes in " home studios" equipped to simulate the sound quality of commercial 16 and 24 track studios.

Four Song Maximum

Record company personnel who listen to tapes are very busy and listen to many tapes in a day's work. Don't discourage them with a tape that has too many selections.

Song Names & Order Identified on Tape Container

The name of the selection and the order of performance should be clearly written or typed on the tape box. Make it easy for the listener to name the song he likes. Other important information includes whether Dolby noise reduction is used; and the person to contact about the tape (personal manager, attorney or band leader).

The other components of the physical package that can significantly enhance the listener's evaluation and should accompany the demo tape are:

Lyric Sheets

Lyric sheets tend to involve the listener in the music. While the ears follow the sounds, the eyes follow the words.

Photographs/Videotape

If an artist has a "look" or "image," the record company should know about it. A professional and attractive appearance is a valuable asset in today's music industry. Record companies are increasingly interested in an artist's visual impact due to the development of MTV and videotape markets, and the growing interrelationship between motion pictures, television, and records. Some recording acts have been signed on the strength of a videotape of a live performance sent in lieu of or in addition to a demo tape. For an act with significant visual appeal, a videotape, if economically feasible, should be considered.

Biographical Information

A succinct, factual statement of an artist's credentials and background helps to explain the music to the listener and to distinguish the artist from others. The "bio" is analogous to a resume in other professions: it informs the reader of the qualifications of the applicant.

Reviews And/Or Itinerary

Favorable reviews tell the reader that the artist has stage experience and is enjoyable to hear. If the artist can excite an audience or has a following, the record company will want to know about it because live performance is an important method of promoting records. If a number of impressive gigs have been played, or if the artist is regularly working, an itinerary should be enclosed to communicate that the talent is stage-wise and has an additional source of income.

By paying attention to the details of the physical package, an aura of professionalism can be projected to the record company by the artist, the music, and people that advise and work with him or her. A clever, enticing physical package will merit special attention by its recipient. With so many contenders vying for a deal, the effort to create an appealing physical package is warranted.

THE HUMAN PACKAGE

Most successful artists are members of a team. A critical issue in a record company's decision whether to sign an act is who will "carry the ball" after a record is released. If an act has inexperienced, incompetent or no personnel to support and direct it, the record company's job in selling records will be difficult and/or hampered. An artist will substantially improve the chance of securing a recording agreement if he or she is part of a functioning, well-organized business machine that can work with the company towards the common goal of generating income.

The Personal Manager

The personal manager is the most important member of the human package. If the would-be recording artist is able to arrive at the doorstep of a desired record company arm-in-arm with a highly regarded manager, the record company will be more easily swayed to invest its monies. Record company executives feel secure when an artist's career-recording duties, public performance, songwriting, and other professional activities are being coordinated on a day-to-day basis by a professional.

The artist must be extremely selective in choosing a personal manager. Some managers are persona non grata because of their pushy and demanding demeanor, unsavory reputation, or incompetence. If a would-be recording artist associates with such a personal manager, it may result in a case of guilt (and rejection) by association.

Talent Agent

The human package can include a talent agent who is successfully booking the artist in live engagements. The artist with a talent agent offers the record company an added inducement for making a deal because it will be able to rely upon a skilled professional to book the artist into live engagements before, during and after the release of the artist's album. This will promote record sales.

The artist with a talent agent offers the record company an added inducement for making a deal because it will be able to rely upon a skilled professional to book the artist into live engagements before, during and after the release of the artist's album.

Attorney

The attorney is an important member of the human package because of their contacts at record companies and elsewhere in the industry through the clients they represent. It is predominantly lawyers, managers, music publishers, and record producers who shop record deals to the major labels. An artist should have the guidance of a professional to assist in any legal needs and in helping to select the other members of the human package.

Business Manager

A business manager, or anyone with a strong relationship to executives at a label can also function as part, or in the place, of some members of the human package.

Record Producer/Production Company

A record producer and/or production company (an entity which finances and shops record deals) is another route to a deal. One caveat must be stated with regard to the artist who approaches the record company already signed to (via a "production deal," a kind of recording agreement) or firmly allied with a record producer. The record company may be unimpressed with such producer's talent or track record. If the artist cannot or refuses to work with another producer, this consideration may be a "deal-breaker," i.e., end any chances of a recording agreement with that company.

METHOD OF PRESENTATION: DEMO TAPE AND/OR LIVE PERFORMANCE

There are two ways of presenting the total package to a record company. The first is to have a representative of the record company see the artist perform live; the second is to present or send a demo tape to the record company. An artist will usually have to do both in order to clinch a deal. What you want to present are credits and creditability. Write a hit song and the doors are wide open. If the critics love the show, this may be all the "buzz" that is needed.

Showcases and Live Performances

Record companies want to sign artists who perform well on stage. Performing live, by "showcase" (an act performed primarily for representatives of record companies) or other live engagement, can be an effective way of attracting the attention and interest of a record company. If an artist's stage performance is a knockout, this will measurably enhance the prospects of a record deal or a future demo tape at the company's expense.

It is not easy to induce a record executive involved with talent acquisition, such as A & R personnel, to attend a gig or showcase. If the artist is performing in, say, Seattle, Washington, the chances of getting a record company person to attend the performance are poor. New York City, Los Angeles and Nashville are the main cities where record companies are located, and it is still very tough to get executives to turn out for a show.

Invitations to attend a showcase or gig should be in writing and delivered or mailed to each invitee. A follow-up telephone call the day before or on the day of the performance is the best reminder. Be certain that the names of all who have been invited are on the guest list.

Demo Tapes

The most effective way of presenting a demo tape is through a personal meeting with the individual to whom the tape is to be given. If this cannot be arranged, the demo tape should be accompanied by a concise, clearly typed letter stating the purpose for which the tape is sent, the level of production of the tape (4, 8-, 16-, or 24- track), whether the songs are original, and who the members of the human package are. The record company will, if it finds the tape worthy of further consideration, usually request an itinerary of live performances by the artist so that it can have a choice of when to attend.

Because of the problems with live engagements and showcases, the artist in search of a deal should seriously consider providing the record company with both a demo tape and an invitation to a subsequent showcase or gig. As a practical note, demo tapes, as opposed to showcases, are the most common method of approaching a record company.

Occasionally, a record company will request other material or that the artist return with subsequently written material. Some companies will pay for recording sessions to make additional demonstration tapes.

If the record company accepts the demo tape, in most cases it will be referred to a listener in the A & R department. This person listens to thousands of tapes a year, and most tapes grace the heads of the recorder for less than two minutes.

SHOPPING THE PACKAGE

Assuming the total package is ready to be shopped, it must be decided who will perform this function and who will be approached. If an invitation to a showcase is sent by an individual unknown to the record company, it will probably be ignored. If a demo tape is sent solo to a record company - through the mail with a letter of introduction by the artist, the probable response of the record company will be to reject it and return it to the sender. If the record company accepts the demo tape, in most cases it will be referred to a listener in the A & R department. This person listens to thousands of tapes a year, and most tapes grace the heads of the recorder for less than two minutes. The listener is a filter for the rest of the A & R department with a mandate to say, "No."

The artist should bypass individuals on the lower rungs of the record company and attempt to get his package presented to the president of the record company, the chairman of the board or the head of the A & R department, persons who have the authority to commit the record company to signing an artist. Many companies work on a committee basis, and most signings occur via the A & R department. Other members of the A & R hierarchy and employees in other departments of the company, such as promotion or marketing, may be approached also. The higher the person approached in the management of that department, the better the chances of serious consideration by the head of the A & R department or other executive involved with talent acquisition. Many acts have been signed as a result of recommendations from local or regional promotion men who have noticed an act in a city other than New York or Los Angeles.

There is, in the usual situation, but one avenue of reaching someone at the record company who wields substantial influence or who is in a decision-making position to sign an artist: personal contact. An invitation to a showcase/gig will be favorably answered and the demo tape will get serious consideration only if they are sent or referred by someone who is recognized and respected by the person receiving such invitation or tape. This doesn't mean that the person sending such invitation or tape need be famous within the music industry, he or she simply needs to be credible. The adage that it is not what you know, but who you know, definitely applies to the music business.

A number of personal managers, producers, lawyers and publishers, because of their success and power, can induce the president or chairman of the board of a record company to listen to a tape. Each member of the human package should be called upon to present the package to those with whom they are acquainted at the record company. Because personal contacts are so important in the industry, an artist who wishes to secure a recording agreement should attempt to get to know as many people in the music business as possible. The young promotion man at a record company today may be the head of the A & R department tomorrow. An artist friendly with a promoted person may, on the strength of that contact, have both a friend and a business acquaintance who will be helpful in advancing the artist's career.

A number of music attorneys are well connected throughout the industry. Many of these attorneys will "run a tape," doing so for anywhere from a flat fee ($250 to $5,000 or more!) to a percentage (of the initial advance or the entire deal and all music publishing revenues earned from compositions on sound recordings subject to the record deal), to a percentage of the artist's earnings derived from the record deal, should one be secured.

The human package must operate at the same level of professionalism as the physical package. Any person presenting the total package must have a good relationship with and be enthusiastic about the artist, know and understand the music, be aware of the long-term career goals of the artist, and most importantly, be able to communicate with and be credible to the record company being approached. Finally, the best method of "attacking" a record company is the "flying wedge" approach: a strong manager, attorney, publisher, producer and agent all working for an artist will eventually succeed.

CHOOSING A RECORD COMPANY

Equally important to the preceding concerns is which record company to contact. Record companies all press, distribute and promote records, but there the similarity ends. The artist must carefully investigate the business structure, the standing in the industry, and the marketing philosophy of any record company being pursued. An artist in search of a record deal needs a company that is both committed to the artist and has the organization to support that commitment.

Most artists want a company that is, or is part of, a strong and successful worldwide enterprise. This does not mean that an artist need pursue only the big companies. The artist should be looking for a capable company that has the organization and financial wherewithal to exploit records successfully throughout the world. CBS (Columbia, Epic and Portrait), WEA (Warner Brothers, Atlantic and Elektra/Asylum), RCA, MCA, A & M, Capitol/EMI America, Polygram, Motown, Geffen, Arista, Virgin and Chrysalis are the largest and most successful companies in the United States and have substantial worldwide organizations. Know which companies support the music you make. If it is jazz or new age, then approach those companies which specialize in those genres.

READ THE TRADES

Billboard is the industry magazine charting the events of the music business on a week-to-week basis. Any artist who wants to obtain a record deal in today's competitive music business should read it to become aware of the trends and developments in the industry and to keep track of key executives.

CONCLUSION

Talent alone will not guarantee a record deal, and seeking one can be a discouraging and fruitless crusade. (There are only a few hundred deals a year available; lottery odds are probably better.) To those who have tried but have not as yet been able to secure a recording agreement, and to those who wish to secure one, and never will, be aware that those individuals who are evaluating music at record companies are asked to make extremely difficult decisions: determining what music will be commercially viable. No amount of hype can sell a demonstration tape or a performance that doesn't have it "in the grooves," yet no reliable definition of this phrase has ever been articulated.

Moreover, an artist who is seeking a record deal should do so only if he or she is ready, dedicated, and willing to spend years in the studio and on the road. The effort necessary to launch a career is enormous.

However, with enthusiasm, hard work and perseverance, a talented artist can achieve the goal of a record deal. Sure, rejection is commonplace, but there is only one person who really matters —the executive who says "Yes." That executive wants to find you as much as you want to find him or her. Keep at it!

Have a backup plan. There are labels overseas which may be interested in your music and may be more receptive. Consider attending MIDEM, the annual music business convention at the end of each January in Cannes, France where music publishers and record executives congregate. I know of at least 30 U.S. acts that have foreign deals and whose records are imported into the United States. There are other conventions where one can "network" and make contacts. The biggest convention is the New Music Seminar in New York City, but there are other conventions in Austin, Chicago and other cities which should be considered.

Finally, you can always release your own record. Regardless of its sales, it is at least a start to putting you on the map and getting the attention of the right person.

An alternative to seeking a major recording contract or raising funds to produce your own recording is to approach independent record companies. Within the last decade, independent record labels specializing in particular styles of music have become very successful in reaching and developing niche markets. By researching these labels, you may find one that successfully markets music that fits your style and is interested in producing, manufacturing and/or distributing your record. Some of these independent labels have been very successful and have become subsidiaries to major recording labels, such as GRP (MCA), Narada (MCA) and Tommy Boy (Warner Bros.), or have developed strong relationships with major label branch distribution, such as Windham Hill and Private Music.

SMALL LABEL ADVANTAGES

The chief advantages of releasing your album with independent record labels are similar to the reasons for signing with major labels. They generally have a distribution mechanism in place. They are organized to handle the time and costs of financing and administering the production, manufacture, marketing and distribution of records. They can better absorb the financial risks and have more leverage in collecting money from the wholesalers and retailers of records. In addition, the company may have developed a reputation in the music community for a certain style of music and can move a great volume of records in a wide geographical territory.

Bear in mind, however, that if a small label invests time and money in your career and is successful in generating a reasonable level of income for you, you should carefully weigh the benefits of signing with a major label if asked (where you probably will be one of many)—against staying with the smaller one (where you may be the star!) Far too often, the benefits of a smaller label are discovered only after an unhappy relationship with a major recording label occurs. Much depends on the style of music involved, for example, pop and rock may get more attention from a major label than a style of music aimed at more narrow and focused audiences, such as jazz, new age, children's music, or Yiddish folk songs. Both small and large labels have demonstrated effectiveness at heavy metal and dance music.

CONTRACTS

Although contracts with independent labels can be very similar to those negotiated with major labels, smaller independent companies sometimes work out arrangements that do not mirror these standards. For example, these companies may be willing to step away from obtuse and confusing language to create a contract in plain English that is balanced between the interests of the record company and those of the artist, namely, to more equitably share the economic benefits realized from the skills and talents of the artist and the business expertise and mechanisms of the recording company. With increasing frequency, however, on artist recording agreements, the smaller labels are reflecting the contractual style and approach of the major labels, perhaps because of the investment costs and financial risks incurred in developing an artist and wanting to be secure that the contract with the artist is sufficiently strong that a larger label will not be in a position to tempt the artist to switch labels without the smaller label participating in the benefits of that switch. Many smaller labels also insist on participating in some or all of the music publishing of the artist. That is an issue that needs to be carefully examined, and if it occurs should be the subject of a separate deal.

If a small label invests time and money in your career and is successful in generating a reasonable level of income for you, you should carefully weigh the benefits of signing with a major label (where you probably will be one of many)—against staying with the smaller one (where you may be the star!) Far too often, the benefits of a smaller label are discovered only after an unhappy relationship with a major recording label occurs.

Here are some options not usually available to musicians signing with major labels:

Distribution Deals

In this type of deal, you deliver an agreed amount of fully manufactured and packaged records, cassettes or compact discs to a record company. Some labels may only distribute product, while you do the marketing and promotion; others may do everything.

In a distribution only deal, the record label will either contract directly with stores or deal with networks of independent distributors or both, selling to them at wholesale prices.

If the company only distributes your record, you will receive a sum equivalent to the wholesale price, minus a fee of 20-30% and other direct expenses that you authorize the company to spend, but you pay for all the manufacturing costs and all associated marketing and promotion costs. A standard contractual agreement is that you will receive money only on records actually sold and paid for.

These types of deals often have resulted after bands release recordings for a regional audience, find themselves with growing popularity, and use the added leverage to make a deal that will broaden their audiences.

Unlike major recording labels, independent labels sometimes encourage the sale of records, cassettes or compact discs at performances or to fan mailing lists. In this case, a clause can be added to the standard recording contract that will state that the musician can buy product at a low wholesale price. This inventory may be provided as an "advance" against the royalties or other fees that will be owing. This practice is actively discouraged by most major recording labels.

Pressing and Distribution Deals (P&D Deals)

In P&D deals, you deliver a fully mixed recording master and artwork to the record label, which then assumes the responsibility of manufacturing and distributing your records, cassettes or compact discs. If the label advances the manufacturing costs, it will reimburse itself out of the sales proceeds of your phonorecords, plus, perhaps, some value for the use of its money, in addition to the distribution fee.

If the recording label also picks up promotion, publicity and marketing, then the deal is usually structured as a royalty deal that will leave the recording label with a sufficient margin to cover all of its costs and make a reasonable profit. The royalty is sometimes higher than in standard recording contracts because you have already invested in the costs of recording and producing. That is not always the case, however. When negotiating this type of deal, ask that any royalty percentages be specified as net cents per unit.

As an alternative, if marketing and promotional duties are involved, these expenses could be deducted as direct costs also, along with the distribution fee and manufacturing costs, with the balance paid to you, but more likely the deal will be structured on a royalty basis, with a royalty of anywhere from 10-18% of retail, plus mechanical royalties.

Production Deals

In this type of deal, you sign as an artist with a production company. The company is responsible for recording your music and for obtaining distribution through independent distributors or a record company. In many cases, contracts for these deals are structured similarly to record contracts because the production company will typically make a pressing and distribution deal with a record label that also includes marketing and promotion and then contract with you for a percentage of the royalty paid to it by the record company.

For example, a production company may have a deal with a record company that pays 14-18% of the retail selling price on records sold, depending in part on whether the recording costs are paid by the production company or advanced by the record company. It might then contract with the artist to pay a royalty from between 6% and 10% of the retail selling price.

Obtaining a recording contract is one of the most important goals for a musical artist. In addition to royalties from the sale of records, which can be very substantial, records generate radio airplay and other media exposure and lead to higher live performance income and other opportunities. The recording contract, therefore, may be the most important agreement an artist signs during his or her career. For that reason we have included on the following pages a very detailed discussion of the most important provisions of a typical recording agreement.

Before turning to that agreement, a few preliminary points should be made. The form of agreement reproduced and discussed here is derived from a first draft contract submitted by one of the major record labels. Since certain clauses may not be identical with that company's standard form, we have chosen to use the fictional name, Label Records, Inc. However, the agreement is representative of the kind of agreement a major label would present an artist as they commence negotiating a first recording contract.

Although the following discussion points to a number of areas where the artist will seek to change the agreement, this is not to suggest that this form of agreement is unusually bad or one-sided. The artist should never expect any record company to deliver initially a recording agreement which the artist can sign without negotiating changes. It is the artist's and his or her adviser's responsibility to negotiate the agreement until it is satisfactory to them. The degree to which the record company will improve its initial draft depends in large measure on how badly it wants the artist to sign with it. An artist making his or her first record deal will obviously have less leverage than a Bruce Springsteen. There are many points, however, which a record company is willing to concede if the issues are raised. The artist's representative should ask for all points that he or she feels the record company could reasonably be expected to agree to, and perhaps even a few more. The artist should not fear being branded as a troublemaker simply because he or she thoroughly negotiates the recording contract. If anything, negotiation reflects that the artist is taking the commitment seriously and is handling it in a professional manner. However, the artist and the artist's representatives must not lose sight of the forest for the trees.

Since recording contract negotiations can involve heated bargaining over many different points, and since recording contracts have grown more and more complex in recent years, particularly due to the MTV "revolution," it is a practical necessity for the artist to engage an attorney or other experienced representative to handle the actual negotiations. This will also insulate the artist from any possible personal friction with the record company personnel, with whom the artist will need to have a smooth, working rapport. Still, even if the artist is not participating in the head-to-head negotiations, he or she should monitor their progress and ask to be consulted on all significant points.

When aspiring recording artists dream of getting a recording contract, they envision a deal with a major record label: CBS (whose labels include Columbia and Epic), WEA (Warner Brothers, Elektra/Asylum, and Atlantic), Capitol, RCA, Polygram, MCA, A&M, EMI, Motown, Arista, or Geffen. Quite often, however, it will not be a major record company which offers the artist a first recording deal. Instead it may be a production company.

Production companies take a variety of forms—from one-person operations to major companies that are essentially record labels—but they all serve basically the same function. They try to put together a "package" for a record company. This package normally consists of an artist, musical material, and a producer. Some well-established production companies have ongoing deals with record companies to provide a specified number of packages per year. These production companies may deliver a completed master tape to the record company which then simply releases and promotes the album. Other production companies will be searching for a deal with a record company. In these cases the production company may approach a record company simply on the basis of demos by the artist; it may offer the record company a package including the artist and a producer; or alternatively, the production company may produce a master tape and then attempt to shop it to a label for release and distribution.

Whether the production company already has a deal or is looking for one, it will usually seek to put the artist under contract as part of its effort to assemble a package for the record company. The form of the recording agreement presented to the artist will be very similar to the one offered by the record label, but the artist will be under contract to the production company, not the label. The production company, in turn, will furnish the artist's services to the label under a separate agreement, known as a "production" contract, negotiated between the production company and the record company.

As far as the recording artist is concerned, the production company is a middleman, standing between the artist and the record company. Undoubtedly it collects more from the record company than it pays the artist. Whether the production company deserves that share depends entirely on how valuable a service it can provide. The question for the artist is: can the production company get a deal that I would be unable to get on my own? Some production companies have a strong enough track record so that they have no difficulty making a deal for any artist they sign. Entering a contract on reasonable terms with a company like that can make a great deal of sense. In other cases an artist may sign an exclusive recording contract with a production company and find the production company is unable to make a deal. The artist then may be trapped — too legally entangled for anyone else to make a deal directly with the artist but still under a binding multiyear contract to a production company that cannot get a record contract. In these circumstances the artist has made his or her position worse by becoming involved with a production company.

The artist's strategy must be different when he or she negotiates with the production company from when negotiating directly with a record label. The point to remember is that the production company is only useful to the artist if it can get a deal and even then its usefulness is a function of how good a deal it makes. It is crucial to find out if the production company has a prearranged deal with a record company and what that deal is. If there is no deal, the agreement should provide that unless the production company obtains a production contract meeting specified standards within a certain time period, the artist will be freed from all obligations to the production company.

Production companies that do not already have deals with recording labels may try to justify a one-sided recording contract by claiming that they have to eliminate the references to "Lender," (see below) cannot predict what kind of terms they will be able to obtain from the record company, and therefore they cannot make certain concessions to the artist because the record company may not be willing to accept those terms. The result can be an extremely unfair contract. The artist should always seek to have a clause included providing that the artist will have the benefit of any provisions in a deal between the production company and the record company which are more favorable than the provisions the artist obtains from the production company. The artist will also want a provision in the agreement with the production company that the record company will directly pay the artist his or her royalties and that the artist will receive copies of royalty statements from the record company.

One final point: the recording agreement appearing below deals only with the artist's services as a performer on records. Where an artist writes material as well as performs, the rights in the material are properly handled in a separate publishing agreement. Formerly it was the almost universal practice of record companies to demand that performers grant rights to a publishing company affiliated with the record company. This practice has generally been discontinued by the major record labels, although many production companies will still seek to obtain publishing rights.

Please note that the recording contract which follows is in the form of what is known as a "loan-out corporation" owned and controlled by the artist. Loan-out corporations are generally used to take advantage of certain tax benefits which might not be available if the artist conducted business as an individual or as a partnership of individuals, whether a formal partnership (i.e., under a written partnership agreement) or informally (most bands operate as informal partnerships). The most significant benefit is in the area of pensions.

In the following recording contract, however, the "Lender" is a partnership consisting of the members of a group artist. There is no legal significance to the use of the concept of a "Lender" in this case. We could have simplified the form to eliminate the references to "Lender," but chose not to do so. We hope it does not hinder your understanding of the contract and discussion which follows.

EXHIBIT 1: EXCLUSIVE RECORDING AGREEMENT

This Agreement ("Agreement") is entered into this _____ day of ____________, 199_ by and between Label Records, Inc. ("Label") and ____________, a California partnership ("Lender") for the exclusive services of _______________, _____________, collectively and professionally known as "_____________" ("Artist") in connection with the production of records.

1. ENGAGEMENT AND TERM

(a) Label hereby engages, and Lender hereby agrees to provide to Label throughout the Territory (as defined in Paragraph 14 hereof), the exclusive personal services of Artist as vocalists and/or instrumental musicians in connection with the production of records, on the terms and conditions of this Agreement. The term of this Agreement shall be for an Initial Period commencing on the date hereof, which Initial Period shall continue until eight (8) months following the date of the release in the USA of the album derived from the LP-Master to be delivered in the Initial Period as specified in the OPTION PERIODS AND MASTER SCHEDULE set forth below. Lender hereby grants Label three (3) options, each to renew this Agreement for that period specified beside each option period in the "Duration" column of the OPTION PERIODS AND MASTER SCHEDULE, said options to run consecutively beginning at the expiration of the Initial Period. Each option may be exercised, if at all, by Label's giving Lender written notice of such exercise at any time prior to the expiration of the then-current period.

(b) With respect to the Initial Period and each Option Period hereunder, Label may, by giving written notice to Lender at any time prior to the expiration of such Period, increase the Minimum Number of Masters in such Period(s) by one (1) LP-Master ("Overcall LP-Master"), in which event the term of the applicable Period shall continue until the last day of the eighth (8th) month following the release in the USA of the album derived from the Overcall LP-Master in the applicable Period.

> ***Commentary:*** *This sets forth one of the key points of any recording contract, namely the minimum number of master recordings ("masters") which the Label is required to pay for the artist to record and the maximum number of masters which the artist is required to record. These are almost always different. In this case, Label is required to allow the artist to record only one LP, while the artist is obligated to record, should Label so require, up to ten LPs. Label is never obligated to commit to more than one LP at a time. This is quite typical for a new artist recording contract. In some cases, the Label's commitment may be to record only two masters (i.e., the "A" and "B" sides of a single). This is most common when the artist's recordings are intended to be marketed primarily in the area of 12-inch "rap" or dance singles, or where the Label simply doesn't have a great deal of faith in the artist. In other cases, the Label's commitment may be for two or more albums at a time, either initially or in the option periods. This is most generally limited to contracts for established top selling acts, but can sometimes be attained by new acts, particularly where there is strong interest from more than one record company, thereby giving the artist increased bargaining power.*
>
> *The Label's commitment to more than one album gives the artist additional security, both financially and creatively, in that the artist knows he has a second bite at the apple if his first album is not a commercial success.*

OPTION PERIODS AND MASTER SCHEDULE

Period of This Agreement	Duration	Minimum Number of Masters
Initial Period	From the date of this Agreement through and including the eighth (8th) month following the date of release in the USA of the album embodying the LP-Master specified for the Initial Period.	One (1) LP-Master*
First Option	From the commencement of First Option Period until eight (8) months following the release in the USA of the album embodying the LP-Master specified for the First Option Period.	One (1) LP-Master*
Second Option	From the commencement of Second Option Period until eight (8) months following the release in the USA of the album embodying the LP-Master specified for the Second Option Period.	One (1) LP-Master*
Third Option	From the commencement of the Third Option Period until eight (8) months following the release in the USA of the album embodying the LP-Master specified for the Third Option Period.	One (1) LP-Master*

*Subject to increase pursuant to Paragraph 1(b)

The "term" of the contract is entwined with the "recording commitment." For many years, the "standard" new artist recording contract consisted of an initial term of one year followed by four one-year options, with a recording commitment of one album plus an optional "overcall" album in each period, making a maximum ten albums. The so-called Olivia Newton-John case [MCA Records, Inc. v. Newton-John, 90 Cal. App. 3d 18 (1979)] forced record companies, at least those operating in California, to change the "term" of their contracts so that it would expire not by the passage of time (e.g., one year deal with four one-year options), but on the delivery of product (e.g., a one album deal with nine additional options for one album each). This is because the Newton-John court appeared to have ruled that a "standard" one year plus four one-year options contract could not be enforced to prevent the artist from recording for a third party after the expiration of five calendar years from its commencement, even though the contract contained the usual standard clause allowing the record company to "suspend" the running of the term of the contract if Ms. Newton-John failed to fulfill her recording commitment before the end of the applicable year. I say "appeared" because there is still widespread disagreement in the legal community as to the meaning and precedential value of the court's statements on this point in the Newton-John case.

Under the new contract structures now used by nearly every record company, the "term" is never "suspended" or "extended" by reason of the artist's failure to deliver an LP; it merely runs until the required number of LPs have been delivered. California law limits the enforceability of all personal service contracts to seven years, i.e., after seven years the record company cannot prevent the artist from recording for another record company for breach of contract if the artist performed for a third party record company prior to delivery of the required number of albums. This seven year limitation is implied in every recording contract governed by California law.

2. LENDER'S RECORDING OBLIGATIONS

In each period of this Agreement Lender shall record and deliver to Label at least the number of masters shown in the "Minimum Number of Masters" column in the OPTION PERIODS AND MASTER SCHEDULE. Lender shall be responsible for the timely delivery to Label of the required number of masters hereunder pursuant to the terms of this Agreement, including, without limitation, Paragraph 4 hereof. Notwithstanding the foregoing, nothing contained in this Agreement shall obligate Label to manufacture, distribute or sell records derived from masters recorded hereunder or to have Lender, in fact, record or deliver the "Minimum Number of Masters" specified in the OPTION PERIODS AND MASTER SCHEDULE for any period hereunder. Label shall fulfill its entire obligation (including advance payments, if any) to Lender as to undelivered masters by notifying Lender in writing not to record and/or deliver the particular masters and by paying Lender Artist's applicable minimum union scale for each of the Minimum Number of Masters not delivered in the particular period.

Commentary: *The last two sentences of this paragraph completely undo Label's "recording commitment," as discussed above. These sentences constitute a so-called "pay or play" clause, which allows Label to renege on its commitment to allow the artist to record an album by merely paying the artist minimum union scale. As minimum union scale for a royalty artist is a mere pittance, this is not adequate compensation for the Label's reneging on its commitment to record an album. This clause is almost never a "deal point" (i.e., specifically agreed upon by parties in making the deal before a formal contract is submitted), but is generally buried in the "boilerplate" for unsuspecting artists and, when discovered, is defended by the record company on the grounds of "policy."*

This clause, as drafted, should never be accepted by the artist or his representative. Whatever the Label's commitment is, whether one single, an album or several albums, it should be stated straightforwardly, not given with one clause and taken back with another.

3. RECORDING FUND

(a) Prior to the recording of each master to be recorded hereunder, Lender or Producer (as the term is defined in Paragraph 9 hereof) shall submit to Label for approval a written proposal for the recording of each such master ("Proposed Budget"). The Proposed Budget shall be in substantially the form attached hereto as Exhibit "A" (NOT INCLUDED IN THIS BOOK) and shall specify (i) the number of vocalists and/or musicians to be employed; (ii) an estimate of the costs of recording masters ("Recording Costs"), which Recording Costs shall include, without limitation, applicable union scale to Artist, vocalists, musicians, conductors, arrangers (including "sketchers"), orchestrators and copyists; Producer fees and advances, if any; Artist advances, if any; studio rental (including without limitation editing, mixing and remixing time), instrument rentals, transportation, accommodations, mastering costs, and all other costs relating to the recording and editing of masters hereunder up to and including the final lacquer and/or metal master; and (iii) the proposed time, date and place of the recording sessions.

Commentary: *Due to space limitations, Label's budget form is not reproduced. As a practical matter, the producer will prepare and submit the budget, so the artist need not be overly concerned about the mechanics of its preparation and submission, but only with the bottom line. Generally, the particulars are not closely scrutinized by record companies, so long as the total does not exceed the amount approved by the Label, although some record companies resist approving multiple scale payments to session players.*

(b) Lender shall not commence the recording of any masters pursuant to this Agreement unless and until Label has approved in writing the Proposed Budget with respect to such masters. If Label has not approved the Proposed Budget within ten (10) business days after its submission, the Proposed Budget shall be deemed disapproved and Lender shall promptly consult with Label to arrive at a satisfactory Proposed Budget. Upon Label's written approval, the Proposed Budget shall become the "Approved Budget." In the following "Recording Fund Schedule," the total dollar amount of the particular Proposed Budget for the LP-Masters listed in Column "A" (inclusive of Producer's fees and advances, if any, and Artist's advances, if any) shall not exceed the corresponding amounts in Column "B") ("Approved Recording Fund"); provided, however, that with respect to the Overcall LP-Master in the Initial Period and the LP-Master(s) in the Option Periods, if any, the Approved Recording Fund for the applicable LP-Master shall be the amount derived by applying the Formula [as defined in Paragraph 3 (c)] to said LP-Master. Notwithstanding the foregoing, in no event shall the applicable Approved Recording Fund be less than the amount designated in Column "B" nor exceed the amount designated in Column "C", with respect to the applicable LP-Master:

RECORDING FUND SCHEDULE

Column "A"	Column "B"	Column "C"
Initial Period		
First LP-Master	$ ______	$ ______
Overcall LP-Master, if any	$ ______	$ ______
First Option Period:		
First LP-Master, if any	$ ______	$ ______
Overcall LP-Master, if any	$ ______	$ ______
Second Option Period:		
First LP-Master, if any	$ ______	$ ______
Overcall LP-Master, if any	$ ______	$ ______
Third Option Period:		
First LP-Master, if any	$ ______	$ ______
Overcall LP-Master, if any	$ ______	$ ______

(c) The word "Formula" shall refer to the derivation of an Approved Recording Fund for each applicable LP-Master ("Applicable LP-Master") by computing an amount equal to sixty-six and two-thirds percent (66-2/3%) of the net royalties accrued to Lender hereunder with respect to net sales in the USA of Full Price Units (as that term is defined in Paragraph 15 hereof) of albums manufactured from the last LP-Master delivered hereunder immediately preceding the Applicable LP-Master ("Preceding Album") during the period commencing upon the date of the release in the USA of the Preceding Album ("Release Date"), and ending on the earlier of (i) the last day of the ninth (9th) full calendar month following the Release Date or (ii) the date of the commencement of recording the Applicable LP-Master, whichever occurs first ("Applicable Period"), less a reasonable reserve for returns. Neither "Best of" nor "Live" lp-masters shall be construed as constituting either an Applicable LP-Master or a Preceding Album.

Commentary: *In nearly all record deals with major record companies today, the company's financial commitment to the artist is made by way of an all-inclusive "recording fund." This replaces the older approach of allocating a "recording budget" for each album and a separate cash advance to the artist for each album. In the recording fund, the budget and artist advance are combined, with the result that if the budget is exceeded for any reason, the artist's advance is automatically reduced. Accordingly, where the artist needs some portion of the recording fund for living expenses during the period of preproduction and production of the album, he or she should arrange to have some portion of it paid to him or her as an advance (see subparagraph (f) below). The artist or artist's manager must attempt to control the actual recording costs. Generally this is done by contracting with the producer to produce the album for a budget which is less than the amount of the fund and by requiring the producer to assume the cost of budget overruns.*

However, as a practical matter, producers will accept liability only for cost overruns due solely to their own fault (i.e., blatant foul-ups), not for the usual causes (e.g., delays, faulty equipment, endless takes, etc.) and generally, the producer will not reach into his own pocket to pay any overruns; usually, the most that can be extracted from the producer is that he may forfeit the second half of his advance which is normally paid upon delivery of the completed masters.

(d) Lender or Producer shall conduct the recording sessions in accordance with the Approved Budget for the masters specified therein and shall make all arrangements for such sessions. All Recording Costs paid or incurred by Label shall be deemed advances to Lender, shall be deducted from the applicable Approved Recording Fund, and shall be recoupable from any royalties payable to Lender by Label pursuant to this Agreement. If any of the Recording Costs are not direct charges to Label but are instead incurred at facilities owned or controlled by Label or a parent, subsidiary or affiliate of Label, such Recording Costs shall be computed pursuant to Label's then-current "Schedule of Standard Costs." If Lender and/or Artist should delay the commencement of, completion of, or if Artist should be unavailable for, any recording session hereunder for any reason whatsoever, Lender agrees to pay all expenses and charges incurred or paid by Label by reason thereof.

***Commentary**: It is the custom in the industry that while the Label initially advances the recording costs, those costs must be "recouped" (i.e., paid back) out of royalties earned by the artist. If the artist's records are successful, the artist ultimately pays the cost of recording them. All record companies define recording costs in essentially the same way. They include not only the obvious things such as costs of recording studios, producers' and engineers' fees, etc., but also any amounts which may be advanced by the Label to the artist, producer or other personnel performing at the sessions for transportation, lodging and "per diems" (i.e., a daily payment to cover out-of-pocket expenses such as meals, cab fares, etc.). Accordingly, the artist or his manager must take the responsibility for carefully reviewing the budget and trying to keep these incidental costs as low as possible.*

(e) Lender agrees that there will be no liens, encumbrances or obligations upon or in connection with masters recorded hereunder, and in connection with the recording and/or delivery of such masters all applicable government taxes shall be paid in full by Lender.

(f) Solely with respect to the First LP-Master in the Initial Period, Label shall pay Lender the following amounts as advances which shall be fully recoupable from royalties otherwise payable by Label to Lender hereunder:

(i)__________Dollars ($_________) from the Approved Recording Fund for the First LP-Master in the Initial Period within fourteen (14) days following the full execution of this Agreement;

(ii) With respect to up to five (5) of the calendar months immediately preceding the commencement of the recording of the First LP-Master in the Initial Period, and upon Lender's written request therefor, Label shall advance to Lender the sum of ____________Dollars ($_________) per month for Lender's use in connection with preproduction costs of the First LP-Master in the Initial period. Such advance shall reduce the Approved Recording Fund for the First LP-Master in the Initial Period in the amount advanced to Artist during said preproduction period.

Commentary: *This paragraph seems to have been specifically tailored to a new artist, since it not only provides for a portion of the recording fund for the first album to be paid upon execution of the agreement, but also provides for a monthly "allowance" to be deducted from the fund to cover the preproduction costs (e.g., rehearsals and living expenses) that a new artist very often cannot afford.*

(g) Each LP-Master shall be recorded under Label's recording license, and the following provisions shall apply:

(i) The applicable LP-Master to be recorded and delivered hereunder will be recorded under Label's current Phonograph Record Labor Contract with the American Federation of Musicians ("AFM") and all musicians who render services in connection with the recording of such masters (including instrumentalists, if any) will be paid by Label, on Lender's behalf, the scale set forth in the said Labor Contract and label, on Lender's behalf, shall pay the contributions to the Pension Welfare Fund required by Exhibit "B" (NOT INCLUDED IN THIS BOOK) thereto.

(ii) All American Federation of Television and Radio Artists ("AFTRA") members whose performances are embodied in the masters will be paid by Label, on Lender's behalf, the rates applicable under the current AFTRA Code of Fair Practices for Phonograph Recordings. Lender agrees to be solely responsible for and to pay all royalties and/or other sums payable to Artist, other performers, Producer(s) and any other persons whose performances are embodied on applicable masters recorded hereunder. Lender warrants and represents that Artist is or shall become a member in good standing of AFTRA subject to and in accordance with the applicable union security provisions of the AFTRA National Code of Fair Practice for Phonograph Recordings. Label shall, on Lender's behalf, if necessary, also pay to the AFTRA Pension and Welfare Fund any contribution required to be made under the AFTRA Code based on compensation to other performers whose performances are embodied on the applicable masters recorded hereunder.

(iii) The foregoing representations and warranties are included for the benefit, respectively, of the AFM, AFTRA, and the AFM and AFTRA members whose performances are embodied in the applicable masters, and for the benefit of Label, and may be enforced by AFM and/or AFTRA or their respective designees, as the case may be and by Label.

(iv) Lender shall furnish or shall cause the applicable Producer to furnish Label with copies of all union contracts and/or union session reports so that all payments may be made by Label, on Lender's behalf, in a timely fashion to the proper parties thereunder; and if Lender fails to do so with the result that Label is required to pay any penalty sum for making a late payment under the applicable union agreements, such payments shall be a direct debt from Lender to Label which, in addition to any other remedy Label may have, Label may recover from any monies otherwise payable to Lender. Lender hereby agrees to indemnify Label against, and hold Label harmless from, any claims arising out of Lender's breach of any of the material terms and provisions contained in this Paragraph.

(v) Label shall be responsible for payments to the AFM Music Performance Trust Fund and Special Payments Fund arising from the manufacture and sale of records embodying masters recorded hereunder.

(vi) Lender shall cause all bills incurred with respect to masters recorded hereunder pursuant to the applicable Approved Recording Fund to be sent promptly to Label after having placed on such bills (a) sufficient identification so that Label may ascertain the particular Recording Fund involved and the nature of the bills, and (b) written authorization for Label to pay such bills. If Lender fails to do so and if as a result thereof, Label is required to pay any penalty sum for making untimely or late payments, such penalty payments shall be deemed a direct debt from Lender to Label which, in addition to any other remedy Label may have, Label may recover from any monies otherwise payable to Lender hereunder.

(vii) Label shall pay the Recording Costs, on Lender's behalf, in connection with the recording of the applicable masters hereunder up to the amount of the applicable Approved Budget and Lender shall be responsible for any excess. In the event that Label pays any such excess, such payments shall be a direct debt from Lender to Label which Label may, in addition to any other remedy Label may have, recover such excess from any monies payable to Lender under this or any other agreement between Label and Lender.

(viii) Following payment by Label of the Recording Costs as provided herein, Label shall pay to Lender the balance, if any, remaining of the Approved Recording Fund for the applicable LP-Master as follows: If the total expenses, inclusive of Recording Costs, advances and fees payable to Lender, paid by Label relating to the recording of the applicable masters do not exceed the applicable Approved Recording Fund, the difference between such total expenses and the applicable Approved Recording Fund will be paid to Lender with thirty (30) days following delivery of the applicable masters to Label; provided, however, that Label may retain a reasonable reserve with respect to unpaid Recording Costs. Said reserve shall be payable to Lender by Label within sixty (60) days following delivery of the applicable LP-Master, provided that all Recording Costs shall have theretofore been paid in full.

Commentary: *This paragraph sets forth standard provisions pertaining to union requirements, which are general handled as a matter of course by the producer. Subparagraph (vii) is a standard clause which provides that if the recording costs exceed the approved budget, the artist must pay those out of his pocket. Obviously, this applies only where the entire Recording Fund has been exceeded. As a practical matter, in most instances the record company will not seek to enforce this provision literally, because budget overruns are generally not the result of misconduct by the artist, but often occur even if the artist and pro-*

ducer are working together smoothly and efficiently. They are likely to occur particularly with first time recording artists who are unfamiliar with the experience of recording and who probably would not have the money to repay to the Label in any event. Generally, these cost overruns are simply added to the artist's unrecouped balance and, if the artist's records are successful, the Label will ultimately recoup them.

(h) Label shall charge all amounts paid or costs incurred by Label pursuant to this Paragraph 3 against and recoup the same from royalties otherwise payable by Label to Lender hereunder; provided, however, that all amounts paid or costs incurred by Label pursuant to this Paragraph 3 which are expressly deemed herein to be direct debts from Lender to Label shall be chargeable against and recoupable from all monies otherwise payable by Label to Lender hereunder.

Commentary: *This provides an alternative to royalties as a source for the Label to recoup the cost overruns, namely subsequent album recording funds, mechanical royalties and other payments which may be due to the artist under the agreement.*

4. LENDER'S MASTER DELIVERY OBLIGATIONS

(a) Lender shall cause the masters required hereunder to be delivered to Label as follows:

(i) the First LP-Master in the Initial Period shall be delivered no later than eight (8) months after the execution of this Agreement;

(ii) the Second LP-Master in the Initial Period shall be delivered no earlier than eight (8) months and no later than twelve (12) months following the delivery to Label of the First LP-Master in the Initial Period.

(iii) the First LP-Master in each Option Period, if any, shall be delivered no later than four (4) months following the commencement of the applicable Option Period.

(iv) the Overcall LP-Master, if any, in each Option Period shall be delivered no later than four (4) months following Label's request therefor.

Commentary: *The delivery schedule should be realistic. Generally, a record company wants to get a new album from the artist every twelve months. Some artists record a little more frequently than that, but most record at about that pace or even less frequently, particularly if the artist tours heavily. If the last album is continuing to sell, the record company will be content.*

Once the artist is no longer being heard on the radio and the records are no longer moving in the stores, the record company wants new product. However, the frequency of delivering albums does not usually become a problem unless there are other problems in the relationship. The best way to handle potential problems in advance is to require that the Label give the artist written notice and a reasonable opportunity to cure before the Lender may terminate the agreement for nondelivery. Such a clause would be added to paragraph (c) below.

(b) Lender shall not commence recording with the intention of completing an LP-Master (i) without Label's prior written consent and (ii) until Lender has delivered the immediately preceding LP-Master to Label.

(c) In the event Lender fails to deliver any master required hereunder when such master was due as aforesaid, Label, in addition to any other rights or remedies which it may have, may elect to terminate this Agreement by giving written notice thereof to Lender and thereby be relieved of any liability in connection with undelivered masters.

(d) Masters shall not be deemed to be delivered hereunder until such time as the following items have been delivered to and have been accepted by an authorized employee of Label at the address for purposes of serving notices on Label or at such other location as Label may advise Lender by written notice from time to time: (i) Fully equalized, edited two-track stereophonic tape copies of such masters acceptable to Label as commercially satisfactory for the manufacture and sale of records, and ready for the manufacture of final lacquer masters, and (ii) fully proofed final reference discs of such masters, and (iii) all elements necessary for Label to have complete "label copy" information with respect to such masters (including, without limitation, (A) the title of each selection embodied on the masters, (B) the timing of each such selection, (C) the publisher(s) of each such selection, (D) any other information that is to appear on labels and/or liners of records embodying such masters, (E) all "sideman" clearances, (F) all mechanical licenses for each musical composition embodied in the masters, at the rates specified in Paragraph 10 hereof, and (G) all other elements and approvals required by Label). Lender further agrees to irrevocably direct in writing the person who has possession of any and all tapes of masters or digital masters recorded hereunder that all such tapes and masters are Label's property and that such person shall be obligated to deliver such tapes and masters to Label upon Label's written request.

Commentary: *This paragraph is full of potential pitfalls. To the layman, "delivery" of an album would seem to be a very simple thing, i.e., the producer hands over the completed master tape to the record company.*

Generally the artist thinks he is finished before this has even happened. However, the Label views it differently. It insists that a host of other things, none of which the artist is directly involved with, must be completed for the album to be considered "delivered." Again, as a practical matter, this is generally not a problem except where there are other problems in the relationship. For example, if the Label is not thrilled with the album it has just been given or if a dispute later arises as to whether the Label timely exercised an option, the Label's attorneys will look to this clause to find some requirement which was not met by the artist. Accordingly, it is helpful to provide some kind of outside date (e.g., 10 days after the artist's notice that it has delivered the master tapes) for the album to be deemed delivered unless the Label has notified artist of some element within the artist's control which the artist has failed to deliver.

Also, subclause (i) requires that the masters be "commercially satisfactory" to Label. This clause is always the subject of a battle between the artist's representatives and the record company's representatives. The record company insists that this is necessary for them to get what they bargained for, whereas the artist's representatives see this as an improper infringement upon the artist's creativity and an improper attempt to guarantee what simply cannot be guaranteed, i.e., a commercially successful album. Five years ago nearly every artist other than a new artist could get a "technically satisfactory" (i.e., that from an engineering perspective they sound well, without regard to commercial or creative judgements) standard. In today's contracts only superstars are afforded a "technically satisfactory" standard.

Who pays the costs of re-recording if the Label does not like what it hears? Under this contract, the artist must pay, and these costs may exhaust what the artist had expected to put in his pocket upon delivering the album. Accordingly, the artist's lawyer should try to require the Label to pay the costs of any re-recording it requires once a technically satisfactory album has been delivered. Keep in mind, however, that the Label is normally reluctant to second guess what the artist and the producer have decided upon. This is particularly true where an outside producer (i.e., not the artist) has been used, and even more so, where the record company has selected or approved the producer and selected or approved the material. Most record company representatives will tell you that in all of their years they can only remember one instance of having rejected an album as being not commercially satisfactory, and their example is always one where the artist pulled a fast one on the company, such as an album of kazoo music. However, getting the record company to limit in the contract their right to reject the album to instances such as their bad faith example is generally impossible.

Generally the outcome is a matter of relative bargaining strength; however, a resourceful attorney can come up with any number of different ways to prevent the Label from arbitrarily requiring the artist to re-record.

(e) With the exception of Paragraph 10 hereof, for the purposes of this Agreement, more than one (1) lp-disc intended to be initially used in the manufacture of an album shall nevertheless be deemed to be one (1) LP-Master and there shall be no so-called "live" recording without the prior written consent of Label.

Commentary: *This clause is standard and with good reason. With rare exceptions, multiple disc albums can only be sold for slightly more than single disc albums and generally do not sell as well as single disc albums due to their higher price. Live albums, with rare exceptions, do not sell nearly as well as studio albums.*

(f) Times of delivery of masters as provided hereinabove are of the essence of this Agreement.

5. LABEL'S OWNERSHIP OF MASTERS AND RELATED RIGHTS

Lender acknowledges that Label is the sole, exclusive, and perpetual owner of all masters from inception, which ownership entitles Label among other things to:

(a) The exclusive and perpetual ownership of all duplicates of the masters and records manufactured therefrom and the right to use and control the same and the performances embodied therein.

(b) The exclusive and perpetual right throughout the Territory to manufacture, advertise, sell, lease, license, synchronize with any medium, or otherwise use or dispose of masters and records manufactured from or embodying all or any part of the contents of the masters, or to refrain therefrom, in any and all fields of use throughout the Territory upon such terms and conditions as Label may determine.

(c) The perpetual right to use and publish and to permit others to use and publish the names (including any professional names heretofore adopted), likenesses of, and biographical material concerning Artist and all the performers who recorded the masters, for advertising and trade purposes in connection with the sale and exploitation of the masters and records produced from the masters, or to refrain therefrom.

(d) The right to release records manufactured from the masters under the name of "Label" or such other trade name or mark as Label may elect.

(e) The right to sell and exploit records manufactured from the masters on which performances by other artists are coupled and to sell records manufactured from the masters in albums, which albums may contain pictures, prose and verse, and records embodying performances of other artists.

(f) Label's ownership and rights with respect to the masters shall extend to all tapes and other physical devices embodying performances made at recording sessions held pursuant to the terms of this Agreement.

(g) Label shall have the exclusive right to use and license others to use any artwork created by Label in connection with albums, singles, twelve inch (12") singles, and mini-LPs manufactured from masters delivered hereunder in connection with merchandise of any sort. Label shall also have the exclusive right to use and license others to use any other materials created by or furnished by Label and any materials paid for, in whole or in part, by Label, in connection with merchandise of any sort. Label shall pay to Lender fifty percent (50%) of all "net receipts" received by Label in respect of any such merchandise uses. As used herein, "net receipts" shall mean gross receipts less all expenses incurred by Label in connection therewith and any third party payments, such as payments to copyright proprietors.

Commentary: *Subparagraphs (a) through (f) contain standard grants of rights. Subparagraph (g) is less customary. It grants Label the exclusive merchandising rights with respect to artwork created (i.e., paid for) by Label. This clause is reflective of a current trend in recording contracts for the record company to attempt to acquire merchandising rights. The major record companies recently reawakened to the fact that merchandising rights with respect to rock artists can be extremely lucrative and several major record companies, beginning with CBS, have begun to insist on acquiring merchandising rights as part of their form recording contract. Their rationale is that the sale of records creates the demand for an artist's merchandise and that, therefore, they are entitled to share in merchandising revenue. The degree of exclusivity which they require varies from company to company. Since CBS reportedly acquired a 50% interest in Winterland Productions, the nation's largest concert tour merchandiser, CBS insists on the exclusive rights to sell merchandise of the artist at the artist's concerts, at least in deals with new artists. The clause in this form is much less onerous, since it is limited to artwork and similar materials paid for by the Label.*

It is typical in these clauses for the record company to agree to split net receipts evenly with the artist. However, if the artist were not required to give these rights to the record company, the artist could obviously get 100% of the receipts payable by the licensee and, moreover, this would mean cash in hand to the artist, as opposed to a credit to his royalty account, which may be very substantially unrecouped.

Until the record companies' recent demands for merchandising rights, record companies generally allowed artists to use album artwork created and paid for by the record company for the artist's own merchandising purposes, although in most instances the record company required that the artist reimburse them all or half of the costs of creating such artwork as a pre-condition to using it. Whenever possible, the artist should insist, as a deal point, that no merchandising rights will be conveyed. For a more complete discussion about merchandising see the chapter entitled "Merchandising in the Music Industry."

(h) During the term of this Agreement, including all renewals, extensions, days of suspension, and all periods added by amendments or by other agreements, (i) Lender will not authorize or permit Artist to perform, and Artist will not perform, for the purpose of making records for anyone other than Label; and (ii) neither Lender nor Artist will authorize or permit the use of Artist's name, likeness, or other identification for the purpose of distributing, selling, advertising, or exploiting records for anyone other than Label.

Commentary: *This is a typical clause which provides that the artist's recording services, name and likeness are exclusive to the record company. Certain exceptions are routinely granted, e.g., rights to perform as a "sideman" on records by other artists and rights to produce other artists. Less commonly, a right may be given to the artist to perform on a limited number of soundtrack albums or cast albums released by other record companies, subject to certain restrictions, such as the reservation of the exclusive rights to release singles and prohibitions against using the artist's likeness in any manner or using the artist's name in advertising.*

However, a good degree of bargaining power or other special circumstances are required for a record company to allow this exception, since soundtrack albums have proven to be tremendously lucrative.

6. SOUND RECORDING COPYRIGHT

(a) With respect to any person whose services are furnished by Lender in connection with masters recorded hereunder, including without limitation Artist and any person engaged to act as Producer, Lender has or shall have a contract in which such person acknowledges that each master embodying the results and proceeds of his services prepared within the scope of Lender's engagement of his personal services is a work made for hire, or is prepared as part of an LP-Master which constitutes a work specially ordered by Lender for use as a contribution to a collective work and shall be considered a work made for hire. Lender further agrees that Lender shall cause each such person to execute and deliver to a Label a "Declaration Re Collective Work and Power of Attorney" in the form attached hereto as Exhibit "C" (NOT INCLUDED IN THIS BOOK).

(b) With respect to each master recorded hereunder and all "sound recordings," "phonorecords," and "copies" manufactured therefrom (individually and collectively called the "Work"), Lender hereby grants, assigns and transfers to Label exclusively, perpetually and throughout the Territory all right, title and interest in and to such Work, including but not limited to the ownership of the Work and all rights of the owner of copyright specified in 17 U.S.C. 106. Lender hereby grants to Label a power of attorney, irrevocable and coupled with an interest, to execute for Lender and in Lender's name all documents and instruments necessary or desirable to effectuate the intents and purposes of this Paragraph and to accomplish, evidence and perfect the rights granted to Label pursuant to this Paragraph, including, but not limited to Exhibit "C" (NOT INCLUDED IN THIS BOOK) attached hereto and documents to apply for and obtain all registrations of copyrights in and to any such Work, and documents to assign such copyrights to Label.

Commentary: *Paragraph 6 contains a very standard and unobjectionable declaration that the record company owns the sound recording copyrights, as distinguished from the copyrights in the underlying musical compositions recorded by the artist.*

7. ROYALTY PROVISIONS

In consideration of (i) the copyright ownership provided herein, (ii) Label's right to use Artist's name and likeness as provided herein, and (iii) the other agreements, representations and warranties contained herein, Label agrees to pay Lender in connection with records manufactured from masters recorded hereunder a royalty on net sales of records manufactured from the masters delivered hereunder at the applicable rates specified in the Royalty Schedule below. Such royalty shall include royalties due to Artist and Producer and all other artists, musicians, performers, producer(s), and A&R personnel other than those employed by Label which become or may become due by reason of Label's exploitation of the masters delivered hereunder.

Commentary: *This contract contemplates what is known as an "all-in" royalty rate. While this clause suggests that royalties may be payable to outside musicians and A&R personnel, this term means in essence that the royalties stated as payable to the artist are inclusive of the royalty payable to the individual producer. This was originally done in instances where the artist was expected to be the producer as well. However, it has become more prevalent in recent years as a means for the record company to fix its total expenditure for royalties. Since the producer's royalty comes out of the artist's royalty, the artist should have the right to approve the royalty rates payable to the producer.*

ROYALTY SCHEDULE USA & CANADA

LP-	7" Singles & Mini-LP's	12" Singles	All Other records
1st and 2nd LP-Masters	______ %	______ %	______ %
LP-	7" Singles & Mini-LP's	12" Singles	All other records
3rd and 4th LP-Masters, if any	______ %	______ %	______ %
5th and 6th LP-Masters, if any	______ %	______ %	______ %

Commentary: *Since these rates are always negotiated specifically, I did not wish to create the impression that there were "standard" rates by filling any specific rates in.*

Generally in negotiations the royalty rate for albums sold through normal retail channels (i.e., records sold at a top-line price for resale in retail stores) in the United States is the basic cornerstone of the royalty structure. The royalty rates for 7" singles and 12" singles are generally lower than the royalty rates for albums. This is because the costs of promoting singles have been so high, particularly in recent years when record companies have been paying enormous sums to independent promotion men to obtain radio airplay of records. This may be changing due to recent criminal investigations into the business of independent record promotion. If this practice should be more than temporarily stopped, singles royalty rates may escalate again.

The lower rate on 12" singles is due to the fact that the manufacturing cost of a 12" single is identical to that of an album, while the wholesale price is much lower, and to the fact that 12" singles generally do not achieve a very high volume of sales.

Note that in Label's royalty structure, the royalty rate for Canada is the same as that for the United States. Normally, Canada is treated as a foreign territory in record company contracts, although the royalty rate is often slightly higher (typically 85% of U.S. rate) than the royalty rate for other so-called "major" foreign territories (typically 66.7%-75% of U.S. rate).

FOREIGN

TERRITORY	ALL RECORDS
Major Territories	_____percent (__%) of applicable USA royalty rate as specified above in the Royalty Schedule.
Rest of the World	_____percent (__%) of applicable USA royalty rate as specified above in the Royalty Schedule.

* Subject to increases, decreases and adjustments as set forth hereinbelow.

Commentary: *Historically, royalty rates for records sold in foreign territories have been substantially lower than royalty rates for records sold in the United States. There may or may not have been economic justifications for paying a reduced royalty rate in foreign territories, but at this point in time the predominant reason for this is the history or custom of the business. In many contracts, particularly older ones and ones with small record companies or for new artists, the artist would be paid one-half of the artist's United States royalty rate for sales in any country outside the United States and Canada. Generally, the foreign rate is specified as, or negotiated as, a percentage of the United States rate. This is largely a matter of convenience, ease of negotiation and consistency for the record company. Generally, the record company will agree to pay a larger percentage, e.g., 3/4 or 2/3 of the United States royalty rate in the so-called "major" territories and a lesser royalty rate, usually one-half, in the rest of the world. This is justifiable because there are naturally more profits where the volume of sales is higher.*

However, in recent years, there has been in certain foreign territories an abandonment of the use of "suggested retail list prices" in favor of "constructed" retail prices nego-

tiated between the local societies which collect mechanical royalties and the representatives of the record companies in that territory as the basis upon which mechanical royalties will be computed. In certain territories these "constructed retail prices" are yielding in favor of a straight wholesale price, i.e., the price at which the record companies sell the records to distributors or dealers. Because of this trend, it may be that at least for certain foreign territories, major recording artists will begin to secure royalty rates which approach or perhaps even exceed their domestic royalty rates (although computed on a wholesale rather than a retail basis), and this would then gradually affect foreign royalty rates for artists of lesser stature. Keep in mind that wholesale and retail prices of records in foreign territories are generally higher than in the United States.

Royalties payable hereunder shall be computed and paid as follows:

(a) (i) Royalties will be computed and paid upon net sales of records. Label shall be entitled to withhold from payments otherwise due from time to time reserves against anticipated returns, rebates and credits.

Commentary: *It is customary for record companies to allow their customers (i.e., retail stores, distributors, subdistributors, etc.) to return records for full credit long after they are initially sold. Record companies report that returns come in as late as two years after they were sold. Consequently, the record companies hold reserves for anticipated returns. Some companies have an automatic, standard formula for computing, maintaining and liquidating reserves which they will, if requested, set forth in the contract. Other companies tailor their reserves on an artist-by-artist, statement-by-statement basis and will only state that their reserves will be "reasonable." Generally, reserves held on albums are in the range of 25% to 30% of albums shipped for resale, while reserves held on singles are in the range of 40% to 50% of singles shipped for resale since returns of singles are usually higher. Generally, companies will liquidate reserves over 3-4 semi-annual accounting periods. Record companies are usually inflexible about their contractual provisions regarding reserves, but the artist should attempt to clarify and limit the reserves which may be taken and have the record company provide for a schedule for their liquidation. It is also important to clarify that returns will be applied first in reduction of reserves being held.*

While this may seem obvious, since the reserves are held in anticipation of returns, most record companies insist that they may apply returns first against current sales. This obviously penalizes the artist. It is instructive to note that the Copyright Office regulations, which govern compulsory mechanical licenses, require that returns be applied first against reserves.

(ii) The royalty rate applicable to (A) budget-line records, (B) records sold through a record club distribution plan owned or controlled by Label or Label's licensees outside the USA who distribute Label's top line records ("Primary Licensees"), and (C) records sold through a special markets plan owned or controlled by Label or a Primary Licensee shall be fifty percent (50%) of the otherwise applicable rate specified in the Royalty Schedule above.

(iii) No royalties will be payable on records

(A) furnished as free and/or bonus to members or other participants in a record club distribution plan for special markets plan; or

(B) given away for promotional purposes to disc jockeys, radio and television stations or networks or others; or

(C) distributed as a sales inducement or otherwise and invoiced on a "no charge" basis to independent distributors, subdistributors, dealers and others; or

(D) licensed or distributed for airline, background use or other transportation use; or

(E) sold as scrap.

Commentary: *Generally record companies do not pay royalties on records for which they are not paid, and generally artists do not quarrel with that position. However, just as the record company is in business to sell records, the artist is in business to earn royalties on his records which are purchased by the public, and there are situations in which records are purchased by the public but are not considered royalty-bearing records by the record company. Subclause (A) deals with "free goods" in record club distributions. As we all know, record clubs give away a number of records in order to induce customers to join the club and thereafter purchase a minimum number of records at full prices, which prices are generally higher than you would pay if you went to the store to buy the same record. Record companies do not pay royalties on those records given away. However, if one artist's records are entirely given away and another artist's records are only available for purchase at full price, there would obviously be an inequitable result in royalty payments. Accordingly, most record companies will agree that the artist will be paid on at least as many of his records as are given away (i.e., 50% free and 50% sold).*

The record club free goods limit is much higher than the free goods limit in connection with normal sales, which is referred to in subclause (C). This is the key clause here. It is customary for record companies to give away certain quantities of records to dealers or distributors as a means of discounting the price of those records. These records are sold by the retail store for the same prices that the records for which they pay are sold, but the artist is not paid a royalty on these "free" records, known as "free goods." Most companies have a "standard" free goods program pursuant to which all of their records are shipped.

Although these policies differ from company to company, a typical policy is to give away 15 albums for every 85 albums sold and 30 singles for every 100 singles sold. The particular record company's free goods policy must be known in order for the artist to really know what his net royalty will be for each record that is bought by a consumer. The artist's representative attempts to negotiate the specific free goods limits and to provide that these are fixed limits which cannot be exceeded without the artist's being entitled to be paid his full royalty rate on the excess freebies. In many contracts, particularly with new artists, the record company will state what its current free goods limits are, without agreeing that these limits may not be changed in the record company's discretion. This does not provide the artist much security. Generally, record companies will agree to fix their free goods for the entire term at the current limits then in effect.

In addition to the "standard" free goods there are "special programs," which consist of short-term incentives, normally four to six weeks in duration, during which the Label will offer a further discount in order to stimulate sales of particular albums or its entire catalog. Again, these additional free goods are royalty free, but most record companies will agree to put a "cap" on them, with the artist being entitled to be paid royalties on records given away free in excess of the agreed upon free goods limits.

(iv) No royalties will be paid on sales made to anyone at prices fifty percent (50%) or more below the otherwise regular price to subdistributors ("Closeout Sales").

(v) As to records sold by a licensee of Label through a special markets plan or record club distribution plan; or as to soundtrack albums (other than soundtrack albums distributed by Label or licensed by Label to be distributed by Primary Licensees) where the consideration payable to Label is based on a flat fee, cent rate or a percentage basis, then in lieu of any other royalty specified in this Agreement, Lender's royalty shall be fifty percent (50%) of the net royalties received by Label from such licensee with respect to (a) such sales of records of (b) such other use of the applicable masters , as the case may be, computed on the same quantity, basis and in the same manner as Label is paid. For purposes hereof the term "net royalties" shall mean the gross monies received by Label from the applicable licensee with respect to either:

(A) net sales of records, or

(B) where record sales are not involved, the use of the records or masters, as the case may be, by said licensee, less any amounts Label is required to pay to third parties with respect to the net sales or use, as the case may be, of such records or masters, other than any amounts that Label may be obligated to pay a Producer. Any portion of monies received by Label hereunder which Label may be obligated to pay a Producer of masters hereunder shall be deducted solely from Lender's share of net royalties.

(b) As to records manufactured under this Agreement and sold in the USA by Label, royalties will be based upon the retail selling price per record (less all excise, sales and use taxes and other similar taxes, however designated, if any), and shall be computed on net sales of such records within the USA, except as hereinafter provided.

Commentary: *In this agreement "retail selling price" is defined as being less Label's "container charges", which are set forth in the definition in paragraph 14 below.*

At the present time there are no taxes deducted from the retail selling price for purposes of computing royalties on records sold in the United States.

(c) As to records manufactured under this Agreement and sold in Canada, royalties will be the same number of Canadian pennies as USA pennies would be payable if the same records had been sold in the USA, except that, as to records sold by licensees of Label's Canadian affiliate ("Label-Canada"), royalties based on percentage will be computed upon the same quantity, on the same basis, and in the same manner as fees payable to Label-Canada are computed. All royalties applicable to this Agreement received from Canada shall be computed in the national currency of Canada and shall be paid in USA currency at the same rate of exchange as Label is paid or credited.

Commentary: *As mentioned above, Label pays the same royalty rate on Canadian sales as they do on sales in the United States, whereas most companies will pay 80% to 85% of the U.S. royalty rate for sales in Canada. Keep in mind that "free goods" are generally not distributed to dealers and distributors in Canada, and this must be taken into account in arriving at a true comparison of the royalty rates offered by competing companies.*

(d) As to records manufactured under this Agreement and sold outside the USA and Canada:

(i) Royalties will be based on the retail selling price per record (less excise and other applicable taxes) for retail sales in the country of manufacture or the country of sale (depending upon the basis upon which Label was paid) on net sales of records, except as hereinafter provided.

(ii) Except as provided in Paragraph 7 (h) below, only records for which payment is received by Label in the USA or for which Label's account has been credited shall be deemed sold.

(iii) All royalties will be computed in the national currency of the country to which the retail selling price so elected applies and will be paid in USA currency at the same rate of exchange as Label is paid.

(iv) All royalties applicable to this Agreement received from foreign sources shall be subject to and reduced by that portion of all withholding and/or monetary transfer or export taxes, if any, charged to or paid by Label's licensees on Label's behalf which are attributable to income to Label which would otherwise be payable as a royalty to Lender hereunder.

(v) Royalties on records packaged in jackets, in boxes, on reels, or in or on similar "containers" shall be computed on the retail selling price less the container deductions charged to Label by Label's licensee. That portion of the retail selling price of the record attributed to the "container" and any tax on the "container" will be excluded in said computation.

(vi) Royalties applicable to records sold under special merchandising plans or otherwise at less than the regular wholesale price applicable to the initial release of the records and/or applicable to records of that type in the record industry shall be reduced in the same proportion as the regular wholesale price was reduced on such sales.

(vii) Notwithstanding anything to the contrary contained in the Royalty Schedule, the royalty rate applicable to records manufactured under this Agreement and sold in Greece, Denmark, Ireland, Italy, Luxembourg, the Netherlands, Germany, the United Kingdom, France, Belgium, Japan, and Australia ("Major Territories") shall be equal to seventy-five percent (75%) of the applicable USA royalty rate specified in the Royalty Schedule for records manufactured under this Agreement and sold in the USA ("Major Territory Rate") subject to all other terms and conditions of this Agreement in connection with the records manufactured hereunder and sold outside the USA and Canada; provided, however, that the escalation provisions applicable to the USA royalty rate as specified in Paragraph 7 (n) hereof shall not be applicable to the Major Territory Rate hereunder.

(viii) Notwithstanding anything to the contrary contained in the Royalty Schedule, the royalty rate applicable to records manufactured under this Agreement and sold outside the USA, Canada, and the Major Territories shall be equal to sixty-five percent (65%) of the applicable USA royalty rate specified in the Royalty Schedule for records manufactured under this Agreement and sold in the USA ("Row Rate") subject to all other terms and conditions of this Agreement in connection with records manufactured hereunder and sold outside the USA and Canada; provided, however, that the escalation provisions applicable to the USA royalty rate as specified in Paragraph 7 (n) hereof shall not be applicable to the Row Rate hereunder.

Commentary: *The computation of royalties for records sold outside the United States and Canada is more intricate and difficult to understand than the accounting for records sold in the United States and Canada. This is for a number of reasons. First, different U.S. record companies have different relationships with their foreign licensees. Some own their foreign licensees; some are owned by their foreign licensees; and others have arms-length arrangements with unrelated licensees.*

The foreign licensing network of several major record companies is a mixture of these three possibilities. Therefore, in many respects the artist will be accounted to in the same manner as the U.S. record company is accounted to.

Second, in many countries "suggested retail list prices" have been abolished and "constructed retail prices" or "dealer prices" (i.e., wholesale prices) are used in lieu thereof as the royalty base price. Third, in many countries value-added taxes are included in the price of the records and must be deducted from those prices to arrive at the royalty base price. Fourth, in many countries there are "transfer" or "withholding" taxes assessed on the amount of royalties to be paid. The amount of these taxes can range from 10% to as high as 50% in some countries. Whether the artist gets the benefit of income tax deductions taken by the U.S. record company, as well as the detriment of having his royalties proportionately reduced by these taxes, can be a substantial issue with respect to a high selling artist.

Additionally, the artist's royalties from foreign sales are subject to currency exchange fluctuations. A detailed analysis of these portions of the agreement is beyond the scope of this treatise, and generally for a new artist the most that can be expected is to secure foreign royalty rates which bear a good relationship to the artist's U.S. royalty rate. Interestingly, the list of "Major Territories" in subclause (vii) above is more inclusive than the list used in most record companies' agreements. Territories most commonly regarded as being major Territories are Germany, France, Holland, United Kingdom, Japan and Australia.

(e) With respect to records sold or distributed as premiums or in connection with the sale or distribution of any other product, commodity or service, the royalty rate shall be fifty percent (50%) of the otherwise applicable royalty rate set forth in the Royalty Schedule hereinabove, and shall be applied to the amount per record actually received by Label, less the container deduction provided for herein, applicable taxes, and shipping and delivery expenses, rather than to the retail selling price.

(f) Royalties applicable to records sold in any territory at prices in excess of "closeout" prices, but less than the normal wholesale price applicable to records of that type in such territory, shall be reduced in the same proportion as the regular wholesale price was reduced on such sales.

(g) The specified percent royalty rate for a given master recorded hereunder embodied on a particular record shall be equal to a fraction of the applicable royalty, the numerator of which is one (1) and the denominator of which is the total number of master recordings (including the master) embodied on said record.

(h) If royalties are not paid to Label by a licensee because the currency of the relevant country is "blocked," Label may elect to accept payment of royalties in the currency of such country, in which case Label will deposit to Lender's credit (and at Lender's expense) in such foreign currency in a depository selected by Label any payments so received as royalties applicable to this Agreement and will notify Lender thereof promptly. Deposit in accordance with the foregoing shall fulfill Label's obligations under this Agreement as to record sales to which such royalty payments are applicable.

(i) It is understood and agreed that Label shall have the right, at its sole option, to calculate royalties payable to Lender on a wholesale basis, in which event the royalty rates at which royalties are payable hereunder shall be adjusted by Label such that, at the time of the adjustment, the royalty, in pennies, payable on a wholesale basis shall equal the royalty, in pennies, otherwise payable hereunder.

(j) Notwithstanding anything to the contrary contained herein, Label shall have no obligation to pay royalties to Lender upon records sold by Label to a person who is licensed to manufacture records outside the USA ("Foreign Associate") utilizing masters owned by Label on which sales Label does not collect a royalty, pressing or other license fee ("Ex Fee Record") until the Foreign Associate sells the Ex Fee Record to its customer; and for royalty computation purposes hereunder the sale of such Ex Fee Record shall be deemed made at the time when and in the country where the Foreign Associate made its sales. The sale to a Foreign Associate of an Ex Fee Record which embodies any Owned Composition (as "Owned Composition" is defined in Paragraph 15 hereof) shall not give rise to an obligation to pay USA mechanical license royalties, but such Ex Fee Record shall be subject to the payment of mechanical license royalties by the Foreign Associate at the rate applicable in the country of sale when and if the Foreign Associate sells the applicable Ex Fee Record to its customer.

(k) Notwithstanding anything to the contrary contained herein, with respect to sales of records hereunder by Label's licensees in Germany, Hungary, Czechoslovakia, Poland, the U.S.S.R., Romania and Bulgaria, Label's obligation to pay royalties to Lender shall be limited to fifty percent (50%) of gross hard currency receipts actually received by Label from Label's applicable licensees with respect to such sales, provided that in no event shall such royalty exceed that which would be payable in the event the other applicable royalty provisions contained in this Agreement applied to such sales.

(l) As to each master recorded hereunder jointly ("Joint Master") with another artist whose compensation for such recording is based on a royalty payable by Label ("Other Royalty

Artist") and as to records that are manufactured therefrom, the applicable royalty rate under any other provision of this Agreement shall be reduced on a prorata basis based upon the total number of Other Royalty Artists participating in the recording of such Joint Master. No Joint Master shall be recorded absent Label's prior written consent.

(m) Notwithstanding anything to the contrary contained in this Agreement, Label agrees to pay Lender in connection with net sales of Compact Discs (as that term is defined in paragraph 15 hereof) distributed hereunder which are manufactured from masters recorded hereunder a royalty ("Compact Disc Royalty") calculated in accordance with and subject to the terms, conditions and provisions contained in this Agreement, provided that such royalty will be the same number of pennies as would be payable if the masters embodied in the Compact Disc were embodied in the corresponding analogue tape-type record.

Commentary: *The royalty rates payable on compact discs are currently a very hot item of negotiations between artists and record companies. Normally, for an album with a suggested retail list price of $8.98, the royalty base price will be approximately $8.08 after deducting a 10% container charge, although many labels will charge a 20% container charge on cassettes. In order to launch a new technology such as compact discs, tremendous start-up costs are involved. These occur not only in the actual development of the technology and manufacturing capacity, but also in marketing and selling the product. Accordingly, in the early 1980's the record companies asked their artists to give them a break in the royalty rates on compact discs until such time as compact discs could establish a substantial market share.*

Different companies did this in slightly different ways, but the formula generally used was to pay the artist the same royalty percentage rate as for a vinyl disc album, but to compute it on the same royalty base price as for a vinyl disc album, as opposed to using the suggested retail list price for the compact disc itself. This was coupled with a "most favored nations" clause in some instances, which provides that if the record company pays any artist in a more favorable way with respect to compact discs, then the particular artist must also be paid in that same more favorable way.

The "start-up period" during which the record company was to get the benefit of reduced royalties on compact discs varied from company to company. In the case of Warner Brothers Records, their agreements with their artists provided that this period would end on June 30, 1986. On July 1, 1986, Warner Brothers began to pay the artist's normal royalty percentage rate based on the actual suggested retail list price of the applicable compact disc, less a 25% "container charge", as opposed to the 10% charge they normally use for disc albums and the 20% charge they normally use for cassettes.

Companies have generally not been designating a suggested retail list price on their compact discs. However, as compact discs have been selling in retail stores for as high as $15.98 it is likely that the suggested retail list price of the compact disc will average $14.98. This price would result in a royalty base price of $11.25, compared to $8.08 for a single disc top line album or $7.18 for the cassette equivalent. Accordingly, the artist's royalties for a compact disc under this formula would be almost 40% higher than the artist's royalty for the equivalent vinyl disc and almost 57% higher than for the equivalent cassette.

According to recent surveys taken by the Recording Industry Association of America, compact disc sales accounted for approximately 33% of total record sales in volume and 45.7% in dollar value. Compact discs are now firmly established in the marketplace and their market share will continue to grow. While it is still unclear whether other record companies will follow

Warner Brothers' example, competition and artist representatives will be putting pressure on them to move to a similar position. However, for the moment, most other record companies are continuing to attempt to get a concession from artists to allow them to continue to pay at a rate that is disproportionately lower for compact discs relative to their retail prices when compared to the retail prices of cassettes. Similar issues most likely will apply to digital audio-tape (DAT), as those mediums are introduced to the consumer market. However, this clause continues to be a very fertile source of negotiations for the next few years, since the impact on the artist's royalty earnings is quite substantial.

(n) Notwithstanding anything to the contrary contained in the Royalty Schedule hereinabove, and with respect to each album, seven inch (7") single, twelve inch (12") single, and mini-lp derived solely from an LP-Master delivered to Label during the term hereof, the royalty rate to be applied to net sales in the USA of Full Price Units (as that term is defined in Paragraph 14 hereof) of each such album, seven inch (7") single, twelve inch (12") single, and mini-lp pursuant to the terms hereof shall be the royalty rate specified in the following Royalty Escalation Schedule:

ROYALTY ESCALATION SCHEDULE

LP-Master	Net USA Sales of Full Price Units		
	0-500,000	500,000- 1,000,000	1,000,000+
1st and 2nd LP-Masters			
Albums	____ %	____ %	____ %
Seven Inch (7") Singles	____ %	____ %	____ %
Twelve Inch (12") Singles	____ %	____ %	____ %
3rd and 4th LP-Masters, if any			
Albums	____ %	____ %	____ %
Seven Inch (7") Singles	____ %	____ %	____ %
Mini-LP's	____ %	____ %	____ %
Twelve Inch (12") singles	____ %	____ %	____ %
5th and 6th LP-Masters, if any			
Albums	____ %	____ %	____ %
Seven Inch (7") Singles	____ %	____ %	____ %
Mini-Lp's	____ %	____ %	____ %
Twelve Inch (12") singles	____ %	____ %	____ %

Commentary: *Royalty escalations are often, although certainly not always, given at these levels of sales. Likewise, sometimes, but not always, it occurs that royalty escalations are tied to the album or contract period of the term. It is unusual for there to be escalations on sales of term. It is unusual for there to be escalations on sales of mini-LP's and 12" singles, as these are generally not high volume sellers. Generally, royalty escalations come 1% or 1/2% at a time. I have intentionally not filled in royalty rates, as I do not wish to imply that any particular royalty rate in normal, standard, average or fair.*

(o) Lender agrees to be solely responsible for accounting to and paying Artist and Producer any and all advances and royalties in connection with masters delivered to Label hereunder.

(p) Notwithstanding anything to the contrary contained herein, royalties for records sold at armed forces post exchanges ("PX Sales") irrespective of where the initial transaction occurs, shall be based upon the published PX retail selling price for such PX Sales in the USA (less all excise, sales use and other similar taxes, however designated, if any, and the applicable container deduction, which deduction shall be computed upon the published PX retail selling price for such records in accordance with the provisions of Paragraph 14 hereof.)

***Commentary**: Royalties on PX sales are often paid at a reduced rate. Here the full rate is used, but it is based upon the published PX retail selling price, which is normally substantially below the suggested retail list price for the same album sold in any normal retail store. However, this may not be fair to the artist, as the record company is generally paid substantially the same wholesale price for records sold to the PX as they are for records sold through other retail stores.*

8. AUDIT PROVISIONS

(a) Label will compute royalties payable hereunder, and shall furnish Lender with a statement thereof, within sixty (60) days after the first day of April and October of each year (or such other semi-annual payment dates as Label may adopt) for the preceding six (6) month period and will pay such royalties, less reserves and any then unrecouped advances or other recoupable payments within sixty (60) days.

(b) Provided that Lender shall have theretofore notified Label in writing of its objections to such statement, specifying with particularity each element of such statement to which objection is made, Lender may, at any time within one (1) year after any royalty statement is due to Lender hereunder, notify Label in writing of Lender's intention to examine the books and records of Label described below with respect to such objections. Such examination shall be commenced at a mutually convenient time and conducted at Lender's sole cost and expense, by an independent certified public accountant designated by Lender who is not then engaged in an outstanding examination of Label's books and records on behalf of a person other than Lender and who certifies (i) that he will conduct such examination in accordance with the then current rules and regulations of the applicable society of Certified Public Accountants, and (ii) that such examination shall be made in accordance with generally accepted accounting principles. Such examination shall be made during Label's usual business hours at the place where Label maintains the books and records which relate to Lender and which are necessary to verify the accuracy of the statement of statements specified in Lender's notice to Label, and Lender's examination shall be limited to the foregoing. Lender's sole right to inspect Label's books and records shall be as set forth in this Paragraph, and Label shall have no obligation to produce such books and records more than once with respect to each statement rendered to Lender nor more than once in any calendar year. Without limiting the generality of the foregoing, Label shall have no obligation to furnish Lender with any books and/or records that do not specifically show sales or gratis distributions of phonograph records as to which royalties may be payable to Lender hereunder. Except with respect to objections made by Lender in accordance with the first sentence of this Paragraph, each royalty statement rendered to lender shall be final, conclusive and binding on Lender and shall constitute an account statement. Lender shall be foreclosed from maintaining any action, claim or proceeding against Label in any forum or tribunal with respect to any statement or accounting due hereunder unless such action, claim or proceeding is commenced against Label in a court of competent jurisdiction within three (3) years after the date of such statement or accounting.

(c) If at the time any royalties would otherwise be payable under this Agreement, there are recoupable payments, charges or advances which have been paid or incurred hereunder but which have not theretofore been recovered from royalties as set forth herein, Label may recoup such payments, charges and/or advances from royalties otherwise payable hereunder prior to paying any royalties hereunder.

Commentary: *Most record companies account and pay royalties on a semi-annual basis, although a few account and pay royalties on a quarterly basis. Generally, the record company will account 60 to 90 days after the close of the accounting period. Each record company has its own unique accounting practices. The information supplied by one record company on its statements may vary tremendously from the information supplied by another record company, particularly as it relates to foreign sales. Very often it is difficult to ascertain anything from the foreign royalty statements other than the net amount of money which the record company claims the artist has earned. However, despite the problems which this may cause an artist who has to account to third parties such as producers, record companies adamantly refuse to specify in the contract what information they will provide and often the information cannot be obtained except on audit.*

Advances paid and charges incurred after the close of a period but before the statement is rendered for that period should not be deducted from that statement, but many contracts, such as this one, would permit the record company to do that. Most record companies will agree to change this, but some absolutely will not.

With respect to audits, companies initially offer artists the right to audit within one year after statements are rendered. Two to three years is more reasonable, since it is simply too expensive to audit every year, and the increased time is generally agreed to Contracts often require specific objection to be made in writing prior to commencing an audit, but as a practical matter it is often impossible to be specific until the auditors have examined the record company's books. Record companies also resist showing the artist's auditors books and records that do not specifically show sales or distributions of free goods, e.g., general ledgers and manufacturing records.

However, it is important that the artist's auditors be able to see these books and records in order to verify the accuracy of the statements rendered. Very often there are substantial quantities of records which simply cannot be accounted for which the record company will claim to have been promotional distributions. This can be a source of very heated negotiations in attempting to conduct and settle an audit.

9. INDIVIDUAL PRODUCER OF MASTERS

Notwithstanding anything to the contrary contained herein, each individual producer of masters hereunder ("Producer") shall be subject to the written approval of Label. Lender shall be solely responsible for the payment of royalties and advances to each Producer of masters hereunder and agrees to indemnify and hold Label harmless from any claims and expenses (including reasonable attorney's fees) arising from Lender's breach or claimed breach of such obligation. In the event Label agrees to pay any royalties and/or advances to a Producer, Label shall reduce Lender's royalty hereunder and the Approved Recording Fund for the applicable LP-Masters by the royalty and advances payable to such producer and by the full amount of all royalties accrued for payment by Label to such Producer. If at the time a particular Producer is paid royalties by Label, any advance or other recoupable payment made by Label hereunder has not been fully recouped by Label from royalties otherwise payable to Lender, then any such royalties paid to such Producer shall be deemed a direct debt from Lender to Label which, in addition to any other rights and remedies available to Label, Label may recover from royalties or any other payments to be made by Label to Lender under this Agreement. Lender shall cause each Producer to sign and deliver to Label a producer's Declaration in the form attached to this Agreement as Exhibit "D" (NOT INCLUDED IN THIS BOOK) prior to utilizing such Producer's services hereunder and Lender shall have no right to utilize any Producer's services absent such executed Producer's Declaration.

Commentary: *One of the most critical creative points in a recording contract is the selection of the individual producer. Most commonly the producer must be mutually approved by the artist and the record company. Certain artists have the clout to designate the producer without the company's approval, and for certain artists the company will demand the right to make the final decision in the event of any disagreement as to who the producer should be. The most difficult stalemates to resolve in this area occur when the artist wishes to self-produce, but the record company wants an outside producer. Self-producing is generally not a viable option for a new recording artist.*

One disadvantage of the "all in" recording contract, such as this one, is that when the record company takes the position that the artist or the Lender, as the case may be, is totally responsible for the payment of royalties and advances to the producer. Whereas the advances are simply deducted from the recording fund for the particular album, and while the royalty rate is simply deducted from the artist's royalty rate, a problem arises when the artist's account is unrecouped, as it usually is. In that case the record company may not agree to pay the producer royalties, but may insist that the artist must pay the royalties to the producer. As a practical matter, this is often impossible for the artist to do. Consequently, the artist's representative must attempt to get the record company to agree to account and pay royalties to the producer when the producer's account is recouped, even though the artist's account is not. Obviously, a producer of stature will not produce a recording artist whose account is substantially unrecouped if he has to rely on that artist to pay him royalties. Producers of stature rightfully insist on getting direct accountings and payments from the record company. If they are not paid, they want to be able to proceed directly against the record company and not against the artist who may be insolvent. Although it is sometimes difficult to get record companies to agree to do this in the contract, once it is time to hire a producer they often have no choice but to do so.

10. MECHANICAL LICENSE PROVISIONS

(a) Lender agrees that with respect to each different selection embodied in a record manufactured from masters recorded hereunder and sold at Label's invoiced price and not returned, Lender shall grant to Label, or cause the publisher(s) to grant to Label, a mechanical license for the USA and Canada at the statutory rate for a musical composition with a playing time of five (5) minutes ("Standard Musical Composition") current at the time any record embodying such selection is first manufactured hereunder ("Statutory Rate"); provided, however, that in no event shall the combined rates for all of the different selections in an album manufactured from one (1) LP-Master exceed the total of ten (10) times the Statutory Rate; and provided further that in no event shall the combined rates for all selections in a single record sold and not returned exceed two (2) times the Statutory Rate; and provided further that in event shall the combined rates for all of the different selections in a mini-lp record sold and not returned exceed three (3) times the Statutory Rate. For purposes of computing mechanical royalties hereunder, different versions of a musical composition, including without limitation vocal versions, instrumental versions, remixed, re-edited, and/or re-arranged versions, and versions of different durations shall nevertheless be deemed to be the same selection. Notwithstanding the foregoing, if a particular selection recorded hereunder is embodied more than once in a particular record, Label shall pay mechanical royalties in connection therewith at the Statutory Rate as though the selection was embodied therein only once.

(b) Notwithstanding anything to the contrary contained in Paragraph 10 (a) above, the following provisions shall apply with respect to each Owned Composition (as defined in Paragraph 15 hereof) embodied in a record sold at Label's invoiced price and not returned: Lender shall grant or cause the applicable publisher(s) thereof to grant to Label a mechanical license for the USA for each different Owned Composition embodied in such record at seventy-five percent (75%) of the Statutory Rate; and with respect to mechanical licenses for Canada, Lender shall grant or cause the publisher thereof to grant to Label a mechanical license for Canada at the minimum statutory rate required by the laws of the Commonwealth of Canada; provided, however, that in no event shall Label be obligated to pay for a mechanical license in Canada in excess of an amount equal to seventy-five percent (75%) of the Statutory Rate in the USA. Label shall pay mechanical royalties only for selections embodied in records sold at Label's invoiced price and not returned.

(c) Lender agrees to indemnify and hold Label harmless from rates in excess of the applicable amounts specified in Paragraphs 10 (a) and 10 (b). If Label pays any such excess, such payments shall be a direct debt from Lender to Label which Label may recover from royalties or any other payments to be made by Label to Lender pursuant to this Agreement.

> ***Commentary***: *Since the minimum statutory mechanical royalty rate payable under the compulsory license provisions of the United States Copyright laws increased from 2-3/4¢ prior to 1986 to (as of January 1, 1990) 5.7¢ for songs of 5 minutes or less, and 1.1¢ per minute for songs greater than 5 minutes, mechanical royalty provisions have been among the most hotly debated provisions in recording contracts. Further, as of January 1, 1992, 1994, and 1996, the rates automatically will increase based on the U.S. Consumer Price Index. After that, Congress is required to re-examine whether to adjust the mechanical rate up or down, or to stabilize it.*

As of this date it is virtually impossible for any new artist to sign with any record company unless the artist agrees to give the record company a 3/4 rate on "Controlled Compositions." Moreover, some record companies will break off negotiations with even a well-established artist who will not grant them a 3/4 rate on Controlled Compositions. The definition of a "Controlled Composition" can also be a hotly debated matter. Most record companies insist that if any song is written in whole or in part by any member of the artist, the entire song is a Controlled Composition. If, therefore, a song is written 50% by a member of artist and 50% by an outside writer, and if the outside writer insists on being paid at the statutory rate, as he usually will, the artist may find himself reduced to a one-half rate (i.e., 5.7¢ x 3/4 = 4.275¢ - 2.85¢ = 1.425¢). Also, many companies insist that all compositions written in whole or in part by the producer are Controlled Compositions.

Record companies also insist on maximum rates for albums and singles. In this contract, the requested maximum is 10 times the minimum statutory rate for an album and 2 times the minimum statutory rate for a single. These are reasonable maximums.

However, if companies insist on a 3/4 rate from the individual producers or from everyone, as some companies do, the artist must bear out of his royalties or out of his pocket the extra 25% payable to any producer or outside writer who will not agree to the 3/4 rate. This can result in a tremendous reduction in the artist's royalties and may be deducted out of the next advance payable to the artist. Accordingly, it is economically not feasible for the artist to deliver an album containing more than 10 tracks.

Keep in mind that medleys are treated by the record company as being one composition, but are treated by outside publishers and under the copyright laws as being however many compositions are actually used in the medley, regardless of the duration of each segment. The full statutory rate is payable for each different composition used in the medley, even if only for a few seconds, unless a reduced rate is agreed between the publisher and the record company. There can be no assurance that such an agreement will be reached. Accordingly, medleys are a potential financial disaster for both the artist and the record company. This is why many contracts will require the record company's approval in advance of recording any proposed medley.

This agreement also addresses the problem raised by multiple versions of the same song being embodied on a record. Most commonly this happens on 12" singles. While the record company's position that all versions constitute one use may have some merit, it would seem fair that all the so-called "long-song" statutory rate (currently 1.1 cents per minute of playing time, or portion thereof) rather than at the minimum statutory rate.

Another important area for negotiation is payment of mechanical royalties on "free goods." Nearly all new artist's contracts will state that the record company does not pay on any records for which royalties are not payable. However, most record companies will agree to pay mechanical royalties on 50%, or if the artist has clout, 100% of album free goods and, if the artist has clout, on 50% or more of singles free goods. Additionally, some record companies will attempt to get a reduced rate, i.e., 1/2 or 3/4 on records sold other than through normal retail channels, e.g., midpriced, budget, record club, premiums, etc.

Patrick Moraz, composing his Star Peace Symphony on his Macintosh midi-based Kurzweil and Korg Synthesizer systems. Photo by Linda Sullivan.

11. AUDIOVISUAL

From time to time during the term hereof, at Label's request, Lender shall cause Artist to perform at sessions for the purposes of embodying Artist's performances on videotape and/or film ("Tapes").

(a) Label and Lender hereby agree to the production of one (1) Tape in connection with the first (1st) album released hereunder during the term of this Agreement. The budget for said Tape shall not exceed ________Dollars ($________). Thereafter, the production of any other Tape will be at the sole election of Label. Label and Lender hereby agree that all Tapes produced hereunder shall be subject to the terms and conditions of this Paragraph 11.

(b) Lender agrees that Label is the sole, exclusive and perpetual owner of the Tapes from inception including, but not limited to, the sole, exclusive and perpetual owner of all copyrights of any nature whatsoever in and to the Tapes.

(c) Lender consents to the exhibition and exploitation of the Tapes by Label and its licensees for such purposes, at such times and places, and in such media as determined by Label and its licensees.

(d) (i) Lender agrees that Label and its licensees shall have the right to use all Owned Compositions embodied in Tapes with no further payment for the use of such Owned Compositions, provided that in the event that any Owned Composition is embodied on videograms distributed to the home video market, Label shall pay a mechanical royalty equal to four percent (4%) of the distributor price for each videogram actually sold in the USA and Canada by companies wholly-owned by Label and a royalty of twelve and one-half (12-1/2%) of Label's net receipts on each videogram actually sold or rented in the USA and Canada by any Lender. With respect to all sales of videograms outside the USA and Canada, a royalty will be negotiated in good faith between Label's licensees and the applicable subpublisher or mechanical rights collecting society in the particular country.

(ii) Lender agrees to use its best efforts to cause the publisher of any non-Owned Composition embodied in a Tape hereunder to grant synchronization licenses at the rates specified in Paragraph 11 (d) (i).

(iii) Lender agrees to hold Label harmless from rates in excess of those specified in this Paragraph 11 (d). If Label pays any such excess, such excess payments shall be a direct debt from Lender to Label which, in addition to any other remedies Label may have, Label may recover from royalties and/or any other payments to be made by Label to Lender.

(e) (i) With respect to the commercial exploitation of the Tapes by means of theatrical distribution, nontheatrical distribution (as that term is defined below), on television (including free, pay, subscription, cable and CATV) and any other commercial exploitation of the Tapes with the exception of the types of exploitation of the Tapes specified in Paragraph 11 (g) hereinbelow, Label agrees to pay Lender fifty percent (50%) of Label's adjusted gross receipts (as that term is defined below).

(ii) With respect to the exploitation of the Tapes, or any portion thereof, in generic television commercials (as defined herein), Label agrees to pay to Lender twenty-five percent (25%) of Label's net revenues from such exploitation of the Tapes. The words "generic television commercial(s)" as used herein, shall mean advertisements for radio stations, on television, using visual and/or audiovisual portions of the Tapes.

(f) In the event that any Tapes are combined with older tapes to create a videotape program ("Program"), all payments arising from the distribution and/or exploitation of the Tapes included in the Program (including, without limitation, payments to Lender, publishers of all selections embodied on the Tapes, video directors and audio producers) shall be calculated and paid from a pro-rata share of Label's adjusted gross receipts from the Program ("Tape Share"). The Tape Share shall be determined by multiplying Label's adjusted gross receipts from the Program by a fraction the numerator of which shall be the playing time of the Tapes and the denominator of which shall be the aggregate playing time of the portion of the Program, inclusive of the Tapes.

(g) In the event that Label embodies any Tape(s) produced hereunder on videograms distributed to the home video market, Lender shall be paid a royalty of ten percent (10%) of the distributor price (less taxes) on sales of each videogram by Label companies and fifty percent (50%) of Label's net receipts from sales and rentals of such videograms by non-Label companies.

(h) Label shall reduce Lender's royalty arising from the distribution of videograms and all other forms of exploitation of the Tapes the amount of all royalties paid to third parties in connection with the distribution of videograms and all other forms of exploitation of the Tapes, including, without limitation, audio producers, video directors, publishers and unions (or a reasonable reserve with respect thereto).

(i) No royalties shall be payable to Lender with respect to Tapes produced hereunder until such time as Lender's Liability Share (as hereafter defined) has been fully recouped pursuant to Paragraph 11 (m) hereinbelow.

(j) Except as otherwise expressly set forth to the contrary in this Paragraph 11, Label's manufacture, distribution, sale, advertising, promotion, marketing and other exploitation of the Tapes and records derived therefrom shall at all times be subject to all of the other terms and conditions contained in this Agreement. Label shall have the right to embody Tapes produced hereunder with videotapes embodying the performances of other artists.

(k) In connection with the Tapes, Label's sole royalty obligation to Lender is to make the payments specified in this Paragraph 11.

(l) For purposes of this Paragraph 11 the term "commercial exploitation" shall mean those uses of the Tapes for which Label receives money which is allocated or is reasonably allocable to the Tapes produced hereunder, with the exception of the use provided for in Paragraph 11 (g) hereof.

(m) Notwithstanding anything in the foregoing to the contrary Label shall create an account ("Tape Account") which shall be (1) credited with all sums payable to Lender pursuant to this

Paragraph 11 in connection with Label's exploitation of the Tapes ("Lender's Revenue Share"); and (2) debited with one hundred percent (100%) of all Production Costs (as hereinafter defined) in connection with the Tapes ("Lender's Liability Share"). Lender's Liability Share shall be fully recoupable from Lender's Revenue Share. To the extent that Lender's Liability Share is not recouped from Lender's Revenue Share, one hundred percent (100%) of Lender's Liability Share shall be recoupable from Lender's audio record royalty account hereunder.

(n) The words "nontheatrical distribution" shall mean any use of the Tapes on airlines, ships at sea, or in institutions, churches, etc., but shall specifically exclude the types of exploitation of the Tapes specified in Paragraph 11 (g) hereof.

(o) The words "adjusted gross receipts" shall mean Label's gross receipts relating to the exploitation of the Tapes with the exception of the exploitation set forth in Paragraph 11 (g) hereof less (1) a distribution fee equal to thirty-five percent (35%) of Label's gross receipts from such exploitation of the Tapes; or if higher, the distribution fee charged Label by a subdistributor plus ten percent (10%).

(p) The words "gross receipts" shall mean all sums received by Label in connection with the exploitation of the Tape (with the exception of the exploitation as specified in Paragraph 11 (g) after deducting any taxes paid or payable arising from the aforesaid exploitation of the Tape.

(q) The words "net receipts" shall mean all sums received by Label from non-Label companies in connection with the distribution of videograms to the home video market.

(r) Label shall have the right to charge as a Production Cost, interest on unrecouped Production Costs incurred and/or paid by Label hereunder, which interest shall be (i) deemed to be a Production Cost in connection with the Tape; (ii) recoupable by Label from royalties otherwise payable to Lender hereunder; and (iii) computed for each accounting period and calculated at one percent above the prime bank lending rate of the Hollywood Main Office of the Bank of America in effect on the last day of such production accounting period.

(s) For the purpose of this Paragraph 11 Production Costs shall be deemed to include all costs incurred and/or paid by Label in connection with the production of the Tape(s) including but not limited to (i) video master tape duplication costs; (ii) broadcast system transfer charges; (iii) shipping and freight charges; (iv) synchronization fees paid to publishers of selections embodied on the Tape(s); (v) assemblage costs; (vi) artwork costs; and (vii) all other payments to third parties, exclusive of those payments specified in Paragraph 11 (h) hereof.

(t) The word "videogram" shall mean videotape cassettes, videodiscs or similar or future devices on which the Tape(s) may be replicated for the Home Video Market as defined hereinafter.

(u) The words "Home Video Market" shall mean the sale, lease or rental of videograms to individuals for private viewing the home, and not for viewing at a place open to the public or any place where a substantial number of persons outside the social circle of the family or its acquaintances is gathered, or where admission charge is made, or for viewing beyond the immediate place of exhibition, or for viewing over any television broadcast or transmission system.

(v) In the event that videograms embodying Tapes are (i) distributed through record clubs owned and/or controlled by Label companies; or (ii) embodied on budget videograms distributed by Label companies; or (iii) embodied on EP videograms distributed by Label companies; or (iv) distributed by companies through special markets plans, the otherwise applicable royalty rates arising from the distribution of videograms embodying Tapes by Label companies shall be reduced by one-half (1/2).

(w) For the purpose of this agreement the words "budget videogram" shall mean those bearing a retail selling price at the date of release of seventy-five percent (75%) or less of the then current retail selling price for the substantial number of top line videograms in that category.

(x) For purposes of this Agreement the words "EP videogram" shall mean a videogram embodying thereon not less than three (3) nor more than five (5) selections.

Commentary: *Everyone knows what a profound impact videos have had on pop music over the last five years. They have had an equally great impact on the difficulty of negotiating recording contracts. For years record companies and artists had acknowledged the unpredictability of this area and had generally agreed to "freeze" the situation by providing that while "audiovisual devices" were defined to be "records," they would not be exploited by either party without the other party's consent.*

No longer are there such simple solutions. Some companies' contracts take up to 20 pages just for the audiovisual provisions; others with presumably no less strong a belief in the power of videos handle them in 2 or 3 paragraphs. This particular contract form falls in the middle. Nevertheless it is so intricate that careful analysis might leave the reader unable to see the forest for the trees. Accordingly, let me discuss the basic considerations of record companies and artists with respect to videos.

First, videos cost a tremendous amount of money. The average cost of a video released by a major record company in 1990 was at least $75,000.00. The average cost of the underlying master sound recording would be less than 1/3 that amount. It is not uncommon for a single video to cost in the hundreds of thousands of dollars. Who pays the cost? Generally, as with sound recordings, the record company will initially pay the production costs. Accordingly, there must be an approved budget. Generally, the first draft recording contract will provide that the artist should be responsible for overbudget costs, but most record companies will limit the artist's responsibility to costs incurred due to the artist's negligence or fault or due to matters within the artist's control or the like. This is critical, because budget overruns on videos can be astronomical. Equally important, however, the artist must assure that the written contract with the production company engaged to produce the video provides that the production company will be liable for all cost overruns on the project. If the record company insists on holding the artist liable for excess costs, the artist should insist on entering into a contract with the production company, so that the artist can contractually shift this risk to the production company.

Sometimes the artist wants a more expensive video than the record company is willing to finance. In such a case the record company may agree to pay up to a certain amount and the artist must pay the rest. This must be taken into account in determining how the recoupment of production costs is to be implemented, as well as the split of income derived from the video.

Second, because costs of videos are so high, record companies insist on their right to recoup the costs of the video from all sources. However, despite some notable commercial successes, most videos do not generate nearly enough money to recoup their production costs. They serve as promotional vehicles primarily, not as expected sources of profits. Accordingly, artists have always felt that at least some portion of their costs should be treated as non-recoupable, in the same way that other promotional expenditures made by the record company are not recouped from the artist's royalties. The almost universally accepted basic recoupment formula is that 50% of the record company's expense for production costs is recoupable out of the artist's record royalties and whatever is not recouped out of the artist's record royalties may be recouped out of receipts from the exploitation of the video.

The manner in which receipts from the exploitation from the video are applied to recoupment of recording costs and, assuming recoupment occurs, the manner in which the excess monies are split between the artist and the record company are subject to variation. I have often taken the position that gross receipts from exploitation of the video should be applied 100% to recoup the production costs of the video and, once recouped, the artist and record company should split the excess 50% to each. However, record companies do hire people to administer the creation, marketing and distribution of promotional videos, and many record companies feel they are entitled to recoup such "distribution expenses" off the top before receipts are applied to recoupment of production costs.

The recoupment of distribution expenses is a concept borrowed from the motion picture industry, which is not surprising, since the video is, by definition, a melding of a phonograph record and a motion picture. Some companies may, therefore, take the right to recoup their out-of-pocket "distribution expenses" or "transaction costs" in servicing television stations, clubs, etc. with promotional videos and/or take a "distribution fee," i.e., a percentage of gross receipts, usually from 15 to 35%, to cover their overhead.

Some companies, not surprisingly, do not agree with my approach to the recoupment of production costs and, instead, insist that only the artist's 50% share of net receipts, after distribution fees and expenses have been taken off the top, and after the record company has put the other 50% in its pocket, should be applied to recoup production costs. This means that the artist will be required to recoup the entire production costs of the video out of the artist's own share of video receipts. This has some logical support in that the entire cost of making the sound recording is recouped only from the artist's royalties, not from the gross receipts of the record company. However, the practical effect is that the artist's "video account" may never recoup. Should this be a big concern for the artist? Probably not, at least until such time as the artist begins to sell substantial quantities of "videograms."

The third basic aspect of video royalty provisions for the artist to understand is that the revenue to be derived from them by an artist is not very great compared to revenue from records. It is only quite recently that record companies have begun to receive payments from MTV and some other users of videos for the rights conveyed to them to broadcast the videos. Some record companies still do not command such payments. In the case of major record companies who have entered into agreements with MTV giving MTV exclusive premiers of their videos, the sums payable by MTV in respect of the catalog can be quite substantial. However, it is as yet unclear whether any substantial sums will trickle down to popular video artists on these labels. Most record companies now are refusing to allow the artist to share in video revenues generated from any "promotional" uses of their videos, which generally means all broadcast uses and sometimes means all uses other than on "videograms" (i.e., videodisc and videocassettes) sold to the public. The reason is that revenues from "promotional uses" are relatively small and the administrative costs, as well as the costs of producing all of those videos, are very high. Royalties from the sale of videograms can be substantial if the artist has produced an entire "video album" or "video EP."

While sales of these programs are, on the average, a small percentage of what the equivalent record album would sell, prices have been decreasing, sales of hardware have been increasing, and sales volume of these type of programs have been increasing significantly. By far the largest number of these kinds of programs on the market are "live," "in-concert" video programs and compilation videos consisting of a number of videos produced initially for promotional purposes. Often the live or in-concert videos are produced initially for pay television at the expense of a company such as HBO, with the artist being given the rights to sell videograms of the program without any participation by HBO in the proceeds. However, if the artist has entered into a recording contract such as this one, the company, and the record company's consent will be required before the program can be released as a videogram. Since the "live," in-concert program will not have been produced at the record company's expense, the artist should be able to strike a deal with the record company whereby the record company gets a reasonable percentage of the artist's revenues from the sale of videograms and the artist gets the remainder free and clear of any unrecouped balance in his recording contract. However, the record company may insist that the entire artist's share of revenue be applied to the artist's royalty account in order to first recoup any unrecouped balance. Accordingly, whenever an artist plans to do a video recording of a live concert, his representative should negotiate up front with the record company to sort out all of these considerations.

If the record company accumulates enough videos of the artist to compile a video album or EP, royalties will be computed in the manner set forth in the agreement and applied to the artist's account. Given the high cost of producing videos, sales of these videograms will have to be quite high before the artist's video account is likely to be recouped. Even then, if excess royalties from the video account merely spill over into the record royalty account, rather than being paid directly to the artist, there is even less likelihood that the artist will get these royalties in hand. However, if the artist's video royalty account is recouped, the artist's record royalty account will probably also be recouped, in which case the monies would flow out immediately to the artist.

Recently there have been indications that record companies may be reevaluating their belief in videos as a cost effective marketing tool, primarily because of the extraordinarily high cost of production. It is truly in the best interests of both the artist and the record company to cooperate in keeping these production costs to a minimum.

12. PERSONAL APPEARANCES

(a) From time to time at Label's request, Lender shall cause Artist to: (a) appear for photography, artwork and similar reasons under the direction of Label or its duly authorized agent; (b) appear for interviews with such representatives of newspapers, magazines and other publications, and of publicity and public relations firms as Label may arrange; (c) confer and consult with Label regarding Artist's performances hereunder and other matters which may concern the parties hereto. Lender shall also, if requested by Label, cause Artist to be available for personal appearances on radio and television and elsewhere, and to record taped interviews, spot announcements, trailers and electrical transcriptions, all for the purpose of advertising, promoting, publicizing and exploiting records hereunder and for other general public relations and promotional purposes related to the record business of Label or its subsidiary and related companies. Neither Lender nor Artist shall be entitled to any compensation from Label for such services, other than minimum union scale to Artist if such payment is required by applicable agreements.

(b) Label may recover from all royalties otherwise payable to Lender all costs incurred or paid by Label in connection with the following: tours, personal appearances, television appearances or other performances by Artist including, but not limited to, agency fees, costs of transportation, costs of accommodations, instrument rental, costumes and other costs related to such appearances.

> ***Commentary:*** *It is customary for the record company to require the artist to cooperate in publicity and promotional appearances. Normally the record company will agree to pay any out-of-pocket costs incurred by the artist in making these promotional appearances and paragraph (b) needs to be clarified to provide that a company will pay and not recoup these expenses when the appearances are made at the company's request primarily for promotional purposes.*

13. OTHER TERMINATION RIGHTS

(a) If Artist's ability to perform as vocalists or musicians should be materially impaired, or if Lender or Artist should fail, refuse or neglect to comply with any of their respective obligations hereunder, then, and in addition to any other rights or remedies which Label may have, Label may elect to terminate this Agreement by notice in writing and shall thereby be relieved of any liability in connection with undelivered masters.

(b) No termination of this Agreement (whether by Lender or by Label) shall in any way limit or curtail any of Label's rights, title, interest or privileges to or in connection with any of the results and proceeds of Lender's and/or Artist's endeavors under this Agreement or any rights or privileges of Label which continue after the term of this Agreement ends.

> ***Commentary:*** *The record company's rights to terminate the contract under any circumstances obviously must be carefully reviewed. In general, the artist should always be given a certain period of time in which to cure any cause for termination, whether for failure to timely deliver an album, for other breach of contract or reasons beyond the artist's control. Usually the cure period allowed is 30 days, but for failure to deliver an album, 60 or 90 days is more realistic.*

14. DEFINITIONS

(a) The word "selection" means a single musical work (including a medley), story, poem or similar work, irrespective of length.

(b) The word "master" means any original recording of a selection not theretofore recorded by Artist which is commercially acceptable to Label for the manufacture and sale of records and which embodies a performance by Artist of a selection approved by Label. Masters shall not contain selections designed to appeal to a specialized or limited market including, but not limited to, gospel, Christmas and/or children's music. Further, Artist's performances on masters hereunder shall be of the same quality and style as those recordings of Artist which originally induced Label to enter into this Agreement with Lender for the services of Artist. The word "master" includes the original recording and all derivatives therefrom, including, without limitation, mix-down tapes and lacquer masters produced therefrom. There shall be no so called "live" recording hereunder in the absence of Label's consent.

(c) The noun "record" means any device by which sound may be recorded for later transmission to listeners, whether now known or unknown and howsoever used, whether embodying sound alone or synchronized with or accompanied by visual images. The noun "record" does not include a "master" as defined above.

> ***Commentary:*** *Always remember that "records" are now defined to include audiovisual devices. It is almost always futile to attempt to limit the definition of records to those embodying sound alone, even if the record company will not agree to make a commitment to produce a video.*

(d) The words "tape record" mean a record recorded on magnetic tape, whether reel-to-reel, continuous loop or otherwise.

(e) The term "lp-disc" means a 12 inch, 33-1/3 rpm, long playing disc-type record or its tape equivalent, embodying thereon not less than eight (8) selections and not more than twelve (12) selections.

(f) The term "LP-Master" means a set of masters sufficient to constitute a lp-disc.

(g) The word "album" means one (1) or more lp-discs released in one (1) package, or the tape record or compact disc equivalent thereof.

(h) The words "single record" or "single" mean a disc-type record, regardless of size or playing speed embodying therein not more than two (2) different selections, or the tape record equivalent thereof.

(i) The words "seven-inch single record" or "seven-inch single" mean a 7", 45 rpm, disc-type record, embodying not more than two (2) different selections, or the tape record equivalent thereof.

(j) The words "twelve-inch single record" or "twelve-inch single" shall mean a 12", 33-1/3 rpm, disc-type record embodying not more than two (2) different selections or the tape record equivalent thereof.

(k) The words "mini-lp" shall mean a 12-inch, 33-1/3 rpm, long-playing disc-type record or the tape equivalent thereof, embodying therein not less than three (3) selections and not more than five (5) selections.

(l) The words "mini-lp master" means a set of masters sufficient to constitute a mini-lp.

(m) The term "Compact Disc" shall mean a 120mm. diameter (or such other size) disc record primarily reproducing sound (whether or not together with visual images), the signals of which are read and transmitted from such disc by means of laser, such disc being commercially suitable in the opinion of Label for release to the public.

(n) The words "budget line record" mean a record which bears a retail selling price at the date of release of three-quarters (3/4) or less of the then current retail selling price for the substantial number of top line records in that particular category.

(o) The term "Owned Composition" shall mean each musical composition that is written by Artist in whole or in part, or owned or controlled, directly or indirectly, by Lender and/or Artist in whole or in part, or by a publishing Lender owned or controlled by Lender and/or Artist directly or indirectly, in whole or in part.

> ***Commentary:*** *As mentioned above, it is important to attempt to get the definition of "Owned Compositions" also known as "Controlled Compositions" to be limited to the part actually written or owned by the artist and to exclude the part written by an outside writer. If this is not done, the artist's own rate will be liable to be reduced below the agreed-upon basic rate, even if that is a 3/4 rate. This record company does not include compositions written or owned by the individual producer as "Owned Compositions," which is merciful to the artist.*

(p) The word "royalties" as used in this Agreement include only royalties payable under this Agreement.

(q) The word "person" means a person, firm, association or corporation.

(r) The letters "USA" mean the United States of America, its territories and possessions.

(s) The word "Territory" shall mean the universe, including without limitation, the Solar System.

(t) The term "Major Territories" shall mean Greece, Denmark, Ireland, Italy, Luxemburg, the Netherlands, Germany, the United Kingdom, France and Belgium, Japan, and Australia.

> ***Commentary:*** *This is an expansive list of major territories. Generally, Greece, Denmark and Ireland are not considered major territories. Italy is sometimes considered a major territory, but not usually. Holland (the Netherlands) is generally regarded as a major territory, but Belgium and Luxembourg often are not; it is beneficial to the artist to lump them together under the common name "Benelux" and request that sales in those territories be paid at the major territories' rate.*

(u) The phrase "net sales of records" shall refer, in the case of sales by Label, to eighty-five percent (85%) of the aggregate number of records sold for which Label has been paid or credited, in each applicable royalty category, after deducting returns, rebates and credits on records returned in each royalty category; or, in the case of sales by Label's licensees, to the same quantity of records for which Label is paid or credited.

(v) (i) The phrase "retail selling price" shall be deemed to mean the retail selling price, as defined in Paragraph 15 v (ii) below, less all taxes and a container deduction equal to twelve and one-half percent (12-1/2%) of the retail list price for albums in a single-fold cover, mini-LPs, twelve-inch (12") singles and seven-inch (7") singles in other than standard sleeves;

seventeen percent (17%) for albums in a double-fold cover or including a special insert; and twenty percent (20%) for tape records and compact discs.

Commentary: *This paragraph sets forth the record company's "container charges" or "packaging deductions." These vary slightly from company to company. The higher the charge, the lower the artist's net royalty will be. Whereas this company's deductions are 12 1/2%/17%/20%, the most common formulation is 10%/15%/29%. These charges are largely arbitrary, because while the charge for a cassette is twice that for a normal vinyl disc package, the cost of producing a cassette is less than the cost to produce an ordinary vinyl disc. However, record companies refuse to negotiate their packaging deductions, except that if an artist has clout, the company may agree to "pass through" their own lower charges on foreign sales. To the extent that the record company is basing its compact disc royalty rate on the vinyl disc rate, the corresponding packaging deduction should only be the vinyl disc deduction not the higher deduction applicable to tapes.*

(ii) The words "retail selling price" shall mean (A) the retail price suggested by the manufacturer in the USA for records sold in the USA; (B) the retail price suggested by the manufacturer in Canada for the records sold in Canada; and (C) in countries outside the USA and Canada, the retail price suggested either by the manufacturer in the country of manufacture or by the seller in the country of sale, depending upon which such price Label's reporting licensee utilizes in computing record royalties payable to Label.

(iii) Notwithstanding the foregoing, if, at the end of a period for which royalties are being computed hereunder, no retail price for the particular record is suggested or recommended by the manufacturer in the relevant country, then for royalty accounting purposes hereunder with respect to that country the basis upon which royalty computations shall be made ("Base"), shall be determined by the method then in general use in the phonograph record industry in that country for arriving at a Base such as (A) utilizing the retail price agreed upon by the phonograph record industry generally and the local mechanical rights society for copyright accounting purposes; (B) determining the prices at which various classes of phonograph records are customarily available to purchasers through retail outlets in that country by means of an averaging or sampling of data gathered through a survey undertaken by or for the phonograph record industry; or (C) applying a percentage retail markup to the wholesale prices for various classes of records established by a similar process. If at that time no method is in general use in the phonograph record industry in that country for arriving at a Base, then Label or its applicable licensee will establish the Base by use of one of the methods described in the preceding sentence but applied only to such licensee's own various classes of Label's phonograph records and not on an industry-wide basis. From the Base as determined above, there shall be deducted such sales or other taxes levied on sales as are recovered directly or indirectly as part of the selling price and the appropriate container deduction provided for elsewhere in this Agreement unless in the determination of the Base those deductions were previously made. In no event shall the Base for sales by the applicable licensee of Label in a given country be lower than the Base utilized by such licensee in that country in accounting for fees payable to Label.

(iv) Notwithstanding the foregoing to the contrary, if with respect to sales in any territory other than the USA and Canada, Label is paid by its licensee on the basis of the so-called "base price to dealer" instead of the retail selling price, Label shall compute that percentage of the "base price to dealer" which, in the currency of such territory, equals the monetary amount otherwise payable hereunder based on the retail price ("B.P.D. Rate"). Label shall notify Lender in writing of the B.P.D. Rate based upon the "base price to dealer" (less all applicable taxes) in the territory of sale, instead of at the rate set forth in the Royalty Schedule based upon retail selling price. Royalties payable at the B.P.D. Rate shall be subject to all other terms and provisions of this Agreement.

Commentary: *As mentioned above, the definition of "retail selling price" is relatively simple with respect to the United States. Outside of the United States, it has been the subject of significant changes over the last decade.*

Due to the time lag in accounting for foreign sales, the infrequency of auditing, and the record companies' refusal to allow auditors to audit their foreign licensees, it is only now becoming clear that foreign royalty base prices must be carefully analyzed in order to assure that the artist is getting a "fair" royalty rate, i.e. the royalty rate he bargained for. Clause (iii) above basically says that if the suggested retail list price has been abandoned in a territory, the price generally in use in such territory as the retail price will be substituted. Generally this is the price agreed upon by representatives of the record industry and the local mechanical rights society. It is generally computed by applying an agreed upon percentage factor to the dealer price referred to in clause (iv) as the "base price to dealer" or B.P.D. Rate to increase it to a retail price level. In some territories this factoring process has been eliminated entirely and instead the mechanical rights societies are now paid a higher percentage of the B.P.D. Rate than they were paid previously.

If the artist were to be paid the same royalty percentage rate on the B.P.D. Rate that they were paid on the suggested retail list price or the "constructed retail price," the artist will obviously suffer a substantial reduction in the effective royalty. Clause (iv) seems to provide that when the artist's agreed upon royalty rate for the territory is based upon the B.P.D. Rate, the artist's agreed upon royalty rate will be increased by a factor which will result in the same monetary amount being paid to the artist as before the B.P.D. Rate went into effect.

This should be clarified, and the artist should request the record company to supply a schedule setting forth the royalty base prices and any adjusting factors in each of the major territories, along with the common prices for albums and singles in those territories and the net amount of the artist's royalty calculated in the local currency. Only if this is done will the artist know what effective royalty he can expect to receive, subject to currency fluctuations, which are, or course, beyond the control of both the artist and the record company.

(w) The words "special markets plan" mean a marketing plan designed for ultimate distribution of all types of records to consumers through such methods including, but not limited to, methods commonly known in the recording industry as "direct mail to consumers" and "key outlet marketing." Distribution of records on top-line or budget-line through usual channels of distribution, or through a record club distribution plan and/or as premiums are hereby excluded from the foregoing definition.

(x) The words "Full Price Units" shall mean records (in specified configurations) sold through Label's (or, if outside the USA, Label's licensee's) normal channels of retail distribution in the designated territory, and shall specifically exclude sales (a) through a record club distribution plan or special markets plan (b) to wholesalers solely for export to customers outside the designated territory, (c) of budget-line and mid-line records, (d) of premium records and (e) to military post exchanges.

15. SPECIAL RECORDING GROUP PROVISIONS

(a) If any member of Artist refuses, neglects or fails to perform with the other member(s) of Artist hereunder, Label may, by notice in writing to Lender, terminate the term of this Agreement, or the engagement of the member of Artist who so refuses, neglects or fails to perform. Further, upon the mutual Agreement of Label and Lender, Lender shall have the right to terminate the engagement of any member(s) of Artist during the term hereof. If the term of this Agreement is not terminated entirely as aforesaid, (i) the member of Artist whose engagement is terminated shall not use the Artist's professional name in any commercial or artistic endeavor; (ii) Artist's professional name shall be and remain the property of the member(s) of Artist whose engagement is not terminated; and (iii) any person(s) engaged to replace the member of Artist whose engagement is terminated shall be mutually agreed upon by Label and Lender and if such agreement cannot be reached, Label may thereafter terminate the term of this Agreement by notice in writing to Lender.

(b) No changes in the members of Artist may be made without Label's prior written consent. If any such change is made, the member of Artist released shall be subject to the restrictions specified in items (i) and (ii) of Paragraph 15 (a) above. If any such change is made without Label's consent, Label may terminate this Agreement upon written notice to Lender and thereby be relieved of any liability in connection with undelivered masters.

(c) If any member ceases to be a member of Artist ("Leaving Member") then in addition to all of its other rights and remedies, Label may, by notice in writing to Lender at any time within sixty (60) days following the date Label consented in writing to such Leaving Member ceasing to be a member of Artist, elect to require said Leaving Member to record for Label individually upon the same terms and conditions set forth in this Agreement (as such terms may be or have been suspended or renewed) relating to Artist, including without limitation the remaining minimum number of LP-Masters required to be recorded, and the royalty rates payable with respect to net sales of records derived from such LP-Masters; provided, however, that (i) Artist shall record the first LP-Master embodying the solo Performances of the Leaving Member upon all of the terms and conditions that are applicable to the first LP-Master in the Initial Period hereunder; (ii) advances shall not exceed $5,000.00 for each applicable LP-Master by any Leaving Member(s); (iii) the recording of any and all LP-Masters subsequent to the Leaving Member's first LP-Master shall be at Label's sole option; (iv) Label shall have the right to select the individual Producer of masters to be recorded by the Leaving Member; and (v) Label shall establish a separate account with respect to records manufactured from masters embodying the performances of the Leaving Member from and after the date such Leaving Member commenced recording pursuant to this Paragraph 15 (c) and such account shall be cross-collateralized on a pro-rata basis with the royalty account relating to Artist hereunder and vice versa. Label shall have all of the rights set forth above in this Paragraph with respect to any and all Leaving Members, with the further right to record two (2) or more Leaving Members as a new group.

(d) If any member of Artist ceases to be a member of Artist, such member shall continue to look solely to Lender for payment of all applicable royalties and/or fees.

Commentary: *See the chapter entitled "Group Breakups" by Peter T. Paterno.*

16. RELEASE

(a) Provided that Lender and Artist are not then in breach of any of their respective obligations under this Agreement, or any part hereof, Label shall release an album derived from each LP-Master delivered and accepted by Label hereunder in the USA and Canada within one hundred twenty (120) days of the delivery and acceptance of the LP-Master from which such album was derived, excluding the months of November and December. If with respect to any LP-Master delivered to and accepted by Label, Label fails to release such album derived from such LP-Master in the USA and Canada as provided herein, and if Label fails to cure such failure within sixty (60) days after receipt of written notice of Lender's objection to such failure to release ("Notice of Objection"), then Lender may preclude Label from further exercising Label's options to extend the term of this Agreement by giving Label written notice of such preclusion on or before the seventieth (70th) day following the date of the Notice of Objection. Lender's Notice of Objection, to be effective, shall be given to Label no sooner than one hundred twenty (120) days and no later than one hundred fifty (150) days after Label's acceptance of the applicable LP-Master.

(b) provided that Lender and Artist are not then in breach of any of their obligations under this Agreement, or any part hereof, then, with respect to each album required to be released in the USA as set forth hereinabove, Label shall cause its licensees to release such album in the Major Territories within ninety (90) days following the date of the release of such album in the USA, excluding the months of November and December. If with respect to any LP-Master delivered to and accepted by Label, Label fails to cause such album derived from such LP-Master to be released in a Major Territory as provided herein, and if Label fails to cure such failure within sixty (60) days after receipt of written notice of Lender's objection to such failure to release ("Notice of Objection"), then Lender may preclude Label from further exercising Label's options to extend the term of this Agreement by giving Label written notice of such preclusion on or before the seventieth (70th) day following the date of the Notice of Objection. Lender's Notice of Objection, to be effective, shall be given to Label no sooner than ninety (90) days and no later than one hundred twenty (120) days after Label's release of the album derived from the applicable LP-Master in the USA. Notwithstanding the foregoing to the contrary, in the event an album is not commercially released by a Label licensee as aforesaid, Label shall have the right to import the subject album, from another market, to the nonreleasing country in sufficient quantities to satisfy initial orders and thereby meet, or cure its prior failure to meet Label's release commitment with respect to the nonreleasing country.

Commentary: *The Label giveth and the Label taketh away. Strangely enough, it is important for the artist to obtain a release commitment from the record company, i.e., that the record company agrees to release each album that the artist records. Since the release of albums would seem to be the point of the recording contract, it is strange to think that you have to specify this as a deal point in order to get it, but you do. Even when you do get a release commitment, the record company always insists on the right not to release the album. However, the company will* *agree that if they don't release the album in the United States, the artist can terminate the deal, at least after written notice and an opportunity for the record company to cure.*

If the artist is fortunate enough to have a recording commitment for more than one album, it is even more important to obtain a release commitment for each album with the right to terminate if it is not released. It is also helpful, but difficult, to obtain the right to buy the album back and avoid having to re-record it should a new deal be made with another record company.

Foreign release commitments are much more difficult to obtain from record companies. Records which are successful in the United States are not necessarily successful in other territories, even the major ones. Accordingly, only artists with substantial bargaining power or a proven track record are able to get foreign release commitments. However, foreign release commitments are always expressly limited so that the artist cannot terminate the contract entirely if an album is not released in a particular foreign territory. That territory should revert to the artist free and clear, i.e., the artist would have the right to license that album (and perhaps subsequent albums) to a third party and retain the royalties without the label sharing in them. Instead, they usually insist that if the artist finds a willing licensee, they will enter into the license with that licensee and all monies paid by the licensee will flow through the record company as if they had timely released the record through their own channels. They feel that if the record is right for the particular foreign market, their own licensee will release it. Other reasons for this reluctance are that most record companies simply cannot control their foreign licensees and therefore will not be held responsible for their failures. Unless the artist has tremendous bargaining power, the artist can really only hope that his album will be so successful that it will in fact be released in all the major territories without undue delay.

17. LENDER'S REPRESENTATIONS AND WARRANTIES

Lender represents, warrants and agrees as follows:

(a) Lender has a written contract with Artist (as amended by the Artist Declaration attached hereto as Exhibit "E") (NOT INCLUDED IN THIS BOOK), wherein Artist has agreed to perform exclusively for Lender upon such terms and conditions, including a term of sufficient duration, as will enable Lender to perform all of its obligations under this Agreement ("Artist Recording Contract").

(b) Artist is the sole owner throughout the Territory of the professional name "__________" (sometimes referred to herein as the "name"). During the term of this Agreement, no other person has or will have the right to use the name (and/or any other name that may be used by Artist upon the mutual agreement of Label and Lender) or to permit such names to be used in connection with records. Lender has the authority to grant Label the right to use the name and any other name that may be used by Artist upon the mutual agreement between Label and Lender will not infringe upon the legal rights of any third parties.

(c) Lender agrees that Label may cause a search to be instituted to determine whether there have been any third party uses of the name for record purposes. Lender further agrees that Label may cause an application for USA federal registration of the name to be made in favor of Artist for record and/or entertainment purposes. Lender agrees that any amounts expended by Label pursuant to this Paragraph will be deemed to be advances against and recoupable by Label from royalties otherwise payable to Lender hereunder. If the aforesaid search indicates that the name should not be used for phonograph record and/or entertainment purposes hereunder, Label and Lender shall mutually agree upon a substitute name for Artist. Nothing contained herein shall release Lender or Artist from their warranty to Label with respect to Label's use of Artist's name as specified herein, nor from their indemnification of Label with respect to any breach of such warranty.

(d) The Artist Recording Contract authorizes Lender to record masters for Label on all of the terms and conditions of this Agreement.

(e) In the Artist Recording Contract, Artist acknowledged and agreed that Artist's services in the record field are of a special, unique, unusual, extraordinary and intellectual character which gives them a peculiar value, the loss of which cannot reasonably or adequately be compensated for in damages in an action at law and that a breach of Artist's obligations under the Artist Recording Contract will cause irreparable injury and damage to Lender, entitling Lender to injunctive and other equitable relief.

(f) Artist shall execute the Artist's Declaration in the form attached hereto as Exhibit "E" (NOT INCLUDED IN THIS BOOK), and incorporated herein by reference, and Lender shall furnish the same to Label no later than the date of execution hereof.

(g) In the Artist Recording Contract, Artist granted Lender the right to authorize Label to enforce the provisions of the Artist Recording Contract against Artist directly, either in Lender's name or in Label's own name, and Lender does so authorize Label.

(h) Lender shall pay each member of Artist compensation for his services at the rate of not less than Six Thousand Dollars ($6,000.00) per annum during the term hereof. If the law of the jurisdiction by which this Agreement is governed is amended to provide that to be enforceable by injunction the minimum compensation under a personal services contract theretofore entered into shall be a sum greater than Six Thousand Dollars ($6,000.00) per annum, this Paragraph shall be deemed automatically amended to require annual compensation in the amount specified by such amended statute. During each year of this Agreement, Lender shall provide documentation, in a form satisfactory to Label, that the aforesaid payments have been paid by Lender. Lender agrees that Label shall have the right at any time, and from time to time during the term hereof, to pay the minimum compensation specified above directly to each such member on Lender's behalf. Any such payment made by Label shall reduce dollar for dollar any royalties, advances and any other amounts otherwise payable to Lender hereunder.

Commentary: *This clause is the direct result of California Civil Code §3423 which provides that in order for a company which contracts for the personal services of an individual to be able to enforce that contract, that contract must guarantee that the individual employed thereunder is paid at least $6,000 per year. Most major record companies will insert this clause in any contract with California residents, even if they operate out of New York, in order to protect themselves should the artist bring suit against the company in a California court. For contracts with major recording artists the requirement is not particularly onerous. However, if it is a new artist which happens to be a group composed of several members, it may be a substantial burden for the record company to agree that each member will receive at least $6,000 per annum during the term.*

This statute has been the subject of some very interesting litigation, e.g., MCA Records, Inc. v. Olivia Newton-John, 90 Cal.App.3d 18 (1979). In the Olivia Newton-John case, her attorneys argued that MCA could not obtain an injunction against her to prevent her from recording for another record company, because they had not guaranteed her $6,000 per annum. MCA had provided, however, for a recording fund of $200,000 per album, and MCA's attorneys prevailed in their arguments that, since Ms. Newton-John controlled all aspects of the production of her records, there was sufficient money guaranteed to her for her to put $6,000 in her pocket. However, the same result might not occur in the case of a new group artist composed of several members signed to a contract providing a fund which is controlled by the record company or which is less than $200,000.

However, if you are an artist who is exclusively signed to a contract with a small production company which does not guarantee each member $6,000 per year, don't be so quick to sign with a new record company. Although the company to which you are signed may not be able to obtain an injunction to prevent you from recording for a new record company, it may be able to sue you and your new record company for damages arising from your breach of contract should you jump to the new record company before the term of your contract has expired. See a lawyer instead.

(i) Artist is under no disability, restriction or Prohibition respecting musical works that Artist can record for Label except to the extent, if any, set forth in the Schedule of Restricted Musical Works attached hereto as Exhibit "F" (NOT INCLUDED IN THIS BOOK).

(j) Lender shall perform all duties and obligations under the Artist Recording Contract.

(k) Lender has the right to enter into this entire Agreement and all terms, covenants and conditions hereof, and Lender has not done or permitted to be done anything which may curtail or impair any of the rights granted to Label herein.

(l) Lender will not authorize Artist to perform, and Artist agrees that Artist will not perform, any selection embodied in a master recorded hereunder for the purpose of making records for anyone other than Label until the later of (i) seven (7) consecutive years after delivery of the applicable master to Label hereunder; or (ii) seven (7) consecutive years after the expiration or termination of this Agreement.

Commentary: *This is an example of what is known as a re-recording restriction. Every recording contract has such a clause. However, the general formula is that the restrictions expire on the later of five years after the date of recording the composition for the Label or two years after the expiration of the term of the contract. The artist's representative should also try to get a waiver of this restriction as to recordings which are not commercially released during the term or one (1) year thereafter.*

(m) Each member of Artist is a member of the American Federation of Musicians ("AFM") or the American Federation of Television and Radio Artists ("AFTRA"), as applicable, in good standing or if not now a member in good standing of either of said unions as required, shall become a member in good standing of said unions subject to and in accordance with the applicable union security provisions of the AFM Phonograph Record Labor Agreement and the AFTRA National Code of Fair Practice for Phonograph Recordings.

18. NOTICES

(a) All notices which Label may be required or desire to serve upon Lender may be served by depositing same, postage prepaid, in any mail box, chute or other receptacle authorized by the USA Post Office Department for mail addressed to Lender at the address below its signature, or at such other address as Lender may from time to time designate by written notice to Label to the attention of the Secretary. The date of service of any notice, statement or payment so deposited shall be the date of deposit. Statements and payments may be mailed to Lender at the address below its signature.

(b) All notices which Lender may be required or desire to serve upon Label shall be served upon Label by depositing the same, certified or registered mail, return receipt requested, postage prepaid, in any mail box, chute or other receptacle authorized by the USA Post Office Department for mail addressed to Label at the address below its signature, attention Vice President, Business Affairs, and at the address set forth in Subparagraph 18 (c) below, or at such other address as Label may from time to time designate by written notice to Lender. The date of service of any notice so deposited shall be the date of deposit.

(c) Label Records, Inc.
(Address)

19. FORCE MAJEURE

If at any time during the term hereof by reason of any act of God, fire, earthquake, flood, explosion, strike, labor disturbance, civil commotion, act of Government, its agencies or officers, any order, regulation, ruling or action of any labor union or association of artists, musicians, composers or employees affecting Label, its subsidiaries or affiliates or the industry in which it or they are engaged or any shortage of or failure or delays in the delivery of materials, supplies, labor or equipment, or any other cause or causes beyond the control of Label, any affiliate or subsidiary, whether of the same or any other nature; (a) the enjoyment by Label, its subsidiaries or affiliates of any rights, privileges or benefits hereunder, including, without limitation, the recording of masters or the manufacture, sale or distribution of records, is delayed, hampered, interrupted or interfered with, or otherwise becomes impossible or impracticable, then Label may upon notice to Lender suspend the term of this Agreement for the duration of any such contingency. The duration of the term of the Agreement shall be extended by a number of days equal to the total of all such days of suspension.

20. INDEMNIFICATION BY LENDER

Lender agrees to indemnify Label against, and hold Label harmless from, any and all claims, liabilities, causes of action, damages, expenses, costs of defense (including reasonable attorney's fees and court costs) and other costs arising out of or in any way related to any breach or claimed breach of any representation, warranty or agreement by Lender contained in this Agreement. Lender agrees that Label may withhold sums otherwise due Lender hereunder in amounts reasonably related to such claim(s) until such time as such claim(s) are reduced to a final judgement by a court of competent jurisdiction or are settled.

Commentary: *This indemnity clause is a standard "boilerplate" provision, which should be left in the hands of your lawyer to negotiate the normal and customary protections. The same advice applies with respect to the rest of this Agreement.*

21. ATTORNEYS' FEES

If any action or proceeding is instituted between the parties hereto to enforce any of the terms and conditions of this Agreement, and if a party makes a written settlement offer to the other party ("Settlement Offer") in such action or proceeding, the offering party shall be entitled to recover reasonable attorneys' fees and costs incurred after the date of the Settlement Offer in the event a judgement is later entered the monetary terms of which are more favorable to the offering party than the monetary terms of the Settlement Offer. In the event no such Settlement Offer is made the prevailing party in any such action or proceeding shall be entitled to recover reasonable attorney's fees and costs.

22. CONSENTS

Wherever the consent of Lender is required by the provisions of this Agreement, such consent shall not be unreasonably withheld or delayed; and Lender's failure to respond in writing within five (5) business days to a written request from Label for consent shall be conclusively deemed to constitute Lender's consent to such request.

23. TAX WITHHOLDING

Lender agrees and acknowledges that Label shall have the right to withhold from royalties payable hereunder such amount, if any, as may be required under the applicable provisions of the Internal Revenue Code of the United States and/or the California Revenue and Taxation Code, and Lender and Artist agree to execute such forms and other documents as may be required in connection therewith.

24. INDEPENDENT CONTRACTOR RELATIONSHIP

The relationship between Label and Lender hereunder shall at all times be that of independent contractor; and nothing contained herein shall render or constitute the parties joint venturers, partners or agents of each other. Neither Label nor Lender shall hold itself out to third parties other than as set forth herein. Neither party shall have the right to execute any contract, or incur any obligation for which the other may be liable, or otherwise bind the other; and neither party shall be liable for any representation, act or omission of the other. This Agreement is made for the sole benefit and protection of the parties hereto and not for the benefit of any third party. No person not a party to this Agreement shall have any right of action hereunder.

25. WAIVER

No waiver by Label of any breach by Lender of any term or condition of this Agreement shall operate as a waiver by Label of any subsequent breach by Lender of any term or condition of this Agreement.

26. SEVERABILITY

If the payments provided by this Agreement shall exceed the amount permitted by any present or future law or governmental order or regulation, such stated payments shall be reduced while such limitation is in effect to the amount which is so permitted; and the payment of such amount shall be deemed to constitute full performance by Label of its obligations to Lender hereunder with respect to compensation during the term when such limitation is in effect. If any part of this Agreement is determined to be void, invalid, inoperative or unenforceable by a court of competent jurisdiction or by any other legally constituted body having jurisdiction to make such determination, such decision shall not affect any other provisions hereof, and the remainder of this Agreement shall be effective as though such void, invalid, inoperative or unenforceable provision had not been contained herein.

27. CLAUSE HEADINGS

The clause headings in the Agreement are for reference only and do not form a part of this Agreement.

28. WHOLE AGREEMENT

The terms set forth in this Agreement and all attachments hereto, constitute the entire agreement between Label and Lender, all prior negotiations and understandings being merged herein. Lender represents that no person acting or purporting to act on behalf of Label has made any promises or representations upon which Lender has relied except those expressly found herein. This Agreement may only be altered by an instrument executed by both Lender and Label. No failure by Label to perform any of its material obligations under this agreement shall be deemed a material breach of this Agreement until Lender has given Label written notice of such breach and such breach has not been corrected within forty-five (45) days after the giving of such notice. Label may assign this Agreement or any part hereof or any rights hereunder to any person. Lender may not assign this Agreement or any rights hereunder to any person without the prior written consent of Label.

> *While prohibitions on contract assignments by the lender or artist are common, with the Label being permitted to assign the contract, it is advisable for the Lender/Artist to negotiate that the Label restrict its assignment of the contract to transfers of the Label's stock or assets as a whole, thus prohibiting the assignment of the contract alone (excepts, perhaps, to an affiliated label, e.g. Warner Bros. Records to Reprise Records).*

29. EFFECTIVE DATE

This Agreement shall become effective only when executed by an authorized agent of Lender and an authorized signer on behalf of Label. It shall be deemed to have been made in the State of California and its validity, construction, breach, performance and operation shall be governed by the law of the State of California applicable to contracts made and to be performed in the State of California.

> ***Commentary:*** *Although it is highly unlikely that a record company will change its choice of law provision, you should know that California law favors the artist and, wherever possible, try to stick to California law.*

WHEREFORE the parties have executed this Agreement as of the day and year first above written.

"LENDER"

By: ______________________________ ________________, Partner

Title: ______________________________ ________________, Partner

An Authorized Signer

________________, Partner

After the recording artist, the record producer is one of the most important individuals involved in creating recordings. Although not as widely known to the general public as the artists they produce, certain producers are well known within music industry circles and are sought out by recording artists because they believe that the producer can assist them in creating the "sound" that will help them achieve record sales at platinum or multi-platinum levels.

This article focuses upon the situation in which the producer is engaged to produce a master recording for use on an album by an artist who already has a recording agreement with a record company.

PRODUCER COMPENSATION

The producer of master recordings for an artist with a record deal generally receives as compensation for his or her services, a sum of money as an advance that is recoupable (i.e., must be earned back) from future royalties that may become payable to the producer under the producer agreement. Generally (although the country music area is often an exception), the artist's recording agreement with the record company will provide that the artist receives an "all-in" royalty on net sales of the artist's records. An all-in royalty means that the artist must pay the producer's royalty out of the royalty that is set forth in the recording agreement as being payable to the artist. In most cases, the record company will agree to pay the producer directly, after receiving a "letter of direction" from the artist requesting direct payment to the producer. Thus, if the artist's all-in royalty rate is 12% of the retail selling price (after deduction of a packaging charge) on net sales of records sold through normal retail channels in the United States, and the producer's royalty rate on such sales is 3% of the retail price (with appropriate reductions), the royalty rate that the artist is really entitled to is 9% of the retail price. However, the artist and the producer must both bear in mind that they will not receive royalties from the moment the first record is shipped from the record company to the record store (or other purchaser). The record company only pays royalties on "net sales," which are some portion of the records that are sold and not returned, with no royalties payable on "free goods" (see the article on recording agreements for an explanation of free goods). Furthermore, the artist and the producer will not receive royalties until they have recouped (i.e., earned back) certain recording costs and advances from royalties earned in connection with sales of records embodying the relevant master recordings. The artist and the producer will have to recoup different sums at different royalty rates. The concept of recoupment for record producers is discussed below in paragraph 6 of the "Sample Producer Agreement."

WHO CHOOSES THE PRODUCER?

When the artist receives an all-in royalty, the artist's recording agreement will generally specify that the artist is responsible for engaging the producer; how-

Captured during the "Dial & Oatts" project, left to right Dick Oatts, conductor Carlos Franzetti and producer Tom Jung at Clinton Recording Studio in New York City. Courtesy Mix Magazine. Photo by Dave King.

ever, the record company usually retains the ultimate control over determining which producer will be engaged. The artist's attorney should always attempt to obtain for the artist the right to approve the producer; however, the recording agreement for a new artist will generally provide that the record company and the artist will mutually approve the producer and if the record company and the artist disagree as to the appropriate producer, the record company's decision will prevail. As the artist's career becomes more successful, the record company will probably allow the artist more control over creative decisions, including the selection of the producer.

In some cases, a producer who is a member of the staff of the record company will produce the album. Many recording agreements contain provisions relating to the minimum compensation (usually $1,500 per master or $15,000 per album and a 3% of retail royalty) that would be payable if a record company staff producer produces any master recording for the artist. The artist's attorney should require that a provision be included in the recording agreement stating that a staff producer can only be engaged with the artist's consent and that the advances and royalties that are payable to the staff producer would be prorated (i.e., reduced proportionately) if there are co-producers on the master recordings or if there are other master recordings on the album that are not produced by the staff producer.

When the producer is not on the staff of the record company and is not the artist, a producer agreement is generally prepared. When the artist is responsible for engaging the producer, the artist's attorney will generally prepare the producer agreement; however, it is not uncommon for the record company to prepare the producer agreement as an accommodation to the artist. The producer agreement provided below is an agreement that was prepared by an attorney for a record company. With slight modifications, the producer agreement could just as easily have been prepared by the artist's attorney as an agreement between the artist and the producer rather than an agreement between the record company and the producer.

Since most producer agreements (including the one below), are prepared to favor the artist or the record company and not the producer, I will review the provisions of the following producer agreement from the perspective of the attorney who is negotiating on behalf of the producer:

EXHIBIT 1: SAMPLE PRODUCER AGREEMENT

The subject matter of this Agreement is your services to us as the producer of [Insert #] master recording (s) ("Master(s)") embodying performances by ____________________ ("Artist"). You and we agree as follows:

1. The term of this Agreement ("Term") shall commence as of the date hereof and shall continue until the Master(s) are completed to our satisfaction and delivered to us or until we terminate the Term upon written notice to you. During the Term, you shall render your services as the producer of the Master(s) in cooperation with us and Artist, at times and places designated or approved in writing by us. You shall produce the Master(s), and you shall deliver the Master(s) to us or our designee promptly after the Master(s) are completed. All elements for the creation and production of the Master(s), including, without limitation, the compositions to be recorded in the Master(s) and other individuals rendering services in connection with the production of the Master(s), shall be designated or approved by us in writing. We shall pay or cause to be paid all costs to produce and record the Master(s) in an amount not to exceed a recording budget therefor which is designated or approved by us in writing. If the costs to produce and record the Master(s) exceed the recording budget for reasons within your control or which you could have avoided, then you shall, upon our demand, pay to us the amount of those excess costs, and we may, at our election, deduct the amount of those costs from any royalties or other monies payable to you under this Agreement.

Commentary: *The producer agreement should contain a more definite completion standard than "completed to our satisfaction." The producer's attorney should attempt to obtain a "technically satisfactory" delivery standard (i.e., the masters must be of suitable sound quality from a sound engineer's perspective); however, if (as most current recording agreements provide) the artist's recording agreement contains a "technically and commercially satisfactory" delivery standard, the artist's or record company's attorney should not provide a more favorable provision to the producer than "until the completion of technically and commercially satisfactory Masters as determined by the record company."*

The artist and/or record company will generally retain a right of approval over the elements for the creation and production of the masters. If the producer intends to use his or her own studio, a statement that the producer's studio is approved as the studio for recording the masters should be included in the producer agreement in order to avoid any doubt about what studio will be used. Also, if the musical compositions to be recorded are known at the time the agreement is prepared, the titles of those compositions should be included in the agreement as well.

This agreement provides that the record company will pay the recording costs. (In some instances the producer's agreement will provide that the producer will receive an all-in advance, that is a lump sum of money that may be paid in 2 or 3 installments during the recording of the masters and that includes the money to pay the recording costs for the masters as well as the producer's advance.)

The producer should be certain to find out the amount of money available to record the masters before agreeing to take on the project. If the recording costs for the masters exceed the amount of the authorized budget, those excess costs may be charged against monies payable to the producer and; accordingly, the producer may lose part of their advance or may be delayed or prevented from receiving royalties as a result of the excess costs.

The worst case scenario is that many agreements provide that any excess recording costs will constitute a direct debt from the producer to the artist or record company and that any excess costs must be repaid by the producer on demand. The producer's attorney should attempt to delete the record company's and/or artist's right to request repayment directly from the producer and should limit the record company's and/or artist's rights to recover the excess costs caused by situations that were within the producer's control. If the excess costs were caused by situations within the producer's control, the excess costs should be recoverable from any producer royalties or advances payable to the producer under the specific producer agreement in question. In any event, the producer should be aware at the beginning of the project how much money is available to record the masters and should constantly bear this figure in mind while working. Although the record company may, in some cases, come up with additional monies to pay excess recording costs, the producer should make every effort to complete the masters within the originally approved budget.

2. From the inception of the recording of the Master(s), we shall own the entire worldwide right, title and interest, including, without limitation, the copyright, in and to the Master(s), the performances embodied therein and the results and proceeds of your services hereunder, as our employee for hire for all purposes of the applicable copyright laws, free of any claims by you or any person, firm or corporation. Alternatively, you grant to us the entire worldwide right, title and interest derived from you, including, without limitation, the copyright, in and to the Master(s).

> ***Commentary:*** *This language is very standard in producer agreements and would not be subject to negotiation by the producer's attorney. The artist and record company want the masters created by the producer to be "works made for hire" as that phrase is defined in the United States Copyright Act of 1976. The benefit to the artist and record company of this classification is that, unlike the creator of a work that is created and then sold to another person or company, the creator of a work made for hire has no right to terminate the transfer of his work and re-acquire the copyright at a later date. Nevertheless, since there is some question as to whether the masters created as the result of the producer's services under the producer agreement would qualify as "works made for hire," the agreement also contains language stating that alternatively, the producer grants all rights in the masters to the artist or record company. To protect the artist's or record company's interests better, this agreement should state that the last sentence of paragraph 2 would apply only if the masters were determined not to be works made for hire.*
>
> *If the producer wrote all or part of any of the compositions embodied in the masters, a statement should be included in the agreement excluding the compositions written by the producer from the provisions of this paragraph.*

3. You hereby grant to us and our designees the worldwide right in perpetuity to use and to permit others to use, at no cost, your name, likeness and biographical material concerning you in connection with any and all phonograph records and other reproductions made from the Master(s), the advertising in connection therewith and institutional advertising. We shall accord you appropriate production credit on the jackets, labels or liner notes of all records embodying the Master(s), which you agree may be in substantially the following form: "Produced by ______________________." Any failure to comply with the provisions of this paragraph shall not be a breach of this Agreement. Your sole right and remedy in that event shall be to notify us of that failure, after which we shall use reasonable efforts to accord that production credit to you on records manufactured after the date we receive that notice.

> ***Commentary:*** *The producer should have a right of approval over all photographs, likenesses and biographical material concerning him or her that is used under this paragraph. "Institutional advertising" should be limited to the record company's institutional advertising. Producer credit should be placed on all record labels and on jackets or liner notes on all records in all configurations (including compact disc and tape packaging). The producer should receive credit in all one-half page or larger trade and consumer advertisements featuring a master produced by the producer. The producer's attorney should attempt to obtain a "favored nations" provision relating to credit so that the producer's credit will be of similar size and placement as any other producer's credit on the album and will appear in advertising relating to the album if another producer is credited (unless the advertisement features a master that is produced by another producer). The agreement should state that the credit will be in the following form: "___________," not "<u>may</u> be in substantially the following form."*
>
> *The failure to provide the credit should not be a material breach of the agreement provided that the record company and/or artist uses its best efforts to cure the failure on records (in all configurations) manufactured after receipt of the notice of the failure from the producer and in advertisements authorized after the receipt of such notice.*

4. In full consideration for your entering into and executing this Agreement and your fulfilling all of your obligations hereunder, you shall be paid __________ Dollars ($__________), payable one-half (1/2) promptly after the later of the execution of this Agreement or the commencement of recording sessions for the Master(s) and one-half (1/2) promptly after the later of the completion and delivery to us of all Master(s) or our determination of the aggregate costs to record the Master(s). Those monies payable to you shall be an advance recoupable from royalties earned by you hereunder.

Commentary: *The producer's attorney may wish to delete the word "full" in the first sentence since the possibility of the producer receiving royalties under the agreement is also "consideration" to the producer. ("Consideration" is a legal concept that requires that in order for a contract to be binding upon the parties, one party must give or do something of value in exchange for receiving something of value from the other party.) Additionally, the word "material" should be added before the word "obligations" because the producer should still receive his or her advance even if there is some kind of failure to fulfill a minor, "nonmaterial" obligation under the agreement. The agreement should specify that the advance is nonreturnable once it is paid.*

The amount of the advance can vary widely based upon the experience and reputation of the producer. A producer advance for a single master would generally not be less than $1,000, with a more common figure being approximately $3,000. A producer advance of $5,000 would be a very good advance for an established producer. Of course, there will always be exceptions, with a few "superstar" producers receiving $10,000 or $12,500. As mentioned previously, this agreement presents the situation where the record company pays the recording costs and pays a separate advance to the producer. In the all-in advance situation, the producer would receive a sum of money from which the producer would have to pay the recording costs and any remaining monies would be retained by the producer. The all-in advance situation often works best for a producer who has his or her own studio and can, therefore, keep recording costs down. In the all-in advance situation the producer is required to pay recording costs and may, therefore, have a real need to obtain the advance monies more quickly than as set forth in this agreement.

One method of payment of the all-in advance could be one-half upon the commencement of recording, one-fourth upon the producer's delivery of a rough mix of the master, and the final one-fourth upon delivery of the completed master. A typical all-in advance for a producer producing a master for a new "pop" artist on a major label might be anywhere from $12,000 to $15,000. A more established producer producing a more established artist might receive an all-in advance of $20,000 or $25,000. All of the foregoing figures vary widely, with lower figures for producers who do not have an established track record, producers producing newer artists, producers producing artists on smaller record labels and producers producing artists who record in areas other than pop and rock. For example, the monies available for the recording budget for a new jazz artist at a major label might be about one-fourth of the monies available to a new pop artist at the same label.

Another point in paragraph 4 that the producer's attorney should raise is to limit the time period that the artist or the record company has in which to determine the aggregate costs to record the masters. I am aware of at least one situation in which the record was released and on the charts for several months and the record company's attorney still claimed that the recording costs had not yet been determined, notwithstanding the fact that all re-

cording was conducted in the artist's own studio. The time period in which to determine the aggregate recording costs should not exceed thirty days after delivery of the masters.

5. Conditioned upon your full and faithful performance of all the terms hereof, you shall be paid a royalty on reproductions and exploitations of the Master(s) at the following rates in accordance with the following terms:

Commentary: *The word "material" should be inserted before the word "terms" in the first sentence of this paragraph. The producer should request to be paid directly from the record company rather than from the artist. A "letter of direction" in the record company's standard form directing the record company to pay the producer royalties directly should be signed by the artist and attached to the producer agreement as an exhibit.*

(a) (i) On sales of full-priced, top-line long-playing phonograph records embodying solely Master(s) (in the form of conventional vinyl-discs and cassette tapes) which are sold through normal retail distribution channels in the United States ("Base Rate") of _________ percent (___%) of the suggested retail list price ("SRLP") of those Base Rate Records (or the equivalent). Your Base Rate on Base Rate Records shall be prorated, calculated, adjusted and paid on the same percentage of net sales of Base Rate Records as Artist's royalty rate on sales of Base Rate Records is prorated, calculated, adjusted and paid under the recording agreement between us and Artist ("Artist Agreement"). On sales in and outside of the United States of all records other than Base Rate Records, you shall be paid a royalty at a rate equal to the Base Rate but which is prorated, calculated, proportionately reduced, adjusted and paid on the same percentage of net sales as Artist's base royalty rate on sales of Base Rate Records is prorated, calculated, proportionately reduced, adjusted and paid under the Artist Agreement; and

Commentary: *A producer royalty rate generally ranges between 2% and 4% of the suggested retail list price of "Base Rate Records" (as defined in the producer agreement), with a few top producers receiving 5%. A typical royalty rate to a producer would be 3% of the retail price of records. If two producers co-produce a master they might each receive a royalty at the rate of 1 1/2% or 2% of the retail price of records embodying the master. If the artist's royalty under the artist's recording agreement is computed on the basis of the wholesale price of records, rather than the retail price, then the producer's royalty would be computed based on the wholesale price of records. In that event, the producer's royalty rate would be approximately twice the rate as the royalty rate computed based on the retail price of records (e.g., approximately 6% of wholesale rather than 3% of retail). Many producers receive increased royalties if the record that they produce sells a certain number of units. A fairly typical royalty rate structure would be a 3% of retail royalty rate escalating 1/2% to 3 1/2% on all sales of the record in excess of 500,000 units and escalating an additional 1/2% to 4% on all sales in excess of 1,000,000 units.*

The producer's royalty is generally reduced, adjusted and paid on the same basis as the artist's royalty is reduced, adjusted and paid. In the situation where the artist has a recording agreement with a production company and the production company in turn has an agreement with the record company whereby the production company agrees to provide the artist's services to the record company, the producer's attorney should attempt to have the producer's royalty reduced, adjusted and paid on the same basis as the production company's royalty from the record company is computed, adjusted and paid. Note that this agreement states that the producer's royalty is to be prorated on the same basis as the artist's royalty - this is not technically correct: the producer's royalty is prorated (i.e., reduced proportionately) based on the number of masters produced by the producer that are on the particular record, and the artist's royalty is prorated based upon the number of masters recorded by the artist on the record. For example, if the producer produced 5 out of 10 masters on Artist A's most recent album and the producer's basic royalty rate was 3% of the retail price of records comprised entirely of masters produced by the producer, the producer's royalty on Artist A's album would be reduced from 3% to 1.5% because the producer only produced half of the masters on that album. The artist's royalty rate on the same album would not be reduced in this fashion since the album was entirely comprised of masters embodying the artist's performance.

Many established producers obtain a special exception to the proration provisions in their producer agreements. This special exception is known as "A-side protection." "A"-side protection applies only to singles where the "A"-side of the single is produced by one producer and the "B"-side of that single is produced by another producer. If a producer who does not have "A"-side protection has a 2 1/2% of retail royalty rate on singles and has a master that he or she produced on the "A"-side of a single with a master not produced by that producer on the "B"-side of that single, that producer's royalty rate on the single would be one and one-quarter percent (i.e., 1/2 of 2 1/2%). The producer with "A"-side protection does not receive this royalty rate reduction on singles where that producer's master appears on the "A"-side of the single. The reason that a producer who produced the "A"-side of a single may receive "A"-side protection and be paid as if he or she produced both sides of the single is that the vast majority of people who buy a single buy it because of the master embodied on the "A"-side. Since few people buy a single for the "B"-side, the theory is that the royalty of the producer of the "A"-side should not be reduced because of that "B"-side.

(ii) On exploitations of the Master(s) for which Artist is paid a percentage of our net royalty or net flat fees under the Artist Agreement, you shall be paid a royalty equal to ____________ percent (_____%) of our net flat fees or net royalties on such exploitations. On exploitations of the Master(s) embodied in audiovisual devices (such as videodiscs and videocassettes), however, you shall be paid a royalty equal to _________ percent (_____%) of our net flat fees or net royalties on those exploitations;

Commentary: *When the artist is paid based on a percentage of the record company's net royalty or net flat fee, then the producer should be paid a percentage of the amount received by the artist computed by dividing the producer's basic royalty rate (without regard to escalations) by the artist's basic all-in royalty rate (without regard to escalations). For example, if the producer's basic royalty rate is 3% of retail and the artist's basic all-in royalty rate is 12% of retail, the producer would receive 25% of any monies that the artist received as a percentage of the record company's net royalties or net flat fees. On net receipts from the exploitation of audiovisual devices, the producer would generally receive one-half of the otherwise applicable net receipts royalty.*

Thus, in the foregoing example, the producer would receive 12.5% (rather than 25%) of the monies the artist received from the record company for the exploitation of audiovisual devices. Again, if the artist is signed to a production company instead of directly to the record company, the producer's attorney should attempt to have the producer's royalty calculated based upon the royalties payable by the record company to the production company rather than based on the royalties payable from the production company to the artist; however, the producer's attorney should be aware that this may be a difficult concession to obtain.

In any event, subparagraphs 5(a)(i) and 5(a)(ii) make it clear that in order for the producer to have a clear idea of what producer royalties may be payable on a particular project, he or she must know the terms of the royalty provisions of the artist's recording agreement. Accordingly, a copy of the royalty provisions relating to the applicable album and the definitions provisions of the artist's (or, if applicable, the production company's) recording agreement should be attached as an exhibit to the producer agreement.

(b) Your royalty rate on records and other devices embodying Master(s) and other master recording shall be the otherwise applicable royalty rate multiplied by a fraction, the numerator of which is the number of Master(s) embodied in that record or other device and the denominator of which is the total number of master recordings (including Master(s)) embodied in the record or other device;

Commentary: *This paragraph sets forth the appropriate proration of the producer's royalty. The words "royalty-bearing" should be inserted after the words "total number of" towards the end of the sentence.*

(c) Your royalty rates hereunder shall not be increased due to increases in Artist's royalty rates under the Artist Agreement based on record sales; and

Commentary: *The producer does not generally share in sales escalations received by the artist; however, as discussed in subparagraph 5(a)(i), the producer or the producer's attorney can often negotiate for escalations in the producer's royalty rate based on sales, which escalations in the producer's royalty rate would be separate from the sales escalations received by the artist.*

(d) Your royalties hereunder shall be reduced by the royalties payable by us for the services of any other person to produce or complete the production of the Master(s) until they are satisfactory to us.

Commentary: *The producer's attorney should request that the producer be accorded the first opportunity to do any mixing, remixing, editing or other material altering of the masters produced by the producer. If any other person performs these services, the producer should have the right, at the producer's sole discretion, to remove his or her name from the master. Also, if another person is engaged to perform production work on the master, the producer's royalty should not be reduced unless the producer is in material breach of the agreement. The producer's attorney should require that a provision be included in the agreement stating that if a mixer is engaged to mix the masters, any royalties payable to the mixer should be borne one-third by the record company, one-third by the artist and one-third by the producer. If the record company refuses to bear any of the royalties payable to the mixer, the royalties to the mixer (usually 1% of retail) should be borne one-half by the artist and one-half by the producer.*

6. No royalties shall be credited to your account hereunder unless and until the aggregate of recording costs of the Master(s) and advances and fees payable to you for the Master(s) are recouped from royalties on reproductions and exploitations of the Master(s) at the "Net Artist Royalty Rate." The term "Net Artist Royalty Rate" shall mean the aggregate royalty rate payable to Artist and the producers on reproductions of the Master(s), less the aggregate royalty rate payable to the producers on reproductions and exploitations of the Master(s). After that recoupment, your royalty account shall be credited with royalties earned by your hereunder on all exploitations of the Master(s) retroactive to the first record sold. We shall account for and pay royalties earned by you hereunder within ninety (90) days after the end of each of our then-current six-month accounting periods, currently ending on June 30 and December 31. Accountings and statements for royalties earned by you on reproductions and exploitations of the Master(s) shall be based upon our receipt in the United States of an accounting and payment or final credit for the actual reproductions and exploitations of the Master(s) in the accounting period for which a statement is rendered. We shall have no obligation to account for or pay to you any royalties unless and until we receive in the United States an accounting for and payment of or final credit for royalties on actual reproductions and other exploitations of the Master(s). All statements and accountings rendered to you shall be binding and not subject to any examination, audit or objection for any reason unless you shall notify us in writing of your specific objection thereto within one (1) year after the date the statement is rendered or was to be rendered. No action, suit or proceeding regarding any royalty statement or accounting rendered to you may be maintained by or on behalf of you unless commenced in court within one (1) year after the date the statement is rendered or was to be rendered. We may deduct from any amounts payable to you hereunder that portion hereof required to be deducted under any statute, regulation, treaty or other law, or under any union or guild agreement.

Commentary: *The first three sentences of this paragraph deal with recoupment of the recording costs and the producer advance and/or fees. The producer will not receive royalties until the recording costs and advances and fees to the producer for the masters produced by that producer are recouped (i.e., earned back) from royalties earned at the Net Artist Royalty Rate (i.e., the artist's royalty rate minus the producers' royalty rate) from sales of records embodying the master produced by the producer. The producer's attorney should attempt to exclude any advances or fees to the artist from the recording costs for the purposes of determining recoupment by the producer. Furthermore, the advances to the producer should be excluded as well since paragraph 4 states that the advance to the producer will be recouped from royalties payable to the producer. A failure to exclude the producer advance from this provision may result in "double recoupment" of the producer advance and, accordingly, may delay (or prevent) the producer's receipt of royalties.*

Once the appropriate costs are recouped at the Net Artist Royalty Rate, the producer's royalty account is credited with all royalties earned at the producer's royalty rate from the first record that was sold. These royalties will be paid to the producer after deduction of the amount of the advance previously paid to the producer. This provision is favorable to the producer. The artist receives royalties "prospectively" after recoupment of all recording costs for the album at the artist's all-in rate. This means that if the appropriate costs are recouped after sales of 200,000 units, the artist will receive royalties for the 200,001st unit and future units sold, as long as the artist's royalty account remains in a recouped position; however, the artist will not receive any royalties on the first 200,000 units sold prior to recoupment.

If the producer is entitled to receive royalties "retroactively from the first record sold" and the cost chargeable against the producer's account are recouped after sales of 100,000 units, the producer's account would be credited with the producer's royalty on units 1 through 100,000 and these royalties would be paid to the producer after deduction of the advance previously paid to the producer. The producer would then be paid royalties on all sales in excess of 100,000 units. In some cases, the producer agreement will state that the producer is only to be paid prospectively after recoupment of the recording costs. In that event, the producer's attorney should request that the producer be paid retroactively from the first record sold after recoupment of the appropriate costs at the Net Artist Royalty Rate. This is an important deal point that should not be overlooked in any producer agreement.

As mentioned previously, the producer should be paid directly from the record company. Accounting statements and payments (if any) should be sent to the producer at the same time that the artist is sent accounting statements. If the record company fails or refuses to send accounting statements directly to the producer, the artist should be required to send such statements and payments (if any) within thirty days after the artist receives the corresponding accounting statement from the record company. The producer should have a minimum of 2 years after the date a statement is rendered (delete "or was to be rendered") to audit the artist and/or record company and to object to that statement, and 2 1/2 years from the date the statement was rendered in which to file a lawsuit based on that statement.

7. You warrant, represent, covenant and agree as follows:
(a) You have the right and power to enter into this agreement, to grant the rights granted by you to us hereunder and to perform all the terms hereof; and

(b) No materials, ideas or other properties furnished or designated by you and used in connection with the Master(s) will violate or infringe upon the rights of any person, firm or corporation.

Commentary: *This is a standard provision in producer agreements. Subparagraph 7(b) should be limited to elements "furnished" by the producer, not "designated" by the producer. The producer's attorney should require a warranty from the artist or record company be included in the agreement similar to subparagraph 7(b) stating that all elements not furnished by the producer will not violate or infringe on the rights of others.*

8. You hereby indemnify, save and hold us and any person, firm or corporation deriving rights from us harmless from any and all damages, liability and costs (including legal costs and attorneys' fees) arising out of or in connection with any claim, demand or action by us or by any third party that is inconsistent with any of the warranties, representations, covenants or agreements made by you in this Agreement. You shall reimburse us, on demand, for any loss, cost, expense or damage to which the foregoing indemnity applies. Pending the disposition of any claim, demand or action to which the foregoing indemnity applies, we shall have the right to withhold payment of any monies payable to you hereunder and under any other agreement between you and us or our affiliates.

Commentary: *This paragraph is called an "indemnity" provision. Under this provision, if the artist or record company was sued (or sued the producer) based on any facts (or purported facts) that were inconsistent with any of the promises made by the producer in the producer agreement, the record company and/or artist could look to the producer to pay all costs incurred in connection with that lawsuit or claim.*

The producer's attorney should limit the producer's indemnity of the artist and/or record company to claims reduced to final judgment by a court of competent jurisdiction or settlements with the producer's consent. The word "reasonable" should be inserted before the words "attorneys' fees" in the first sentence of this paragraph. This provision should also state that monies will not be withheld in an amount exceeding the producer's probable liability under the producer agreement, would be held in an interest bearing account, and would be released if no action was taken on the claim during a 1 year period. The following phrase at the end of the paragraph should be deleted: "and under any other agreement between you and us or our affiliates." The artist or record company should indemnify the producer with respect to materials not furnished by the producer to the same extent that the producer indemnifies the artist or record company pursuant to this paragraph.

9. The respective addresses of you and us for all purposes hereunder are set forth on page 1 hereof, unless and until notice of a different address is received by the party notified of that different address. All notices shall be in writing and shall either be served by certified mail return receipt requested or by telex, in each case with all charges prepaid. Notices shall be deemed effective when mailed or sent by telex, all charges prepaid, except for notices of a change of address, which shall be effective only when received by the party notified. A copy of each notice to us shall be sent to: (______________ Attorney's name and address).

Commentary: *This is a standard provision. If the producer is represented by an attorney, the attorney should receive a copy of any notice sent to the producer so that the attorney can advise the producer whether any action needs to be taken on any notices received by the producer.*

10. We may, at our election, assign this Agreement or any of our rights hereunder or delegate any of our obligations hereunder, in whole or in part, to any person, firm or corporation. You may not delegate any of your obligations hereunder.

Commentary: *The record company's right to assign its rights and/or obligations under the producer agreement should be limited to a person, firm or corporation that acquires all or substantially all of its stock and/or assets. If the agreement is with the artist, the artist's right to assign his or her rights under the agreement should be limited to assigning it to a record company. Any assignment by the artist or record company should not relieve them of liability for their obligations to the producer under the producer agreement.*

11. During the Term and for three (3) years thereafter, you shall not produce or co-produce any recording for any person, firm or corporation other than us embodying, in whole or in part, the musical selections recorded in the Master(s).

Commentary: *This provision is called a "re-recording restriction". The restriction period should be reduced from 3 years to 2 years.*

12. You acknowledge and agree that your services hereunder are of a special, unique, intellectual and extraordinary character which gives them peculiar value, and that if you breach any term hereof, we will be caused irreparable injury which cannot adequately be compensated by money damages.

Commentary: *This language assists the artist and/or record company in obtaining an injunction against the producer should the producer engage in activities that violate the terms of the producer agreement. An injunction is a court order that demands that an individual or firm stop doing something. An injunction could prevent the producer from working for someone else. Since issuing an injunction is such a drastic action, a court will not issue an injunction in the situation where a person is rendering personal services unless there is a showing that the person's services are unique and that the injured party would not be made whole by the payment of money. The language contained in paragraph 12 is almost always contained in the artist's recording agreement, but is not as common in a producer agreement. The producer's attorney should attempt to delete the paragraph or, at a minimum, to modify it by inserting the word "material" before the word "term" and by substituting the word "may" for "will" and the word "may not" for the word "cannot."*

13 (a) This document sets forth the entire agreement between you and us with respect to the subject matter hereof and may not be modified except by a written agreement signed by the party sought to be bound. Except as expressly provided herein to the contrary, you are performing your obligations hereunder as an independent contractor;

(b) In the event of any action, suit or proceeding arising from or based upon this Agreement brought by either party hereto against the other, the prevailing party shall be entitled to recover from the other its attorneys' fees in connection therewith in addition to the costs of that action, suit or proceeding;

(c) The validity, construction, interpretation and legal effect of this Agreement shall be governed by the laws of the State of California;

(d) Nothing contained in this Agreement or otherwise shall obligate us or any other person, firm or corporation to reproduce or exploit the Master(s) in any manner or media;

Commentary: *These provisions are all very standard. In subparagraph 13(b), the word "reasonable" should be inserted before the words "attorneys' fees."*

(e) We may terminate the Term for any reason, with or without cause, on the date of our notice to you terminating the Term;

Commentary: *This subparagraph should be deleted. If the subparagraph is not deleted it should be limited to the situation in which the producer is in material breach of the producer agreement and has failed to cure that breach within 30 days after the artist or record company provides written notice to the producer of that breach. In any event, the producer should receive the advances and royalties that he or she is otherwise entitled to under the agreement.*

(f) We shall not be in breach of any of our obligations under this Agreement unless and until you notify us in writing in detail of our breach or alleged breach and we fail to cure that breach or alleged breach within thirty (30) days after our receipt of that notice from you; and

Commentary: *This subparagraph should be made mutual (i.e., the artist or record company should have to provide notice and a 30 day cure period to the producer prior to the*

producer being placed in breach of the agreement). The cure period for the artist or record company should be reduced to 15 days if the artist or record company fails to pay any monies owing to the producer.

(g) You have been represented by independent counsel or have had the unrestricted opportunity to be represented by independent counsel of your choice for purposes of advising you in connection with the negotiation and execution of this Agreement. If you have not been represented by independent legal counsel of your choice in connection with this Agreement, you acknowledge and agree that your failure to be represented by independent legal counsel in connection with this Agreement was determined solely by you.

Commentary: *This paragraph is a standard provision in producer agreements. Due to the complexity of issues involved in the negotiation of a producer agreement, the producer is advised to seek an attorney's advice in the negotiation and execution of any agreement.*

If the foregoing sets forth your understanding and agreement with us, please so indicate by signing in the space provided below.

Very truly yours,	Agreed and accepted
By: ______________________	By: ______________________
	Soc. Sec. No.: ______________

Commentary: *The foregoing agreement covers most of the issues that are included in most producer agreements. If the producer wrote all or part of any of the musical compositions embodied in the masters produced by the producer, the producer agreement would almost certainly contain a provision requiring the producer to grant a reduced rate "mechanical license" granting to the record company the right to reproduce the compositions on records (in all configurations) in exchange for the payment to the producer/songwriter of mechanical royalties at the rate of 75% of the minimum statutory rate on a specified date (usually either the date of the commencement of recording or the date of delivery of the master to the record company - the later the date the better for the producer). The producer's attorney should attempt to revise this provision to provide for payment of 100% of the minimum statutory rate (as of January 1, 1990 that minimum statutory rate in the United States is 5.7 cents for each record sold embodying one use of a composition that is 5 minutes or less in length); however, many record companies refuse to negotiate on this issue unless the producer has some clout. The provision in the producer agreement relating to the licensing of musical compositions may also contain a requirement that the producer/songwriter issue a free "synchronization license" to the record company. A synchronization license is an agreement that grants the right to "synchronize," or use a musical composition in the soundtrack of an audiovisual work (e.g., the right to use a song in a music video or television program). The producer who writes the composition recorded in the master that he or she produces should only be required to grant a free synchronization license for the use of the composition in MTV type free promotional videos. Since the terms of a producer agreement relating to the licensing of musical compositions written by the producer can be very complex, these provisions should be reviewed very carefully by the producer and his or her attorney.*

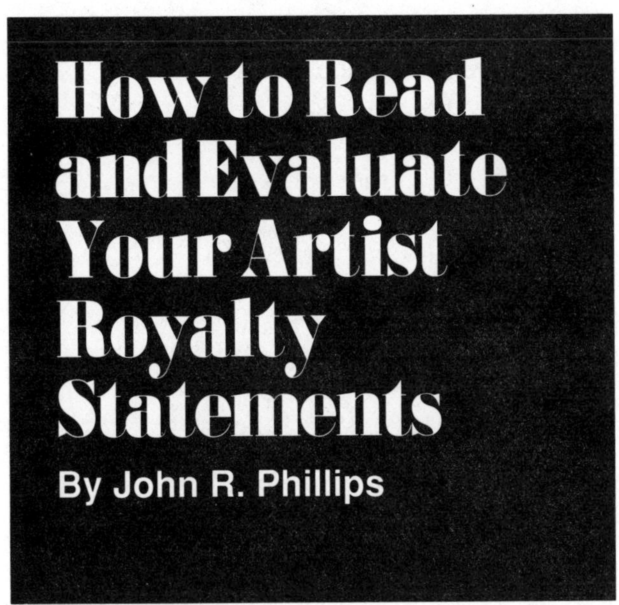

Suppose you are a newly successful artist with a hit album on your hands. In August Billboard shows your album has gone "gold" which means" . . . sales of 500,000 units or more." In early September you receive your first royalty statement, which, when you finally distinguish between the album and single of the same name, seems to add up to only about 200,000 units.

Have you been taken? Not necessarily.

DISCREPANCIES? DON'T PANIC

First of all, the 500,000 unit criteria for gold albums can include record club sales, which may be communicated from the club to the record company for certification purposes well before the record club remits the money due on the sales. Additionally, the 500,000 unit criteria probably include sales plan and special program free goods which can range from 15% to 20% of the units counted for certification, although royalties by agreement are not normally paid on them. Also by agreement, your royalties may only be payable on a percentage of net sales, say 85% or 90%. Usually this lower unit base is offset by a royalty rate higher than the record company would pay using a 100% unit royalty base. Your contract may also allow a reserve for returns in calculating royalties which can amount to 25% or more. You will eventually receive royalties on units in reserve to the extent returns do not deplete them. Lastly, don't forget, some of the 500,000 units could be from the period between your royalty statement period end, for example June 30th, and the Billboard edition in August.

Similar situations can occur with the reporting of royalties on your foreign sales. Suppose a friend from London has told you what a megahit your album is there, only for you to find zero royalties for the United Kingdom. The problem is probably a matter of time lag. The English affiliate or licensee record company has a normal accounting period to accumulate, process and report the sales and royalties to your record company in the U.S., which should report it on your next statement.

ARTIST ROYALTY STATEMENT FORMAT

Not only are each record company's royalty statements different, but the royalty statements of the individual labels of a record company group, may differ. Often, preceding the details may be a summary of the various types of earnings, including domestic, which may or may not include Canada, domestic licensee sales such as record clubs, and foreign licensee sales, which may actually be affiliates. Additionally, the summary will often give the previous statement balance and payment, if any, reserves currently held and prior reserves released, recording costs and advances deducted, charges, including session costs, video costs, advances, producer royalty deductions, miscellaneous adjustments and an ending balance.

DOMESTIC ROYALTIES

The common thread between record companies in reporting domestic royalties is the presentation of at least selections, units, royalty rates and amounts. The selections, or titles, are usually identified by a number and the title. Presently, the three primary configurations of an album, i.e.; LP (long playing disc), MC (music cassette tape) and CD (compact disc) are usually identified by the addition of a prefix or suffix letter or number, for example 1 = LP, 2 = CD and 4 = MC. 7" 45 RPM singles may be identified by a 7 prefix. Generally you can tell the difference between the product by the royalty cent rate. For example, the CD might have the highest rate to correspond with the highest price. However, in the past this may not have been so if your contract permitted CD's to be paid at the same rate as black vinyl disc LP's, as was common. The MC, although it may have been sold for the same price, generally has a slightly lower cent rate than the LP because the packaging allowance deducted from the price, 20%, is higher than the LP's, 10% to 15%. 45's generally have the lowest rate. To confuse things, however, there may be 12" vinyl singles, CD singles and cassette singles, in between. Ultimately, your record company may have to be consulted to identify some or all of the selections, particularly if titles are not given.

As mentioned previously, the record companies differ widely in their presentation of data. Some, for example, Record Company X (RCX) disclose all the elements used to calculate royalties for normal domestic sales, i.e.; catalog number, title description, configuration code, royalty percentage rate, packaging deduction percentage, the suggested retail list price (SRLP), royalty cent rate, quantity base (if other than 100%), quantity of royalty units, royalty amount for each configuration and a total for the catalog number. Since it would be beyond the intended scope of this article to cover all the variations between record companies, we will utilize RCX as an example for further discussion. To calculate your royalty in this case, you multiply the SRLP, i.e.; $8.98 by the reciprocal of the packaging percentage, i.e.; 90% (100% - 10%), times the royalty percentage, e.g.; 12%, equals $.96984 which would be rounded to $.9698. This cent rate multiplied by the number of units gives the royalty amount.

Simple? Not exactly, as you will see.

Prices

RCX, our example record company, negotiates contractually to pay royalties on the suggested retail list price basis. Other companies may use a wholesale basis, or variation thereof.

In the latter part of 1989, RCX's prices (SRLP's) for full priced normal retail channel sales were $15.98 for CD's, about to go to $13.98 except for superstars, and $8.98 for LP's and MC's, with a premium price of $9.98 for some new releases. It appears that $9.98 will soon be the normal full price with $10.98 the premium price for new releases by superstars. 12" singles usually are priced at $4.98, CD singles at $3.98, cassette singles at $2.49 and 45's at $1.99. Frequently of late, albums are being released only on MC and CD. It seems that vinyl discs are headed the way of 8-Track tapes. If you have some older releases you may see them at midprice, such as $11.98 for CD's and $6.98 for LP's and MC's.

Military sales through post exchanges (PX's) and ship's stores etc., have lower list prices, generally $11.95 for CD's, $6.75 for MC's and $6.50 for LP's. New releases from superstars generally are priced for PXs at $7.50 for MC's and $7.25 for LP's.

Price changes should be properly reflected in your royalties. Suppose, unlike RCX which retains a "dollar" reserve for returns, a record company has held a "unit" reserve on your first album. Two years, and two albums later, the first album is reduced to midprice. Any reserves still held on the first album relating to sales at the higher price should be reported at the higher royalty than the current midprice sales. For another illustration, assume all LP's and MC's go to a $9.98 price. To the extent that there are any returns after the price increase which relate to sales at the old price they should be segregated and charged back at the old, lower royalty rate.

Packaging Deductions

Packaging allowances are customarily deducted to arrive at a royalty base price on which your royalty percentage rate is applied. Generally, they approximate 10% for LP's, 20% for MC's and 25% for CD's. If you have a double fold LP, a greater deduction may be allowed, possibly 12 1/2% or 15%. Sometimes the agreement may be that the higher LP packaging allowance may apply if there are "special elements," i.e. something other than plain white sleeves. Special elements are, hopefully, clearly defined in your agreement. Additionally, your agreement may allow a 10% packaging deduction for 7" and 12" singles in four color sleeves, 20% for cassette singles and 25% for CD singles. You may, as has been common, have agreed to be paid royalties for CD's on a black vinyl disc LP basis for a certain time period. In that case, usually the 25% CD packaging is superseded by a provision for the same cent rate to be paid as for the LP.

Royalty Percentage

Typically, for the progressive albums of your commitment there are higher rates. There may also be increases of royalty percentage rates, or "escalations," for reaching plateaus of sales levels. Suppose your album came out and within the first six month royalty statement period 600,000 units were reported. Assume an escalation from 12% to 13% was required by your contract at 500,000 units. Suppose further that the sales were equally distributed between LP's, MC's, and CD's, i.e., 200,000 of each. So, in our example, 33,333 units of each should receive 1% more, i.e.:

CD's:	$15.98 x	75%	x	1% =	$.1199 x	33,333	=	$3,996.63
LP's:	$ 8.98 x	90%	x	1% =	$.0808 x	33,333	=	$2,693.31
MC's:	$ 8.98 x	80%	x	1% =	$.0718 x	33,334	=	$2,393.38
						100,000		$9,083.32

However, record companies often claim that their systems are not capable of prorating unit sales between the different configurations. Therefore, one configuration is counted first, another second and the third last. In this case the last one only would fall over the plateau and get the entire escalation. Curiously, record companies, when faced with the dilemma of which configuration to choose, usually escalate the cassettes, i.e.:

MC's: $.0718 x 100,000 = $7,180.00

If this was the case, since MC's have the lowest base price, you would have been underpaid by $1,903.32.

Your agreement may also allow the record company royalty relief for albums sold at midprices. For example, by contract you may receive 75% of your normal royalty rate for albums sold at SRLP's between 66.6% and 80% of the normal full price. Obviously, $6.98 divided by $8.98 equals 77.7% and therefore qualifies. However, if your contract defines midprice as between 66.6% and 75%, it would not qualify. In that case you should have received your full royalty percentage rate.

In another instance, suppose because of the downward trend on CD prices all of your CD's are priced at either $13.98 or $11.98. In this case just the full royalty percentage rate should be used despite $11.98 having formerly qualified for consideration as a midprice when the full CD price was $15.98.

Your agreement may also state, that your approval must be obtained for midpricing or that a certain amount of time must have passed since the initial full-priced release.

PX sales are often paid at a reduced royalty percentage rate, as are singles, record club and foreign sales. You need to summarize the differing percentages from your contract and compare them to what is shown on the statement. For record companies where just a cent rate is presented, it is more difficult to check. In this case knowing your contractual royalty percentage rate and packaging, you can check if the price is reasonable. For example, your agreement specifies a 12% rate and 10% packaging for the LP version of your album. Your royalty statement simply shows a royalty cent rate of $.9698 for the LP. $.9698 divided by 12%, divided by 90% (100% less the 10% packaging allowance) equals $8.98. Seems reasonable. If it doesn't work out, you question why. Perhaps the producer's royalty is being paid directly from the record company and deducted from yours?

Quantity

Since only net units payable are usually shown on the statements, not much can be done to check the quantities reported without access to the record company's internal records. Primarily, you can check reasonableness and make inquiries about an omission of product you know is out in the market. Considering all possible reasons, if quantities still appear too low, you may want to consider a royalty examination by professionals.

Record Club and Other Domestic Licensees

Our example record company, RCX, gives details of the U.S. Record Club reportings amongst its foreign detail. Often artists receive one-half of receipts from the club as their share of royalties. Sometimes you might notice a record club name, i.e.; CBS, followed by F/G. This is most likely your one-half share of the record club's reporting of excess bonus and free units distributed, usually made at the end of a contract period, often three years or more. If you don't have a percentage of receipts club provision you should check if your agreement allows club royalties to be paid on less than 100% of net sales. Often clubs pay on a reduced unit basis, for example 85%.

A special product licensing arrangement may also have occurred for which you are receiving a 50% of receipts royalty. These are the "K-tel" type compilation albums which usually have an intense media advertising campaign and a short life. Normally the royalties are prorated between the tracks included based on their share of the total number of tracks. If artist approval was required by the contract you have a means of checking for unreported product. However, the approval may have been obtained and then the track may not have been included or the product never released.

FOREIGN ROYALTIES

Record companies vary widely in their presentation of foreign royalties. While some simply report an amount due you for each territory, our example record company, RCX, gives a substantial amount of detail. However, even RCX shows only a U.S. dollar equivalent base price i.e., the local currency suggested retail list price, (SRLP) or constructed price if there is no SRLP, has already been reduced by taxes and packaging allowances and a conversion rate applied. The conversion rate may have been adjusted for withholding taxes in the territory. All these actions are probably permitted by your contract. However, you can't tell if they have been done correctly. For example, to "construct" the retail price, the foreign dealer price may have been incorrectly marked up or not marked up at all. The local territories' copyright royalty collection organization, upon whose requirements the constructed price may be based, may have followed the trend and negotiated for a mechanical royalty based directly on the dealer price, called the PPD (published price to dealers). The taxes deducted may also be incorrect. Suppose you received a royalty based on wholesale (dealer) prices and the foreign tax was calculated applying the correct tax rate, but to the higher constructed price. The packaging allowance may have been calculated applying the correct percentage incorrectly to a price including taxes. The packaging deductions made may also have been conformed to the local copyright society's allowances, which may differ from your agreement.

Unfortunately, it would require prohibitively detailed statements to give all the necessary information to check all of these concerns. Once again, however, you can check for reasonableness and inquire about what looks really odd. For example, if you are now supposed to be paid on the SRLP for CD's you should see the premium CD price being reflected in foreign territories as well, unless you agreed otherwise. Prices generally are higher in foreign territories, so you should not normally see a significant number of your albums being sold at an equivalent U.S. price which is notably lower than $8.98. However, it could be a territory which has runaway inflation. It may also be your older album(s) being mid or budget priced, if allowable. To test for reasonableness you should see if the older album(s), if any, which is being reported at the contractually reduced midprice rate fits the price criteria required. It should not be reported, for example, at a price which is 90% of the full priced latest album.

You can also check that your rates specified in the contract are being correctly utilized in reporting. If you are to receive 75% of your normal 12% domestic rate for major foreign territories you would expect to see 9% for the U.K., Germany, etc., as major is defined in your agreement. Also, if your recordings are generally successful overseas, you might want to inquire into significant missing territories for any of your selections.

PREVIOUS STATEMENT BALANCE

Surprisingly, sometimes the amount labeled "Previous Balance Forward" on your current statement does not agree with the balance on the previous statement. Perhaps an undetailed adjustment has been made which should be queried.

Payment dates for the statement balance are usually contractually specified, usually within 60 or 90 days of the royalty statement period end. If you are receiving payment directly, no doubt you will notice a delinquency. If payment goes to your business manager, and you expect it to be substantial, there is no harm in you checking if it has been received. Usually the large record companies are quite reliable in getting their statements and payments out.

RESERVES

A record company can withhold the normally allowed reserve for returns and credits in two ways: in units or in dollars. In the former instance you may or may not see the reserve quantities on your royalty statement. If not, you should request and your record company should easily supply this information, at least for domestic sales.

Sometimes record companies may withhold a percentage of "royalties otherwise payable. . ." as a reserve. This will usually be shown on the royalty statement. Your contract may limit the percentage of allowable reserves and specify a time schedule for release. With the necessary information at hand, you can readily see if the limits are being exceeded, or that the release schedule is not being adhered to.

Many contracts permit the record company to hold "reasonable" reserves in their best business judgment. If you are a new artist and they have pushed your product out into the stores, you can expect a high reserve percentage. About all you can do is reason with them for a reduction. Perhaps you're about to deliver another album. Also, if you have several releases which are cross-collateralized, i.e., negative royalties from net returns on one are offset against positive royalties otherwise payable on another, there is a good deal less justification for a high reserve percentage. High reserves on foreign royalties are a possibly objectionable area as well. Returns are not as readily accepted overseas. Normally, 5% to 10% is the maximum actually accepted.

CHARGES AGAINST ROYALTIES

Session charges, other recording costs and advances are usually the largest charges on your royalty statements, at least your initial royalty statement. Combined with producer fees and advances and some miscellaneous charges, these elements usually make up a recording fund as defined in your agreement.

It's important to remember that typically, record companies desire to foster artists' good will by cooperating and providing explanations and reasonable support for any significant charges you have questions about. The amount of details involved with sessions will prohibit total disclosure in your royalty statement. If any detail is given on sessions, it is likely to be invoice dates, descriptions, maybe just the vendor name and amounts. Presuming you have been in the studio recently, about all you can do with this information is to look for familiar company and individual names.

The record company is normally contractually allowed to charge all recording costs up to the point where the recording is ready for manufacture. Thus, sometimes you will note remix costs for example for a 12" single, or remastering costs, for an old album being readied for release on CD. When you see these types of charges, you should expect to see some new product released soon after the date charged.

Also you may notice miscellaneous charges for hotels and per diems, limo's, gold record copies, etc. Despite the erroneous assumption that sometimes these items are being given free, it is normal for them to be charged against your royalties. Normally, you can only prevail on something that was not in your control, unless your contract specifically states otherwise.

The recording fund for your album may, after the first album, be based on the results of your previous album. For example, your agreement may say that the current recording fund will amount to 66.6% of the net royalties earned on the last album. Producer fees and advances, along with the recording costs and your advances, will normally equal the current fund, i.e., the delivery advance will be adjusted to make it so.

Videos, because of their high cost and modest independent earning power in the past, have developed their own customary treatment. Typically, 50% of the cost is chargeable against your royalties from audio recordings. You should be aware of the budget and check that no more than 50% is charged to your royalty account, unless contractually permitted.

Currently, even with a commercially exploited video for home viewing, it is not likely for the video to earn more than production costs. However, you might check if your contract allows your record company to apply 100% of earnings to the 50% share of costs not charged to you. In other words, the earnings, however modest, should be shared 50/50 from the first dollar unless the contract allows the record company to first recoup their share. Additionally, as MTV, VH1, etc., revenues increase, you may question how the record company distributes the earnings between the videos submitted. For example, some record companies may receive large catalog guarantee advances periodically, with no identification of the airplay of individual videos. Therefore, they may simply apportion a share equally to all videos submitted, which would be detrimental to you if your's received a great deal of airplay.

Producer Royalty Deductions

Producer royalty deductions are shown on your statement in one of three ways: 1. the producer's royalty cent rate may be deducted from yours and just a net rate shown; 2. the producer deduction is shown by a repetition of a line showing the unit sales, etc., but using the negative producer cent rate to calculate the amount to be deducted; or 3. the total producer royalties payable could be deducted in a lump sum on the summary page. In the last case, you should request a copy of the producer's statement, which gives the details of the calculation. You will want to check that the producer is not being paid a higher rate than appropriate.

Also there is the concern as to when the producer royalty starts to be payable. You need to consult your agreement as to whether the producer royalty should commence only when your account is recouped and whether the costs and advances should be recouped at rates inclusive or exclusive of the producer's rate. Also, check whether the producer is then paid from record one, or just after recoupment. In addition, if the producer has received an advance charged to you, then you should not see any producer deductions until his advance is recouped from his royalties. At that point, only royalties in excess of his advance, should be deducted from yours.

Miscellaneous Adjustments

After receiving more than one royalty statement, you may notice adjustments on the current statement correcting errors made by the record company on previous statements rendered. If, for example, a rate is being corrected, you should agree the applicable quantities adjusted coincide to your previous statement. Analyzing your rate, as discussed previously, should reveal if the correction is appropriate.

CONCLUSION

If you have applied all of the procedures discussed herein, you have gained some satisfying comfort that your royalty statements contain no glaring improprieties, or you are contemplating a royalty examination. If an examination appears warranted, and routine periodic examinations are usually warranted after several releases/royalty statements, you should consult your contract concerning any limitation on the time period to object to your statements. Record companies normally put a great deal of effort into making timely and accurate royalty accountings. However, errors do occur and contracts often contain language which can be interpreted in various ways.

EXAMPLE OF AN ARTIST ROYALTY STATEMENT SUMMARY

Period 07/01/89 to 12/31/89

BALANCE FORWARD	$467,246.00
ROYALTY PAYMENTS	(467,246.00)
PRIOR RESERVES HELD	75,698.78
BEGINNING BALANCE	$75,698.78
EARNINGS	
DOMESTIC SALES	$669,629.64
MILITARY SALES	49,306.20
LICENSEE SALES	478,969.62
LICENSEE CLUB SALES	7,043.74
LICENSEE MISCELLANEOUS SALES	1,250.00
TOTAL EARNINGS	1,206,199.20
CHARGES	
ADVANCES	($200,000.00)
SESSION CHARGES	(348,790.18)
MISCELLANEOUS CHARGES	(74,512.88)
TOTAL CHARGES	(623,303.06)
RESERVES	(241,239.84)
BALANCE PAYABLE	$417,355.08
LESS: PRODUCER DEDUCTION (ALBUM 2)	(62,154.09)
BALANCE ENDING PAYABLE	$355,200.99

ARTIST ROYALTY STATEMENT
EXAMPLE OF SUMMARY OF DOMESTIC EARNINGS

CAT	NUMBER	DESCRIPTION	CFG	ROY%	PACK%	SRSP	$RATE	QUANTITY	AMOUNT	NET PAYABLE
RCX	000001	SINGLE #1	1	12.000		$1.99	0.23880	2,133	$509.36	
RCX	000001	SINGLE #1 (PRODUCER)	1	-3.000		$1.99	0.05970	2,133	(127.34)	
RCX	000001	SINGLE #1	2	12.000	25.00	$3.49	0.31410	4,908	1,541.60	
RCX	000001	SINGLE #1(PRODUCER)	2	-3.000	25.00	$3.49	0.0785	4,908	(385.43)	
RCX	000001	SINGLE #1	4	12.000	20.00	$2.49	0.23904	11,117	2,657.41	
RCX	000001	SINGLE #1 (PRODUCER)	4	-3.000	20.00	$2.49	0.05976	11,117	(664.35)	$3,531.25
RCX	000002	SINGLE #2	1	12.000		$1.99	0.23880	75,248	$17,969.22	
RCX	000002	SINGLE #2	2	12.000	25.00	$3.49	0.31410	48,962	15,378.96	
RCX	000002	SINGLE #2	4	12.000	20.00	$2.49	0.23904	157,658	37,686.57	$71,034.75
RCX	001001	ALBUM #1	1	13.000		$8.98	1.16740	2.133	$2,490.06	
RCX	001001	ALBUM #1 (PRODUCER)	1	-3.000		$8.98	-0.26940	2.133	(574.63)	
RCX	001001	ALBUM #1	2	13.000	25.00	$13.98	1.36305	4,908	6,689.85	
RCX	001001	ALBUM #1(PRODUCER)	2	-3.000	25.00	$13.98	-0.31455	4,908	(1,543.81)	
RCX	001001	ALBUM #1	4	13.000	20.00	$8.98	0.93392	11,117	10,382.39	
RCX	001001	ALBUM #1(PRODUCER)	4	-3.000	20.00	$8.98	-0.21552	11,117	(2,395.94)	$15,047.92
RCX	001002	ALBUM #1	1	12.000		$9.98	1.19760	104,558	125,218.66	
RCX	001002	ALBUM #1	1	13.000		$9.98	1.29740	4,106	5,327.12	
RCX	001002	ALBUM #2	2	12.000	25.00	$15.98	1.43820	108,855	156,555.26	
RCX	001002	ALBUM #2	2	13.000	25.00	$15.98	1.55805	4,275	6,660.66	
RCX	001002	ALBUM #2	4	12.000	20.00	$9.98	0.95808	286,587	274,573.27	
RCX	001002	ALBUM #2	4	13.000	20.00	$9.98	1.03792	11,254	11,680.75	$580,015.72
				TOTAL DOMESTIC SALES						**$669,629.64**

Period
07/01/89
to
12/31/89

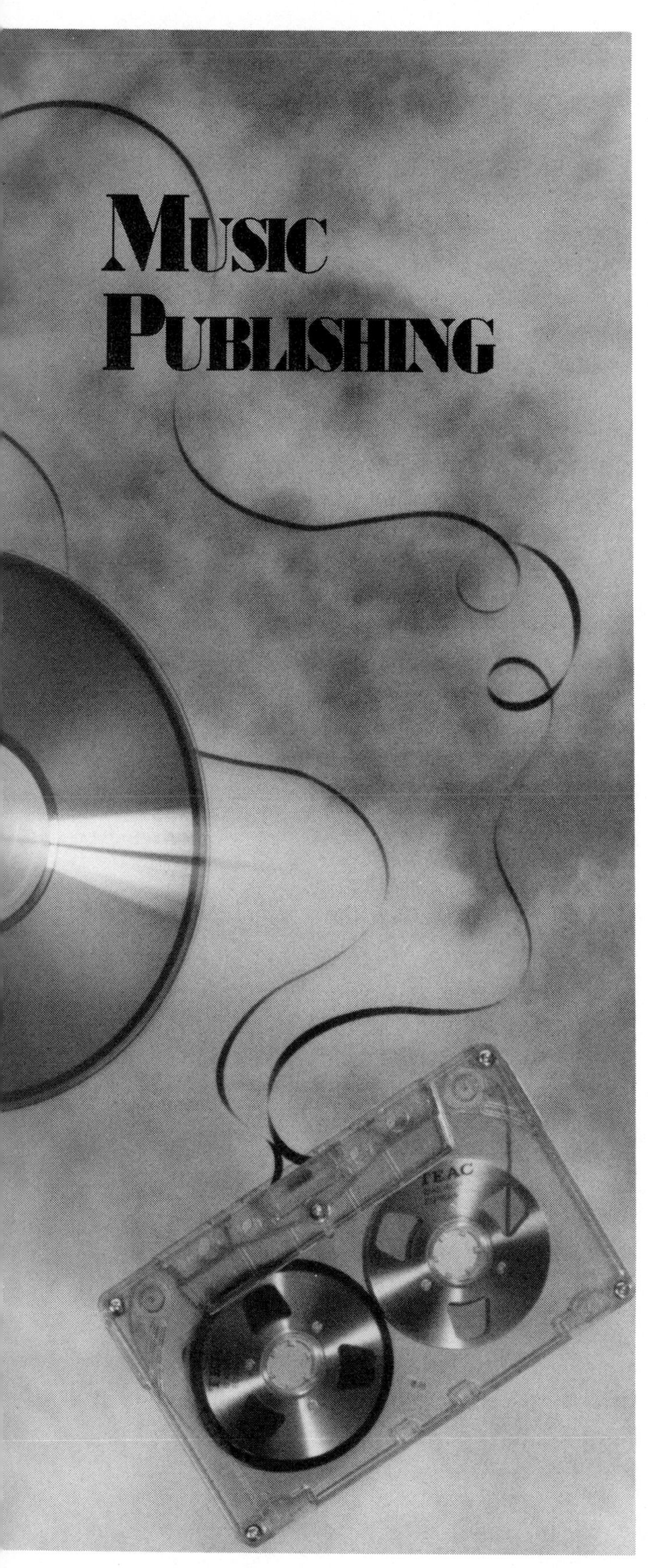

- Music Publishing
- Analysis of a Single-Song Agreement
- Analysis of an Exclusive Term Songwriter Agreement
- Music Clearance: The Clearing House, Ltd.

Music Publishing

By Neville L. Johnson

Every songwriter should know the dynamics and economics of the exploitation of a song. This essay explores the types of income that are generated in the music publishing industry and the kinds of deals that are commonly struck between publishers and songwriters. The attributes of a good publisher are summarized, suggestions for obtaining a publisher are made, and a typical music publishing agreement is examined.

Music publishing has been the major source of revenue for songwriters since the turn of this century when vaudeville was the primary outlet through which songs were exploited. Music publishers of that era attempted to persuade entertainers to publicly perform musical compositions to stimulate the sale of printed editions and player piano rolls. Over the years, the technology for merchandising music expanded with such inventions as radio, the phonograph record, television, motion pictures, videotape, and most recently, compact discs. Songwriters and publishers benefited from the by-products: new sources of income. As the complexity and size of the music publishing industry increased, so also did the amounts of income capable of being earned within it. Today, one hit song can make someone a millionaire.

TYPES OF INCOME

There are four general categories of revenue in the music publishing industry: public performance income, mechanical rights income, sheet music income, and synchronization income.

Performance Income

The copyright laws in the United States and similar laws in virtually every other country of the world require that compensation be paid to copyright owners for the public performance of their music. In practical terms, radio stations and television stations, theater halls, nightclubs, and discotheques throughout the world make payments to performing rights organizations, which, in most cases, are nonprofit companies. These organizations, after deducting their costs of administration, distribute their revenues to publishers and composers. These performing rights organizations exist because it would be impractical for music publishers to license separately the right to publicly perform their compositions to all radio and television stations and every concert hall and nightclub.

The United States has three performing rights organizations. ASCAP (American Society of Composers, Authors and Publishers) and BMI (Broadcast Music Incorporated) are both nonprofit organizations, while SESAC (formerly Society of European Stage Authors and Composers) has been a family owned company for nearly fifty years and has no significant presence in the marketplace. ASCAP and BMI are the organizations that most songwriters and composers join. (A composer should meet with representatives of both organizations before signing with one.) These organizations perform the difficult task of collecting public performance income and distributing it in proportion to the success of each composition licensed by the organizations.

These organizations also license public performance rights to sister performing rights organizations which exist in other territories of the world.

Music publishing performance income is paid by performing rights organizations in two varieties: The "writer's share" and the "publisher's share." Under these headings, the performing rights organizations segregate the income on an equal basis so that 50% of their payable public performance revenue on any composition is paid directly to its composer and 50% paid to its publisher.

Mechanical Income

An important source of income to songwriters is that earned from the manufacture and sale of sound recordings, and commonly referred to as "mechanical income." The rate payable for each recording of a composition distributed is currently 5.7 cents for songs of 5 minutes or less; or 1.1 cents per each minute or fraction thereof above that. (The rates are set by the Copyright Royalty Tribunal and will be periodically increased in 1992, 1994, and 1996 based on changes in the U.S. Consumer Price Index.) Thus, for a recording containing 10 compositions of 5 minutes or less, 57 cents is paid in mechanical income to the publisher(s) of the compositions. If 100,000 albums are sold, $57,000 is paid to the publisher(s) of the compositions contained on such a record. In a typical publishing deal the songwriter will receive half this amount, or $28,500.

In the United States, mechanical income is paid to the publisher of a composition by the record company manufacturing recordings of the composition pursuant to a contract between them called a "mechanical license." Usually the record company is required to account to the publisher on a quarterly basis.

In most countries of the world, mechanical rights income is computed differently than in the United States. Instead of a flat rate per song, the royalty is computed on a basis that is usually 6 to 8 percent of the retail selling price of recordings sold in such territories. Mechanical income in such locales is allocated evenly among the compositions contained on the record or tape to which the formula is applied. Usually, this income is collected by mechanical rights societies that exist in most countries of the world. Such mechanical rights societies remit the monies they have collected to the publisher of the composition earning such revenue.

The closest entity in the United States to a mechanical rights society is the Harry Fox Agency, Inc. headquartered in New York City. Although many American publishers issue their own mechanical licenses, many prefer to use this company, which, for a 3% fee, issues mechanical licenses to American record companies, and conducts audits of such companies to insure that proper payments are made.

Print Income

Sheet music has always contributed substantially to the earnings of a songwriter. Today the industry is concentrated in a few companies that manufacture and distribute sheet music across the United States. A publisher who does not print and manufacture sheet music, but licenses such rights to another company, can be paid 75 cents or more per single edition sold, but the writer usually receives only 8-12 cents per single edition.

Synchronization Income

Synchronization income refers to those monies which are paid by motion picture and television production companies for the right to use compositions in motion pictures or dramatic presentations on television. The "synch right" for a composition contained in a major motion picture may cost $25,000 and can stimulate the generation of revenue from those areas discussed in the above three sections.

Foreign Income

The foregoing sources of income occur throughout the world. Domestic publishers enter into foreign licensing or subpublishing agreements with music publishers who operate outside the United States and Canada. The shrewd and successful commercial songwriter often retains his foreign rights and makes his own subpublishing deals, which often provide substantial income to the songwriter-publisher.

MUSIC PUBLISHING AGREEMENTS

There are three types of contracts pertaining to songwriters: standard agreements, co-publishing agreements, and administration agreements.

Standard Agreements

These transactions come in two species—single-song agreements and long-term agreements (which are discussed in separate articles). Under these agreements, the income is generally split as follows:

Mechanical Income
Publisher collects all mechanical income and pays 50% to composer.

Performance Income
Publisher collects and retains all of "publisher's share" of performance income. Writer is paid income directly by his performing rights organization and retains all such "writer's share" of performance income.

Print Income
Publisher collects all revenue and pays writer 10 cents per printed edition.

Synchronization Income
Publisher collects income and splits 50/50 with composer.

Foreign Income
Net receipts (that amount received by or credited to publisher from subpublisher) are split 50/50 with composer.

In a single-song deal, the publisher owns the copyright in the composition for the term of its copyright, subject to the possibility of its reversion to its composer thirty-five years after its publication (its first commercial distribution) or forty years after its assignment (transfer), which ever is earlier. Some long-term songwriter's agreements provide that compositions created pursuant to such agreements are "works for hire" for the publisher and, hence, incapable of being recaptured by the composer. Normally such agreements last for one year, with two to four one-year options held by the publisher. All compositions created by the songwriter during the term are owned by the publisher.

Under most such agreements, the writer is paid an advance on signing and with each option pickup, or a weekly salary ($18,000 to $25,000 per year is the average for a fledgling writer). Single-songwriter agreements are entered into with or without advances paid to the songwriter: there is no common industry practice or standard.

Under both types of agreement, the publisher administers the compositions subject to them. That is, the publisher issues all documents and contracts affecting such compositions and collects all income, other than the writer's share of performance income, earned by the compositions.

Co-publishing Agreements

Co-publishing agreements differ in two material respects from standard agreements described above. Under co-publishing agreements, as in standard agreements, the publisher administers the compositions subject to such agreements. However, the songwriter not only receives the writer's share of publishing income, or roughly 50% of the gross revenues of the composition, but also shares in that portion of what traditionally was the publisher's share of music publishing income. Thus, under such agreements, the songwriter is ordinarily paid 75% of the mechanical income, print income, and synchronization income derived from the composition and, in addition to the writer's share of performance income, receives 50% of the publisher's share of performance income. Also, under co-publishing agreements the copyrights to the compositions usually are owned jointly by the publisher and songwriter.

Co-publishing agreements can encompass one song, a number of stated songs, or cover all compositions written over a period of years, as in the case of a long-term songwriter's agreement.

Administration Agreements

The most advantageous arrangement for a songwriter is an administration agreement. Under this type of agreement, the administrative activities of a songwriter's company are conducted by another publisher, which performs such functions as issuing mechanical licenses, registering compositions with performing rights organizations, and collecting its income throughout the world. The administrator collects all income but remits at least as much as a co-publisher's share, and often a higher percentage, to the songwriter's administered publishing company (15% of the publisher's gross revenues is the percentage normally retained by an administrator).

Such agreements extend for periods varying from three to five years, at the close of which periods all administrative rights to the compositions revert to the administered company. In practice, such agreements are difficult to obtain for songwriters who have no independent means of exploiting compositions that would be subject to such an arrangement. For singer-songwriters who have recording deals, or songwriters who can get their songs "covered" (recorded by others) such transactions are often the most beneficial and these are done frequently.

Points of Negotiation

Royalties are always negotiable, as are advances. A songwriter should always attempt to obtain a reversion of any composition subject to a single-song, long-term publishing, or co-publishing agreement when any such composition has not been commercially exploited within a time period specified in any such contract. A composer should allow translations of or the addition of new lyrics to any composition only with his or her prior consent as in some countries a translator or lyricist may register and receive income from a translation which is never performed, sold, or even recorded.

Points in publishing contracts vary in importance among publishing companies. Similarly, songwriters differ on the priorities of the numerous issues involved in a songwriting agreement. Songwriters must become expert or have advisors, such as attorneys, personal managers, and business managers, to counsel them on the best methods of navigating the narrows of music publishing.

Self-publishing

Some composers are capable not only of creating but also of administering their catalogues. The music publishing industry is not so difficult that its mechanics would confound an attentive student. It is difficult, however, to obtain commercially exploited versions of compositions. For the composer interested in and capable of properly administering and promoting the products of his or her artistry, self-publishing is a viable alternative to the traditional business arrangements with publishers, but in practice, few writers are successful going it alone.

When a record is released on an independent label, financed by the artist, self-publishing makes sense. Universal copyrights are valuable assets - don't transfer or lessen rights to them without a good reason.

FINDING A GOOD PUBLISHER

Music publishers play an important role in today's music industry. First, they have the best success at securing "covers." Moreover, a songwriter usually needs a middleman, critic, cheerleader, and businessman. A good music publisher, in fulfilling these needs of a songwriter, will: be enthusiastic and knowledgeable about the artist and his or her music; have a good royalty department and a reputation for honesty; pay or advance money for demos; have an aggressive professional department—e.g. professional managers who will attempt to get songs to record producers and their artists; be responsive to the needs of the songwriter and to suggestions and questions.

Songwriters, with their advisors, should work out a strategy to find a good publisher and to enter an advantageous agreement with such a publisher. Some personal managers of songwriters are capable of finding reputable publishers and subsequently obtaining agreements that are satisfactory to both parties. The songwriter's music attorney often can open the door to publishing companies. Representatives of ASCAP and BMI can be helpful, as can the recommendations of other songwriters. Information and guidance is available at the National Academy of Songwriters (NAS) and the Los Angeles Songwriters Showcase (LASS), both of which are nonprofit organizations.

Because music publishing agreements can be extremely technical, a music attorney should always be consulted to review most agreements a composer is requested to sign (in the case of "single-song agreements," composers should master all salient points of negotiation and negotiate for themselves, or should obtain someone expert in the subject to advise them or liaise on their behalf.) Most importantly, composers should investigate carefully before choosing their advisors and business partners.

Single-song agreements come in a wide variety of forms: there is no standard form of agreement. There is no written agreement that cannot be modified before it is executed - be wary of printed forms, and be sure to understand what is being signed. The agreement below is representative of one that while not slanted in favor of the songwriter, is not a "total rip-off."

SINGLE-SONG AGREEMENT

AGREEMENT effective __________ day of ________________
19____, by and between ________________________________
hereinafter referred to as "PUBLISHER," and ________________
hereinafter (collectively) referred to as "WRITER."

1. ASSIGNMENT OF WORK

Writer hereby sells, assigns and delivers to Publisher, its successors and assigns, the original musical composition written and composed by Writer (hereinafter referred to as the "Composition" now entitled ____________) including the title, words and music thereof, and all worldwide rights therein, and all copyrights and the rights to secure copyrights and any extensions and renewals of copyrights therein and in any arrangements and adaptations thereof, and any and all other rights that Writer now has or to which he may be entitled, whether now known or hereafter to become known.

Commentary: *The composition should revert to the songwriter at a stated time if the publisher cannot get the song covered. 1 to 2 years is fair.*

2. USE OF COMPOSITION

Publisher shall have the free and unrestricted right to use the Composition in any way that Publisher may desire, and Writer hereby consents to such changes, adaptations, versions, dramatizations, transpositions, translations, foreign lyric substitutions, parody lyrics for commercial purposes, editing and arrangements of the Composition as Publisher deems desirable. In the event that the Composition is an instrumental composition, then Writer hereby irrevocably grants to Publisher the sole and exclusive right and privilege to cause lyrics to be written for the Composition by a lyricist or lyricists designated by Publisher, and in such event, one-half (1/2) of the royalties provided for herein shall be payable to Writer.

Commentary: *Advocates for songwriters attempt to limit this type of clause as much as possible. First, writers generally resist changes made to their music without their consent. Moreover, the songwriter may suffer a substantial decrease in his or her share of the revenue if another writer is added at the unilateral discretion of the publisher. Translations are a special problem, as songwriters frequently lose substantial portions of revenue to* *translators who write versions that are not successful commercially. Translations should not be registered with any foreign performing or mechanical rights society until a commercial recording of the translation has been released. All major changes and additions should be made with the consent of the songwriter.*

3. WARRANTIES AND REPRESENTATIONS

Writer hereby warrants and represents that the Composition is an original work, that neither the Composition nor any part thereof infringes upon the title, literacy or musical property of copyright or in any other work nor the statutory, common law or other rights (including rights of privacy) of any person, firm or corporation, that he is the sole writer and composer and the sole owner of the Composition and of all the rights therein, that he has not sold, assigned, transferred, hypothecated or mortgaged any right, title or interest in or to the Composition or any part thereof or any of the rights herein conveyed, that he has not made or entered into any contract with any other person, firm or corporation affecting the Composition or any right, title or interest therein or in copyright thereof, that no person, firm or corporation other than Writer has or has had claims or has claimed any right, title or interest in or to the Composition or any part thereof, or any use thereof or any copyright therein, that the composition has never been published, that where no copyright registration information has been given in paragraph 1 of this Agreement, the Composition has never been registered for copyright, and that the Writer has full right, power and authority to make this present instrument of sale and transfer.

Commentary: *This is typical "boilerplate." Of course, the song must be noninfringing and not the property of someone else - this is the heart of the agreement. Virtually all publishing agreements contain language of the above nature. In any event, if the song is infringing or has been previously sold to a third party, the composer is liable.*

4. ROYALTIES

Publisher shall pay or cause to be paid to Writer the following sums with respect to the Composition:

(a) 5 cents per copy on all regular piano-vocal sheet music sold, paid for and not returned in the United States and Canada.

Commentary: *Songwriters have long received less than a fair share of print music income. Many publishing companies now split this revenue equally with the songwriter, rather than using a penny rate. A songwriter should receive a minimum of 15 cents per single edition, and the payment should increase with inflation. The increase can be tied to the Consumer Price Index.*

(b) 10 percent of the net wholesale selling price for each copy of all other editions sold, paid for and not returned in the United States and Canada.

Commentary: *"Net wholesale selling price" is ambiguous. What are the deductions from "gross" (which means all amounts received) to arrive at "net"? These deductions should be specified. Most contracts, unlike this one, provide that the songwriter will be paid on the suggested retail selling price of the edition. The royalty commonly paid is*

10% of any such selling price. Again, 50% of what the publisher receives is what the songwriter should ask.

(c) If the Composition is included in any song book, folio or similar publication issued by Publisher or its affiliates in the United States or Canada, a proportionate share of the royalty set forth in paragraph (b) above, which the number "one" bears to the total number of copyrighted musical compositions or arrangements of works on which royalties are payable included in such publications. If pursuant to a license granted by Publisher to an unaffiliated licensee, the Composition is included in any song book, folio or similar publication in the United States or Canada, the proportionate share of fifty percent (50%) of the net sums actually received by Publisher from said licensee, which the number "one" bears to the total number of Publisher's Compositions included in any such publication.

Commentary: *This is fair as the split is equal.*

(d) Fifty percent (50%) of any and all sums actually received (less any costs for collection) by Publisher from mechanical rights, electrical transcription and reproducing rights, motion picture and television synchronization rights and all other rights therein (except as provided for in subparagraph (e) hereof), in the United States and Canada.

Commentary: *It should be specified that the songwriter be paid 50% of any advances paid to the publisher with respect to the composition. Costs of collection, such as Harry Fox Agency fees, should be charged against publisher's share. It is the publisher's job to administer.*

(e) Writer shall have no claim whatsoever against Publisher for any royalties received by Publisher from any performing rights society or other similar organization which makes payment directly (or indirectly other than through Publisher) to writers, authors and composers.

Commentary: *The writer is paid performance income directly by ASCAP or BMI, not through the publisher.*

(f) Fifty percent (50%) of any and all sums, after deduction of foreign taxes, actually received in the United States (less any costs for collection) by Publisher from sales and uses directly related to the Composition in countries outside of the United States and Canada (other than public performance royalties as hereinabove set forth in paragraph (e). This provision shall not apply to copies of printed music shipped from the United States to such countries, to which the rates set forth in subparagraphs (a), (b), and (c) above shall apply.

Commentary: *No subpublisher (licensee of original publisher) should be permitted to take a percentage greater than 25% to collect the income, or 50% of the income "at source" (i.e., where the revenue is earned) if he secures a cover record. This is an important provision and can involve substantial income for the writer. Also, the writer should be paid when monies are credited to the subpublisher, not just received.*

(g) It is agreed that no royalties are to be paid for professional copies, copies disposed of as new issues, or copies distributed for advertising purposes. It is also distinctly understood

that no royalties are payable on consigned copies unless paid for, and not until such time as an accounting therefor can properly be made.
(h) Except as herein expressly provided, no other compensation, royalties or monies shall be paid to Writer.

Commentary: *This is a superfluous statement and should be deleted and replaced by a 50% "catch-all" provision. See Evanne L. Levin's commentary below.*

Commentary: *Evanne L. Levin from "Analysis of an Exclusive Term Songwriter Agreement." Provision should be made for advances to be paid to the writer under any term songwriter agreement. The publisher is requiring the writer to write exclusively for it and in exchange is paying the writer only the royalties noted above, while retaining complete ownership of the songs and keeping 100% of the publisher's share of income. Nor is there any guarantee that the publisher will successfully exploit any of the writer's material, in which case the writer will see no income.*

Advances are typically paid (i) in one lump sum on execution of the agreement and at the beginning of each succeeding year of the term, and/or (ii) in regular installments over the term, like a weekly or semi-monthly paycheck. $20,000 - 24,000 for the first year is not an unusual amount for a large publishing company to pay; small, independent publishers typically pay less but contend that more time will be devoted to promoting its staff writers since they have fewer staff. The amount of the advance typically escalates 10 - 20% for each succeeding year of the term, and may be further boosted by additional advances triggered by a song's commercial success. This is commonly done by tying increases to Billboard Chart positions achieved or sales levels reached by previous albums. All advances are recoupable from both the writer's share and publisher's share of royalties otherwise payable to the writer (ASCAP/BMI royalties excluded).

A publisher who pays an advance to the writer will require the delivery of a specified minimum number of compositions written by the writer. 15 to 20 "Wholly Owned Compositions" is typical, with songs co-written receiving partial credit. For example, if the writer writes a song with two other writers, the publisher will give the writer credit for 1/3 of a Wholly Owned Composition toward the minimum delivery requirement. If the writer fails to deliver the minimum number of songs required during any contract year, the publisher will have the right to extend the term without having to increase the advances beyond the agreed amount until a sufficient number of songs are delivered. The writer should object to any provision giving the publisher the right to suspend advances in addition to extending the term.

(i) Notwithstanding anything to the contrary herein contained in this Agreement, Publisher shall have the right to deduct ten percent (10%) of all sums received in the United States from all sources throughout the world as administration fees, before computing the compensation payable to Writer hereunder.

Commentary: *This clause is unfair and would reduce the writer's share by 5% of gross revenues. There is no justification for such a split - the publisher's job is to administer the composition, and he or she is well paid for it without this so-called "administration fee."*

5. ACCOUNTING

Royalty statements shall be rendered to Writer quarterly within forty-five (45) days following the close of each such quarterly period. Each statement shall be accompanied by a remittance of such amount as may be shown thereon to be due and payable. All royalty statements rendered by Publisher to Writer shall be binding upon Writer and not subject to any objection by Writer for any reason unless specific objection is made, in writing, stating the basis thereof, to Publisher within one (1) year from the date rendered. Writer shall have a reasonable right to audit those portions of the books and records of Publisher pertaining to the Composition.

> ***Commentary:*** *Statements are rendered quarterly, which is nice, but the time should be stated more clearly (for example, within 90 days after each calendar quarter). Most agreements provide for semiannual accounting. The writer should have at least a two year period to audit and object, and preferably three years.*

6. ASSIGNMENT OF COPYRIGHT

Writer hereby expressly grants and conveys to Publisher the copyright in the Composition, together with renewals and extensions thereof, and the right to secure any and all rights therein that Writer may at any time be entitled to. Writer agrees to sign any and all other papers which may be required to effectuate this Agreement, and hereby irrevocably authorizes and appoints Publisher, its successors or assigns, his attorneys and representatives in their names or in his name to take such actions and make, sign, execute, acknowledge and deliver all such documents as may from time to time be necessary to secure the renewals and extensions of the copyright in the Composition, and to assign to Publisher, its successors and assigns, said renewals and extensions of copyrights and all rights therein for the term of such renewals and extensions.

> ***Commentary:*** *The first sentence is redundant: the songwriter assigned the copyright in paragraph 1. The rest of the paragraph is boilerplate and irrelevant now - copyrights are not capable of being renewed.*

7. TRANSFER OF AGREEMENT

Writer agrees that he will not transfer nor assign this Agreement nor any interest therein nor any sums that may be or become due hereunder without the written consent of Publisher, and no purported assignment or transfer in violation of this restriction shall be valid to pass any interest to the assignee or transferee.

> ***Commentary:*** *Prohibiting the assignment of income is unjustifiable and unlawful under laws in some states which discourage agreements that prohibit assignment of monies.*

8. ACTIONS AND INDEMNITIES

Writer hereby authorizes Publisher at its absolute discretion and at Writer's sole expense to employ attorneys and to institute or defend any action or proceeding and to take any other proper steps to protect the right, title and interest of Publisher in and to the Composition and every portion thereof acquired from Writer, pursuant to the terms hereof and in that connection to settle, compromise or in any other manner dispose of any matter, claim, action or proceeding and to satisfy any judgment that may be rendered and all of the expense so incurred and other sums so paid by Publisher. Writer hereby agrees to pay to Publisher on demand, further authorizing Publisher, whenever in its opinion its right, title or interest to any of Writer's compositions are questioned or there is a breach of any of the covenants, warranties or representations contained in this contract or in any other similar contract heretofore or hereafter entered into between Publisher and Writer, to withhold any and all royalties that may be or become due to Writer pursuant to all such contracts until such questions shall have been settled or such breach repaired, and to apply such royalties to the repayment of all sums due to Publisher with respect thereto.

> ***Commentary:*** *This is a very tricky area. Too much control over litigation resides in the publisher. The publisher should be required to protect the copyright and to prevent and stop infringements, and should bear all costs of doing so. That is a risk of doing business.*
>
> *When sued by third parties, the writer should have the right to have his or her own attorney and to consent to all settlements. Monies should not continue to be withheld unless a lawsuit is brought within six months after such monies are first withheld; any monies withheld should bear interest.*

9. COLLABORATION

The term "Writer" shall be understood to include all the authors and composers of the Composition. If there be more than one, the covenants herein contained shall be deemed to be both joint and several on the part of all the authors and composers, and the royalties hereinabove specified to be paid to Writer shall, unless a different division of royalty be specified in paragraphs 2 and/or 14 hereof, be due to all the authors and composers collectively to be paid by Publisher in equal shares to each. This Agreement may be executed by the authors and composers in several counterparts.

> ***Commentary:*** *If a lyricist and composer have written the song, their respective contributions should be delineated. The lyricist should not suffer if the music is infringing and vice versa with respect to the composer if the lyrics infringe. Further, it is the lyricist, not the composer, who may suffer a loss in income from translations, which the composer may not wish to share.*

10. USE OF NAME

Writer hereby grants to Publisher the perpetual right to use and publish and to permit others to use and publish Writer's name (including any professional name heretofore or hereafter adopted by Writer), likeness and biographical material, or any reproduction or simulation thereof and the title of the Composition in connection with the printing, sale, advertising, distribution and exploitation of music, folios, recordings, performances, player rolls and otherwise concerning the Composition, and for any other purpose related to the business of Publisher, its associates, affiliates and subsidiaries, or to refrain therefrom.

> ***Commentary:*** *The clause "any other purpose related to the business of Publisher, its associates, affiliates and subsidiaries," is too general and should be deleted.*

11. ASSIGNMENT

Publisher shall have the right to assign this Agreement and any of its rights hereunder and to delegate any of its obligations hereunder, in whole or in part, to any person, firm or corporation. Without limiting the generality of the foregoing, Publisher shall have the right to enter into subpublishing, collection, print or other agreements with respect to the Composition with any person, firm or corporation for any one or more countries of the world.

Commentary: *Publisher should be allowed to assign only to a person or entity acquiring all or substantially all of the assets of publisher. Writer should be allowed to purchase the song at the same price at which it is sold to any third party (if it is part of a catalogue, an independent appraiser can be appointed), but few publishers will agree to this.*

12. DISPUTES

This contract shall be deemed to have been made in the State of California, and its validity, construction and effect shall be governed by and construed under the laws and judicial decisions of the State of California applicable to agreements wholly performed therein.

Commentary: *In the event of a dispute, the prevailing party should be entitled to reasonable attorney's fees and costs of suit. Oftentimes it costs as much to fight about the song as the amount at stake. Further, arbitration before the American Arbitration Association, which has offices across America, may be the most economical method of dispute resolution - it's generally less expensive and faster than the court system.*

13. ENTIRE AGREEMENT

This Agreement contains the entire understanding between us, and all of its terms, conditions and covenants shall be binding upon and shall inure to the benefit of the respective parties and their heirs, successors and assigns. No modification or waiver hereunder shall be valid unless the same is in writing and is signed by the parties hereto.

14. ROYALTY DIVISIONS

Royalties payable to Writer hereunder shall be divided among the parties below in the proportions following if otherwise than provided for in paragraph 9 herein.

WRITER	PERCENTAGE
______________________	________________
______________________	________________
______________________	________________

IN WITNESS WHEREOF, the parties hereto have executed this Agreement as of the day and year first above written.

____

WRITER ________________

ADDRESS ________________

____

PUBLISHER ________________

ADDRESS ________________

____

The agreement which follows is an example of an exclusive term songwriter agreement entered into between an unestablished songwriter (Writer) and a music publisher (Publisher) which provides that 100% of the ownership (Copyright) in the compositions written during a stated period of time will belong to the publisher.

Although a songwriter is required to relinquish part or all ownership in the musical compositions covered by this type of agreement, songwriters seek term agreements for two basic reasons. First, the annual advance and/or weekly salary paid to the writer provides the financial foundation enabling the songwriter to dedicate more time and energy to writing and, with the assistance of the publisher's professional staff, develop the professional writing skills shared by successful songwriters. Second, the publisher's contacts introduce the writer's material to a broad network of performers and record producers, increasing the likelihood the songs will be recorded.

Like the single-song agreement analyzed earlier, there is no standard term agreement. Even a term agreement which may be a particular publisher's standardized form is subject to modification by your legal representative. The term agreement is distinguished from the single-song agreement most notably by the addition of provisions not applicable to single-song agreements. These include advances payable to the songwriter, a period of time the songwriter is employed to write and deliver original songs, the writer's exclusivity to the publisher, a guaranteed annual minimum compensation option, and the scope of the writer's earnings withheld for claims brought by others against the publisher. Many of the other provisions are essentially the same as those in the chapter titled "Analysis of a Single-Song Agreement."

Given the complexity of and variations in this type of agreement, it is recommended that a writer not sign a term agreement without first seeking the advice of an attorney familiar with the subject matter.

EXCLUSIVE TERM SONGWRITER AGREEMENT

AGREEMENT effective ______________day of ____________
19__, by and between ________________________________
hereinafter referred to as "PUBLISHER," and ____________
hereinafter (collectively) referred to as "WRITER."

WITNESSETH: In consideration of the mutual covenants and undertakings herein set forth, the parties do hereby agree as follows:

1. SERVICES

Publisher hereby engages Writer to render his or her services as a songwriter and composer and otherwise as may be hereinafter set forth. Writer hereby accepts such engagement and agrees to render such services exclusively for Publisher during the term hereof, upon the terms and conditions set forth herein.

Commentary: *Although the writer is not the publisher's employee, for the term of the agreement the writer is considered like an exclusive employee of the publisher, and as such, cannot write for anyone else.*

2. TERM

The term of this Agreement shall commence with the date hereof and shall continue in force for a period co-terminus with the term of that certain Exclusive Recording Artist Agreement of even date between Writer and Publisher, as same is renewed, extended, amended or substituted.

Commentary: *Often performers who record their own material will enter into a term songwriter agreement with the record label's affiliated publishing company. In these instances, the writer should limit the term of the songwriter agreement to the length of the term of the record deal. Once the recording agreement is over the writer will want new material written to be available to possibly "throw into the pot" to negotiate a stronger agreement with the next record company, and by that time may be in a better position to keep some or all of the copyright in the new songs and a portion of the publisher's share of income. In instances where the songwriter agreement is not tied to a record deal, the term is usually three years with an initial term of one year and two one-year options, exercisable by the publisher. The songwriter may want to try to obtain some measure of performance by the publisher, such as obtaining a certain number of cover recordings, especially if little or no advances are paid, as a condition to the publisher's exercise of its option to extend the term. As a practical matter, the greater the advances, the less likely an option to extend the term will be exercised unless the publisher has been successful in exploiting the material.*

There are pros and cons to a performer-writer entering into a songwriting agreement with the record company's publishing affiliate. Since the publishing company knows that the writer's material will be recorded and released by its affiliate record company, it is not taking a great risk that it will not earn back advances paid. Moreover, since the parent company will be earning money from two sources with each record sold (profits on the record and the publisher's share of mechanical royalties for the writer's compositions on the record), the writer should be able to negotiate a more favorable advance in exchange for the publisher's share of the compositions. The writer may also insist that in exchange for signing with the affiliated publishing company, the record company must pay a full mechanical royalty rather than the usual 3/4 rate on the writer's compositions included on the record. The publishing company will also benefit to the extent it has acquired a copyright in the recorded songs. Finally, the affiliated companies have a "two-pocket" incentive to promote the writer and material.

Other considerations may suggest that the writer's best interests would be served by entering into a term songwriter agreement elsewhere. The record company's publishing arm may not be offering the best terms, or may not be the best publisher for that writer's material. Are the recording contract and term songwriter contract cross-collateralized in any way, so that advances or other costs incurred by one company under one contract can be recovered from the writer's income under the other contract? How do the different pub-

lishing companies measure up in various territories? The writer may be one whose material has tremendous foreign income potential in certain major markets where a different publisher would do a better job for the writer. The writer may even wish to consider refraining from entering into any exclusive term songwriter agreement until the record is released, to be in a position to negotiate a better deal with competing suitors (if the record catches on).

Many times, however, the writer has cash flow problems and is anxious to receive the publisher's advance, so cannot or will not adopt perhaps a riskier but potentially more profitable "Let's wait and see what happens" posture.

3. GRANT OF RIGHTS

(a) Writer hereby irrevocably and absolutely assigns, transfers, sets over and grants to Publisher, its successors and assigns each and every and all rights and interests of every kind, nature and description in and to the results and proceeds of Writer's services hereunder, including but not limited to the titles, words and music of any and all original musical compositions in any and all forms and original arrangements of musical compositions in any and all forms, and all rights and interests existing under all agreements and licenses relating thereto, together with all worldwide copyrights (and any renewals or extensions thereof), which musical works have been written, composed, created or conceived, in whole or in part, by Writer alone or in collaboration with another or others, and which may hereafter, during the term hereof, be written, composed, created or conceived by Writer, in whole or in part, alone or in collaboration with another or others, and which are now owned or controlled and which may, during their term hereof, be acquired, owned or controlled, directly or indirectly, by Writer, alone or with others, or as the employer or transferee, directly or indirectly, of the writers or composers thereof, including the title, words and music of each such composition, and all worldwide copyrights (and renewals and extensions thereof), all of which Writer does hereby represent, are and shall at all times be Publisher's sole and exclusive property as the sole owner thereof, free from any adverse claims or rights therein by any other person, firm or corporation.

Commentary: *Note that the writer is assigning 100% of the compositions to the publisher even if co-written or owned with others. The writer should be required to give the publisher only the writer's share, since the co-writer(s) or joint owner(s) will want the right to decide what to do with their share, and may even have their own term songwriter agreement with another publisher which contains an identical provision. Unless the other writers give you permission to give your publisher their share of the copyright, you may be in breach of your agreement with your publisher if you cannot grant 100% of the copyright in songs you co-write. The prudent way to handle this common dilemma is to limit the publisher's ownership in the material to your share. It would also be acceptable to require you to use "reasonable efforts" to obtain the co-writer's copyright share.*

Requiring the writer to also give the publisher ownership of all songs written before the term is unfair, unless the publisher is paying additional money for these. The writer should at least be entitled to have the copyright in these songs returned if the publisher fails to commercially exploit them within a reasonable period of time - 1 1/2 to 2 years would be fair. A similar reversion should also apply to songs written during the term if the advances are low. Advances refers to both money received by the writer at the beginning of each year of the contract and money paid out on a regular basis like a paycheck.

A concept having far-reaching effects on writers' future rights in their compositions is embedded in this provision. It is most significant that this provision, while assigning the writer's copyright in the compositions for the minimum copyright term, does not include specific language describing the writer as creating the compositions "within the scope of Publisher's employment of Writer's personal services" whereby the writer would be deemed the publisher's so-called "employee for hire" and the publisher would be "deemed the author of the Compositions initially created during the Term." When this language is used the compositions are deemed "works made for hire" under U.S. Copyright laws. The publisher is treated as if it wrote the compositions and as the original copyright owner. This would preclude the writer from having any right to reclaim the copyright in these songs after 35 years, which the writer can do if they have written the material predating the term of the Exclusive Term Songwriter Agreement or the language of the Agreement provides for the writer to assign copyrights to the publisher without saying more about the publisher being considered the "author" from the outset or including the "works made for hire" language.

If the publisher agrees to allow the writer to keep a share of the copyright, or publisher's share of income (roughly 50¢ on each $1.00 generated from exploiting the composition) it is generally handled by the writer first assigning the entire copyright to the publisher and the publisher then assigning back to the writer a part of the copyright, or publisher's share of income if the publisher wants to maintain sole ownership and control of the copyright, but is willing to share part of the 50% income that comes to the copyright owner. This can be accomplished by adding a provision to the end of this agreement assigning back to the writer a percentage of the copyright and/or providing for payment to writer of a percentage of the publisher's share of income.

(b) Writer acknowledges that, included within the rights and interests hereinabove referred to, but without limiting the generality of the foregoing, is Writer's irrevocable grant to Publisher, its successors, licensees, sublicensees and assigns, of the sole and exclusive right, license, privilege and authority throughout the entire world with respect to the said original musical compositions and original arrangements of compositions in the public domain, whether now in existence or hereafter created during the term hereof, as follows:

Commentary: *This is a more detailed version of Paragraph 2 of the sample single-song agreement already commented on. The publisher should also have to give the writer the first opportunity to make changes in the material.*

(i) To perform said musical compositions publicly for profit by means of public and private performance, radio broadcasting, television or any and all other means, whether now known or which may hereafter come into existence;

(ii) To substitute a new title or titles for said compositions and to make any arrangement, adaptation, translation, dramatization and transposition of said compositions, in whole or in part, and in connection with any other musical, literary or dramatic material as Publisher may deem expedient or desirable;

(iii) To secure copyright registration and protection of said compositions in Publisher's name or otherwise as Publisher may desire, at Publisher's own cost and expense and at Publisher's election, including any and all renewals and extensions of copyrights, and to have and to hold said copyrights, renewals, extensions and all rights of whatsoever nature thereunder existing, for and during the full term of all said copyrights and all renewals and extensions thereof;

(iv) To make or cause to be made, master records, transcriptions, sound tracks, pressings, and any other mechanical, electrical or other reproductions of said compositions, in whole or in part, in such form or manner and as frequently as Publisher's sole and uncontrolled discretion shall determine, including the right to synchronize the same with sound motion pictures and the right to manufacture, advertise, license or sell such reproductions for any and all purposes, including, but not limited to, private performances and public performances, by broadcasting, television, sound motion pictures, wired radio and any and all other means or devices whether now known or which may hereafter come into existence;

Commentary: *Writers can protect the integrity of their music by requiring prior consent to its use in X-rated films or those taking an overt political, religious or moral stand.*

(v) To print, publish and sell sheet music, orchestrations, arrangements and other editions of the said compositions in all forms, including the right to include any or all of said compositions in song folios or lyric magazines with or without music, and the right to license others to include any or all of said compositions in song folios or lyric magazines with or without music; and

(vi) Any and all other rights of every and any nature now or hereafter existing under and by virtue of any common law rights and any copyrights (and renewals and extensions thereof) in any and all of such compositions.

(c) Writer grants to Publisher, without any compensation other than as specified herein, the perpetual right to use and publish and to permit others to use and publish Writer's name (including any professional name heretofore or hereafter adopted by Writer), likeness, voice and sound effects and biographical material, or any reproduction or simulation thereof and titles of all compositions hereunder in connection with the printing, sale, advertising, distribution and exploitation of music, folios, recordings, performances, player rolls and otherwise concerning any of the compositions hereunder, and for any other purpose related to the compositions hereunder, and for any other purpose related to the business of Publisher, its affiliated and related companies, or to refrain therefrom. This right shall be exclusive during the term hereof and nonexclusive thereafter. Writer will not authorize or permit the use of his name, likeness, biographical material concerning Writer, or other identification of Writer, or any reproduction or simulation thereof, for or in connection with any musical composition or works, in any manner or for any purpose, other than by or for Publisher. Writer further grants to Publisher the right to refer to Writer as a "Publisher Exclusive Songwriter and Composer" or other similar appropriate appellation.

Commentary: *The clause "any other purpose related to the business of Publisher, its associates, affiliates and subsidiaries," is too broad and should be deleted. All uses of Writer's name and likeness reasonably related to their compositions has already been cov-*

ered. In addition, the prohibition against writers allowing their names or information about them to be used in connection with any composition not covered by this agreement is overreaching and unfair since the agreement may not cover pre-existing material or new material not accepted by the publisher. The designation "Publisher Exclusive Songwriter and Composer" is merely descriptive of the writer's status and is standard in exclusive term agreements.

4. EXCLUSIVITY

From the date hereof and during the term of this Agreement, Writer will not write or compose, or furnish or dispose of, any musical compositions, titles, lyrics or music, or any rights or interests therein whatsoever, nor participate in any manner with regard to the same for any person, firm or corporation other than Publisher, nor permit the use of their name or likeness as the writer or co-writer of any musical composition by any person, firm or corporation other than Publisher.

Commentary: *This exclusivity provision should be qualified to state the writer retains ownership material written before the term of the agreement. In addition, the material written during the term should be evaluated by the publisher and either accepted or rejected as commercially viable within a reasonable period of time after delivery —30 to 60 days is fair. Those songs which are rejected should be given back to the writer to do with as he or she wishes since the publisher has already indicated that it does not believe in them and therefore will not promote them.*

5. WARRANTIES AND REPRESENTATIONS

Writer hereby warrants and represents to Publisher that:

(a) Writer has the full right, power and authority to enter into and perform this Agreement and to grant to and vest in Publisher all the rights herein set forth, free and clear of any and all claims, rights and obligations whatsoever.

(b) All the results and proceeds of the services of Writer hereunder, including all of the titles, lyrics, music and musical compositions, and each and every part thereof, delivered and to be delivered by Writer hereunder are and shall be new and original and capable of copyright protection throughout the entire world.

(c) No part thereof shall be an imitation or copy of, or shall infringe any other original material.

(d) Writer has not and will not sell, assign, lease, license or in any other way dispose of or encumber the rights herein granted to Publisher.

Commentary: *This is essentially the same as the boiler plate language of Paragraph 3 of a single-song agreement.*

6. ATTORNEY IN FACT

Writer does hereby irrevocably constitute, authorize, empower and appoint Publisher, or any of its officers, Writer's true and lawful attorney (with full power of substitution and delegation) in Writer's name, and in Writer's place and stead, or in Publisher's name, to take and do such action, and to make, sign, execute, acknowledge and deliver any and all instruments or documents which Publisher, from time to time, may deem desirable or necessary to vest in Publisher, its successors, assigns and licensees, any of the rights or interests granted by Writer hereunder, including but not limited to such documents required to secure to Publisher the renewals and extensions of copyrights throughout the world of musical compositions written or composed by Writer and owned by Publisher, and also such documents necessary to assign to Publisher, its successors and assigns, such renewal copyrights, and all rights therein for the terms of such renewals and extensions for the use and benefit of Publisher, its successors and assigns.

> ***Commentary:*** *This common boiler plate provision gives the publisher the authority to act on behalf of the writer to secure and protect the rights it has obtained from the writer.*

7. ROYALTIES

Provided that Writer shall faithfully and completely perform the terms, covenants and conditions of this Agreement, Publisher hereby agrees to pay Writer for the services to be rendered by Writer under this Agreement and for the rights acquired and to be acquired hereunder, the following compensation based on the musical compositions which are the subject hereof.

(a) Eight (8¢) cents per copy for each and every regular piano copy and for each and every dance orchestration sold by Publisher and paid for, after deduction of each and every return, in the U.S.

> ***Commentary:*** *This rate is far too low; 10 cents per single edition is reasonable, with increases tied to the Consumer Price Index. In the alternative, and more beneficial to the songwriter, many publishers now split their receipts from single editions with the songwriter.*

(b) Ten (10%) percent of the wholesale selling price upon each and every printed copy of each and every other arrangement and edition thereof printed, published and sold by Publisher and paid for, after deduction of each and every return, in the United States, except that in the event that such composition shall be used or caused to be used, in whole or in part, in conjunction with one or more other musical compositions in a folio or album, Writer shall be entitled to receive that proportion of said ten (10%) percent which the subject musical composition shall bear to the total number of musical compositions contained in such folio or album.

> ***Commentary :*** *The writer should try for 50% of what the Publisher receives, but in any event at least 15% of the wholesale selling price, or its retail equivalent.*

(c) Fifty (50%) percent of any and all net sums actually received (less any costs for collection) by Publisher from mechanical rights, electrical transcription and reproduction rights, motion picture synchronization and television rights and all other rights (excepting public performing rights) therein, including the use thereof in song lyric folios, magazines or any other editions whatsoever sold by licensees of Publisher in the U.S.

> ***Commentary:*** *While the equal split stated is fair, the agreement should also provide that the writer receive 50% of any nonreturnable and earned advances the Publisher receives with respect to the composition(s). Also, since the Publisher is the administrator of the compositions, collection costs should be charged against the Publisher's share rather than the writer's share, if possible. This comment applies wherever collection costs are referred to in the agreement. The writer should see to it that he or she is paid on monies credited to*

the Publisher wherever the agreement refers to the writer receiving a share of monies "received" by the Publisher.

(d) Writer shall receive his public performance royalties throughout the world directly from his own affiliated performing rights society and shall have no claim whatsoever against Publisher for any royalties received by Publisher from any performing rights society which make payment directly (or indirectly other than through Publisher) to writers, authors and composers.

Commentary: *This is correct. The writer's performing rights society (usually ASCAP or BMI, but occasionally SESAC) pays the writer's share of public performance income directly to the writer.*

(e) Fifty (50%) percent of any and all net sums, after deduction of foreign taxes, actually received (less any costs for collection) by Publisher from sales and uses directly related to subject musical compositions in countries outside of the United States (other than public performance royalties as hereinabove mentioned in Paragraph 7(d).

Commentary: *Income generated through subpublishers (licensees of original Publisher) or foreign affiliates of the Publisher may far exceed United States income; it is important to establish ceilings that a subpublisher or affiliate of Publisher can charge. The collection fee charged by a subpublisher for obtaining a cover record (local version) of the writer's composition is usually greater than the fee charged for mechanical license and other income generated from the original recording in the territory involved. The fee should not exceed 30-40% (depending on the territory) of what the Publisher would otherwise receive before paying the writer for income attributable to the cover recording, and 20-25% for original recording income. The split between the Publisher and subpublisher (i.e. before the writer's share is computed) is often stated in songwriter agreements as "80/20", "75/25", etc., representing the Publisher and subpublisher's shares of gross income from its origin.*

(f) Publisher shall not be required to pay any royalties on professional or complimentary copies of any copies or mechanical derivatives which are distributed gratuitously to performing artists, orchestra leaders, disc jockeys or for advertising or exploitation purposes. Furthermore, no royalties shall be payable to Writer on consigned copies unless paid for, and not until such time as an accounting therefor can be properly made.

(g) Royalties as specified hereinabove shall be payable solely to Writer in instances where Writer is the sole author of the entire composition, including the words and music thereof. If this Agreement with Publisher is made and executed by more than one person in the capacity of Writer, the royalties as hereinabove specified shall be payable solely to the particular Writer or Writers who are the authors of the entire composition, including words and music thereof, and such royalties shall be divided equally among the particular Writers of such composition unless another division is agreed upon in writing between the Writers. However, in the event that one or more other songwriters are authors along with Writer on any composition, then the foregoing royalties shall be divided equally between Writer and the other songwriters of such composition unless another division of royalties is agreed upon in writing between the parties concerned.

(h) Except as herein expressly provided, no other royalties or moneys shall be paid to Writer.

Commentary: *Provision should be made for advances to be paid to the writer under any term songwriter agreement. The publisher is requiring the writer to write exclusively for it and in exchange is paying the writer only the royalties noted above, while retaining complete ownership of the songs and keeping 100% of the publisher's share of income. Nor is there any guarantee that the publisher will successfully exploit any of the writer's material, in which case the writer will see no income.*

Advances are typically paid (i) in one lump sum on execution of the agreement and at the beginning of each succeeding year of the term, and/or (ii) in regular installments over the term, like a weekly or semi-monthly paycheck. $20,000 - 24,000 for the first year is not an unusual amount for a large publishing company to pay; small, independent publishers typically pay less but contend that more time will be devoted to promoting its staff writers since they have fewer staff.

The amount of the advance typically escalates 10 - 20% for each succeeding year of the term, and may be further boosted by additional advances triggered by a song's commercial success. This is commonly done by tying increases to Billboard Chart positions achieved or sales levels reached by previous albums. All advances are recoupable from both the writer's share and publisher's share of royalties otherwise payable to the writer (ASCAP/BMI royalties excluded).

A publisher who pays an advance to the writer will require the delivery of specified minimum number of compositions written by the writer. 15 to 20 "Wholly Owned Compositions" is typical, with songs co-written receiving partial credit. For example, if the writer writes a song with two other writers, the publisher will give the writer credit for 1/3 of a Wholly Owned Composition toward the minimum delivery requirement. If the writer fails to deliver the minimum number of songs required during any contract year, the publisher will have the right to extend the term without having to increase the advances beyond the agreed amount until a sufficient number of songs are delivered. The writer should object to any provision giving the publisher the right to suspend advances in addition to extending the term.

In any event, (h) is meaningless and should be deleted, since the rest of Paragraph 7 provides for payment to the writer for all types of uses.

8. ACCOUNTING

Publisher will compute the royalties earned by Writer pursuant to this Agreement within ninety (90) days after the first day of January and the first day of July of each year for the preceding six (6) month period, and will remit to Writer the net amount of such royalties, if any, after deducting any and all unrecouped advances and chargeable costs under this Agreement, together with the detailed royalty statement, within such ninety (90) days. All royalty statements rendered by Publisher to Writer shall be binding upon Writer and not subject to any objection by Writer for any reason unless specific objection is made, in writing, stating the basis thereof, to Publisher within one (1) year from the date rendered. Writer shall have the right, upon the giving of at least thirty (30) days written notice to Publisher, to inspect the books and records of Publisher, insofar as the same concerns Writer, at the expense of Writer, at reasonable times during normal business hours, for the purpose of verifying the accuracy of any royalty statement rendered to Writer hereunder.

> ***Commentary:*** *Mechanical income should be paid on a quarterly basis since record companies usually account for mechanical income quarterly. Forty-five to sixty days after the close of an accounting period should be enough time for statements to be rendered. The writer should have at least two years from the time rendered to object to a statement.*

9. COLLABORATIONS

Whenever Writer shall collaborate with any other person in the creation of any musical composition, any such musical composition shall be subject to the terms and conditions of this Agreement and Writer warrants and represents that prior to the collaboration with any other person, such other person shall be advised prior to the collaboration with any other person, such other person shall be advised of this exclusive agreement and that all such compositions must be published by Publisher in accordance with the terms and provisions hereunder. In the event of such collaboration with any other person, Writer shall notify Publisher of the extent that such other person may have in any such musical composition and Writer shall cause such other person to execute a separate songwriter's agreement with respect thereto, which agreement shall set forth the division of the songwriter's share of income between Writer and such other person, and Publisher shall make payment accordingly. If Publisher so desires, Publisher may request Writer to execute a separate agreement in Publisher's customary form with respect to each musical composition hereunder. Upon such request, Writer will promptly execute such agreement. Publisher shall have the right, pursuant to the terms and conditions hereof, to execute such agreement on behalf of Writer hereunder. Such agreement shall supplement and not supersede this Agreement. In the event of any conflict between the provisions of such agreement and this Agreement, the provisions of this Agreement shall govern.

> ***Commentary:*** *This language is not consistent with the reality that writers do collaborate without regard to existing exclusive writer agreements, and is detrimental to the natural collaborative creative process. The better approach would be to require that the publisher be entitled to all of its own writer's ownership share of the song, and perhaps also the ownership share of any co-writer not similarly signed to a publisher. Moreover, it should state that "Writer shall 'use best efforts to' cause such other person to execute a separate songwriter's agreement" with respect to co-written compositions. Finally, writers should never authorize others to sign agreements in their name, except possibly to the extent necessary to allow the publisher to secure and protect the copyright share obtained from them, as discussed in Paragraph 6 above.*

10. DEMOS

Writer will deliver a manuscript copy of each musical composition hereunder immediately upon the completion or acquisition of such musical composition. Publisher shall advance reasonable costs for the production of demonstration records and one-half (1/2) of such costs shall be deemed an advance which shall be deducted from royalties payable to Writer by Publisher under this Agreement. All recordings and reproductions made at demonstration recording sessions hereunder shall become the sole and exclusive property of Publisher, free of any claims whatsoever by Writer or any person deriving any rights from Writer.

> ***Commentary:*** *It is unfair, but traditional, for publishers to recover 1/2 the demo costs from the writer's royalties. The writer should try to get this deleted, especially if they aren't also receiving part of the publisher's share of income. The writer should be able to keep copies of demos of songs that are rejected by the publisher and can offer to reimburse*

publisher the unrecouped share of demo costs if they are successful in exploiting the song on their own.

11. GUARANTEE OPTION: INJUNCTION

(a) Services Unique. Writer acknowledges that the services rendered hereunder are of a special, unique, unusual, extraordinary and intellectual character which gives them a peculiar value, the loss of which cannot be reasonably or adequately compensated in damages in an action at law, and that a breach by Writer of any of the provisions of this Agreement will cause Publisher great and irreparable injury and damage. Writer expressly agrees that Publisher shall be entitled to remedies of injunction and other equitable relief to prevent a breach of this Agreement or any provision hereof, which relief shall be in addition to any other remedies, for damages or otherwise, which may be available to Publisher.

Commentary: *This standard provision allows the publisher to get a court order preventing the writer from writing for any other publisher if the writer becomes dissatisfied and wants to terminate the deal with the current publisher and write for someone else. It is doubtful, however, that a court would issue an injunction just because this clause is in the contract.*

This provision should only allow the publisher to seek an injunction from the court so that the publisher would be required to prove that a money judgment would not be sufficient. In addition, this kind of relief should be available only if the writer's action or failure goes to the essence of the agreement, such as the writer's failure to deliver the songs required, or refusal to turn over the demos to the publisher.

(b) Annual Guarantee Option. Publisher may, by notice in writing to Writer given at any time during the term of this contract, elect to revise this contract so that Publisher shall be obligated to pay Writer compensation at the rate of not less than Six Thousand Dollars ($6,000.00) per annum during each consecutive twelve (12) month period during the remaining term of this contract for services rendered by Writer during each such period. Prior to the end of the contract year during which Publisher makes this election, and prior to the end of each subsequent twelve (12) month period during the term hereof, Publisher will pay to Writer the difference, if any, between any amounts theretofore received by Writer as royalties hereunder during each such contract year or twelve (12) month period, as the case may be, and Six Thousand Dollars ($6,000.00). Such payment shall be deemed a nonreturnable advance against royalties accruing under this contract and any other agreement between Writer and Publisher or any of their respective related or affiliated companies. Notwithstanding the foregoing, in the event that a rate of compensation in excess of Six Thousand Dollars ($6,000.00) is required during the term hereof under the laws of the State of California for the purpose of obtaining injunctive relief, then the figure of Six Thousand Dollars ($6,000.00) set forth in the first two sentences of this paragraph shall be automatically increased to such higher rate of compensation as of the effective date of such new law.

(c) Injunctive Relief. If Publisher exercises its option pursuant to the foregoing paragraph, then Writer acknowledges and confirms that their resulting agreement is intended to preserve the right to seek injunctive relief to prevent the breach of this contract by Writer and, accordingly, it is Writer's and Publisher's mutual intention that their such obligation be interpreted and construed in such a manner as to comply with the provisions of California

Civil Code Section 3423 (Fifth), and California Code of Civil Procedure Section 526 (second paragraph 5), concerning the availability of injunctive relief to prevent the breach of a contract in writing for the rendition of personal services.

> ***Commentary:*** *This provision is commonly referred to as "the Six Thousand Dollar Provision." As applied to this type of contract, California law provides that a publisher acquiring the exclusive writing services of a writer cannot prevent that person from writing elsewhere, regardless of the number of options the publisher may have to continue the writer's term, unless the publisher guarantees the writer at least $6,000 for each year.*
>
> *For years publishers were getting away with providing for an option in the agreement to pay the difference between the total that a writer actually made during the year and $6,000, so the publisher didn't have to spend the money unless it decided at the end of the year that it wanted to continue the contract. However, the California Court of Appeals decided in 1984 in the "Teena Marie" case that an option to pay the minimum did not meet California's requirement of a guaranteed minimum and would not prevent the artist from going elsewhere.*
>
> *The recording contract requiring exclusive personal services with only an option to pay the $6,000 was not "just and reasonable," and therefore did not meet the minimum standard of fairness required by the court to enforce the exclusivity clause. Note that the sample provision provides only for an option, so could no longer be enforced by the publisher to prevent the writer from going elsewhere. The publisher can, however, still sue the writer for breach of contract and recover money determined lost by the writer's action.*
>
> *For term songwriter agreements entered into and governed by the law of states other than California the writer should seek the advice of an attorney to determine whether that state has a similar law.*

12. ACTIONS; INDEMNITY

(a) Publisher may take such action as it deems necessary, either in Writer's name or in its own name, against any person to protect all rights and interest acquired by Publisher hereunder. Writer will at Publisher's request, cooperate fully with Publisher in any controversy which may arise or litigation which may be brought concerning Publisher's rights and interests obtained hereunder. Publisher shall have the right, in its absolute discretion, to employ attorneys and to institute or defend any action or proceeding and to take any other proper steps to protect the right, title and interest of Publisher in and to each musical composition hereunder and every portion thereof and in that connection, to settle, compromise or in any other manner dispose of any matter, claim, action or proceeding and to satisfy any judgment that may be rendered, in any manner as Publisher in its sole discretion may determine. Any legal action brought by Publisher against any alleged infringer of any musical composition hereunder shall be initiated and prosecuted by Publisher, and if there is any recovery made by Publisher as a result thereof, after the deduction of the expense of litigation, including but not limited to attorneys' fees and court costs, a sum equal to fifty (50%) percent of such net proceeds shall be paid to Writer.

(b) If a claim is presented against Publisher in respect to any musical composition hereunder, and because thereof Publisher is jeopardized, Publisher shall have the right thereafter, until said claim has been finally adjudicated or settled, to withhold any and all royalties or other sums that may be or become due with respect to such compositions pending the final adjudication or settlement of such claim. Publisher, in addition, may withhold from any and all royalties or other sums that may be due and payable to Writer hereunder, an amount which Publisher deems sufficient, to reimburse Publisher for any contemplated damages, including court costs and attorneys' fees and costs resulting therefrom. Upon the final adjudication or settlement of each and every claim hereunder, all moneys withheld shall then be disbursed in accordance with the final adjudication or settlement of said claim.

Commentary: *This version is more fair to the writer in several respects than the indemnity provision appearing in the single songwriter agreement in the previous chapter. It clarifies that the writer shares in any recovery obtained against infringers, limits the amount of money withheld from the writer to a sum related to the anticipated cost of the claim and continues payment to the writer for income from compositions not involved in the claim. Since many "claims" are made by third parties that are not pursued, the agreement should also provide that any monies withheld from the writer by the Publisher when a claim is made against the Publisher bear interest and be released to the writer if not formal lawsuit is filed within six months after the monies are first withheld. The writer should also have the right to be represented by his or her own attorney and to consent to at least those settlements in excess of a few thousand dollars. In addition, since the Publisher has acquired the copyright and controls the compositions, the Publisher should have not only the right but the obligation to protect the copyrights by taking action against infringers, and bearing all costs of defending or instituting claims.*

13. NOTICES

Any written notice, statement, payment or matter required or desired to be given to Publisher or Writer pursuant to this Agreement shall be given by addressing the same to the addresses of the respective parties referred to herein, or to such other address as either party shall designate in writing, and such notice shall be deemed to have been given on the date when same shall be deposited, so addressed, postage prepaid, in the United States mail, or on the date when delivered, so addressed, toll prepaid, to a telegraph or cable company.

Commentary: *Be sure that the contract includes complete addresses for both parties. A copy of notices given by the publisher should also be sent to the writer's attorney so she or he can answer any questions that might arise from the notice. Notices exercising an option or claiming that a breach has occurred should be by certified mail with a return receipt.*

14. ENTIRE AGREEMENT

This Agreement supersedes any and all prior negotiations, understandings and agreements between the parties hereto with respect to the subject matter hereof. Each of the parties acknowledges and agrees that neither party has made any representations or promises in connection with this Agreement or the subject matter hereof not contained herein.

15. MISCELLANEOUS

This Agreement may not be cancelled, altered, modified, amended or waived, in whole or in part, in any way, except by an instrument in writing signed by both Publisher and Writer. The waiver by Publisher of any breach of this Agreement in any one or more instances, shall in no way be construed as a waiver of any subsequent breach (whether or not of a similar nature) of this Agreement by Writer. If any part of this Agreement shall be held to be void, invalid or unenforceable, it shall not affect the validity of the balance of this Agreement. This Agreement shall be governed by and construed under the laws of the State of New York applicable to agreements executed in and to be wholly performed therein.

> ***Commentary:*** *These boiler plate provisions are like Paragraphs 12 and 13 of the single-song agreement. If the writer and/or attorney reside in California it would be better for California law to apply since it is more familiar and may be more favorable to the artist inasmuch as this state's legislature and courts have adopted a role somewhat more protective of artists than other states.*

16. BREACH; NOTICE

No breach of this Agreement on the part of Publisher shall be deemed material, unless Writer shall have given Publisher notice of such breach and Publisher shall fail to discontinue the practice complained of (if a practice of Publisher is the basis of the claim of breach) or otherwise cure such breach, within sixty (60) days after receipt of such notice, if such breach is reasonably capable of being fully cured within such sixty (60) day period, or, if such breach is not reasonably capable of being fully cured within such sixty (60) day period, if Publisher commences to cure such breach within such sixty (60) day period and proceeds with reasonable diligence to complete the curing of such breach.

> ***Commentary:*** *The writer should be given the same opportunity to cure breaches.*

17. ASSIGNMENT

This Agreement may not be assigned by Writer. Subject to the foregoing, this Agreement shall inure to the benefit of and be binding upon each of the parties hereto and their respective successors, assigns, heirs, executors, administrators and legal and personal representatives.

> ***Commentary:*** *Publisher should be allowed to assign only to a person or entity acquiring all or substantially all of the assets of publisher. Writer should be allowed to purchase the song at the same price at which it is sold to any third party (if it is part of a catalogue, an independent appraiser can be appointed), but few publishers will agree to this.*

IN WITNESS WHEREOF, the parties hereto have executed this Agreement as of the day and year first above written.

________________________ **MUSIC (ASCAP)**

AGREED TO AND ACCEPTED:

BY: ________________________ ____________________________

("WRITER")

________________________ **MUSIC (BMI)**

EXHIBIT 1
MECHANICAL LICENSE AGREEMENT

Date:

Re:

By:

To:

Gentlemen:

We own or control the mechanical recording rights in the copyrighted musical composition referred to above (hereinafter referred to as "the Composition"). You have advised us that you wish to use the Composition pursuant to the terms of the Compulsory License provisions of the United States Copyright Act (Title 17), as varied herein, upon parts of instruments serving mechanically to reproduce the Composition. We accede to such use, upon condition that except as such rights and obligations are specifically varied herein, we shall have all of the rights and obligations of proprietors and you shall have all of the rights and obligations of users of copyrighted works pursuant to the Copyright Act.

1. You shall pay royalties and shall render detailed accounting statements required by the Copyright Act, except that they need not be rendered under oath and they need only be rendered quarterly, within forty-five (45) days after each March 31, June 30, September 30, and December 31 for the calendar quarter year just concluded, whether or not royalties are due and payable for such period.

2. You shall pay us at the following rate for each part embodying the Composition manufactured by you, distributed and not returned (except for promotional copies distributed without charge to radio and television stations) :

for "single" recording

for "extended play" recording

for "long play" recording

for each pre-recorded tape

3. This variance is limited solely to the recorded performance of the Composition which is identified as follows:

Record No. :

Artist:

Label:

This variance shall not supersede or in any way affect any prior licenses or variances now in effect with respect to recordings of the Composition.

4. In the event that you fail to comply with all the provisions of the Copyright Act, except as varied herein, or with all of the terms hereof, we shall have the right to revoke this variance by service of written notice thereof.

5. You need not serve or file the notices required by the Copyright Act.

6. This variance is specifically limited to the use of the Composition, and the sale of the recording within the United States of America, unless we grant you written permission to the contrary.

7. On the label affixed to each part manufactured by you, you will include the title of the Composition, our name as Publisher, the name of the performing rights society with which we are affiliated ( ), and the last name of the composer and lyricist.

8. You will not use or authorize the use of the title of the Composition in any manner whatsoever on the label cover, sleeve, jacket, or box in which the recording is sold, except in a list of musical compositions contained thereon and then only in print of size, type and prominence no greater than that used for the other musical compositions contained thereon.

Very truly yours,

By: ______________________ ______________________

We acknowledge the receipt of a copy hereof and the accuracy of the terms contained herein:

By: ______________________

The Clearing House, Ltd. (TCH) deals with a vital and complicated area of copyright practice called "music clearance." Only if music is "cleared" (when permission to use it has been secured) can a producer proceed with the distribution or broadcasting of its production.

TCH represents a wide variety of clients and arranges for their right to use music in television programs, feature films, home video projects, live stage musicals, nontheatrical or nonbroadcast productions, and so forth. While there are producers who negotiate these transactions for themselves, many prefer to use the services of a company dedicated to performing these transactions on their behalf. TCH is the foremost music rights clearance organization in the country.

More specifically, TCH negotiates on behalf of its producer clients for their right to record music on the soundtracks of their productions. In production industry terms, these rights are referred to as "synchronization rights" because the music is being recorded in synchronization with film or video images. These clearance negotiations take place between TCH and the publishers who own the songs, or with the publishers' representatives (The Harry Fox Agency, lawyers, etc. as the case may be). When pre-existing recordings are to be cleared, TCH negotiates with the record companies which own the masters.

This music clearance process is important because a producer, program distributor or broadcaster could be held liable for infringing copyrights if the music it uses or broadcasts has not been properly cleared. In addition, producers have contractual obligations to a number of parties, including those who have paid for the program to be produced, and the companies who insure the program in the event its exhibition violates the rights of any third party. These contractual obligations require that the program be delivered for broadcast or other exhibition with all rights secured and free of any restrictions which could limit the exploitation of the program. This is why producers are careful to consider alternatives to songs which may be difficult to clear for any reason. This is especially so because of the short time period between when a song is considered for use, and the actual taping or broadcasting of the program. If the ownership of a song cannot be determined and an acceptable fee negotiated within that short time frame, few producers will be willing to run the risk of possible legal consequences or massive re-editing of a production if negotiations cannot be consummated.

CLEARING THE RIGHTS

An explanation of how the clearance process works and the rules regarding what songs must be cleared and when is well beyond the scope of this short discussion, because complex legal and business affairs issues affecting producers, publishers, distributors and broadcasters are involved. It would be instructive, however, to identify the steps that TCH goes through in representing its clients. Remember that ultimately, this process of "clearing" the rights is of great importance to composers, songwriters and their publishers because the recording of a song in a television or film production generates synchronization license revenues, and the broadcast of the program may generate significant performance income as well.

Generally, it is TCH's function to help producers get the music that they feel will enhance their productions. This may involve helping to arrange for a composer to create an original score, a songwriter to create new songs, or suggesting the use of a prerecorded music cue library. Most importantly though, is the function of securing permission to use popular songs and recordings which for one reason or another cannot be cleared upon terms acceptable to the producer.

Who Owns the Material?

If popular songs and recordings are to be used, the first step in the clearance process is to determine who owns the material. This is not a simple process because several writers can collaborate in creating a single song, and a copyright can be divided into separate parts with each part owned either individually or by several parties. Additionally, the people who own copyrights frequently transfer the right to grant permission and the right to collect royalties to outside agencies who do the collecting and paperwork (administration) for them. In order to quickly determine who owns and/or controls the rights in a song or recording, TCH maintains an extensive database of song ownership information specifically for television and film synchronization licensing purposes.

Fee Negotiation

Next, TCH will contact the parties controlling the various copyrights and negotiate the fees which must be paid for the right to use the song or recording in the production wherever it will be exhibited or distributed. TCH supervises the process of having contracts executed for each such "licensing" transaction and distributes the license fees to the publishers and record companies from its producers' trust account.

Music Cue Sheets

Generally, it is also TCH that prepares and distributes the music cue sheet for each of its clients' productions after actually viewing the production. A music cue sheet is a very important document which lists, in order of performance, each song or portion thereof which has been used in the production along with the composers, publishers, performing rights affiliations (ASCAP or BMI), usage and timing of each song. It is these documents which ASCAP and BMI use to determine who will receive royalties for the public performance of the music on television stations and in theaters outside the United States.

Film
Transfer
INCLUDES
COMPACT DISCS

Film, Television, Jingle Music and Music Merchandising

- Music Licensing for Television & Film: A Perspective for Songwriters
- Pop Soundtrack Music for Film
- Analysis of a Jingle Contract
- Merchandising in the Music Industry

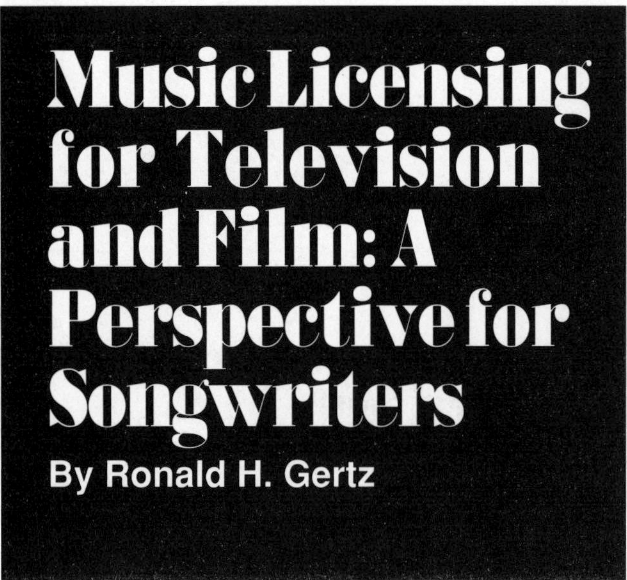

This chapter will discuss, in general terms, how music is licensed or acquired by television and film producers. These media are important and accessible vehicles for generating exposure for the writer's works and developing immediate and long term revenue sources.

Songwriters generally want to receive the greatest amount of income possible from the exploitation of their creations. One of the major sources of income for a songwriter is from the performance of the songwriter's works in feature films and in network, syndicated, cable and pay television programs. A significant portion of ASCAP and BMI revenues are collected from television broadcasters; therefore, the opportunity for songwriters to have their music used in a television program should not be overlooked since each performance can become a significant revenue source. The royalties received from public performances of music in television and film soundtracks can far exceed the "up-front" money paid to composers for services in creating original songs or musical scores.

FOR THE SONGWRITER WHO IS JUST STARTING OUT

If you are a songwriter or performer starting out in the business, you will be happy to know that there are television and film producers who actively look for new material for their projects in order to capture the latest sounds and styles. Some producers may be looking for hot new talent, while others may just want inexpensive music. Whatever the reason, the net effect for the songwriter is that the use of a song in a television or film program means exposure; the chance to be seen, heard and paid. Producers know that exposure is what the new songwriter is looking for and for that reason the producer will probably be in the driver's seat when it comes to negotiating a deal.

If a producer is interested in using a songwriter's music, the producer will require the songwriter to sign a contract which usually gives the producer the right to use the material in any way the producer desires. This is called "licensing the rights." The songwriter must remember that such documents will usually require certain warranties and representations (guarantees) about the ownership of the material, because the producer must be sure to license the rights from the true owner of the song. An attorney's help in understanding the rights and obligations would probably be a good idea.

THE PUBLISHER AND THE PRODUCER

The producer who wishes to use pre-existing music in a program must secure a license to do so from the owner of the song. On first impression, this may seem like a simple and obvious statement. However, the way a song is owned can cause complications because of the number of parties who can own it. If a song has been co-written by several writers, each writer may legally own an undivided pro rata share of the copyright. In the absence of an agreement to the contrary, if two people co-write a song, each will own 50% of the copyright or if three writers collaborate each will own 33.33%. Each of the writers may have assigned all or a portion of their rights to various parties (or publishers) in different territories of the world. For these and other reasons (which are beyond the scope of this discussion) several parties may have the right to determine how a song is licensed, or if it is to be licensed at all, and at what price.

These issues can make the licensing process a very lengthy one and can work against both new and established songwriters because music decisions are made very quickly in the TV and film business. Songwriters are well advised to make sure that a producer who wants the right to use the writer's song in a production can get the rights quickly and easily. All things being equal, the producer will usually license the song which is easiest and cheapest to use.

As the exclusive owner of the bundle of rights that comprise a copyright, a publisher can generally prevent anyone from using a song without first having obtained a license to do so. There are four instances where the publisher is required to grant a license under the compulsory license provisions of the copyright law (the law sets out the license terms, rather than the parties themselves). However, those instances (dealing with cable retransmissions and public television broadcasts and records on jukeboxes) have little present impact on songwriter's royalty distributions from the television and film industries.

The producer, on the other hand, must acquire whatever rights are necessary, depending on the kind of performance contemplated, directly from the publisher or the publisher's agent. Since the producer is ultimately liable if rights are not secured properly, the producer must be sure to deal with the true owner of the composition, that the publisher has the legal right to grant the license, and that all rights are "cleared." The clearance process, in simplest terms, involves determining whether the copyright owner of the song will allow the producer to use the song in the way the producer intends, and negotiating the fee that the producer will have to pay for the right to use the song.

Now, we'll examine the organizations involved in the music licensing process, by looking at the rights which the publisher controls and which the producer must acquire. When we talk about rights, we are referring to certain privileges which the copyright law gives to the owner of a copyright. By licensing those rights to those who wish to use the music, creative people are hopefully able to earn a living and provide for their families. This provides an incentive for those creative people to create more works for the enjoyment of the general public.

THE PERFORMING RIGHTS ORGANIZATIONS

In the copyright law, one of the exclusive rights granted to the owner of a composition is the right to perform that composition publicly, subject to certain exemptions. In this context, "perform" is a term of art which means the singing, dancing, playing, broadcasting or exhibiting of a song. Broadcasters traditionally secure licenses from the organizations that represent songwriters and publishers which allow them to broadcast programs containing music.

Three organizations in the United States act as agents for composers and publishers in licensing public performing rights. The American Society of Composers, Authors and Publishers (ASCAP), Broadcast Music, Inc. (BMI), and SESAC. They function as central agencies for the licensing of performance rights to broadcasters. It must be noted that there are differences in the working processes of each of these organizations, and a composer seeking affiliation with one of them should consult knowledgeable industry sources to help in making a choice. For a more complete discussion on these organizations, see the chapters titled "Performing Rights Organizations: An Overview" and "ASCAP/BMI Primer."

The producer who wishes to use pre-existing music in a program must secure a license to do so from the owner of the song. On first impression, this may seem like a simple and obvious statement. However, the way a song is owned can cause complications because of the number of parties who can own it.

The performing rights organizations make their entire catalogs of compositions available to broadcasters upon the payment of a fee. The fees paid by broadcasters give them the right to perform all of the songs in the catalog of the performing rights organization without having to contact each publisher directly. After deducting the costs of administration, these monies are divided between the writers and publishers based upon the number of performances logged by the performing rights organization.

Each of the performing rights organizations log and keep track of performances and calculate disbursements in different ways. However, the performance of a song on a prime time network television program (when millions of viewers are watching) should generate more income than a performance on a local independent station at 4:00 AM (when most people are sleeping). It is important to remember that while the performing rights organizations collect fees from television and radio broadcasters, night clubs, stores, etc., they normally only make disbursements to songwriters and publishers whose songs are performed and logged on television and radio broadcasts. This is, of course, another reason why television uses are so important to songwriters.

A songwriter is well advised to understand the performance rights licensing process, become a member of one of these societies, and register all songs written. A producer will not usually take a chance on using unregistered material because of the likelihood that the rights may not be available. With skyrocketing costs of production, producers cannot afford to put something on film or tape that they might not be able to use. For the writer, it would be a shame to lose royalties simply because a clerical registration function was not performed properly.

SYNCHRONIZATION RIGHTS

Another major source of royalties for the songwriter comes from licensing the right to reproduce music. The right to reproduce (like the right to perform) is another exclusive right that the copyright law grants to the owner of the copyright in a song. A mechanical license, which refers to the right to mechanically reproduce music in the form of audio records and tapes, for distribution to the public, is an example of one type of reproduction. In the television and film business, music is reproduced when it is recorded on the soundtrack of a production. The industry has come to refer to the right to do this as a synchronization right, because the music is being reproduced on the soundtrack in synchronization with the pictures. Unlike performance royalties, which the performing rights organizations traditionally collect from broadcasters on some form of blanket basis, synchronization rights are a matter of individual negotiation for each composition used. Rights are secured by the producer or their representative directly from the publisher or the publishers agent.

In addition, there are organizations such as The Harry Fox Agency, Inc., and Finell-Brunow and Associates which represent publishers in the negotiation and collection of synchronization fees.

Synchronization licenses are required in most situations where the composition is reproduced on film or videotape. The limited exceptions to this rule are very complicated and refer generally to certain network and regional television programs and live telecasts.

PRODUCER'S REPRESENTATIVES

The producer's side of the licensing equation is handled in one of several ways. Producers will either negotiate for themselves, or through their attorneys or in-house music department, or use the services of an outside organization maintaining extensive internal files on the copyright ownership and licensing history of most popular songs. The largest organization of this kind is The Clearing House, Ltd., which represents television and feature film producers and distributors in the research, clearance and licensing of music rights and in the supervision, production and packaging of musical scores. For a more complete discussion, see the chapter titled "Music Clearance: The Clearing House, Ltd."

USE OF A SONG ON A TELEVISION PROGRAM

We are now going to follow what happens when a song is actually used on a television program. Let's assume that Fred Composer, Wilma Words and Lydia Lyric have co-written a song called "Sing It High" which a young crooner would like to warble on the finals of the TV series "You Too Can Hit It Big." Fred wrote the music while Wilma and Lydia wrote the words. Through their attorneys, an agreement was worked out which provided that they would divide all performance income equally, but that because Fred owned the studio in which they produced the demo, Fred would receive half of the publishers' share of income and Wilma and Lydia would each receive 25%. They also agreed that each would separately administer their own shares. Synchronization rights for Fred Composer Music Publishing are administered by The Harry Fox Agency, Wilma Words Music is administered by the law firm of Abdulla and Steinmetz, and the affairs of Lydia Lyric's publishing company Aidyl Time Music are handled by her manager. All of the above (for the sake of simplicity) are affiliated with BMI.

Let us first consider the public performance rights issues. The producer or the producer's agent (e.g. The Clearing House, Ltd.) will make sure that "Sing it High," Fred, Wilma, Lydia and their respective publishing companies are registered and affiliated with a performing rights organization. If registered, the rights to publicly perform "Sing It High" will be covered under the terms of the blanket licenses secured by the broadcasters. A blanket license allows a broadcaster to broadcast any and all songs in the catalog of the performing rights organization. As stated earlier, the songwriters and publishers will be paid a portion of the fees collected by BMI from the individual broadcasters for the privilege of performing all the songs in the BMI catalog.

The performing rights organizations have reciprocal agreements with similar organizations in foreign territories. Therefore, if the program is broadcast outside of the U.S. the foreign performance rights organization (after deducting a fee) will eventually remit the revenue generated from foreign performances of "Sing It High" to BMI, which will in turn pay these additional monies to all the parties. (This may not be the most efficient way to collect foreign revenues.)

It is important to note here that ASCAP and BMI license only nondramatic (small) performing rights, where the performance consists of a singer or instrumentalist in modern clothes, on a basic set, doing a straight performance. A dramatic performance, in simple terms, involves a dramatization of the story line of the song, perhaps with the aid of such things as sets, costumes, or props. Dramatic performing rights are not licensed by ASCAP or BMI. Therefore, the use of these rights must be negotiated directly with the publisher. Just what is or is not a dramatic performance has never been fully decided in the courts, and is a subject of disagreement among producers, publishers, and attorneys.

There is another important performance rights issue which bears discussion at this point. That is the issue of "direct" or "source licensing." In recent years, the broadcasting and cable TV industries have objected to the rate structures which the performing rights organizations are seeking from free television and pay, cable and subscription television broadcasters. As a result, there has been litigation challenging the legality of blanket licensing. The litigation so far has been unsuccessful, but in the recent past television broadcasters have lobbied for legislation that would shift the burden of seeking performance rights from television broadcasters to program producers (the "source") who would be required to go directly to the publisher for performance rights. Both sides of the controversy cite strong economic and practical reasons for their positions. If such legislation passes, the performing rights organizations feel that their writer and publisher members will face the loss of a substantial portion of their total revenues. The television broadcasters, on the other hand, are seeking a system which they feel would more fairly allow them to pay for the music they actually use. As of this writing, the legislative effort has not been successful, however, the parties are currently litigating the issue of rates in a federal court proceeding.

The producer must also acquire a synchronization license from each of the publishers because each controls its own share of the rights. As mentioned earlier, the synchronization license refers to the right to reproduce "Sing It High" on the soundtrack of "You Too Can Hit It Big" in synchronization with the video portion. The territories and term of distribution rights are a matter of negotiation between the parties, reflecting the producer's needs. However, synchronization licenses may run for a period of one, three or five years, and may cover only the territories in which the producer feels the program can be distributed. If a producer feels that the program will have a long life in syndication he may try to secure these rights for worldwide distribution of the program, in perpetuity (forever). A five-year worldwide television synchronization license allows the program on which a song is used to be broadcast throughout the world for an unlimited number of times over a five-year period (assuming that the station over which the program is broadcast is duly licensed by a performing rights organization).

The amount of money paid for the sync license depends upon the way in which the song is used. For example, a use with a singer on camera (visual vocal) or with a musician playing an instrument on camera (visual instrumental), may be more expensive than music that is used for background purposes only. Prices are also determined by the running length of the song, and whether the program is produced for network television for syndication, or otherwise. Since a network program telecast in prime time may have a higher budget than a syndicated program, the fees may be negotiated accordingly. ASCAP and BMI also pay more money for performances in prime time, on the theory that more people are watching the programs.

Synchronization fees for television uses are traditionally modest (rarely over a few hundred dollars), since publishers are usually willing to give producers a break on the price in order to have the song performed on television and generate performance revenue. Remember that public performance fees are paid by the broadcasters and have no effect on the production budget. However, synchronization fee payments are the responsibility of the producer and directly effect the producer's bottom line profit. Therefore, producers fight hard to limit costs for synchronization licenses, knowing that the songwriter and publisher stand to make a considerable amount of money and receive exposure from the television performance.

Since Fred Composer Music Publishing is represented by The Harry Fox Agency, the producer or his agent would negotiate with The Harry Fox Agency for a license covering Fred's 50% interest. The producer would also have to negotiate a deal with Wilma's law firm and with Lydia's manager for their respective interests. It is imperative that the producer be able to contact all of the representatives and negotiate acceptable license fees prior to taping of the program. Imagine what might happen if Lydia and her manager were on tour in Europe. Since television programs are produced on short production schedules, time can become a factor in whether a song will be used.

USE OF A COMPOSITION IN A FEATURE FILM

Now let's suppose that "Sing it High" is proposed for use in a feature film. Many of the same rules apply with respect to clearing the use of the composition. However, the fees for use of music on theatrical films can be dramatically higher than those for television programs. This is for several reasons. A complete package of rights and media are involved (discussed below) and these rights are always secured for the duration of the copyright in the composition. Also, theatrical films are usually produced on a much higher budget than television programs. As a result, the producer requires a broad license with the right to exploit the film in all media in order to at least recoup the cost of the film.

First, the producer must secure a United States theatrical performing rights license. When a film with music on its soundtrack is exhibited in a movie theater, a public performance occurs for which the composers and their publishers are entitled to receive performing royalties. However, motion picture exhibitions in the United States do not generate royalties for the performing rights organizations. It is a violation of United States antitrust laws for ASCAP and BMI to charge theater owners a license fee for the right to publicly perform the music included in the films. As a result, the film producer must go directly to the publishers to negotiate the fee for these rights.

The process is completely different outside the United States, where the United States antitrust laws do not apply. Theater owners in foreign countries are required to pay a percentage of box office receipts to the local performing rights organizations. These monies eventually filter through to the domestic performing rights organizations by virtue of their agreements with the foreign performing rights organizations. These foreign performance royalties are a major source of publishing revenue, and can mean thousands of dollars to the songwriter and publisher.

While producers will be very serious about all of the legal ramifications, they still have important creative needs. Their need for good music is an opportunity for both new and experienced songwriters to generate revenue and provide the exposure that may lead to other successes.

The producer must also secure worldwide synchronization rights. As in television, these rights are obtained by dealing with the publishers, and are obtained for duration of copyright in the composition. As a practical matter, both the worldwide synchronization rights and the United States theatrical performing rights are negotiated in one package deal in one license agreement.

Along with worldwide synchronization rights and United States theatrical performing rights, the film producer will also secure a package of rights referred to in industry terms as the "broad rights." The broad rights include the right to exhibit a program in essentially all possible media, including free television, cable, subscription or pay television, and closed circuit television, and in film and video trailers and advertisements for the promotion of the film.

Producers also secure home video (video cassettes and discs) rights. The actual structure of home video rights negotiations may take several forms and an adequate discussion for television, film and "made for" home video programs would go far beyond the scope of this chapter. However, most feature film producers have been adamant about securing what is called a "buy out" of home video rights (a one time flat fee payment). For the most part they have been successful in securing buy outs and will generally not use a song which requires any form of continuing royalty. With television programs, or programs made specifically for the home video market which use a substantial amount of music, it is more likely that some kind of per unit royalty may be negotiated.

No producer worth his salt will allow "Sing It High" to be used in a feature film unless the producer receives what is tantamount to nonexclusive rights to the music in all possible media of distribution of the film, with no restrictions or limitations. This is because a motion picture studio might not distribute a film if the right to do so could be enjoined (prohibited by court order) by a music publisher because all rights were not secured. The film companies have too much money at stake to allow a song to restrict their right to distribute.

In some situations the producer may require what is called a "hold back" in future licensing of a song. For example, if "Sing It High" is expected to be a prominent song in the film, the producer may want to restrict other producers from using it for any purpose for a certain period of time so as not to compete with his own film. This may increase the cost of the license because the publisher will have to turn down other license requests during the hold back period. Hold backs occur more typically where a song is written for a film, or where a song is used in television commercials (the song becomes identified with a product).

CONCLUSION

This brief explanation of television and film music licensing does not include all of the possible exceptions and nuances. The licensing process can become complicated in the extreme. The legal and business ramifications for the producer involve, among other things, the producer's distribution agreements, insurance policies, and contractual obligations to broadcasters and exhibitors, etc.

While producers will be very serious about all of the legal ramifications, they still have important creative needs. Their need for good music is an opportunity for both new and experienced songwriters to generate revenue and provide the exposure that may lead to other successes.

Pop Soundtrack Music for Film

By Mark Halloran and Thomas A. White

In recent years, successful pop/rock songwriters and recording artists have moved, seemingly *en masse*, into motion picture soundtrack songwriting and performing. In some recent films writers/performers have also had star acting roles, such as Prince in *Purple Rain*, Sting in *Stormy Monday*, Madonna in *Desperately Seeking Susan*, and most recently, Phil Collins in *Buster*. However, these are exceptions. Typically, songwriters and recording artists are hired by film studios during or after the film is shot to write and record individual musical compositions specifically for the film. The songs are then synchronized with the picture, possibly used in promotional trailers and television spots, included in a soundtrack album, and may even be released as singles and MTV promotional videos. This chapter examines relevant issues when nonacting writers/performers are commissioned to create new film music. The primary focus is on practices at major Hollywood studios, although we also compare practices at the nonmajors as well. (When we say "major Hollywood studios" we mean 20th Century Fox, Orion, Warner Brothers, MCA/Universal, Columbia Pictures Entertainment (Columbia and Tri-Star), Paramount, and Disney.) The chapter does not cover the licensing of preexisting music, which has numerous separate issues, or composers who write orchestra scores or "concert films." (MTV has seemingly killed concert films. The latest victim is U2's *Rattle and Hum*. Another recent failure was Sting's *Bring on the Night*. Rock concert films may be joining the ranks of film documentaries, with very limited audience appeal.)

BRIEF HISTORY: POP SONGS IN FILM

1920s to Late 1970s

Popular songs have been important to films since the late 1920s. However, with the explosion of rock music in the 1950s and the resultant growth of the modern record industry, filmmakers began to use rock songs in their films. The resulting soundtrack records became best sellers. The first film to use a rock and roll soundtrack was *Blackboard Jungle* (1957), featuring Bill Haley's *Rock Around the Clock*. Other early rock uses included Elvis Presley's string of films and the Beatles' *A Hard Day's Night* (1964) and *Help* (1965). Another breakthrough rock n' roll film was George Lucas' *American Graffiti* (1973), which featured a 1950s nostalgia soundtrack of licensed preexisting music, with no orchestral underscore. *Graffiti* spawned numerous imitative soundtracks which still abound today.

More typical of the use of contemporary pop music in today's films was *The Graduate* (1968), featuring tunes written and performed by Simon and Garfunkel, some of which were already released by the duo in record form *(Scarborough Fair, Sounds of Silence)*, but at least one song was commissioned specifically for that film *(Mrs. Robinson)*. *Saturday Night Fever* (1978) spawned numerous top ten singles and was the largest-selling album in history before Michael Jackson's *Thriller*.

1980s

The 1980s have witnessed an explosion of original pop music specially written and performed for use in film soundtracks, soundtrack albums, and in MTV-type videos featuring the artist's performance intercut with film footage. An increasing number of major studios are seeking to exploit the huge pop music market (U.S. record shipment revenues exceeded $6 billion in 1988).

More than 125 soundtrack albums were released in 1988 and again in 1989. In 1988, the most successful pop soundtrack LP, with United States sales of 10 million copies, was *Dirty Dancing,* which finished second in the year-end *Billboard* Top Pop Albums charts, the highest any soundtrack album has finished since 1978 when *Saturday Night Fever* and *Grease* were No. 1 and No. 2. The second most popular soundtrack, coming in at No. 18 on the *Billboard* pop LP charts, was - you guessed it - *More Dirty Dancing,* with United States sales of 3 million copies. Year-end Top 100 albums also included *Good Morning Vietnam* (No. 62) and *Cocktail* (No. 74).

The top pop soundtrack singles for 1988 were Eric Carmen's *Hungry Eyes* from *Dirty Dancing* (No. 25), the Bangles' remake of Simon and Garfunkel's *Hazy Shade of Winter* from *Less Than Zero* (No. 35), Bobby McFerrin's *Don't Worry, Be Happy* from *Cocktail* (No. 37), and The Beach Boys' *Kokomo* from *Cocktail.*

The most successful pop soundtrack albums for 1989 were *Beaches* (No. 14); *Cocktail* (No. 32); *Soundtrack Batman* (No. 40) and *Ghostbusters* (No. 98).

The top pop soundtrack singles for 1989 were Bette Midler's *Wind Beneath my Wings* from *Beaches* (No. 7); Bobbie Brown's *On Our Own,* from *Ghostbusters II* (No. 19); Prince's *Batdance* from *Batman* (No. 44); Michael Damian's *Rock On* from *Dream a Little Dream of Me* (No. 45); Cher and Peter Cetera's *After All,* love theme from *Chances Are* (No. 79); and Ann Wilson's and Robin Zander's *Surrender to Me* from *Tequila Sunrise* (No. 98).

Studios now enthusiastically pursue soundtrack records not only as a source of additional income, but more importantly as *marketing* devices - a hit single, preferably with the same title as the film, generates tremendous free publicity from radio airplay. Promotional videos, aired by MTV (with over forty million subscribers in the United States alone), the eighty other domestic music television outlets, and a large number abroad offer the studio the opportunity to have a catchy song together with highlights from the film promoted to millions worldwide. Both new and established artists are therefore anxious to expand their careers into theatrical films.

CURRENT PRACTICE IN WRITING AND RECORDING SOUNDTRACK MUSIC

Let's assume you are asked by a studio to write and record an original song for a motion picture. There are many fundamental business and legal concerns. How much money will you be paid initially? How will your music publisher and record label be involved in the deal? What controls concerning the use of the song and the recording will you have? How much money can you later expect from the exploitation of the song and the recording? First, let's look at the studio viewpoint to better understand its motives.

Who Chooses The Songs And Performers?
The Creative Choices

Studios now enthusiastically pursue soundtrack records not only as a source of additional income, but more importantly as marketing devices - a hit single, preferably with the same title as the film, generates tremendous free publicity from radio airplay.

The choice of songs and performing artists is usually made by the filmmaking team - the studio, the producer and the director - collectively trying to reach a creative and business consensus. Most major studios have music departments that are headed by creative music executives who, combined with the filmmaking team, represent the studio's music interests and are available to its producers for consultation referrals and other general music services. Absent a creative consensus, the amount of clout the individual members of the filmmaking team wield determines the choice of songs and performers. When dealing with high-powered, experienced, successful film producers and directors, the studio will often defer to their creative choice, but will still insist on consultation or approval of both the musical talent and their deal. Some directors have so-called final cut of the film, which may or may not include final determination of musical talent and their product in the film.

In some instances another team member is hired, the music supervisor, who reports to the director and producer and represents their interests. Music supervisors have gained prominence as filmmakers have recognized the effect successful records have in stimulating box office sales and the necessity for a bridge between the filmmakers, the music community, the studio, and the soundtrack record label. Soundtrack singles are routinely released in advance of the picture so that its opening coincides with demand created by the label's record marketing efforts and the studio's film advertising, which, ideally, are coordinated to maximize public awareness of the film and its music. The music supervisor has varying degrees of involvement in the music that is commissioned or selected for the film. The extent of this job is frequently defined by how the filmmakers perceive their own abilities as music experts. Music supervisors are almost never delegated decision-making authority, but rather gather and present choices to the filmmakers.

The role a music supervisor plays is subject to varied interpretation. Some supervisors offer only creative services (e.g., suggesting possible songs and artists; record producing). Others provide primarily business or sales services (e.g., publishing administration, music clearance, soundtrack placement, music production coordination). Business affairs (i.e., deal making) services are usually handled by the studio music business affairs department or filmmaker's music counsel. There are generally no professional qualification prerequisites for music supervisors. Although film music is a diverse and specialized field, virtually anyone who has ever worked in the music business may (and frequently do) offer their services as a music supervisor. Consequently, competence varies greatly. Because the market has an excess of prospective music supervisors, most practitioners are not engaged in such services on an exclusive, full-time basis.

The main concern of the filmmaking team is whether the choice of the song and artist will enhance the dramatic and commercial impact of the picture. They in effect cast the songwriters and performers as they would theatrical talent by subjectively evaluating whether the writer or act's musical contribution will enhance the look, feel, and profit of the picture.

Budgets

In commissioning soundtrack songs, the established trend is for major studios to stick with top pop writers whose songs have sold millions of records and have had successful chart histories. The independent motion picture companies, however, have less financing available than do the majors and are prone to use less recognized writers and artists who have not had hit records. Accordingly, they pay less money.

Exhibit 1 compares the amount of money that is typically spent by the recognized independents, mini-studios and major studios. The bottom line is that nonmajors pay less up-front money than the major studios. Major studios are frequently tied in with labels owning national branch distribution systems and invest far greater sums than nonmajors in promoting their films and their music. Back-end revenue potential is therefore usually higher at major studios than nonmajors.

Even studios which defer to the creative choice of filmmakers must approve the writer/performer deal because of the large studio investment. One thing an artist should keep in mind is that the studio intends to protect a multi-million-dollar investment, of which music is an important, but relatively minor, part. Average production budgets of major studios are around $17 million; exploitation budgets (principally ads) often approach $8-10 million. Although music budgets vary widely, they are usually 2 to 5% of the film budget.

Probably the most pervasive myth regarding songs that are written for soundtracks is that in some cases the studio makes more money from the music than they do from distribution of the film. Although it has been true in certain cases that an unsuccessful film has spawned a successful album, the authors are unaware of any case in which the amounts generated to a studio from a film have been less than those generated from the film music. In contrast to this myth, there are some basic truths. One is that ultimately studios view film music, except in the rarest cases (perhaps *Flashdance*), as a less integral part of the film and more of a promotional tool and an ancillary (as opposed to primary) market for the film. If a teenager has $6 to spend for entertainment and has a choice between seeing a film or buying the soundtrack album, the studio would much rather have the teenager spend the money on a theater ticket. The studio can expect to receive approximately half the $6 spent on the theater ticket, but is lucky if it nets 30 cents to 50 cents from the sale of each album. On the film revenue side, the $3 net to the studios is calculated at 50% of $6. In other words, the theater remits one-half the ticket price to the studio. On the music revenue side, we assume that the studio would retain 2-5% of retail (14 - 35 cents per LP) and would receive 10 cents as a publishers share of mechanical royalties on five songs.

It should be noted that, as of late, studios have found it very difficult to successfully market music-based films, even with superstar acts as focal points. Michael Jackson's *Moonwalker* went straight to home video in the United States, although it was released theatrically abroad. U2's *Rattle and Hum* disappointed at the box office, as did *Imagine: John Lennon* and *Bird*, Clint Eastwood's homage to Charlie Parker. *Rattle and Hum* did domestic (United States and Canada) box office of $7,778,875 as of

November 20, 1988. *Imagine: John Lennon* did $3,510,629 as of October 30, 1988, and *Bird* did $1,501,022 as of November 13, 1988.

The studio also protects its investment by insisting that broad exploitation rights be obtained in the song and the recording. A studio's incentive for acquiring all rights to songs and recordings include: (1) complete freedom of use and exploitation (including royalty-free use in other studio productions) without consultation, approval or further payment; (2) optimum duration of copyright ownership; (3) avoidance of third-party claims and controls; (4) actual profit from music revenues; (5) increased cash flow; and (6) the building of a publishing catalog as a perennial, liquid, and saleable asset.

Probably the most pervasive myth regarding songs that are written for soundtracks is that in some cases the studio makes more money from the music than they do from distribution of the film.

Limiting The Studio's Investment: Spec Writing And Spec Writing Deals

Studios and filmmakers like to have the opportunity to choose songs that are not specifically commissioned and that require no guaranteed upfront payment. There is quite a lot of speculative songwriting for film soundtracks. By speculative we mean songs that are written or reworked for the film and submitted for consideration without the studio being committed to use or pay for the song. If the studio likes the song, a deal is negotiated. Some songwriters will not write *spec* songs since their time is valuable and they consider it an insult to their artistic integrity to be asked to write a song without a financial commitment. On the other hand, many name and nonname songwriters are happy to have their song considered in this manner.

A variation of spec writing is the so-called songwriter's *step* or *option* deal. This means there will be an intermediate step after the song is written but before it is used in the film when the studio can decline to proceed further by not making further payment for the song. For example, in a step deal the studio will pay the songwriter $5,000 for a song to be written and demoed, with an option to buy the song. If the studio approves the song and synchronizes it in the movie, the writer receives another $20,000 for a total songwriting creative fee of $25,000. If the studio thinks the song inappropriate and it cannot be satisfactorily rewritten, the rights to the song are usually retained by the writer, sometimes with conditions attached.

Probably the most contentious point on step deals is whether or not the writer gets back rights to rejected songs, and under what conditions. Although the usual outcome is that the songwriter keeps the rights, sometimes studios take the position that they will return the song, but only provided the song is subject to a lien on the song for recovery of the amount the studio has invested. In the example above, if the studio were to reject the song and the song reverted to the songwriter, and the song were subsequently exploited, the studio would receive the first $5,000. Another variation of this is that the studio may retain a continuing financial participation in the publisher's share of music income, irrespective of recoupment of the studio investment. Alternatively, the writer may buy back the rights by reimbursing the studio its out-of-pocket costs.

EXHIBIT 1
TYPICAL MUSIC ACQUISITION PRACTICES FOR EACH COMMISSIONED SONG

	Major Studios	Mini Studios	Recognized Independents
Songwriter's fee	up to $25,000	up to $15,000	$500 to $5,000
Participation in publisher's share of income	zero to 50%	zero to 50%	zero to 100%
Writer/Artist recognition level	Major label (recently signed) to superstar	Unsigned to recognized label artists	Mostly unsigned
Artist's fee (off-camera)	Not less than $10,000	Zero to $15,000	$200 to $500 or scale
Recording budget	$15,000 to $50,000+	$5,000 to $10,000	$500 to $2,000
Copyright proprietor (occ. writer)	Major studio*	Mini studio	Independent
Artist's & producer's soundtrack royalty (subject to proration)	12% to 14% (foreign reduced to 1/2 or 3/4)	6% to 12% (foreign reduced to 1/2 or 3/4)	6% to 8% (if any, with 1/2 on foreign)
Copyright administrator	Major studio	Mini studio or its licensee	Outside publisher
Music producer's fee (if negotiated separately)	$4,000 to $10,000	Somewhat lower than major studios	None (usually artist or supervisor produced)

**Note: a major studio is defined as one with branch distribution systems; a mini-studio is one without branch distribution systems; and an independent is one whose films are released through independent distributors.*

STUDIO/RECORD LABEL DEAL

The studio makes the basic arrangement for the production and distribution of the soundtrack with the label. Assuming a pop soundtrack rather than an orchestral one, the following list delineates the basic issues:

Advance

Advances typically reflect the record companies' perception of anticipated sales in the domestic territory, and can range from $0 to, in extraordinary cases, $1 million. What makes the negotiations difficult is that soundtrack albums are usually "one-shots," and the label cannot recover losses from subsequent product. Another difficulty when the deal is made is that typically, the final music choices have not yet been made. A graduated scale is created to remedy this, e.g., $150,000 with an additional $50,000 per platinum-certified artist and $25,000 per gold-certified artist, with a cap of $300,000.

Royalty Rate

Again, royalty rate negotiation is very similar to that for a normal recording artist. The range is from a basic royalty of 10% on the low end to 19% on the high end. The studio hopes to maintain a minimum royalty override in the 4-6% range; thus, in a 16% of retail deal, 10-12% of royalty would be available to third parties.

Product

The record company is going to want to know what they are buying. Also, the record company would prefer a pop soundtrack with a potential single rather than an orchestral soundtrack, although in many cases the two are combined.

Promotion Fund

Oftentimes the record company will look to the studio to put up a matching fund for promotion under the theory that both the studio and the record company will profit.

Singles

The releasing label will always want singles rights. The singles are used as promotional tools to sell the LPs, which is where the real money is. If singles rights are not available, the record company will probably cut its advance.

Guaranteed Release

Studios will often insist that as long as the necessary materials are delivered on time, the record company will be required to release the LP no later than the theatrical release of the film, with singles preceding by six weeks.

Ownership

The studio will continue to own the underlying musical compositions and the sound recording embodied in the film. The record company will want to assert ownership over the sound recording as embodied in records. The record company will want worldwide rights. Split territory deals with major labels are almost nonexistent.

ARTIST VIEWPOINT: PREEXISTING AGREEMENTS

The following are major concerns when you are approached by a studio to write and perform a soundtrack song. The threshold issue is whether you can grant to the studio the rights in the song and the recording that the studio requires.

Preexisting Term Songwriter's Agreement

If you are signed to a term songwriting deal, the publisher has the exclusive right to the songwriter's services during the term and owns and administers songs the songwriter composes or co-writes during the term, subject to paying the usually inviolate writer's share of music income. However, studios have music publishing holdings too. In these agreements, administration means the management of the copyright for purposes of collection and distribution of income. Like other music publishers, studios often insist on copyright ownership and administration of the song, and they normally retain all or part of the publisher's share of music income. Usually any conflict of rights between the songwriter's publisher and the studio is settled during initial discussions. In some cases, the studio's publishing arm and the songwriter's publisher will split the publisher's share of music income between the writer's publisher, film production company, and studio.

In order to avoid potential publisher/studio conflict and to freely shop their songs for soundtracks, a very few established writers have negotiated a fixed number of songs per year which are excluded from their exclusive term songwriting deal. If you are not signed to a term songwriting deal, have negotiated an exclusion, or have already reached the maximum number of songs required under the term songwriting deal, you are free to work out whatever arrangements you desire with the studio.

If you do not have a lot of clout, the studio will end up owning and administering the song, and you will be entitled to approximately 50% of the income generated from the song as the writers share, plus whatever nonrecoupable creative fee is negotiated. (Note the studio will grant itself a free synchronization license in connection with the use of the song in the film and in-home video devices, so you will receive no further synchronization income from these sources.) Studios typically insist on free synchronization licenses for product based on the initial film, such as remakes, sequels, and television programs that they produce or distribute, and even for totally unrelated properties that they produce or distribute. However, the writer retains the writer's share of public performance rights.

Preexisting Recording Agreement

If you are signed to a term or multiple album recording contract, the label typically has the right to your exclusive recording services during the term for master recordings and phonograph records. Recording contracts usually define phonograph records as including "sight and sound devices," so unless you are the rare superstar artist who has a soundtrack exclusion (i.e., a provision excluding soundtrack recordings from the record deal) the label must grant a waiver of its services exclusivity for theatrical synchronization, home video, and phonograph records.

Record companies are understandably jealous of the services of their artists. Major record companies can invest up to $1 million or more to break in a new recording act. It is estimated that minimum sales of 300,000 LP units, or its equivalent in the current configuration mix of vinyl LPs, CDs and cassettes, are necessary for a major label to break even on typical artist investment. Such costs include advances and royalties to artist, producer, and production companies; recording costs; manufacturing and distribution; marketing, including record promotion and advertising; mechanical licenses; video clip production; general overhead; legal expenses; salaries and taxes; product returns; etc.

Record companies are understandably jealous of the services of their artists. Major record companies can invest up to $1 million or more to break in a new recording act. It is estimated that minimum sales of 300,000 LP units, or its equivalent in the current configuration mix of vinyl LPs, CDs and cassettes, are necessary for a major label to break even on typical artist investment.

In order to receive a return on their investments, some record companies will insist on an "override" royalty (a royalty in addition to or to be deducted from the recording artist's royalty) from the studio as a condition to granting permission for the artist's soundtrack services. For example, if your deal with the studio is a basic album royalty of 10% of retail prorated, and you have two of ten cuts on a soundtrack album, the label may ask for a 1% override on your 2% of retail royalty. In terms of pennies, your royalty will be about 18 cents per LP, and the label's royalty will be about 9 cents per LP.

Most studios, however, insist that the artist and the label work out the royalty arrangement between themselves. Some labels may require a 75 (artist)/25 (label) split of the prorated royalty for the sales of soundtrack records. The label retains its share and either credits the artist's share to their royalty account or pays the 75% directly to them irrespective of the artist royalty account. For an illustration, see Exhibit B. Also, just as major studios are music publishers, some major studios have record company divisions. MCA/Universal (MCA Records) and Warner Communications (Warner Bros. Records) are the two leading examples.

In some cases, major labels insist that the entire royalty (and even part or all of the artist's up-front cash creative fee) be paid directly to them for their services exclusivity waiver, especially if the royalty account is unrecouped. However, the artist more typically keeps the cash creative fee from the studio, which is deemed a fee for motion picture services rather than a recording advance.

RECORDING ARTIST AND STUDIO ISSUES

Assuming the artist and label make their arrangement, the next step is to sort out the soundtrack recording issues between the record company and its artist on the one hand and the studio on the other hand. These issues are:

Marketing Fund

A guaranteed marketing fund to be spent by the studio (and perhaps a matching amount by the label) to promote the soundtrack album and/or singles, the aggregate of which can be in the $100,000-$500,000 range if on a 50 (studio)/50 (label) matching basis.

Video Ownership

Irrespective of the investment issue, both studios and labels compete for music video ownership. The studio wants to control the exploitation of the video, especially in conjunction with marketing the film, although promotion of the video is often a joint effort by the label and studio. Because of uncertainty about the impact of commercial exploitation under union agreements, studios rarely give record companies commercial exploitation rights if the video contains film clips and try to limit the non-commercial exploitation to the period when the film is in active distribution.

No Singles Rights

The principal issue centers around prohibition of release of the recording as a single by any label other than the artist's label. Since the label distributing the soundtrack LP wants to use singles as a selling tool for the LP, retention of singles rights by the artist's nondistributing label can diminish the attractiveness of the LP to the distributing label. Additionally, the studio is anxious to use the single to promote the theatrical release of the film. One recent example of a master that the soundtrack distributing label did not have singles rights to was *I Want Your Sex* by George Michael, for *Beverly Hills Cop II.* CBS, not MCA Records, the soundtrack LP label, distributed the single. In rare cases, no singles rights are granted, as for the song *Say You, Say Me* by Lionel Richie on the *White Knights* soundtrack. This noncompetition restriction allows the artist and the label to reap full benefit by ensuring that a potential single used in a film is included on and stimulates the sale of the artist's own album, rather than a soundtrack album containing other artist's recordings which yields a prorated royalty to each.

Home Video Royalty

Home video device royalty overrides to the label by the studio are rarely, if ever, granted. Studios with unaffiliated home video distribution now typically receive 20 percent of the wholesale price as a royalty for cassettes. For an $89.95 cassette, the average wholesale price is about $50, so the studio receives $10 per cassette from the distributor, from which it must pay its costs and royalties. If, for example, the artist's label wanted a 10% home video override, the studio would have to pay approximately $5 per cassette to the label, i.e., 10% of $50, or $5. CBS (Song) Records reportedly demanded a very high video override for the use of Bruce Springsteen masters in *Mask*, so Universal declined and used Bob Seeger masters instead.

THE ARTIST/STUDIO DEAL: MAJOR DEAL POINTS

The following is a list of the major deal issues which will be discussed between artist's counsel and the studio commissioning a song and record. Exhibit 1 provides a comparison on typical deals for major studios, mini-studios, and recognized independents.

Cash Creative Fee

Compensation for writing and recording can be structured either as a cash creative fee, not including recording costs, or an all-inclusive recording *fund* including writing, performing, producing, and recording costs. Writing fees per song range from $0 for an unknown to $30,000 for a superstar's work. Recording fees may be in the range of $10,000 per track for major performers.

If the deal is structured as a recording fund, the studio will pay a flat sum for delivery of the song and master, with the artist being responsible for all recording costs, keeping the balance as, in effect, the creative fee. The *all-in* fee per song for a top writer/performer ranges from $50,000 to $75,000, and for a midlevel writer/performer from $20,000 to $35,000. New acts may receive in the range of $7,500 to $15,000. The all-in structure is an inducement for the artist to limit recording costs, and also caps the studio's investment. However, the studio has no contractual assurance the money is being allocated judiciously. Problems sometimes arise when the studio is dissatisfied with the song or recording and asks the artist to rework it. Recording fund deals are particularly attractive to acts who own recording studios and/or computer-based music technology.

Song Royalties

The writer's share of royalties for songwriting services is negotiated the same as a nonfilm song agreement, i.e., the writer basically receives 50% of the income, except for sheet music, which is typically about 8 to 12 cents per piano copy and 10-12 1/2% of wholesale for nonpiano copies. The writer may seek to guarantee a full statutory mechanical rate for the soundtrack LP or single (currently 5.25 cents per song or one cent per minute of playing time, whichever is greater). Most studios resist guaranteeing a full mechanical rate since the label will seek to limit the mechanical rate for LPs to 10 times 3/4 statutory (now 39.375 cents per LP, 3.94 cents per song) and for singles to 3/4 statutory for each side.

If you have a lot of clout or are signed exclusively to a publisher, you may be able to structure a co-publishing agreement in which song ownership and administration may be shared, thus allowing the artist and/or the publisher to participate in a percentage of the publisher's share of music income. Independent motion picture companies - such as Atlantic Releasing Corporation, Crown International, and Transworld Entertainment-which typically pay less up-front money and do not have affiliated music publishing arms are more likely than major studios to agree to grant a participation in the publisher's share. Assuming a 50/50 participation arrangement, the client will receive approximately 75% of the total music income (the full writer's share and half of the publisher's share).

The split of copyright known as co-publishing is considerably less common than financial participation in the publisher's share of income. In participation deals, the participant has little or no control over the use or exploitation of the copyright. Major writers/performers receive a participation in the publisher's share of income that ranges from zero to 50%.

Also, the publisher's share of income that is subject to participation is reducible if the studio or its music publishing arm charges an administration fee on income, if collected. For example, if there is a 15% administration fee, the net publisher's share would be reduced to about 42.5% of the total income derived from the song.

In extraordinary cases, superstars who both write and perform have been able to keep both copyright ownership (and administration) and all the publisher's share of music publishing income, subject always to a free synchronization license to the studio for use of the song in the film and home video devices.

Major writers/artists are much more likely to share in publishing revenue than writers who do not perform their own material, since successful artists are perceived to add great promotional value to the song and the film. However, to the extent the artist participates in the publisher's share of income, the upfront cash fee may decline correspondingly, because the studio is forgoing all or a portion of the publisher's share of income from which they hope to recover their investment and some profit. However, for superstars, studios have a hard time reducing the cash creative fee, even if the publisher's share is relinquished or split.

Record Royalties

Record royalties, like music royalties, are negotiated much in the same manner as a normal recording agreement. However, there are a few points that are particularly important in soundtrack agreements.

All-In Royalty. Studios usually insist that the artist royalty be all-in, i.e., inclusive of all others who might be entitled to royalties with respect to the artist's recording, such as the record producer and the artist's label.

Proration. The royalty is usually subject to two forms of proration. First, it will be prorated for length, either by playing time or more typically by number of cuts. For example, if you have 2 out of the 10 cuts on the album, and receive a prorated 10% of retail royalty, your basic royalty will be .2 x 10%, or 2%. Second, the royalty is prorated by the number of artists on the cut. For example, if on the cuts the act performs together with a second recording act, the act's royalty will be cut in half (1/2 x .2 x 10% or 1%).

LP Override

Heavyweight artists ask for an album override, e.g., an additional 2% on the entire LP, regardless of proration. This may be fair when the soundtrack LP consists of *filler* that doesn't sell records or promote the film.

Royalty Allocation

Studios try to keep the aggregate artist royalties in check so they retain an appropriate net portion of the overall royalty from the soundtrack LP. For example, if the studio gets 16% of retail from the record company, they may allocate 10-12% to all royalty participants, retaining 4-6% for themselves. One way the studios try to contain royalties is to give the same *most favored nations* royalty deal to every artist, e.g., 10-12% prorated.

Singles

The artists who anticipate release of their master as an A-side single may try to insulate themselves from royalty reduction for the B-side of the single to assure a full single record royalty. Singles royalties are not as heavily negotiated as LP royal ties. In many respects singles are purely a promotional tool to sell albums.

EXHIBIT 2
ARTIST'S ROYALTY STATEMENT

Sales for original soundtrack of "Century City Blues" cat. no. 14899

Statement Date:	September 30, 198
Country of Sale:	United States
Period of Sales:	Second-Half 1988
Release Date:	April 5, 1988
Distributing Label:	Megabite Records, Inc.
Film Company	Behemoth Studios, Inc.

	Prorata Per Unit						
Configuration	Pkg. Deduct.	SLRP	Royalty	Share	Royalty	Sales	Earnings
Vinyl 7" singles	10%	1.98	8%	2 on 2	.14256	1,000,000	$142,560
Vinyl 12" singles	20%	4.98	8%	2 on 2	.31187	100,000	31,872
Cassette single	20%	3.98	8%	2 on 2	.25472	5,000	3,820
CD singles	25%	4.98	8%	4 on 4	.29880	2,500	747
Vinyl album	10%	9.98	10%	2 on 10	.17964	300,000	53,892
Cassette album	20%	9.98	10%	2 on 10	.15968	450,000	71,856
CD album*	25%	15.98	10%	2 on 10	.14970	250,000	37,425

Gross Earnings This Period	$342,172
Less Soundtrack Conversion	-6,000
TOTAL PAYABLE THIS PERIOD	$336,172

$252,129 remittance to artist (75%) enclosed
$84,043 remittance to artist's label (25%)

*Although top-line compact discs generally retail for $15.98, current record company practices vary as to royalty rate and method of calculation. Our example is based upon a typical accounting using the normal vinyl/cassette album rate with a higher packaging deduction.

The studio's attitude is "we own what we pay for." The studio likely will insist on acquiring the song and master recording copyrights as "works made for hire." As discussed above, superstars may occasionally succeed in sharing ownership and administration of the song and/or master recording.

Recoupment

Smart artist representatives insist that the only recording costs the studio or label can recoup from the artist royalty account before royalties are paid are those paid solely in connection with the soundtrack LP, as opposed to the picture, since the studio pays recording costs whether or not there is a soundtrack LP. These nonpicture recording costs are called "soundtrack conversion costs" and usually include guild new use fees, and occasionally remixing. This point can have a major financial impact on the artist royalty. If not limited to nonpicture costs, the artist royalty account could be charged with film-related recording costs. For example, if the act's royalty is 10% of retail prorated on a cut, and they have 1 cut of 10, the royalty per LP sold would be .1 x 10%, or 1% of retail (about 7 cents/LP). If the label sells 100,000 LP units, the artist's royalty account would be credited with $7,000. To the extent the studio recoups costs, they are *deducted* from the royalty. Recoupment of recording creative fees from the artist's royalty account is negotiable. New acts often have their creative fee recouped from their royalties; established acts face this less often.

SONG AND MASTER OWNERSHIP

The studio's attitude is "we own what we pay for." The studio likely will insist on acquiring the song and master recording copyrights as "works made for hire." As discussed above, superstars may occasionally succeed in sharing ownership and administration of the song and/or master recording. Artist ownership of master recordings may be allowed in rare cases when a superstar's recording services are furnished by their own production companies, e.g., Paul McCartney's MPL Communications, Ltd. or David Bowie's Main Man Productions, Inc.

Use Of Master On Artist's Label

Some acts succeed in getting a license from the studio for use of the master recording on the acts' own records. The master might then be released both on the soundtrack album and the artist's own album. As a condition to granting the license, the studio may ask for an override royalty from the artist's label on records embodying the master. In any event, the studio will insist that any release of such master by the artist's label not compete with the studio's soundtrack records by conditioning the licensing grant on a *holdback* from release. This holdback mostly applies from four to twelve months after release of the soundtrack album, so that the record-buying public associates the soundtrack song and master with the film and is motivated to buy the soundtrack LP. Studios are finding it more difficult, at least with major acts, to negotiate a holdback on the release of the master on the artist's home label.

Approval of Record Producer

Many established acts produce themselves or insist on using a record producer they approve. Studios rarely try to interfere with the artist's producer selection or the artist/producer creative relationship, especially if the deal is the typical recording fund deal, which makes the artist responsible for the producer's compensation. However, if the studio separately pays the producer's cash advance or royalty, they insist on approving the producer deal.

Credits

As long as the song is used in the film, most studios will agree to give an "end title" screen credit in the form of "[Song Title], written by [Artist], performed by [Artist]." Sometimes credit in the form of, "courtesy of [Label]" is accorded the artist's record company. Only rarely does an artist receive main title credit (where the writer, director, producer, and other major creative elements get credit). However, Huey Lewis and the News received main title credit in *Back to the Future* for their song *Power of Love*. This may be desired by superstar artists.

Paid ad credits that promote the film, e.g., credits in newspapers, magazines, and the like, are usually not granted to writers/performers by major studios, except for main title songs such as Lionel Richie for *Say You, Say Me* in *White Nights*, or when the prestige of the soundtrack artist is considered a significant marketing benefit. Independents tend to grant paid ad credits to writers/performers more frequently than major studios.

Record jacket credit is a different matter. Studios rarely refuse to give the recording act credit on the jackets of soundtrack LPs or CDs and on the jacket of singles since these are selling tools. Sometimes, if there are multiple recording artists, all the acts get credit in alphabetical order. In contrast to the normal competition among actors, directors, and producers for large and prominent credit, the act and label may try to keep the credit small so the soundtrack LP does not look like it is the act's own LP, which might compete with and thereby diminish sales of the act's own records. This makes sense because the act receives the entire royalty on their own LPs (subject to recoupment of recording costs by the label) and, if they write, they receive the mechanical royalties on the entire LP (always the writer's share and sometimes a portion of the publisher's share).

Additional Artist/Studio Deal Points

One issue to consider is that the studio will also insist on a provision whereby they are not obligated to use the song or the recording (whether in the film, soundtrack LP, or as a single), although they may have to pay whether or not they use the song. The filmmaking team must be allowed the freedom to add and subtract songs and recordings with impunity.

Also, since music videos are an important selling tool, studios normally insist that the act provide music video services, usually at no additional cost or at minimum union scale. MTV prefers concept videos (such as Billy Ocean's *When the Tough Get Going* from *Jewel of the Nile*) to film-clip-only videos (such as Madonna's *Into the Groove* from *Desperately Seeking Susan*).

Finally, songwriters and soundtrack performers who do not perform onscreen are never granted a participation in the nonmusic receipts of a film. These participations are usually divided between the actors, director, and producers on the one hand, and the studio on the other. However, music artists have a distinct

EXHIBIT 3
ROUGH INCOME SUMMARY

The following rough income summary is designed to alert you to sources of income rather than to provide exact figures (although we have done our best to be reasonably accurate).

A. Writer

1. Writing Fee (nonrecoupable)	$ 25,000
2. Song Synch License For Film	0
3. Performance Income (worldwide)	
(a) From Film In Theatres	
(i) United States	0
(ii) Foreign	$20,000
(b) Radio Performances	$100,000
(c) Home Video	0
(d) Pay TV	*
(e) Free TV	
(i) United States Network TV (two runs)	$3,000
(ii) U.S. Syndicated TV (two runs 150 stations	$600
(iii) Foreign	$5,000
4. Sheet Music (40,000 copies @ 10 cents/copy)	$4,000
5. Mechanicals	
(a) United States (3/4 statutory)	
(i) Single (A side only) (1,000,000 x 1.969 cents)	$19,690
(ii) LP (500,000 x 1.969 cents)	$9,845
(b) Foreign	
(i) Single (750,000 x 2.25 cents)	$16,875
(ii) LP (375,000 x 2.25 cents)	$8,438
Total	**$212,448**

B. Recording Artist

1. Recording Fee (nonrecoupable)	$ 25,000
2. Master License For Film	0
3. United States Record Sales	
(a) Singles A-side only (1,000,000 copies)	$ 76,500
(b) LPs (500,000 copies)	$49,401
4. Foreign Record Sales	
(a) Singles (750,000 copies)	$ 47,81
(b) LPs (375,000 copies)	$ 27,225
less soundtrack conversion costs	- $3,000
Total	**$222,938**

*Figures presently unavailable.

advantage as to the payment of royalties - they do not have to wait until the studio earns back its investment before songwriter royalties are paid. The same is true for artist royalties from the soundtrack LP. Usually only relatively minimal nonpicture soundtrack conversion costs are recouped before the artist is paid for record sales.

INCOME

Let's assume you make a deal at Paramount, you are a writer/performer/producer who writes a title song and records a title song master. You are paid $25,000 for the song and $25,000 to record. You retain the writer's share but Paramount retains the publisher's share. You receive a 12% retail United States record royalty, prorated, on LPs, and 9% on singles. Your master is 3 minutes long. The picture is a blockbuster; your single sells 1,000,000 copies in the United States, 750,000 foreign, and hits No. 1 on *Billboard's* Hot 100 Pop Chart. The soundtrack LP, on which you have 1 of the 10 cuts, sells 500,000 copies in the United States and 375,000 copies overseas. Exhibit 3 gives you a rough idea of what your earnings might be.

CONCLUSION

The writing and recording of songs by pop writers and performers involves complex financial and business arrangements with studios, record labels, and music publishers. The advantages to both new and established songwriters and recording acts in participating in soundtracks are numerous. The song and its recording will be exposed to millions of people, it may be included in the soundtrack album, and, in the best case, be released as a single and MTV video. The down side is that ultimately the artist has very little, if any, input as to how the song is used in the film. You may write and record a beautiful four-minute ballad which is blared from a radio for only a few seconds, but that's the risk you take.

The most important advice to a new writer or recording act, however, is to not play prima donna if approached by a studio to work on a soundtrack. Only major acts have this luxury. Your goal should be to get the song considered and accepted. Nonestablished writers/performers should not expect the same sort of terms that Paul McCartney gets. The bottom line: Don't blow the deal. Once you get your foot in the door and make a positive contribution to a soundtrack, you may well have taken a substantial step in both your film and nonfilm writing and performing careers.

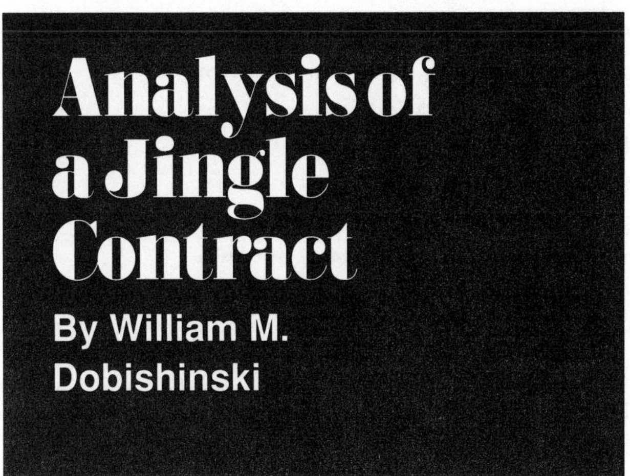

Analysis of a Jingle Contract

By William M. Dobishinski

Advertising music is an integral part of the music world today, with some industry estimates that advertising music represents over 1/3 of all music broadcast on television. Many successful advertising music composers (i.e. Barry Manilow) have also achieved prominence in pop, television and film music.

Sponsors, advertising agencies and music suppliers are the three principals in the creation of advertising music. Sponsors are located nationwide, while the major agencies and music suppliers are based primarily in New York, Chicago and Los Angeles.

Sponsors (referred to as "Client" in the following jingle contract) typically request their advertising agencies (referred to as "Agency" in the contract) to design and produce their advertising campaigns, including contracting with music suppliers to provide the music for the commercials. These campaigns can range from national television broadcasts for a well known client via local television stations throughout the United States (national spot) or network television stations, to one-city radio broadcasts for a local business. Advertising music suppliers (referred to as "Supplier" in the contract) range from one man shops to "jingle houses" representing several composers. In addition to composing the composition, the supplier is also responsible for hiring the producer, musicians and vocalists used in the composition recording sessions. Often, suppliers produce and perform the composition themselves.

There are primarily three types of compositions used as advertising music:
(1) an original jingle written specifically for a particular advertising campaign;
(2) existing compositions in the form of:
(a) popular compositions (either in their original form or adapted for the commercial); or
(b) stock music

JINGLES

Typically, the agency will supply lyrics for the jingle and request a bid from the supplier to compose, arrange and produce an original musical composition for the commercial. In order to secure a contract to supply music for a commercial, suppliers may have to compete with one another by submitting "demos" of the music to the agency at production cost only. Thus, although some suppliers write over one hundred jingles a year, many jingles never go beyond the "demo" stage. Once a demo is selected by the agency for the final production, the supplier should consider the desired length of the music and commercials, the number of compositions and/or arrangements, the number of required performers and the broadcast mediums in setting creative fees and production costs. A creative fee for one 30 second commercial can range from $1,500 to $15,000. Production costs vary, depending primarily upon studio rental rates and the number of musicians hired (the current approximate hourly union rates are as follows: off-camera television solo vocalists - $250; off-camera group vocalists - $150; and television and radio studio musicians - $75).

Although the agency usually pays the supplier a moderate upfront fee for the music, the supplier usually receives most compensation in the form of union residuals (i.e., "back end" compensation paid, pursuant to union requirements, according to different types of use of the recorded music.) Depending on the success of a commercial, residuals can range from a modest few hundred dollars to many thousands of dollars. These residuals are paid by the agency on behalf of the client (usually, musicians are represented by the American Federation of Musicians; television vocalists by the Screen Actors Guild; and radio vocalists by the American Federation of Television and Radio Artists). A smaller amount of additional back end compensation may also be paid to the composer and publisher of the composition by ASCAP or BMI in the form of performing rights royalties. (See "Rider to Agreement" section of the following jingle contract.)

Musician and vocalist residual payments (at 75% of the recording session payments) are based on 13-week broadcast cycles, starting with the second 13-week cycle of the commercial. Solo vocalists may also be paid substantial additional residuals based on the number of individual station broadcasts. Thus, while the supplier is awarded the account based on skill as a composer, they can maximize income by performing as a vocalist and/or musician during the production.

EXISTING POPULAR MUSIC

In some instances, the agency may wish to use an easily recognizable popular composition (e.g. "Anticipation" for Heinz ketchup) or a popular composition with a variation for the client's purposes (e.g. Elton John's "Sad Songs Say So Much" to "Sassons Say So Much" for Sasson jeans).

If the agency uses the original master recording of the composition, both a synchronization license from the publisher and a master use license from the record company must be obtained. If the agency re-records the composition, only the synchronization license from the publisher is required. Synchronization license fees vary, depending upon the popularity of the composition, advertising medium and market, term of use, exclusivity in certain product types or for commercials generally, and parody arrangement. Publishers may charge in excess of $100,000 for a synchronization license for use of a popular composition in a national commercial, while a master use license may cost between $5,000 to $10,000.

STOCK MUSIC

In many instances where music is considered less important or budgets are low (most often in regional or one-city campaigns), the agency will license existing music directly from a music library or indirectly from a post-production house for use as an underscore to evoke a certain mood in the commercial. "Library music" rarely has any individual popular recognition and is composed and recorded specifically as "background music." Further, it is recorded in nonunion sessions (often overseas) to avoid paying residuals. License fees for library music are generally very inexpensive (approximately $100 for use in a network television commercial; less for local television and radio) for a nonexclusive buy out arrangement for the master use license to the recording of the composition (with no residuals payable) and the synchronization license to the composition itself.

Agencies often use post-production houses to secure the desired synchronization license, and to edit and synchronize the music to the film portion of the commercial. In addition to the synchronization license fee, post-production houses charge the agency for the editing and synchronization services. The fees for these services may range up to $1,000 or more. Agencies with their own facilities to edit and synchronize music to the film often obtain the synchronization license from the music library.

In practice, agency agreements are often not signed (payment invoices are often considered sufficient) or signed with little negotiation of the form contract points as long as the basic deal is correct (i.e. the blanks to be filled in).

Atlanta Session Players and members of the Atlanta Symphony Orchestra photographed at Doppler Studios. Courtesy Mix Magazine and Doppler Studios. Photo by Roger Macuch.

EXHIBIT 1: SAMPLE JINGLE CONTRACT

SUPPLIER
COMPOSITION*
CLIENT/PRODUCT

DATE
JOB NUMBER

**As used in the following contract, "composition" refers to television commercials. Television commercials have traditionally run for 30 seconds and radio commercials for 15 seconds, although the current television trend is also toward 15 second spots. In rare instances, television commercials may also run for 10, 45, 60, or 90 seconds.*

This contract is entered into between ________as agent for Client, and Supplier, on the above date under the following terms and conditions.

Commentary: *Agreements of this type are three party arrangements between the agency, on its own behalf and as an agent for the sponsor (referred to in the agreement as "client"), and the supplier, relating to the composition and its recording.*

1. WARRANTY

Supplier warrants and represents that

(a) It is the sole author as an "employee for hire" of the Composition, a copy of which is hereby annexed;

(b) The Composition has never been published;

(c) No application has been made to register the Composition for copyright as either a published or unpublished work;

(d) Supplier has full right, power and authority to make and enter into this agreement, and the rights granted to Client hereunder will not violate the legal or equitable rights of any person, firm or corporation;

(e) No assignment has been made of any of the rights in the Composition.

Commentary: *Most advertising music agreements are entered into with the supplier as an "employee for hire" of the client. The agreement might more properly be deemed to relate to a "specially commissioned audio-visual work" under the 1976 Copyright Act. Under these terms, the client owns the copyright to the composition, which allows him to control all rights regarding the use and exploitation of the composition. Clause 2 infra refers to a copyright assignment, probably to insure that the client will retain all rights in the composition if the "employee for hire" status is not enforceable or is one day contested. The remaining warranties and representations provide additional "insurance" for the client.*

2. GRANT OF RIGHTS

Supplier hereby sells, transfers and assigns to Client, its successors, assigns and licenses, in perpetuity, all rights of whatsoever kind, nature and description, that are presently known or hereafter ascertained, in and to the Composition, including, but not limited to the right to secure copyright therein and all renewals thereof throughout the entire world, without any restriction whatsoever as to use. Supplier further sells, transfers and assigns to Client all recordings made of the Composition. Supplier will execute, without charge or expense, any additional documents Client or Agency deem necessary to further evidence such transfer of ownership, establishment of copyright or renewal of copyright in the Composition.

> ***Commentary:*** *When the supplier composes advertising music for the agency as an "employee for hire," the agency acquires all rights in the composition and may use the composition in any medium and form it chooses. The supplier may request a right of first refusal to write and produce all arrangements of the composition (enabling the supplier to charge additional fees as arranger, performer and producer). Sometimes, the supplier may also negotiate an "artificial" residual to be paid if the composition is arranged, produced or otherwise altered by anyone other than the supplier. In this situation, the supplier is paid as if he or she were a vocalist or musician on the arrangement, production or alteration, enabling collection of residuals tied into the respective union rate even though he or she provided no services as a vocalist or musician.*

3. OWNERSHIP

The commercials or other productions hereunder, shall be and remain the absolute property of Client forever. Without limiting the preceding sentence, it is understood that Client shall have the right during the term hereof, to use any production produced hereunder for broadcasting and telecasting over any network or networks, station or stations, in any country or countries, at any time and from time to time and for programs, spots, or on any other basis whatsoever, as well as the right to revise the picture and/or sound therefor.

> ***Commentary:*** *Although the client is granted the right to use the composition without restriction during the term of the agreement, the broadcast lifetime of most jingles is generally no more than one year. Eventually, the composition will become part of the public domain when the copyright expires.*

4. SPECIAL PROVISIONS

Subject to Rider to Agreement. (Examples of typical ASCAP and BMI riders are to be found at the end of this contract.)

5. CONSIDERATION

In full consideration of Supplier's performance hereunder, and for all rights granted by Supplier herein, Client agrees to pay Supplier and Supplier agrees to accept the following:

(a) For the Composition, $______________

(b) For all Artists, the minimum scale under the code of the applicable union having jurisdiction over their services, $______________

(c) For the studio facilities, Supplier's substantiated out-of-pocket costs,
$______________ Total Cost $______________

Commentary: *Compensation depends on many factors, including on the length of the music and commercial, broadcast medium (local television, radio, network television), number of compositions written for the advertising campaign and the supplier's reputation. Generally, 50% of the compensation is paid up front and the balance paid upon satisfactory completion of the project.*

6. INDEMNITY

Supplier hereby agrees to defend, indemnify and hold harmless Client, Agency and their respective associated or affiliated companies, successors, assigns and licensees (hereinafter called "Indemnitees") from and against any and all damages, costs, charges, legal fees, recoveries, judgments, penalties and expenses or losses of whatsoever kind or nature which may be obtained against, imposed upon or suffered by the Indemnitees by reason of any infringement or claim of infringement of copyright, or violation or claim of violation of any other rights resulting from any use made by the Indemnitees, of the Composition or the recording. Agency will similarly indemnify Supplier and hold Supplier harmless with respect to any alterations or additions Agency makes to the Composition.

Commentary: *Under this indemnity provision, the supplier agrees to reimburse the agency for damages resulting from any claims of copyright infringement. Sometimes, supplier may request that his liability to the agency be limited to the amount of creative fees paid to the supplier under the agreement since extensive production costs, media buys and other costs could form an enormous liability (e.g., if a copyright infringement problem resulted in the cancellation of a commercial). If possible, the supplier should have his own Errors and Omissions insurance policy (although he may also have some coverage under the agency's policy).*

In a situation where the supplier is arranging a popular composition, the agency may indemnify (i.e., protect from damage or loss) the supplier from claims by the original publishing company since the supplier is relying on the agency to properly clear the rights to the composition that the supplier is arranging.

Even in those instances where the agency requests the supplier to compose a jingle that is original but has the same "feeling" as a popular composition, agency may be asked to indemnify supplier for any copyright infringement problem that arises despite supplier's best efforts to avoid it.

Further, recent claims that "soundalike" recordings (i.e., recordings imitating a performer's style) for commercials violate applicable law (even when a synchronization license has been obtained) may cause supplier to transfer to agency all liability for work in connection with popular songs (i.e., composing, arranging and recording).

7. SERVICES

Supplier will cause the Artists to render all of their services hereunder in a competent, painstaking and artistic manner and to the best of their ability. They will attend and participate in all rehearsals, conferences and such other meetings that shall be deemed necessary or advisable by Agency in connection with the rendition of their services hereunder. All of their services shall be subject to Agency approval, direction and control at all times and Supplier will cause them properly to comply with whatever reasonable instructions, suggestions and recommendations which Agency may give them in connection with rendition of their services. The final tape must meet all requirements of broadcasting stations.

Commentary: The agency is usually responsible for paying union residuals upon receipt of union contracts for each performer submitted by the supplier to the agency. The agency will typically submit the contracts to a company that specializes in talent and residuals to administer the payments.

8. MATERIAL FURNISHED

Supplier will record such Composition as Agency directs with the selected Artist(s) and furnish to Agency 35mm Mag Stripe with a 7 1/2 IPS AND 15 IPS tape transfer of the one-quarter inch final music tape ready for audio mixing, embodying the Composition and the services and/or materials which meet Agency approval. Agency and Client shall have the right to send one or more representatives to each rehearsal and recording session.

9. UNIONS

Not withstanding any provision in this agreement to the contrary, Supplier agrees that only union personnel will be used.

10. COMMISSIONS

It is agreed that Agency shall be under no obligation for the payment of any commissions to or for Supplier on account of this agreement.

11. INJUNCTIVE RELIEF

It is agreed that the services of Supplier and those of each Artist selected hereunder are special, unique, unusual, extraordinary and of an artistic character giving them a peculiar value, and are impossible of replacement and that any breach of this agreement by Supplier will cause Client and Agency irreparable damage. Therefore, Client and Agency shall be entitled as a matter of right, and without notice, to equitable relief by way of injunction or otherwise, in the event of any violation of the provisions of this agreement.

Commentary: It is doubtful that any court would enforce an injunction without notice and simply as a matter of right.

12. OBLIGATION LIMITED TO PAYMENT

Client and Agency shall be under no obligation to cause the commercial(s) made hereunder to be broadcast or to use Artist(s) services, it being understood that the only obligation is for Client to make the payments required under this agreement.

13. LIABILITY

Supplier hereby agrees to indemnify, defend and hold harmless Client and Agency from and against any liability arising out of Supplier's breach of warranties and representations hereunder.

Commentary: The liabilities addressed in this clause are similar to those mentioned in Clause 6 above.

14. NO WAIVER

Failure to exercise the rights granted herein upon the occurrence of any of the contingencies set forth in this agreement shall not in any event constitute a waiver of such rights upon the recurrence of any such contingencies.

15. ENTIRE AGREEMENT

This agreement constitutes the entire understanding between the parties with respect to the subject matter of this agreement and supersedes all prior agreements. No waiver, modification or addition to this agreement shall be valid unless in writing and signed by the parties hereto. This agreement shall be construed pursuant to the laws of the State of ____________.

Your signature, together with ours, shall constitute this a binding agreement between us.

AGREED: AS AGENT FOR:

BY____________________ ____________________ BY: Broadcast Manager

Your signature, together with ours, shall constitute this a binding agreement between us.

SUPPLIER INVOICES WILL NOT BE APPROVED FOR PAYMENT WITHOUT A SIGNED CONTRACT, AFM CONTRACT AND LEAD SHEET RETURNED TO BROADCAST BUSINESS MANAGER.

EXHIBIT 2
RIDER TO JINGLE CONTRACT
(ASCAP) (BMI) MODIFICATION OF AGREEMENT OF COMMISSIONED WORK

This agreement is being entered into in order to modify the agreement, dated __________, executed by ______________ (hereinafter referred to as Author) and __________ (hereinafter referred to as Agency), pertaining to the "musical composition" entitled__________.

Notwithstanding anything to the contrary contained elsewhere in the agreement, dated ______________, it is expressly agreed that although the composition is a "work for hire," the performing rights have been assigned back to the Author. The right to "use" said composition shall not mean or be deemed to mean the right to "perform," which right shall belong exclusively to the author.

Author is a member of ASCAP (BMI) and the "composition" is part of the ASCAP (BMI) repertory. The parties acknowledge that the right to perform the "composition" publicly has been reserved exclusively to Author for licensing only through ASCAP (BMI). ASCAP's (BMI's) agreement with Author permits Author, hereafter, to grant a nonexclusive license to perform the "composition" and, if Author shall later do so, Author must promptly notify ASCAP (BMI). In the event any such license is granted, the "composition," the Author would not then be entitled to be paid by ASCAP (BMI) for surveyed performances.

The undersigned warrant and represents as follow:

1. ______________________________ (Name(s) of composer(s)) has (have) composed the music and ______________________________ (Name(s) of lyricist(s) has (have) written the lyric for a musical work entitled ________________ (Name of musical work) to be used as part of broadcast commercial announcements by________________ (Name of sponsor) for the product ________________________(Name of product) (which announcements are herein called "the commercials") and that ______________________________ (Name of publisher(s)) is (are) the publisher(s) thereof.

2. The work has not been written as a "work made for hire" or pursuant to any other agreement which would prevent the licensing of performing rights in the work by BMI pursuant to the writer(s) and/or publisher(s) agreement(s) with BMI.

3. The agreement among the parties provides for the division of writer and publisher performance royalties as follows:

______________	__________	______________	__________
writer	share	publisher	share
______________	__________	______________	__________
writer	share	publisher	share

4. The work is and will be used for at least 15 seconds or more as the sole auditory focus of audience attention in the course of the commercials.

5. Attached are a lead sheet and tape of the work as used in the commercials and an accurate list of broadcast time bought for the commercials by the sponsor or the undersigned agency on behalf of the sponsor for the period from ________ to ______________.

6. It is understood by all parties that payments to the writer(s) and/or publisher(s) of the work will be made by BMI in reliance on the representations made in this notice and the documents attached hereto.

Dated ______________________

____
Writer

____
Writer

____
By Agency (or sponsor)

____
Publisher

____
By (Title)

____
By (Title)

____
Publisher

____
By (Title)

THIS DOCUMENT MUST BE SIGNED BY EACH WRITER AND PUBLISHER CLAIMING RIGHTS AND BY THE APPROPRIATE REPRESENTATIVE OF THE ADVERTISING AGENCY OR SPONSOR.

Commentary: *If the suppliers do not obtain an express performing rights provision granting the nondramatic public performance rights in the composition (such as the attached riders suggested by ASCAP and BMI), they will be unable to collect performing rights royalties. Both ASCAP and BMI have unique requirements for jingles, including BMI's requirement that a commercial have a total of a certain number of seconds of music without voice-over before paying any performing rights royalties. The amount of potential performing rights royalties for jingles varies, depending on the medium of broadcast and the respective performing rights society. ASCAP has recently paid $68 (combined writer and publisher shares) for each prime time network television performance of advertising music, and BMI has recently paid $60 (combined writer and publisher shares) for each network performance. Local television and radio rates are substantially less.*

REPORT OF STATION TIME BOUGHT FOR COMMERCIAL

Entitled ______________________ For ______________________
Name of Sponsor

Station or Network	Broadcast Dates	Number of Performances per day

EXHIBIT 3
ASCAP LETTER AND CHECKLISTS FOR ACCURATELY IDENTIFYING AND CREDITING SURVEYED PERFORMANCES OF WORKS USED IN COMMERCIALS AND PROMOTIONAL OR PUBLIC SERVICE ANNOUNCEMENTS

Dear Member:

This letter and the attached materials are intended to advise you of the information ASCAP needs in order to accurately identify and credit surveyed performances of your works used in commercials and promotional or public service announcements.

For your convenience, we have prepared two checklists for you to use when you are indexing your works which will be performed as commercials or promotional ("promo") or public service announcements ("psa").

Checklist "A" should be used when your work has been created to be performed as a commercial, promo or psa.

Checklist "B" should be used when your work has been created for another purpose, but has been licensed subsequently for commercial, promo, or psa use.

Regardless of the type of information you submit, it is essential for ASCAP to receive these indexing materials from you IN ADVANCE OF THE FIRST AIRING of these works. We may not be able to identify your works in our radio and local television sample surveys unless we are aware of your claim when these performances are on the air.

We believe that most of the information requested on both checklists is self-explanatory. However, one area where members frequently have questions concerns the content of agreements with the sponsor or advertising agency. When a work is written specifically for use in a commercial, promo, or psa, the contract with the agency or sponsor frequently contains a direct grant of the performing rights. In order for you to receive royalties from ASCAP, it must be clear that you have expressly reserved the performing rights to your works for licensing through the Society. ASCAP, therefore, must see the relevant contract to determine whether or not a grant of these rights has been made.

While the Society cannot give individual members advice with respect to the drafting of these contracts, ASCAP is prepared to review these agreements before they are executed in order to assist the parties in drafting the appropriate language if it is the intention of the parties that the performing rights be reserved for licensing through the Society.

One item on the checklists that may not be familiar to you is the reference to "Industry Standard Coding Identification ('ISCI')#." This is an identifying code used in the advertising industry, which is made up of four letters and four numbers (e.g., GENM4333). Each commercial produced is assigned a unique ISCI code, which identifies the commercial, both to the agency and the broadcaster, for airing and billing purposes. Since performance reports from the television networks (ABC, CBS, NBC) refer to this code, having this information will greatly enhance ASCAP's ability to credit you with these performances. These code numbers should be available from the advertising agency or sponsor. In addition to each ISCI code #, please be sure to include on the checklist the title of each commercial that includes your music.

We hope this information will be helpful, and that you will not hesitate to be in touch if you have any questions or need additional information.

Sincerely yours,

CHECKLIST "A"
WORKS CREATED AS COMMERCIALS, PROMOS, PSA'S

TO ASSIST ASCAP IN CREDITING YOU FOR SURVEYED PERFORMANCES OF THESE WORKS, PLEASE COMPLETE THE FOLLOWING ITEMS:

Author(s): ________________________________ Publisher(s):
Sponsor: ________________________________ ____________
Product: ________________________________ ____________
Title of commercial: ______________________ ____________
Industry Standard Coding Identification (ISCI) #: ______

(Please list all #'s for each commercial) __________
Song Title (if different): ________________
First air date: __________________________

Term of agreement:
Media: Networks TV___ Local TV___ Cable TV___ Radio___
(check all that apply)

PLEASE SUBMIT THE FOLLOWING ITEMS:

*Lead sheet and lyrics ___ or ___ *Lead sheet (for instrumental performances)

Advertising copy

(*Please submit a cassette tape if a lead sheet is unavailable.)

Copy of agreement with the sponsor or advertising agency whereby the ASCAP members-in-interest retain performing rights for licensing through ASCAP _____

Index registration card _____

FOR NETWORK (ABC, NBC OR CBS) PERFORMANCES ONLY, PLEASE SUBMIT ONE OF THE FOLLOWING AIRING SCHEDULES

Advertising agency report ___

Talent and residual report ___

Other ____

CHECKLIST "B"
WORKS CREATED FOR ANOTHER PURPOSE BUT SUBSEQUENTLY LICENSED AS COMMERCIALS, PROMOS, PSA'S

TO ASSIST ASCAP IN CREDITING YOU FOR SURVEYED PERFORMANCES OF THESE WORKS, PLEASE COMPLETE THE FOLLOWING ITEMS:

Author(s) ____________________ Publisher(s) ____________________
Sponsor ____________________ ____________________
Product ____________________ ____________________
Song Title ____________________
Industry Standard Coding Identification (ISCI) # ____________________

(Please list all #'s for each commercial)
Title of commercial (if different) ____________________
First air date ____________________

Term of agreement: ____________
Media: Network TV___ Local TV___ Cable TV___ Radio___
(check all that apply)
Work is ____Instrumental ___Original Lyric ___Parody Lyric

PLEASE SUBMIT THE FOLLOWING ITEMS:

FOR NETWORK (ABC, NBC OR CBS) PERFORMANCES <u>ONLY</u>, PLEASE SUBMIT ONE OF THE FOLLOWING AIRING SCHEDULES

Advertising agency report___

Talent and residual report___

Other___

EXHIBIT 4
INSTRUCTIONS FOR BMI COMMERCIAL CLEARANCE FORM

Dear Affiliate:

Thank you for your recent inquiry regarding royalty payments for commercials. Enclosed is the appropriate clearance form. When completed, please sent it to us marked ATTN: COMMERCIAL JINGLES. An audio tape of the commercial as broadcast, NOT a studio tape, must be submitted with each clearance form. (In the case of TV, the audio portion alone is sufficient.)

Only one clearance form needs to be submitted for each commercial or commercial version. If use continues after the initial time period covered by the form, a letter from the agency to our Commercial Jingle Department referring to the original form and updating the time buy information, is adequate.

Please do not submit Public Service Announcements, Station or Network Promos. Background music used in TV network commercials may qualify for payment. Qualification for other uses requires the music to be the sole focus of audio attention for at least 15 seconds in a commercial announcement. And, in all cases, if the writer has assigned his/her rights away, please let us know to whom they were given.

In order to receive payment in the next commercial distribution, all material relating to qualifying commercials broadcast between July 1, 1988 and June 30, 1989 must be received by us before November 1, 1989.

Please feel free to call me if you have any questions.

Sincerely yours,

*BMI reserves the right to request additional information regarding submitted material.

EXHIBIT 5
BMI COMMERCIAL CLEARANCE FORM

TITLE: ONLY ONE VERSION OF EACH WORK PER FORM

List Writer(s)

Name(s) Social Sec. # Share%

__________ __________ __________

__________ __________ __________

List Publisher(s) Share%

____________________ __________

____________________ __________

Was work composed originally for commercial or adapted from existing work?
(Check one) Original ________ Adaptation ________

If adaptation, give original title and writer(s):

____

No part of this work - original or as adapted - has been written under any agreement that would prevent BMI from licensing the performing rights.

FOR PUBLISHER	FOR AGENCY OR SPONSOR
Signature __________ Date _____	Signature __________ Date _____
Print name _______________	Print name _______________
Title _______________	Title _______________
Firm Name _______________	Firm Name _______________
Address: _______________	Address _______________
City/State/Zip _______________	City/State/Zip _______________

NOTE: AN OFF-AIR TAPE OF WORK LISTED ABOVE AND AN AGENCY (OR SPONSOR) SUPPLIED SCHEDULE OF PURCHASED BROADCAST TIME FOR THE ABOVE COMMERCIAL MUST BE PROVIDED TO US. PAYMENT CANNOT BE PROCESSED WITHOUT BOTH. (SEE LISTING ON OTHER SIDE FOR BROADCAST INFORMATION REQUIRED.)

BROADCAST INFORMATION

Author's note: Since many agencies and/or sponsors prefer to use forms of their own design to maintain their media buy information, the following form is only a suggested form. If you find it convenient to use, please feel free to copy it or let us know and we will provide you with a supply. Regardless of the form you choose to use in reporting, however, we do require that it contain ALL of the information called for above.

Title of Work:

_______________________ _______________________

Name of Agency (or Sponsor) Name of Product (or Commercial)

____

Address of Agency (or Sponsor)

COMMERCIAL PLACEMENT INFO (See note above)

TV NETWORK (full/region) (F OR R)	SYNDICATED PROGRAM	LOCAL SPOTS	USED DURING WHAT CALENDAR QUARTER (example: 3Q/90)	NUMBER OF BUYS IN (pls use separate line for each type)	RADIO OR TV (R OR T)
SAMPLE					
F			1Q/87	3	T
	X		1Q/87	14	R

NOTE: ALL RADIO USES SHOULD BE LISTED AS LOCAL SPOTS. TV NETWORKS ARE ABC, CBS OR NBC ONLY. (NON ABC, CBS OR NBC USES ARE EITHER SYNDICATED OR LOCAL SPOTS.)

_______________________ _______________________

Signature of Agency (or sponsor) representative Date

____

Print Name and Title

Merchandising in the Music Industry

By Lawrence J. Blake

Even as recently as Woodstock, the sale of T-shirts at a rock concert consisted of occasional fanatics printing up their own unauthorized designs for the appreciation of a handful of others only slightly less fanatical than themselves. Today, merchandising companies regularly pay in excess of $100,000 for the right to sell T-shirts and other merchandising products at the concerts of artists who have just released their first record on a major record label and may spend millions of dollars to secure those rights with respect to superstars. Having triumphed in what is often a fierce competition for the rights to a particular artist, the merchandising company faces even tougher competition in the form of legions of unauthorized sellers of bootleg T-shirts who could not care less about the music, but are quick to seize the opportunity to cash in on an artist's popularity.

Merchandising agreements are big business. A superstar in the merchandising field can earn royalties in excess of $4 per attendee at his concerts. Artists of this caliber include Michael Jackson, The Rolling Stones, Bruce Springsteen, Guns N' Roses, Motley Crue, Metallica, New Kids On The Block, etc. On the other hand, there are countless artists who sell large quantities of records or who have received critical acclaim who are not superstars in the merchandising arena, where success is dependent on the type of music (hard rock and heavy metal sell well; pop, R&B, and jazz do not; rap is beginning to sell well), the demographics of the audience, and the image, visual appeal and sex of the artist. With the notable exception of Madonna, most successful female artists have not had commensurate success in the merchandising arena.

MERCHANDISING AGREEMENTS

Merchandising agreements are lucrative not only for established superstars, but also for new artists. In my practice we have a virtually nonstop flow of merchandising agreements being drafted and negotiated. Very often these are for artists who have just made their first record album or, in the case of foreign artists, who are about to tour the United States for the first time. Merchandising agreements commonly provide the critical seed money for paying the start-up expenses of an artist's tour. In most instances the recording fund or advance provided to a new artist by its record label is entirely depleted by the time the album has been delivered. Often the album has gone over budget and the record company has been advancing, on a noncontractual basis, additional funds to pay the band's living expenses while waiting for the record to be released. Once the album is released, the artist needs to tour extensively and often needs additional money for new equipment and other expenses to get that tour going. All too often, however, the record company is so far unrecouped that it is unwilling to advance additional sums for tour support.

Funding Sources.

Generally speaking, the two most likely sources for additional funding are a publishing agreement and/or a merchandising agreement. There is absolutely no doubt that a merchandising agreement should be the artist's first choice. With a customary exclusive songwriting and co-publishing agreement, there are substantial and long-term downsides (e.g., the giving up of a substantial portion of publishing income from the sale of the artist's own records without any beneficial service having been necessarily performed by the publisher), in merchandising agreements there typically are no such downsides. The deals are relatively short-term and are essentially risk free.

Of course, it is possible, at least for new artists, to sell their own T-shirts at their own concerts without the intervention of a third party company, and many artists have done this. In such a case, the artist will obviously make a greater per shirt profit than when a third party merchandising company sells the shirts. However, as a practical matter, it is not possible to sell T-shirts and other merchandise on one's own in larger venues, and the additional burdens of manufacturing, trucking, and selling the shirts militate toward making a deal with an established merchandising company and leaving the hassles of selling the merchandise to them. In any event, if the primary goal of the merchandising agreement is to create start-up money to fund a tour, the artist cannot act as their own merchandiser.

When Should A Merchandising Agreement Be Made?

Generally speaking, the first time that an artist is in a position to make a merchandising deal with a major merchandising company is when the artist is about to release or has just released a first album through major record label distribution and is about to embark on a substantial tour or, when the artist has released an album or albums through independent distribution channels which have gathered sufficient attention such that the artist can establish a nationwide tour as a headliner of first rate clubs or is invited to open a nationwide tour for another headline act.

With Whom Does The Artist Make A Merchandising Deal?

As of this writing there are only a handful of merchandising companies which control the rock n' roll merchandising business in the United States. By far, the two largest such companies are Winterland Productions, a company founded by Bill Graham, operating out of San Francisco and now owned by MCA, and Brockum Company, a company owned and operated out of Toronto, Canada by the BCL Entertainment Group, which is also very active in the field of concert promotion, both in the United States and Canada. Considerably smaller, are the Great Southern Company, which has an affiliation with Polygram Records, and Nice Man Merchandising, Inc. which is independently owned. While the smaller companies may lack the financial resources to compete with the giants for superstar acts, they pride themselves on the quality of their products and their attention to the needs and desires of their artist rosters. As this is being written, Irving Azoff has just started his own merchandising company which is expected to compete vigorously with Winterland and Brockum for a substantial share of the marketplace. Because it is so much easier to evaluate an artist's worth in the merchandising arena than it is in the record contract arena, any given deal is often shopped to all of the major companies and, although there are numerous instances in which the decision is made on the basis of personal rapport or personal relationships between the artist and the representatives of a particular company, in most cases, the artist goes with what is the best deal on paper.

Should Artists Give Their Merchandising Rights To The Record Company Or Production Company To Which They Are Signed?

Certain companies, as part of their standard recording contract, require the artist to grant to them exclusive or nonexclusive merchandising rights. While a grant of nonexclusive merchandising rights would certainly be less problematic than a grant of exclusive merchandising rights, it is almost never in the artist's best interest to grant merchandising rights to any company pursuant to an unrelated contract such as a recording contract.

The primary reasons for that are that if the company is not directly involved as a major merchandising company (i.e., it does not have a substantial merchandising company as a related division), it will have to license the rights it obtains from its artists to a third party merchandising company, in which event the intermediary record company will obviously take a share of the monies which the real merchandising company would otherwise have been willing to pay directly to the artist. This means that the artist makes less money.

Second, the merchandising royalties which would be earned by the artist pursuant to the clause in that recording contract would normally be cross-collateralized with the artist's record royalty account, meaning that royalties which would otherwise be payable to the artist from the sale of merchandise would be subject to being applied toward any unrecouped balance of recording costs and other advances in the artist's account. This is extremely disadvantageous.

Unfortunately, there appears to be a developing trend of record companies that are trying to get into the merchandising business, which will mean that these companies will want to have guaranteed access to recording artists and may choose to impose requirements that new artists who are entering into recording contracts also grant their merchandising rights to the record company as a condition of the record contract. There are, however, serious concerns that such activity on the part of record companies would constitute an illegal tie-in in violation of applicable antitrust laws. A detailed discussion of that issue is beyond the scope of this article. Suffice it to say that the artist should never give up merchandising rights other than to a real merchandising company unless it is unavoidable.

TOUR MERCHANDISING AGREEMENTS AND RETAIL MERCHANDISING AGREEMENTS

Merchandising agreements are basically divided between tour merchandising agreements and retail merchandising agreements. Tour merchandising agreements are strictly limited to the right to sell merchandise at the artist's concerts, except for sell-off rights after the term of the agreement has expired, as to which products may be sold through retail channels. Retail merchandising agreements encompass retail sales (i.e., sales made at a wholesale price for ultimate sale to the consumer in department stores, record shops, T-shirt shops and other retail outlets), mail order sales (direct to the consumer through advertisements in magazines, television and radio, or through "bounce-backs" placed in record albums), and licensing (which consists of the licensing by the merchandising company to third party licensees of rights to produce specific types of merchandise which the primary company does not customarily manufacture and sell through its own channels, e.g., calendars, tapestries, key chains, towels, lunch boxes, drinking glasses, etc.). Reprinted in this book is a copy of a form Tour Merchandising Agreement which is used by one of the major merchandising companies. We have not felt the necessity to reprint that company's standard retail merchandising agreement, since most of the clauses are duplicative and the royalty provisions are already contained in the sell-off provisions of the tour merchandising agreement.

KEY CONTRACT CLAUSES: TOUR MERCHANDISING DEAL

Term (Including Options, Matching Rights, Buy Out Rights, Etc.)

From the lawyer's perspective, the term of the merchandising agreement is the most critical element of the agreement. Often merchandising agreements are made in principle by managers on behalf of their artist. Managers, particularly managers of new artists, are often not aware of the intricacies of structuring the term, any options or matching rights and buy out rights and it is important to have a lawyer experienced with these types of agreements negotiate these points so that the artist retains as much freedom as possible to renegotiate their agreement when they achieve greater success or to change merchandising companies should that become necessary or desirable.

The term of nearly all tour merchandising agreements made today is the longer of some specified period of time or until recoupment of all advances paid to the artist. Most typically the fixed time component is one "album tour cycle" or some fixed period of time which approximates a typical album tour cycle, e.g., from the release of one album until the commencement of recording of the next album or the completion of all touring in connection with that album, but the essential concept is the same. The reason for using the album tour cycle concept as a measuring stick is each time an artist releases a new album in today's market, they need, almost without exception, to tour in support of that album in order to increase its sales. A specific line of merchandise is usually developed to be sold in conjunction with that particular tour, utilizing album cover artwork and graphics which specifically identify the particular tour. As the release of each album marks a new stage in the artist's development, it makes good business sense for the contract to be structured along the lines of album tour cycle so that at the designated milestones the parties can reevaluate their relationship, decide whether to pick up options or to buy out of one agreement and try to make an agreement with a competitor, and so on. It is very awkward to accomplish a changeover from one merchandising company to another merchandising company in the middle of a tour cycle, which is another reason for the term to be keyed to the beginning and ending of album tour cycles.

Merchandising business today is somewhat of an artist's market. The merchandising companies aggressively compete with each other to sign artists, the artists are able to negotiate the highest advances which the market is willing to bear, and the merchandising companies pay royalty rates which are relatively high and which leave them with a profit margin which is relatively low, compared to the rates of royalties payable to artists and the profit margins left to the record companies. The relationship between the merchandising company and the artist is similar to the relationship between a record company and an artist. Unless the artist dies, retires from touring, or, in the case of a group artist, breaks up, the merchandising company will eventually recoup its advance. However, the cost of money is also a very important consideration to the merchandising company, and the time within which it expects to recoup or be repaid its advance is always taken into consideration in determining the size of the advance and under what circumstances it may become repayable.

In recent years, many tour merchandising agreements were limited to the longer of a single album tour cycle or recoupment. Thus, if at the end of the album tour cycle, the artist was recouped, he was free to make a new deal upon the release of his next album with a competitor of the original merchandising company. Companies began to cut back on the free agent, "artist's market" mentality of these deal structures by insisting on "matching rights" to the artist's next album tour cycle. Such rights are also commonly referred to as "rights of last refusal" or sometimes also, although less accurately, as "rights of first refusal." Although these rights can be written in somewhat different ways, the fundamental principal is that the artist is not free to make a new deal with a different merchandising company unless he comes back to his current merchandising company and offers them the right to match whatever deal he was willing to accept from a third party. If the original merchandising company agrees to match that deal, the artist must re-sign with that original merchandising company.

This matching rights mechanism is, generally speaking, more favorable to the artist than a structure whereby the merchandising company has one or more options to acquire the rights for subsequent album tour cycles, since the rights to the particular tour cycle are negotiated at the time that the tour cycle is about to happen, which makes the artist in effect a free agent able to negotiate their fair market value, rather than allowing the merchandising company to acquire the rights pursuant to terms set at the time the original deal was made when, generally speaking, the artist would have had less bargaining power.

However, the trend in the merchandising industry toward consolidation of power into the hands of a couple or few very strong, highly competitive merchandising companies, the trend towards ownership by record companies, and the frustration and embarrassment of having an artist who has been supported by a merchandising company when he was starting out switch allegiances to that company's rival at the time the artist breaks into stardom, are all contributing toward a new trend for merchandising companies to demand longer terms on their contracts, with built in options. In short, it is my expectation that the term of a typical merchandising agreement will grow ever closer to the term of a typical recording contract.

Because merchandising contracts were structured so that they continue until recoupment of advances, the artist's attorney typically negotiates for buy out rights. This basically means that when a tour cycle comes to an end, if the artist's royalty account is unrecouped, the artist has the right to pay the unrecouped balance to the merchandising company and thereby terminate the contract. In some instances, the payment price may include interest on the unrecouped balance or may include a payment for unsold inventory. The reasons for this are that the merchandising company does not want to merely to be made "whole" i.e., so that it does not suffer a loss, but wants to wind up having made some positive return on its investment. Of course, profits can and are generally made by merchandising companies even when the artist has barely recouped and often times even when the artist has not recouped, but in relatively small deals, the merchandising company considers itself to have broken even, i.e., made a minimally satisfactory return on its investment, when it has recouped.

Buy out rights, if agreed to by the merchandising company, are generally made subject to the company's matching rights, so that the artist can buy out only if the merchandising company has declined to match a third party's offer. Generally the buy out payment is made by or through the merchandising company which has outbid the original merchandiser.

For the reasons discussed above, merchandising companies are often reluctant to grant buy out rights, particularly when the amount of the unrecouped balance is a substantial percentage of the advances made by them.

Territory

The territory covered by a typical tour merchandising agreement entered into in the United Sates can be for the United States only, for North America, or for the entire world. At this time all of the major merchandising companies have worldwide operations, so that it is not a significant concern as to whether the merchandising company will be able to perform adequately in foreign territories. The only major territory which is often useful to withhold from the merchandising agreement made in the United States is Japan, because Japanese promoters often insist on acquiring the merchandising rights themselves and are often prepared to pay a very significant advance for those rights. The reason for that is in recent years the per capita gross sales for a typical rock star touring in Japan are often well in excess of their per capita sales in the United States or elsewhere, due chiefly to the value of the yen.

However, if the artist is making an agreement with a company other than one of the major merchandising companies, for whatever reason, it is important to inquire as to how the merchandising rights will be administered in the foreign territories and to be sure that the royalties payable in respect of those foreign territories will be competitive rates computed at the source, i.e., on the basis of the gross sales price in the territory in which the sale is made, as distinguished from royalties based on the amount paid by the local merchandising company to the United States merchandising company with whom the artist entered into the contract.

Advances

In most merchandising deals the amount of the initial advance is the single most important element of the deal and the one which determines which merchandising company will acquire the rights.

In comparing offers from different companies, it is important to analyze the timing of when advances are payable, simply because deals are often structured such that a portion of the total advance, usually one-quarter to one-half, is payable upon signing of the contract, a similar portion upon commencement of a tour, and often the balance is payable only after the artist has played a certain number of shows or played before a certain number of attendees or when a certain level of gross sales has been achieved.

Wherever advances are deferred until the performance of a certain number of shows, the attainment of a certain number of attendees or the receipt of a certain amount of gross dollars, the use of the term advance is somewhat misleading. For example, if a $25,000 advance installment is payable when $100,000 in gross receipts have been generated, then, assuming the artist has a 30% royalty rate, it is somewhat misleading to call that $25,000 an advance, as the artist earns $30,000 in royalties in respect of that $100,000 in gross receipts. In almost all cases, even without a specific contractual requirement, the merchandising company will advance the artist royalties which have already been earned but which are technically not yet payable (due to customary allowances for time needed to process accounting statements). Therefore, the real issue is how far ahead is the merchandising company willing to put the artist or, stated another way, how far unrecouped is the merchandising company agreeing to put itself.

Is the biggest advance always the best? Generally it is, but since the issue of whether the artist is obligated to the merchandising company for the future often turns on the point of whether or not the artist's account is unrecouped, an argument can certainly be made that the artist should not accept an advance which he cannot reasonably expect to recoup by the end of the current tour cycle, if so doing will obligate him to the merchandising company for the next tour cycle without the ability to buy out of the contract.

Two other issues are indirectly raised by an advance which is too large to be recouped from the sales likely to be made during the current tour cycle. First, does the manager commission the entire advance if it is received during the current tour cycle but the manager is no longer the manager during the next tour cycle in which some portion of the advance is still being recouped? Second, what if one of the band members were to leave the group prior to the advance having been fully recouped? Is there an agreement, e.g., a partnership agreement, among the band members which provides that the leaving member must repay his share of the unearned advance remaining as of the time such individual becomes a leaving member?

Royalty Rates: Tour Merchandise

Generally this is the second most important deal point, although if the artist expects to recoup the advance and can afford to take a longer perspective, e.g., where there is little or no need for a quick influx of cash to mount a tour, this could be the most important point. Royalties on merchandise sold at the artist's concerts are paid on gross sales at the venue less, in most cases, only sales taxes and customs duties, if applicable. Royalties for new artists for sales at concerts in the United States, stated as a percentage of gross less taxes, are generally in the range of the high 20's to the low 30's. Royalties for superstars in the merchandising field can be significantly higher and often involve more sophisticated calculations. Assuming a T-shirt sells for $18 at the artist's concert, with a royalty of 30%, that yields a royalty of $5.40. By comparison, the same artist would probably have to sell five records at full price to earn the same in record royalties.

Royalty rates for sales outside the United States are generally slightly lower, due to the fact that sales volume is generally lower, and therefore the gross profit margins to the merchandising company are lower.

Royalties for sales of tour merchandise are generally the same for all items except for high-priced (generally over $30) items, such as designer sweatshirts and jackets, and tour programs. Due to the high start-up cost of producing a tour program, the major companies have begun to shift from paying a royalty in gross sales to paying a percentage of the company's net profits, generally 70% to 75%.

Royalty Rates: Retail Merchandise

Royalties from retail sales of merchandise, i.e. sales through T-shirt shops, record stores, department stores, etc. are generally stated as a percentage of wholesale, i.e. the price at which the merchandising company sells the shirts to its own customers, namely the retail stores or, in some cases, subdistributors who in turn sell to the retail stores. These royalty rates are much lower. For example, retail royalties on T-shirts run in the range from 10% of wholesale to 15% of wholesale in the United States. This is true even for superstar artists. Accordingly, the royalty which an artist makes from the sale of one T-shirt at a department store is only a small fraction of the royalty the artist would receive if that T-shirt had been sold at his concert. Most commonly, the royalty on a T-shirt selling for $18 in a department store would be approximately 45¢ to 60¢, as compared to the tour merchandising royalty of $5.40. The primary reason for this is the large markup taken by department stores and other retail outlets. However, this is not to say that a great deal of royalties cannot be earned from the retail merchandising market. Artists as diverse as Guns N' Roses and New Kids on the Block have reportedly earned millions of dollars from the sale of retail merchandise. While these artists are certainly the exception, they have had the effect of starting up interest in the retail sale of artist's merchandise and the penetration into the department store market which is likely to have a very significant trickle down effect to a wide range of other artists.

A much greater variety of merchandise is sold through retail channels than is sold on tour. Generally, tour merchandise is limited to a few categories of top selling items, namely T-shirts, sweatshirts (in season), tour programs (if the artist is a substantial headliner), posters and buttons. In the retail market, however, all kinds of different merchandise may be offered for sale. Many of these are sold only through sublicensees which specialize in those particular types of products. A major merchandising company may have a number of different sublicensees to whom it licenses the rights to the various types of products. Generally, the merchandising company will pay the artist a large percentage of the merchandising company's own receipts from the sublicensee. This essentially amounts to the merchandising company taking a licensing fee, generally 20% to 25% of the gross receipts, and remitting the balance to the artist.

Generally, royalties from retail merchandising sales are cross-collateralized with tour merchandising royalties. Although it is generally better for the artist if different types of sales are not cross-collateralized, it is often not critical in merchandising agreements, because the structure is such that the artist is generally tied to the merchandising company until all advances paid to the artist have been recouped, and therefore it is in the artist's interest to allow the merchandising company to recoup those advances from any royalties. However, there will be some instances where it will be beneficial for an artist not to have tour merchandising royalties cross-collateralized with retail merchandising royalties, and it will be up to the artist's lawyer to determine whether it is important under the particular circumstances to eliminate cross-collateralization, assuming the artist has the clout to get this point.

Performance Guarantee

In nearly all merchandising contracts, the artist must guarantee the merchandising company either that the artist will perform to a certain minimum number of people within a certain period of time after the execution of the contract or, alternatively, will perform at least a specified number of concerts in a specified territory or territories within a certain period of time. The merchandising company calculates the advance which it is willing to pay to the artist primarily on the basis of the tour itinerary which the artist provides to the merchandising company in the contract negotiations.

Generally, the merchandising company will take a very close look at the proposed tour, including the geographic locations, the venues to be played, the other acts on the bill, and the artist's past history of merchandise sales on its concert tours, if any, in order to determine how large of an advance to offer. The merchandising company then generally requires that the artist warrant that they will perform to at least the number of people indicated on the tour itinerary or perform at least the number of concerts indicated on the tour itinerary in venues of a certain minimum size. A deadline is usually specified in the contract for the performance by the artist of this minimum guarantee.

The consequences of the artist's failure to perform this minimum guarantee are that the merchandising company may elect to require a repayment to the merchandising company of either the entire unrecouped balance or, if the artist's attorney has successfully negotiated this point, the lesser of that number or a pro rata portion of the total advances, based upon the short fall in the number of attendees or the number of concerts played, as the case may be. Often interest is tacked on to the principal amount as of the deadline for meeting the performance guarantee. As a practical matter, however, in most cases, the major merchandising companies are willing to let the unrecouped balance ride even if the artist has not completely met the performance guarantee, and, generally speaking, the merchandising company will not demand repayment unless the company believes that the artist is not likely to recoup in the foreseeable future. However, the merchandising company often will insist on charging interest on the unrecouped balance, generally starting as of the missed deadline for the performance guarantee.

Creative Matters/Approvals

Generally speaking, artists are given strong rights of approval in connection with their merchandise. As a practical matter, and even as a contractual matter in those instances where the merchandising company has a pre-existing relationship with the artist or its representatives, the merchandising company will not sell any product unless the artist has specifically approved the product and its design. Most merchandising companies are also willing to allow the artist to submit designs and concepts rather than just pick from those which the merchandising company's own designers create. This allows the artist to have a great deal of control, fun and satisfaction in the creative process.

LEGAL ELEMENTS

Aside from contract law, the legal foundations upon which merchandising agreements rest are the trademark laws, laws with respect to right of publicity and, to a somewhat lesser extent, the copyright laws.

Artist's Name

The most important element requiring legal protection in order to exploit merchandising rights is the artist's name. In cases of solo artists using their own legal names, this generally does not present any problems, although if the artist's name happens to coincide with the name of a company which sells T-shirts, there could be a serious problem requiring the help of a lawyer. For all artists who use fictional names, however, it is quite important that they choose a name which is sufficiently distinctive so that they will avoid lawsuits and threatened lawsuits from companies or other artists with similar names. It is a good idea to conduct a trademark search, which costs a few hundred dollars, before selecting a fictitious name, and, once a suitable name is found and is begun to be used, to file for state and/or federal trademark registration. For a complete discussion of trademarks, see the chapter titled "Entertainment Group Names: Selection and Protection." If the artist believes that they will be successful, then it is worth the money to take the necessary steps to protect the artist's rights in the fictitious name.

Ownership of Artwork

Another important consideration is the ownership of the artwork which will be used on the merchandise. Generally, merchandising contracts require the artist to provide to the merchandising company a reasonable selection of photographs or other artwork from which the merchandising company can prepare the designs for the merchandise. Sometimes the artwork consists of the artist's album cover and related publicity shots owned by the record company. In that case, the artist must be sure that he may use those photographs or designs without the need for separate approval by the record company. Often the record company will agree to allow the artist to use this artwork, but only upon payment to the record company of all or a portion of its costs of producing the applicable artwork. If the artwork comes from some other source, for example, a photographer or a graphic designer hired by the artist, a friend of the band or any other source, the artist must be sure to have a written agreement with the creator of the artwork which specifically allows the artist to reproduce that artwork on merchandise. In such event, the creator of the artwork may negotiate for a royalty or a flat fee payment. Generally speaking, the artist will have to pay any such fees or royalties, although in some instances the merchandising company may, if requested, agree to pay all or a portion of the costs of acquiring the rights to use a certain piece of artwork. The most important thing is to be sure that there is an agreement in writing for each piece of artwork used. Otherwise the artist may end up on the wrong end of a very expensive lawsuit.

Rights And Obligations Of Individual Group Members

An important legal issue is how, if at all, the contract deals with the rights and obligations of the various group members in the case of a group artist. In nearly all agreements, all members of the group must agree to be jointly and severally liable for any sums which the artist may be obligated to pay back to the merchandising company. This creates a possible problem should the group disband with an unrecouped balance or should a member leave and be replaced by a new member at a time when there is an unrecouped balance. This is an issue for the artist's lawyer to handle.

Rights of Solo Artists

Another issue is whether the merchandising company has any rights with respect to the individual members apart from the group. In most instances, the merchandising company will not have and should not have these rights, but in some cases the merchandising company may feel that in order to protect their investment in the group, they must have rights to sell merchandise pertaining to an individual or individuals as solo artists, but generally this should be limited to cases where the group breaks up at a time when it has an unrecouped balance.

If the artist and the merchandising company intend for the merchandising company to sell certain items which feature the individual group members apart from the group, some provision will have to be made among the group members as to how to take that into account in computing the group members' individual shares of the total merchandising royalties, particularly if advances have already been paid in equal shares, but have not yet been totally recouped. This would normally require an internal accounting among the group members which might result in one or more of the group members paying royalties over to one or more of the other group members in order that the royalties be shared in proportion to the actual earnings. These kinds of problems are addressed not in the merchandising agreement itself, but in a partnership or similar agreement among the band members.

Commercial Tie-ins

Another area which must be carefully scrutinized is the possible conflict between merchandising agreements and commercial tie-ins or endorsements. As artists become stars, they are often presented with numerous opportunities for commercial tie-ins and endorsements, all or some of which will involve the sale or promotional distribution of merchandise with the artist's name and/or likeness on it. Although merchandising contracts generally contain broad language which addresses this issue, for the most part they do not adequately cover the variety of situations which can occur. Accordingly, the artist's lawyer should carefully try to negotiate these provisions up front to be sure that they will give the artist maximum flexibility in making commercial tie-ins and endorsements. However, whenever an artist has a merchandising agreement and is subsequently approached to do some kind of a commercial tie-in or endorsement, the artist's attorney must be certain to review the merchandising agreement to be sure that the activities proposed do not conflict with the rights of the merchandising company. If they do, it is best to advise the merchandising company at the deal making stage in order that any misunderstandings and potential breaches of contract can be avoided and the relationship between the artist and the merchandising company can be maintained as a mutually beneficial and amicable one.

EXHIBIT 1
SAMPLE TOUR MERCHANDISING AGREEMENT

Gentlepersons:
The following will confirm the understanding between you (hereinafter "Licensor"), and ___________ (hereinafter "Licensee"):

1.(a) Licensor hereby grants Licensee the exclusive right to utilize the name, symbols, emblems, designs, likenesses, visual representations, service marks, copyrights in graphic designs, and/or trademarks of the musical group and all of the individual members thereof, both as members of and, subject to the provisions of subparagraph 1(c) below, as individual artists and its individual members hereinafter referred to as "Artist" (such name, symbols, etc. hereinafter referred to as the "Licensed Property") in connection with the manufacture, advertisement, distribution, and sale by Licensee of any products utilizing the Licensed Property (hereinafter "Licensed Products"), including but not limited to the pre-approved merchandise listed as Exhibit "A" attached hereto, in and about the premises and environs of and at any and all live concerts given by Artist throughout the world (such premises and environs hereinafter referred to as the "Licensed Area"). Notwithstanding anything to the contrary, the grant hereunder shall include the exclusive right to sell all nonfood and nonbeverage items at Artist's concerts in the Licensed Area for a period beginning with the congregation of the audience outside Artist's concert sites and ending with the dispersement of the audience after Artist's concerts. No other licenses exist which would permit the distribution and/or sale of Licensed Products during the Licensed Term in the Licensed Area, and Licensor warrants that it has not entered into and will not enter into any other license agreements which would permit the sale of products bearing the Licensed Property during the Licensed Term in the Licensed Area without Licensee's written consent. All rights and interests with respect to the Licensed Property not specifically granted to Licensee herein shall be and are specifically reserved to Licensor and/or its licensees without limitation during the term hereof.

(b) Notwithstanding anything to the contrary contained herein, Licensee shall be entitled during the Licensed Term to sell the following merchandise through Licensee's retail distribution network at the royalty rates set out in paragraph 6(a) of the merchandising agreement of even date herewith (hereinafter "Merchandising Agreement"):

(i) Licensed Products no longer offered for sale at Artist's concerts; and

(ii) all Licensed Products (if Artist does not perform at a live concert in the Licensed Area for a period of thirty (30) consecutive days at any time during the Licensed Term).

(c) Notwithstanding anything to the contrary contained in this agreement, in addition to having the exclusive right to utilize the Licensed Property with respect to the members of Artist as members of ________________, Licensee shall have the exclusive right to utilize the names, symbols, emblems, designs, likenesses, visual representations, service marks, and/or trademarks of each of the individual members of Artist other than as members of _________ (e.g., as solo artists, members of other musical groups, etc.) until recoupment of all advances payable hereunder.

2. (a) For the license granted herein, Licensee will pay Licensor the advances, deposits, and royalties set out in Exhibit "B" attached hereto.

(b) Licensor's representative shall have the right to be present at all load-ins and load-outs of Licensed Products at Artist's concert sites and during all settlements with halls. The night after each concert, Licensee shall furnish licensor with complete and accurate statements showing the following with respect to Licensed Products sold by Licensee during the previous concert: quantity and gross selling price of each of the Licensed Products, as well as the hall fees, vendor fees, and sales taxes paid by Licensee with respect to its sale of the Licensed Products in connection with such concert.

(c) The night after each concert, Licensor shall furnish Licensee with complete and accurate attendance counts for the previous concert, specifying both the number of paying and nonpaying attendees for such concert.

(d) Every two (2) weeks, Licensee shall furnish Licensor with summary statements for such two-week period based upon the information provided in the nightly statements furnished pursuant to subparagraph 2(c) above.

(e) Within thirty (30) days after the later of:

(i) the last date of the Licensed Term; or

(ii) Licensee's receipt of a statement of bona fide, paid attendees (as defined in Exhibit "B" and in accordance therewith) or other attendance which may affect bona fide, paid attendees for all live concerts given by Artist for which a statement is due;

Licensee shall furnish Licensor with a royalty statement setting forth in reasonable detail the following with respect to Licensed Products sold on the tour for which royalties are paid as a percentage of gross sales: quantity and gross selling price of all such Licensed Products; hall fees, vendor fees, and sales taxes paid by Licensee with respect to its sale of the Licensed Products in connection with such tour. Such statement shall be accompanied by payment of royalties earned hereunder and due Licensor, less any advances paid hereunder.

(f) Within sixty (60) days after the later of:

(i) the last date of each leg of a Tour; or

(ii) Licensee's receipt of a statement of bona fide, paid attendees or other attendance which may affect bona fide, paid attendees for all live concerts given by Artist for which a statement is due; and again within sixty (60) days after the later of:

aa. the last date of the Licensed Term; or

bb. Licensee's receipt of a statement of bona fide, paid attendees or other attendance which may affect bona fide, paid attendees for all live concerts given by Artist for which a statement is due;

Licensee shall furnish Licensor with a royalty statement setting forth in reasonable detail the following with respect to Licensed Products sold during the Licensed Term for which royalties are paid as a percentage of net profits: quantity and royalties are paid as a percentage of net profits: quantity and gross selling price of all Licensed Products, hall and vendor fees, freight and trucking expenses (equipment and personnel), insurance on goods shipped outside the United States, customs duties, mutually approved costs of production, mutually approved bootleg security and direct legal costs incurred with respect to same, road staff expenses (including without limitation salaries, per diems, and travel directly related to services hereunder), a mutually agreeable royalty payable with respect to designer garments (i.e., garments which sell for more than $35), and other mutually approved expenses. Such statement shall be accompanied by royalties earned hereunder and due Licensor, less any unrecouped advances paid hereunder. Within forty-five (45) days after the last date of the Licensed Term, Licensee shall furnish Licensor with payment representing a good faith estimate of such royalties due, with reasonable reserves withheld for charges incurred but not yet paid.

(g) Licensee will compute any royalties due Licensor relative to sales hereunder in the currency of the country earned, and:

(i) with respect to earnings in Europe, same shall be converted to pounds sterling when the monies are transferred to the United Kingdom. Such transfer shall be effected as quickly as practicably possible, but in any event, within fourteen (14) days of Licensee's receipt thereof unless governmental instrumentalities prevent such transfer, in which case, said monies shall be converted at the rate in effect at the actual time of transfer;

(ii) any earnings in Europe so converted to pounds sterling, as well as earnings in the United Kingdom, shall be converted to United States dollars as of the day such earnings are received or deemed received in the United Kingdom;

(iii) with respect to earnings in the remainder of the Licensed Area, monies shall be converted to United States dollars at the exchange rate received by Licensee when such funds are transferred from the country in which earned to the United States. Licensee shall use its reasonable efforts to have such monies remitted to the United States as soon as practicably possible, it being understood that Licensee shall not be held responsible for delays in such remittance due to reasons beyond Licensee's control.

If Licensee is required by a foreign governmental instrumentality, to deduct taxes based on Licensee's receipts from merchandise sales hereunder, Licensee may deduct a proportionate amount of such taxes (based on Licensor's royalty rates hereunder) from Licensor's accrued earnings with respect to such sales only; if such governmental instrumentality requires deduction of any other taxes on Artist or Licensor's behalf due to Artist or Licensor's liability in such territory, payment to such instrumentality shall be from Licensor's accrued earnings. Licensee shall provide tax certificates in Artist or Licensor's name with respect to such deductions. If any law or governmental ruling of any country places a maximum limit on the amount Licensee may pay Licensor, Licensee shall pay Licensor the lesser of (aa) such maximum; or (bb) the amount earned hereunder. If the amount earned hereunder is greater than such maximum, Licensee shall, if permissible, deposit the difference between such amounts in an account in Licensor's name in the country of such law or ruling. For accounting purposes, such deposit shall constitute royalty payment hereunder. Licensee shall notify Licensor immediately of any such governmental intervention relative to payment of monies to Licensor. If Licensee is unable to remove Licensor's royalties earned hereunder from the country in which earned and Licensor's account is in a fully recouped position, Licensee shall notify Licensor of such inability, then at Licensor's request and expense and if Licensee is able to do so, Licensee shall deposit such earnings in Licensor's name in a foreign depository selected by Licensor in the country in which such royalties were earned and in the currency thereof. For accounting purposes, such deposit shall constitute royalty payments to Licensor.

3. During the Licensed Term, Licensor shall supply Licensee with a list of Artist's proposed live concerts setting out the date, city, venue, and hall capacity (as scaled for each such live concert) of any and all such concerts by facsimile (FAX) to FAX number ______________ (or such other FAX number as Licensee may direct), attention: tour department, by the earliest of the following:

(a) the date any such live concerts have been booked and confirmed through a booking agent and concert promoter; or

(b) the date tickets for such live concerts have been placed on sale; or

(c) the date fourteen (14) days prior to such live concerts.

Licensor shall notify Licensee within twenty-four (24) hours of the cancellation or postponement of any live concerts of which Licensee has previously been notified.

4. The term of this agreement (hereinafter "Licensed Term") shall consist of an Initial Term, as set out in subparagraph 4(a) below, and an Option Term (if exercised by Licensee), as set out in subparagraph 4(b) below.

(a) The Initial Term shall commence upon execution and continue until the later of:

(i) one (1) year after Artist's first Performance (as defined in Exhibit "B" attached hereto) in the Licensed Area; or

(ii) recoupment of all advances payable hereunder.

(b) Licensee shall have the option to extend the Licensed Term (hereinafter "Option"), exercisable only by notice in writing given to Licensor by the earlier of:

(i) fourteen (14) days after Licensor's notice of the United States commercial release of Artist's second as-yet unrecorded, unreleased studio album following the date hereof (hereinafter "Option Term Album"); or

(ii) thirty (30) days after the end of the Initial Term; or for an additional period (hereinafter "Option Term") commencing on Licensee's exercise of the Option and terminating the latest of:

aa. one (1) year after Artist's first Performance in the Licensed Area in support of the Option Term Album; or

bb. completion of all touring by Artist in support of the Option Term Album; or

cc. recoupment of the Option Term Advances (including the unrecouped balance of advances previously paid).

As used herein, "album" shall specifically exclude record albums consisting of re-released or "live" material. If, for any reason, Licensor fails to provide Licensee with such notice, Licensee may exercise the Option at any time.

c. Notwithstanding the foregoing, if:

(i) recoupment of all advances payable hereunder occurs while a tour by Artist is in progress in the Licensed Area; and

(ii) the Licensed Term would otherwise expire on such recoupment; the Licensed Term shall automatically be extended upon such recoupment until completion of such tour.

(d) In the event that Licensee elects not to exercise the Option, Licensor shall have the option to terminate the Licensed Term by repaying to Licensee the full amount of all unrecouped advances theretofore paid and purchasing Licensee's inventory of Licensed Products remaining and on hand, calculated at Licensee's cost (up to a cost of ________). Such option to terminate the Licensed Term must be exercised in writing by Licensor no later than the earlier of:

(i) the date seventy-four (74) days after the United States commercial release of the Option Term Album; or

(ii) the date of execution of a tour merchandising agreement with respect to Artist's tour in support of the Option Term Album between Licensor and a third party.

Upon such payment and purchase by Licensor, this agreement shall terminate.

(e) Notwithstanding the foregoing, if the advances paid hereunder are unrecouped by the later of the dates set out in subparagraph 2(f)aa or 2(f)bb above, Licensor shall have the option to terminate the Licensed Term by repaying to Licensee the full amount of all unrecouped advances theretofore paid and purchasing Licensee's inventory of Licensed Products remaining and on hand, calculated at Licensee's cost (up to a cost of ____________). Such option to terminate the Licensed Term must be exercised in writing by Licensor no later than ninety (90) days after the date set out in subparagraph 2(f)aa or 2(f)bb above, as the case may be. Upon such repayment and purchase by Licensor, this agreement shall terminate.

5. During the Licensed Term and for a period of two (2) years thereafter, Licensee will keep and maintain at its principal place of business true and accurate records of all transactions which relate to or affect this agreement or any provision thereof, which books and records, together with supporting vouchers, shall be open for inspection by Licensor or its representative during regular business hours upon seventy-two (72) hours' written notice, but no more than once with respect to any period to be examined. At such time, copying of books and records relating directly to monies due Licensor hereunder will be allowed.

6. (a) At its sole cost and expense, Licensor shall supply Licensee with artwork embodying the Licensed Property as reasonably requested by Licensee, including but not limited to a sufficient number of suitable photographs for a complete tour program and for other reasonable artwork needs. Licensor shall use its best efforts to grant Licensee the rights to artwork from Artist's most recent EP, and if Licensor is so able, it shall provide same to Licensee at Licensor's sole cost and expense no later than thirty (30) days after execution hereof. Licensor shall use its best efforts to grant Licensee the rights to artwork from any of Artist's albums subsequently released during the Licensed Term, and if Licensor is so able, it shall provide same to Licensee at Licensor's sole cost and expense no later than thirty (30) days after such release.

(b) All artwork and products shall be mutually agreed upon prior to the manufacture, and Licensee shall furnish samples of each of the Licensed Products, as well as the packaging therefor, to Licensor for its approval as to quality, style, and cost (which approval shall not be unreasonably withheld). Licensor shall use its best efforts to provide such approval or disapproval within seven (7) days of receipt of such samples. In the event that Licensor does not provide written approval of any of same in whole or in part within seven (7) days after receipt thereof, such failure shall automatically constitute disapproval by Licensor.

(c) Notwithstanding the above, Licensee shall be obligated only to use its best efforts to obtain mutually agreed upon unprinted T-shirts, and in the event it is unable to secure adequate quantities of same as a result of limited supply and the special nature of the shirts, Licensor and Licensee shall mutually agree on alternate unprinted T-shirts.

(d) Promptly after initial shipment of the Licensed Products, Licensee will so notify Licensor and supply Licensor with twenty (20) samples of each such Licensed Product, at no cost to Licensor. Licensor may purchase reasonable additional quantities of Licensed Products at the prices set out on Exhibit "D" attached hereto, but such merchandise shall not be offered for resale.

7. During the Licensed Term, Licensor shall not, by itself or through third parties, engage in any premiums, giveaways, or promotional tie-ins of merchandise utilizing the Licensed Property, including but not limited to souvenirs, booklets, T-shirts, wearing apparel, posters, stickers, programs, visors, and shorts, which are specifically related to Artist's concert appearances (e.g. radio station and tour-sponsor promotions) and which would result in the advertisement or distribution of the above described merchandise at any concert site or other location within twenty (20) miles of such concert and less than forty-eight (48) hours prior thereto, nor shall Licensor, by itself or through third parties, engage in any other distribution or sale of such merchandise within two (2) miles of such concert and less than forty-eight (48) hours prior thereto. Notwithstanding the foregoing, nothing herein shall preclude standard, record industry promotion by __________(name of record company) or its distributors in support of album releases by Artist.

8.(a) Licensee represents and warrants that the Licensed Products will be of high standard in style, appearance, and quality, and that no liability will attach to Licensor for merchandise manufactured or sold by Licensee.

(b) Licensee recognizes the value of the publicity and goodwill associated with the Licensed Property, and with respect thereto, acknowledges that, as between Licensor and Licensee, such goodwill belongs exclusively to Licensor. In addition, Licensee acknowledges that the Licensed Property has a secondary meaning in the mind of the purchasing public.

9. (a) Licensee shall print, stamp, or mold the copyright and/or trademark notice designated by Licensor as Exhibit "C" attached hereto on all Licensed Products and on each package or container used in connection therewith, and shall print such notice on each label, advertisement, and promotional release concerning the Licensed Products, all in accordance with instructions from Licensor, including but not limited to instructions with respect to position and letter size.

(b) (i) If Licensee fails to affix proper copyright and/or trademark notice on all Licensed Products and such failure does not result from:

aa. Licensor's failure to provide proper copyright and/or trademark notice; or

bb. Licensor changing the copyright and/or trademark notice during the Licensed Term or Sell-Off Period (as defined in paragraph 15 below); and

(ii) If such failure results in any Licensed Product being adjudicated as having fallen into the public domain; Licensor shall have the right to terminate this agreement within fifteen (15) days of such adjudication upon thirty (30) days' written notice to Licensee.

10. Licensor agrees to assist Licensee to the extent necessary in the procurement of any protection or to protect any of Licensee's rights to the Licensed Property, and if it so desires, Licensee may, at its own expense and with Licensor's prior approval, commence or prosecute any claims or suits in its own name or in the name of Licensor, or it may join Licensor as a party thereto (but all such actions undertaken by Licensee shall be at Licensee's sole expense). Each party shall provide the other with written notice of any infringements or limitations by others of the Licensed Property on articles similar to those covered by this agreement which may come to its attention. In the event any sums are recovered as a result of any judgment or settlement from prosecution of any claim or suit, Licensor shall receive ______ percent (___%) of the net amount recovered, after deduction from gross amounts recovered of all related legal fees (from litigation only) incurred by Licensee, subject to other arrangements on a suit-by-suit basis. With Licensor's approval and after submission of a budget therefor, Licensee shall obtain seizure orders at various concert sites during a tour to combat bootleggers during such tour. Licensee may treat as a recoupable advance _______ percent (___%) of the cost of each such seizure order, including legal fees and court costs (which costs shall be allocated on a reasonable basis among Licensor and all other artists who are the subject of such seizure order), and ____ percent (___%) of the cost of security actually paid by Licensee and may recoup same from Licensor's accrued royalties. The preceding sentence applies only if Licensor's royalties are calculated on the basis of gross sales. Licensee shall allocate legal costs between programs (if applicable) and all other Licensed Products, and shall not take double deductions for such costs.

11. Licensor warrants and represents that it is free to enter into and fully perform this agreement, and that use of the Licensed Property hereunder will not infringe upon or violate any third party's rights of any nature whatsoever. Licensor will at all times indemnify and hold Licensee and those with whom Licensee has contractual arrangements with respect to the Licensed Property harmless from and against any and all claims, damages, loss of profits, liabilities, costs, and expenses, including reasonable attorneys' fees, arising out of any breach by Licensor herein. The above indemnification shall apply only to final judgments entered by a court of competent jurisdiction thereof or settlements entered into with Licensor's written consent, which shall not be unreasonably withheld.

12. (a) Licensor represents and warrants that it is the sole owner of the professional name "________________" (hereinafter "Name") and that to the best of Licensor's knowledge, no other musical artist or entertainer has or will have the right to use the Name or permit the Name to be used in connection with phonograph records, entertainment services, or clothing. Licensor has the authority to grant Licensee the right to use the Name as provided herein and warrants that Licensee's use of the Name will not infringe upon the rights of any third parties.

(b) Licensor agrees that Licensee may cause a search to be instituted at Licensee's expense to determine whether there have been any third party uses of the Name in connection with phonograph records and/or entertainment and/or clothing and other merchandise.

(c) Licensor warrants and represents that it has made an application for United States registration of the Name in Licensor's name for phonograph records, entertainment services, and clothing, or that it shall file such an application within thirty (30) days of execution of this agreement and promptly provide Licensee with a copy of such application. Licensor further agrees that if Licensee has not received a copy of such application within sixty (60) days of execution of this agreement, Licensee may cause such application to be made in Licensor's name for phonograph record purposes, entertainment services, and clothing. Licensor agrees that any amounts expended by Licensee pursuant to this paragraph shall be deemed to be advances against and recoupable by Licensee from royalties otherwise payable to Licensor hereunder. Nothing contained in this paragraph shall release Licensor and/or Artist from their indemnification of Licensee with respect to Licensee's use of Artist's name as specified herein.

13. (a) Licensor hereby acknowledges and agrees that it and each member of Artist have fully complied with all necessary laws, statutes, or regulations and have taken any action required to exempt Licensee from reporting, withholding, or paying so-called "withholding" taxes, which include the following without limitation: federal and state income taxes, federal social security tax, and California unemployment insurance tax (hereinafter "Withholding Taxes").

(b) Licensor warrants that all members of Artist are United States citizens. If, at any time during the Licensed Term, a non-United States citizen is a member of Artist, Licensor shall promptly notify Licensee thereof, and Licensor acknowledges and agrees that in any such case, it shall fully comply with all necessary laws, statutes, or regulations, and shall take any action required to exempt Licensee from reporting, withholding, or paying Withholding Taxes and any federal withholding taxes on nonresident aliens. Notwithstanding the foregoing, in such case, Licensee shall withhold the appropriate amount from payments to nonresident aliens (whether individuals or corporations) as required by Sections 1441 and 1442 of the Internal Revenue Code unless Licensor provides Licensee with appropriate documentation relieving Licensee of such responsibility.

14. Subject to paragraph 11 above, Licensee will at all times indemnify and hold Licensor harmless from and against any and all claims arising out of the use or possession of any Licensed Products manufactured, advertised, distributed, or sold. At its own expense, Licensee will maintain throughout the Licensed Term an insurance policy for products liability in a form acceptable to Licensor, naming Licensor and Artist (as well as their employees, agents, and representatives, if the insurance company so permits) as additional insureds. Such policy shall have the following minimum limits:

(a) basic coverage in the amount of $______ per occurrence; and

(b) umbrella coverage in the amount of $________.

15. Upon expiration of this agreement, all rights granted to Licensee herein shall forthwith revert to Licensor, with the following consequences:

(a) Licensor shall thereafter by free to use and license others to use the Licensed Property in connection with the manufacture, advertisement, distribution, and sale of items identical or similar to the Licensed Products.

(b) Licensee shall not thereafter manufacture, advertise, distribute, or sell Licensed Products in any place whatsoever. However:

(i) for a period of one hundred twenty (120) days (hereinafter "Sell-Off Period") and in accordance with all the terms and conditions contained in this agreement, Licensee may continue to sell any Licensed Products previously manufactured and on hand on a nonexclusive basis; and

(ii) in connection with the Sell-Off Period, Licensee may manufacture during the Sell-Off Period sufficient quantities of Licensed Products which come in different sizes to restore the ratio of Licensee's inventory to the following ratio per dozen: 1 small, 3 medium, 5 large, 3 extra-large. The quantities of Licensed Products so manufactured during the Sell-Off Period shall not exceed ____ percent (___%) of quantities previously manufactured pursuant to this agreement.

(c) The royalties payable with respect to Licensed Products sold through wholesale distribution during the Sell-Off Period shall be at the rates set out in paragraph 6(a) of the Merchandising Agreement. Notwithstanding the foregoing, no royalties shall be payable to

Licensor for Licensed Products sold during the Sell-Off Period at a price less than ____ percent (___%) of Licensee's listed wholesale price for quantities of eighteen (18) dozen or less of such items (fifteen [15] dozen for sales of jerseys only).

(d) Licensee shall notify Licensor of the quantity of unsold Licensed Products remaining at expiration of the Licensed Term, and Licensor shall have the right to purchase all such unsold merchandise from Licensee at its cost in lieu of permitting Licensee to exercise its "sell-off" or manufacturing rights granted under this paragraph.

(e) If:

(i) for any reason, fifteen (15) or more concerts about which Licensee has been notified are cancelled and not made up during the Licensed Term; and

(ii) Licensee has manufactured Licensed Products in anticipation of the occurrence of such concerts; and

(iii) Licensee has not, subsequent to notification of such cancellation, manufactured any Licensed Products which are overstocked because of such cancellation; the Sell-Off Period shall be one hundred eighty (180) days instead of one hundred twenty (120) days.

16. In the last one hundred twenty (120) days of the Licensed Term, Licensee shall not manufacture, in anticipation of the Sell-Off Period, quantities of Licensed Products greater than those necessary to meet reasonably anticipated demand therefor during the remainder of the Licensed Term.

17. Nothing contained herein shall be construed to constitute a partnership or joint venture between the parties hereto, and neither Licensee nor Licensor shall become bound by any representation, act, or omission of the other.

18. (a) This agreement and all matters or issues collateral thereto shall be governed by the laws of the State of California applicable to contracts performed entirely therein.

(b) Any controversy or claim arising out of or relating to this agreement or the making, performance, or interpretation hereof shall be settled in accordance with the rules of the American Arbitration Association in Los Angeles, California, but the choice of an arbitrator shall be subject to agreement of the parties hereto, not the rules of said Association, and judgment upon the arbitration award may be entered in any court having jurisdiction over the subject matter of the controversy. The prevailing party in any such arbitration or litigation related to such controversy or claim shall be entitled to its reasonable attorneys' fees and court costs in addition to any award received.

19. (a) The entire understanding between the parties hereto relating to the subject matter hereof is contained herein, and no warranties, representations, or undertakings are made by the parties hereto except as are expressly provided herein.

(b) This agreement cannot be modified or amended except by a written instrument executed by the parties hereto, and any prior or contemporaneous agreement of the parties hereto, whether oral or in writing, pertaining to the subject matter hereof, shall be deemed merged herewith.

(c) Neither party shall be deemed to have waived any of its rights hereunder except by a written instrument executed by such waiving party.

20. Licensor agrees to the terms of, and shall propose in all its contracts with promoters for concerts at which Artist is the major headliner, a provision in substantially the following form, and Licensor shall use its best efforts to insure inclusion of such provision in the final version of all such contracts:

Promoter agrees that artist's designee __________(name of merchandiser) shall have the sole and exclusive right to sell all nonfood and nonbeverage items, including but not limited to souvenir books, phonograph recordings, wearing apparel, posters, stickers, programs, and other items of merchandise, at or about the venue on the day of artist's concert and prior to, during and after each concert, whether or not such items bear artist's name and/or likeness.

Promoter shall provide adequate space for artist's designee to vend such material, and promoter agrees that artist's designee shall, as it may require, have access to any hall facilities and any and all areas adjacent to the venue.

Promoter further agrees to use its best efforts to prevent and stop the sale or distribution of any merchandise sold by any person other than artist's designee at artist's concerts, whether inside or outside the venue. It is understood that no person or entity other than artist's designee shall have the right to sell or distribute any nonfood and nonbeverage items at the engagement without the express written consent of ___________(name of merchandiser).

Promoter further agrees to use its best efforts to obtain the lowest possible hall and vendor fees payable to the venue for the sale of artist's merchandise hereunder, and promoter represents and warrants that it will receive no interest or fee, either directly or indirectly, from the proceeds of sales of artist's merchandise.

21. Licensee may assign or sublicense this agreement or any portion hereof to a subsidiary or affiliated company or to any person, firm, company, or entity owning or acquiring a substantial potion of Licensee's stock or assets, provided that Licensee remains primarily responsible for its obligations hereunder. Notwithstanding the foregoing, Licensee may assign or sublicense this agreement, any part hereof, or any rights hereunder, other than those relating to the United States, to any person or entity who is or may be a parent, subsidiary, or affiliate. "Affiliate" shall mean any person or entity with whom Licensee enters into an agreement with respect to rights hereunder or with respect to any other merchandising agreement outside the United States. Licensor may assign this agreement to any party, provided that Licensor remains primarily liable for its obligations hereunder. Any other attempted or purported assignment or other transfer, sublicense, mortgage, or other encumbrance of this agreement by either party without prior approval of the other shall be void and have no effect.

22. All notices required to be given hereunder shall be in writing and shall be delivered personally, by facsimile (FAX), or by certified or registered mail, return receipt requested, postage prepaid, as follows:

(a) if to Licensor, at the address set out above, with a courtesy copy to

____

(b) if to Licensee, at the address set out above, with a courtesy copy to

____

Any notice so given shall be deemed effective upon receipt by any party to whom it is addressed. Either party may change the address to which notice is to be sent by giving written notice of such change of address to the other party as provided herein. Notwithstanding the foregoing, either party's failure to send a courtesy copy of notices pursuant to subparagraph 22(a) or 22(b) above, as the case may be, shall not be deemed a material breach of this agreement.

23. If Licensor believes Licensee to be in default, Licensor shall provide Licensee with written notice thereof as provided in paragraph 22 above and Licensee shall have fifteen (15) days within which to cure said default before Licensor may pursue other remedies.

24. Concurrently with execution hereof, Licensor shall attach a schedule hereto as Exhibit "E" with respect to any other licenses for the Licensed Products and/or heat transfers and/or any other retail merchandising or mail order licenses, which schedule shall include the following with respect to each license: licensor; licensee; duration of licensed term; licensed products; and licensed area. In addition, Licensor shall submit a sample of any item licensed pursuant to any license set out above concurrently with attachment of Exhibit "E".

25. This agreement has been the result of negotiations between the parties. Each party and its counsel have reviewed this agreement. Accordingly, the rule of construction embodied in California Civil Code §1654 (or in the laws of any other jurisdiction), to the effect that uncertainty in a contract is to be resolved against the drafting party, shall not be employed in the interpretation of this agreement.

26. This agreement may be executed in any number of counterparts, each of which shall be deemed to be an original and all of which together shall be deemed to be one and the same agreement.

ADDENDUM TO MERCHANDISING CONTRACT ROYALTIES (EXHIBIT "B")*

For the license granted herein, Licensee shall pay Licensor the following and Licensor shall make the warranties set out herein to secure such payment:

1. ADVANCES/DEPOSITS

(a) Initial Term: Licensee shall pay Licensor the following Initial Term Advances and Initial Term Deposits:

(i) an Initial Term Advance of _____ plus an additional sum of _____ to buy out Licensor's outstanding merchandising deal, within five (5) business days after execution of this agreement;

*NOTE: EXHIBITS "A", "C" ,"D" AND "E" REFERRED TO IN THE MERCHANDISING AGREEMENT ARE LISTS OF PRODUCTS, COPYRIGHT NOTICES AND VARIOUS PRICES OF MERCHANDISED PRODUCTS AND ARE NOT INCLUDED HERE.

(ii) an Initial Term Advance of _____ within five (5) business days after gross sales hereunder exceed _____.

(iii) after recoupment of the prior advances, Licensee shall pay Licensor an Initial Term Deposit equal to ___ of Licensor's projected earnings for the remainder of the Initial Term (but in no event more than _____) if, in Licensee's good faith business judgment, it is anticipated said sum will be earned hereunder, which earnings shall be calculated by Licensee on the basis of merchandise sales up to the date of such recoupment, anticipated attendance for the remainder of the Initial Term, the venues to be played and venue location, and geographic sales patterns, and Licensee shall pay Licensor a deposit equal to ___ of Licensor's projected earnings each time the prior deposit is recouped if calculations of projected earnings as set out above so warrant in Licensee's good faith business judgment. The initial deposit hereunder shall be paid within five (5) days after recoupment of the prior deposit. If, by expiration of the Initial Term, any portion of said deposits has not been recouped by Licensee from Licensor's accrued royalties, Licensor shall repay Licensee the full unrecouped amount thereof within five (5) business days of said expiration or when otherwise subject to repayment under this Exhibit "B";

(iv) notwithstanding anything to the contrary contained herein, if Artist fails by August 1, 19__ (hereinafter "Initial Term Scheduled Commencement Date"), to commence a tour of the United States and Canada consisting of at least thirty (30) Performances scheduled during the Initial Term within a period of approximately eight (8) weeks (such tour hereinafter referred to as an "Initial Term US Tour"), Licensor shall be charged an amount equal to ____ per annum on the unrecouped balance of advances theretofore paid (such charge of ___ per annum hereinafter referred to as a "Delayed Performance Fee"), which shall be charged between the Initial Term Scheduled Commencement Date and the actual commencement of an Initial Term US Tour and shall be treated as an additional Initial Term Advance paid hereunder. It is acknowledged that Artist commenced an Initial Term US Tour.

(b) Option Term: Licensee shall pay Licensor the following Option Term Advances and Option Term Deposits:

(i) an Option Term Advance equal to the greater of:

aa.____________; or

bb. an amount equal to ___ of Licensor's earnings during the Initial Term, less the unrecouped balance of advances and deposits theretofore paid (but in no event more than _______), payable as follows:

I. ________ (___) on Licensee's exercise of the Option;

II. _______ (___) on the first Performance of a tour by Artist of the United States and Canada consisting of a series of at least thirty (30) Performances scheduled within a period of approximately eight (8) weeks (such tour herein after referred to as an "Option Term US Tour");

III. __________ (__) when gross sales during the Option Term exceed ________;

(ii) after recoupment of the prior advances and deposits, Licensee shall pay Licensor an Option Term Deposit equal to ___ of Licensor's projected earnings for the remainder of the Option Term (but in no event more than ________) if, in Licensee's good faith business judgment, it is anticipated said sum will be earned hereunder, which earnings shall be calculated by Licensee on the basis of merchandise sales up to the date of such recoupment, anticipated attendance for the remainder of the Option Term, the venues to be played and venue location, and geographic sales patterns, and Licensee shall pay Licensor a deposit equal to ___ of Licensor's projected earnings each time the prior deposit is recouped if calculations of projected earnings as set out above so warrant in Licensee's good faith business judgment. The initial deposit hereunder shall be paid within five (5) days after recoupment of the prior advances and deposits, and each subsequent deposit shall be paid within five (5) days after recoupment of the prior deposit. If, by expiration of the Option Term, any portion of said deposits has not been recouped by Licensee from Licensor's accrued royalties, Licensor shall repay Licensee the full unrecouped amount thereof within five (5) business days of said expiration or when otherwise subject to repayment under this Exhibit "B";

(iii) notwithstanding anything to the contrary contained herein, if Artist fails to commence an Option Term US Tour by the date four (4) months after the United States commercial release of the Option Term Album (hereinafter "Option Term Scheduled Commencement Date"), Licensor shall be charged a Delayed Performance Fee, which shall be charged between the Option Term Scheduled Commencement Date and the actual commencement of an Option Term US Tour and shall be treated as an additional Option Term Advance paid hereunder.

(c) The advances and deposits payable pursuant to this agreement shall be recoupable from the royalties payable pursuant to paragraph 15(c) of the main body of this agreement, paragraph 2 below, and from royalties earned pursuant to the Merchandising Agreement.

(d) Licensee shall have the right to deduct from any payment of monies due Licensor hereunder the amounts shown to be due all of Licensee's outstanding invoices, if any, to or on behalf of Licensor or any member of Artist.

2. ROYALTIES PAYABLE

The advances and deposits shall be recouped and/or royalties paid as follows:

(a) on sales of Licensed Products (other than tour programs and specialty items, in the event Licensor and Licensee mutually agree to market same hereunder) in the United States:

(i) at concerts where Artist performs as a sole headliner before at least 1,500 bona fide, paid attendees, ___ of gross sales on gross sales from _____ to_____, and ___ of gross sales on gross sales in excess of ________;

(ii) at concerts where Artist performs in all other capacities:
aa. before at least 1,500 bona fide, paid attendees, _____ of gross sales on gross sales from ___ to _____, ___ of gross sales on gross sales from_____ to _____ and _____ of gross sales on gross sales in excess of _____.

For the purpose of all calculations in this agreement, "gross sales" shall exclude sales tax, value-added tax, or any equivalent taxes;

(b) on sales of Licensed Products (other than tour programs and speciality items, in the event Licensor and Licensee mutually agree to market same hereunder) in the United Kingdom and Germany, ____ of gross sales;

(c) on sales of Licensed Products (other than tour programs and specialty items, in the event Licensor and Licensee mutually agree to market same hereunder) in the remainder of the Licensed Area, ____ of gross sales;

(d) on sales of tour programs, in the event Licensor and Licensee mutually agree to market same hereunder, throughout the entire Licensed Area, of net profits; as used in this subparagraph 2(d), "net profits" shall mean gross sales of programs hereunder less mutually approved costs of production, other mutually approved expenses, and a pro rata share of the following expenses attributable to programs: value-added tax or its equivalent, freight and trucking expenses (equipment and personnel), hall and vendor fees, insurance on goods shipped outside the United States, customs duties, mutually approved bootleg security and direct legal costs incurred with respect to same, road staff expenses (including without limitation salaries, per diems, and travel directly related to services hereunder);

(e) on sales of specialty items, including designer garments (i.e., garments which sell for more than ___), ___ of net profits; as used in this subparagraph 2(e), "net profits" shall mean gross sales of specialty items hereunder, less mutually approved costs of production, other mutually approved expenses, a mutually agreeable royalty payable with respect to specialty items and a pro rata share of the following expenses attributable to specialty items: hall and vendor fees, freight and trucking expenses (equipment and personnel), insurance on goods shipped outside the United States, customs duties, mutually approved bootleg security and direct legal costs incurred with respect to same, and road staff expenses (including without limitation salaries, per diems, and travel directly related to services hereunder);

(f) Notwithstanding the foregoing, on sales of tour programs and specialty items, in the event Licensor and Licensee mutually agree to market same hereunder, in Japan and Australia, the royalty rate set forth in subparagraph 2(c) above shall apply.

(g) Royalties on sales of Licensed Products in Northern Ireland and the Republic of Ireland shall be payable at the rate for Europe, rather than the rate for the United Kingdom.

(h) The royalties set out above only apply to Licensee's standard blank stock for and style and design of the Licensed Products listed on Exhibit "A".

(i) Notwithstanding anything to the contrary contained herein, if Licensee is required by a foreign governmental instrumentality to deduct taxes based on Licensee's receipts (due to Licensor or Artist's liability in such territory, not to Licensee's income tax liability, if any) and/or Licensor's earnings from merchandise sales hereunder or if such governmental instrumentality requires deduction of any other taxes on Licensor or Artist's behalf due to Licensor or Artist's liability in such territory, Licensee may:

(i) deduct the full amount of any such taxes actually paid or estimated to be required for payment to such instrumentality; and/or

(ii) in the event the advances paid hereunder by Licensee to Licensor are unrecouped, Licensor shall pay Licensee the amount of such taxes paid by Licensee to such instrumentality on presentation of appropriate proof of payment by Licensee. Notwithstanding anything contained in this subparagraph 2(i), Licensee shall notify Licensor as soon as reasonably possible after having been contacted by any governmental instrumentality with respect to the taxes described above. If Licensor or Artist itself makes the payments of any such taxes, Licensee may not avail itself of the remedies set out in subparagraphs 2(i) (i) and 2(i) (ii) above, provided that the governmental instrumentality involved has recognized such payment by Artist or Licensor and has provided Licensee, prior to the time its payment to the governmental instrumentality is due, with its appropriate governmental notification that it need not make the payment with respect to Licensor or Artist's taxes. Licensee shall provide Licensor with suitable confirmation of any such taxes paid by Licensee.

3. PERFORMANCE MINIMUM

(a) Initial Term:

(i) In order to induce Licensee to pay the Initial Term advances, deposits, and royalties set out above, Licensor warrants that between the date of this agreement and August 1, 19__ (hereinafter "Initial Term Performance Minimum Period"), Artist shall perform live musical concerts at shows:

aa. held in the United States;

bb. where Artist is the sole headliner or second-billed act supporting an artist for which Licensee is the tour merchandiser;

cc. before at least 500 bona fide, paid attendees; and

dd. not given in conjunction with another nonmusical public performance, air, or amusement event, unless a separate admission price is charged for Artist's concert;

[concerts satisfying the above criteria hereinafter referred to as a "Performance(s)"] before a minimum of 66,000 bona fide, paid attendees as set out on the attached itinerary or at venues comparable in location and capacity to those listed thereon (hereinafter "Initial Term Performance Minimum"). A "bona fide, paid attendee" shall mean a person who has paid the full ticket price for admission to a Performance [with the exception of Stadium Shows, for which the number of bona fide, paid attendees shall be counted pursuant to subparagraph 3(a) (ii) below] and actually attended such Performance and whose attendance is verified by facility drop counts supplied to Licensee. Licensor and Licensee agree that in the event Artist plays before bona fide, paid attendees during the Initial Term Performance Minimum Period in excess of the Initial Term Performance Minimum, the Initial Term shall include the dates at which Artist performs before such excess number of bona fide, paid attendees. Licensor also warrants that when Artist performs as a headliner, there will be at least one (1) intermission and one (1) opening act at each Performance;

(ii) Notwithstanding the foregoing, with respect to concerts during the Initial Term Performance Minimum Period at venues with capacities in excess of 22,000 people at which three (3) or more musical artists perform (hereinafter "Stadium Shows"), the number of bona fide, paid attendees to be counted for purposes of fulfilling the Initial Term Performance Minimum shall be the following:

(Licensor's gross sales of Licensed Products or individual Stadium Show)

DIVIDED BY

(Licensor's average gross sales of Licensed Products per bonafide, paid attendee at Performances [other than Stadium Shows] during Initial Term Performance Minimum Period) =

Number of bona fide, paid attendees to be counted for such Stadium Show (but the number to be inserted shall not exceed the actual number of full-playing attendees at such Stadium Show).

(iii) Notwithstanding anything to the contrary contained herein, in the event that Artist fails at any Performance during the Initial Term Performance Minimum Period to substantially perform, the number of bona fide, paid attendees to be counted at such Performance toward fulfillment of the Initial Term Performance Minimum shall be calculated as follows:

(Licensor's gross sales of Licensed Products for such Performance)

DIVIDED BY

(Licensor's average per-head gross sales of Licensed Products at Performances during Initial Term Performance Minimum Period at which Artist does substantially perform) =

Number of bona fide, paid attendees to be counted (but the number to be inserted shall not exceed the actual number of bona fide, paid attendees at such Performance) As used herein, to "substantially perform" shall mean to play at least sixty (60) minutes of live music when Artist is a headliner and thirty (30) minutes of live music when Artist is not a headliner.

(iv) If the Initial Term Performance minimum is not met and the advances and deposits then paid have not been recouped by Licensee from Licensor's accrued royalties, Licensor shall pay Licensee the lesser of I or II within five (5) business days of Licensee's request therefore:

I

$$\frac{(66{,}000 - \textit{bona fide, paid attendees}}{66{,}000}$$

X (Advances paid by Licensee) = Sum due Licensee

OR

II

(Advances paid by Licensee) - (Licensor's accrued royalties when repayment requested) = Sum due Licensee

(v) If Artist fails to commence an Initial Term US Tour by September 1, 19__, or there is a gap of at least thirty (30) days between Performances during the Initial Term, Licensee may invoke the terms of subparagraph 3(a) (iv) above by letter, in which event, the repayment shall be due within five (5) business days of Licensor's receipt of such notice.

(b) Option Term:

(i) in order to induce Licensee to pay the Option Term advances, deposits, and royalties set out above, Licensor warrants that during the period of one (1) year after Licensee's exercise of the Option (hereinafter "Option Term Performance Minimum Period"), Artist shall give Performances before a minimum number of bona fide, paid attendees equal to the following (hereinafter "Option Term Performance Minimum"):

$$\frac{\textit{Option Term Advance}}{\textit{Average Per-Head Gross Sales x Option Term Royalty Rate}}$$

where "Average Per-Head Gross Sales" means Licensor's aggregate gross sales of Licensed Products during the Initial Term divided by the aggregate number of bona fide, paid attendees at Artist's concerts in the Licensed Area during the Initial Term, and "Option Term Royalty Rate" means the royalty rate payable during the Option Term at Performances during the Option Term Performance Minimum Period.

Solely by way of example, if the Option Term Advance is ____, Average Per-Head Gross Sales are ____, and the Option Term Royalty Rate is _____, the Option Term Performance Minimum will be _____ bona fide, paid attendees, calculated as follows:

Licensor and Licensee agree that in the event Artist plays before bona fide, paid attendees during the Option Term Performance Minimum Period in excess of the Option Term Performance Minimum, the Option Term Performance Minimum shall include the dates at which Artist performs before such excess number of bona fide, paid attendees. Licensor also warrants that when Artist is a headliner, there will be at least one (1) intermission and one (1) opening act at each Performance during the Option Term;

(ii) Notwithstanding the foregoing, with respect to Stadium Shows during the Option Term Performance Minimum Period, the number of bona fide, paid attendees to be counted for purposes of fulfilling the Option Term Performance Minimum shall be the following:

(Licensor's gross sales of Licensed Products for individual Stadium Show)

DIVIDED BY

(Licensor's average gross sales of Licensed Products per bonafide, paid attendee at Performances [other than Stadium Shows] during Option Term Performance Minimum Period) =

Number of bona fide, paid attendees to be counted for such Stadium Show (but the number to be inserted shall not exceed the actual number of full-paying attendees at such Stadium Show).

(iii) Notwithstanding anything to the contrary contained herein, in the event that Artist fails at any Performance during the Option Term Performance Minimum Period to substantially perform, the number of bona fide, paid attendees to be counted at such Performance toward fulfillment of the Option Term Performance Minimum shall be calculated as follows:

(Licensor's gross sales of Licensed Products for such Performance)

DIVIDED BY

(Licensor's average per-head gross sales of Licensed Products at Performances during Option Term Performance Minimum Period at which Artist does substantially perform) =Number of bona fide, paid attendees to be counted (but the number to be inserted shall not exceed the actual number of bona fide, paid attendees at such Performance).

As used herein, to "substantially perform" shall mean to play at least sixty (60) minutes of live music when Artist is a headliner and thirty (30) minutes of live music when Artist is not a headliner.

(iv) If the Option Term Performance Minimum is not met and the advances and deposits then paid have not been recouped by Licensee from Licensor's accrued royalties, Licensor shall pay Licensee the lesser of I or II within five (5) business days of Licensee's request therefore:

I

$$\frac{(\text{Option Term Performance Minimum} - \text{bona fide, paid attendees}}{\text{Option Term Performance Minimum}}$$

X (Advances paid by Licensee) = Sum due Licensee.

OR

II

(Advances paid by Licensee) - (Licensor's accrued royalties when repayment requested) = Sum due Licensee.

(v) If Artist fails to commence an Option Term US Tour within four (4) months after the release of the Option Term Album or there is a gap of at least thirty (30) days between Performances during the Option Term, Licensee may invoke the terms of subparagraph 3(b) (iv) above by letter, in which event, the repayment shall be due within five (5) business days of Licensor's receipt of such notice.

(c) If any lawsuit is filed to collect the amount set out in subparagraph 3(a) (iv), 3(a) (v), 3 (b) (v) above, the prevailing party shall be entitled to full court costs and attorneys' fees incurred in connection with such effort.

(d) Any sum due Licensee pursuant to subparagraph 3(a)(iv), 3(a)(v), 3(b)(iv), or 3(b)(v) above, if not timely paid, shall accrue interest from the date due at the rate of ten percent (10%) per annum.

(e) If a fee is charged by another entertainer for Licensee's right to sell merchandise, Licensor, rather than Licensee, shall pay such fee.

(f) Licensor hereby warrants that at each of Artist's concerts during the Licensed Term, including but not limited to support dates with __________, Licensee will be permitted to sell Artist's merchandise.

(g) Notwithstanding anything contained in this agreement, the Licensed Term shall continue until the repayment due, if any, plus interest thereon, pursuant to subparagraph 3(a)(iv), 3(a)(v), 3(b)(iv), or 3(b)(v) above is received by Licensee. Repayment of all sums owed by Licensor to Licensee pursuant to the terms of subparagraph 3(a)(iv), 3(a)(v), 3(b)(iv), or 3(b)(v) above shall result in termination of this agreement upon the date of such repayment.

Your signature, together with ours, shall constitute this a binding agreement between us.

AGREED: DATE:

BY____________________(Licensor) BY____________________ (Licensee)

THE END

As with a marriage, the best time to plan for a group breakup is at the outset of the relationship. Practically speaking, however, very few people are concerned with planning a breakup when things are going well. This chapter will discuss the kinds of problems which arise at the time of a breakup (or, more commonly, at the time a member of the group chooses to leave), and will describe some planning devices which can help avoid these problems.

MEET THE RUMMIES

The Rummies are a successful recording group on the White Noise label. The Rummies consist of the following four individuals:

Richie, the drummer, a former butcher who wouldn't know one chord from another, but is tough on the back beat.

John, the bass player, a former session player with the creativity and stage presence of a cadaver.

David, a flashy lead guitarist who writes about half of the group's material.

Fred, the lead singer and occasional rhythm guitar player who writes the rest of the group's material.

THE INITIAL BREAKUP

John, the bass player decides to leave the group to become a Moonie (the religious organization, not the rock group). At this point, the group is required to notify White Noise that John has decided to leave the group (Section 2.01.2 (a) (i) of Exhibit 1, Group Artist Rider).

The remaining members of the group decide to find a new bass player. After a quick search, the group settles upon Floydine, a bass player for a local punk rock group. White Noise, quite concerned that this new bass player will affect the Rummies bubble gum sound, refuses to allow Floydine to join the group. The group is outraged, and wants to know what right White Noise has to keep them from letting whomever they choose join their group. Unfortunately, the Rummies have not read their contract. The contract essentially provides that White Noise has a right to veto any replacement members selected by the group (Section 2.01.2 (a) (i) of Exhibit 1, Group Artist Rider). While White Noise may have been willing to give up this right in initial negotiations, the Rummies' lawyer never raised the point, and the Rummies are now paying the price.

In fact, under the provisions of the "Group Artist Rider," the record company retains the right to split up the group in the event of a leaving member situation and may thereafter treat each member of the group as a leaving member (Section 2.01.2 (a) ii of Exhibit 1, Group Artist Rider). Provisions such as these give the record company considerable leverage in a leaving member situation. They permit the record company to threaten to break up the group and keep certain members. (It should be pointed out that it is unlikely that a record company would actually try to assert this right.) In any event, some foresight by the group's lawyers would probably result in the tempering of much of this language.

White Noise and the Rummies eventually agree on a replacement bass player named Craig. Craig will become bound to the terms of the Rummies' recording contract with White Noise (Section 2.01.2 (a) (1) of Exhibit 1, Group Artist Rider). Although White Noise has the right to retain John's services as a solo recording artist (Section 2.01.2 (b) of Exhibit 1, Group Artist Rider), it is quite satisfied, given John's distinct lack of creative talents, to let John sign with the Moonies.

CRAIG SIGNS ON

With the departure of John and the addition of Craig, the Rummies have some fairly complicated financial problems to think about. John is entitled to receive his share of the group's royalties on all albums on which he participated. In general, however, a record company will keep all royalties earned by a recording artist until such time as the artist has "paid back" all advances made to him, including any recording costs incurred by the artist in making records. Until those advances are paid back, the artist is "unrecouped." The advances are not actually returnable — i.e., the artist has no general obligation to pay them back — but the record company has the right to recoup them from any royalties earned by the artist. As a result, an artist can have significant record sales, and still not receive any royalties from those sales. It might be that advances to the group and recording costs, both incurred after John's departure, will place the group in an unrecouped position with White Noise. If subsequent earnings are not ample enough to recoup these advances, the group may not have sufficient funds with which to pay John his share of royalties for the records on which he participated.

Craig faces the opposite side of this problem. It may be that when Craig joins the group, the Rummies' royalty account is in a seriously unrecouped position. Craig may prove to be the catalyst the band needs to obtain massive commercial success, which will lead to large royalties. Craig may feel, however, that his share of the royalties should not be used to recoup advances and recording costs in which he did not share.

The best way to handle the problems outlined above is for the group to enter into a formal partnership agreement or to incorporate: this should be done as early in the group's career as is financially possible. The partnership agreement, or, in the case of an incorporation, the bylaws or shareholders' agreement, should contain buy out and buy in provisions, and will usually provide an adequate vehicle for dealing with the legal and financial ramifications of a leaving member situation. These are sophisticated agreements, which require considerable legal expertise to prepare, and a discussion of their specific terms is beyond the scope of this article. References below to a partnership agreement will apply with equal force to a shareholders' agreement — the choice of entity (i.e., partnership or corporation) will not affect the basic terms which should be in these agreements. Consult your attorney to determine which will work best for your group.

TREATMENT OF THE LEAVING MEMBER

After receiving a large advance, the Rummies spend six months in the studio recording their next album. The album is an incredible stiff. Fred believes the group is not a proper forum for exhibiting his talent and decides to leave. Once again the group notifies White Noise of the leaving member situation (Section 2.01.2 (a) (1) of Exhibit 1, Group Artist Rider).

White Noise is interested in keeping Fred as a solo recording artist. It therefore exercises the leaving member option to which it is entitled under its recording contract with the Rummies (Section 2.01.2 (b) of Exhibit 1, Group Artist Rider). By exercising its rights under the leaving member clause of its contract with the Rummies, White Noise will now have the exclusive right to Fred's services as a solo recording artist. Unfortunately, the terms of Fred's contract with White Noise are not very favorable to Fred. Generally, the terms of a leaving member contract will be the standard terms contained in the record company's form contract (Section 2.01.2 (b) of Exhibit 1, Group Artist Rider). The number of renewal terms of that contract will usually be the number of renewal terms remaining at the time the member becomes a leaving member (Section 2.01.2 (b) (1) of Exhibit 1, Group Artist Rider), no advances will be provided, the royalty rate will be significantly lower than the group's royalty rate (Section 2.01.2 (b) (2) of Exhibit 1, Group Artist Rider), the recording commitment may be lower (Section 2.01.2 (b) (2) of Exhibit 1, Group Artist Rider), and most deal points negotiated in the group's contract will be deleted from the leaving member's contract. Fred, who considers himself a major talent and a superstar but for White Noise's lack of support, is not pleased with this state of affairs. There are, however, several reasons for having leaving member provisions which are worse than the provisions of the group's recording contract.

Initially, the record company does not want to provide, in a group's contract, an incentive for a member to leave the group. For instance, if, instead of splitting advances and royalties 3 or 4 ways, a member could receive the same advances or royalties as the group does and keep them entirely for himself, he might be more inclined to leave the group. In addition, when a record company retains a leaving member, it often has no idea how that member will fare as a solo artist. Accordingly, it will not wish to risk as much money on or commit to record as many records with the leaving member. At the time a leaving member leaves the group, the record company will want as few obstacles as possible standing in the way of its decision as to whether or not to retain that leaving member, since it is taking a risk the leaving member will be able to generate the same quality and chemistry with a new band as he did with the old.

Knowing these justifications does not make Fred feel any better, however. Having just left the group, he is staring at a contract which he does not feel is fit for an artist of his stature. Often, if the record company is interested enough in an artist to exercise its leaving member option, it will be interested enough to renegotiate his leaving member contract. Just incidentally, this willingness to renegotiate will arise to some extent from the record company's lack of certainty as to its rights under the leaving member clause, and its desire to coerce additional product out of the artist. The leaving member will invariably leave at a time when there are less than the customary 7 or 8 option LPs left for the record company to exercise. By exercising its option to retain Fred, White Noise is committing itself to Fred's new career. If White Noise is going to spend the time and money necessary to develop Fred as a solo artist, it will want to be assured of receiving the maximum amount of product in return for its commitment. In any event, White Noise will probably elect to renegotiate. However, since the terms of the leaving member contract are so onerous, Fred will likely be renegotiating from a position of weakness, unless the amount of product he owes White Noise at the time of his departure is quite small (e.g., if there are only 1 or 2 LPs left in the Rummies' contract).

Another problem Fred faces arises from the fact that, because of the group's disastrous last album, the Rummies are, when Fred leaves, in a seriously unrecouped position. White Noise may try to recoup the Rummies' deficit position from Fred's earnings as a solo artist. Thus, if Fred is quite successful, and the Rummies fade, Fred's initial platinum album may go entirely towards paying off the Rummies' unrecouped royalty account.

If White Noise retains the right to recoup the Rummies' deficit from Fred's royalties as a solo artist (this is known in the record industry as "cross-collateralization"), Fred would have been much better off if White Noise had dropped him and let him sign with another record company. White Noise would then have had no right of recoupment against Fred's subsequent royalties (since the royalties would have been earned with another record company) and would have been left solely with the Rummies' earnings to recoup the Rummies' deficit balance. At best, Fred should be treated by White Noise as a new artist who has signed a new contract and should be given a fresh start and a fresh, zero-balance royalty account. At worst, Fred should be responsible for no more than his pro rata share of any deficit incurred by the Rummies. To the extent that Fred's earnings are used to pay the Rummies' deficit balance, Fred should later be credited with any royalties the Rummies do manage to accumulate. It should be noted, however, that the group has an interest in whether or not Fred's earnings can be used to recoup their deficit. Since Fred received his share of the group's advances and recording costs, the group might be justified in requesting some recoupment out of Fred's earnings.

In many record contract negotiations, the leaving member provisions of the contract are given short shrift. More attention should be paid to these provisions, and to the extent that the group is able, it should attempt to make the leaving member provisions as favorable to the group as possible.

There is a familiar solution to the problems a leaving member will face in his contractual relations with the record company which retains his services as a recording artist - proper planning by the group and its lawyer. In many record contract negotiations, the leaving member provisions of the contract are given short shrift. More attention should be paid to these provisions, and to the extent that the group is able, it should attempt to make the leaving member provisions as favorable to the group as possible. Not only will this provide a leaving member with better contract terms if he is forced to perform under the leaving member clause, but it will also provide the leaving member with a stronger bargaining position in the event of a renegotiation.

The financial problems of a leaving member situation can be minimized through preplanning. The cross-collateralization problem discussed above can probably be satisfactorily resolved in initial negotiations for the group's record contract. Intragroup problems of recoupment should be dealt with in the group's partnership agreement.

UP FROM THE ASHES

The Rummies, *sans* Fred, decide to continue on as a power trio. A little later, Richie is reading the trades when he notices that a group called "John and the Rummies" is playing revival meetings throughout the Midwest. After a little research, the group discovers that John has gone back to playing music and is actively seeking a recording contract. The group is disturbed by this development since John is doing a lot of their old hits and the public believes that John and the Rummies is the same group as the Rummies. White Noise is also quite concerned, since it does not want a group on a competing label using the Rummies' name and possibly hurting the Rummies' sales. Many record companies have provisions in their contracts preventing leaving members from using the group name as long as any members of the group are still under contract to the record company. Unfortunately, the same lawyer who negotiated the Rummies' contract with White Noise originally drafted the White Noise form recording agreement, and did not cover this point.

White Noise and the Rummies file suit against John to keep him from using the Rummies' name, but, given the absence of any clearly defined rights regarding the group name, the lawsuit will be over at about the same time the Electric Prunes have their next hit. The entire problem could have been avoided, however, if the group had included provisions dealing with the ownership of the group name in their partnership agreement.

DOWN FOR THE COUNT

David discovers that his dog loves Richie more than it loves him. He cannot stand the competition and decides to leave the group. White Noise Records exercises its leaving member option and keeps David as a recording artist (Section 2.01.2 (b) of Exhibit 1, Group Artist Rider). However, White Noise decides that its mail room staff has more talent than the remaining members of the Rummies, and it decides to drop the group (Section 2.01.2 (a) (2) of Exhibit 1, Group Artist Rider). Richie and Craig realize they have no future as rock and roll stars and decide to join the A&R department at White Noise Records. However, the group has pending litigation against John, payments to make on the group bus, a lawsuit from a Bakersfield promoter on a concert for which they did not show, and a large quantity of equipment which Richie, David and Craig all think they own. David consults his lawyer at Pig, Pork, Swine & Razorback regarding the impending lawsuit over these items. David asks the lawyer how he can avoid some of these problems in his new group. After discussing David's situation, the lawyer sits down and prepares a draft of a partnership agreement for David's new group which resolves the critical partnership issues. Now, all his bases covered, David lies in bed, safe and secure. He reads his partnership agreement and the leaving member clause of his contract with White Noise, and dreams of the day when his new group can break up.

SUMMARY OF CRITICAL 'LEAVING MEMBER' ISSUES TO BE SETTLED BY AGREEMENT

The orderly withdrawal of old members from and addition of new members to a group.

The equitable division of advances and royalties among old and new members, with an eye towards the recoupment problems discussed above.

The ownership of the group name.

The complete breakup and dissolution of the group.

Language which may provide the record company with an absolute veto power in the selection of replacement members.

Provisions which may provide the record company the unfettered right, in a leaving member situation, to break up the group and treat all the members as leaving members.

Provisions which may allow the record company to cross-collateralize advances and charges under the particular recording contract against charges and advances under other agreements between the record company and the group or its members.

Unfavorable provisions (e.g., lower royalty rates, lower advances and reduced recording commitment) in the leaving member's contract.

EXHIBIT 1
GROUP ARTIST RIDER

Author's note: This 'rider' is commonly appended to recording contracts or incorporated into the contract. See contract provision 16 in the chapter "Analysis of a Recording Contract."

GROUP ARTIST RIDER annexed to and made part of the agreement dated ________, between ________ (name of record company) and the ________(name of Artist or group).

The provisions of this Rider shall be deemed to be part of the aforesaid (recording) agreement. To the extent that anything in said agreement is inconsistent with any provisions of this Rider, the latter shall govern. Numerical designations in this rider refer to the related provisions of the aforesaid agreement.

2.01.1 (a) The Artist's obligations under this agreement are joint and several and all references herein to the "Artist" shall include all members of the group inclusively and each member of the group individually, unless otherwise specified.

(b) Notwithstanding any change in the membership of the group,________ (name of record company) shall continue to have the right to remit all payments under this agreement in the name of the ________ (name of Artist/group).

2.01.2 If any member of the Artist shall cease to perform as a member of the group:

(a) (i) You shall promptly notify ________ (name of record company) thereof and such leaving member shall be replaced by a new member, if you and ________ (name of record company) so agree. Such new member shall thereafter be deemed substituted as a party to this agreement in the place of such leaving member and, by performing hereunder, shall automatically be bound by all the terms and conditions of this agreement. Upon ________ (name of record company)'s request, you will cause any such new member to execute and deliver to________ (name of record company) such documents as ________ (name of record company), in its judgement, may deem necessary or advisable to effectuate the foregoing sentence. Thereafter, you shall have no further obligation to furnish the services of the leaving member for performances hereunder, but you (and such leaving member individually) shall continue to be bound by the other provisions of this agreement, including, without limitation, subparagraph 2.01.2(b) below.

(ii) Notwithstanding anything to the contrary contained herein, ________ (name of record company) shall have the right to terminate the term of this agreement with respect to the remaining members of the Artist by written notice given to you at any time prior to the expiration of ninety (90) days after ________ (name of record company)'s receipt of your said notice to (name of record company). In the event of such termination, all members of the Artist shall be deemed leaving members as of the date of such termination notice, and paragraph 2.01.2(b) hereof shall be applicable to all of them, collectively or individually, as ________ (name of record company) shall elect.

(b) ________ (Name of record company) shall have, and you and the Artist hereby grant to __________ (name of record company), an option to engage the exclusive services of such leaving member as a recording artist ("Leaving Member Option"). Such Leaving Member Option may be exercised by ________ (name of record company) by notice to such leaving member at any time prior to the expiration of ninety (90) days after the date of: (1) ______ (name of record company)'s receipt of your notice provided for in section 2.01.2(a) (i), or (2) ______ (name of record company)'s termination notice pursuant to section 2.01.2(a)(ii), as the case may be. If ________ (name of record company) exercises such Option, the leaving member concerned shall be deemed to have executed ________(name of record company)'s then current standard form of term recording agreement for the services of an individual artist containing the following provisions:

(1) A term consisting of an initial period of one year commencing on the date of __________ (name of record company)'s exercise of such Leaving Member Option, which term may be extended by (name of record company), at its election exercisable in the manner provided in paragraph 1.01., for the same number of additional periods as the number of option periods, if any, remaining pursuant to paragraph 1.02 at the time of ____ (name of record company)'s exercise of the Leaving Member Option;

(2) A Minimum Recording Commitment, for each Contract Period of such term, of <u>two (2)</u> satisfactory Sides, or their equivalent; and

(3) A basic royalty at the rate of <u>five percent (5%)</u> in respect of phonograph records embodying performances recorded during such term.

______________ (Name of record company), a division of

______________ (Name of record company), Inc.

By:______________________

RESOURCES, SERVICES AND BIBLIOGRAPHY

Compiled by Marianne P. Borselle, Esq. and edited by Gregory T. Victoroff, Esq. Based on the Original Version Compiled by Harris E. Tulchin, Esq. and earlier supplemented version by Debra J. Graff, Esq.

TRADE AND CONSUMER PUBLICATIONS

Bam
5951 Canning Street
Oakland, CA 94609

Billboard
1515 Broadway, 39th Floor
New York, NY 10036

Cashbox
157 West 57th Street, Suite 1402
New York, NY 10019

Circus
419 Park Avenue South
New York, NY 10016

Classical
128 East 56th Street
New York, NY 10022

Country Music Magazine
342 Madison Avenue, Suite 2118
New York, NY 10173

Creem
4735 Sepulveda Boulevard
Suite 249
Sherman Oaks, CA 91403

Daily Variety
1400 North Cahuenga Boulevard
Hollywood, CA 90028

Dance Music Report
33-39 22nd Street
Long Island City, NY 11106

Down Beat
180 West Park Avenue, Suite 105
Elmhurst, IL 60126

Entertainment Law Reporter
2210 Wilshire Boulevard, #311
Santa Monica, CA 90403

Gig
17042 Devonshire Street
Suite 209
Northridge, CA 91325

Guitar Player
20085 Stevens Creek Boulevard
Cupertino, CA 95014

Guitar World
1115 Broadway
New York, NY 10010

Hit Parader
Charlton Building
Derby, CT 06418

Hollywood Reporter
6715 Sunset Boulevard
Hollywood, CA 90028

Home And Studio Recording
22024 Lassen Street, Suite 118
Chatsworth, CA 91311

International Musician
1501 Broadway, Suite 600
New York, NY 10036

Jazziz
P.O. Box 8309
Gainesville, FL 32605

Jazztimes
8055 13th Street
Silver Springs, MD 20910

Keyboard
20085 Stevens Creek Boulevard
Cupertino, CA 95014

Mix Magazine
6400 Hollis Street, #12
Emeryville, CA 94608

Modern Drummer
870 Pompton Avenue
Cedar Grove, NH 07009

Modern Recording
15 Columbus Circle
New York, NY 10023

Music City News
50 Music Square West, Suite 601
P.O. Box 29275
Nashville, TN 37203

Music Connection Magazine
6640 Sunset Boulevard, Suite 201
Hollywood, CA 90028

Music Trades
80 West Street
P.O. Box 432
Englewood, NJ 07631

Music Week
Greater London House
Hampstead Road
London, NW1 7QZ
England

Musician
1515 Broadway, 39th Floor
New York, NY 10036

Performance
1203 Lake Street, Suite 200
Fort Worth, TX 76102

Pollstar
4838 N. Blackstone Avenue
2nd Floor
Fresno, CA 93726

Pro Sound News
2 Park Avenue, Suite 1820
New York, NY 10016

Probe
41 Valleybrook Drive
Toronto, Ontario M3B 2S6
Canada

Radio And Records
1930 Century Park West
Los Angeles, CA 90067

Recording Engineer/Producer
9221 Quivira Road
Box 12960
Overland Park, KS 66215

Record Week
216 Carlton
Toronto, Ontario
Canada

Rock And Soul
441 Lexington Avenue
New York, NY 10017

Rolling Stone
745 Fifth Avenue
New York, NY 10151

RPM
6 Brentcliffe Road
Toronto, Ontario M4G 3Y2
Canada

Rythym
22024 Lassen Street, Suite 118
Chatsworth, CA 91311

Songtalk
6381 Hollywood Boulevard
Hollywood, CA 90028

Spin
6 West 18th Street
New York, NY 10011

Variety
475 Park Avenue South
2nd Floor
New York, NY 10016

DIRECTORIES AND REFERENCE MATERIALS

Billboard Publications, Inc.
1515 Broadway, New York, NY 10036
(212) 764-7300, or
9107 Wilshire Boulevard, Suite 700,
Beverly Hills, CA 90210
(213) 273-7040

Billboard International Talent And Touring Directory

Billboard International Buyer's Guide
(Lists all music publishers and record and video companies and industry services, associations, licensors and music libraries.)

Billboard's Country Music Sourcebook And Directory
(Record companies, artists, agents and managers, radio stations, leading music publishers, key facilities, concert promoters, independent promoters, associations.)

Billboard International Recording Equipment And Studio Directory

Billboard International Directory Of Manufacturing And Packaging

Billboard Book Of Top 40 Hits, 1955 - Present - Joel Whitborn.

Billboard Book Of Number One Hits - Fred Bronson.

Performance Magazine Annual Guides
Talent/Personal Management
Booking Agencies
Promoters/Clubs
Concert Production
Facilities
Transportation/Accommodations
Services/Personnel
International

The Recording Industry Sourcebook
Fuchs, Michael, ed.
8800 Venice Boulevard,
Los Angeles, CA 90034
Ascona Communications, Inc., 1990,
(213) 841-2702 or
(800) 969-7472

Phonolog
Music Department
10996 Torreyana Road
San Diego, CA 92121

GUILDS AND LABOR ORGANIZATIONS

American Federation Of Musicians (AFM)*
1501 Broadway
Paramount Building, Suite 600
New York, NY 10036
(212) 869-1330

1777 Vine Street
Hollywood, CA 90028
(213) 461-3441

Local 47
817 Vine Street
Hollywood, CA 90028
*Other Offices Nationwide

American Federation Of Television And Radio Artists (AFTRA)*
260 Madison Avenue
New York, NY 10016
(212) 532-0800

6922 Hollywood Boulevard
8th Floor
Hollywood, CA 90028
*Other Offices Nationwide

PERFORMING RIGHTS ORGANIZATIONS AND TRADE ASSOCIATIONS

Academy Of Country Music
6255 Sunset Boulevard
Suite 923
Hollywood, CA 90028
(213) 462-2351

American Society Of Composers, Authors, And Publishers (ASCAP)
One Lincoln Plaza
New York, NY 10023
(212) 595-3050

6430 Sunset Boulevard
2nd Floor
Hollywood, CA 90028
(213) 466-7681

2 Music Square West
Nashville, TN 37203
(615) 244-3936

American Society Of Music Arrangers
P.O. Box 11
Hollywood, CA 90028

Broadcast Music Incorporated (BMI)
320 West 57th Street
New York, NY 10019
(212) 586-2000

8730 Sunset Boulevard
Hollywood, CA 90069
(213) 469-9109

10 Music Square East
Nashville, TN 37203
(615) 259-3625

Country Music Association (CMA)
7 Music Circle North
Nashville, TN 37202
(615) 244-2840

Country Music Society Of America
One Country Music Road
P.O. Box 2000
Marion, OH 43306
(800) 669-1002

Electronic Industries Association (EIA)
2003 I Street N.W.
Washington, D.C. 20006
(202) 457-4900

Gospel Music Association
P.O. Box 23201
Nashville, TN 37202
(615) 242-0303

Music and Entertainment Industry Educators Association, (MEIEA)
Director, Music Industry Progam
State University College
Oneonta, N.Y. 13820
(607) 431-3425

National Association Of Independent Record Distributor and Manufacturers (NAIRD)
P.O. Box 568
Maple Shade, NJ 08052-0568
(609) 547-3331

National Association Of Record Merchandisers (NARM)
10008 F. Astonia Boulevard
Suite 200
Cherry Hill, NJ 08034
(609) 427-1404

National Music Publishers Association
110 East 59th Street
New York, NY 10022
(212) 754-1930

Recording Industry Association Of America, Inc. (RIAA)
1020 19th Street, N.W.
Suite 200
Washington, D.C. 20036
(202) 775-0101

SESAC
10 Columbus Circle
New York, NY 10019
(212) 586-3450
9000 Sunset Boulevard
Los Angeles, CA 90069
(213) 274-6814

SUPPORT GROUPS AND OTHER ORGANIZATIONS

Association Of Independent Music Publishers
P.O. Box 1561
Burbank, CA 91507
(818) 842-6257

Beverly Hills Bar Association
300 South Beverly Drive, # 201
Beverly Hills, CA 90212
(213) 553-6644

California Lawyers For The Arts (CLA)
315 West Ninth Street
11th Floor
Los Angeles, CA 90015
(213) 623-8311
Fort Mason Center
Building C, Room 255
San Francisco, CA 94123
(415) 775-7200

The Clearing House, Ltd.
6605 Hollywood Boulevard
Suite 200
Hollywood, CA 90028
(213) 469-3186

The Harry Fox Agency
205 East 42nd Street
New York, NY 10017
(212) 370-5330

Los Angeles Songwiter's Showcase (LASS)
1209 North Orange Grove
P.O. Box 93759
Hollywood, CA 90093
(213) 654-1666

Los Angeles Women In Music
8489 West Third Street
Los Angeles, CA 90048
(213) 653-3662

Mix Bookshelf/The Recording Industry Resource Center
6400 Hollis Street, #12
Emeryville, CA 94608
(415) 653-3307

Musician's Referral Service
1655 McCadden Place
Hollywood, CA 90028

National Academy Of Recording Arts And Sciences (NARAS)
Atlanta Chapter
1227 Spring Street N.W.
Atlanta, GA 30309
(404) 875-1440

Chicago Chapter
1946 North Hudson
Chicago, IL 60614
(312) 440-1350

Los Angeles Chapter
4444 Riverside Drive, Suite 201
Burbank, CA 91505
(213) 843-8253
Nashville Chapter
2 Music Circle South
Nashville, TN 37203
(615) 255-8777

New York Chapter
157 West 57th Street, #902
New York, NY 10019
(212) 245-5440

San Francisco Chapter
245 Hyde Street
San Francisco, CA 94102
(415) 441-0662

National Academy Of Songwriters (NAS)
6381 Hollywood Boulevard
Suite 780
Hollywood, CA 90028
(213) 463-7178

Society of Composers, Authors and Music Publishers of Canada (SOCAN)
41 Valley Brook Drive
Don Mills, Ontario M3B 2S6 Canada
(416) 445-8700

The Songwriter's Guild Of America
276 Fifth Avenue
New York, NY 10001
(212) 686-6820

6430 Sunset Boulevard
Los Angeles, CA 90028
(213) 462-1108

Trademark Register Of The United States
454 Washington Building
Washington, D.C. 20005

United States Copyright Office
Library Of Congress
Washington, D.C. 20559
(202) 707-6850

SELECTED BIBLIOGRAPHY

Anderton, Craig, MIDI for Musicians, New York, Music Sales Corp., 1987.

Bagehot, Richard. Music Business Agreements. New York; Pergamon, 1989.

Bartlett, Bruce. Recording Demo Tapes At Home. Indiana: Howard W. Sams and Co., 1989.

Bartlett, Bruce. Introduction To Professional Recording Techniques. Indiana: Howard W. Sams and Co., 1987.

Baskerville, David, Ph.D. Music Business Handbook And Career Guide. 5th Ed. Los Angeles: Sherwood, Co., 1990.

Berger, Robert A. Songwriting: A Structured Approach. San Diego, California: Beer Flat, 1983.

Blume, August G. Music Business Directory 1987-1988. California: Blume And Associates, 1988.

Braheney, John. The Craft And Business Of Songwriting. Cincinnatti, Ohio: Writer's Digest Books, 1988.

Burton, Gary. A Musician's Guide To The Road. New York: Watson-Guptill Books, 1981.

Carter, Walter. The Songwriter's Guide To Collaboration. Cincinnati, Ohio: Writer's Digest Books, 1988.

Chapple, Steve And Garofalo, Reebee. Rock 'N' Roll Is Here To Pay (The History And Politics Of The Music Industry). Chicago: Nelson-Hall, 1978.

Connelly, Will. Musician's Guide To Independent Record Production. Chicago: Contemporary Books, 1981.

Curcio, Louise. Musician's Handbook. New York: J. Patelson Music, 1968.

Davis, Sheila. The Craft Of Lyric Writing. Cincinnati, Ohio: Writer's Digest Books, 1985.

Dearing, James. Making Money Making Music. Cincinnati, Ohio: Writer's Digest Books, 1990.

Dorf, Michael; Appel, Robert. Gigging: The Musician's Underground Touring Directory. Cincinnati, Ohio: Writer's Digest Books, 1989.

Dranou, Paula. Inside The Music Publishing Industry. White Plains, New York: Knowledge Industry Publications, 1980.

Drews, Mark. New Ears: A Guide To Education In Audio And The Recording Sciences. Syracuse, New York: New Ears Productions, 1989.

Erickson, J. Gunnar; Hearn, Edward R.; and Halloran, Mark. Musician's Guide To Copyright. New York: Charles Scribner's Sons, 1983.

Evans, Marc. The Music Of The Movies. New York: Hopkinson & Blake, 1975.

Fink, Michael. Inside the Music Business. New York: MacMillan Publishing, 1989.

Frascogna and Hetherington. Successful Artist Management. New York: Billboard Books, 1990.

Garvey, Mark. Songwriter's Market. Cincinnati, Ohio: Writer's Digest Books, 1978.

Gere, Don. The Record Producer's Handbook. Los Angeles: Acrobat Books, 1978.

Gibson, James. Getting Noticed: A Musician's Guide To Publicity And Self-Promotion. Cincinnati, Ohio: Writer's Digest Books, 1987.

Gibson, James. How You Can Make $30,000 A Year As A Musician Without A Record Contract. Cincinnati, Ohio: Writer's Digest Books, 1987.

Goldfield, Paul, Ed. by Peter L. Alexander. Recording, Syncing And Synths. Newbury Park, California: Alexander Publishing, 1988.

Hagen, Earle. Scoring For Films. New York: Criterion Music, 1971.

Hall, Tom T., Rev. Ed. Songwriter's Handbook. Nashville, Tennessee: Rutledge Hill Publishers, 1987.

Hurst, Walter E., and Hale, William Storm. Record Industry Book: Stories, Text, Forms, Contracts. 7th Rev. Ed. Hollywood, California: Seven Arts Press, 1974.

Hurst, Walter E., and Hale, William Storm. Music Record Business And Law: Your Introduction To Music, Record, Copyright, Contracts And Other Business And Law. Hollywood, California: Seven Arts Press, 1974.

Jahn, Mike. How To Make A Hit Record. Scarsdale, New York: Bradbury Press, 1976.

Josefs, Jai. Writing Music For Hit Songs. Cincinnati, Ohio: Writer's Digest Books,1989.

Keller, Fred. How To Pitch And Perform Your Songs. Cincinnati, Ohio: Writer's Digest Books, 1988.

Klavens, Kent J. Protecting Your Songs And Yourself. Cincinnati, Ohio: Writer's Digest Books, 1989.

Krasilovsky, William M. and Shemel, Sidney. This Business Of Music (Revised And Enlarged). New York: Billboard Publications, Inc., 1990.

Krasilovsky, William M. and Shemel, Sidney. More About This Business Of Music (3rd Edition, Revised And Enlarged). New York: Billboard Publications, 1989.

Liggett, Mark & Cathy. The Complete Handbook Of Songwriting: An Insider's Guide To Making It In The Music Industry. New York: New American Library, 1985.

Lindey, Alexander. Lindey On Entertainment, Publishing & The Arts: Agreements And The Law. New York: Clark Boardman Co., Ltd., 1963-1969 (Includes Cumulative Supplements).

Livingston, Robert Allen. How To Reduce Your Taxes Legally: Songwriters, Musicians, Performers. California: GLGLC Music, 1982.

Livingston, Robert Allen. Livingston's Complete Music Industry Business And Law Reference Book. Cardiff By The Sea, California: La Costa Music Business Consultants, 1985.

Livingston, Robert Allen. Livingston's Complete Music Industry Business Reference, Vol I And II. California: GLGLC Music, 1987.

Livingston, Robert Allen. Music Publisher Directory. California: GLGLC Music, 1986.

Livingston, Robert Allen. Music Attorney Directory. California: GLGLC Music, 1986.

Livingston, Robert Allen. Recording Contract. California: GLGLC Music, 1986.

Livingston, Robert Allen. Recording Studio Directory - East. California: GLGLC Music, 1986.

Livingston, Robert Allen. Recording Studio Directory - West. California: GLGLC Music, 1986.

Livingston, Robert Allen. Record Company Directory, California: GLGLC Music, 1986.

Livingston, Robert Allen. Record Promotion, Radio Station Directory. California: GLGLC Music, 1985.

Livingston, Robert Allen. Recording Artist Management. California: GLGLC Music, 1986.

Livingston, Robert Allen. Songwriter-Publisher Contract. California: GLGLC Music, 1985.

Livingston, Robert Allen. Sound Basics. California: GLGLC Music, 1985.

Livingston, Robert Allen. Trademarks. California: GLGLC Music, 1985.

Livingston, Robert Allen. The Tax Deduction Checklist: Songwriters, Musicians, Performers. California: GLGLC Music, 1982.

Lustig, Milton. Music Editing For Motion Pictures. California: Hastings, 1980.

Mandell, Jim. The Studio Business Book. Los Angeles, CA: First House Press, 1990.

Martin, George, ed. Making Music: The Guide To Writing, Performing And Recording. New York: W.M. Morrow & Co., 1983.

Mclan, Peter and Wichman, Larry. The Musician's Guide To Home Recording. P.O. Box 1168, Studio City, California: Noteworthy Press, 1988.

Monaco, Bob and James Riordan. The Platinum Rainbow. 5445 Ventura Boulevard, #10, Sherman Oaks, California: Swordsmen Press, 1980.

Murray, Lyn. Musician: Hollywood Journal Of Wives, Women, Writers, Lawyers, Directors, Producers And Music. Secaucus, New Jersey: L. Stuart, 1987.

Nimmer, Melville. Nimmer On Copyright. New York: Matthew Bender & Co., 1966.

Oland, Pamela P. You Can Write Great Lyrics. Cincinnati, Ohio: Writer's Digest Books, 1989.

Orobko, William. Musician's Handbook: A Practical Guide To The Law And Business Of Music. Costa Mesa, California: ISC Publications, 1985.

O'Shea, Shad. Just for the Record. P.O. Box 11333, Cincinnati, Ohio 45211, 1989.

Papalos, Janice. The Performing Artist's Handbook. Cincinnati, Ohio: Writer's Digest Books, 1988.

Pettigrew, Jim, Jr. The Billboard Guide to Music Publicity. New York: Billboard Books, 1989.

Pincus, Lee. The Songwriter's Success Manual, 2nd Ed. New York: Music Press, 1978.

Pohlmann, Ken. Principles of Digital Audio. Indiana: Howard W. Sams & Company, 1987.

Prendergast, Roy M. Film Music: A Neglected Art. New York: Norton, 1977.

Rachlin, Harvey. The Songwriter's Handbook. New York: T.Y. Crowell, 1977.

Rachlin, Harvey. Encyclopedia Of The Music Business. New York: Harper & Row, 1981.

Rachlin, Harvey. Songwriter's And Musician's Guide To Making Great Demos. Cincinnati, Ohio: Writer's Digest Books, 1988.

Rapaport, Diane Sward. How To Make & Sell Your Own Record: The Complete Guide To Independent Recording. Rev. 3rd Ed. Jerome, Arizona: Jerome Headlands Press, 1988.

Rappoport, Victor. Making It In Music. New York: Prentice-Hall, Inc., 1979.

Riordan, James and Monaco, Bob. Making It In The New Music Business. Cincinnati, Ohio: Writer's Digest Books,1988.

Riordan, James and Monaco, Bob. The Platinum Rainbow: How To Succeed In The Music Business Without Selling Your Soul. Chicago: Contemporary Books, 1988.

Rogers, Kenny and Epand, Len. Making It With Music. New York: Harper & Row, 1978.

Rohrlich, Chester. Organizing Corporate And Other Business Enterprises (5th Edition). New York: Matthew Bender & Co., 1985.

Roth, Ernest. The Business Of Music: Reflections Of A Music Publisher. New York: Oxford University Press, 1969.

Rudolph, Thomas E. Music And The Apple II: Applications For Music Education, Composition And Performance. Philadelphia, Pennsylvania: Unsinn Publications, 1984.

Shankman, Ned, And Thompson, Larry A. How To Make A Record Deal And Have Your Song Recorded. New York: Hastings House Publishers, 1975.

Siegel, Alan H. Breaking Into The Music Business. New York: Cherrylane Books, Rochester, 1988.

Shoemaker, Joanie, Ed. Note by Note: A guide to Concert Production, Oakland, Ca: Redwood Cultural Work, 1989.

Skiles, Marlin. Music Scoring For TV And Motion Pictures. Summit, Pennsylvania: Tab Books, 1976.

Smalley, Jack. Lyrics, Lyrics, Lyrics And How To Write Them. California: STS, 1987.

Spitz, Robert Stephen. The Making Of A Superstar: Artists And Executives Of The Rock Music World. New York: Anchor Press, 1978.

Taubman, Joseph. Performing Arts Management And Law, Sound Copyright/Music Publishing. New York: Law Arts Press, 1981.

Taubman, Joseph. Performing Arts Management And Law Forms. Books IV, V, VI, VII: Sound Copyright/Music Publishing. New York: Law Arts Press, 1981.

Taubman, Joseph. In Tune With The Music Business. New York: Law-Arts Publishers, 1980.

Telton, Geary. Music And The Macintosh. Atlanta, Georgia: Midi America, 1989.

Thomas, Tony. Music For The Movies. New York: A.S. Barnes, 1973.

Viera, John David And Thorne, Robert. Entertainment Publishing And The Arts Handbook. New York: Clark Boardman Co., Ltd., Annually.

Wadhams, Wayne. Sound Advice: Musicans' Guide to the Record Industry. New York: Schirmer Books, 1990.

Wadhams, Wayne. Sound Advice: Musician's Guide to the Recording Studio. New York: Schirmer Books, 1990.

Warner, Jay. How To Have Your Hit Song Published. New York: Music Bank Publishers, Inc., 1978.

Weissman, Dick. The Music Business-Career Opportunities And Self-Defense. NewYork: Crown Publishers, 1979.

Whitburn, Joel. Music And Video Yearbook. Wisconsin: Record Research, 1987.

Whitfield, Jane. Songwriters Rhyming Dictionary. Los Angeles: Wilshire Book Co., 1974.

Williams III, George. Ed. by Bill Dalton. The Songwriter's Demo Manual and Success Guide. Dayton, Nevada: Tree by the River Publishing/Music Business Books, 1984.

Wootton, Richard. Honky Tonkin': A Guide to Music U.S.A. North Carolina: East Woods Press, 1980.

Woram, John. Sound Recording Handbook. Indiana: Howard W. Sams and Co., 1989.

Young, Jean and Jim. Succeeding in the Big World of Music. Boston: Little Brown, 1977.

Zalkind, Ronald. Getting Ahead in the Music Business. New York: Schirmer Books, 1978.

Zalkind, Ronald and Stein, Howard. Promoting Rock Concerts. New York: Schirmer Books, 1979.

LEGAL PUBLICATIONS

Forum on the Entertainment and Sports Industries
American Bar Association
750 North Lake Shore Drive
Chicago, IL 60611

The Entertainment and Sports Lawyer

Recording, Management and Agency Contracts in the Music Industry, 1988

Legal and Business Aspects of the Music Industry, 1987

Music Publishing and the Law, 1986

Beverly Hills Bar Association
300 South Beverly Drive, #201
Beverly Hills, CA 90212
(213) 553-6644

Film Music: Hit Records to Dramatic Underscore: Legal, Business and Creative Aspect (Talent acquisition agreements, music clearance procedures, album agreements and aspects of film music).

Artists v. Managers v. Labor Commissioner (This three volume set is a major authority in the regulation of entertainer's representatives with a review of leading cases and authorities).

Hollywood in Arbitration (A unique publication containing pleadings and samples of labor contracts of the various guilds in the industry).

Actor's Manual (Overall way to get started - how to audition, casting, choosing your medium, agreements with managers, etc.).

Visual Artists' Manual (Two volumes discuss how to choose a representative, agreements with galleries, estate planning, artists' rights, art collecting and much more).

Writer's Legal and Business Guide (Discusses manuscript submission, lawyers, contracts, privacy and other aspects. A 1989 publication).

The Fundamentals of Copyright, by Lionel S. Sobel, Esq. (The book is an overview of all phases of copyright law. It deals with exclusive rights, transfers, infringement, remedies, etc.).

Fundamentals of International Copyright (Covers all aspects of the subject and is a basic reference publication for all practitioners involved in international copyright matters. Printed in conjunction with a seminar taught by Paul Edward Geller, David Nimmer and Lionel S. Sobel).

California Lawyers for the Arts
Fort Mason Center
Building C, Room 255
San Francisco, CA 94123
(415) 775-7200

The Art of Deduction: Income Tax for Performing, Visual and Literary Artists

Dispute Resolution for the Arts Community, by Alma Robinson (Columbia/VLA Journal of Law and Arts Reprint).

Performing Arts Issues With Small Claims Court Guide

Financing An Independent Recording

Using Trademarks

Practicing Law Institute
810 Seventh Avenue
New York, NY 10019
(Annual Publication)

Counseling Clients in the Entertainment Industry

CONTRIBUTORS

STEPHEN BIGGER, a graduate of Yale Law School, is a partner in the New York law firm of Weiss, David, Fross, Zelnick & Lehrman. He authors the "Notes from Other Nations" column in The Trademark Reporter.

LAWRENCE J. BLAKE received his law degree from Harvard Law School in 1976. He now practices law as a partner with the Los Angeles firm of Manatt, Phelps, Rothenberg, Tunney & Phillips, specializing in record business law and related areas.

JOHN BRAHENY is co-founder/director of the Los Angeles Songwriters Showcase (LASS), a national BMI-sponsored nonprofit service organization founded in 1971. He's the author of The Craft and Business of Songwriting (Writers Digest Books; 1988), director of the Advanced Songwriting Program at the Grove School of Music, a board member of the California Copyright Conference and has produced the annual Songwriters' Expo since 1976. He's been a musician, folksinger, recording artist, commercial jingle music writer/producer, film music composer and publisher of the Songwriters Musepaper, a monthly magazine for songwriters with a circulation of 20,000.

WAYNE C. COLEMAN, C.P.A. is a business management partner at Gelfand, Rennert & Feldman (a division of Coopers & Lybrand). Formerly in charge of the firm's royalty examination division, Wayne still coordinates the international activities of that group while taking care of his client's many other business needs. Wayne is a graduate of Mississippi State University. He has been Marshall Gelfand's partner for nearly twenty years.

WILLIAM DOBISHINSKI is an attorney specializing in music entertainment law relating to commercials, television and motion pictures. Mr. Dobishinski is the performing rights administrator for many composers throughout the United States, and has written and lectured extensively on performing rights and other matters.

ROBERT M. DUDNIK is a partner in the firm of Paul, Hastings, Janofsky & Walker, which has offices throughout the United States and in Tokyo. Mr. Dudnik, whose office is at the firm's Santa Monica location, chairs the firm's Entertainment Practice Group. That Group, which functions on a nationwide basis, handles both litigation and transactional matters covering all aspects of the entertainment and related industries, including theatrical motion pictures, television, recorded music and broadcasting. The Group's litigation practice deals with intellectual property and business related disputes of all types, and handles matters in various state and federal courts, as well as a broad range of arbitrations. Mr. Dudnik is a graduate of Cornell University and the Yale Law School, where he graduated cum laude and was a member of the Order of the Coif. Mr. Dudnik practiced and taught law in Cleveland, Ohio from 1964 to 1969. Since he moved to Los Angeles in 1969, his practice has been primarily related to the handling of entertainment litigation matters and providing prelitigation counseling to clients in all areas of the entertainment industry.

RICHARD FLOHIL runs his own music business publicity and promotion company in Toronto, Canada; he has edited music magazines, managed bands, organized industry seminars, helped run folk festivals, travelled incessantly, and learned to live out of a very small suitcase. He acknowledges the bright ideas and suggestions of Ralph Alfonso, a brilliant, experienced Canadian road manager, expressed in an article written for The Canadian Composer (which Flohil was formerly the editor of) in May, 1988.

STEVEN GARDNER is a partner in the Century City (Los Angeles) law firm of Cohon and Gardner, which specializes in the entertainment field, and is a founding member of the Committee for the Arts. He is past-president of the Beverly Hills Bar Association Barristers and past-chairperson of the Committee for the Arts. He is currently a member of the Board of Governors of the Beverly Hills Bar Association and President of the Beverly Hills Bar Association Foundation.

MARSHALL M. GELFAND, C.P.A. is the managing partner of the international business management firm of Gelfand, Rennert & Feldman (a division of Coopers & Lybrand), one of the largest and renown of firms specializing in this area. Marshall is a graduate of Syracuse University and New York University Law School.

BRAD GELFOND began as an agent at Regency Artists, Ltd., (a specialized agency) and is now currently a senior agent at Triad Artists, Inc. (a full service agency).

RONALD H. GERTZ, founder of The Clearing House, Ltd. and Studio Music Department, was trained as a classical vocalist and guitarist, and performed professionally in many rock tours. He received his bachelor's degree in Finance from California State University, Northridge, and his law degree from the University of San Fernando Valley College of Law. Mr. Gertz's legal practice began with the representation of clients in the television, publishing and recording fields. He eventually joined EMI Videograms, Inc. as general counsel and Director of Business Affairs, concentrating on the production and acquisition of home video product. Mr. Gertz has written and produced songs for a number of recording artists.

The Clearing House, Ltd. and The Studio Music Department represent television and film producers in the acquisition of music rights for feature film, television and video markets, and in the production and supervision of musical scores.

Mr. Gertz is currently President and CEO of Media Reports, Inc. (MRI), a joint venture between The Clearing House, Ltd. and the broadcast industry. MRI maintains the "Broadcast Performance Date Base," including information on music used and programs broadcast in the United States.

A frequent speaker at colleges, law schools and seminars throughout the country, Mr. Gertz has written articles for the Los Angeles Daily Journal, Billboard Magazine, the Century City Bar Association Journal, the Beverly Hills Bar Association Journal, The Entertainment Law Journal, Entertainment Publishing and the Arts, and Soldier of Fortune.

Currently, Mr. Gertz is on the Board of Directors of the Intellectual Property Section of the Los Angeles County Bar Association.

MARK HALLORAN, is a principal in a law firm, Halloran & Powell, and in a production company, Cine/Disc Entertainment.

Halloran & Powell represent film and television writers producers, directors, actors, recording artists, film composers and songwriters. Halloran & Powell also represent independent production companies in such areas as financing, business affairs, business planning and entertainment management. Cine/Disc is involved in motion picture, television, music and stage production.

Halloran joined MCA/Universal from Orion Pictures in 1985 as a business affairs executive and served as Vice President of Business Affairs from 1986 until 1990. At Orion Pictures, Mark was involved in the soundtrack for "Woman in Red" (Stevie Wonder) and "The Falcon and the Snowman" (David Bowie and Pat Metheny). During his tenure at Universal he was involved in contract negotiations for such films as "Out of Africa," "Parenthood," and "Sea of Love."

Halloran is coauthor of the Musician's Guide to Copyright, and he frequently writes and lectures on the entertainment business. He co-chaired the USC/Beverly Hills Bar Association Annual Entertainment Law Institute in 1989 and 1990, and received the Lawrence J. Black award for outstanding service to the Beverly Hills Bar Association Barristers in 1986.

EDWARD (NED) R. HEARN is in private law practice with offices in San Jose, Palo Alto and San Francisco. Mr. Hearn's practice concentrates on the entertainment and computer software businesses. He is director of the Bay Area Lawyers for the Arts, an organization that provides legal assistance to musicians and other artists, Board President of the Northern California Songwriter's Association, coauthor of the Musician's Guide to Copyright, and lectures on music business and legal issues.

NEVILLE L. JOHNSON has been an entertainment attorney since 1975 and is based in Hollywood, California. He represents numerous music publishers, record companies, artists and personal managers throughout the world. He frequently lectures and writes about the music industry, and is the author of a definitive law review article on personal managers.

EVANNE L. LEVIN graduated with honors from UCLA and Loyola Law School in her native Los Angeles. Since 1974 she has specialized in the music and entertainment law fields and she has been associated with the law firm of Mason & Sloane, where she represented clients such as Motley Crue, Olivia Newton-John, Kenny Rogers, and Sammy Hagar, and with Ervin, Cohen & Jessup as attorney to the California Jam II which attracted 250,000 concert-goers. Her in-house legal and business affairs experience includes Twentieth Century Fox, Orion Pictures, Paramount and ABC. She currently maintains her own practice in Los Angeles. Ms. Levin was a founding member and co-chair of the Beverly Hills Bar Association Committee for the Arts, and chaired its annual symposium that produced the written materials subsequently edited and appearing in the Musician's Manual you are currently reading. She has also served on the board of directors of the Hollywood Women's Coalition and Los Angeles Women in Music, and is currently a member of the UCLA Executive Advisory Committee for Entertainment Programs. In addition to offering personal management, music publishing and television courses at institutions including UCLA, Ms. Levin has contributed to numerous music and entertainment publications.

LINDA A. NEWMARK is an entertainment attorney with the law firm of Cooper, Epstein & Hurewitz in Beverly Hills. She received her B.A. degree, summa cum laude, from UCLA in 1984 and her J.D. degree, with distinction, from Stanford Law School in 1988. She is a member of the California bar and a member of Phi Beta Kappa. During law school, she was an extern law clerk in the Business and Legal Affairs Department at MCA Records, Inc. Her essay, "Performance Rights in Sound Recordings: An Analysis of the Constitutional, Economic and Equitable Issues," which has been published by Columbia University Press in ASCAP Copyright Law Symposium Number Thirty-Eight (1989), won National Fourth Prize in the 1988 Nathan Burkan Memorial Competition sponsored by the American Society of Composers, Authors and Publishers (ASCAP) and second prize in the 1988 Nathan Burkan Memorial Competition at Stanford Law School. She is a panel attorney for California Lawyers for the Arts, a nonprofit organization that provides legal services to individuals and organizations with arts-related legal problems.

PETER T. PATERNO, a 1976 graduate of UCLA Law School, formerly practiced law as a partner with Manatt, Phelps, Rothenberg, Tunney & Phillips in Los Angeles, specializing in music law. He is now President of Hollywood Records.

JOHN R. "JACK" PHILLIPS is the partner-in-charge of royalty and participation examinations at the Los Angeles headquarters office of Gelfand, Rennert & Feldman (a division of Coopers & Lybrand). Jack received a BBA and MBA from Iona College and Graduate School in New York. For over twelve years he and his staff have performed royalty examinations in all of the major territories around the world.

DIANE SWARD RAPAPORT is a former artist manager with Bill Graham Productions and pioneer in the field of music business pedagogy. She is currently president of Jerome Headlands Press, her own publishing and public relations firm in Northern Arizona. Ms. Rapaport is the author of *How To Make and Sell Your Own Record*, a widely respected guide to independent recording. She is an Adjunct Professor of Music Management at the University of Colorado, Denver.

JAMES A. SEDIVY is an attorney specializing in entertainment law and civil litigation. He is currently co-chairman of the Committee for the Arts of the Beverly Hills Bar Association Barristers, as well as President of the Beverly Hills Bar Association Barristers. He is a graduate of Syracuse University and Gonzaga University School of Law.

ALFRED SCHLESINGER has been a music business attorney for the past thirty years. Prior to becoming an attorney, he had his own record and music publishing companies. His entire practice is now, and has been, in the field of music, representing record companies, music publishing companies, recording artists, record producers, songwriters, personal managers, talent agents and disc jockeys. In addition to his activities as an attorney, he was the personal manager of the recording group "Bread", from its inception in 1968 to its dissolution in 1978. He is a past president of the California Copyright Conference, a past president of the Los Angeles Chapter of the National Academy of Recording Arts and Sciences (NARAS) and has just concluded his second year as National Chairman of the Board of said organization. He is also a past recipient of Billboard Magazine's Entertainment Attorney of the Year. Mr. Schlesinger has written articles for the Beverly Hills Bar Journal, the National Academy of Songwriters (of which he is a founding member), the Association of International Entertainment Attorneys (of which he is a charter member) and various educational institutions throughout the United States. He has also taught courses on the music business, and been a guest lecturer and panelist for many educational institutions and music oriented organizations.

GREGORY T. VICTOROFF has been an entertainment litigation attorney since 1979, representing clients in the music, film, and fine art businesses in Los Angeles. He is currently practicing with the offices of Stephen F. Rohde and is a frequent author and lecturer on copyright and art law and co-chairman of the Committee for the Arts of the Beverly Hills Bar Association Barristers. As an orchestral musician he has backed artists such as Huey Lewis and the News, Santana, Bobby McFerrin, Jefferson Starship, and Graham Nash.

THOMAS A. WHITE is a consultant in the record and music publishing industries based in Beverly Hills, California. He is the author of "The Crisis of A&R Competence and Record Industry Economics" and other analytical articles. Mr. White headed the Artist Development Department at CBS Records (Epic, Portrait and the CBS Associated Labels), West Coast, was President of the European label CBO Records Inc., and President of Harmony Gold Music Inc.

INDEX

ABOUT JEROME HEADLANDS PRESS

Jerome Headlands Press, based in Jerome, Arizona, designs and produces music business books for the working musician and business professional. How to Make and Sell Your Own Record, it's first book, helped revolutionize the recording industry by providing musicians with the information needed to produce, market and sell records, cassettes and compact discs outside the major label networks. Called "A Bible for Musicians,' the book has sold over 100,000 copies since it was first published in 1980. A comprehensive new edition is currently being written by Diane Rapaport for publication by Prentice Hall in 1992.

Diane Rapaport, founder and President of Jerome Headlands Press, has been a pioneer in the field of music business education. "We provide business information and training for musicians that helps them to make a living from their art and avoid costly mistakes. Until musicians learn to cope with their art as a business, they will sign bad contracts and earn monies less than equal to their level of training, skill and experience."

We are seeking manuscripts in the field of music business education and audio technology. Please contact us with a letter describing your project, a working table of contents and sample chapter.

Diane Rapaport
Jerome Headlands Press
PO Box N
Jerome, Arizona 86331